The Soviet Army, 1939–1980

The Soviet Army, 1939–1980:

A Guide to Sources in English

Myron J. Smith, Jr.

With a Historical Introduction
by John Erickson

ABC-Clio, Inc.
Santa Barbara, California
Oxford, England

Library of Congress Cataloging in Publication Data

Smith, Myron J.
  The Soviet Army, 1939–1980.

  (The War/peace bibliography series; #11)
  Includes index.
  1. Soviet Union. Army—Bibliography. 2. Soviet Union—History, Military—1917– —Bibliography.
  3. Soviet Union—Military policy—Bibliography.
  I. Title. II. Series.
  Z6725.S68S54 1982 [UA772] 016.355'00947 82-4107
  ISBN 0-87436-307-1   AACR2
  10 9 8 7 6 5 4 3 2 1

ABC-Clio, Inc.
2040 Alameda Padre Serra, Box 4397
Santa Barbara, California 93103

Clio Press Ltd.
Woodside House, Hinksey Hill
Oxford OX 1 5BE, England

Manufactured in the United States of America

in memory of West Virginia boys killed in Indochina

Other Bibliographies
By Myron J. Smith, Jr.

Navies in the American Revolution. Vol. I of the American Naval Bibliography Series.

The American Navy, 1789–1860. Vol. II of the American Naval Bibliography Series.

American Civil War Navies. Vol. III of the American Naval Bibliography Series.

The American Navy, 1865–1918. Vol. IV of the American Naval Bibliography Series.

The American Navy, 1918–1941. Vol. V of the American Naval Bibliography Series.

The European Theater. Vol. I of *World War II at Sea: A Bibliography of Sources in English.*

The Pacific Theater. Vol. II of *World War II at Sea: A Bibliography of Sources in English.*

General Works, Naval Hardware, Home Fronts, Special Studies, and the "All Hands" Chronology (1941–1945). Vol. III of *World War II at Sea: A Bibliography of Sources in English.*

General Works, European and Mediterranean Theaters of Operations. Vol. I of *Air War Bibliography, 1939–1945: English-language Sources.*

The Pacific Theater: Airpower, Strategy, and Tactics; Escape, Evasion, Partisans, and POW Experiences. Vol. II of *Air War Bibliography, 1939–1945: English-language Sources.*

Multi-theater Studies and the Air Forces. Vol. III of *Air War Bibliography, 1939–1945: English-language Sources.*

The Aircraft. Vol. IV of *Air War Bibliography, 1939–1945: English-language Sources.*

World War I in the Air: A Bibliography and Chronology.

Air War Southeast Asia, 1961–1973: An Annotated Bibliography and 16mm Film Guide.

The War Stories Guide: An Annotated Bibliography of Military Fiction.

Intelligence, Propaganda and Psychological Warfare, Resistance Movements, and Secret Operations, 1939–1945: Vol. I of *The Secret Wars.*

Intelligence, Propaganda and Psychological Warfare, Covert Operations, 1945–1980. Vol. II of *The Secret Wars.*

International Terrorism, 1968–1980. Vol. III of *The Secret Wars.*

Cloak-and-Dagger Bibliography: An Annotated Guide to Spy Fiction, 1937–1975.

The Salem College Guide to Equestrian Studies: A Bibliography and 16mm Film Guide.

The Sea Fiction Guide. With Robert C. Weller.

The War/Peace Bibliography Series

RICHARD DEAN BURNS, EDITOR

About the War/Peace Bibliography Series

With this bibliographical series, the Center for the Study of Armament and Disarmament, California State University, Los Angeles, seeks to promote a wider understanding of martial violence and the alternatives to its employment. The Center, which was formed by concerned faculty and students in 1962–63, has as its primary objective the stimulation of intelligent discussion of war/peace issues. More precisely, the Center has undertaken two essential functions: (1) to collect and catalogue materials bearing on war/peace issues; and (2) to aid faculty, students, and the public in their individual and collective probing of the historical, political, economic, philosophical, technical, and psychological facets of these fundamental problems.

This bibliographical series is, obviously, one tool with which we may more effectively approach our task. Each issue in this series is intended to provide a comprehensive "working," rather than definitive, bibliography on a relatively narrow theme within the spectrum of war/peace studies. While we hope this series will prove to be a useful tool, we also solicit your comments regarding its format, contents, and topics.

RICHARD DEAN BURNS
SERIES EDITOR

Contents

Kirill A. Meretskov   Joseph Stalin
Kirill S. Moskalenko   Semen K. Timoshenko
Ivan G. Pavlovskiy   Mikhail N. Tukhachevskiy
Vladimir Petrov   Dimitriy F. Ustinov
Petr A. Pirogov   Aleksandr M. Vasilevskiy
Markian M. Popov   Nikolai F. Vatutin
Vladimir Rodinov   Fred Virski
Konstantin K. Rokossovskiy   Andrei A. Vlasov
Boris M. Shaposhnikov   Nikolai N. Voronov
Nikolay A. Shchelokov   Kliment E. Voroshilov
Sergei L. Sokolov   Aleksey A. Yepishev
Vasiliy D. Sokolovskiy   Matvey V. Zakharov
Mikhail Soloviev   Georgiy K. Zhukov

"The Russian Army is a wall which, however far it may retreat, you will always find in front of you."

— Jomini to Marshal Canrobert
Crimean Campaign, 1854

Preface

Background

THE GROWTH OF Soviet Army activity has been one of the most dramatic war/peace developments to occur in the post–World War II period. Today, the Soviet Union possesses the best equipped, second-largest (after China), and well-trained ground force in the world. Unlike the Soviet Navy, Air Force, or Strategic Rocket Force, the Soviet Army already is superior in might to its Western counterparts. As events in Afghanistan have demonstrated, there are flaws, however, in the Russian juggernaut which, while not fatal, may prove embarrassing if it is ever employed against a modern adversary.

The development of the Soviet Army since 1917 is a story filled with ups and downs reminiscent of a soap opera. Down periods have included the years immediately after the Revolution, the time of the Great Purges, and the dark days of 1941–1942 following the German invasion. The Soviet Army, called the Red Army until 1946, saw good times in the 1930s and again from late 1943 to the time of Khrushchev, who saw the nuclear missile as an end-all in military strategy and therefore ignored and humbled the army, including its most famous marshal, Georgiy K. Zhukov. After Khrushchev's retirement, the new and current Soviet leadership sought balanced force components and a new buildup which saw the Soviet Army emerge as a powerful agent second in influence only to the Strategic Rocket Force.

The impressive growth of a first-rate nuclear umbrella and the development of a formidable conventional army able to operate offensively under a variety of conditions and over different terrains has given the Soviet Union a sense of security and foreign policy flexibility once enjoyed by the United States alone. To a great extent, Russian activity in the Third World may be directly attributed to this growth in confidence and military-projection capability. Events in Africa, the Persian Gulf, Afghanistan, and around Poland may be taken as indications of Soviet ability and willingness to influence situations in a more forceful manner now than in the past. These events, coupled with continuing large-scale arms expenditures and transfers and an apparent breakdown in détente, have given rise to new Western concerns for the future.

Objectives

THIS GUIDE, the first on its subject, is intended to serve as a working bibliography of English-language sources concerning the Soviet Army. While aimed primarily at scholars, and especially graduate and undergraduate students, it should also prove useful to librarians, general readers, journalists, policymakers, and such military enthusiasts as wargamers.

The guide is not definitive, but it covers virtually all factors concerning Russian ground forces, including the Soviet Navy–administered naval infantry and marines. As a reference tool, it will permit its user to quickly determine what material is available and help him to establish a basis for further research. In general, the items cited are those the user might reasonably expect to find in large university, public, or government libraries. If not immediately available, almost every citation can be obtained through interlibrary loan, details of which can be provided by any library.

This volume is the third in a series of resource guides devoted to the Russian military, published by ABC-Clio, the first two being *The Soviet Navy, 1941–1978: A Guide to Sources in English* and *The Soviet Air and Strategic Rocket Forces, 1939–1980: A Guide to Sources in English*. The criteria for selection in this compilation are the same as those employed for them. The following types of published material are represented: books and monographs; scholarly papers, including appropriate numbers from the RAND Corporation and the International Institute for Strategic Studies; periodical and journal articles, including translations such as the *Soviet Military Review* and the U.S. Joint Publication Research Service's *Soviet Military Translations* and *Translations on USSR Military Affairs;* U.S., British, and Soviet government documents, the last in translation; doctoral dissertations, masters theses, and research projects, including several from private firms as well as many from the American military. A list of journals consulted will be found in Appendix I.

Although much has been included, it was necessary to draw a line somewhere and omit certain kinds of information. Excluded material includes fiction, obvious children's works, newspaper articles (unless reprinted in anthologies or translations), and poetry.

The context, content, and emphasis of English-language literature on Soviet ground forces activity has changed greatly over the past four decades. Except in the U.S.S.R., where great emphasis is placed on the "lessons" of earlier conflicts, much of what has been published is now outdated or "historical." In that respect, much of this guide can be considered "historical," in that many of its citations will be dated by the time the book is published. To keep abreast of new works and current events as they concern our topic, the user will find it necessary to continuously consult the reference works provided in section 1.

Arrangement

THE FIVE MAIN sections in the table of contents, with their subsections, form a classified subject index to this guide and the key to the manner in which the book is laid out. Within the text, each section and many subsections have introductions, following which material is arranged alphabetically under the headings "Books," "Articles," and "Documents, Papers, and Reports." At the conclusion of each subsection, the user will find a note on further references within the book designed to guide him to related information.

Each citation has an entry number. These entry numbers run consecutively throughout the guide. An author index keyed to entry numbers is provided.

Acknowledgments

FOR THEIR ADVICE, assistance, or encouragement in the formulation, research, and completion of this endeavor, the following persons and libraries are gratefully acknowledged:

> Mr. Robert B. Lane, Director, and the reference staff of the Air University Library, Maxwell AFB, Alabama.
>
> LTC Howard Wright, USAF (ret.), Washington, D.C.
>
> Mr. David James Ritchie, Simulations Publications, New York.
>
> Ms. Penny Underdal, Freedom of Information Act Officer, U.S. Department of Defense, Defense Intelligence Agency, Washington, D.C.
>
> Mr. Ben Russak, *Conflict Magazine,* New York.
>
> Mr. James G. Steuard, La Puente, California.
>
> Mrs. Dianne S. Tapley, Head, Public Services Section, U.S. Army Infantry School Library, Fort Benning, Georgia.

Mr. Lester L. Miller, Jr., Supervisory Librarian, Morris Swett
    Library, U.S. Army Field Artillery School, Fort Sill, Oklahoma.
Mr. Ray Merriam, *Military Journal,* Bennington, Vermont.
Library, U.S. Army Military History Institute, Carlisle Barracks,
    Pennsylvania.
West Virginia University Library, Morgantown, West Virginia.

Special appreciation is reserved for my colleagues and students at
Salem College, without whose backing and aid this project would still be
undone. President James C. Stam, Dean Ronald O. Champagne, and
Dean Gary S. McAllister provided continuous support and the encour-
agement to proceed. Margaret Allen, Jacqueline Isaacs, Sara Casey, Stu
Godfrey, and Janet Underwood of the Benedum Learning Resources
Center staff provided support, bibliographic help, and interlibrary
loan assistance. The students in my modern civilization class learned
more about the Soviet Army than they cared to know, especially Ms.
Mary Roe, who assisted in the compilation of Appendix II, "Selected
Soviet Military Lives."
Finally, hearty thanks is due to Professor John Erickson of the Defence Studies Center at the University of Edinburgh for his splendid
foreword and to series editor Dick Burns for his support, guidance,
and kind words.

Myron J. Smith, Jr.
Salem, West Virginia

Historical Introduction:
The Soviet Ground Forces, 1941–1960

IN THE EARLY HOURS of 22 June 1941, on the *Führer's* orders, the *Wehrmacht* launched Operation BARBAROSSA, the massive surprise attack which signaled the German invasion of the Soviet Union and which initiated the greatest land campaign in the history of the world. The Red Army was at once engulfed in a merciless war that stretched ultimately into 1,426 grueling days. The Soviet-German war ended in May 1945, but Soviet forces added a further tally of 23 operational days with their brief *blitzkrieg* campaign in the Far East directed against the Japanese Kwantung Army. The Soviet-German war, otherwise called the "Great Patriotic War of the Soviet Union," commands the most compelling statistics and reflects in most fearsome fashion the magnitude and scope of the school of sustained war through which the Red Army passed, from the first calamitous defeats of 1941–1942 to its final vengeful victories in 1945, to emerge on the morrow of these triumphs as the *Soviet Army*.[1]

The Soviet-German war raged across battlefronts that spanned distances ranging from 3,000–6,000 kilometers. In the 47 months of war the Red Army passed through three phases: the first (June 1941–November 1942) involved desperate attempts to check the German advance into Soviet territory, but was not without shocks to German arms such as those delivered before Moscow and Stalingrad; the second (Novenber 1942–December 1943) marked the huge bloodletting at the battle of the Kursk salient in 1943 and the ultimate Soviet success in breaking the offensive power of the German armies in the east; the third period (January 1944–May 1945) brought the Red Army crashing across the Soviet frontiers, blasting its way into southeastern and central Europe and through East Prussia to the glittering prize of Berlin itself, the very "lair of the Fascist beast."

In terms of intensity of warfare these three periods bear some small investigation. The first (1941–1942) lasted for 516 days, 485 of which saw the Red Army fully committed operationally (94 percent of

xxiii

the time was taken up with active operations, leaving a mere 31 days of relative quiet). The second phase (1943) saw the only period of extended pause throughout the war (66 days), marking the strange, even eerie lull which preceded the mighty confrontation in the Kursk salient in the high summer of 1943 and the massive armored jousting of German *Panzers* and Soviet tank forces. The third phase (1944–1945) lasted 500 days, 451 of them operationally active, yielding a percentage of active engagement time of 90 percent, a little short of the intensities of the first phase of the war. In all, the Red Army was operationally active for 88 percent of the total duration of war, leaving only 146 days of relative quiet.

Measured in terms of manpower, human effort, and human sacrifice, the Soviet-German front consumed no less than 70 percent of total German strength in 1941 (153 out of 217 divisions), a proportion that remained more or less constant until the end of 1942. In 1943 the number of divisions actually increased to 196 (rising to a peak of 201 in January 1944), although the percentage of German divisions so committed began to fall to just over 60 percent and thence to 57 percent by January 1945. At the cost of its own horrendous losses, the Red Army destroyed or took prisoner 290 enemy divisions and 25 brigades, with 93 divisions surrendering at the end of the war, when the Soviet Armed Forces numbered 11,365,000 men. Just over 6 million German soldiers were killed, wounded, or posted missing in the *Ostfeldzug*. The pitiless scale of Soviet losses—although never precisely calculated—soared past the 12–13 million mark, with perhaps 10 million lost forever, plus the melancholy toll of 10 million civilians who were enslaved, massacred, or simply hapless victims of a gigantic war. The heaviest toll was exacted during the first 20 months of battle, including the terrible plummeting in strength in the late autumn of 1941 due to staggering tallies of prisoners taken by the German Army.

Weapons and equipment were also consumed at a colossal rate, confirming Stalin's view that war would be won—or lost—in the machine shops. The Soviet Union, aided by Lend-Lease, won this industrial war with the outlay of 104,000 tanks and self-propelled (SP) guns (with 78,000 tanks and 16,000 SP guns going to the field armies), 110,000 lorries, 10,000 armored cars, and 30,000 motorcycles, along with additional supplies of 17,000 million rounds of small arms ammunition, 427 million artillery and mortar rounds, 13 million tons of fuel, 40 million tons of food, and 73 million army tunics (Table 1).

The six Soviet tank armies, the first of which suffered a fiery test almost to destruction in 1942, but lived to fight another day and become the pride and joy of the Red Army, carried through 64 offensive operations at Front (Army Group) level or acted as "mobile groups"

Table 1

Soviet Tank/SP Artillery Production:
1941–1945 (to June)

Year	Total Tanks / SP guns	Types			Tank Diesel Engines
		Heavy	Medium	Light	
1941	6,590	1,358	3,014	2,218	4,867
1942	24,719	2,553	12,578	9,588	16,890
1943	24,006	1,423	17,192	5,391	22,955
1944	28,983	4,762	17,066	7,155*	28,120
1945	15,097	3,030	8,505	3,562	14,498
Totals	99,395**	13,126	58,355	27,914	87,330

*SP guns only
**representing only tanks/SP guns accepted from factories
For details of Soviet Tanks/SP guns see *German Military Documents* (GMD).
GenStdH/FHO(IId) reports to *Chef der Heeresrüstung:* T-78/Roll 478 6461092-1200.

attached to Soviet Fronts.[2] There is no better illustration of the transformation in Soviet capabilities, when comparing the first half (1942–1943) of the war with the second, than the rapid growth of this armored striking power and Soviet recourse to the armored offensive, *tankovyi udar.* Out of a grand total of 67 operations conducted by Soviet tank armies, only 11 could be counted within that first phase of the war (producing a mere 236 operational days for tank army operations), while in the second and final periods Soviet armor mounted 56 operations (including the Far Eastern offensive with the 6th Guards Tank Army) amounting to no less than 1,081 operational days expended by the 'homogeneous' *(odnorodnyi sostav)* tank armies consisting of one or two tank corps and a mechanized corps. Manpower hovered around the 35,000–50,000 mark with a complement of 550–700 tanks. In 1945 the Soviet command had at its disposal no less than 15,000 tanks and self-propelled guns.

For all the dramatic expansion and diversification of Soviet armored forces after 1942–1943, the same process—especially the increase in fire-power—affected the entire Red Army, making of it a startlingly different military machine at the end of the war as opposed to its structure and capabilities at the beginning. At first sight huge and seemingly formidable, the Red Army discovered to its grievous cost in 1941 that the rifle division (with an establishment of 14,483 officers and men) was too cumbersome, lacking both mobility and effective communications (signals), and although committed in theory to "maneuver warfare" was wholly unfitted for such a role. Worse still, no proper rear services (logistics) organization existed at the outbreak of war; staffs handled both operations and supply as part of their competence. The armored forces were in little better shape. Soviet plans called for the creation of 20 mechanized corps, but realization of these plans required 30,000 tanks (including 16,600 new KV and T-34 tanks) and 7,000 armored cars needing no less than four to five years for completion in the opinion of the Soviet General Staff. Like the rifle formations, the mechanized elements suffered a drastic shortage of transport (lorries, tractors, and motorcycles).

The savage mauling suffered by the Red Army in the autumn of 1941 and the impact of fearsome losses forced immediate reorganization (Table 2). The manpower level of the rifle formations dropped sharply, although they were more tightly packed with automatic weapons, antitank weapons, and mortars. Between July and December 1941, 124 rifle divisions were disbanded, but 308 divisions (including 24 "militia" divisions) were brought into the order of battle with revised establishments. Perhaps the most decisive move, indeed that which may have saved the Red Army from total destruction, was stripping the artillery from the rifle divisions (leaving only a single artillery regiment with 24 guns per division) and concentrating artillery resources for direct fire under centralized artillery command. The *rifle corps* was abolished and the *rifle brigade* (4,000–6,000 men, 3 rifle battalions, 2 artillery batteries, and a section of tommy gunners) became more widespread. Manpower was cut by at least 50 percent, but firepower increased by 64 percent and 82-mm mortars boosted by a colossal 360 percent in rifle units.

The same fate befell the ill-starred *mechanized corps*. In June 1941 the Red Army—on paper at least—could count the administrations for 29 mechanized corps, 31 motorized divisions, and 61 tank divisions,[3]

Table 2

Rifle Division Establishments (Manpower)	
Date	1941–1945 Establishment
April 1941	14,483
July 1941	10,859
December 1941	11,626
March 1942	12,795
July 1942	10,386
December 1942	9,435
July 1943	9,380
December 1944	11,706
June 1945	11,780

but on the ground the picture was vastly different, with too few formations fully equipped and trained. Worse still, the blight of obsolescence had crept over almost the whole Soviet tank-park. In battle these gross and unwieldy corps with their aged tanks—mounting "pea shooters" as gun armament—proved wholly unfitted to cope with the swift and nimble German *Panzer* divisions, while massive Soviet tank losses further debilitated Soviet performance. Within a month the Soviet command decided to disband the mechanized corps. The tank divisions were subordinated to army commanders and the motorized divisions converted into rifle formations, while 10 tank divisions were hurriedly formed from the remaining mechanized corps in the interior of the Soviet Union. In August 1941 the tank brigade appeared in the order of battle, but even this brigade organized with regimental structure proved to be too cumbersome and was replaced by the brigade with a battalion structure (3 battalions), plus the independent tank battalion assigned to work with rifle units.

A battered and bloodied Red Army nevertheless summoned up sinew enough to deal the *Wehrmacht* a stunning reverse in the winter of 1941–1942, thrusting the German divisions back from Moscow. Corps administrations had been reduced to only six, but the number of combined-arms armies had grown from 27 to 58, with an army fielding on average 5–6 rifle divisions to furnish mobility. The Red Army put no less than 82 cavalry divisions in the field, while the armored forces proper consisted at this time of 7 tank divisions (4 in the Far East), 76 independent tank brigades, and 100 independent tank battalions. In the winter of 1941–1942 the Red Army acquired its first experience of conducting large-scale offensive operations, which damaged but did not mortally wound the German army in the east. In that same spring (1942) the Red Army slowly expanded and diversified, reintroducing the tank corps and the rifle corps (34 of which existed at the end of 1942, including Guards rifle corps and Guards rifle armies). Rifle formations also received tank regiments and independent tank breakthrough regiments (21 heavy tanks) as infantry support. The number of guns and mortars rose from 44,900 to 77,800 and tanks from 3,900 to 7,350.

Soviet tank forces slowly clambered back with more powerful tactical unities. In March 1942 four tank corps were reformed (each with two tank brigades), even if these new unities still lacked "operational-tactical self-sufficiency." In May–June 1942 the first Soviet *tank armies* appeared on the scene, together with the refurbished mechanized corps (Tables 3 and 4). Although of mixed establishment (rifle, tank, and cavalry divisions, plus artillery and multiple rocket launchers, or MRLs) and in spite of being roughly handled by the *Panzers* in the summer of 1942, the new tank armies proved their worth

Table 3

Tank Army: Establishments 1943–1945

	1943	1944	1945
Personnel	46,000	48,000	50,000
Tanks	450–560	450–620	700
SP Guns	25	98–147	250
Guns/mortars	500–600	650–750	850

Tank Corps: Establishments 1942–1945

	1942	1943	1944	1945
Personnel	7,800	10,977	12,010	11,788
Tanks (total)	168	208	207	228
Light	70	–	–	–
Medium	90	208	207	207
Heavy	–	–	–	21
SP guns	–	49	63	42
Tanks +				
SP guns (total)	168	257	270	270
Guns	12	12	36	56
Mortars	18	48	94	94
MRLs	8	8	8	8

in the Soviet counteroffensive at Stalingrad in the following winter. At the same time the Red Army began to concentrate and expand its artillery resources, introducing the artillery division in November 1942 with eight regiments and a total of 168 guns; once again, the innovation justified itself during the Stalingrad counteroffensive. It also led to the vast accretion of the artillery reserves of the Supreme Command (RVGK), a potent instrument which added massive firepower to the "shock power" so ardently desired by Soviet commanders.

Thus, through these red mists of war, the modern, battle-tested Red Army began to take shape with its greater effectiveness in combined-arms organization and operation. At first sight and in view of the early wartime disasters, it seemed that basic Soviet military doctrine based on the principles of combined-arms *(obshchevoiskovoi boi)* and operations in depth *(glubokaya operatsiya)*—developed in the 1936 Field Service Regulations (PU-36) and bearing all the hallmarks of Marshal Tukhachevskii's acknowledged brilliance[4]—might be intrinsically faulty, but the Soviet command learned in painful fashion that this doctrine would not work until the requisite "armament norms" were met. The lack of artillery and the shortage of tanks inhibited battlefield performance from the outset, and there was also the problem of working out effective methods of combat deployment and echeloning

Table 4

Mechanized Corps: Establishments 1942–1945				
	1942	1943	1944	1945
Personnel	13,559	15,018	16,442	16,318
Tanks (total)	175	204	183	183
Light	75	42	–	–
Medium	100	162	183	183
Heavy	–	–	–	–
SP guns	–	25	63	63
Tanks +				
SP guns (total)	175	229	246	246
Guns	36	36	80	80
Mortars	54	72	154	154
MRLS	8	8	8	8

(operativnoe postroenie). Inefficient deployments weakened the assault force by making it unable to attack to sufficient depth or hold enemy counterblows. More tanks, particularly for infantry support, improved the situation, as did greater holdings of artillery. The interaction *(vzaimodeistivie)* of armor with infantry proceeded via trial and error, with error largely predominating, where armor and artillery were too often used in "penny packets" (or "spattered," to use Marshal Zhukov's term). Frequent changes in missions and regrouping weakened the assault groups and snagged the mobile groups (armor/cavalry), thereby dissipating what Soviet commentators called *kompaktnost*. Much effort went into keeping those mobile groups intact and not draining them to provide infantry support, which may have stiffened the initial assault but hampered interaction once in the depth of the enemy defenses.

Artillery support came increasingly to the fore, with the concept of the "artillery offensive" making its appearance in 1942, designed to mass fire resources and to furnish fire support for the assault to the full depth of enemy positions. The shortcomings to be overcome included insufficient fire support to the depth of the enemy defenses, poor planning, and lack of planned fire support when mobile formations were introduced into the breach in the German defenses. Improvements in the course of 1942–1943 brought in the long-range artillery groups (at army level), together with heavy bombardment groups *(razrushenie)*, MRL divisions, and antiaircraft groups. At divisional level artillery support for the rifle elements was distributed among the first echelon rifle regiments. The artillery offensive usually lasted for some 70–80 minutes, with the "heavy bombardment" phase (neutralization and destruction shoots) increased from 20 to 65 minutes, while rolling barrages were extended to a depth of 1.5 kilometers to give greater support to the infantry attack. Artillery support for the mobile groups (tank formations) was assigned to the long-range artillery groups operating to a depth of 10–12 kilometers. As artillery resources grew in the later stages of the war, army artillery groups were split into subgroups to facilitate cooperation with rifle troops, while the appearance after 1943 of heavily fortified and substantially engineered German defensive systems brought the Soviet "heavy bombardment/demolition artillery group" *(gruppa artillerii razrusheniya)* into existence. However, it was not until 1944 that the various artillery groups were given standardized organization, based mainly on their operational-tactical roles (regimental/RAG, divisional/DAG,[5] corps, army support, and so forth).

While the *decisiveness of artillery* in the combined-arms battle became justifiably something of an article of faith, the role of *tactical air support* and the organization of *frontovaya aviatsiya* (FA) added its own complexity in the move away from the early, primitive scattering of air elements throughout combined-arms armies with *ad hoc* units. The advent of the air army *(vozdushnaya armiya)* in 1942 helped to stabilize the situation, but the allocation of the air effort needed urgent resolution. Too often tactical bombing assigned to targets in the depth of the enemy defenses bore little relation to and lacked coordination with "direct support" (close air support). Before 1943 the air effort was usually planned to cover only the first day of offensive operations, largely ignoring the organization of air support as the attack developed through the depth of the enemy positions. Later in the war the air offensive was standardized in two phases, the "air preparation" *(aviatsionnaya podgotovka)* followed by "air support" *(soprovozhdenie)* during the course of the offensive. An army would have as many as three to five air divisions for support, while the mobile group was supported by one *shturmovik* (ground-attack)[6] air division and one fighter division. Bomber divisions were also used in support of Front and army operations.

Soviet experience confirmed that the combined-arms approach was indispensable to meeting the requirements of operations in depth, whether in the form of the systematic breakthrough operation or in relation to the meeting engagement (or any combination of both). For the breakthrough, the surprise "fire blow" *(ognevoi udar)* was decisive, followed by launching attacks across the entire frontage of an army. Effectiveness in the breakthrough operation depended on *tempo* (not simply speed), the exploitation of maneuver, and timely repulse of enemy counterblows mounted with tactical reserves. After 1943 the Red Army was able to use the *corps* to facilitate echeloning, while the production of growing numbers of self-propelled guns allowed artillery to accompany the assault force and tackle enemy antitank guns and strong points, thus freeing the infantry-support tanks to carry out their primary mission, namely, the neutralization of enemy fire directed against Soviet infantry.

After 1943 the Soviet command made substantial improvements in employing both second echelons and reserves. In general, the second echelon was used to break through the depth of the defensive positions off the march, being committed after the breaching of the second line of enemy defenses, although the second echelon could be used to complete the entire destruction of the tactical defensive system. Second echelon formations were also used to develop success by mounting fresh attacks, to widen breaches in the defenses, and to cover the flanks of Soviet shock groups. In the absence of a second echelon, the army reserve (one rifle division) was committed to these tasks. Equally, the *meeting engagement* demanded greater skills from the Red Army. Unlike prewar Soviet doctrine which saw the meeting engagement as the collision of vanguards and an advance to contact—German and Soviet forces were already "in contact"—the wartime meeting engagements developed out of the movement of the assault formations into "operational depth" after breaching the tactical defenses, or else as a result of the defender's maneuver of operational reserves to launch counterblows. The trend in the later stages of the war was for larger mobile forces to be committed in *more intensive* actions (Table 5), with the depth

Table 5

Mobile Groups: Composition Army Mobile Groups
and Depth at Which Committed

Operation	Army	Mobile Group	Tanks SP Guns	Distance from FEBA (km.)	Day of Operation
Byelorussia	11 Guards Army	2 GTkC	252	3–4	1
	65 Army	1 GTkC	252	3–4	1
Jassy-Kishinev	37 Army	7 Mech Corps	197	9–10	2
East Prussia	2 Shock Army	8 GTkC	252	3–4	1
	65 Army	1 GTkC	235	5–6	1
Vistula-Oder	69 Army	11 TkC	274	4–5	1
	5 Guards Army	31 TkC	252	4–5	1
Khingan-Mukden (Far East)	39 Army	61 Tk Div	164	–	1

GTkC = Guards Tank
Tk Div = Tank Division
Mech Corps = Mechanized Corps

at which the meeting engagements were initiated constantly increasing—not infrequently to as much as 135 kilometers—and at a point
when Soviet assault forces were losing their *kompaktnost* due to losses in
manpower (10–15 percent) and armor (45–70 percent) incurred in the
actual breakthrough.

It was not until 1943 (or even 1944) that the combined-arms army
proper came into existence (Table 6). The early 1941 combined-arms
formation consisted largely of rifle divisions with some mechanized
and air support. In 1943–1944 the establishment of the combined-
arms army settled at or about 3 corps, 8–12 rifle divisions, and 4
artillery regiments, plus infantry support tanks and self-propelled
guns, the average manpower strength wavering around the 110,000–
120,000 mark. After 1943 the combined-arms army was increasingly
reinforced with 1–2 artillery breakthrough divisions, 3 field artillery
regiments, 3 antitank brigades, 3–4 tank and self-propelled gun regiments, and at least 10 independent tank regiments and possibly 2
antiaircraft artillery divisions. The mobile group attached to the army
and air support was formed by 1–2 tank (or mechanized) corps and was
supplied by several (3–5) aviation divisions. Heavier tanks were used
for the infantry support role with the object of enabling the tank/
infantry team to operate at greater depths within enemy defensive
systems (Table 7). Soviet calculations estimated that a combined-arms
army, operating as an element within a Front, could destroy between
3–6 enemy divisions and penetrate to a depth of 100–150 kilometers.

The essence of the combined-arms battle became, in theory at
least, *fire, shock power/attack, maneuver.* Soviet efforts, therefore, concentrated continuously on increasing the "tactical densities" *(plotnost)* involved in the combined-arms mix of infantry, armor, artillery, SP guns,

Table 6

Combined-Arms Armies: 1941–1945

Army	Manpower	Guns / Mortars	AT Guns	AA Guns	MRLs	Tanks	SP Guns	Aircraft
30A(41)	72,000	303	77	25	19	21	–	–
20A(42)	70,000	444	79	4	40	96	–	–
6A(42)	101,000	1,004	149	55	24	445	–	145
31A(42)	89,000	1,128	154	52	426	267	–	–
11 GdsA(43)	135,000	2,652	468	255	144	615	33	–
53A(43)	77,000	1,698	390	80	48	291	11	–
11 GdsA(44)	122,000	2,087	192	148	360	293	191	–
3A(44)	93,000	2,108	370	78	232	319	225	–
2 ShA(45)	102,000	1,910	327	104	388	306	125	–
5 GdA(45)	81,000	2,400	217	124	456	420	217	–

Table 7

Density of Infantry Support Tanks
Examples (1944–1945)

Operation	Formation	Tanks	SP Guns	Total	Density per 1 km frontage
Byelorussia	5 Army	135	136	271	22
	3 Army	83	120	203	16
	65 Army	22	85	107	13
Jassy-Kishinev	37 Army	55	43	98	17
East Prussia	2 Shock Army	96	83	179	30
	65 Army	91	84	175	25
Berlin	5 Shock Army	178	128	306	44
	5 Guards Army	84	23	107	14
Harbin-Hirin (Far East)	5 Army	260	149	409	34

engineers, and communications (signals). In the last stage of the war (1944–1945), in the course of breakthrough operations, five to seven rifle battalions, 200–250 guns, 20–30 tanks, and two to four combat engineer companies were concentrated for each kilometer of the attack sector, with similar densities elaborated both for the meeting engagement and for defensive actions. As for inter-arms cooperations and coordination, the 1943 Field Service Regulations *(Polevoi ustav/1943)* stipulated that this process should be managed in the interests of the infantry, although it became increasingly plain that fire—*ognevoi boi*—was becoming the arbiter of the battlefield, be the action defensive or offensive. Without massive artillery and air support, the tank/infantry team could not carry out its mission to any depth. For all practical purposes, fire *(ogon)* came to exercise total sway over the battlefield. The diversification of the combat arms, however, inevitably complicated the interaction/co-ordination process, which added to the significance of maneuver, both "maneuver with fire power" *(manevr ognem)* and "troop maneuver," all culminating in the fusion of *maneuver with assault/attack.*

That same diversification was readily apparent in Red Army structure and organization after 1943. Tank and mechanized corps proliferated. The tank corps had 3 tank brigades, 1 motor-rifle brigade, 2–3 SP gun regiments, mortar and antiaircraft gun regiments, in all 11,000 men, 209 T-34 tanks, 49 SP guns, and 152 guns and mortars. The mechanized corps had more men (16,369) but fewer tanks (197), while the *artillery corps* consisted of 2 artillery breakthrough divisions and one Guards mortar division (MRL[7] units capable of delivering 3,456 rounds with a salvo weight of 320 tons). The tank armies either raised or reorganized in 1943 consisted of 2 tank and 1 mechanized corps with 2 antitank gun, 2 mortar (MRL), 2 antiaircraft, and 2 self-propelled gun regiments, plus, on occasions, a howitzer regiment. At the close of 1943 Soviet armored forces comprised 5 army HQs (tank armies), 24 tank and mechanized corps, 80 independent tank brigades, 106 independent tank and SP gun regiments, plus numerous battalions. Combat engineers were similarly expanded and diversified, amounting to 58 brigades, 9 regiments, and more than 1,000 battalions at the end of 1943.

At the beginning of 1944, in preparation for the "ten decisive blows" about to be rained on the German Army in the east, the Red Army mustered 5,987,000 men (419,000 of them held in reserve) with 92,650 guns and mortars (with 5,000 in reserve), 5,357 tanks and self-propelled guns (271 in reserve) and over 8,000 combat aircraft, in all 461 rifle and motor-rifle divisions, 76 artillery/mortar divisions, and 124 aviation divisions. In June 1944 Red Army strength topped the 6 million mark, the tank-park had grown to 7,753 (with SP guns, reserves amounting to 2,323 machines) and the strength of combat aircraft boosted to 13,428 (Tables 8 and 9). To direct these formations and units the vast network of Soviet training establishments turned out no less

Table 8

Front-line and Reserve Strength: January 1944			
	Field Armies, Fleets	*Stavka* Reserve	Total
Red Army	5,568,000	419,000	5,987,000
Air Force (including Long-Range Aviation: ADD)	331,000	77,000	408,000
Navy	266,000	–	266,000
Airborne Troops	–	75,000	75,000
Total	6,165,000	571,000	6,736,000
Divisions/brigades			
Rifle, motor-rifle, cavalry, airborne divisions	461	19	480
Independent brigades	38	17	55
'Fortified districts' (URs)*	32	–	32
Tank/mechanized corps	23	12	35
Independent tank brigades	42	4	46
Artillery/mortar divisions	76	4	80
Aviation divisions	124	4	128
Weapons			
Guns and mortars	92,650	5,040	97,690
Tanks and SP guns	5,357	271	5,628
Aircraft	8,506	312	8,818

*Firepower equivalent to a rifle division.

Table 9

Front-line and Reserve Strength: June 1944

	Field Armies, Fleets	*Stavka* Reserve	Total
Red Army	5,691,000	386,000	6,077,000
Air Force (including Long-Range Aviation: ADD)	337,000	70,000	447,000
Navy	357,000	–	357,000
Airborne Troops	–	58,000	58,000
Total	6,425,000	514,000	6,939,000
Divisions/brigades			
Rifle, motor-rifle, cavalry, airborne divisions	453	23	476
Independent brigades	17	–	17
'Fortified districts' (URs)	19	–	19
Tank/mechanized corps	22	15	37
Independent tank brigades	36	1	37*
Artillery/mortar divisions	72	11	83
Aviation divisions	132	21	153
Weapons			
Guns and mortars	92,557	4,493	97,050
Tanks and SP guns	7,753	2,232	9,985
Aircraft	13,428	1,359	14,787

*Including two SP gun brigades

than 317,000 officers in the course of 1944. Front commands now consisted of 6–9 combined-arms armies, 1 air army and, not infrequently, 1 or 2 tank armies, while the combined-arms army itself expanded to include 3–4 rifle corps (9–12 rifle divisions), 1–3 tank brigades, and the possible additive of a tank or mechanized corps for particular operations. Artillery strength continued to bound ahead, although more than one-third of the divisions and brigades were held as Supreme Command reserves, facilitating the centralized direction and maneuver of powerful artillery assets as well as enabling the Soviet command to mass artillery in the requisite densities on decisive sectors and axes of advance.

From the outset, on German admission alone, the Russians proved to be first-class fighters; in time, they learned the business of being first-class soldiers. But bravery and the traditional qualities of the Russian infantryman would not of themselves meet the demands of the modern battlefield. *Upravlenie voiskami*, troop control, had to be developed under the most searching conditions, amid a shortage of the basic means of communications, such as radios, and even where radios did exist *radioboyazn* (wireless-fear) took hold among commanders unused to or suspicious of these new-fangled devices. A first and necessary step involved reducing the overblown staffs of cumbersome formations (at army and division), as well as splitting responsibility for operational and rear services (logistics) matters. The post of Chief of Rear Services was established at the end of July 1941, with corresponding positions at Front and army level.

Centralization, strict centralization, was (and remains to this day) the dominant mode. Operational direction of the field armies devolved on the *Stavka* (General Headquarters) of the High Command (adapted as the Supreme Command), with the General Staff acting as the operational channel to the fronts and Front commands. This super-centralization, however, even with regionalized high commands as an intermediate echelon, proved to be too inflexible, while the *Glavkoms* (the regional high commands) lacked adequate staffs and communications facilities. In effect, higher staffs were mere information-collecting agencies passing information upwards to the *Stavka,* which became overloaded as it struggled with strategic decisions, operational questions, and even tactical handling. Coordination and communications broke down; five Fronts were activated in June 1941, but within a matter of months the *Stavka* was wrestling with a battlefront expanded from 2,000 to 4,000 kilometers, and involving eight Fronts and four independent armies. The intermediate high command echelon *(Glavkoms)* did not endure throughout the war (although the method was revived briefly for the Far Eastern operations in 1945). While maintaining the centralized system, indeed as a means of reinforcing it and even as Stalin kept the tightest grip on both strategic and operational matters, the General Staff sent its own representatives to field commands (down to division, in many instances). The *Stavka* also despatched *predstavitelii*—representatives with enormous authority and sweeping powers—to Front commands, or else to coordinate the operations of several Fronts, a procedure which soon earned the label of the "flying circus" as Marshal Zhukov, Marshal Vasilevskii, or Artillery Marshal Voronov descended on Front commanders, communicating the scope of the specific *Stavka* directive, reporting directly to Stalin, and steering Front (and army) commanders towards particular operational decisions and solutions fitting the prime directive.

Although the quality of leadership and strategic direction at the highest levels steadily improved, owing not a little to Stalin restraining his intemperate urge for the single "war-winning" offensive, to the talents of the Marshals Zhukov and Vasilevskii within the *Stavka* and at the Fronts, and to the skills of Front commanders such as Koniev, Rokossovskii, Bagramyan, Vatutin, Malinovskii together with armored commanders in the mould of Rotmistrov and Katukov, the Red Army's performance and effectiveness still gave rise to frequent concern. In the first phase of the war, as the high command struggled to develop a system of command, control, and coordination, performance was subject to the drastic constraints of weapons and equipment shortages, lack of available reserves (or reserves heedlessly squandered), the shortcomings of hastily improvised mobile groups, and the lack of tactical skills at lower levels. Armies and divisions were simply expended wholesale in defense and attack. Over-tasking, brute expenditure of major formations without reinforcements, and *total attrition* over time, plus calamitous losses among junior officers, accelerated defeat in the field.

In general, massive losses were due to physical annihilation (encirclement *en masse* after ineffective linear defense tactics), over-tasking in time and space, loss of command and control, the lack of operational reserves, and tactical inflexibility. The *Field Service Regulations* of 1942 introduced valuable correctives, but Soviet performance continued to suffer from inadequate initial force (due to shortage of time or shortage of resources) committed to operations, leading to the rapid erosion of combat capability compounded by poor reconnaissance. All too often artillery simply fired by squares and had no effective interaction with infantry and armor. As the war progressed, the Soviet command learned that maintaining combat capability *(boesposobnost)* depended on uninterrupted troop control; replenishment of formations with men, weapons, and equipment; organizational measures (to preserve the initial structure of the unit); good morale; and speedy replacement of damaged equipment. Total attrition occurred most frequently in the early phases of the war, but inadequate performance due to the weakness of the *initial force* persisted throughout 1943–1945. Most operations proceeded with "on-line" forces with the reserve battalions and field reinforcement used to maintain the core of the formation. Losses fell into two categories: high initial loss (as when the assault was stopped cold, frequently during the first 12 hours of an attack), and losses over time arising out of the constant employment of forces whereby battalion strengths were almost negligible and divisional strengths on occasion ground down to a skeletal 350 men.[8]

Manning levels and reinforcement capability obviously affected *small-unit* performance. In 1944–1945 Soviet rifle division strength hovered about the 6,000-man mark, enabling rifle companies to be built up to some 70–80 men, but replacements were usually untrained and simply filling out companies did not guarantee tactical effectiveness. It was not unusual, therefore, for Soviet divisions to cream off their experienced soldiers in order to form mobile lead battalions. Meanwhile, over-tasking persisted, although loss of or deterioration in combat capability could be traced in many instances to a *logistical* failure, with divisions outrunning their supplies and outdistancing artillery support in spite of all the efforts to motorize Soviet artillery. As losses mounted, the political officer (replacing the military commissar, whose watchdog functions were abolished in 1942 along with the post of commissar) came into play and his role cannot be discounted in maintaining fighting spirit and sheer doggedness in the face of heavy casualties. Finally, in the closing stages of the war, offensive operations in built-up areas and the great assaults on cities such as Budapest and Berlin imposed very heavy losses on rifle and armored forces alike (Tables 10 and 11), demanding constant regrouping and improvisation in tactical organization.

The provision and maintenance of the required tactical densities (in men and weapons) could reduce losses and preserve the cohesion *(kompaktnost)* of formations operating on divergent axes of advance and with open flanks, while special attention was directed to maintaining the cohesion of the small units—even in the face of heavy losses—and, above all, the integrity of command and control, *upravlenie voiskami*. *Upravlenie voiskami* was perhaps one of the most critical measures of performance and effectiveness. The Soviet aim consisted of coordinating all the elements of a full combat deployment *(boevoi poryadok)* to effect the *rapid exploitation of the fire assault.*[9]

After a calamitous start, the Red Army made a remarkable recovery. Many of its victories were won in bludgeoning fashion, but this should not obscure the elements of mastery showed by Soviet commanders at all levels, not to mention the quality of Soviet weapons and the sturdiness of Soviet equipment. In many respects, Soviet performance was a paradox; centralization and inflexibility gave way to improvisation and rapid adaptability, doggedness to deftness, the unimaginative and the stolid to boldness and even dash. For all its shortcomings, the Red Army proved to be no mean precursor to the modern Soviet Army, which became at once the beneficiary of experience, tradition, and competence so dearly bought.

* * *

AT THE BEGINNING of 1946, as the first of more than 8 million men demobilized from the wartime armies made their way homewards, Stalin and the *Politburo* embarked on a comprehensive review of the Soviet wartime experience and a thorough appraisal of the structure of the Soviet armed forces. At the same time, they weighed the scope and nature of the military threat presented by the "imperialist powers"—so recently wartime allies of the Soviet Union. Demobilization of the massive wartime armies went hand in hand with reorganization and the introduction of significant changes into the Soviet high command. The three fighting services—army, navy, and air force—were not separately identified and were placed under a single unified command, the Minis-

Table 10

Loss Analysis/Tank Army Operations

Army	Operation	No. of tanks/ SP guns Initial Strength	Duration (days)	Total Units	Recycling rate: % initial strength	Total *write-off* losses	
						Nos.	% of initial strength
1 Gds Tk A	Belgorod-Kharkov	562	29	1,040	185	289	51.4
	Prokurov	549	36	1,317	240	523	95.2
	Lvov-Sandomierz	419	12	429	102.4	121	28.8
	E. Prussia	584	8	149	24.6	49	8.4
2 Gds Tk A	Orel	371	9	415	111.8	78	21.9
	Vistula-Oder	838	16	302	36	84	10
3 Gds Tk A	Vistula-Oder	922	19	520	56.4	183	19.8
4 Tk A	Orel	735	10	551	75	252	34.3
	Lvov	464	14	456	98	122	26.3
	Vistula-Oder	750	13	423	56.4	118	15.7
5 Gds Tk A	E. Prussia	585	25	421	72	210	35.9
Averages:		613	17	547	89.2	184	30

Table 11

Distribution/Characteristics of Tank Army Losses (Offensive Operations)

Operation	Army	Losses (in %)				
		Arty. Fire	Mines	due to Air Attack	'Faust-* patrone'	Various
Orel (43)	2 TA	76	14	10	–	–
	4 TA	68.5	8	17.7	–	5.8
Kiev (43)	3 Gd TA	94.8	2	.5	–	2.7
Lvov-Sandomierz (44)	3 Gd TA	80	6	14	–	–
	4 TA	91.8	3	3.4	–	1.8
Vistula-Oder (45)	3 Gd TA	88.5	2	9.5	–	–
	1 Gd TA	63.1	5.3	10.5	20	1.1
	2 Gd TA	79.5	2	1.5	–	17
	4 TA	78.5	9.5	1.0	6.2	4.8
Berlin (45)	2 Gd TA	58.7	5.8	6.6	24	4.9
	3 Gd TA	67.1	6.6	10.3	16	–

*Bazookas

try of the Armed Forces *(Ministerstvo Vooruzhennykh Sil)*, formally established in March 1946.[10] The "collegiate" supervision of the Ministry was vested in a Supreme Military Council *(Vysshii Voennyi Sovet)* with its membership drawn from the *Politburo*, the Central Committee, and senior military commanders. The wartime command agencies, the State Defense Committee (GKO) and the *Stavka*, had ceased to function as of September 1945. Immediate control of the three services devolved upon their respective Commanders-in-Chief and the Main Staffs. Command of the newly designated Soviet Army in the spring of 1946 went—not surprisingly—to Marshal Zhukov, unrivaled in his military skills and competence as the first soldier of the Soviet Union, but within months, and at Stalin's behest, Zhukov was unceremoniously shunted out of this post and bundled off to the Odessa Military District; his place as Ground Forces commander was assumed by his arch-rival Marshal Koniev.

Stalin's lesson to the Soviet senior command was blunt, immediate, and menacing. Any move toward political independence on the part of the armed forces, any thought of garnering the fruits of victory after this fashion, would not be tolerated. Even less would Stalin contemplate a "national," Russian army, a notion which may have accounted for the eclipse of General Gordov. Stalin evidently had not forgotten the 1942–1943 "rebellion" against political control in the interests of enhanced military efficiency, because when the war had been won he pursued his vindictive "purge of the heroes" which engulfed senior air force and naval officers (to mention but Novikov and Galler).[11] The consequence was rigidity and immobilism within the senior ranks, not only in terms of personal advancement but within the sphere of military doctrine and innovation, for Soviet commanders perforce subscribed to all the tenets of "Stalinist military science," nothing less than inflexible dogma which relegated surprise to the category of a "temporary" factor in modern war and which denigrated not only the atomic weapon but also "capitalist" capability as incapable of implementing the "permanent operating factors" adumbrated by Stalin and thus predetermining the defeat of such capitalist foes. Yet Stalin's public scorn of the atomic bomb did not preclude a desperate effort to produce a comparable Soviet weapon. The dilemma facing the Soviet command was how to integrate the new weapons produced by Soviet scientists into the framework of what was summarily ordained, Stalin's own "military science."

The enormous wartime army slowly dispersed in six demobilization stages that ultimately released all 33 age groups mobilized for war service. The first two releases occurred in 1945; the third main demobilization came in 1946 and was followed by the return of all older age groups to civilian life by 1947. Although careful planning and deliberate selection ensured that key men were retained and only 2.5 percent of those officers with higher military (or military-political) education were allowed to leave, the vast wartime tally of 520 divisions shrank steadily to 175 divisions, a diminution in numbers which was nevertheless accompanied by major reorganization designed to produce a more flexible and mobile force with greater shock power. In like fashion the number of military districts (MDs) organized within Soviet territory dwindled after discharging their role in the demobilization process much as they had previously managed mobilization. At the end of the war 33 military districts were operational; by the end of 1946 this number had fallen to 21. The Soviet Far East was something of an exception. In 1945 three military districts were created on the basis of wartime Fronts: the TransBaikal-Amur, the Maritime Provinces, and the Far Eastern MDs. This arrangement was further transformed in May 1947 when the TransBaikal MD became the command base *(upravlenie)* of the Commander-in-Chief Far Eastern Forces with operational control over the Maritime Provinces, the Far Eastern MDs, the Pacific Fleet, and the Amur Naval Flotilla—a TVD.[12]

Official Soviet figures set postwar strength after demobilization at 2,874,000 men, a figure which excluded frontier guards and internal security troops.[13] Substantial Soviet forces remained on station beyond the Soviet frontiers, with 29 divisions deployed in east-central and southeastern Europe, in the Soviet zone of Germany, in Poland, Hungary, Austria, Rumania, Bulgaria, and in the Far East in North Korea. Not only did these divisions guard the Soviet perimeter in a pattern of extended deployment stipulated by Stalin, but they were also instrumental in ensuring the installation of the various "People's Democracies" in eastern Europe and guaranteeing the eventual transition to one-party systems, all under the watchful guns of the Soviet Army. In Bulgaria Biryuzov's 37th Army kept up the pressure on Greece; in East Germany Soviet troops clamped on the Berlin blockade (1948–1949); in North Korea Chistyakov's 25th Army screened preparations for the attack that finally erupted into the Korean War.

Soviet forces within the Soviet Union proper were organized and deployed within the military districts (MDs). Divisions deployed abroad were designated "Groups of Forces," of which the largest in the western theater was that installed in East Germany, initially the Group of Soviet Occupation Troops in Germany (GSOVG), which became the Group of Soviet Forces in Germany (GSVG) with the creation of the German Democratic Republic (DDR) in 1949. GSOVG/GSVG was organized into six armies with a strength of 22 divisions (10 mechanized, 8 tank, and 4 rifle).[14] The Northern Group in Poland comprised 2 divisions (1

mechanized, 1 tank), while the Central Group (including Soviet occupation troops in Austria, as well as lines of communication forces in
Hungary and Rumania) amounted to 5 divisions (1 rifle division in
Austria, 2 mechanized divisions in Hungary, and 2 in Rumania), in all
29 divisions in this forward deployment. Behind the Soviet frontiers a
further force of 60 divisions was stationed in the western MDS, 40
divisions were deployed in the Soviet Far East, and the remaining 45
divisions were stationed in the Transcaucasus, the Central Asian regions, and the strategic interior.

Numbers alone, however impressive, did not represent the full
scene. The Soviet Army, the mainstay of the Soviet military system at
this time, and Stalin's deterrent against the American nuclear
monopoly, was undergoing major restructuring, incorporating both
the lessons of the recent war and the advances in military technology.
The rifle (infantry) component of the Soviet Army was based on the
combined-arms army *(obshchevoiskovaya armiya)* and on armored forces
reorganized into mechanized armies *(mekhanizironannye armii)*, replacing the wartime tank armies. The highest tactical entity within the
combined-arms army became the rifle corps; the basic tactical entity
became the rifle division, and the tank and mechanized corps were now
reorganized as tank and mechanized divisions. The corps echelon
disappeared in the armored forces, producing a mechanized army
consisting of two tank divisions and two mechanized divisions. The
combined-arms army could include three rifle corps, each corps having
three rifle divisions (or two rifle divisions and a mechanized division). A
brief profile of these postwar Soviet divisions demonstrates the degree
to which wartime lessons were being absorbed.[15]

RIFLE DIVISION

Horse drawn transport was replaced by motorization, the 1948 establishment providing 1,488 lorries, prime movers, and armored troop carriers as
compared to 419 in the establishment of 1944. A medium tank/self-
propelled gun regiment was added along with SP gun troops in the rifle
regiments, providing a tank strength of 52 tanks and 34 SP guns.

TANK DIVISIONS

This was a highly mobile formation of 252 medium and heavy tanks,
furnished with adequate motorized infantry to hold ground seized by the
armor and to provide protection for the armor, with an extra medium tank
battalion, but fewer rifle units, when compared with the mechanized division.

MECHANIZED DIVISION

These were fully motorized and embodied the lessons of the infantry/tank
team of the war; the mechanized regiment contained three rifle battalions

and a tank battalion, while the medium tank regiment and the heavy tank/SP gun regiment each had a rifle component of one motorized rifle battalion.

ARTILLERY DIVISION
These varied in manpower strength from 9,000 to 12,000 (for the heavy breakthrough divisions), with artillery complements to suit the particular operational assignments. These complements were composed of a light gun brigade, a howitzer brigade, a medium howitzer regiment, a medium gun regiment, an MRL brigade, and a heavy mortar brigade in various combinations. *Antiaircraft divisions* of 2,500 men and four regiments were included in the tally of artillery divisions.

CAVALRY DIVISION
These were retained on strength but not developed and were phased out in 1955.

Clearly the impress was upon mobility and firepower, with the tank and mechanized divisions receiving more tanks and greater artillery resources. The rifle divisions were reinforced with more tanks, SP guns, prime movers, and transport. All this was reflected in the revised postwar establishments (Tables 12, 13, and 14).

RIFLE DIVISION
manpower: 11,013
three rifle regiments,[16] a medium tank/SP gun regiment,
a gun and howitzer regiment,
52 medium tanks (T-34/85), 18 SU-76 (SP),
16 SU-100 (SP), 36 122-mm howitzers,
12 160-mm mortars, 18 120-mm mortars,
162 medium machine guns, 511 light machine guns,
6,208 rifles, 279 antitank rifles

TANK DIVISION
manpower: 10659
three medium tank regiments, a heavy tank/SP gun regiment, a motorized rifle regiment, a light AA and mortar regiment, a howitzer battery, 44 heavy tanks, 208 medium tanks, 21 heavy SP guns, 1,362 vehicles, 12 122-mm howitzers, 42, 120-mm mortars, 52 82-mm mortars, 405 light machine guns, and 6,112 rifles (the medium tank regiment consisted of 65 tanks and 3,660 men)

MECHANIZED DIVISION
manpower: 14,485
three mechanized regiments, a medium tank regiment, a heavy tank/SP gun regiment, a howitzer regiment, a mortar regiment, a light AA regiment and MRL battery, 21 heavy tanks, 183 medium tanks, 44 heavy SP guns, 1,667

Table 12

RIFLE DIVISION

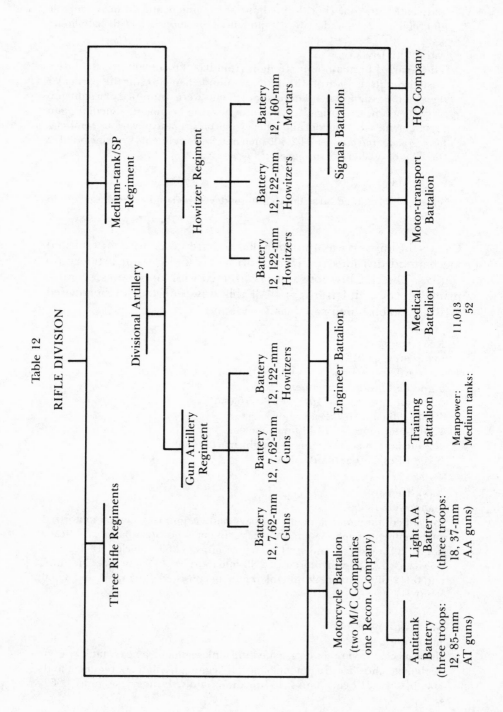

Manpower: 11,013
Medium tanks: 52

Table 13

TANK DIVISION

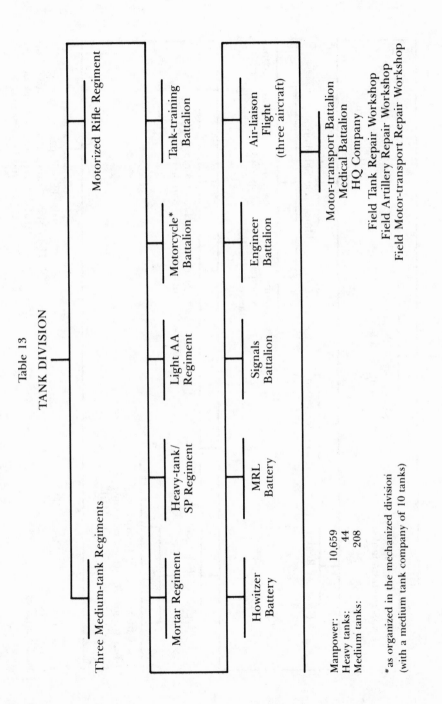

Three Medium-tank Regiments

Motorized Rifle Regiment

Mortar Regiment | Heavy-tank/SP Regiment | Light AA Regiment | Motorcycle* Battalion | Tank-training Battalion

Howitzer Battery | MRL Battery | Signals Battalion | Engineer Battalion | Air-liaison Flight (three aircraft)

Motor-transport Battalion
Medical Battalion
HQ Company

Field Tank Repair Workshop
Field Artillery Repair Workshop
Field Motor-transport Repair Workshop

Manpower: 10,659
Heavy tanks: 44
Medium tanks: 208

* as organized in the mechanized division
(with a medium tank company of 10 tanks)

Table 14

MECHANIZED DIVISION

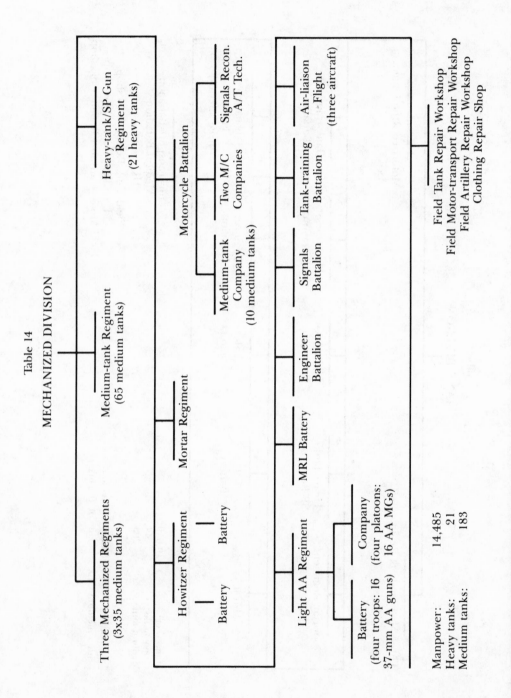

Three Mechanized Regiments
(3x35 medium tanks)

Medium-tank Regiment
(65 medium tanks)

Heavy-tank/SP Gun
Regiment
(21 heavy tanks)

Howitzer Regiment

Battery   Battery

Mortar Regiment

Motorcycle Battalion

Medium-tank
Company
(10 medium tanks)

Two M/C
Companies

Signals Recon.
A/T Tech.

Light AA Regiment

MRL Battery

Engineer
Battalion

Signals
Battalion

Tank-training
Battalion

Air-liaison
Flight
(three aircraft)

Battery   Company
(four troops: 16   (four platoons:
37-mm AA guns)   16 AA MGs)

Field Tank Repair Workshop
Field Motor-transport Repair Workshop
Field Artillery Repair Workshop
Clothing Repair Shop

Manpower: 14,485
Heavy tanks: 21
Medium tanks: 183

vehicles, 8 MRLS, 24 122-mm howitzers, 54 120-mm mortars, 100 82-mm mortars, 611 light machine guns, and 7,645 rifles

(the mechanized *regiment* consisted of 2,711 men and three motorized rifle battalions, a medium tank battalion with 35 T-34/85s, 257 vehicles, 6 120-mm mortars, 30 82-mm mortars, and 1,510 rifles)

In general composition, the Soviet Army was built around some 50–60 tank or mechanized divisions and 80–100 rifle and artillery divisions. One hint of the shape of things to come was the formation in July 1946 of the first Soviet rocket troop unit, formed from a Guards mortar regiment (MRL regiment).[17]

The huge wartime production of tanks, guns, and aircraft had already ceased to flow, but Soviet industry continued to turn out 5,000 tanks per year and 10,000 aircraft, including the first prototype jet fighters. In addition, the Soviet Army could draw on its very substantial tank-park, many of them the latest models such as the formidable IS-2 and IS-3 heavy tanks mounting a 122-mm gun with the even more advanced IS-4 waiting in the wings. Production of the IS-2 and the IS-3 continued through the 1940s, with later models utilizing the V-54 engine which came to be fitted to subsequent tank designs. Expansive though these resources were, Stalin pressed ahead with the updating and the modernization of a wide range of weapons and equipment for the ground forces, with armored fighting vehicles (AFVs) taking pride of place, tank modernization in the mid-1940s laying down the pattern of development for the coming decades. Already in 1944 the T-44 tank had appeared as a replacement for the T-34/85, involving changes in the turret design, hull area, and suspension (using a torsion bar arrangement)—a tank with a lower silhouette, powerful armament, substantial armor, and transversely mounted transmission system. An improved version of the T-44, the T-44M, was developed, but the attempt to fit the new tank with the D-10T 100-mm gun did not meet with unqualified success and only confirmed the limitation of the T-34 turret style. It was literally "back to the drawing board."

Expectations that the future would lie with the heavy tank proved to be mistaken. Recourse to the drawing board paid off when in 1947 the T-44M hull was modified to take a larger turret ring and with it a redesigned turret housing for the D-10T gun. This compared very favorably with the D-25T 122-mm gun of the IS series and was eminently capable of dealing with existing enemy armor. The modified hull, redesigned turret, and 100-mm gun made a triumphal entry upon the scene in 1947–1948 as the T-54, providing Soviet tank and mechanized units in 1949 with a highly advanced medium tank that became the forerunner of a whole series of Soviet main battle tanks. As such, the T-54 deserves more than passing mention. With a combat weight of 35 tons, the T-54 had a cross-country speed of 31 mph. It was manned by a crew of four, the commander and gunner occupying the left half of the turret, the loader the right half in a severely constricted space. The stadiametric system for fire control reduced accuracy at longer ranges, while reloading the gun meant maximum elevation followed by resighting. In a number of respects the T-54 represented the lessons learned from the improved transmission of the T-44M and the hull and turret configurations of the IS tanks. As for the distinctive turret, in early models the crab shell shape had a rear overhand (plus numerous shot traps), although this was eliminated in the third production version.

In addition to the new tanks, the ground forces at this time received a wide variety of updated and modernized equipment, not least improved artillery and heavy mortars. Artillery units acquired the new 85-mm D-48 antitank gun, the D-74 122-mm gun, the M-46 130-mm field gun, the M-47 152-mm gun, and the 240-mm mortar.[18] Rifle units were issued the new Kalashnikov machine carbine and the Goryunov heavy machine gun, plus recoilless antitank hollow charge weapons. Two new regimental armored personnel carriers were introduced, the BTR-40 and the BTR-152 (although the latter took some time to achieve series production). Based on the German Sd. Kfz.-247 four- and six-wheeled models, the BTR-40 was based on the GAZ-63A lorry and the BTR-152 on the ZIL-151 truck. IS hulls were also converted to a troop carrying role. To manage the increased number of vehicles and transport, the independent Auto-Tractor Service (*Avtotraktornya sluzhba*) was set up in 1949, a sign that motorization was making considerable progress. Artillery prime movers received new equipment in place of the older wartime tracked vehicles, thereby increasing the speed of movement from 6–10 km/h to 25–30. In 1950 the AT-T artillery tractor came into service; it was the largest such tractor available and was subsequently adapted as a prime mover for tactical missiles, the BAT bulldozer, and the BTM trench digger. Antiaircraft artillery was also updated with the introduction of the newer models of the 57-mm and 100-mm guns, while the celebrated Katyushas—MRLS— emerged as the BM-14 and the BM-24 to replace the wartime M-8 and M-13.

Inevitably Soviet commanders saw their operational-tactical requirements through the prism of the recent war. Offensive operations assumed pride of place, with major offensives conducted by groups of Fronts, where a Front might consist of three to four combined-arms armies or mechanized armies with an air army in support. An encirclement operation would normally be carried out by two Fronts with a third committed in the final state. Combined-arms armies were assigned to break the enemy line on the flanks of the force to be encircled; mechanized elements moved through the gap and completed their pincer movement to be followed in turn by rifle divisions forming an inner perimeter as the mechanized forces drove out to establish the outer perimeter. This constituted the double encirclement operation. Equally, a Front would breach the enemy defenses at a number of points, with armor committed once operational depth had been attained—the armor striking to a depth of 200 miles.

Leaning on and learning from wartime "superiority norms," the Soviet Army turned to improving on them in the postwar period, envisaging tactical densities of 304 rifle battalions, 180–240 guns, and 20–30 tanks (of SP guns) for each kilometer of the breakthrough sector. Above all, the number of tanks had to be increased, hence the inclusion within the rifle division of a tank/self-propelled gun regiment and the adding of a mechanized division to the rifle corps. Similarly, the frontage for offensive operations of a division was increased to four kilometers, that of a regiment to two kilometers. Deep echeloning also became the order of the day as the equipment piled up. Lead detachments *(peredovye otriady)*[19] now assumed greater importance as small, combined-arms, mobile elements for increasing *tempo*. The war had also indicated that committing tank and mechanized formations to completing the breaching of the main defensive positions appreciably increased tempo, although these forces suffered substantial losses in the process. Postwar practice, therefore, assigned this task to the rifle corps suitably reinforced with a mechanized division. In sum, postwar operational-tactical doctrine envisaged expanding the depth of the simultaneous neutralization of the defensive system, a general spatial expansion of the battle, an increase in the role of tactical air in providing fire resources and augmenting the shock power and mobility of divisional and corps second echelons, together with using these elements along the lines of army mobile groups and developing the means to conduct offensive operations off the march. Nor did Soviet tacticians neglect defensive operations, with special emphasis on increasing depth, densities, and antitank measures.

It was assumed that Front offensive operations would begin with breaching prepared defenses, or a breakthrough into hastily prepared defensive positions or, yet again, breaking into fortified districts, although *meeting engagements* either at the outset or during the course of these operations were not excluded. Breaching the enemy defenses was assigned to the rifle divisions, with tank and mechanized divisions in the first echelon only where the defenses had been hastily *(pospeshno)* erected. The assault would be initiated with infantry support tanks, artillery, and ground-attach (close support) aircraft, with mechanized divisions forming the second echelon of the rifle corps and assigned to complete the breakthrough of the main defensive positions. The second defensive line would be taken off the march. The enemy tactical defensive positions would be breached on the first day of offensive operations. The breakthrough into operational depth would be effected by the Front mobile group consisting of a mechanized army to be committed on the second day of the offensive on a frontage of 8–12 kilometers and operating with artillery and air support. Properly supplied with combat engineer support, the mechanized army would break away from the main assault force, smash enemy reserves and close the encirclement ring in cooperation with other Front mobile groups and with airborne drops. Airborne troops in divisional strength might well be employed to seize bridgeheads and key river crossing points, sections of coastline, road junctions, aerodromes, and command/communications centers.

Formidable though the Soviet Army appeared to be, looming over Europe with its assembly of divisions, it was in fact rather thinly stretched, maintaining at Stalin's command ground and tactical air forces from the Elbe to the Kurile Islands. Nominal order of battle was undoubtedly impressive, with scores of Soviet divisions apparently squaring off to a mere nine Western divisions (American, French, and British) at the time of the Berlin blockade, but closer inspection reveals that many of these Soviet divisions had been "hollowed out" to mere regimental strength at a time of reorganization and reequipping. The myth that all the Russians needed to reach the Channel was boots had begun to be perpetuated, an unconscious tribute to the deterrent effect of the Soviet Army as it held Western Europe hostage to any US atomic assault on the Soviet Union and thus fending off preventive war.

Not that the Soviet Army neglected the task of organizing and equipping its allies. By 1949, with communist governments firmly in power in Eastern Europe, Stalin embarked on the expansion and "Sovietization" of these regional military forces, imposing the Soviet military pattern on these disparate and even disorganized armies. Substantial Soviet military missions assumed both staff and command functions in Eastern Europe, supervising the introduction of the quantities of Soviet military equipment shipped to these armies. In Poland Marshal Rokossovskii became Minister of Defense and directed the restructuring of the Polish Army. The 10th Section of the Soviet General Staff, charged initially with supervision of the bilateral security treaties signed with the East European states and also responsible for monitoring the situation in East Germany, took charge of this coordination program and laid the groundwork of what was to become the Warsaw Pact. Military integration made little progress at this time, with the possible exception of air defense, but at least the East European officer corps were shaped more nearly to Soviet requirements and some 50 divisions added to a nominal order of battle, although less than half of these could be considered at all battleworthy.

In 1946 the Soviet Army withdrew from Manchuria, taking with it large quantities of machines and industrial equipment as the spoils of war, and allowing the Chinese communists only relatively small amounts of tanks and aircraft available from captured stocks. With the end of the civil war in China and the advent of a communist government, the Soviet Union and China signed a treaty of friendship and mutual assistance, after which a Soviet military mission and 3,000 Soviet advisers were despatched to China. The Soviet aid program was as expensive as it was extensive, involving the Chinese in heavy debts to the Soviet Union. Even more complicated was the situation over the Korean War, which the Chinese had not initiated but in which they became deeply involved and for which they had to pay. Chinese officers supplied the Soviet mission with their information about and impressions of US military capability. American assets included close battlefield coordination between infantry, artillery, and tactical air; effective artillery and tactical air support; powerful long-range artillery support; high maneuvrability with artillery resources; and on the battlefield at large, infantry well equipped with automatic weapons and good troop control. On the debit side was the flabbiness of the infantry in attack and the sloppiness in defense, reluctance to operate without air and artillery support, little stomach for either hand-to-hand fighting or night operations, and fear of being outflanked or encircled. American soldiers attacked frontally with the tanks well up in close support. Whatever the value of these lessons, the Soviet command bought them cheaply and at second hand from Chinese commanders.[20]

In spite of the burst of modernization undertaken after the war, it became apparent towards the end of Stalin's life in 1952 that a certain blight was creeping over the Soviet military establishment. The creation of NATO and the assertion of American military power in Korea had given even Stalin cause to think. The Soviet high command was in disarray; Shtemenko proved to be a monumental flop as Chief of the General Staff and Koniev had been removed from command of the ground forces. In a reported attempt to subdue rebellious Yugoslavia, Shtemenko at the General Staff and Koniev in the Carpathian Military District worked out a plan for military operations which Marshal Zhukov—drawn back from his exile in the Urals Military District—tore to shreds for its unworkability and dangerous incompetence. Stalin replaced Shtemenko with Marshal Sokolovskii as Chief of the General

Staff and countenanced the readmission, if it can be called that, of Zhukov. Bit by bit the Soviet ground forces were called in from their remote billets.

On 1 March 1953 Stalin succumbed to a stroke and died within days, dispelling the nightmare of the "Doctors' plot" which hung menacingly over the heads of senior Soviet commanders. The new leadership at once redistributed posts within the high command, merging the Ministries of War and the Navy once again into a unified Ministry of Defense under Marshal Bulganin.[21] Marshal Vasilevskii and Marshal Zhukov became First Deputy Ministers of Defense. Shtemenko, erstwhile Chief of the General Staff, was actually demoted. Above all, the Soviet command "discovered" the nuclear weapon, hidden hitherto under the verbal wraps of Stalin's military dogma. More to the point, the Soviet Union exploded its own hydrogen bomb in August 1953, thus giving added urgency to a reappraisal of the Soviet military outlook, one which threw off Stalinist restrictions and led to a revised military doctrine. Preparations had to be made to meet a nuclear war situation, involving a radical review of each element of Soviet capability, not least the ground forces.

With Zhukov at the helm as Defense Minister (from February 1955–October 1957) the ground forces were given a leaner and more mobile look, accompanied by manpower reductions in 1955 advertised by Khrushchev as part of a unilateral Soviet move towards disarmament. The completion of the State Treaty of 1955 with Austria was the signal to announce the transfer to the reserve of a number of men equal to the number to be withdrawn from Austria (estimated at 50,000). The equivalent of one to two divisions moved henceforth into Hungary which became the main base for the Soviet Southern Group of Forces. During the period 1955–1957, 1,840,000 men were released from the armed forces, although it was only later that Khrushchev revealed that total Soviet strength was 5.7 million before this demobilization, thus disclosing a very substantial mobilization during the Korean War period.[22] Soviet announcements intimated that "63 divisions and independent brigades" had been disbanded, although no hint was offered as to the manner in which this affected the order of battle.

In the years 1954–1959 nuclear weapons thrust themselves to the forefront of Soviet attention, demanding changes in structure and tactics. Marshal Koniev again assumed command of the ground forces in 1955, but the master plan for radical change was developed and implemented by Marshal Zhukov himself. The reduction in manpower, whatever its political and economic advantages, assisted appreciably in this new rationalization and further modernization. To fit the nuclear battlefield, Zhukov required more mobile and flexible formations, eliminating the corps as an intermediate echelon between army and division and restructuring Soviet rifle and armored/mechanized formations. The mechanized army and the mechanized division disappeared, the latter being apparently too unwieldy for the fast moving operations envisaged by Zhukov. Henceforth, the ground forces would consist of only two main types of division, the *motor-rifle division* (MR division, *motostrelkovaya diviziya,* MSD) and the *tank division,* with tank armies comprising three to four tank divisions and combined-arms armies formed with three to four motor-rifle divisions and a tank division, and with air support for both types of army coming from tactical air resources under Front control. The tank came to predominate as never before, with a combined-arms army having more than 1,000 tanks and the tank army almost 1,500.

With the nuclear weapon fully admitted into the Soviet arsenal and its effects generally recognized, tactical requirements were drastically revised, particularly the relationship between fire, shock power, and maneuver. Hitherto, maneuver had been largely a matter of the speedy positioning of forces to mount their own blow or to parry an enemy blow, but the nuclear weapon employed on the battlefield now transformed maneuver into the process of exploiting the nuclear strike to the fullest degree in order to make the deepest penetration into the depth of enemy defenses or, conversely, to counter-maneuver by moving Soviet troops out of range of any impending nuclear blow.[23] In brief, the battlefield had expanded, increasing attack frontages, the depth of assigned missions, and the *tempo* of offensive operations. The radiation environment was now a factor of great importance and thus amplified the role of reconnaissance, as well as the tactics of operating in an irradiated battlefield. In offensive operations, the breakthrough could now be effected not only from positions maintained in direct contact with the enemy, but also off the march, where tactical densities (men and weapons) were appreciably reduced. Artillery and air support would be combined into a single mode of fire preparation, although the duration of this support must inevitably decline.

Tactical deployment had also to be reviewed against the requirement of maximum exploitation of both the nuclear strike and conventional fires. This did not preclude the general principle of mounting a massive fire assault throughout the depth of enemy defenses and constantly intensifying the weight of the assault, although the tank was, if anything, singled out for special attention, for it could fill gaps torn in the assault forces or even take over the role of the first echelon decimated by nuclear strikes. Equally, lead detachments and airborne units could be used to exploit the nuclear strike with the "tactical air landing operation" designed either to eliminate enemy mass destruction weapons or to close breaches opened by enemy nuclear strikes.

The *meeting engagement*[24] now became a focus of Soviet attention, since it could develop in the course of *all* types of military operations. It was essential to organize combat groups capable of forestalling the enemy's recourse to nuclear weapons or use of conventional weapons, the deployment of the main body of his forces, and the launching of an attack. Lead detachments should under these circumstances be reinforced with tactical airborne forces. In line with standard Soviet doctrine that in the meeting engagement the enemy forces were best eliminated "in packets," both frontal and flank attacks should be directed against those gaps in the enemy lines already opened by nuclear strikes. Under modern nuclear conditions, the meeting engagement would be marked by substantial dispersion in combat deployment and the order of march, the use of tactical airborne forces, the limitation of *time* available in which to organize the operation and implement interaction *(vzaimodeistvie)*, and reliance on *frontal attack* as the most effective way of "winning time" and splitting enemy forces into separate pockets. As for defensive tactics, Soviet practice presupposed extending defensive frontages (including battalion and even company "defensive sectors," prepared positions, and trenches dispersed to reduce losses), deepening and dispersing the echelon system, and developing the stability of antinuclear defense.[25]

One immediate consequence was an increase in "armament norms," particularly tanks and armored personnel carriers, whose annual production was running at 5,000–6,500 and 10,000 respectively, with 20 tank factories working for the ground forces and supported also by "shadow factories" with tank workshops capable of rapid expansion and volume production. In 1955 a new version of the T-54, the T-54A with an improved gun (the D-10TG 100-mm) was unveiled. The gun was now gyrostabilized and had power elevation, while some vehicles had snorkel equipment and additional fuel capacity. In 1957–1958 yet another version of the T-54, the T-54B, entered service equipped with a two-plane stabilizer for the improved D-10T2S gun, infrared night vision devices, and full snorkel equipment. The T-54X acted as a bridge between the T-54 and the T-55 series, the T-55 incorporated the improved V-54 engine, an improved transmission, and a rotating turret floor. Although heavy tank divisions had become a thing of the past, the heavy tank received a boost with the advent of the T-10.[26] Weighing 49 tons and with a crew of four, the T-10 mounted the D-25T 122-mm gun and two 14.5-mm machine guns. Both the newer motor-rifle divisions and the tank divisions were receiving increased numbers of tanks and APCs, a tank-heavy development which ultimately gave the motor-rifle division the look of a semiarmored division.

With the introduction of tactical missiles, the short-range rocket FROG (free rocket over ground) as a divisional weapon, a tactical ballistic missile with a range of some 150 miles, and a cruise missile (range up to 300 miles), the role of conventional artillery was inevitably reduced but by no means eliminated.

The modernization of the Soviet ground forces, which extended over almost a whole decade, proceeded in circumstances both uneasy and turbulent, due in no small degree to the personality and the policies of Nikita Khrushchev. In 1956, as de-Stalinization began to bite, the Soviet Army was flung into limited conventional warfare in Hungary, crushing the revolution which had begun with a severe military reverse inflicted on two Soviet mechanized divisions. At Zhukov's command, Soviet forces returned in force to crush popular resistance in bloody fighting. Here was both tragedy and irony, for it was only months before, in May 1955, that signing of the Warsaw Treaty ushered in the framework of a socialist military alliance under the aegis of the Warsaw Pact, with the Joint Command headed by Marshal Koniev. Khrushchev's mind, however, was scarcely fixed on "socialist military integration." The launching in 1957 of the first Soviet ICBM and the first ever artificial satellite, the famous Sputnik, implanted in him the notion of the primacy of nuclear weapons and strategic missiles— finally unveiled in the military "new look" he announced in January 1960. Within the *Politburo* he succeeded in displacing Marshal Zhukov, stripping the Marshal simultaneously of his Central Committee membership and replacing him as Defense Minister with Marshal Malinovskii. A.A. Grechko, hitherto Commander-in-Chief of GSVG, took over the ground forces.

These two events had profound consequences for the ground forces. Although Malinovskii continued Zhukov's modernization policy by cutting down manpower, increasing mobility and firepower, phasing out mechanized formations, and replacing the mechanized army with the tank army, the eclipse of Zhukov allowed Khrushchev a much freer hand in shaping military policy and facilitated a tighter political control over the armed forces at large, while the newly emergent senior command group was linked to Khrushchev through personal and wartime, professional ties. The ground forces were being steadily slimmed down to a total of 140 divisions in place of the bloated total of 175, even as two successful nuclear weapons tests in 1958 seemingly infused Khrushchev with confidence enough to pin his faith on strategic weapons, deposing the ground forces as "queen of the battlefield" and installing the Strategic Missile Forces (formally established in 1959) as the primary arm. To the consternation of many commanders but to the plaudits of others, Khrushchev at the beginning of 1960 broke through all doctrinal taboos by insisting unequivocally on the strategic *decisiveness* of nuclear weapons; the conventional ground forces, the surface navy, and the tactical air forces would be cut by *one-third*.

Notes

1. The designation *Raboche-Krest'yanskaya Krasnaya Armiya (RKKA)*, the Red Army (and the general abbreviation of *Krasnaya Armiya*), spanned the years 1918–1946. The term Soviet Army, *Sovetskaya Armiya (SA)* was introduced in 1946. The postwar reorganization defined three branches *(vid)* of the Soviet Armed Forces, the Ground Forces *(Sukhoputnye voiska)*, Air Force *(Voenno-vozdushnye sily)*, and Navy *(Voenno-morskoi flot)*. It is worth noting that "Soviet Army" is sometimes used to denote the Soviet Armed Forces at large.

2. The first tank armies (with "mixed" establishments, including rifle troops) were raised between May 1942–January, 1943. The 5th Tank Army in this phase was *twice* constituted—in May 1942 and again in August 1942. The first of the "homogeneous" tank armies (comprising tank and mechanized corps) was 2d Tank Army raised on 28 January 1943 and followed two days later by 1st Tank Army. The last of these tank armies, the 6th, was established in January 1944.

3. The *mechanized corps* was made up of two tank and one motorized division, the *tank division* of two tank and one motor-rifle regiment, the *motorized division* of two motor-rifle and one tank regiment.

4. Marshal of the Soviet Union M.N. Tukhachevskii was executed with other senior Soviet commanders in 1937 in Stalin's military purge.

5. RAG (regimental artillery group), DAG (divisional artillery group).

6. The Ilyushin Il-2 low-level ground-attack aircraft equipped these formations, the TsBB-55 or BsH-2 *(bronirovannyi shturmovik)* flying first as a prototype in 1938, entered serial production in March 1941 as the Il-2, some 35,000 being produced as the war progressed. *Shturmovik* is often rendered as *stormovik*.

7. The *Katyusha* multiple-rocket launchers (also christened "Stalin's organ pipes") were organized into Guards mortar regiments (GMCh), equipped with the BM-8-48, BM-13, and BM-31-13 MRLs. The first MRL battery was organized on 29 June 1941 (7 launchers, 3,000 missiles) and went into action on 14 July 1941; in Jaunary 1945 the Red Army had 500 MRL battalions (2,993 launchers).

8. As reported by the Soviet 3d Army, Byelorussian operations, July 1944.

9. This coordination involved the first echelon with the second, with a combined-arms reserve, and with the antitank (artillery) reserve and artillery groups. It also included cooperation with neighboring units, as well as *internal* coordination between infantry and artillery and armor and combat engineers, and the battlefield interaction of the infantry/tank team with artillery and tactical units.

10. The People's Commissariat for the Armed Forces briefly replaced the *two* wartime Commissariats (Defense and Navy), giving way in turn like all Commissariats to the redesignation as "Ministries" enacted on 15 March 1946.

11. Air Chief Marshal Novikov was Commander-in-Chief of the Soviet Air Force, Admiral Galler Chief of the Main Naval Staff.

12. A theater of operations *(teatr voennykh deisty)* command, the only one to exist in the peacetime USSR.

13. For one of the very few detailed discussions of Soviet demobilization, see V.N. Donchenko, "Demobilizatsiya Sovetskoi Armii i reshenie problemy kadrov v pervye poslevoennye gody," *Istoriya SSSR* (1970, no. 3), pp. 96–102, particularly the "resettlement" aspects.

14. These six armies were the 3d Shock, 3d and 8th Guards Armies, 1st, 3d, and 4th mechanized Armies, supported by the 24th Air Army.

15. Airborne forces were, in June 1946, subordinated directly to the Armed Forces Ministry, with parachute and air-landing (glider) elements formed from airborne brigades and select rifle divisions.

16. As Soviet sources point out, the rifle regiment now included a battery of SU-76 SP guns (six guns) and otherwise consisted of three rifle battalions (1,668 men). The rifle regiment had a total strength of 2,108 men, 194 vehicles, 27 82-mm mortars, and 1,263 rifles.

17. This was at the insistence of M.I. Nedelin, Chief of Staff/Soviet Artillery, who selected the best artillery specialists from wartime days and particular Guards mortar regiments to form further missile units, and who established a special staff to study the problems of organization and operational use for the new weapons.

18. Apart from these new pieces, the Model 1944 85-mm divisional gun, the 100-mm field gun, and the Model 1938 122-mm howitzer, together with the 120-mm and the 160-mm mortars were improved and updated for current service.

19. Also translated as "forward detachments" or "advanced detachments" or even "spearheads." See Captain Stephen Shervals Jr, USAF, "'Forward Detachments' and the Soviet Nuclear Offensive," *Military Review* (April 1979) pp. 66–71.

20. For an account of the Soviet Military Mission to China, see Lieutenant-General G.G. Semenov, *Tri goda v Pekine*, Moscow: "Nauka," 1978, p. 102 on discussions of the Korean War.

21. In February 1950 Stalin split the Armed Forces Ministry into two separate ministries, the War Ministry *(Voenno Ministerstvo)* and the Navy Ministry *(Voenno-morskoe Ministerstvo)*. The new combined Defense Ministry set up in March 1953 had the Main Military Council *(Glavnyi voennyi sovet)* as its collegiate body, reviving a designation from the immediate prewar years (1938–1941).

22. This is to assume that the 1948 figure for the Soviet military establishment was, in fact, correct at 2,874,000 men.

23. "The *anti-nuclear manoeuvre* stands out separately among the known forms of manoeuvre as the newest form of manoeuvre, consisting of organized movements of troops to take them out of range of the enemy's nuclear attack and give them freedom to perform their missions," *Manoeuvre in Modern Land Warfare*, p. 35.

24. Note the two terms, *vstrechnyi boi* and *vstrechnoe srazhenie*, the former tactical (and comparable to the hasty attack), the latter at the operational level (armies, Fronts). The tactics rely upon rapid deployment from the line of

march with artillery and antitank reserves well forward, providing a firm fire base, the object being to deploy and defeat the enemy rapidly before he can deploy his forces into attack formation.

25. For a contemporary survey, see V. Pozdnyakov, "Atomic Defense in the Soviet Army," *Bulletin* (Munich) (August 1955, no. 8), pp. 13–19, with summaries of Soviet instructions on reconnaissance, radiation detection, and decontamination.

26. The T-10 was originally the IS-10 and the culmination of experiments with the IS models IS-6/7/8/9 as well as the realization that the IS-3M required upgrading in the light of lessons learned in Korea.

1 / Reference Works

Introduction

THE PURPOSE OF this section is twofold: first, to present tools that should prove useful in updating this guide and for additional research into the complexities of the Soviet Army; and second, to point out those titles that have, in different ways, a general impact either on the topic or on the formation of background knowledge useful to those who wish to deal with it.

Current and retrospective English-language sources on the Russian ground forces may be located in the bibliographies, abstracts, and indexes cited in parts A, B, and C. Data on the operational and political impact of these land troops are reviewed in citations in parts D and E. Terminology useful in interpreting language or concepts in some of the works cited in this book can be found in the dictionaries numbered in part F. General biographies of people of importance involved in some fashion with Soviet military power during our period are included among the citations in part G. Users should also be certain to check footnotes and bibliographies in any of the materials cited in the various other sections and parts of this guide.

A. Bibliographies

1.   *ABS Guide to Recent Publications in the Social and Behavioral Sciences.* New York: American Behavioral Scientist, 1965.

2.   *ABS Guide to Recent Publications in the Social and Behavioral Sciences: Supplements.* Beverly Hills, Calif.: Sage, 1966–.

3.   Albrecht, Ulrich, et al. *A Short Research Guide on Arms and Armed Forces.* New York: Facts on File, 1980. 112p.

4.   *American Bibliography of Russian and East European Studies.* Bloomington: Indiana University Press, 1960–. v. 4–.

1

5.   *American Bibliography of Slavic and East European Studies.*
Bloomington: Indiana University Press, 1956–1959. v. 1–3.

6.   *American Book Publishing Record.* New York: R. R. Bowker,
1960–. v. 1–.

7.   American Historical Association. *Writings on American History.*
Washington, D.C.: U.S. Government Printing Office, 1947–
1961.   This valuable research tool was not published during World
War II.

8.   _____ . *Writings on American History, 1962–1973.* 4 vols. New
York: Kraus Reprint, 1975.

9.   _____ . *Writings on American History, 1974–.* New York: Kraus
Reprint, 1976–.

10.   _____ . Committee for the Study of War Documents. *Guides
to German Records Microfilmed at Alexandria.* Washington, D.C.: U.S.
National Archives and Records Service, 1958–. no. 1–.

11.   American Security Council Foundation. Center for International Security Studies. *Quarterly Strategic Bibliography.* Boston, Mass.,
1976–. v. 1–.

12.   Armstrong, John A. "Recent Soviet Publications on World War
II." *Slavic Review* 31 (September 1962), 508–519.

13.   Attar, Chand. *Bibliography of Indo-Soviet Relations, 1947–1977.*
New York: Sterling Publications, 1978. 152p.

14.   Bayliss, Gwyn M. *Bibliographic Guide to the Two World Wars: An
Annotated Survey of English-Language Reference Materials.* London and
New York: R. R. Bowker, 1977. 578p.

15.   *Bibliography of Asian Studies.* Ann Arbor, Mich.: Association for
Asian Studies, 1957–. v. 1–.

16.   Bloomberg, Marty, and Hans H. Weber. *World War II and Its
Origins: A Select Annotated Bibliography of Books in English.* Littleton,
Colo.: Libraries Unlimited, 1975. 311p.

17.   "Books and Ideas." *Air University Review.* Maxwell AFB, Ala.:
Air University, 1959–. v. 10–.

18.   *Books on Demand Subject Guide: 84,000 Selected Books Available as
On-Demand Reprints.* Ann Arbor, Mich.: University Microfilms International, 1977. 786p.

19.   *British Books in Print: The Reference Catalogue of Current Literature—Author, Title, and Subject Index.* London and New York: R. R. Bowker, 1967–. v. 1–.

20.   Burns, Richard D., and Susan Hoffman, comps. *The SALT Era: A Selected Bibliography.* Political Issues Series, v. 6, no. 1. Rev. ed. Los Angeles: Center for the Study of Armament and Disarmament, California State University, 1979. 59p.

21.   Burt, Richard. *Congressional Hearings on American Defense Policy, 1947–1971: A Bibliography.* Lawrence: University Press of Kansas, 1974. 377p.

22.   Byrnes, Robert F. *Bibliography of American Publications on East Central Europe, 1945–1957.* Slavic and East European Series, no. 12. Bloomington: Indiana University Press, 1958. 213p.

23.   Conover, Helen F., comp. *The Defense of Leningrad, 1941–1944: Writings Published in America.* Washington, D.C.: General Reference and Bibliography Division, Library of Congress, 1946. 26p.

24.   Cooling, B. Franklin, 3d, and Alan Millett. *Doctoral Dissertations in Military Affairs: A Bibliography.* Bibliography Series, no. 10. Manhattan: Kansas State University Library, 1972. 153p.   Updated in the April issue of *Military Affairs,* 1973–.

25.   Council on Foreign Relations. *The Foreign Affairs 50-Year Bibliography: New Evaluations of Significant Books on International Relations, 1920–1970.* New York: R. R. Bowker, 1970. 936p.

26.   Craig, Hardin. *A Bibliography of Encyclopedias and Dictionaries Dealing with Military, Naval and Maritime Affairs, 1577–1971.* 4th rev. ed. Houston, Tex.: Rice University, 1971. 134p.

27.   *Cumulative Bibliography of Asian Studies.* 2 vols. Boston, Mass.: G. K. Hall, 1969–1972.

28.   *The Cumulative Book Index.* New York: H. W. Wilson, 1939–.

29.   Dallin, Alexander, comp. *The German Occupation of the USSR in World War II: A Bibliography.* External Research Paper. Washington, D.C.: Office of Intelligence and Research, U.S. Department of State, 1955. 96p.

30.   DeVore, Ronald M. *The Arab-Israeli Conflict: A Historical, Political, Social, and Military Bibliography.* War/Peace Series, no. 5. Santa Barbara, Calif.: ABC-Clio, 1976. 273p.

31.   Draughon, Donnie W. *The Central Intelligence Agency's Reference Aid Series: A List.* Washington, D.C.: Document Expediting Project, Exchange and Gift Division, Library of Congress, 1979. 6p.

32.   Enser, A. G. S. *A Subject Bibliography of the Second World War: Books in English, 1939–1974.* Boulder, Colo.: Westview Press, 1977. 592p.

33.   Erickson, John. "The Soviet Union at War, 1941–1945: An Essay on Sources and Studies." *Soviet Studies* 14 (January 1963), 249–274.

34.   Foreign Affairs, Editors of. *Foreign Affairs Bibliography: A Selected and Annotated List of Books on International Relations, 1919–1962.* 4 vols. New York: Harper, 1933–1962.   Readers should also consult the new titles section in each quarterly issue of *Foreign Affairs.*

35.   *Forthcoming Books.* New York: R. R. Bowker, 1966–. v. 1–.

36.   Freidel, Frank, ed. *Harvard Guide to American History.* Rev. ed. 2 vols. Cambridge, Mass.: Harvard University Press, 1974.

37.   Funk, Arthur L., comp. *The Second World War, a Bibliography: A Select List of Publications Appearing since 1968.* Gainesville, Fla.: American Committee on the History of the Second World War, 1972. 32p.

38.   Garrison, Lloyd W., ed. *ABC POL SCI: A Bibliography of Contents: Political Science and Government.* Santa Barbara, Calif.: ABC-Clio, 1969–. v. 1–.

39.   Gordon, Colin. *The Atlantic Alliance: A Bibliography.* New York: Nichols Publishing, 1978. 216p.

40.   Great Britain. British Museum. Department of Printed Books. *Catalogue of Printed Books: Additions.* London: Clowes, 1963–. v. 1–.

41.   _____ . *Subject Catalogue of Modern Books Acquired, 1941–1945.* London: H.M. Stationery Office, 1953.

42.   Great Britain. Public Records Office. *The Second World War: A Guide to Documents in the Public Records Office.* Handbook, no. 15. London: H.M. Stationery Office, 1972. 303p.

43.   Halasj de Beky, I. L. *A Bibliography of the Hungarian Revolution, 1956.* Toronto, Ont.: University of Toronto Press, 1963. 179p.

44.   Hammond, Thomas T., ed. and comp. *Soviet Foreign Relations and World Communism: A Selected, Annotated Bibliography of 7,000 Books in 30 Languages.* Princeton, N.J.: Princeton University Press, 1965. 1,240p.

45.   Higham, Robin, ed. *Official Histories: Essays and Bibliographies from Around the World.* Manhattan: Kansas State University Library, 1970. 644p.

46.   _____ , and Donald J. Mrozek, eds. *A Guide to the Sources of United States Military History: Supplement I.* Hamden, Conn.: Shoe String Press, 1981. 416p.

47.   Holler, Frederick L., comp. *Information Sources of Political Science.* 3d ed. Santa Barbara, Calif.: ABC-Clio, 1981.

48.   Horecky, Paul L., ed. *East Central Europe: A Guide to Basic Sources.* Chicago, Ill.: University of Chicago Press, 1969. 956p.

49.   _____ . *Southeastern Europe: A Guide to Basic Sources.* Chicago, Ill.: University of Chicago Press, 1969. 755p.

50.   Icks, Robert J. "Books about Armor." *Armor* 81 (January 1972), 53-58; (April 1972), 43–45.

51.   *International Bibliography of Political Science.* Chicago, Ill.: Aldine, 1952–. v. 1–.

52.   *International Information Service: A Quarterly Annotated Index of Selected Materials on Current International Affairs.* Chicago, Ill.: Library of International Affairs, 1963–. v. 1–.

53.   Kanet, Roger E. *Soviet and East European Foreign Policy: A Bibliography of English- and Russian-Language Publications, 1967–1971.* Santa Barbara, Calif.: ABC-Clio, 1974. 208p.

54.   Kennedy, James R., Jr. *Guide to Reference Sources on Africa, Asia, Latin America and the Caribbean, Middle East and North Africa, Russia and East Europe: Selected and Annotated.* Williamsport, Pa.: Bro-Dart, 1972. 73p.

55.   Kuehl, Warren F., comp. *Dissertations in History: An Index of Dissertations Completed in History Departments of United States and Canadian Universities, 1873–1970.* 2 vols. Lexington: University Press of Kentucky, 1972.

56.   Lang, Kurt. *Military Institutions and the Sociology of War.* Beverly Hills, Calif.: Sage, 1972. 337p.

57.   Michel, Henri, and Jean Marie D'Hoop. *The Two World Wars: Selective Bibliography.* New York: Pergamon, 1964. 246p.

58.   "The Military Library." *Military Affairs.* Washington, D.C., and Manhattan, Kans.: American Military Institute, 1939–. v. 3–.

59.   Miller, Lester L., Jr., comp. *Combat Support: A Bibliography.*
SB-55. Fort Sill, Okla.: U.S. Army Field Artillery School Library, 1979.
23p.

60.   _____ . *Desert Operations: A Bibliography.* SB-61. Fort Sill,
Okla.: U.S. Army Field Artillery School Library, 1979. 11p.

61.   _____ . *Gunnery Laying by the Direct and Indirect Method.*
SB-44. Fort Sill, Okla.: U.S. Army Field Artillery School Library, 1977.
7p.

62.   _____ . *Mountain Warfare—Its Preparation and Execution: A
Bibliography.* SB-62. Fort Sill, Okla.: U.S. Army Field Artillery School
Library, 1979. 21p.

63.   _____ . *Night Warfare—Its Preparation and Pursuit: A Bibliography of Periodical Articles.* SB-57. Fort Sill, Okla.: U.S. Army Field
Artillery School Library, 1978. 18p.

64.   _____ . *Russia at War—Imperial or Soviet: A Bibliography of
Periodical Articles.* SB-71. Fort Sill, Okla.: U.S. Army Field Artillery
School Library, 1980. 11p.

65.   _____ . *Winter War: A Periodicals Bibliography.* SB-65. Fort
Sill, Okla.: U.S. Army Field Artillery School Library, 1979. 9p.

66.   Morton, Louis. "World War II: A Survey of Recent Writings."
American Historical Review 75 (December 1970), 1987–2009.

67.   New York Public Library. Research Libraries. *Subject Catalog of
the World War II Collection.* 3 vols. Boston, Mass.: G. K. Hall, 1977.

68.   Nyman, Kristina, comp. *Finland's War Years, 1939–1945: A List
of Books and Articles.* Helsinki, Finland: Society of Military History, 1973.
259p.

69.   *Paperbound Books in Print.* New York: R. R. Bowker, 1955–.
v. 1–.

70.   Parrish, Michael, comp. *The 1968 Czech Crisis: A Bibliography,
1968–1970.* Bibliography, no. 12. Santa Barbara, Calif.: ABC-Clio,
1971. 41p.

71.   _____ . *The Soviet Armed Forces: Books in English, 1950–1967.*
Hoover Institution Bibliographical Series, no. 48. Stanford, Calif.:
Hoover Institution Press, 1970. 128p.

72.   Remington, Robin A. *International Relations of Eastern Europe:
A Guide to Information Sources.* International Relations Information
Guide Series, no. 8. Detroit, Mich.: Gale Research, 1978. 273p.

73. Rubner, Michael, comp. *Middle East Conflict from October 1973 to July 1976: A Selected Bibliography.* Political Issues Series, v. 4, no. 4. Los Angeles: Center for the Study of Armament and Disarmament, California State University, 1977. 82p.

74. *Russian Studies, 1941–1958: A Cumulation of the Annual Bibliographies from the Russian Review.* Ann Arbor, Mich.: Pierian Press, 1974. 279p.

75. Rzheshevsky, Oleg. "Survey of Some Bourgeois Presentations of the Second World War." *World Marxist Review* 23 (May 1980), 57–61.

76. Schulz, Ann. *International and Regional Politics in the Middle East and North Africa: A Guide to Information Sources.* International Relations Information Guide Series, no. 6. Detroit, Mich.: Gale Research, 1977. 244p.

77. Scott, William F. *Soviet Sources of Military Doctrine and Strategy.* New York: Published for the National Strategy Information Center by Crane, Russak, 1975. 72p.

78. Simon, Reeva S. *The Modern Middle East: A Guide to Research Tools in the Social Sciences.* Modern Middle East Series, no. 10. Boulder, Colo.: Westview Press, 1978. 283p.

79. Smith, Myron J., Jr. *Air War Bibliography, 1939–1945: A Guide to Sources in English.* Manhattan, Kans.: Military Affairs/Aerospace Publications for the USAF Historical Foundation, 1976–. v. 1–.

80. _____. *Air War Southeast Asia, 1961–1973: An Annotated Bibliography and 16mm Film Guide.* Metuchen, N.J.: Scarecrow Press, 1979. 298p. In addition to general sources, both of the above contain references to airborne/airmobile forces and equipment.

81. _____. *The Secret Wars.* War/Peace Bibliography Series, nos. 12-14. 3 vols. Santa Barbara, Calif.: ABC-Clio, 1980. See especially vol. 1, *Intelligence, Propaganda and Psychological Warfare, Resistance Movements and Special Operations, 1939–1945.*

82. *Sources: A Guide to Print and Nonprint Materials Available from Organizations, Industry, Government Agencies, and Specialized Publishers.* Syracuse, N.Y.: Gaylord Professional Publications, 1977–. v. 1–.

83. *Soviet Analyst.* London: Castle Press, 1971. v. 1–.

84. *Subject Guide to Books in Print.* New York: R. R. Bowker, 1957–. v. 1–.

85. Tapley, Dianne S., comp. *Asia, Southwest.* SB-5. Fort Benning, Ga.: Learning Resources Division, U.S. Army Infantry School, 1980. 24p.

86.   _____ . *Opposing Forces Bibliography.* SB-1. 3 pts. Fort Benning, Ga.:Learning Resources Division, U.S. Army Infantry School,
1978.

87.   Thompson, Anthony. *Russia/USSR.* World Bibliography
Series. Santa Barbara, Calif.: ABC-Clio, 1979. 289p.

88.   Turner, Frederick C. "Professional Reading for the Soviet
Armor Leader." *Armor* 78 (January 1969), 4-13; (April 1969), 4-10.

89.   Union of Soviet Socialist Republics. Ministry of Defense. *Recent Articles on Events in Soviet World War II Operations.* Trans. no. 18281.
Arlington, Va.: U.S. Joint Publications Research Service, 1963. 13p.

90.   United States. Air Force. Air University. Library. *Soviet Military Capabilities: Selected References.* SB-17. Maxwell AFB, Ala.: Air University Library, 1975. 17p.

91.   United States. Central Intelligence Agency. National Foreign
Assessment Center. *CIA Publications Released to the Public, 1972–1979.*
NF80-16009. Washington, D.C.: Document Expediting Service, Ex-
change and Gift Division, Library of Congress, 1980. 20p.

92.   United States. Department of the Army. *U.S.S.R.: Analytical
Survey of Literature.* Bibliographic Surveys of Strategic Areas of the
World. DA 550-6-1. Washington, D.C.: U.S. Government Printing
Office, 1976. 232p.

93.   _____ . Military Academy. Library. *Subject Catalog of the Military Art and Science Collection.* 6 vols. Westport, Conn.: Greenwood Press,
1969.

94.   United States. Department of the Army. Military History Institute. *The Era of World War II.* SB-16. 4 vols.1 Carlisle Barracks, Pa.,
1977–. v. 1–.

95.   United States. Department of the Army. Office of the Chief of
Military History. *Guide to Japanese Monographs and Japanese Studies on
Manchuria, 1945–1960.* Washington, D.C., 1960. 282p.

96.   United States. Department of Defense. Defense Intelligence
Agency. *Bibliography of Unclassified Books and Monographs on the Soviet and
East European Ground Forces.* DIA-DDB-1100-164-78. Washington,
D.C., 1978. 109p.

97.   United States. Department of State. Bureau of Intelligence
and Research. *Soviet Military Doctrine.* External Research Paper, no. 141.
Washington, D.C., 1963. 39p.

98.   United States. Library of Congress. General Reference and
Bibliography Division. *Library of Congress Catalog, Books-Subjects: A*

Cumulative List of Works Represented by Library of Congress Printed Cards. Washington, D.C.: U.S. Government Printing Office, 1939–. v. 8–.

99. _____ . Arms Control and Disarmament Bibliography Section. *Arms Control and Disarmament: A Quarterly Bibliography with Abstracts and Annotations.* 10 vols. Washington, D.C.: U.S. Government Printing Office, 1964–1973.

100. *Verticle File Index.* New York: H. W. Wilson, 1939–. v. 8–.

101. Ziegler, Janet. *World War II: Books in English, 1945–1965.* Hoover Institution Bibliographical Series, no. 45. Stanford, Calif.: Hoover Institution Press, 1971. 224p.

B. Abstracts

102. *Abstracts of Military Bibliography.* Buenos Aires, Argentina: Navy Publications Institute, 1968–. v. 1–.

103. Congressional Information Service. *C.I.S. Annual: Abstracts of Congressional Publications and Legislative Histories.* Washington, D.C., 1969–. v. 1–.

104. *Dissertation Abstracts, Volumes 2-30.* Ann Arbor, Mich.: University Microfilms, 1939–1968.

105. *Dissertation Abstracts International: "A" Schedule.* Ann Arbor, Mich.: University Microfilms, 1969–. v. 1–.

106. Ferri, Albert, Jr., comp. *Selections from the Soviet Military Press, 1968–1971.* SRI Project 8474, Technical Note SSC-TN-8974-70. Menlo Park, Calif.: Stanford Research Institute, 1973. 142p.

107. *Historical Abstracts: Part "B," Twentieth Century Abstracts (1914 to the Present).* Santa Barbara, Calif.: ABC-Clio, 1955–. v. 1–.

108. *International Political Science Abstracts.* Oxford, Eng.: Basil Blackwell, 1952–. v. 1–.

109. *Masters Abstracts.* Ann Arbor, Mich.: University Microfilms, 1962–. v. 1–.

110. RAND Corporation. *Selected RAND Abstracts.* Santa Monica, Calif.: RAND Corporation, 1962–. v. 1–.

111. United States. Air Force. Air University. Library. *Abstracts of Student Research Reports.* Maxwell AFB, Ala., 1949–. v. 1–.

C. Indexes

1. Newspapers

112.   American Association for the Advancement of Slavic Studies. *Index to Pravda.* Columbus, Ohio, 1950–1977.

113.   *California News Index.* Claremont, Calif.: Center for California Public Affairs, 1970–. v. 1–.

114.   *The Christian Science Monitor Index.* Corvallis, Oreg.: Helen M. Cropsey, 1960–. v. 1–.

115.   *Editorials on File.* New York: Facts on File, 1970–. v. 1–.

116.   *The German Tribune.* Hamburg, West Germany: Friedrich Verlag, 1956–. v. 1–.

117.   Joint Committee on Slavic Studies. *Current Digest of the Soviet Press.* Ann Arbor, Mich., 1949–. v. 1–.

118.   *The National Observer Index.* Flint Mich.: Newspaper Indexing Center, 1970–. v. 1–.

119.   New York Times. *New York Times Index.* New York, 1939–.

120.   *Newspaper Index.* Wooster, Ohio: Bell & Howell, 1972–. v. 1–.   Covers *Chicago Tribune, Washington Post, Los Angeles Times,* and New Orleans *Times-Picayune.*

121.   *Reprints from the Soviet Press.* New York: Compass Publications, 1965–. v. 1–.

122.   Times of London. *Index to the Times.* London, 1939–.

123.   *The Wall Street Journal Index.* New York: Dow Jones, 1958–. v. 1–.

2. Periodicals

124.   *Access: The Supplementary Index to Periodicals.* Syracuse, N.Y.: Gaylord Professional Publications, 1975–. v. 1–.

125.   *America: History and Life—A Guide to Periodical Literature.* Santa Barbara, Calif.: ABC-Clio, 1964–. v. 1–.

126.   Botlorff, Robert M., ed. *Popular Periodical Index.* New York, 1973–. v. 1–.

127.   *Humanities Index.* New York: H. W. Wilson, 1975–. v. 1–.

128. *Index to Foreign Legal Periodicals and Collections of Essays.* Chicago, Ill.: Murphy, 1960–. v. 1–.

129. *Index to Legal Periodicals.* New York: H. W. Wilson, 1939–. v. 22–.

130. *Index to the Contemporary Scene.* Detroit, Mich.: Gale Research, 1973–. v. 1–.

131. *Index to U.S. Government Periodicals.* Chicago, Ill.: Infodata International, 1975–. v. 1–.

132. *International Relations Digest of Periodical Literature.* Berkeley, Calif.: Bureau of International Relations, University of California, 1950–. v. 1–.

133. Miller, Lester L., Jr. *Index to the Field Artillery Journal: Author and Title Index, January 1940 –December 1976.* Washington, D.C.: U.S. Government Printing Office, 1978. 141p.

134. _____ . *Index to the Field Artilleryman (Artillery Trends): Author and Subject Index, 1957–1972.* Washington, D.C.: U.S. Government Printing Office, 1978. 53p.

135. *The New Periodicals Index.* Boulder, Colo.: Mediaworks, 1977–. v. 1–.

136. Public Affairs Information Service. *P.A.I.S. Bulletin.* New York, 1939–. v. 24–.

137. *Reader's Guide to Periodical Literature.* New York: H. W. Wilson, 1939–.

138. *Social Science and Humanities Index.* New York: H. W. Wilson, 1939–1974.

139. *Social Sciences Index.* New York: H. W. Wilson, 1975–. v. 1–.

140. United States. Air Force. Air University. Library. *Air University Library Index to Military Periodicals.* Maxwell AFB, Ala., 1949–. v. 1–.

3. Documents

141. Bernan Associates. *Checklist of Congressional Hearings and Reports.* Washington, D.C., 1958–. v. 1–.

142. Congressional Quarterly. *C.Q. Weekly Report.* Washington, D.C., 1945–. v. 1–.

143. _____ . *Congressional Quarterly Almanac.* Washington, D.C., 1945–. v. 1–.

144. Great Britain. *Catalogue of Government Publications.* London: H.M. Stationery Office, 1939–. v. 16–.

145. Newsbank. *Index to the Foreign Broadcast Information Service Daily Report: Soviet Union.* Stamford, Conn., 1977–. v. 1–.

146. *Transdex: Bibliography and Index to the United States Joint Publication Research Service (JPRS) Translations.* New York: C.C.M. Info Corporation, 1961–. v. 1–.

147. United Nations. Dag Hammarskjold Library. *United Nations Documents Index.* New York, 1950–. v. 1–.

148. United States. Department of the Army. Headquarters. Military Publications Division. *Index of Military Publications.* Pamphlet 310. Washington, D.C., 1978–. v. 1–.   Issued monthly.

149. _____ .*Index of Doctrinal, Training, and Organizational Publications.* DA Pam 310-3. Washington, D.C., 1980. 190p.

150. United States. National Technical Information Service. *Government Reports-Announcements.* Springfield, Va., 1946–. v. 1–.

151. United States. Superintendent of Documents. *Monthly Catalog of U.S. Government Publications.* Washington, D.C.: U.S. Government Printing Office, 1939–.

152. *United States Political Science Documents.* Pittsburgh, Pa.: Publications Center, University Center for International Studies, University of Pittsburgh, 1975–. v. 1–.

4. Book Reviews

153. *American Reference Books Annual.* Littleton, Colo.: Libraries Unlimited, 1970–. v. 1–.

154. *Book Review Digest.* New York: H. W. Wilson, 1939–. v. 24–.

155. *Book Review Index.* Detroit, Mich.: Gale Research, 1968–. v. 1–.

156. *Perspective.* Washington, D.C.: Helen Dwight Reid Education Foundation, 1972–. v. 1–.   Other standard reviewing tools include the *New York Times Book Review, Library Journal, Publishers Weekly, Choice, Directions.* Most military journals also review new titles.

D. Encyclopedias and Handbooks

157.   Banks, Arthur S., ed. *Political Handbook of the World, 19 –: Governments, Regional Issues, and Intergovernmental Organizations as of January 1, 19 –.* New York: McGraw-Hill, 1939 –. v. 11 –.

158.   Baudot, Marcel, et al., eds. *The Historical Encyclopedia of World War II.* New York: Facts on File, 1980. 500p.

159.   Chant, Christopher. *The World's Armies.* London: Cassell, 1979. 252p.

160.   *Countries of the World and Their Leaders.* Detroit, Mich.: Gale Research, 1974 –. v. 1 –.

161.   Crow, Duncan, and Robert J. Icks. *Encyclopedia of Armoured Cars and Half-Tracks.* London: Barrie and Jenkins, 1976. 160p.

162.   _____. *Encyclopedia of Tanks.* London: Barrie and Jenkins, 1975. 256p.

163.   Dupuy, R. Ernest, and Trevor N. *The Encyclopedia of Military History.* Rev. ed. New York: Harper & Row, 1976. 1,488p.

164.   Dupuy, Trevor N., Grace P. Hayes, and John A. C. Andrew. *The Almanac of World Military Power.* Rev. ed. San Rafael, Calif.: Presidio Press, 1980. 416p.

165.   Featherstone, Donald, and Keith Robinson. *Battles with Model Tanks.* New York: Hippocrene Books, 1979. 160p.

166.   Florinsky, Michael T., ed. *McGraw-Hill Encyclopedia of Russia and the Soviet Union.* New York: McGraw-Hill, 1961. 624p.

167.   Foss, Christopher F. *The Illustrated Encyclopedia of the World's Tanks and Fighting Vehicles: A Technical Directory of Major Combat Vehicles from World War I to the Present Day.* London: Salamander Books, 1977. 248p.

168.   Hays, Serge. *Profile U.S.S.R.: A National Compendium of Facts, Figures, and Essential Information.* New York: Facts on File, 1980. 576p.

169.   Jones, David R., ed. *Military-Naval Encyclopedia of Russia and the Soviet Union.* 50 vols.1. Gulf Breeze, Fla.: Academic International Press, 1977 –. v. 1 –.

170.   Keegan, John. *World Armies.* New York: Facts on File, 1979. 1,016p.

171.   _____ , ed. *The Rand-McNally Encyclopedia of World War II.* Chicago, Ill.: Rand-McNally, 1977. 256p.

172.   Kurian, George T. *Encyclopedia of the Third World.* 2vols. New York: Facts on File, 1979.

173.   Mallory, Walter H. *Political Handbook and Atlas of the World.* New York: Council on Foreign Relations, 1939–. v. 12–.

174.   *The Marshall Cavendish Illustrated Encyclopedia of World War II.* 25 vols. Hicksville, N.Y.: Marshall Cavendish, 1972–1974.

175.   Menaul, Stewart, et al. *The Illustrated Encyclopedia of the Strategy, Tactics, and Weapons of Russian Military Power.* New York: St. Martin's Press, 1980. 249p.

176.   Morris, Eric, et al. *Weapons and Warfare of the 20th Century: A Comprehensive and Historical Survey of Modern Military Methods and Machines.* London: Octopus Books, 1976. 480p.

177.   Novosti Press Agency, Editors of. *U.S.S.R.—1981.* Translated from the Russian. New York: Harcourt Brace Jovanovich, 1981. 256p.

178.   Paneth, Donald. *Current Affairs Atlas.* New York: Facts on File, 1979–. v. 1–.

179.   Parkinson, Roger. *The Encyclopedia of Modern War.* New York: Stein & Day, 1976. 226p.

180.   Parrish, Thomas, ed. *The Simon and Schuster Encyclopedia of World War II.* New York: Simon & Schuster, 1978. 765p.

181.   Patai, Raphael. *Encyclopedia of Zionism and Israel.* 2 vols. New York: Herzl Press, 1971.

182.   Reid, Alan. *A Concise Encyclopedia of the Second World War.* Reading, Eng.: Osprey, 1974. 232p.

183.   Sellers, Robert C., ed. *Armed Forces of the World: A Reference Handbook.* 4th ed. New York: Praeger, 1977. 288p.

184.   Slusser, Robert M., and Jan F. Triska. *A Calendar of Soviet Treaties, 1917–1957.* Stanford, Calif.: Stanford University Press, 1959. 530p.

185.   Snyder, Louis L. *Encyclopedia of the Third Reich.* New York: McGraw-Hill, 1976. 410p.

186.   Stockholm International Peace Research Institute (SIPRI). *Armaments and Disarmament in the Nuclear Age: A Handbook.* New York: Humanities Press, 1976. 308p.

187.   Union of Soviet Socialist Republics. *The Great Soviet Encyclopedia: A Translation of the Third Edition of Bol'shaia Sovetskaia Entsiklopediia.* London and New York: Macmillan, 1973–.

188.   United States. Department of Defense. Defense Intelligence Agency. *Handbook of Soviet Armed Forces Military Symbols.* DIA-DDB-2680-41-78. Washington, D.C., 1978.

189.   United States. Department of the Army. *Handbook on Soviet Ground Forces.* FM 30-40. Washington, D.C.: U.S. Government Printing Office, 1975. 281p.

190.   Utechin, S. V., ed. *Everyman's Concise Encyclopedia of Russia.* New York: E. P. Dutton, 1961. 623p.

191.   Wieczynski, Joseph L. *The Modern Encyclopedia of Russian and Soviet History.* Gulf Breeze, Fla.: Academic International Press, 1977–. v. 1–.

192.   Wise, Terence. *Military Flags of the World in Color.* New York: Arco, 1978. 184p.

E. Annuals and Yearbooks

193.   *Africa South of the Sahara.* London: Europa Publications, 1970–. v. 1–.

194.   *The Annual Register of World Events: A Review of the Year.* London: Longmans, Green, 1939–. v. 179–.

195.   *Arab Report and Record.* London, 1965–. v. 1–.

196.   Berner, Wolfgang, ed. *The Soviet Union, 1973–.* New York: Holmes and Meier, 1975–. v. 1–.

197.   Crozier, Brian. *Annual of Power and Conflict.* London: Institute for the Study of Conflict, 1973–. v. 1–.

198.   *The Europa Yearbook: A World Survey and Directory of Countries and International Organizations.* London: Europa Publications, 1950–. v. 1–.

199.   Facts on File, Editors of. *News Dictionary.* New York: Facts on File, 1965–. v. 1–.

200.   _____ . *Facts on File Yearbook: The Indexed Record of World Events.* New York: Facts on File, 1941–. v. 1–.

201.   Hoeber, Francis P., David B. Kassing, and William Schneider, Jr. *Arms, Men, and Military Budgets: Issues for Fiscal Year 19 –*. New York: Crane, Russak, 1975 –. v. 1 –.

202.   *Information Please Almanac*. New York: Viking Press, 1946 –. v. 1 –.

203.   Institute of World Affairs. *The Yearbook of World Affairs*. London: Stevens, 1947 –. v. 1 –.

204.   Intelligence International. *Intelligence Digest: A Review of World Affairs*. Cheltenham, Eng., 1938 –. v. 1 –.

205.   International Institute for Strategic Studies. *The Military Balance*. London, 1958 –. v. 1 –.

206.   *The International Yearbook and Statesman's Who's Who*. London: Burke, 1953 –. v. 1 –.

207.   Jones, David R., ed. *Soviet Armed Forces Review Annual*. Gulf Breeze, Fla.: Academic International Press, 1977 –. v. 1 –.

208.   *Keesing's Contemporary Archives*. London: Keesing's Publications, 1939 –. v. 8 –.

209.   Legum, Colin, ed. *Africa Contemporary Record*. New York: Holmes and Meier, 1969 –. v. 1 –.

210.   _____ . *Middle East Contemporary Survey*. New York: Holmes and Meier, 1978 –. v. 1 –.

211.   Marriott, John, ed. *R.U.S.I. and Brassey's Weapons Technology: A Survey of Current Developments in Weapons Systems*. London: Brassey's International, 1975 –. v. 1 –.

212.   *The Middle East and North Africa*. London: Europa Publications, 1953 –. v. 1 –.

213.   Rake, Alan, ed. *New African Yearbook*. New York: Franklin Watts, 1978 –. v. 1 –.

214.   *Reader's Digest 19 – Almanac and Yearbook*. New York: W. W. Norton, 1967 –. v. 1 –.

215.   Royal Institute of International Affairs. *Survey of International Affairs: Post War Series, since 1947*. London: Oxford University Press, 1952 –. v. 1 –.

216.   Scherer, John L., ed. *U.S.S.R. Facts and Figures Annual*. Gulf Breeze, Fla.: Academic International Press, 1977 –. v. 1 –.

217. Starr, Richard F., ed. *Yearbook of International Communist Affairs*. Stanford, Calif.: Hoover Institution Press, 1970–. v. 1–.

218. *The Statesman's Year-Book: Statistical and Historical Information of the States of the World for the Year.* New York: St. Martin's Press, 1939–.

219. Stebbins, Richard P., and Alba Amoia. *The World This Year.* New York: Simon & Schuster, 1971–. v. 1–.

220. Stockholm International Peace Research Institute (SIPRI). *World Armaments and Disarmament: The SIPRI Yearbook.* New York: Humanities Press, 1969–. v. 1–.

221. United States. Congress. House. Committee on Armed Services. *Hearings on Military Posture, etc.* Washington, D.C.: U.S. Government Printing Office, 1961–.

222. ———— . Subcommittee on Department of Defense Appropriations. *Department of Defense Appropriations for Fiscal Year 19 –: Hearings.* Washington, D.C.: U.S. Government Printing Office, 1948–.

223. United States. Congress. Senate. Committee on Armed Services. *Military Procurement Authorization, Fiscal Year 19 –: Hearings.* Washington, D.C.: U.S. Government Printing Office, 1948–.

224. ———— . Subcommittee on Department of Defense Appropriations. *Department of Defense Appropriations for Fiscal Year 19 –: Hearings.* Washington, D.C.: U.S. Government Printing Office, 1948–.

225. United States. Department of Defense. *Report of the Secretary of Defense.* Washington, D.C.: U.S. Government Printing Office, 1948–.

226. *World Almanac and Book of Facts.* Garden City, N.Y.: Doubleday, 1939–. v. 70–.

F. Dictionaries

227. Bruce, George. *Dictionary of Battles.* New York: Stein & Day, 1971. 333p.

228. Carman, William Y. *A Dictionary of Military Uniforms.* New York: Scribners, 1977. 140p.

229. Chochia, Anton P., and A. S. Shcheglov. *English-Russian Dictionary of Motorized Armour.* London: Collet, 1962. 783p.

230. "Concerning Military Rear Service Terminology." *Soviet Military Translations,* no. 318a (September 1966), 31-37.

231. Crowe, Barry. *Concise Dictionary of Soviet Terminology, Institutions, and Abbreviations.* London and New York: Pergamon, 1969. 182p.

232. Gale Research. *Acronyms and Initialisms Dictionary.* 3d ed. Detroit, Mich., 1970. 484p.

233. Garber, Max, and P. S. Bond. *A Modern Military Dictionary.* 2d ed. Washington, D.C.: Bond, 1942. 272p.

234. Hanrieder, Wolfram F., and Larry V. Buel. *Words and Arms: A Dictionary of Security and Defense Terms, with Supplemental Data.* Boulder, Colo.: Westview Press, 1979. 250p.

235. Hayward, P. H. C., comp. *Jane's Dictionary of Military Terms.* London: Macdonald and Jane's, 1975. 201p.

236. Luttwak, Edward. *A Dictionary of Modern War.* New York: Harper & Row, 1971. 224p.

237. Murphy, Paul J. "Glossary of Selected Soviet Naval and Related Terms." In *Naval Power in Soviet Policy.* Studies in Communist Affairs, no. 2. Washington, D.C.: U.S. Government Printing Office, 1978. pp. 314–340.

238. Partridge, Eric, ed. *A Dictionary of Forces' Slang, 1939–1945.* Freeport, N.Y.: Books for Libraries, 1970. 212p.

239. Plano, Jack C., and Milton Greenberg. *The American Political Dictionary.* 5th ed. New York: Holt, 1979. 488p.

240. Plano, Jack C., and Roy Olton. *The International Relations Dictionary.* 3d ed. Santa Barbara: ABC-Clio, 1982. 337p.

241. Quick, John. *Dictionary of Weapons and Military Terms.* New York: McGraw-Hill, 1973. 527p.

242. Raymond, Walter J. *Dictionary of Politics: Selected American and Foreign Political and Legal Terms.* 6th rev. ed. Lawrenceville, Va.: Brunswick, 1978. 956p.

243. Ruffner, Frederick G., Jr., and Robert C. Thomas, eds. *Code Names Dictionary.* Detroit, Mich.: Gale Research, 1963. 555p.

244. Schwarz, Urs, and Laszlo Hadik. *Strategic Terminology: A Trilingual Glossary.* New York: Praeger, 1966. 156p.   Entries in English, French, and German.

245. Segal, Louis. *New Complete Russian-English Dictionary.* 2d ed. London: Lund Humphries, 1943. 1,016p.

246. Smirnitsky, A. I., ed. *Russian-English Dictionary.* Moscow: State Publishing House for Foreign and National Dictionaries, 1961. 1,001p.

247. Smith, R. E. F. *A Russian-English Dictionary of Social Science Terms.* London: Butterworth, 1962. 495p.

248. Taube, Aleksandr M., comp. *Anglo-Russian Dictionary of War and Military Terminology.* London: Collet, 1942. 640p.

249. Taylor, A. Marjorie. *The Language of World War II.* Rev. ed. New York: H. W. Wilson, 1948. 265p.

250. Union of Soviet Socialist Republics. Ministry of Defense. *Dictionary of Military Terms: A Soviet View.* Translated from the Russian. Soviet Military Thought Series, no. 9. Washington, D.C.: U.S. Government Printing Office, 1976. 256p. This volume, like others in the translated "Officer's Library," is published in English under the auspices of the U.S. Air Force.

251. _____ . Frunze Military Academy. *Russian-English Dictionary of Operational, Tactical, and General Military Terms.* Washington, D.C.: Office of Technical Services, Business and Defense Services Administration, U.S. Department of Commerce, 1960. 359p.

252. United States. Department of Defense. *Glossary of Soviet Military and Related Abbreviations.* TM 30–546. Washington, D.C.: U.S. Government Printing Office, 1957. 178p.

253. _____ . Defense Intelligence Agency. *Dictionary of U.S.-Soviet Terms.* DIA-DDI-2200-33-77. Washington, D.C., 1977.

254. _____ . *Glossary of Soviet Military and Related Abbreviations.* DIA-DDB-2600-1585-79. Washington, D.C., 1979. 200p.

255. United States. Department of the Army. *Dictionary of U.S. Army Terms.* Army Reg. 310–25. Washington, D.C., 1972.

256. _____ . *Operational Terms and Graphics.* FM 101-5-1. Washington, D.C., 1980. 124p.

257. _____ . Language School. *Russian: Military Terminology Word List* (English into Russian—alphabetical). Monterey, Calif.: Presidio of California, 1960. 53p.

258. United States. Department of the Army. Ordnance Corps. *Russian-English Small Arms Dictionary.* Washington, D.C., 1956. 91p.

259. United States. Joint Chiefs of Staff. *Department of Defense Dictionary of Military and Associated Terms.* JCS-1. Rev. ed. Washington, D.C.: U.S. Government Printing Office, 1979. 377p.

260.   United States. War Department. *Russian Military Dictionary.* TM 30–544. Washington, D.C.: U.S. Government Printing Office, 1945. 478p.

261.   Young, Peter, and Michael Calvert. *A Dictionary of Battles.* London: New English Library, 1977. 606p.

G. Biographies

1. Collective Biographies

The general biographies provide background information on a large number of Soviet leaders, who, over the years, have had contact with the Red Army. Additional citations relative to this section can be found throughout parts 2:A:1, 2:B:1, 2:C:2: a, b, and d; 3:A, 4:A and E.

262.   Bates, Martin D. "Marshals of the Soviet Army." *An Cosantoir* 18 (July 1958), 302–304.

263.   Berezko, G., et al. *Army of Heroes: True Stories of Soviet Fighting Men.* Translated from the Russian. New York: Universal Distributors, 1944. 171p.

264.   Bialer, Seweryn. *Stalin and His Generals: Soviet Military Memoirs of World War II.* New York: Pegasus, 1969. 644p.

265.   _____ . *Stalin's Successors: Leadership, Stability and Change in the Soviet Union.* Cambridge: At the University Press, 1980. 335p.

266.   *Biography Index.* New York: H. W. Wilson, 1947–. v. 1–.

267.   Blondel, Jean. *World Leaders: Heads of Government in the Postwar Period.* Beverly Hills, Calif.: Sage, 1980. 282p.

268.   Burroughs, E. G. *Who's Who in the Red Army.* Hertsfordshire, Eng.: Farleigh, 1944. 20p.

269.   Carver, Michael, ed. *The War Lords: Military Commanders of the Twentieth Century.* Boston, Mass.: Little, Brown, 1976. 624p.

270.   Clark, Donald L. "Who Are Those Guys?" *Air University Review* 30 (May-June 1979), 47–65.

271.   Cort, David. "Russia's Men on Horseback." *U.N. World* 4 (December 1950), 20–23.

272.   Crankshaw, Edward. "The Men behind Khrushchev." *Atlantic* 204 (July 1959), 27–32.

273.   *Current Biography.* New York: H. W. Wilson, 1940–. v. 1–.

274.   *Current World Leaders.* Pasadena, Calif., 1957–. v. 1–.

275.   *Dictionary of International Biography.* London, 1964–. v. 1–.

276.   Facts on File, Editors of. *Obituaries on File* [1940–1978]. 2 vols. New York: Facts on File, 1979.

277.   "For Whom the Guns Roll: The Men in Command of the Seven Active Fronts." *Time* 42 (September 13, 1943), 26–27.

278.   "Four Horsemen: Generals of the Soviet Armies Hammer the Fleeing Wehrmacht." *Newsweek* 22 (September 13, 1943), 25–27.

279.   Freidman, Leonard R. "Soviet Military and Political Elite [of the Far East Military District]." *Military Review* 46 (April 1966), 68–73.

280.   Heiman, Leo. "Military Background of the New Soviet Leaders." *Military Review* 45 (April 1965), 46–56.

281.   Hellman, Lillian. "I Meet the Front-Line Russians." *Collier's* 115 (March 31, 1945), 11.

282.   Hough, Jerry F. *The Soviet Leadership in Transition.* Washington, D.C.: Brookings Institution, 1980. 175p.

283.   *The International Who's Who.* London: Europa Publications, 1939–. v. 4–.

284.   Keegan, John, and Andrew Wheatcroft. *Who's Who in Military History.* London: Weidenfeld & Nicolson, 1976. 367p.

285.   Levytsky, Borys. *The Soviet Political Elite.* Stanford, Calif.: Hoover Institution Press, 1970. 640p.

286.   Linden, Carl A. *Khrushchev and the Soviet Leadership, 1957–1964.* Baltimore, Md.: Johns Hopkins Press, 1966. 270p.

287.   Martell, Paul, and Grace P. Hayes. *World Military Leaders.* New York: R. R. Bowker, 1974. 268p.

288.   New York Times, Editors of. *New York Times Obituary Index, 1858–1968.* New York: New York Times, 1970. 1,136p.

289.   "Old Soldiers Do Die: Deaths of 12 Russian Generals." *Time* 93 (May 23, 1969), 36.

290.   Pool, Ithiel de Sola. *Satellite Generals: A Study of Military Elites in the Soviet Sphere.* Elites Series, no. 5. Stanford, Calif.: Stanford University Press, 1955.

291.   "Red's Tough Generals." *Newsweek* 21 (February 8, 1943), 23–25.

292.   "Russia's Generals." *Life* 17 (July 31, 1944), 31–32.

293.   Scott, Harriet F. "Top Leaders of the Soviet Armed Forces." *Air Force Magazine* 63 (March 1980), 109–116.

294.   Snow, Edgar. "What Kind of a Man Is a Russian General?" *Saturday Evening Post* 215 (April 17, 1943), 20–21.

295.   Sobel, Lester A., ed. *Russia's Rulers: The Khrushchev Period.* New York: Facts on File, 1971. 394p.

296.   "Soviets Cheer Their Heroes." *Life* 11 (July 21, 1941), 26–27.

297.   Sulzberger, Cyrus L. "Sergei, Red Fighter." *New York Times Magazine* (January 4, 1942), 4.

298.   Thompson, Paul W. "The Nazis' Own Appraisal of the Russian Soldier." *Reader's Digest* 42 (June 1943), 15–18.

299.   Times of London, Editors of. *Obituaries from the Times, 1961–1970.* Reading, Eng.: Newspaper Archive Developments, 1976. 952p.

300.   United States. Central Intelligence Agency. National Foreign Assessment Center. *Appearances of Soviet Leaders, January–December 1978.* CR 79-13337. Springfield, Va.: National Technical Information Service, 1979. 251p.

301.   United States. Central Intelligence Agency. Office of Political Research. *Chiefs of State and Cabinet Members of Foreign Governments.* Reference Aid. Washington, D.C.: Document Expediting Project, Exchange and Gifts Division, Library of Congress, 1972–. v. 1–.

302.   _____ . *A Directory of USSR Ministry of Defense and Armed Forces Officials.* Reference Aid. CR 78-15073. Washington, D.C.: Document Expediting Project, Exchange and Gift Division, Library of Congress, 1978. 109p.

303.   *Who's Who in the Arab World.* New York: International Publications Service, 1968–. v. 1–.

304.   Windrow, Martin, and Francis K. Mason. *A Concise Dictionary of Military Biography.* London: Osprey, 1975. 337p.

2. Specific Biographies

The Soviet Army has seen a lot of important leaders come and go through the years. Some of these have been generals of varying effectiveness, while others have been civilian politicians or arms manufacturers with only the most basic knowledge of military science.

We have listed here in alphabetical order by surname those Russians, regardless of status, in and out of the ground forces, who have had an effect on the army since 1939. Thus the user will find references not only to Malinovskiy and Zhukov, but to Ustinov, Khrushchev, and Brezhnev as well.

The memoirs of a few officers are not cited in this section. Marshal Chuikov's account of the Stalingrad campaign, for example, is noted in 2:C:3:c, while President Brezhnev's reminiscences of service at Novorossissk in 1943 are found in 2:C:3:e. In addition, the differences between Marshal Zhukov and Nikita S. Krushchev are explored not only under their specific biographies but also in section 3:A:2, on the Communist party and the military. Stalin, of course, figures throughout this book, not only under his own heading in this section, but throughout sections 2 (especially 2:C:2:d), 3, and 4. General accounts concerning officers are noted in 4:E:1:c.

IVAN KH. BAGRAMYAN

305.   Dagayev, N. "Marshal of the Soviet Union [I. Kh.] Bagramyan—Biographical Sketch: Translated from *Krasnaya Zvezda,* December 2, 1977." *Translations on USSR Military Affairs,* no. 1339 (March 20, 1978), 8–11.

306.   Vasilevskiy, Aleksandr M. "Biographic Data on Marshal of the Soviet Union I. Kh. Bagramyan: Translated from *Voyenno Istoricheskiy Zhurnal,* December 1977." *Translations on USSR Military Affairs,* no. 1329 (February 10, 1978), 21–27.

SERGEI BIRYUZOV

307.   Chernyshov, M. "Marshal Sergei Biryuzov." *Soviet Military Review,* no. 8 (August 1969), 50–51.

LEONID I. BREZHNEV

308.   Murphy, Paul J. *Brezhnev: Soviet Politician.* Jefferson, N.C.: McFarland, 1981. 363p.

309.   Union of Soviet Socialist Republics. *Leonid I. Brezhnev: Papers from His Life.* New York: Simon & Schuster, 1978. 320p.

SEMEN M. BUDENNYI

310.   "Marshal Semen M. Budennyi." In Walter Yust, ed., *Ten Eventful Years.* Chicago, Ill.: Encyclopedia Britannica, 1947. pp. 447–448.

NIKOLAI A. BULGANIN

311.   Duranty, Walter. "Marshal Bulganin." *Stalin and Company.* New York: Sloane, 1949. pp. 201–205.

312. Salisbury, Harrison E. "Nikolai Bulganin, Bourgeois Communist." *New York Times Magazine* (June 19, 1955), 8.

313. Schwartz, Harry. "Bulganin of the Red Army." *New York Times Magazine* (August 2, 1953), 9.

VASILIY I. CHUIKOV

314. "The Rudest Russian." *Newsweek* 33 (April 11, 1949), 29–30.

DAVID A. DRAGUNSKIY

315. Dragunskiy, David A. *Soldier's Life.* Translated from the Russian. Moscow: Progress Publishers, 1977. 278p.

316. Mosolev, V. "Biographical Data on General David A. Dragunskiy: Translated from *Voyenno Istoricheskiy Zhurnal,* February 1980." *Translations on USSR Military Affairs,* no. 1516 (May 30, 1980), 114–117.

ALEKSANDR V. GORBATOV

317. Gorbatov, Aleksandr V. *Years of My Life: The Memoirs of General of the Soviet Army Aleksandr V. Gorbatov.* Translated from the Russian. New York: W. W. Norton, 1965. 222p.

LEONID A. GOVOROV

318. "Marshal Leonid A. Govorov." In Walter Yust, ed., *Ten Eventful Years.* Chicago, Ill.: Encyclopedia Britannica, 1947. p. 495.

VASILII GRABIN

319. Karnozov, L. "Designer Grabin." *Soviet Military Review,* no. 11 (November 1970), 45–46. Designer of Red Army artillery.

ANDREI A. GRECHKO

320. Benjamin, M. R. "Death of a Survivor." *Newsweek* 87 (May 10, 1976), 55–56.

321. Bialer, Seweryn. "Andrei Antonovich Grechko." In George W. Simmonds, ed., *Soviet Leaders.* New York: Crowell, 1965. pp. 115–121.

322. "Enforcer." *Newsweek* 73 (May 19, 1969), 48.

323. Hubbe, John G. "Grechko: Master of the Soviet Military Colossus." *Reader's Digest* 97 (October 1970), 98–103.

324. "The New Commander of the Warsaw Pact Forces." *East Europe* 9 (September 1960), 32–33.

325. "People of the Week: Marshal Andrei A. Grechko." *U.S. News and World Report* 49 (August 8–12, 1960), 22, 26.

326.   Robinson, Donald B. "Marshal Grechko." *100 Most Important People in the World Today.* New York: G. P. Putnam, 1970. pp. 121–123.

327.   Scott, Harriet F. "The New Soviet Defense Minister." *Military Review* 47 (July 1967), 33–36.

NIKITA S. KHRUSHCHEV

328.   Alexandrov, Victor. *Khrushchev of the Ukraine: A Biography.* Translated from the French. New York: Philosophical Library, 1957. 216p.

329.   Crankshaw, Edward. *Khrushchev: A Career.* New York: Viking Press, 1966. 311p.

330.   Hyland, William G., and Richard W. Shryock. *The Fall of Khrushchev.* New York: Funk & Wagnalls, 1968. 209p.

331.   Kelen, Konrad. *Khrushchev: A Political Portrait.* New York: Praeger, 1961. 271p.

332.   Khrushchev, Nikita S. *Khrushchev Remembers.* Translated from the Russian. Boston, Mass.: Little, Brown, 1970. 639p.

333.   _____ . *Khrushchev Remembers: The Last Testament.* Translated from the Russian. Boston, Mass.: Little, Brown, 1974. 602p.

334.   "Khrushchev: The Real Story of the Man and His Deeds." *U.S. News and World Report* 47 (September 7, 1959), 58–63.

335.   "K[hrushchev] vs. Z[hukov]: How the Rug was Pulled." *Newsweek* 50 (November 11, 1957), 50.

336.   MacGregor-Hastie, Roy. *The Life and Times of Nikita Khrushchev.* London: Hamilton, 1959. 158p.

337.   Medvedev, Roy A., and Zhores A. *Khrushchev: The Years in Power.* New York: Columbia University Press, 1976. 198p.

338.   Page, Martin, and David Burg. *Unpersoned: The Fall of Nikita Sergeyevitch Khrushchev.* London: Chapman and Hall, 1966. 174p.

339.   Paloczi-Horvath, Gyorgy. *Khrushchev: The Making of a Dictator.* Boston, Mass.: Little, Brown, 1960. 314p.

340.   Pistrak, Lazar. *The Grand Tactician: Khrushchev's Rise to Power.* New York: Praeger, 1961. 296p.

341.   Rush, Myron. *The Rise of Khrushchev.* New York: Public Affairs Press, 1958. 116p.

342. Salisbury, Harrison E. "Khrushchev Climbs to the Apex." *New York Times Magazine* (July 14, 1957), 6–7.

IVAN S. KONEV

343. "Marshal Ivan S. Konev." In Walter Yust, ed., *Ten Eventful Years.* Chicago, Ill.: Encyclopedia Britannica, 1947. pp. 804–805.

344. "Marshal Ivan S. Konev, Denouncer of Zhukov." *Newsweek* 43 (November 15, 1957), 20.

345. Robinson, Donald B. "Marshal Konev." *100 Most Important People in the World Today.* New York: Pocket Books, 1952. pp. 122–125.

346. _____ . "Marshal Konev." *100 Most Important People, 1953.* New York: Pocket Books, 1953. pp. 149–152.

347. United States. Library of Congress. Legislative Reference Service. *Who Are They, Pt. 3: Georgi Zhukov and Ivan Konev.* Washington, D.C.: U.S. Government Printing Office, 1957. 7p.

IVAN N. KRYLOV

348. Krylov, Ivan N. *Soviet Staff Officer.* New York: Philosophical Library, 1951. 298p.

P. N. KULESHOV

349. Volkotubenko, I. "Biographical Data on Marshal of Artillery Kuleshov: Translated from *Voyenno Istoricheskiy Zhurnal,* December 1978." *Translations on USSR Military Affairs,* no. 1414 (March 1, 1979), 73–76.

VIKTOR G. KULIKOV

350. Naab, Richard M. *Victor G. Kulikov, Marshal of the Soviet Union: A Dimming Red Star.* New York: U.S. Army Institute for Advanced Russian and East European Studies, 1977. 81p.

PAVEL A. KUROCHKIN

351. Dunayev, P. "Biographical Data on Army General [Pavel A.] Kurochkin: Translated from *Voyenno Istoricheskiy Zhurnal,* November 1980." *Translations on USSR Military Affairs,* no. 1565 (February 5, 1981), 76–79.

KONSTANTIN LIKHOSHERST

352. Likhosherst, Konstantin. "Autobiographical Sketch of Ural MD First Deputy Command: Translated from *Ural,* February 1978." *Translations on USSR Military Affairs.* no. 1359 (June 26, 1978), 8–27.

ALEXANDER LOBOV

353. Lobov, Alexander. "My Two Years in the Red Army." *American Magazine* 155 (March 1953), 24–25.

NIKOLAY G. LYASHCHENKO

354.   Kazakov, K. P. "Biographical Data on General Nikolay G. Lyashchenko: Translated from *Voyenno Istoricheskiy Zhurnal*, May 1980." *Translations on USSR Military Affairs*, no. 1532 (September 10, 1980), 107–110.

RODION Y. MALINOVSKIY

355.   Bialer, Seweryn. "Rodion Iakovlevich Malinovsky." In George W. Simmonds, ed., *Soviet Leaders*. New York: Crowell, 1965. pp. 126–137.

356.   "Fellow Traveler." *Time* 75 (May 30, 1960), 16–19.

357.   "Marshal Rodion Y. Malinovskii." In Walter Yust, ed., *Ten Eventful Years*. Chicago, Ill.: Encyclopedia Britannica, 1947. p. 78.

358.   Noskov, I. "Marshal Malinovskiy." *Soviet Military Review*, no. 11 (November 1978), 34–36.

359.   "People of the Week: Marshal Rodion Malinovskii." *U.S. News and World Report* 43 (November 8, 1957), 19; 48 (June 13, 1960), 25.

VASILIY F. MARGELOV

360.   Lyashchenko, Nikolay G. "Biographical Data on Army General Margelov: Translated from *Voyenno Istoricheskiy Zhurnal*, December 1978." *Translations on USSR Military Affairs*, no. 1414 (March 1, 1979), 69–72.

KIRILL A. MERETSKOV

361.   "Marshal Meretskov." In Walter Yust, ed., *Ten Eventful Years*. Chicago, Ill.: Encyclopedia Britannica, 1947. p. 129.

KIRILL S. MOSKALENKO

362.   "People of the Week: Marshal Kirill S. Moskalenko." *U.S. News and World Report* 49 (November 7, 1960), 26.

IVAN G. PAVLOVSKIY

363.   Lashchenko, P. "Biographical Information on Army General Pavlovskiy: Translated from *Voyenno Istoricheskiy Zhurnal*, February 1979." *Translations on USSR Military Affairs*, no. 1431 (April 30, 1979), 22–26.

VLADIMIR PETROV

364.   Petrov, Vladimir. *My Retreat from Russia*. Translated from the Russian. New Haven, Conn.: Yale University Press, 1950. 357p.

PETR A. PIROGOV

365.   Pirogov, Petr A. *Why I Escaped*. Translated from the Russian. New York: Duell, Sloan & Pearce, 1950. 336p.

MARKIAN M. POPOV

366. "Colonel-General M. M. Popov: Translated from *Pravda,* November 15, 1952." *Current Digest of the Soviet Press* 4 (December 27, 1952), 33.

VLADIMIR RODINOV

367. Dallin, Alexander. "Rodinov: A Case Study in Wartime Redefection." *American Slavic Review* 18 (February 1959), 25–33.

KONSTANTIN K. ROKOSSOVSKIY

368. "Child of the People." *Time* 54 (November 21, 1949), 32–33.

369. Deutscher, Isaac. "Rokossovskiy: Pole or Russian?" *Reporter* 16 (January 10, 1957), 27–29.

370. "General Rokossovskii." In Walter Yust, ed., *Ten Eventful Years.* Chicago, Ill.: Encyclopedia Britannica, 1947. p. 798.

371. Leiser, Edward. "Poland Gets a New Russian Boss." *Saturday Evening Post* 223 (December 9, 1950), 34.

372. "People of the Week: Marshal Konstantin K. Rokossovskii." *U.S. News and World Report* 41 (July 13, 1956), 22; (October 26, 1956), 22; 43 (November 1, 1957), 19.

373. Robinson, Donald B. "Marshal Rokossovskii." *100 Most Important People in the World Today.* New York: Pocket Books, 1952. pp. 126–129.

BORIS M. SHAPOSHNIKOV

374. "Marshal Boris M. Shaposhnikov." In Walter Yust, ed., *Ten Eventful Years.* Chicago, Ill.: Encyclopedia Britannica, 1947. pp. 33–34.

375. Talmadge, I. D. W. "The Man Stalin Couldn't Purge." *Forum* 103 (April 1940), 161–165.

NIKOLAY A. SHCHELOKOV

376. Grushevoy, K. "Biographical Data on Army General [Nikolay A.] Shchelokov: Translated from *Voyenno Istoricheskiy Zhurnal,* November 1980." *Translations on USSR Military Affairs,* no. 1565 (February 5, 1981), 80–83.

SERGEI L. SOKOLOV

377. Binder, David. "Moscow's Man in Afghanistan." *New York Times Biographical Service* 11 (January 1980), 30–31.

VASILIY D. SOKOLOVSKIY

378. "People of the Week: Marshal Vasiliy D. Sokolovskiy." *U.S. News and World Report* 34 (March 6, 1953), 62.

MIKHAIL SOLOVIEV

379.   Soloviev, Mikhail. *My Nine Lives in the Red Army.* Translated from the Russian. New York: David McKay, 1955. 308p.

JOSEPH STALIN

380.   Deutscher, Isaac. *Stalin: A Political Biography.* 2d ed. New York and London: Oxford University Press, 1966. 661p.

381.   Grey, Ian. *Stalin, Man of History.* Garden City, N.Y.: Doubleday, 1979. 547p.

382.   Hingley, Ronald. *Joseph Stalin: Man and Legend.* New York: McGraw-Hill, 1974. 483p.

383.   Hyde, Harford M. *Stalin, the History of a Dictator.* New York: Farrar, 1972. 679p.

384.   Isayev, F. "Stalin's Military Genius." *New Times* [Moscow], no. 52 (December 1949), 21.

385.   Malenkov, Georgiy M. *Comrade Stalin, Leader of Progressive Mankind.* Moscow: Foreign Language Publishing House, 1950. 14p.

386.   Payne, Robert. *The Rise and Fall of Stalin.* New York: Simon & Schuster, 1965. 767p.

387.   Tremain, Rose. *Stalin.* Ballantine's Illustrated History of World War II, War Leader Book, no. 31. New York: Ballantine Books, 1975. 159p.

388.   Ulam, Adam B. *Stalin: The Man and His Era.* New York: Viking Press, 1973. 760p.

SEMEN K. TIMOSHENKO

389.   DeWeerd, Harvey A. "Timoshenko." *Great Soldiers of World War II.* New York: W. W. Norton, 1944. Chpt. 8.

390.   _____ . "Timoshenko and the Defensive Phase of the War." *Infantry Journal* 53 (December 1943), 30–38.

391.   "Marshal Semen K. Timoshenko." In Walter Yust, ed., *Ten Eventful Years.* Chicago, Ill.: Encyclopedia Britannica, 1947. p. 328.

392.   Sulzberger, Cyrus L. "Blitz-Grinder: Marshal Timoshenko, Whose Aim Has Been to Wear Down and Stall the German War Machine." *New York Times Magazine* (October 4, 1942), 5.

393.   Talmadge, I. D. W. "Moscow's Miracle Man: Marshal Timoshenko." *Asia* 42 (June 1942), 344–347.

394.   Wickware, Francis S. "Timoshenko, a Great Defensive Leader, Was the First Victorious Allied General." *Life* 14 (March 29, 1943), 98–105.

MIKHAIL N. TUKHACHEVSKIY

395.   McGranahan, William J. "The Fall and Rise of Marshal Tukhachevskiy." *Parameters* 8 (December 1978), 62–72.

DIMITRIY F. USTINOV

396.   "Biographical Data on Defense Minister Ustinov Related: Translated from *Voyenno Istoricheskiy Zhurnal,* October 1978." *Translations on USSR Military Affairs,* no. 1403 (December 18, 1978), 36–41.

397.   Boll, Michael M. "Soviet Defense Minister Dimitri Ustinov: A Self-Portrait." *Military Review* 60 (December 1980), 10–21.

ALEKSANDR M. VASILEVSKIY

398.   "Marshal Vasilevskiy." In Walter Yust, ed., *Ten Eventful Years.* Chicago, Ill.: Encyclopedia Britannica, 1947. p. 479.

NIKOLAI F. VATUTIN

399.   "General Vatutin." In Walter Yust, ed., *Ten Eventful Years.* Chicago, Ill.: Encyclopedia Britannica, 1947. p. 482.

FRED VIRSKI

400.   Virski, Fred. *My Life in the Red Army.* New York: Macmillan, 1949. 260p.

ANDREI A. VLASOV

401.   Artemiev, Vyacheslav P. "Soviet Volunteers in the German Army." *Military Review* 47 (November 1967), 56–64.

402.   Dallin, Alexander. *The Kaminsky Brigade, 1941–1944: A Case Study of German Military Exploitation of Soviet Disaffection.* Cambridge, Mass.: Russian Research Center, Harvard University, 1956. 122p.

403.   _____. "Soviet Reaction to Vlasov." *World Politics* 8 (April 1956), 307–322.

404.   Fischer, George. "General Vlasov's Official Biography." *Russian Review* 8 (October 1949), 284–301.

405.   _____. *Soviet Opposition to Stalin: A Case Study.* Cambridge, Mass.: Harvard University Press, 1952. 230p.   Reprinted by Greenwood Press in 1970.

406.   _____. "Vlasov and Hitler." *Journal of Modern History* 23 (March 1951), 58–71.

407.		Flanagan, James A. "Hitler's Forgotten Army." *American Legion Magazine* 102 (January 1977), 20.

408.		Hauser, Robert. "The Red Army's Traitor General." *Anthology of True*. New York: Nelson, 1962. pp. 97–104.

409.		Lyons, Edward. "General Vlasov's Mystery Army." *American Mercury* 66 (February 1948), 183–191.

410.		Steenberg, Sven. *Vlasov*. Translated from the German. New York: Alfred A. Knopf, 1970. 230p.

411.		Strik-Strikfeld, Wilfried. *Against Stalin and Hitler: Memoirs of the Russian Liberation Movement, 1941–1945*. Translated from the German. New York: Stein & Day, 1973. 270p.

NIKOLAI N. VORONOV

412.		"Marshal Voronov." In Walter Yust, ed., *Ten Eventful Years*. Chicago, Ill.: Encyclopedia Britannica, 1947. p. 516.

KLIMENT E. VOROSHILOV

413.		Duranty, Walter. "Marshal Voroshilov." *Stalin and Company*. New York: Sloane, 1949. pp. 116–129.

ALEKSEY A. YEPISHEV

414.		Moskalenko, Kirill S. "Biographical Information on Army General A. A. Yepishev: Translated from *Voyenno Istoricheskiy Zhurnal*, May 1978." *Translations on USSR Military Affairs*, no. 1373 (August 29, 1978), 30–37.

MATVEY V. ZAKHAROV

415.		Wolfe, Thomas W. *Note on the Naming of a Successor* [Marshal Zakharov] *to Marshal* [S. S.] *Biruzov*. RAND Paper P-3025. Santa Monica, Calif.: RAND Corporation, 1964. 23p.

GEORGIY K. ZHUKOV

416.		Baldwin, Hanson W. "Russia's Eisenhower Is Preparing, Too." *Collier's* 129 (January 12, 1955), 8–11.

417.		Bialer, Seweryn. "Georgi Konstantinovich Zhukov." In George W. Simmonds, ed., *Soviet Leaders*. New York: Crowell, 1965. pp. 149–164.

418.		"Blow-up in the Kremlin." *U.S. News and World Report* 43 (July 12, 1957), 23–29.		Zhukov's dismissal; for additional relative information, see the biographies of Nikita Khrushchev and Joseph Stalin cited above.

419.   Chaney, Otto P. "The Contribution of Georgi Konstantinovich Zhukov to the Soviet Scene, 1918–1968: A Reappraisal." PhD dissertation, American University, 1969.

420.   _____ . "The Resurrection of an Unperson." *Army* 16 (March 1966), 51–53.

421.   _____ . *Zhukov.* Norman: University of Oklahoma Press, 1971. 512p.

422.   _____ . *Zhukov, Marshal of the Soviet Union.* Ballantine's Illustrated History of World War II, War Leader Book, no. 28. New York: Ballantine Books, 1974. 159p.

423.   Cocks, Paul M. "The Purge of Marshal Zhukov." *Slavic Review* 22 (September 1963), 483–498.

424.   "Cocky Boss and a Headache." *Newsweek* 50 (July 22, 1957), 32.

425.   Colton, Timothy J. "The Zhukov Affair Reconsidered." *Soviet Studies* 28 (April 1977), 185–213.

426.   Conquest, Robert. "Zhukov and the Army, 1953–1957." In Robert Conquest, ed., *Power and Policy in the U.S.S.R.* New York: St. Martin's Press, 1962. pp. 329–345.

427.   Deutscher, Isaac. "Did Zhukov Carry De-Stalinization Too Far?" *Reporter* 17 (November 14, 1957), 15–16.

428.   "Dragoon's Day." *Time* 65 (April 1955), 59–61.

429.   Eisenhower, Dwight D. "Ike on Zhukov: 'We Were Friends.'" *U.S. News and World Report* 38 (February 18, 1955), 88–91.

430.   _____ , and John Foster Dulles. "Meaning of the Kremlin Purge." *U.S. News and World Report* 43 (July 26, 1957), 85–87.

431.   Fischer, Louis. "The Fatal Mistake of Marshal Zhukov." *Reader's Digest* 72 (March 1958), 96–99.

432.   "The General Who Saved Khrushchev's Job." *U.S. News and World Report* 43 (November 19, 1957), 42–44.

433.   "How the Deed Was Done." *Time* 70 (November 11, 1957), 30–31.

434.   "Ike and Zuke." *Time* 65 (February 21, 1955), 11–12.

435.   "In Zhukov's Good Time." *Time* 45 (February 19, 1945), 27–28.

436.   Lauterbach, R. E. "Zhukov." *Life* 18 (February 12, 1945), 94–96.

437.   "Marshal Zhukov." In Walter Yust, ed., *Ten Eventful Years.* Chicago, Ill.: Encyclopedia Britannica, 1947. p. 789.

438.   "Mission to Odessa." *Newsweek* 28 (July 29, 1946), 34. Zhukov's demotion by Stalin, who feared him as a rival.

439.   "New Power in Russia." *U.S. News and World Report* 38 (March 3, 1955), 28–30.

440.   Olshansky, B. "Our Pipe Dream about Zhukov." *American Mercury* 80 (March 1955), 111–115.

441.   "People of the Week: Marshal Georgii K. Zhukov." *U.S. News and World Report* 36 (May 21, 1954), 16.

442.   "Report on the Missing Marshal: What Has Happened to Zhukov?" *Newsweek* 42 (September 7, 1953), 32–34.

443.   Robinson, Donald B. "Marshal Zhukov." *100 Most Important People in the World Today.* New York: Pocket Books, 1952. pp. 118–121.

444.   _____ . "Marshal Zhukov." *100 Most Important People, 1953.* New York: Pocket Books, 1953. pp. 141–144.

445.   Roudakoff, P. P. "Ike and Zhukov." *Collier's* 136 (July 22, 1955), 82–85.

446.   Ruslanov, P. "Marshal Zhukov." *Russian Review* 15 (April-July, 1956), 122–129, 186–195.

447.   _____ . "The Personality and Role of Marshal Zhukov." *An Cosantoir* 17 (July 1957), 307–317.

448.   Salisbury, Harrison E. "Mystery Man of the Red Army." *Collier's* 136 (September 2, 1955), 78–81.

449.   _____ . "Zhukov, Rising Star in the Kremlin." *New York Times Magazine* (May 8, 1955), 14.

450.   Schwartz, Harry. "World-Wide Question: Zhukov's Role." *New York Times Magazine* (October 6, 1957), 16–20.

451.   "They Knew Zhukov When—Interviews with Generals of the West." *U.S. News and World Report* 38 (March 4, 1955), 52–57.

452.   "Top General: Zhukov." *Time* 65 (February 21, 1955), 21.

453.　　"Topsy-Turvy in the Kremlin." *Newsweek* 50 (November 4, 1957), 39–40.

454.　　"Tovarisch." *Newsweek* 26 (October 8, 1945), 48.

455.　　Union of Soviet Socialist Republics. Ministry of Information. "The Ouster of Marshal Zhukov: Text of Announcement, November 2, 1957." *Current History* 34 (January 1958), 50–51.

456.　　United States. Library of Congress. Legislative Reference Service. *Who Are They, Pt. 3: Georgi Zhukov and Ivan Konev.* Washington, D.C.: U.S. Government Printing Office, 1957. 7p.

457.　　Volkov, Leon. "A Hero's Role." *Newsweek* 48 (November 19, 1956), 51–52.

458.　　_____. "Marshal Zhukov to the Top?" *Newsweek* 47 (April 9, 1956), 48.

459.　　_____. "Private Correspondence between Ike and Zhukov." *Newsweek* 45 (May 2, 1955), 18–19.

460.　　_____. "Where Does Zhukov Stand?" *Newsweek* 42 (September 7, 1953), 34.

461.　　Zhukov, Georgiy K. *Marshal Zhukov's Greatest Battles.* Translated from the Russian. New York: Harper & Row, 1969. 304p.

462.　　_____. *The Memoirs of Marshal Zhukov.* Translated from the Russian. New York: Delacorte Press, 1971. 703p.

463.　　"Zhukov Breakthrough." *Time* 70 (July 22, 1957), 21.

464.　　"Zhukov Departs." *New Republic* 137 (November 11, 1957), 5.

465.　　"Zhukov Gets the Boot." *Senior Scholastic* 71 (November 15, 1957), 15.

466.　　"Zhukov, Moving Down." *Senior Scholastic* 71 (November 8, 1957), 15.

467.　　"Zhukov Upended." *America* 98 (November 16, 1957), 183.

2 / The Era of World War II, 1939–1945

Introduction

THIS SECTION, the largest in the book, is divided into four subsections. The first concerns information on general resources relative to the period as a whole. The second deals with events that affected the Red Army in the years immediately before the German invasion. Part 3 details the Red Army and its campaigns throughout the 1941–1945 Great Patriotic War, while part 4 examines the various arms and accoutrements employed by the Soviet soldier.

For most sections, a brief introduction points out the highlights of the events under discussion. Notes on further references will be found at the conclusion of each subsection.

A. General Works, Chronologies, and Atlases

1. General Works

BOOKS

468.   Adams, Henry H. *1942: The Year That Doomed the Axis.* New York: David McKay, 1967. 544p.

469.   _____ . *Years of Deadly Peril: The Coming of the War, 1939–1941.* New York: David McKay, 1969. 559p.

470.   _____ . *Years of Expectation: Guadalcanal to Normandy.* New York: David McKay, 1973. 430p.

471.   _____ . *Years to Victory.* New York: David McKay, 1973. 507p.

472.   Arnold-Foster, Mark. *The World at War.* New York: Stein & Day, 1973. 340p.

473.   Baldwin, Hanson W. *Great Mistakes of the War.* New York: Harper, 1950. 114p.

474.   _____ . *The World at War: Vol. I, The Crucial Years, 1939–1941.* New York: Harper & Row, 1976. 516p.

475.   Barker, Arthur J. *Panzers at War.* New York: Scribners, 1978. 144p.

476.   Blumentritt, Guenther. *Von Rundstedt: The Soldier and the Man.* Translated from the German. London: Odhams, 1952. 288p.

477.   Bradford, George. *Great Tank Battles of World War II: A Combat Diary of the Second World War.* New York: Arco, 1970.

478.   Brownlow, Donald G. *Panzer Baron: The Military Exploits of General Hasso von Manteuffel.* North Quincy, Mass.: Christopher Publishing House, 1975. 176p.

479.   Butler, James R. M., ed. *Grand Strategy.* History of the Second World War: United Kingdom Military Series. 6 vols. in 7. London: H.M. Stationery Office, 1957.

480.   Calvocoressi, Peter, and Guy Wint. *Total War: The Story of World War II.* New York: Pantheon, 1972. 959p.

481.   Carmichael, Thomas N. *The Ninety Days.* New York: Gernard Geiss, 1971. 302p.   October 4, 1942 to January 1, 1943.

482.   Chandler, David G. *The Art of Warfare on Land.* New York: Crown, 1974. 240p.

483.   Churchill, Winston S. *The Second World War.* Boston, Mass.: Houghton Mifflin, 1948–1953.

484.   Collier, Basil. *The Second World War: A Military History, from Munich to Hiroshima.* New York: William Morrow, 1967. 640p.

485.   Davis, Clyde R. *[Ewald] von Kleist, from Hussar to Panzer Marshal.* Houston, Tex.: Lancer Militaria, 1979. 110p.

486.   Detwiler, Donald S., ed. *World War II German Military Studies.* 24 vols. New York: Garland, 1980.   Selected from previously unpublished numbers in the U.S. Army's Foreign Military Studies series.

487.   Downing, David. *The Devil's Virtuosos: German Generals at War, 1940–1945.* New York: St. Martin's Press, 1977. 256p.

488.   Dupuy, R. Ernest. *World War II: A Compact History.* New York: Hawthorn, 1969. 334p.

489.   Dupuy, Trevor N. *European Land Battles.* Vols. I and II of *The Military History of World War II.* 20 vols. New York: Franklin Watts, 1967.

490.   Encyclopedia Americana, Editors of. *A Concise History of World War II*. New York: Praeger, 1964. 434p.

491.   Falls, Cyril. *The Second World War: A Short History*. 3d rev. ed. London: Methuen, 1950. 312p.

492.   Flower, Desmond, and James Reeves, eds. *The Taste of Courage: The War, 1939–1945*. New York: Harper, 1960. 1,120p.

493.   Gardner, Brian. *The Year That Changed the World: 1945*. New York: Coward-McCann, 1964. 356p.

494.   Garrett, Richard. *Clash of Arms: The World's Great Land Battles*. London: Weidenfeld & Nicolson, 1976. 160p.

495.   Guderian, Heinz. *Panzer Leader*. Translated from the German. New York: E. P. Dutton, 1952. 528p.   Reprinted in 1980.

496.   Halder, Franz. *The Halder Diaries*. 2 vols. Boulder, Colo.: Westview Press, 1977.

497.   Hartman, Tom, and Hunt, Robert. *Swastika at War: A Photographic Record of the War in Europe as Seen by the Cameramen of the German Magazine Signal*. Garden City, N.Y.: Doubleday, 1975. 160p.

498.   Hasluck, Eugene L. *The Second World War*. London: Blackie, 1978. 358p.

499.   Heiferman, Ronald. *World War II*. Secaucus, N.J.: Derbibooks, 1973. 256p.

500.   Hogg, Ian V. *Fortress: A History of Military Defense*. New York: St. Martin's Press, 1977. 160p.

501.   Holmes, Richard. *Epic Land Battles*. London: Octopus Books, 1976. 256p.

502.   Holt, Edgar. *The World at War, 1939–1945*. London: Putnam, 1957. 272p.

503.   Hoyle, Martha B. *A World in Flames: A History of World War II*. New York: Atheneum, 1970. 356p.

504.   Irving, David J. C. *Hitler's War*. New York: Viking Press, 1977. 926p.

505.   Jarman, Thomas L. *The Rise and Fall of Nazi Germany*. New York: New York University Press, 1956. 388p.

506.   Jones, James. *World War II*. New York: Grosset & Dunlap, 1975. 272p.

507.   Kahn, David. *Hitler's Spies: German Military Intelligence in World War II.* New York: Macmillan, 1978. 671p.

508.   Keegan, John. *Guderian.* Ballantine's Illustrated History of World War II, War Leader Book, no. 20. New York: Ballantine Books, 1973. 159p.

509.   _____. *Rundstedt.* Ballantine's Illustrated History of World War II, War Leader Book, no. 25. New York: Ballantine Books, 1974. 160p.

510.   Kesselring, Albert. *Kesselring: A Soldier's Record.* New York: William Morrow, 1954. 381p.

511.   *Land Power: A Modern Illustrated Military History.* London: Phoebus Books, 1979. 352p.

512.   Liddell-Hart, Basil H. *The German Generals Talk.* New York: Berkeley, 1958. 252p.

513.   _____. *History of the Second World War.* New York: G. P. Putnam, 1970. 768p.

514.   _____, ed. *World War II: An Illustrated History.* 16 vols. London: Purnell, 1977.

515.   Lukas, John A. *The Last European War.* Garden City, N.Y.: Doubleday, 1976. 562p.

516.   Lyons, Graham. *The Russian Version of the Second World War.* Hamden, Conn.: Shoe String Press, 1976. 142p.

517.   Macksey, Kenneth J. *Guderian: Center of the Blitzkrieg.* New York: Stein & Day, 1976. 226p.

518.   _____. *The History of Land Warfare.* New York: Two Continents, 1974. 248p.

519.   _____. *Panzer Division.* London: MacDonald, 1968. 160p.

520.   _____. *Tank Warfare: A History of Tanks in Battle.* New York: Stein & Day, 1972. 284p.

521.   Maule, Henry. *The Great Battles of World War II.* London and New York: Hamlyn, 1972. 448p.

522.   Mayer, S. L., ed. *Signal: Hitler's Wartime Picture Magazine.* Englewood Cliffs, N.J.: Prentice-Hall, 1976. 200p.

523.   Messenger, Charles. *The Blitzkrieg Story.* New York: Scribners, 1976. 253p.

524.   Michel, Henri. *The Second World War.* Translated from the French. London: Deutsch, 1975. 947p.

525.   Oleck, Howard L., comp. *Heroic Battles of World War II.* New York: Belmont Books, 1962. 189p.

526.   Pitt, Barrie, ed. *Great Battles of the 20th Century.* London: Phoebus Books, 1977. 384p.

527.   Pratt, Fletcher. *The Battles That Changed History.* New York: Hanover House, 1956. 348p.

528.   Preston, Anthony, ed. *Decisive Battles of Hitler's War.* London and New York: Hamlyn, 1977. 256p.

529.   Purnell Publishers. *History of the Second World War.* 96 pts. London, 1966–1967.

530.   Reader's Digest, Editors of. *The Reader's Digest Illustrated History of World War II.* Pleasantville, N.Y., 1969. 528p.

531.   Reeder, Russel P. *The Story of the Second World War.* 2 vols. London: Meredith, 1969–1970.

532.   Revie, Alastair. *The Pictorial History of Land Battles.* London: Marshal Cavendish, 1974. 128p.

533.   Rooney, Andrew A. *The Fortunes of War.* Boston, Mass.: Little, Brown, 1962. 240p.

534.   Rothberg, Abraham. *The Eyewitness History of World War II.* 4 vols. New York: Bantam Books, 1971.

535.   Shirer, William L. *The Rise and Fall of the Third Reich: A History of Nazi Germany.* New York: Simon & Schuster, 1960. 1,245p.

536.   *Signal, Years of Retreat, 1943–1944: Hitler's Wartime Picture Magazine.* Englewood Cliffs, N.J.: Prentice-Hall, 1979.

537.   Snyder, Louis L. *The War: A Concise History, 1939–1945.* New York: Julian Messner, 1960. 579p.

538.   Stamps, T. Dodson, and Vincent J. Esposito, eds. *A Military History of World War II.* 2 vols. West Point, N.Y.: Department of Military Art and Engineering, U.S. Military Academy, 1953.

539.   Stein, George H. *The Waffen SS: Hitler's Elite Guard at War, 1939–1945.* Ithaca, N.Y.: Cornell University Press, 1966. 330p.

540.   Stokesbury, James L. *A Short History of World War II.* New York: William Morrow, 1980. 420p.

541.   Strawson, John. *Hitler's Battles for Europe*. New York: Scribners, 1971. 256p.

542.   Sulzberger, Cyrus L. *The American Heritage Picture History of World War II*. New York: American Heritage, 1966. 640p.

543.   Taylor, Alan J. P., ed. *The Second World War: An Illustrated History*. New York: G. P. Putnam, 1975. 285p.

544.   Time Magazine, Editors of. *Time Capsules: History of the War Years*. 7 vols. in 1. New York: Bonanza Books, 1967.

545.   Toland, John. *Adolf Hitler*. New York: Ballantine Books, 1976. 1,371p.

546.   Von Mellenthin, Friedrich W. *Panzer Battles, 1939–1945: A Study of the Emergence of Armor in the Second World War*. Translated from the German. Norman: University of Oklahoma Press, 1956. 371p.

547.   Whiting, Charles. *Hunters from the Sky: The German Parachute Corps, 1941–1945*. New York: Stein & Day, 1974. 231p.

548.   Wilmot, Chester. *The Struggle for Europe*. New York: Harper, 1952. 766p.

549.   Wise, Arthur. *The Art and History of Personal Combat*. Greenwich, Conn.: Arma Press, 1972. 256p.

550.   Wright, Gordon. *The Ordeal of Total War, 1939–1945*. New York: Harper & Row, 1964. 315p.

551.   Wykes, Alan. *1942: The Turning Point*. London: Macdonald, 1972. 194p.

552.   Young, Peter, ed. *Decisive Battles of the Second World War: An Anthology*. London: Barker, 1967. 439p.

ARTICLES

553.   Batov, Pavel. "Present Day Views of the Lessons of World War II." *World Marxist Review* 23 (May 1980), 21–25.

554.   Gallagher, Matthew P. "Trends in Soviet Historiography of the Second World War." In John Keep, ed., *Contemporary History in the Soviet Union*. New York: Praeger, 1964. pp. 222–242.

555.   Komarov, N. "Instructor Guide for Indoctrination on World War II: Translated from *Kommunist Vooruzhennykh Sil*, June 1979." *Translations on USSR Military Affairs*, no. 1478 (November 29, 1979), 48–54.

556.   Liddell-Hart, Basil H. "The Second World War." In C. L. Mowat, ed., *The Shifting Balance of World Forces, 1898–1945*. Vol. 7 of *The New Cambridge Modern History*. 2d ed. 12 vols. Cambridge: At the University Press, 1968. pp. 735–797.

557.   Patrick, Stephen B. "The Waffen SS." *Strategy and Tactics*, no. 26 (March-April 1971), 10–16.

558.   Werth, Alexander. "The Soviet View of World War II." *Nation* 197 (September 14, 1963), 143–145.

DOCUMENTS, PAPERS, AND REPORTS

559.   Germany. Wehrmacht. Oberkommando. *Blitzkrieg to Defeat: Hitler's War Directives, 1939–1945*. Edited by Hugh R. Trevor-Roper. New York: Holt, Rinehart & Winston, 1964. 231p.

2. Chronologies

BOOKS

560.   Goralski, Robert. *World War II Almanac, 1931–1945: A Political an Military Record*. New York: G. P. Putnam, 1981. 500p.

561.   Rohwer, Juergen, and Gerhard Hummelchen. *Chronology of the War at Sea, 1939–1945*. Translated from the German. 2 vols. New York: Arco, 1973–1974.   Useful for amphibious operations.

562.   Royal Institute of International Affairs. *Chronology of the Second World War, 1938–1945*. London, 1947. 374p.

563.   Smith, Myron J., Jr. *Air War Chronology, 1939–1945*. 8 vols.+. Manhattan, Kans.: Military Affairs/Aerospace Historian for the USAF Historical Foundation, 1977–.   Useful for airborne operations.

564.   Williams, Mary H. *Chronology, 1941–1945*. United States Army in World War II: Special Studies. Washington, D.C.: Office of the Chief of Military History, Department of the Army, 1960. 660p.   Provides valuable coverage of the Russo-German War.

ARTICLES

565.   "Chronology of World War II." *Current History*, ns 8 (June 1945), 492–496.

566.   Galitsan, A. "The Year of Liberation." *Soviet Military Review*, no. 1 (January 1979), 7–9.   Events of 1944.

567.   Smith, Myron J., Jr. "Selected Chronology." *Intelligence, Propaganda and Psychological Warfare, Resistance Movements and Secret Operations, 1939–1945*. Vol. 1 of *The Secret Wars: A Guide to Sources in English*. Santa Barbara, Calif.: ABC-Clio, 1980. pp. xv–li.

568.   _____ . "Selected Chronology." *The Soviet Air and Strategic Rocket Forces, 1939–1980: A Guide to Sources in English.* Santa Barbara, Calif.: ABC-Clio, 1981. pp. xxix–xliv.

569.   "War Chronology: VE-Day to VJ-Day." *Current History,* ns 9 (September 1945), 182–183.

3. Atlases

570.   Banks, Arthur S. *A World Atlas of Military History, 1861–1945.* New York: Hippocrene Books, 1978. 160p.

571.   Chew, Allen P. *An Atlas of Russian History.* Rev. ed. New Haven, Conn.: Yale University Press, 1970. 127p.

572.   Cook, Christopher, and John Stevenson. *The Atlas of Modern Warfare.* New York: G. P. Putnam, 1978. 191p.

573.   Gilbert, Martin. *Russian History Atlas.* London: Weidenfeld & Nicolson, 1972. 146p.

574.   Horrabin, James F. *An Atlas-History of the Second World War.* 10 vols. London and New York: Nelson, 1942–1946.

575.   Williams, John. *World Atlas of Weapons and War.* London: Aldus Books, 1976. 128p.

576.   Young, Peter. *Atlas of the Second World War.* New York: G. P. Putnam, 1974. 288p.

B. Pre-Barbarossa Events, 1939–1941

In the decade following the Bolshevik Revolution, three principal factors influenced the development of the Soviet military. The first was the lack of ready resources or industry to support a large, modern defense establishment. The second was a series of reforms carried out by the energetic Mikhail Frunze, commissar of military affairs. Frunze established a relatively efficient system of military schools and academies, and organized territorial units similar to the American National Guard. He also gave tactical commanders more dignity and responsibility, leading to their eventual brief period of ascendency over the commissars before the Great Purges. The third factor was the acceptance by the CPSU of the idea that the U.S.S.R., as a great power, needed a modern, well-equipped military establishment which would give material strength to its position in world affairs.

When Frunze died in October 1925, he was replaced by a Stalinloyalist and military innocent, Kliment E. Voroshilov. Also about this time the Red Army began a close collaboration with the German Reichswehr. German-Russian arrangements, mutually advantageous to both, continued until 1933. As the Russians sought to modernize, Red Army leaders were able to "lean" on veteran Reichswehr officers for technical and leadership support. For their part, the Germans got space where they could train their men and exploit new technology, contrary to the strict terms of the 1919 Treaty of Versailles.

Stalin, War Commissar Voroshilov, and other Red leaders were extremely displeased with Russia's inability to field new equipment. In October 1928, the first Five Year Plan was launched to remedy this and other industrial ills of the U.S.S.R. By the early 1930's the rapid industrialization which resulted permitted extensive rearmament. Throughout the first half of that decade, the U.S.S.R. developed an effective military establishment; the Red Army, for its part, began to experiment with the use of airborne troops and by 1936 had, perhaps, the largest armored corps in the world.

Beginning slowly around 1934 and building through the later years of the decade, Stalin sought to remove all opposition to his rule through a series of blood purges. In September 1936, Yezhov became head of the NKVD, and under his psychopathic direction, the tempo of the removals reached such proportion that the Soviet people remember that time as the *Yezhovshchina,* or "in the terrible times of Yezhov." In 1938–1939, thousands of Red Army officers of great rank and small were liquidated; the leadership of the armed forces was decimated; and political commissars gained much influence. The Soviet ground forces were no longer able to claim accomplishment or efficiency; rather, they were weak and disorganized with morale and readiness severely damaged.

In the brief interlude between the purges and the German invasion in June 1941, the Soviet army was involved in three minor wars, two of which were relatively well handled, with the third an embarrassment.

In July 1938 there was a small clash with the Japanese in Mongolia known as the Lake Khasan incident. In the following year, however, a series of large-scale battles took place at Khalkin Gol, Manchuria, which resulted in victory for Soviet Russia. Incidentally, it was in the 1939 fighting that General Georgiy K. Zhukov, as commander of the 1st Army Group, first demonstrated his strategic brilliance.

Just as Zhukov's soldiers were defeating the Japanese, Stalin concluded a treaty of nonaggression with Nazi Germany, on August 23, 1939. In a secret protocol, Eastern Europe was to be divided between the two giants, with Russia to receive a chunk of Poland and dominance over the Baltic states.

On September 1, 1939, German troops moved into Poland, setting off World War II. Red Army commanders were surprised at the speed and effectiveness of the Blitzkrieg and hastened to move in for the spoils. The Soviet Byelorussian and Ukrainian fronts attacked the Poles from the rear on September 17, and four days later reached the line of demarcation established in the August 23 treaty.

In September and October, following a quick deal between Stalin and Hitler on adjustment of the Polish boundary, the Soviets, with German blessing, moved on the three Baltic states of Latvia, Estonia, and Lithuania. Each state was forced to sign a mutual defense pact with the Soviets, allowing Red Army troops to be stationed on their soil. Meanwhile in Poland, the NKVD and Red Army began to incorporate Polish territory directly into the U.S.S.R. with phoney elections held to ratify the Russian action.

In the north, Stalin put pressure on Finland, seeking territorial adjustment. Finnish negotiators refused to bow to Soviet demands, and on November 20 the Red Army launched an attack into that Baltic nation.

The early stages of the Russo-Finnish War were quite embarrassing for the Soviet Union. Although the average soldier fought well, the generalship, still suffering the shock of the purges, was poor and Soviet logistics worse. Additional problems were posed by the extreme severity of the 1939–1940 winter and the heroic resistance and military ability of the Finnish defenders. Resistance by the Finns finally crumbled in the spring of 1940, when the Russians committed overwhelming numbers of units. From the experience of the Russo-Finnish War, the Red Army was able to expose and replace a large number of incompetent leaders, and a new generation began to emerge.

The citations in this section detail the above described events. Further references to them are found in the general works cited in part 2:A.

1. Russia: Internal/External Events, Including the Purges

BOOKS

577.   Carmichael, Joel. *Stalin's Masterpiece: The Show Trials and Purges of the Thirties.* New York: St. Martin's Press, 1976. 238p.   For additional insight into the purges, see the biographies of Stalin cited.

578.   Conquest, Robert. *The Great Terror: Stalin's Purge of the Thirties.* Rev. ed. New York: Macmillan, 1973. 844p.

579.   Erickson, John. *The Soviet High Command: A Political-Military History, 1918–1941.* New York: St. Martin's Press, 1962. 889p.

580.   Koblyakov, I. K. *U.S.S.R.: For Peace Against Aggression, 1933–1941*. Moscow: Progress Publishers, 1976. 244p.

581.   Leach, Barry A. *German Strategy Against Russia, 1939–1941*. Oxford: At the Clarendon Press, 1973. 308p.

582.   Lewytzkyj, Borys, comp. *The Stalinist Terror of the Thirties: Documentation from the Soviet Press*. Stanford, Calif.: Hoover Institution Press, 1974. 521p.

583.   McSherry, James E. *Stalin, Hitler, and Europe, 1933–1941*. 2 vols. Cleveland, Ohio: World Publishing, 1968–1970.

584.   Weinberg, Gerhard L. *Germany and the Soviet Union, 1939–1941*. Translated from the German. Studies in East European History, no. 1. Leiden, Switz: E. J. Brill, 1972. 218p.

585.   Wollenberg, Erich. *The Red Army: A Study of the Growth of Soviet Imperialism*. Translated from the German. London: Secker & Warburg, 1940. 400p.   Reprinted by the New York firm of Hyperion Press in 1973.

ARTICLES

586.   Assman, Kenneth. "Stalin and Hitler." *U.S. Naval Institute Proceedings* 75 (June-July 1949), 638–651, 759–773.

587.   Atkinson, Littleton B. "Conflict of Command in the Red Army, 1918–1942." *Military Review* 31 (March 1952), 33–47.

588.   Daynes, V. "Soviet Combined Arms Development, 1929–1941: Translated from *Voyenno Istoricheskiy Zhurnal*, October 1978." *Translations on USSR Military Affairs*, no. 1404 (December 21, 1978), 81–90.

589.   Erickson, John. "The Soviet Military Purge, 1939–1957." *20th Century* 162 (July 1957), 28–40.

590.   Goff, James F. "The 1940 Soviet Tank Divisions: Geographic Order of Battle Analysis." *History, Numbers and War* 2 (Winter 1978–1979), 187–189.

591.   Hudson, George F. "The Red Army Purge of 1937." *Contemporary Review* 175 (May 1949), 289–296.

592.   Khrushchev, Nikita S. "On the Military Consequences of the Purges." In David B. Ralston, ed., *Soldiers and States: Civil-Military Relations in Modern Europe*. Boston, Mass.: D. C. Heath, 1966. pp. 175–177.

593.   Nikitin, Y. "The Buildup of the Soviet Economy to Repulse Aggression, 1939–1941." *Soviet Military Review,* no. 3 (March 1971), 40–42.

594.   Popov, N. "The Use of Tank Forces in Defense on the Eve of the Great Patriotic War: Translated from *Voyenno Istoricheskiy Zhurnal,* March 1979." *Translations on USSR Military Affairs,* no. 1441 (May 24, 1979), 67–73.

595.   "Purges at Home, Expansion Abroad." *Senior Scholastic* 80 (February 14, 1962), 16–18.

596.   Reeves, Earl. "Why Russia Can't Fight: A Secret Service Report Explains Russia's Military Weakness." *Reader's Digest* 36 (March 1940), 60–63.

597.   Schapiro, Leonard. "The Great Purge." In David B. Ralston, ed., *Soldiers and States: Civil-Military Relations in Modern Europe.* Boston, Mass.: D. C. Heath, 1966. pp. 169–172.

598.   Sella, Amnon. "Red Army Doctrine and Training on the Eve of the Second World War." *Soviet Studies* 27 (April 1975), 245–264.

599.   Vannikov, V. L. "The Defense Industry on the Eve of the War: Translated from *Voprosy Istoriy,* October 1968-January 1969." *Translations on USSR Military Affairs,* no. 1337 (March 14, 1978), 1–49.

600.   Voroshilov, Kliment E. "On the State of the Army in 1939." In David B. Ralston, ed., *Soldiers and States: Civil-Military Relations in Modern Europe.* Boston, Mass.: D. C. Heath, 1966. pp. 173–174.

601.   Werth, Alexander. "How Russia Geared for War." *Nation* 166 (March 6, 1948), 273–275.

DOCUMENTS, PAPERS, AND REPORTS

602.   Atkinson, Littleton B. *Dual Command in the Red Army, 1918– 1942.* Documentary Research Study. Maxwell AFB, Ala.: Air University, 1950. 67p.

603.   Germany. Austwärtiges Amt. *Nazi-Soviet Relations, 1939–1941.* Edited by Raymond J. Sontag and James S. Beddie. Department of State Publication, no. 3023. Washington, D.C.: U.S. Government Printing Office, 1948. 362p.

604.   Taylor, Kenneth C. "The Reorganization of the Soviet Command System for Total War, 1939–1941." PhD dissertation, Princeton University, 1973.

2. The Manchurian Incidents

BOOKS

605.   Coox, Alvin D. *The Anatomy of a Small War: The Soviet-Japanese Struggle for Chankufeng/Khasan, 1938.* Westport, Conn.: Greenwood Press, 1977. 409p.

606.   Morley, James W., ed. *Deterrent Diplomacy: Japan, Germany, and the U.S.S.R., 1935–1940.* Translated from the Japanese. New York: Columbia University Press, 1976.

ARTICLES

607.   Odintsov, V. "Khalkhin-Gol Operation—Logistical Support Features: Translated from *Voyenno Istoricheskiy Zhurnal,* September 1980." *Translations on USSR Military Affairs,* no. 1553 (December 29, 1980), 50–57.

608.   "Outer Mongolia: Frontier Incident." *Time* 34 (July 17, 1939), 25–26.

609.   "Rehearsal for War: Japanese and Russians Find Each Other Formidable Foes." *Newsweek* 14 (July 24, 1939), 21–22.

610.   "Small Wars and Border Problems, 1939: The Nomonhan Incident." In Donald S. Detwiler, ed., *War in Asia and the Pacific, 1937– 1949: Japanese and Chinese Studies and Documents.* 15 vols. New York: Garland, 1980. XI, chpt. 1.   For further information, see Marshal Zhukov's memoirs.

611.   Thach, Joseph E., Jr. "Soviet Military Aid to the Chinese Nationalist Government during the Sino-Japanese War, 1937–1941." *Military Review* 57 (September 1977), 49–56.

DOCUMENTS, PAPERS, AND REPORTS

612.   Goldman, Stuart D. "The Forgotten War: The Soviet Union and Japan, 1937–1939." PhD dissertation, Georgetown University, 1970.

3. Poland

BOOKS

613.   Aster, Sidney. *1939: The Making of the Second World War.* New York: Simon & Schuster, 1973. 456p.

614.   Bethell, Nicholas W. *The War Hitler Won: The Fall of Poland, September 1939.* New York: Holt, Rinehart & Winston, 1973. 472p.

615.   Tasca, Angelo. *The Russo-German Alliance, August 1939–June 1941*. Boston, Mass.: Beacon Press, 1951. 218p.

ARTICLES

616.   Adamkiewicz, George. "Hammer and Sickle over Poland." *Contemporary Review* 158 (July 1940), 63–69.

617.   "Dizziness from Success." *Time* 34 (September 25, 1939), 22–24.

618.   "Poland under Occupation." *19th Century* 127 (June 1940), 672–675.

619.   "Soviet Aid in Carving Poland Portends New World Line-up." *Newsweek* 14 (September 25, 1939), 11–14.

DOCUMENTS, PAPERS, AND REPORTS

620.   Berman, Sylvan M. "Hitler: A Study of Ideology and 'Realpolitik' in German-Soviet Relations, 1938–1941." PhD dissertation, American University, 1962.

4. The Russo-Finnish War and the Soviet Occupation of the Baltic States

BOOKS

621.   Chew, Allen P. *The White Death: The Epic of the Soviet-Finnish War*. East Lansing: Michigan State University Press, 1971. 313p.

622.   Coates, William P., and Zelda K. *Russia, Finland, and the Baltic*. London: Lawrence & Wishart, 1940. 144p.

623.   ———. *The Soviet-Finnish Campaign, Military and Political, 1939–1940*. London: Eldon, 1942. 172p.

624.   Condon, Richard. *The Winter War: Russia Against Finland*. Ballantine's Illustrated History of the Violent Century. New York: Ballantine Books, 1972. 160p.

625.   Cox, Geoffrey. *The Red Army Moves*. London: Gollancz, 1941. 278p.

626.   Elliston, Herbert B. *Finland Fights*. London: Harrap, 1940. 398p.

627.   Engle, Eloise, and Lauri Paananen. *The Winter War: The Russo-Finnish Conflict, 1939–1940*. New York: Scribners, 1973. 176p.

628.   Jutikkala, Eino, and Kauko Pirinen. *A History of Finland*. Translated from the Finnish. Rev. ed. New York: Praeger, 1974. 293p.

629.   Kaslas, Bronis J., ed. *The U.S.S.R.-German Aggression Against Lithuania.* New York: Robert Speller, 1973. 543p.

630.   Krosby, H. Peter. *Finland, Germany, and the Soviet Union, 1940–1941.* Madison: University of Wisconsin Press, 1968. 276p.

631.   Langdon-Davies, John. *Invasion in the Snow: A Study of Mechanized War.* Boston, Mass.: Houghton Mifflin, 1941. 202p.

632.   Mannerheim, Carl G. *The Memoirs of Marshal Mannerheim.* Translated from the Finnish. London: Cassell, 1953. 540p.

633.   Paley, Alan L. *The Russo-Finnish War.* Great Events of Our Times, no. 5. Charlotteville, N.Y.: Sam Har Press, 1973. 32p.

634.   Sabaliunas, Leonas. *Lithuania in Crisis: Nationalism to Communism, 1939–1940.* Bloomington: Indiana University Press, 1972. 293p.

635.   Upton, Anthony F. *Finland in Crisis, 1940–1941: A Study in Small Power Politics.* Ithaca, N.Y.: Cornell University Press, 1965. 318p.

636.   ———. *Finland, 1939–1940.* London: Davis-Poynter, 1974. 174p.

637.   Ward, Edward H. H. *Despatches from Finland, January-April 1940.* London: Lane, 1940. 160p.

638.   Warner, Oliver. *Marshal Mannerheim and the Finns.* Helsinki, Finland: Otava, 1976. 232p.

639.   Wuorinen, John H., ed. *Finland and World War II, 1939–1944.* New York: Ronald Press, 1948. 228p.

ARTICLES

640.   Anderson, Albin T. "Origins of the Winter War: A Study of Russo-Finnish Diplomacy." *World Politics* 6 (January 1954), 169–189.

641.   Barclay, Glen St. J. "Diversion in the East: The Western Allies, Scandinavia, and Russia, November 1939–April 1940." *Historian* (May 1979), 483–498.

642.   Bates, Ralph. "Disaster in Finland." *New Republic* 101 (December 13, 1939), 221–225.

643.   Bruce, E. L. "Attack on Finland." *Queen's Quarterly* 47 (February 1940), 48–53.

644.   Bryan, P. H. H. "War in the Artic." *Army Quarterly* 56 (April 1948), 93–102.

645.   Chew, Allen P. "Beating the Russians in Snow: The Finns and the Russians, 1940." *Military Review* 55 (June 1980), 38–47.

646.   Dudin, Mikhail. "An Island in the River of Memory." *Soviet Literature*, no. 9 (September 1977), 38–42.

647.   Eliot, George F. "The Russian Campaign Against Finland." *Life* 8 (January 15, 1940), 26–28.

648.   Elliston, Herbert B. "On the Finnish Front." *Atlantic* 166 (February 1940), 243–249.

649.   Evans, Frederic. "Campaigning in Arctic Russia." *Journal of the Royal United Service Institute* 86 (May 1941), 290–298.

650.   "Finns Prove Themselves the Best Winter Soldiers in the World." *Life* 8 (January 22, 1940), 13–17.

651.   "Flayed by Finns, Russians Muster New Strength, But Still Take Heavy Beating." *Newsweek* 15 (January 15, 1940), 19–20.

652.   Fuqua, Stephen O. "Big and Little Guns on the Finnish Front." *Newsweek* 15 (January 8, 1940), 20.

653.   _____. "Factors in the Russian Slowdown." *Newsweek* 15 (January 1, 1940), 17.

654.   _____. "Has the Red Army Broken the Mannerheim Line?" *Newsweek* 15 (March 4, 1940), 27.

655.   _____. "Russia's Invasion Seesaws over Finland." *Newsweek* 14 (December 25, 1939), 20.

656.   _____. "The Russo-Finnish War in Retrospect." *Newsweek* 15 (March 25, 1940), 30.

657.   _____. "When Spring Comes to Finland." *Newsweek* 15 (February 26, 1940), 22.

658.   _____. "Why the Russians are Taking a Licking." *Newsweek* 15 (February 5, 1940), 23.

659.   "The Gangster Attack on Finland." *Army Quarterly* 40 (April 1940), 32–40.

660.   Gellhorn, Martha. "Blood on the Snow: A Visit to the Front in Finland." *Collier's* 105 (January 20, 1940), 9–11.

661.   Goff, James F. "Winter War: Russo-Finnish Conflict, November 1939–March 1940." *Strategy and Tactics*, no. 33 (July 1972), 27–35.

662. "Lickings Taken by the Red Army Spoil Stalin's Birthday Party." *Newsweek* 15 (January 1, 1940), 14–16.

663. Mydans, Carl M. "War in Winter." *Life* 8 (January 29, 1940), 57–63.

664. "The Northern Theater." *Time* 34 (December 11, 1939), 23–25. Continues in subsequent issues through March 25, 1940.

665. Peitsara, T. "A Short General Survey of the War between Finland and Russia in the Winter of 1939–1940." *Army Quarterly* 43 (October 1941), 45–62.

666. "Red Myth: Prestige of Soviet Juggernaut Deflated in Finnish Invasion." *Newsweek* 14 (December 25, 1939), 21–22.

667. "The Red Push." *Newsweek* 15 (March 4, 1940), 25.

668. "The Red War on Finland." *Current History* 51 (January 1940), 10–11.

669. "Red Waves." *Newsweek* 15 (February 19, 1940), 26–27.

670. "Reds Find Finns and Weather a Tough Combination to Buck." *Newsweek* 14 (December 11, 1939), 21–28.

671. "The Russo-Finnish War." *Fighting Forces* 16 (February 1940), 493–500.

672. Schuler, Emil. "Fighting in the Forests of Finland." *Military Review* 40 (December 1960), 91–97.

673. "The Second Battle of Suomussalni." *Life* 8 (February 12, 1940), 28–32.

674. "The War in Finland." *Round Table* 30 (March–June 1940), 303–311, 506–512.

675. "War on Skis: The Mobile Forces of the North." *Journal of the Royal United Service Institution* 85 (February 1940), 103–104.

676. Westwood, J. N. "Finland: Russia Attacks." In Alan J. P. Taylor, ed., *Purnell's History of the 20th Century.* 10 vols. London: New Caxton Library Service, 1972. VII, 1691-1693.

DOCUMENTS, PAPERS, AND REPORTS

677. Anzulovic, J. V., Jr. "The Russian Record of the Winter War, 1939–1940." PhD dissertation, University of Maryland, 1968.

678.   Condon, Richard W. "The Moscow Parenthesis: A Study of Finnish-German Relations, 1940–1941." PhD dissertation, University of Minnesota, 1960.

C. The Great Patriotic War, 1941–1945

The citations in this section detail the organization and operations of the Red Army during the anti-German phase of World War II.

In addition to a large number of sources relative to the "Eastern Front" as a whole, the user will find references to the make-up of the Soviet ground forces, its leaders, strategy and tactics, partisan operations, and the many campaigns and battles. Later subsections provide citations related to the 1945 Soviet campaign in Manchuria, Lend-Lease and cooperation with the United States and Great Britain, and details of Russian arms, uniforms, medals, and insignia.

Many of the parts in this section have their own introductions and contain cross-reference notes.

1. General Works

BOOKS

679.   Allen, William E. D., and Paul Maratoff. *The Russian Campaigns of 1941–1943*. Harmondsworth, Eng.: Penguin, 1944. 192p.

680.   _____. *The Russian Campaigns of 1944–1945*. Harmondsworth, Eng.: Penguin, 1946. 332p.

681.   Amosoff, Nikolai. *PPG-2266: A Surgeon's War*. Chicago, Ill.: Regnery, 1975. 261p.

682.   Anders, Wladyslaw. *Hitler's Defeat in Russia*. Chicago, Ill.: Regnery, 1953. 267p.

683.   Bann, Peter. *The Invisible Flag*. New York: John Day, 1956. 250p.   A German surgeon's view of the Russian fighting.

684.   Bethell, Nicholas. *Russia Besieged*. World War II Series. Alexandria, Va.: Time-Life Books, 1977. 208p.

685.   Brown, James E. *Russia Fights*. New York: Scribners, 1943. 276p.

686.   Buss, Philip H., and Andrew Mollow. *Hitler's Germanic Legions: An Illustrated History of Western European Legions with the S.S. [in Russia], 1941–1943*. New York: Beekman House, 1978. 160p.

687.   Clark, Alan. *Barbarossa: The Russian-German Conflict, 1941–1945.* New York: William Morrow, 1965. 522p.

688.   Dallin, Alexander. *German Rule in Russia, 1941–1945: A Study of Occupation Policies.* New York: St. Martin's Press, 1957. 695p.

689.   Danishevsky, I., comp. *The Road of Battle and Glory.* Translated from the Russian. Moscow: Foreign Language Publishing House, 1964. 366p.   Personal narratives by Soviet officers and soldiers.

690.   Dunstan, Simon. *Great Tank Battles.* London: Ian Allan, 1979. 112p.

691.   Eremenko, Andrei I. *The Arduous Beginning.* Translated from the Russian. Moscow: Progress Publishers, 1966. 328p.

692.   _____ . *False Witnesses: An Exposure of Falsified [German] Second World War Histories.* Translated from the Russian. Moscow: Foreign Language Publishing House [1964?]. 145p.

693.   Erickson, John. *The Road to Stalingrad: Stalin's War with Germany.* New York: Harper & Row, 1975. 594p.

694.   Gallagher, Matthew P. *The Soviet History of World War II: Myths, Memories, and Realities.* New York: Praeger, 1963. 205p.

695.   *German Experiences in Russia, December 1941–April 1944.* New Martinsburg, W. Va.: Game Marketing, 1974. 160p.

696.   Grossman, Vasiliy S. *The Years of War, 1941–1945.* Moscow: Foreign Language Publishing House, 1946. 451p.

697.   Higgins, Trumbull. *Hitler and Russia: The Third Reich in a Two-Front War, 1937–1943.* New York: Macmillan, 1966. 310p.

698.   Icks, Robert J. *Famous Tank Battles.* Garden City, N.Y.: Doubleday, 1972. 365p.

699.   Jackson, William G. F. *Seven Roads to Moscow.* London: Eyre & Spottiswoode, 1957. 334p.

700.   Kallistov, D. P. *History of the U.S.S.R., Pt. 3: From the Beginning of the Great Patriotic War to the Present Day.* Translated from the Russian. Moscow: Progress Publishers, 1977. 326p.

701.   Kleinfeld, Gerald R., and Lewis A. Tambs. *Hitler's Spanish Legion: The Blue Division in Russia.* Carbondale: Southern Illinois University Press, 1979. 434p.

702.   Kournahoff, Sergei N. *What Russia Did for Victory.* New York: New Century, 1945. 63p.

703.   Krieger, Evgenci G. *From Moscow to the Russian Frontier.* London: Hutchinson, 1945. 136p.

704.   Laqueur, Walter. *Russia and Germany: A Century of Conflict.* Boston, Mass.: Little, Brown, 1965. 367p.

705.   *Letters from the Dead: Last Letters from Soviet Men and Women Who Died Fighting the Nazis, 1941–1945.* Moscow: Progress Publishers, 1965. 236p.

706.   Levinthal, David, and Garry Trudeau. *Hitler Moves East: A Graphic Chronicle, 1941–1943.* Kansas City, Mo.: Sheed Andrews & McMeel, 1977. 95p.

707.   Lucas, James. *War on the Eastern Front, 1941–1945: The German Soldier in Russia.* New York: Stein & Day, 1980. 214p.

708.   Lyons, Graham. *The Russian Version of the Second World War: The History of the War as Taught to Soviet School Children.* Hamden, Conn.: Shoe String Press, 1977. 142p.

709.   Mikhailov, Nikolai N. *The Russian Story.* Translated from the Russian. New York: Sheridan House, 1945. 191p.

710.   Minasyan, M. M., ed. *Great Patriotic War of the Soviet Union.* Translated from the Russian. Moscow: Progress Publishers, 1974. 469p.   The official Russian history of the war was published by the U.S.S.R. Ministry of Defense in the 6-volume 1960 *History of the Great Patriotic War of the Soviet Union*; the U.S. firm of United Translation translated the work into English and a few copies have been distributed to military libraries by the Office of the Chief of Military History, Department of the Army.

711.   Mrazkova, Damela, and Vladimir Remes. *The Russian War, 1941–1945.* New York: E. P. Dutton, 1977. 152p.

712.   ｣Neumann, Peter. *The Black March: The Personal Story of an SS Man.* Translated from the French. New York: Sloane, 1959. 312p.

713.   Pabst, Helmut. *The Outermost Frontier: A German Soldier in the Russian Campaign.* Translated from the German. London: Kimber, 1957. 204p.

714.   Paget, R. T. *Manstein: His Campaigns and His Trial.* London: Collins, 1951. 239p.

715.   Palsokar, R. D. *Manstein, the Master General.* Translated from the German. Poona, W. Ger.: Privately printed, 1970. 176p.

716.   Paneth, Philip. *The Epic of the Soviet Cities.* London: Alliance, 1943. 127p.

717.   Piliar, Iuriy. *It All Really Happened.* Translated from the Russian. Moscow: Foreign Language Publishing House, 1960. 187p.

718.   Polevoi, Boris N. *From Belgorod to the Carpathians: From a Soviet War Correspondent's Notebook.* Translated from the Russian. London: Hutchinson, 1945. 164p.

719.   Poliakov, Aleksandr. *Russians Don't Surrender.* Translated from the Russian. New York: E. P. Dutton, 1942. 191p.

720.   Prueller, Wilhelm. *Diary of a German Soldier.* Translated from the German. New York: Coward-McCann, 1963. 200p. A Wehrmacht lieutenant remembers the Russian front.

721.   Quarrie, Bruce, ed. *Panzers in Russia, 1941–1943.* World War II Photo Album Series, no. 9. New York: Patrick Stephens, 1979. 95p.

722.   _____ . *Panzers in Russia, 1943–1945.* World War II Photo Album Series, no. 12. New York: Patrick Stephens, 1979. 95p.

723.   _____ . *Tank Battles in Miniature, Vol. 2: A Wargamer's Guide to the Russian Campaign, 1941–1945.* London: Stephens, 1975. 200p.

724.   _____ . *Waffen-SS in Russia.* World War II Photo Album Series, no. 3. New York: Patrick Stephens, 1979. 96p.

725.   Reitlinger, Gerald. *The House Built on Sand: The Conflicts of German Policy in Russia, 1939–1945.* New York: Viking Press, 1960. 459p.

726.   Reynolds, Quentin. *The Curtain Rises.* New York: Random House, 1944. 353p.

727.   _____ . *Only the Stars Are Neutral.* New York: Random House, 1942. 298p.

728.   Rudel, Hans-Ulrich. *Stuka Pilot.* Translated from the German. New York: Ballantine Books, 1958. 259p.

729.   *Russians Tell the Story: Sketches of the War on the Soviet-German Front.* London: Hutchinson, 1944. 146p.

730.   Sajer, Guy. *The Forgotten Soldier.* Translated from the French. New York: Harper & Row, 1971. 465p.

731.   Salisbury, Harrison E. *The Unknown War.* New York: Bantam Books, 1978. 219p.

732.   Scheibert, Horst. *Panzers in Russia: German Armoured Forces on the Eastern Front, 1941–1944.* Translated from the German. London: Altmark, 1974. 237p.

733.   Schmidt, Paul K. *Hitler Moves East* [1941–1942]. By Paul Carrell, pseud. Translated from the German. Boston, Mass.: Little, Brown, 1965. 640p.

734.   _____. *Scorched Earth: The Russian-German War, 1943–1944.* By Paul Carrell, pseud. Translated from the German. Boston, Mass.: Little, Brown, 1970. 556p.

735.   Seaton, Albert. *The Russo-German War, 1941–1945.* New York: Praeger, 1971. 628p.

736.   Shaw, John. *Red Army Resurgent.* World War II Series. Alexandria, Va.: Time-Life Books, 1979. 208p.   The Russo-German War through Stalingrad.

737.   Simonov, Konstantin M. *No Question.* Translated from the Russian. New York: L. B. Fischer, 1943. 231p.

738.   Snow, Edgar. *People on Our Side.* New York: Random House, 1944. 324p.

739.   Spielberger, Walter J., and Uwe Feist. *Armor on the Eastern Front.* Armor Series, no. 6. Fallbrook, Calif.: Aero Publishers, 1968. 48p.

740.   Stern, Robert C. *SS Armor.* Warren, Mich.: Squadron/Signal Publications, 1978. 80p.

741.   Strategy and Tactics, Editors of. *War in the East: The Russo-German Conflict, 1941–1945.* Strategy and Tactics Staff Study, no. 1. New York: Simulations Publications, 1977. 186p.

742.   Van Creveid, Martin L. *Hitler's Strategy, 1940–1941.* Cambridge: At the University Press, 1973. 248p.

743.   Von Manstein, Erich. *Lost Victories.* Translated from the German. Chicago, Ill.: Regnery, 1958. 574p.

744.   Von Senger und Etterlin, Fridolin M. *Neither Fear Nor Hope.* Translated from the German. New York: E. P. Dutton, 1964. 368p.   These last two entries are memoirs by German commanders.

745.   Voznesenskiy, Nikolai A. *Economy of the U.S.S.R. during World War II.* New York: Public Affairs Press, 1948. 115p.

746.   Werth, Alexander. *Russia at War, 1941–1945.* New York: E. P. Dutton, 1964. 1,100p.

747.   Ziemke, Earl F. *Stalingrad to Berlin: The German Defeat in the East.* Army Historical Series. Washington, D.C.: Office of the Chief of Military History, Department of the Army, 1968. 599p.

748.   Zubkov, I., ed. *The Second World War.* Translated from the Russian. Moscow: Progress Publishers, n.d. 560p.

ARTICLES

749.   Aldridge, James. "Memory and Duty." *World Marxist Review* 23 (May 1980), 29–31.

750.   Barrows, Frederick M. "The Russo-German War." *Command and General Staff School Quarterly* 21 (October 1941), 43–45.

751.   Bayerlein, Fritz. "With the Panzers in Russia, 1941 and 1943." *Marine Corps Gazette* 38 (December 1954), 46–65.

752.   Brown, Ronald J. "World War II German Success Shows How to Handle Russian Armor." *Marine Corps Gazette* 61 (August 1977), 33–37.

753.   Chaney, Otto P. "The Agony of Soviet Military Historians." *Military Review* 48 (June 1968), 24–28.

754.   Cope, Harley F. "Let's Examine the Russian Military Record." *American Mercury* 89 (November 1959), 128–131.

755.   Dunnigan, James F. "Soviet and German Weapons and Tactics in the East." *Strategy and Tactics,* no. 28 (July-August 1971), *passim.*

756.   Fitzgerald, F. N. "The Russo-German Battles, 1941–1945." *Armored Cavalry Journal* 55 (September 1946), 62–67; (October 1946), 20–24; 56 (January 1947), 24–27.

757.   Glabisz, Kazimierz. "Causes of the German Defeat in the 1941–1945 Russo-German Campaigns." *Military Review* 30 (January 1951), 32–41.

758.   Goodspeed, D. J. "War on the Eastern Front." *Canadian Army Journal* 3 (December 1949), 1–6; (January 1950), 10–14; (February 1950), 4–10; (March 1950), 7–12.

759.   "The Great Victory." *Soviet Military Review,* no. 4 (April 1970), 2–9.

760.   Grechko, Andrei A. "The Great Exploits of the Soviet People—U.S.S.R. Invincible East and West: Translated from *Pravda,* May 9, 1970." *Current Digest of the Soviet Press* 22 (June 9, 1970), 1–6.

761.   ———. "The Great Victory and Its Lessons." *World Marxist Review* 18 (March 1975), 3–16.

762.   Grinyov, V. "On a Wide Frontage." *Soviet Military Review,* no. 9 (September 1979), 10–11.

763.   Guderian, Heinz. "The Experiences of War in Russia." *Military Review* 37 (July 1957), 90–97.

764.   Jessup, John E., Jr. "Soviet-German Operations, 1941–1945." In Thomas Parris, ed., *The Simon and Schuster Encyclopedia of World War II.* New York: Simon & Schuster, 1978. pp. 586–591.

765.   Katukov, Mikhail, and Pavel Batov. "From Moscow to Berlin, 1941–1945: Interviews." *Soviet Military Review,* no. 4 (April 1975), 20–23.

766.   Khrushchev, Nikita S. "The Great Patriotic War." *Life* 69 (December 4, 1970), 48–54.

767.   Kleinfeld, Gerald R., and Lewis A. Tambs. "North to Russia: The Spanish Blue Division in World War II." *Military Affairs* 37 (February 1973), 8–12.

768.   Korkeshkin, A. "Main Front in the Second World War." *Soviet Military Review,* no. 6 (June 1969), 42–45.

769.   Kositsyn, A. "World War II—Sources of Victory Discussed: Translated from *Kommunist Vooruzhennykh Sil,* January 1980." *Translations on USSR Military Affairs,* no. 1520 (June 24, 1980), 1–13.

770.   Lambert, P. C. "The German Defeat in Russia." *Journal of the Royal United Services Institute* 98 (February 1953), 95–101.

771.   Lanza, Conrad H. "The Campaigns in Russia." *Field Artillery Journal* 33 (April 1943), 296–304.

772.   ———. "The Russo-German War." *Field Artillery Journal* 32 (June 1942), 434–440; (July 1942), 512–521; (August 1942), 629–635; (September 1942), 715–722; (October 1942), 767–773; (November 1942), 840–845; (December 1942), 903–910.

773.   "Letters from the Front." *Soviet Literature,* no. 8 (August 1976), 116–121.

774.   Lind, William S. "Some Doctrinal Questions for the United States Army." *Military Review* 57 (March 1977), 54–65.   Includes comments on the Russian front.

775.   Losik, O. A. "The Triumph of the Soviet Art of War: Translated from *Kommunist Vooruzhennykh Sil,* March 1980." *Translations on USSR Military Affairs,* no. 1526 (July 31, 1980), 18–28.

776.   Millar, James R. "Financing the Soviet Effort in World War II." *Soviet Studies* 32 (January 1980), 106–123.

777.   ————, and Susan J. Linz. "The Cost of World War II to the Soviet People: A Research Note, with Rejoinder." *Journal of Economic History* 38 (December 1978), 959–962; 40 (December 1980), 845.

778.   Miller, Jesse W., Jr. "Forest Fighting on the Eastern Front in World War II." *Geographic Review* 62 (April 1972), 186–202.

779.   "New Light on the Russian War." *Fighting Forces* 21 (August 1944), 116–120.

780.   Ogarkov, Nikolay V. "An Immortal Feat: Translated from *Oktyabr,* May 1980." *Translations on USSR Military Affairs,* no. 1528 (August 14, 1980), 60–70.

781.   Petrukhin, V. "The Whole Country Worked for the Front." *Soviet Military Review,* no. 4 (April 1970), 20–23.

782.   Puleston, William D. "Blunders of World War II." *U.S. News and World Report* 38 (February 4, 1955), 106–139.

783.   Rubenstein, Joshua. "World War II—Soviet Style: The Russo-German War." *Commentary* 67 (May 1979), 65–67.

784.   Sandalov, L. "Under the Walls of Tula." *Soviet Military Review,* no. 10 (October 1971), 46–48.

785.   Shutov, Z. "Meeting Engagements of Tank Armies, 1941–1945." *Soviet Military Review,* no. 12 (December 1976), 51–53.

786.   "Soviet Armed Forces—Accomplishments in World War II: Translated from *Voyenno Istoricheskiy Zhurnal,* May 1980." *Translations on USSR Military Affairs,* no. 1532 (September 10, 1980), 1–11.

787.   Tolubko, Vladimir F. "The Great Exploit of the Soviet People: Translated from *Ekonomicheskaya Gazeta,* May 3, 1978." *Translations on USSR Military Affairs,* no. 1355 (May 30, 1978), 48–52.

788. "Treatment of Prisoners-of-War Discussed: Translated from *Voyenno Istoricheskiy Zhurnal,* November 1978." *Translations on USSR Military Affairs,* no. 1404 (December 21, 1978), 55–70.

789. Vel'pukhovskiy, B. "Sources of Victory in the Great Patriotic War: Translated from *Voyenno Istoricheskiy Zhurnal,* May 1980." *Translations on USSR Military Affairs,* no. 1532 (September 10, 1980), 12–21.

789a. Vernon, Graham D. "Soviet Combat Operations in World War II: Lessons for Today." *Military Review* 60 (March-April 1980), 30–40, 42–50.

790. Voloshin, I. "The Majestic Exploit of the Soviet People: Translated from *Kommunist Moldavii,* April 1980." *Translations on USSR Military Affairs,* no. 1528 (August 14, 1980), 52–55.

791. Walters, R. E. "Notes from the Russian Front." *Nation* 213 (September 20, 1971), 248–250.

792. "War in Russia, 1941–1944." *Life* 16 (April 3, 1944), 27–31.

793. "War Years Recalled in Victory Day Articles: Translated from Various Sources, May 9, 1978." *Translations on USSR Military Affairs,* no. 1357 (June 14, 1978), 48–62.

794. Yepishev, Aleksey A. "Results of the Great Feat: Translated from *Moskva,* May 1980." *Translations on USSR Military Affairs,* no. 1528 (August 14, 1980), 71–76.

795. Yuryev, M. "The Principal Stages in the Soviet-German War." *Fighting Forces* 23 (April 1946), 38–39.

796. Zeitzler, Kurt. "Withdrawals of the German Army on the Eastern Front." *Military Review* 40 (August 1960), 73–84.

797. Zhukov, Georgiy K. "The Grandeur of the Soviet Victory and the Impotence of the [German] Falsifiers of History." *Soviet Military Review,* no. 5 (May 1970), 54–60; no. 6 (June 1970), 54–57.

798. Ziemke, Earl F. "The German Defeat in the East, 1942–1945." *Military Review* 45 (May 1965), 33–39.

799. _____ . "'Operation Kreml': Deception, Strategy and the Fortunes of War." *Parameters* 9 (March 1979), 72–83.

DOCUMENTS, PAPERS, AND REPORTS

800. Dallin, Alexander. "German Policy and the Occupation of the Soviet Union, 1941–1944." PhD dissertation, Columbia University, 1953.

801.   Hartmann, Walter. "Principles and Experiences of Position Warfare and Retrograde Movements." Unpublished paper, Foreign Military Studies Program, Historical Division, Headquarters, U.S. Army, Europe, 1947. 39p.

802.   Kravchenko, G. S. *War Economy of the U.S.S.R., 1941*–1945. Translated from the Russian. Translation no. 20701. Arlington, Va.: Joint Publication Research Service, 1963. 340p.

803.   Krueger, Walter. "Conduct of Operations in the East, 1941–1943." Unpublished paper, Foreign Military Studies Program, Historical Division, Headquarters, U.S. Army, Europe, 1949. 20p.

804.   Leach, Barry A. "German Strategic Planning for the Campaign in the East, 1939–1941." PhD dissertation, University of British Columbia, 1968.

805.   Rendulic, Lothar. "Combat in Deep Snow, 1941–1945." Unpublished paper, Foreign Military Studies Program, Historical Division, Headquarters, U.S. Army, Europe, 1947. 17p.

806.   _____. "Diseases of Men and Horses Experienced in Russia." Unpublished paper, Foreign Military Studies Program, Historical Division, Headquarters, U.S. Army, Europe, 1947. 9p.

807.   _____. "The Influence of Terrain, Seasons, and Weather on Operations in Russia." Unpublished paper, Foreign Military Studies Program, Historical Division, Headquarters, U.S. Army, Europe, 1947. 11p.

808.   Schneider, Erich. "Antitank Defense in the East." Unpublished paper, Foreign Military Studies Program, Historical Division, Headquarters, U.S. Army, Europe, 1947. 22p.

809.   Simon, Max. "Experience Gained in Combat Against Soviet Infantry." Unpublished paper, Foreign Military Studies Program, Historical Division, Headquarters, U.S. Army, Europe, 1950. 15p. Reprinted in part 10 of Donald S. Detwiler, ed., *World War II German Military Studies*, 24 vols. (New York: Garland, 1980).

810.   *A Survey of "Quick Wins" in Modern War.* Report no. MDA-903-75-C-0236. Dun Loring, Va.: Historical Evaluation and Research Organization, 1975. 123p.   Includes Operation Barbarossa, 1941, and the Soviet 1945 invasion of Manchuria.

811.   Toppe, Alfred, et al. *Night Combat.* DA Pam 20-236. Washington, D.C.: Department of the Army, 1953. 45p.

812.   Union of Soviet Socialist Republics. Ministry of Defense. *The Soviet Air Force in World War II: The Official History.* Edited by Ray Wagner. Translated from the Russian. Garden City, N.Y.: Doubleday, 1973. 440p.   Provides considerable information on the ground war.

813.   United States. Department of the Army. Office of the Chief of Military History. *Combat in Russian Forests and Swamps: Historical Study.* DA Pam 20-231. Washington, D.C., 1951. 39p.

814.   _____ . *Effects of Climate on Combat in European Russia.* DA Pam 20-291. Washington, D.C., 1952. 81p.

815.   _____ . *The German Campaign in Russia—Planning and Operations, 1941–1942: Historical Study.* DA Pam 20-261a. Washington, D.C., 1955. 187p.

816.   _____ . *German Defense Tactics Against Russian Break-Throughs: Historical Study.* DA Pam 20-233. Washington, D.C., 1951. 80p.

817.   _____ . *Military Improvisations during the Russian Campaign: Historical Study.* DA Pam 20-201. Washington, D.C., 1951. 110p.

818.   _____ . *Operations of Encircled Forces (German Experiences in Russia): Historical Study.* DA Pam 20-234. Washington, D.C., 1952. 74p.

819.   _____ . *Terrain Factors in the Russian Campaign: Historical Study.* DA Pam 20-290. Washington, D.C., 1950. 104p.

820.   United States. Department of the Army. Military Academy. Department of Military Art and Engineering. *Operations on the Russian Front.* 3 vols. in 1. West Point, N.Y., 1945–1946.

821.   Von Bechtolsheim, Anton F. "Blitzkrieg in the East." Unpublished paper, Files of the U.S. Army Military History Institute, Carlisle Barracks, Penn., 1957. 26p.

822.   Von Natzmer, Oldwig. "The Commitment of German Armor, 1943–1945." Unpublished paper, Foreign Military Studies Program, Historical Division, Headquarters, U.S. Army, Europe, 1948. 13p.

823.   Wentzell, Fritz. "Combat Experience in Russia." Unpublished paper, Foreign Military Studies Program, Historical Division, Headquarters, U.S. Army, Europe, 1954. 66p.

824.   _____ . "Combat in the East." Unpublished paper, Foreign Military Studies Program, Historical Division, Headquarters, U.S. Army, Europe, 1952. 96p.

Further References

See also section 2:A.

2. The Red Army

The citations in this section provide general information on the Red Army during the Great Patriotic War and examine four important combat arms: tank troops, artillery, infantry, and airborne troops.

During the defensive period of the war or until late 1943, Moscow had to accomplish its mission with an army composed chiefly of infantry. There was on hand only enough mechanized equipment to spearhead offensive drives. Approximately 10 percent of the Soviet divisions were armored or mechanized; the remainder consisted largely of small infantry divisions with no tanks, little organic artillery, only 100 to 150 trucks, and small allotments of specialized equipment. Later, the situation began to change as more equipment became available from behind the Ural Mountains or from overseas, so that by 1945, in most cases, the Red Army was well supplied with the armor, artillery, and other ingredients necessary to mark "paid" to the German account.

a. GENERAL WORKS

BOOKS

825.   Basseches, Nikolaus. *The Unknown Army: The Nature and History of the Russian Military Forces*. Translated from the Russian. New York: Viking Press, 1943. 239p.

826.   Berchin, Michel. *The Red Army*. By "Benedicoff," pseud. New York: W. W. Norton, 1942. 277p.

827.   Coates, William P., and Z. K. *Why Russia Will Win: The Soviet Military, Naval and Air Power*. London: Eldon, 1942. 104p.

828.   Cole, David M. *The Red Army*. London: Rich, 1943. 156p.

829.   Fedorov, Evgeniy K. *The Red Army, an Army of the People*. Translated from the Russian. New York: Transatlantic Books, 1944. 48p.

830.   Fomichenko, General, ed. *The Red Army*. Translated from the Russian. London: Hutchinson, 1945. 125p.

831.   Foolman, David. *The Red Army on the Eastern Front*. Oxford, Eng.: St. Antony's College [196?]. 52p.

832.   Garder, Michel. *A History of the Soviet Army*. Rev. ed. New York: Praeger, 1966. 226p.

833.   Grechko, Andrei A. *Liberation Mission of the Soviet Armed Forces in the Second World War.* Moscow: Progress Publishers, 1972.

834.   Guillaume, Augustin. *Soviet Arms and Soviet Might: The Secrets of Russia's Might.* Washington, D.C.: Infantry Journal Press, 1949. 212p.

835.   Heisler, J. B. *Russia's Fighting Men.* London: New Europe, 1945. 95p.

836.   Kerr, Walter B. *The Russian Army: Its Men, Its Leaders, and Its Battles.* New York: Alfred A. Knopf, 1944. 250p.

837.   Kournahoff, Sergei N. *Russia's Fighting Forces.* Translated from the Russian. New York: Duell, Sloane & Pearce, 1942. 258p.

838.   Mackintosh, Malcolm. *Juggernaut: A History of the Soviet Armed Forces.* New York: Macmillan, 1967. 320p.

839.   Mayer, S. L., ed. *The Russian War Machine, 1917–1945.* London: Leventhal, 1977. 257p.

840.   Mikhailov, Nikolai A. *Meeting the Challenge: Soviet Youth in the Great Patriotic War, 1941–1945.* Moscow: Progress Publishers, 1970. 326p.

841.   Mints, Isaak I. *The Red Army.* New York: International Publications Service, 1944. 160p.

842.   Montagu, Ivor G. S. *The Red Army at War: Fifty Questions Answered.* London: Russia Today Society, 1943. 32p.

843.   Myers, David, comp. *Unit Organizations of World War II: Tables of Organization and Equipment (TOE).* 2d ed. Milwaukee, Wis.: Z. & M. Enterprises, 1977. 84p.

844.   O'Ballance, Edgar. *The Red Army: A Short History.* New York: Praeger, 1964. 237p.

845.   Snow, Edgar. *The Pattern of Soviet Power.* New York: Random House, 1945. 219p.

846.   White, D. Fedotoff. *The Growth of the Red Army.* Princeton, N.J.: Princeton University Press, 1944. 486p.

847.   White, William L. *Report on the Russians.* New York: Harcourt, Brace, 1945. 309p.

848.   Willis, Ted. *The Fighting Youth of Russia.* London: Russia Today Society, 1943. 15p.

ARTICLES

849.   Antosyak, A. "For Freedom of the European Peoples." *Soviet Military Review*, no. 4 (April 1980), 13–16.

850.   Bobkov, N. "Officer Training during the War." *Soviet Military Review*, no 9 (September 1971), 34–36.

851.   Butsky, I. "Stern Years." *Soviet Military Review*, no. 5 (May 1977), 55–57.   Party-political work in the Red Army, 1941–1945.

852.   Cherednichenko, G. "Wartime Organization of Cooperation at Army Level Discussed: Translated from *Voyenno Istoricheskiy Zhurnal*, October 1978." *Translations on USSR Military Affairs*, no. 1405 (December 29, 1978), 6–16.

853.   Cheremisov, V. "Wartime Indoctrination of Troops Described: Translated from *Voyenno Istoricheskiy Zhurnal*, July 1978." *Translations on USSR Military Affairs*, no. 1476 (November 28, 1979), 103–110.

854.   "Cooperation in the Red Army, as Viewed by the Soviet Press." *Field Artillery Journal* 34 (September 1944), 656–658.

855.   Dement'yev, A. "Troop Control in World War II Discussed: Translated from *Voyenno Istoricheskiy Zhurnal*, July 1978." *Translations on USSR Military Affairs*, no. 1389 (October 24, 1978), 13–18.

856.   DePue, B. E. M. "A History of the Soviet Army." *Military Review* 40 (December 1960), 73–83.

857.   Diyev, D., and V. Drozdov. "Cooperation Born in Battle." *Soviet Military Review*, no. 4 (April 1975), 38–41.

858.   Fay, Sydney B. "The Magnificent Red Army." *Current History*, ns 6 (April 1944), 296–303.

859.   "Fighting Units on the Eastern Front." In Bernard Fitzsimons, ed., *Heraldry and Regalia of War*. New York: Beekman House, 1973. pp. 138–139.

860.   Fuqua, Stephen O. "The Red Army Has the Advangage of Position." *Newsweek* 19 (May 4, 1942), 21.

861.   Galay, Nikolai. "The Soviet Armed Forces' First Half Century: Legends and Reality." *Institute for the Study of the U.S.S.R. Bulletiñ* 15 (February 1968), 5–19.

862.   Garthoff, Raymond L. "Soviet Employment of Ground Forces." *Soviet Military Doctrine*. Glencoe, Ill.: Free Press, 1953. pp. 299–320.

863.   Golubovich, V. "Wartime Operational-Tactical Training of Reserve Armies Described: Translated from *Voyenno Istoricheskiy Zhurnal,* September 1979." *Translations on USSR Military Affairs,* no. 1483 (December 20, 1979), 63–70.

864.   "The Great Russian Army Fights on toward a Second Summer of Growing Power." *Life* 12 (June 22, 1942), 18–19.

865.   Hearnshaw, F. J. C. "The Russians as Fighters." *National Review* 118 (June 1942), 538–544.

866.   Lawrence, William H. "The Mighty Army at Hitler's Back." *New York Times Magazine* (June 11, 1944), 13.

867.   Matsulenko, V. "The Liberating Mission of the Soviet Army." *Soviet Military Review,* no. 6 (June 1968), 6–9.

868.   _____. "Ordeal by Fire." *Soviet Military Review,* no. 11 (November 1977), 53–56; no. 12 (December 1977), 20–31. Rebuilding the smashed Red Army, 1941–1942.

869.   Mitchell, Donald W. "The Red Army Hits Its Stride." *Nation* 156 (January 23, 1943), 126–127.

870.   Nikolaieff, A. M. "The Red Army in the Second World War." *Russian Review* 7 (Autumn 1947), 49–60.

871.   Parry, Albert. "God of War and Moving Forts." *Russian Cavalcade: A Military Record.* New York: Washburn, 1944. pp. 239–257. The Soviet use of artillery and armor.

872.   Pavlovskiy, Ivan G. "The Main Fire and Striking Power." *Soviet Military Review,* no. 2 (February 1975), 8–11.

873.   "The Red Army." *Newsweek* 21 (March 1, 1943), 19–21.

874.   "Red Medicine: A Report on Russian Military Medicine." *Time* 40 (November 23, 1942), 70–71.

875.   "The Russian Soldier in the Great Patriotic War of 1941–1945." *World War Enthusiast, 1939–1945* 1 (January-June, September-October 1974), 5–6, 33–34, 52, 63–64, 124–125, 156–157; 2 (January-February 1975), 4–5, 28.

876.   Ryabov, V. "Road of Courage and Glory." *Soviet Military Review,* no. 2 (February 1968), 14–19.

877.   Salisbury, Harrison E. "The Secret of the Red Army." *Collier's* 114 (December 23, 1944), 14–15.

878.   Sloan, John F. "Soviet Units in World War II: New Data from Soviet Sources." *History, Numbers and War* 1 (Fall 1977), 160–181.

879.   Sobolev, Mikhail G. "Service Chiefs on Lessons Learned in the Great Patriotic War—Deputy Chief Sobolev on Party-Political Work: Translated from *Voyenno Istoricheskiy Zhurnal,* November 1977." *Translations on USSR Military Affairs,* no. 1327 (January 27, 1978), 104–116.

880.   Stowe, Leland. "The Evolution of the Red Army." *Foreign Affairs* 22 (October 1943), 94–105.

881.   Sulzberger, Cyrus L. "Now It Is the Blitz-Grinders' Turn: A New Red Army Faces Hitler Today." *New York Times Magazine* (August 1, 1943), 7.

882.   Vagts, Alfred. "The Foreigner as Soldier in the Second World War: The Military Use of the Foreigner by Russia." *Journal of Politics* 9 (August 1947), 398–404.

883.   Veraksa, Ye. "Co-Operation of Aviation with Land Forces in World War II." *Soviet Military Review,* no. 10 (October 1976), 54–56.

884.   Werner, Max. "Prospects for the Red Army." *New Republic* 150 (November 17, 1941), 647–649.

885.   Williams, A. R. "The Soviet People's Army." *Asia* 43 (January 1943), 10–14.

886.   "The World's No. 1 Army." *Life* 15 (November 29, 1943), 25–31.

887.   Yeroshin, A. "Victory Parade, June 24, 1945." *Soviet Military Review,* no. 5 (May 1975), 38–41.

Documents, Papers, and Reports

888.   Great Britain. War Office. *Tactics and Organization: New Notes on the Red Army.* London: H.M. Stationery Office, 1944. 38p.

889.   Hollidt, Karl. "River Crossings by the Red Army in World War II." Unpublished paper, Foreign Military Studies Program, Historical Division, Headquarters, U.S. Army, Europe, 1949. 135p.

890.   Rendulic, Lothar. "Information on the Russian Army." Unpublished paper, Foreign Military Studies Program, Historical Division, Headquarters, U.S. Army, Europe, 1947. 9p.

891.   Simon, Max. "Soviet Russian Infantry and Armored Forces." Unpublished paper, Foreign Military Studies Program, Historical Division, Headquarters, U.S. Army, Europe, 1953. 10p.

892.   Union of Soviet Socialist Republics. Ministry of Defense. *Field Service Regulations of the Red Army.* Translated from the Russian. RUS-MD-FSR-1944. Washington, D.C.: Department of the Army, 1944. 307p.

893.   United States. War Department. *Handbook of U.S.S.R. Military Forces, 1945.* TM 30-430. Washington, D.C.: U.S. Government Printing Office, 1945. 765p.   Reprinted in 1977 by the Springfield, Va., firm of John Sloan.

894.   ————. General Staff. G-2. *Determination of Fighting Strength, U.S.S.R.* 2 vols. Washington, D.C., 1942.

895.   Von Natzmer, Oldwig, et al. "River Crossings by the Red Army in World War II." Unpublished paper, Foreign Military Studies Program, Historical Division, Headquarters, U.S. Army, Europe, 1949. 190p.

896.   Whiting, Kenneth R. *The Development of the Soviet Armed Forces, 1917–1972.* Documentary Research Study AU-201-72-IPD. Maxwell AFB, Ala.: Air University, 1972. 102p.

Further References

See also sections 2:A and 4:A and C.

b. RED ARMY COMBAT ARMS

(1). Tank Troops

BOOKS

897.   Carver, Lord. *The Apostles of Mobility: The Theory and Practice of Armored Warfare.* New York: Holmes & Meier, 1979. 112p.

898.   Kershaw, Andrew, ed. *Tanks at War, 1939–1945.* Purnell's History of the Second World War Special. London: Phoebus Books, 1975. 64p.

899.   Macksey, Kenneth J. *Tank Tactics.* Warren, Mich.: Squadron/Signal Publications, 1976. 72p.

900.   ————, ed. *The Guinness Book of Tank Facts and Feats: A Record of Armored Fighting Vehicle Achievement.* Enfield, Eng.: Guinness Superlatives, 1972. 240p.

901.   Piekalkiewicz, Janusz. *The Cavalry of World War II.* New York: Stein & Day, 1980. 256p.

902.   Poliakov, Aleksandr. *White Mammoths: The Dramatic Story of Russian Tanks in Action.* Translated from the Russian. New York: E. P. Dutton, 1943. 189p.

ARTICLES

903.   Abolin, F. "Tank Attack with Soviet Sappers." *Armor* 53 (January-February 1944), 66.

904.   Anan'ev, I. "Tank Armies in Offensive Operations." *Military Review* 43 (February 1963), 57–70.

905.   Babadzhanyan, Amazasp K. "Service Chiefs on Lessons Learned in the Great Patriotic War—Babadzhanyan on Armored and Mechanized Troops: Translated from *Voyenno Istoricheskiy Zhurnal,* November 1977." *Translations on USSR Military Affairs,* no. 1327 (January 27, 1978), 84–91.

906.   Busse, Theodor. "Problems in Armored Command." *Military Review* 37 (July 1957), 83–89.

907.   FitzGerald, Charles G. "Armor: Soviet Arm of Decision." *Military Review* 49 (March 1969), 35–46.

908.   Gorodovikov, Colonel. "Vast Soviet Cavalry Armies Forming." *Cavalry Journal* 51 (January-February 1942), 18–21.

909.   Katukov, Mikhail. "Spearhead of the Main Effort." *Soviet Military Review,* no. 9 (September 1976), 1–16.

910.   Kerr, Walter B. "As Long as Fuel Lasts." *Russian Army: Its Men, Its Leaders, and Its Battles.* New York: Alfred A. Knopf, 1944. pp. 116–129.

911.   Kobrin, Nikolai. "A Tank Army in the Offensive." *Soviet Military Review,* no. 1 (January 1976), 47–49.

912.   Krupchenko, I. Ye. "Wartime Employment of Tank Troops Described: Translated from *Voyenno Istoricheskiy Zhurnal,* September 1979." *Translations on USSR Military Affairs,* no. 1483 (December 20, 1979), 53–62.

913.   Losik, O. A. "Wartime Operations—Maneuver of Armored and Mechanized Troops: Translated from *Voyenno Istoricheskiy Zhurnal,* September 1980." *Translations on USSR Military Affairs,* no. 1553 (December 29, 1980), 18–26.

914.   Luttwak, Edward N. "The Strategy of the Tank." *Times Literary Supplement,* no. 3951 (December 16, 1977), 1471–1472.

915.   Malone, Daniel K. "Soviet Armored Warfare." *Ordnance* 56 (January-February 1972), 295–299.

916.   O'Ballance, Edgar. "The Evolution of Soviet Armoured Doctrine." *Army Quarterly* 76 (November-December 1976), 11–17.

917.   Ogorkiewicz, Richard M. "The Evolution of Armored Tactics." *Military Review* 37 (February 1958), 31–39.

918.   Petrov, K. "Wartime Operations—River Crossing by Tank Units: Translated from *Voyenno Istoricheskiy Zhurnal,* September 1980." *Translations on USSR Military Affairs,* no. 1553 (December 29, 1980), 27–34.

919.   Pronin, I. "Soviet Cavalry in World War II." *Cavalry Journal* 56 (July-August 1945), 44–45.

920.   Shorodumov, I. "Wartime Tank Corps Operations Described: Translated from *Voyenno Istoricheskiy Zhurnal,* June 1979." *Translations on USSR Military Affairs,* no. 1466 (October 2, 1979), 29–38.

921.   Shutov, Z. "Troop Control." *Soviet Military Review,* no. 7 (July 1977), 57–59.

922.   Sparkes, Jack. "Early Russian Tank Armies." *AFV-G2* 6 (January-February 1980), 38–40.

923.   "The Story of Soviet Armor." *Armored Cavalry Journal* 59 (March 1950), 40–46; (June 1950), 14–21.

924.   "Tank Wedges." *Infantry Journal* 55 (July 1944), 48–49.

925.   "Tanks in Night Combat." *Military Review* 23 (May 1943), 77–78.

926.   Underhill, Garrett. "Stalin's Men on Horseback." *Infantry Journal* 66 (February 1950), 12–18.

927.   ———. "The Story of Soviet Armor." *Armor* 61 (November-December 1952), 28–38; 62 (January-February 1953), 24–30.

928.   Vassiliev, M. F. "The Evolution of Soviet Armored Principles." *Military Review* 36 (August 1956), 88–93.

929.   Yelshin, N. "Tanks vs. Tanks." *Soviet Military Review,* no. 2 (February 1975), 28–30.

DOCUMENTS, PAPERS, AND REPORTS

930.   "The Russian Armored Command." Unpublished paper, Foreign Military Studies Program, Historical Division, Headquarters, U.S. Army, Europe, 1950. 5p.

931.   Union of Soviet Socialist Republics. Ministry of Defense. *Service Regulations for the Armored and Mechanized Forces of the Red Army, 13 February 1944*. Translated from the Russian. DA-62-TR-F-71-76. Washington, D.C.: Department of the Army, 1952. 159p.

932.   United States. War Department. General Staff. G-2. *Nine Articles on Russian Tank Tactics, Translated from the Journal of Armored Troops, Soviet Army*. Washington, D.C., 1947. Unpaged.

Further References

See also section 2:A and the combat citations in 2:C:3; details on Red armor are found in sections 2:D:4 and 4:F:4.

(2). Artillery

BOOKS

933.   Bidwell, Shelford. *The Mechanics of War: Artillery Tactics, 1939–1945*. Warren, Mich.: Squadron/Signal Publications, 1976. 72p.

ARTICLES

934.   Afanayev, P. "Antitank Action of Soviet Artillery." *Field Artillery Journal* 33 (November 1943), 810.

935.   "Artillery in the Russo-German War." *Field Artillery Journal* 31 (September 1941), 672–673.

936.   "The Artillery Support of the Red Army." *Army Information Bulletin* 4 (December 1944), 4–5.

937.   Chernukhin, V. "Wartime Operations—Reserve Artillery Regroupings: Translated from *Voyenno Istoricheskiy Zhurnal*, June 1980." *Translations on USSR Military Affairs*, no. 1536 (September 26, 1980), 29–38.

938.   DeWatteville, H. G. "Russian Artillery, 1941–1945." *Field Artillery Journal* 37 (May-June 1947), 175, 195–199.

939.   "Duic," pseud. "Armored Artillery in the Soviet Campaign." *Military Review* 23 (October 1943), 72–75.

940.   "Giese," pseud. "Employment of Assault Guns on the Eastern Front." *Military Review* 24 (April 1944), 89–90.

941.   Karelsky, A. "Soviet Artillery Fire." *Field Artillery Journal* 32 (July 1942), 511.

942. Kerr, Walter B. "Death or Insanity." *Russian Army: Its Men, Its Leaders, Its Battles.* New York: Alfred A. Knopf, 1944. pp. 104–115.

943. Luginya, S. "Artillery Counterpreparation for Intermediate Positions." *Field Artillery Journal* 34 (November 1944), 786–787.

944. Maksimov, V. "Wartime Artillery Employment by High Command Discussed: Translated from *Krasnaya Zvezda,* February 12, 1978." *Translations on USSR Military Affairs,* no. 1349 (May 2, 1978), 67–69.

945. Mellano, Pietro. "The Artillery Attack and the German Defeat on the Eastern Front." *Military Review* 31 (August 1951), 97–100.

946. Menshikov, G. "The Use of Feint in Artillery Preparation." *Military Review* 25 (May 1945), 103–105.

947. Nadisov, Georgiy. "The Mass Employment of Artillery." *Field Artillery Journal* 35 (February 1945), 93–94.

948. Nikoforov, N. "Soviet Atillery in Battle." *Coast Artillery Journal* 88 (January 1945), 28–29.

949. Peredl'skiy, G. Ye. "Artillery Employment in World War II Army Operations Described: Translated from *Voyenno Istoricheskiy Zhurnal,* November 1979." *Translations on USSR Military Affairs,* no. 1500 (February 28, 1980), 19–25.

950. _____ . "Service Chiefs on Lessons Learned in the Great Patriotic War—Peredel'skiy on Artillery: Translated from *Voyenno Istoricheskiy Zhurnal,* November 1977." *Translations on USSR Military Affairs,* no. 1327 (January 27, 1978), 79–83.

951. Petrov, Aleksandr. "Soviet Artillery vs. Nazi Artillery." *Field Artillery Journal* 32 (December 1942), 915–917.

952. "Red Army Artillery Trends: 1944." *Field Artillery Journal* 35 (February 1945), 92–93.

953. "The Red Artillery." *Field Artillery Journal* 41 (July 1941), 464–466.

954. "Russian Skill with Big Guns Pays Dividends Against Nazis." *Newsweek* 19 (February 2, 1942), 21–22.

955. Samsonov, F. A. "Artillery in the Breakthrough of a Defense Zone." *Field Artillery Journal* 34 (April 1944), 242–245.

956. _____ . "Artillery in the Offensive." *Field Artillery Journal* 33 (August 1943), 584–585.

957. _____ . "Soviet Artillery Groups." *Field Artillery Journal* 36 (January 1946), 30–31.

958. Smirnov, V. "Self-Propelled Guns in an Offensive." *Field Artillery Journal* 35 (February 1945), 94.

959. Tupakhin, V. "Surprise Artillery Attack." *Field Artillery Journal*, 32 (December 1942), 910.

960. United States. War Department. "Massed Artillery in the Attack: A Report on Soviet Methods." *Military Reports on the United Nations* 23 (November 1944), 33–36.

961. Voronov, Nikolai N. "Getting On with It." *Atlas* 11 (May 1966), 275–277.

962. Young, W. R. "Artillery Offensive: An Examination of the Russian Practice." *Field Artillery Journal* 36 (January 1946), 26–29.

DOCUMENTS, PAPERS, AND REPORTS

963. Berlin, Wilhelm. "Russian Artillery in the Battle for Modlin and German Countermeasures." Unpublished paper, Foreign Military Studies Program, Historical Division, Headquarters, U.S. Army, Europe, 1948. 10p.

964. Brasack, Kurt. "Russian Artillery in the Engagements around Modlin and German Countermeasures." Unpublished paper, Foreign Military Studies Program, Historical Division, Headquarters, U.S. Army, Europe, 1947. 5p.

965. Korobeynikov, F. P. *Gun Drill: A U.S.S.R. Manual.* Translated from the Russian. Ottawa, Ont.: Director of Military Intelligence, Canadian Army, 1952. Unpaged.

966. Marticke, Lieutenant. *Artillery Support of a Tank Attack: The Russian Method.* Translated from the German. Washington, D.C.: U.S. War Department, G-2, 1940. Unpaged.

967. Rickert, Hans-George. "Small Unit Tactics: Artillery." Unpublished paper, Foreign Military Studies Program, Historical Division, Headquarters, U.S. Army, Europe, 1952. 58p.

968. Samsonov, F. A. *Artillery, the Main Striking Force of the Army.* Translated from the Russian. DA-G2-TR-F-6124-A. Washington, D.C.: Department of the Army, 1951. 26p.

969. Thoholte, Karl. "Small Unit Tactics—Artillery." Unpublished paper, Foreign Military Studies Program, Historical Division, Headquarters, U.S. Army, Europe, 1953. 94p.

970.   United States. War Department. General Staff. G-2. "Red Army Artillery." *Military Reports on the United Nations* 7 (June 1943), 15–18.

971.   ———— . "Russian Artillery Counterpreparation." *Tactical and Technical Trends* 36 (October 1943), 9–11.

(3). Infantry

BOOKS

972.   Farrar-Hockley, Anthony H. *Infantry Tactics.* Warren, Mich.: Squadron/Signal Publications, 1976. 72p.

973.   Kershaw, Andrew, ed. *Infantry at War, 1939–1945.* Purnell's History of the Second World War Special. London: Phoebus Books, 1975. 64p.

ARTICLES

974.   Akimov, A. "Fighting Tanks." *Soviet Military Review,* no. 10 (October 1976), 10–13.

975.   Alexeyev, I. I. "The Development of Soviet Antitank Defense." *Field Artillery Journal* 32 (November 1942), 848–849.

976.   Alexeyev, Pavel. "Soviet Sappers on Independent Missions." *Cavalry Journal* 53 (January-February 1944), 67.

977.   Dukov, R. "Fighting Airborne Troops." *Soviet Military Review,* no. 1 (January 1971), 16–17.

978.   Gavrilenko, N. "Immobilizing Tank Maneuvres." *Field Artillery Journal* 32 (November 1942), 846–847.

979.   Isby, David C. "Modern Infantry Tactics, 1914–1974." *Strategy and Tactics,* no. 46 (September-October 1974), 21–40.

980.   Ivanov, V. "Combatting Self-Propelled Artillery." *Field Artillery Journal* 43 (January-February 1975), 54–58.

981.   Kerr, Walter B. "The Infantry." *Russian Army: Its Men, Its Leaders, Its Battles.* New York: Aflred A. Knopf, 1944. pp. 92–103.

982.   Kozlov, A. "Motorized Rifle Division Commander on Combat Traditions: Translated from *Krasnaya Zvezda,* May 9, 1978." *Translations on USSR Military Affairs,* no. 1370 (August 17, 1978), 40–43.

983.   Kozlov, M. "Wartime Operations—Troop Regrouping during the War: Translated from *Voyenno Istoricheskiy Zhurnal,* September 1980." *Translations on USSR Military Affairs,* no. 1553 (December 29, 1980), 9–17.

984.   Maltsev, Nagaiev. "Tactics of Soviet Antitank Riflemen." *Field Artillery Journal* 33 (August 1943), 585-586.

985.   "Mortar Fire by the Red Army." *Infantry Journal* 52 (November 1943), 66-68.

986.   Pope, Vernon. "Russian Commandos." *Collier's* 62 (July 24, 1943), 22-23.

987.   "Russian Antitank Doctrine." *Field Artillery Journal* 31 (August 1942), 618.

988.   "Russia's Messengers of Death: Sappers." *Popular Mechanics* 80 (July 1943), 34-37.

989.   "Soviet Ski Troops." *Command and General Staff School Quarterly* 22 (July 1942), 93-94.

990.   Thompson, Paul W. "Portrait of the Red Soldier." *Infantry Journal* 52 (June 1943), 14-17.

991.   Tsynaklov, A. "Wartime Antitank Operations Described: Translated from *Voyenno Istoricheskiy Zhurnal*, July 1979." *Translations on USSR Military Affairs*, no. 1476 (November 28, 1979), 21-28.

992.   Vorob'yev, I. "Fighting Air Landing Parties." *Soviet Military Review*, no. 10 (October 1971), 10-12.

DOCUMENTS, PAPERS, AND REPORTS

993.   Reinhardt, Hellmuth. "Small Unit Tactics—Infantry." Unpublished paper, Foreign Military Studies Program, Historical Division, Headquarters, U.S. Army, Europe, 1951. 158p.

994.   Rendulic, Lothar. "The Fighting Qualities of the Russian Soldier." Unpublished paper, Foreign Military Studies Program, Historical Division, Headquarters, U.S. Army, Europe, 1953. 10p.
     Reprinted in part 10 of Donald S. Detwiler, ed., *World War II German Military Studies*, 24 vols. (New York: Garland, 1980).

Further References

See also the citations in sections 2:A, 2:C:2:a, 2:C:3, 2:D:3, 4:C:3, and 4:F:3.

(4). Airborne Troops

BOOKS

995.   Galvin, John R. *Air Assault: The Development of Airmobile Warfare.* New York: Hawthorn Books, 1969. 365p.

996.   Gregory, Barry, and John H. Batchelor. *Airborne Warfare, 1918–1945.* London: Phoebus Books, 1979. 128p.

997.   Tugwell, Maurice. *Airborne to Battle.* London: Kimber, 1971. 367p.

ARTICLES

998.   Chant, Christopher. "Eastern Europe." In Philip de St. Croix, ed., *Airborne Operations: An Illustrated Encyclopedia of the Grat Battles of Airborne Forces.* New York: Crown, 1978. pp. 156–163.

999.   Eddy, David. "Wild Men from Heaven: Paraski Troopers." *American Magazine* 133 (June 1942), 20–21.

1000.   Gatley, Matthew J. "Soviet Airborne Operations in World War II." *Military Review* 47 (January 1967), 14–20.

1001.   Kobrin, Nikolai. "In the Enemy Rear." *Soviet Military Review,* no. 2 (February 1972), 40–42.

1002.   Parry, Albert. "Jumping Soldiers of the Air." *Science Digest* 15 (May 1944), 71–74.

1003.   "Reds Take to 'Chutes and Skis to Keep Germans on Defensive." *Newsweek* 19 (January 26, 1942), 20–21.

1004.   Rudakov, V. "Thirty Years of Soviet Airborne Forces." *Military Review* 41 (June 1961), 42–44.

1005.   Samoylenko, Ya. "Wartime Operations—Control of Airborne Landings: Translated from *Voyenno Istoricheskiy Zhurnal,* December 1979." *Translations on USSR Military Affairs,* no. 1508 (March 28, 1980), 20–28.

1006.   Smirnov, Sergei S. "Airborne Troops—Combat Traditions Described: Translated from *Kommunist Vooruzhennykh Sil,* August 1980." *Translations on USSR Military Affairs,* no. 1548 (November 28, 1980), 1–7.

DOCUMENTS, PAPERS, AND REPORTS

1007.   Van Horn, Frederick E. "A Survey of Soviet Airborne History and Missions." MA thesis, U.S. Army Command and General Staff College, 1974. 137p.

Further References

See also sections 2:A, 2:C:2:a, and 4:C:4.

c. The Soviet High Command (Stavka)

On the day following the German invasion, a new organization was established in Moscow to direct the war effort. The General Headquarters of the High Command of the Armed Forces of the U.S.S.R. (*Stavka Glavnovo Komandovaniya Vooruzhennykh Sil S.S.S.R.*), or Stavka, shortly became the vehicle employed by Joseph Stalin to run the Soviet armed forces. Stalin, who took over the duties of defense minister in July 1941, employed this new group via the Commissariat of Defense to direct the General Staff and the staffs of various administrations and service arms. The General Staff, although working through the Stavka, was responsible directly to Stalin, who would often dispatch its chief, Marshal A. M. Vasilevskiy, and his own first deputy, Zhukov, to the field to usurp the authority and prerogatives of local commanders. Thus, in effect, the Stavka became a planning and administrative body with Stalin, like Hitler, calling all of the important—and sometimes less than important—operational shots. Despite later criticism launched against him by Khrushchev and others, Stalin, unlike Hitler, was able to do so well in directing his generals to victory, perhaps a remarkable accomplishment given the confines of the situation he had created.

The citations in this section detail the wartime history of the Soviet high command; many are revisionist in nature and the user should be careful in employing them.

BOOKS

1008.   Bulganin, Nikolai A. *Stalin and the Soviet Armed Forces.* Moscow: Foreign Language Publishing House, 1950. 19p.

1009.   Seaton, Albert. *Stalin as Military Commander.* New York: Praeger, 1976. 312p.

1010.   Shtemenko, Sergei M. *The Soviet General Staff at War, 1941–1945.* Translated from the Russian. New York: Beekman House, 1970. 398p.

1011.   _____ . *The Soviet General Staff at War, 1941–1945.* 2d ed. Moscow: Progress Publishers, 1975. 389p.

1012.   Stalin, Joseph. *War Speeches.* Translated from the Russian. London: Hutchinson, 1946. 140p.

1013.   Voroshilov, Kliment E. *Stalin and the Armed Forces of the U.S.S.R.* Moscow: Foreign Language Publishing House, 1951. 151p.

ARTICLES

1014.　　Bagramyan, I. "Wartime Operations—Role of Supreme High Command Representatives: Translated from *Voyenno Istoricheskiy Zhurnal,* August 1980." *Translations on USSR Military Affairs,* no. 1549 (December 8, 1980), 27–36.

1015.　　Balbin, A. I. "The Communist Party: Inspirer and Organizer of the Soviet People's Victory in the Great Patriotic War of 1941–1945." *International Review of Military History,* no. 44 (1979), 43–58.

1016.　　Berchin-Benedictoff, M. "The High Command of the Red Army." *Russian Review* 2 (Autumn 1942), 10–21.

1017.　　Dallin, Alexander. "Allied Leadership in the Second World War: Stalin." *Survey* 21 (Winter-Spring 1975), 11–19.

1018.　　Erickson, John. "Soviet Command and Control." *Military Review* 52 (January 1972), 41–50.

1019.　　Kavtaradze, A. "Russian Army General Staff Field Operations Described: Translated from *Voyenno Istoricheskiy Zhurnal,* June 1978." *Translations on USSR Military Affairs,* no. 1375 (September 7, 1978), 38–47.

1020.　　Kir'yan, M. M. "The Soviet Strategic Leadership during the War." *Soviet Military Review,* no. 6 (June 1979), 2–5.

1021.　　―――― . "The Strategic Leadership of the Armed Sruggle in the Great Patriotic War." *International Review of Military History,* no. 44 (1979), 59–76.

1022.　　Kulikov, Viktor G. "Strategic Leadership of the Armed Forces: Translated from *Voyenno Istoricheskiy Zhurnal,* June 1975." *Translations on USSR Military Affairs,* (July 8, 1975), 44.

1023.　　Mikhaylovskiy, G. "Development of Supreme Leadership Entities for the Conduct of War: Translated from *Voyenno Istoricheskiy Zhurnal,* April 1978." *Translations on USSR Military Affairs,* no. 1360 (July 3, 1978), 25–39.

1024.　　Morozov, V. P. "Soviet Strategic Leadership in World War II: Translated from *Istoriya S.S.R.,* no. 3, 1975." *Translations on USSR Military Affairs,* (July 21, 1975), 40–41.

1025.　　Panov, B. V. "The Organization of the Soviet High Command during the Great Patriotic War." *International Review of Military History,* no. 47 (1980), 167–179.

1026.   Plyachenko, Pavel. "Officer Describes Work with Supreme High Command in World War II: Translated from *Voyenno Istoricheskiy Zhurnal,* June 1980." *Translations on USSR Military Affairs,* no. 1554 (December 31, 1980), 32-51.

1027.   "Political and Military Problems of Soviet Leadership during the Final Phase of the War." *Military Review* 35 (April 1955), 77-82.

1028.   Portugal'skiy, R. "Improvement in Command Bodies in World War II Traced: Translated from *Voyenno Istoricheskiy Zhurnal,* August 1978." *Translations on USSR Military Affairs,* no. 1391 (October 30, 1978), 135-145.

1029.   Shtemenko, Sergei M. "The General Staff during World War II." *Soviet Military Review,* no. 1 (January 1969), 47-49; no. 2 (February 1969), 46-51; no. 3 (March 1969), 2-5; no. 4 (April 1969), 45-48; no. 5 (May 1969), 50-53; nos. 3-11 (March-November 1974), 58-61, 58-62, 54-56, 52-55, 53-56, 57-61, 55-57.

1030.   _____. "Stalin the Task Master." *Atlas* 11 (May 1966), 273-275.

1031.   _____. "Strategic Leadership during the War." *Soviet Military Review,* nos. 1-2 (January-February 1971), 46-48, 37-39.

1032.   Vasilevskiy, Aleksandr M. "Marshal Vasilevskiy's Views on the High Command in World War II: Translated from *Voyenno Istoricheskiy Zhurnal,* February 1978." *Translations on USSR Military Affairs,* no. 1344 (April 7, 1978), 75-85.

1033.   _____. "On the Question of the Leadership of the Armed Struggle in the Great Patriotic War." *Soviet Military Review,* no. 12 (December 1971), 187-228.

DOCUMENTS, PAPERS, AND REPORTS

1034.   Baird, Gregory C. *Soviet Intermediary Strategic C² Entities: The Historical Experience.* DNA-4355-T3. Washington, D.C.: Defense Nuclear Agency, 1979.

1035.   Neumaier, Erwin. "The Totalitarianism of Stalin and Hitler in Relation to the Army." PhD dissertation, University of Notre Dame, 1971.

1036.   Rendulic, Lothar. "The Russian Command in World War II." Unpublished paper, Foreign Military Studies Program, Historical Division, Headquarters, U.S. Army, Europe, 1951. 28p.   Reprinted in part 10 of Donald S. Detwiler, ed., *World War II German Military Studies,* 24 vols. (New York: Garland, 1980).

1037.   Shtemenko, Sergei M. *The General Staff in the War Years.* Translated from the Russian. JPRS-65733-1 and 2. 2 vols. Arlington, Va.: Joint Publication Research Service, 1975.

Further References

See also the biographies of Marshal Stalin in 1:G:2, and general accounts in 2:A and 2:C:1.

d. PARTISAN OPERATIONS

Nearly every Axis-occupied nation had its bands of partisans moving about the countryside attempting to inflict damage upon the conquerors. These men and women sought to disrupt communications, participated in acts of terrorism or espionage, sabotaged industrial and other targets, and provided refuge to lost soldiers or downed airmen.

Marshal Stalin called for all irregular assistance to the Motherland immediately following the German invasion of June 22, 1941. Despite hard work by the Communist Party of the Soviet Union (CPSU) and the NKVD, efforts to provide effective partisan work were not successful until the spring of 1942. Soviet steadfastness in the Moscow battles gave people renewed hope which, combined with harsh German occupation measures and serious Stavka efforts to encourage guerrilla warfare, began to bear fruit by summer of 1942. By July, there were a large number of partisan bands, some numbering over 1000 participants, with an estimated total of almost 200,000 irregulars.

At first these various groups were isolated, but through the use of radio communications and direct contact with Soviet regular officers, Stavka eventually brought them under control and effectively directed their efforts in the enemy rear, especially behind German Army Groups Centre and North.

Despite harsh antipartisan efforts—or perhaps because of them—German efforts to "win the hearts and minds" of Soviet irregulars and turn them against Stalin were unsuccessful. In several instances, Soviet partisan efforts severely hampered Wehrmacht operations before or during major campaigns. At all times, the Russian irregular was a persistent thorn in the side of the Nazi invader.

BOOKS

1038.   Armstrong, John A., ed. *Soviet Partisans in World War II.* Madison: University of Wisconsin Press, 1964. 792p.

1039.   *Avengers: Reminiscences of Soviet Members of the Resistance Movement.* Translated from the Russian. Moscow: Progress Publishers, 1965. 278p.

1040.   Bailey, Ronald H. *Partisans and Guerrillas.* World War II Series. Alexandria, Va.: Time-Life Books, 1978. 208p.

1041.   *Behind the Front Lines: Being an Account of the Military Activities, Exploits, Adventures and Day-to-Day Life of the Soviet Guerrillas Operating behind German Lines from the Finnish-Karelian Front to the Crimea.* London: Hutchinson, 1945. 160p.

1042.   Blacker, Irwin, ed. *Irregulars, Partisans, Guerrillas.* New York: Simon & Schuster, 1954. 487p.

1043.   Ceck, Jan. *Death Stalks the Forest.* London: Drummond, 1943. 75p.

1044.   Cooper, Matthew. *Nazi War Against Soviet Partisans, 1941–1944.* New York: St. Martin's Press, 1979. 300p.

1045.   Dixon, Cecil A., and Otto Heilbrunn. *Communist Guerrilla Warfare.* New York: Praeger, 1954. 229p.

1046.   Dupuy, Trevor N. *European Resistance Movements.* New York: Franklin Watts, 1965. 88p.

1047.   Ellis, John A. *A Short History of Guerrilla Warfare.* New York: St. Martin's Press, 1976. 220p.

1048.   Fedorov, Aleksei F. *The Underground Committee Carries On.* Translated from the Russian. Moscow: Foreign Language Publishing House, 1952. 517p.

1049.   Foot, Michael R. D. *Resistance: European Resistance to Nazism, 1940–1945.* New York: McGraw-Hill, 1977. 346p.

1050.   Hawes, Stephen, and Ralph White, eds. *Resistance in Europe, 1939–1945: Based on the Proceedings of a Symposium Held at the University of Salford, March 1973.* London: Allen Lane, 1975. 235p.

1051.   Heilbrunn, Otto. *Partisan Warfare.* New York: Praeger, 1962. 199p.

1052.   ————. *Warfare in the Enemy's Rear.* New York: Praeger, 1963. 231p.

1053.   Ignatov, Petr K. *Partisans of the Kuban.* Translated from the Russian. London and New York: Hutchinson, 1945. 212p.

1054.   International Conference on the History of the Resistance Movements [First, Liege, 1958]. *European Resistance Movements, 1939–1945: Proceedings.* London and New York: Pergamon Press, 1960. 410p.

1055.   _____ [Second, Milan, 1961]. *European Resistance Movements, 1939–1945: Proceedings.* New York: Macmillan, 1964. 663p.

1056.   _____ [Third, Karlovy Vary, 1962]. *European Resistance Movements, 1939–1945: Papers.* 13 pts. Karlovy Vary, 1963.

1057.   _____ [Fourth, Vienna, 1963]. *European Resistance Movements, 1939–1945: Papers.* Vienna, 1965. Unpaged.

1058.   Johnson, Brian. *The Secret War: Based on the B.B.C. Television Series.* London: B.B.C. Publications, 1978. 352p.

1059.   Kovpak, Sydir A. *Our Partisan Course.* Translated from the Russian. London and New York: Hutchinson, 1947. 126p.

1060.   Krokhmalwik, Yuriy. *U.P.A. Warfare in the Ukraine: Strategical, Tactical, and Organizational Problems of Ukrainian Resistance in World War II.* New York: Society of Veterans of the Ukrainian Insurgent Army, 1972. Unpaged.

1061.   Laqueur, Walter. *Guerrilla: A Historical and Critical Study.* Boston, Mass.: Little, Brown, 1976. 462p.

1062.   _____ . *The Guerrilla Reader: A Historical Anthology.* New York: New American Library, 1977. 246p.

1063.   Levi, Maxine. *The Communists and the Liberation of Europe.* New York: New Century, 1945. 63p.

1064.   Macksey, Kenneth J. *The Partisans of Europe in the Second World War.* New York: Stein & Day, 1975. 271p.

1065.   Medvedev, Dmitriy N. *Stout Hearts.* Translated from the Russian. Moscow: Foreign Language Publishing House [195?]. 237p.

1066.   Michel, Henri. *The Shadow War: European Resistance, 1939–1945.* Translated from the French. New York: Harper & Row, 1972. 416p.

1067.   Moss, William S. *A War of Shadows.* London and New York: Boardman, 1952. 240p.

1068.   Orbaan, Albert. *Duel in the Shadows: True Accounts of Anti-Nazi Underground Warfare during World War II.* Garden City, N.Y.: Doubleday, 1965. 229p.

1069.   Reitlinger, Gerald R. *The House Built on Sand: The Conflicts of German Policy in Russia, 1939–1945.* New York: Viking Press, 1960. 459p.

1070.   Sanderson, James D. *Behind Enemy Lines*. Princeton, N.J.: Van Nostrand, 1959. 322p.

1071.   Truby, J. David. *Women at War: The Deadly Species*. Boulder, Colo.: Paladin Press, 1979. 100p.

1072.   Whiting, Charles. *The War in the Shadows*. New York: Ballantine Books, 1973. 268p.

1073.   Woodman, Dorothy. *Europe Rises: The Story of Resistance in Occupied Europe*. London: Gollancz, 1943. 154p.

ARTICLES

1074.   "Armies of the Forest." *Time* 42 (November 20, 1943), 25–26.

1075.   "Attack on a Partisan Headquarters: German Anti-Partisan Operations in Russia." *Infantry* 53 (May-June 1963), 29–32.

1076.   Azyasskiy, N. "Wartime Operations—Partisan Actions Against the Germans.: Translated from *Voyenno Istoricheskiy Zhurnal*, February 1980." *Translations on USSR Military Affairs*, no. 1516 (May 30, 1980), 55–63.

1077.   Babakov, A. A. "The Partisan Movement in the Great Patriotic War of the Soviet Union." *International Review of Military History*, no. 44 (1979), 172–180.

1078.   "Battle for Railways." *Newsweek* 21 (March 15, 1942), 22–24.

1079.   Bethell, Nicholas. "The People Strike Back." *Russia Besieged*. World War II Series. Alexandria, Va.: Time-Life Books, 1978. pp. 88–114.

1080.   Bourdow, Joseph A. "Big War Guerrillas and Counter-Guerrillas." *Army* 13 (August 1962), 66–69.

1081.   Brand, Emmanuel. "The Forest Ablaze: A Jewish Partisan Group in the Kovpak Division." *Yad Vasem Bulletin*, no. 2 (December 1957), 16.

1082.   Domank, A. "Partisan and Troop Cooperation in the Ukraine Described: Translated from *Voyenno Istoricheskiy Zhurnal*, November 1979." *Translations on USSR Military Affairs*, no. 1500 (February 28, 1980), 26–32.

1083.   Dupont, Pierre. "Behind Enemy Lines in White Russia." *Free World* 7 (February 1944), 166–169.

1084.   "The Forest Camp: German Antipartisan Operations in Russia." *Infantry* 53 (March-April 1963), 19–21.

1085.   Garthoff, Raymond. "Soviet Employment of Partisan Forces." *Soviet Military Doctrine*. Glencoe, Ill.: Free Press, 1953. pp. 391–411.

1086.   Harvey, A. D. "Wartime Resistance in Peacetime Perspective." *Contemporary Review* 223 (July 1978), 21–28.

1087.   Heiman, Leo. "Guerrilla Warfare: An Analysis." *Military Review* 43 (July 1963), 26–36.

1088.   Hurley, James A. "Soviet Air Support to Insurgents." *Marine Corps Gazette* 47 (January 1963), 13–14.

1089.   Karukin, David S. "Partisans, Guerrillas and War in Depth: A Soviet Tactical Doctrine." *Marine Corps Gazette* 46 (June 1962), 28–31.

1090.   Kobrin, Nikolai. "Moscow Region Partisans." *Soviet Military Review*, no. 10 (October 1971), 41–43.

1091.   Kumanyev, G. A. "On the Soviet Peoples' Partisan Movement in the Hitlerite Invaders' Rear, 1941–1944." *International Review of Military History*, no. 47 (1980), 180–188.

1092.   Kveder, D. "Territorial War: The New Concept of Resistance." *Military Review* 34 (July 1954), 46–58.

1093.   Landwehr, Richard. "Anti-Partisan Forces of the Third Reich: 29 Waffen-Grenadier Division der SS (Roma)." *World War II Journal* 2 (July-December 1975), 31–35, 48–50.

1094.   Makarov, N. "Operation Rail Warfare." *Soviet Military Review*, no. 3 (March 1968), 38–41.

1095.   Moats, Alice L. "Courage to Burn: Russian Partisan Detachments." *Collier's* 108 (September 27, 1942), 24.

1096.   Polyakov, Alexi. "Red Guerrillas: Tough Russians Fight Nazis Far behind the Front Lines." *Life* 11 (November 10, 1941), 126–128.

1097.   Rayleigh, Stevens. "Wasps of War: Guerrilla Fighters Paving the Way to the Eventual Defeat of Hitler and Hirohito." *Saturday Evening Post* 214 (April 25, 1942), 9–10.

1098.   Rizzo, Paul J. "The Soviet Partisan: A Reappraisal." *Infantry* 57 (July-August 1967), 3–6.

1099.   Simpson, Keith. "The German Experience of Rear Area Security on the Eastern Front, 1941–1945." *Journal of the Royal United Services Institute for Defence Studies* 121 (December 1976), 37–46.

1100.   "Soviet Guerrilla Warfare." *Cavalry Journal* 50 (September 1941), 2–10.

1101.   "Soviet Partisan Warfare." *Army Information Digest* 6 (February 1951), 62.

1102.   Szkoda, W. E. "The Red Soldier—Mentality and Tactics: Partisan Warfare." *Armor* 70 (July-August 1961), 34–41.

1103.   Vaupshasov, S. "Enveloped in the Flames of Partisan Warfare." *Soviet Military Review*, no. 4 (April 1970), 24–27.

1104.   Werth, Alexander. "The Partisans in the Soviet-German War." *Russia at War, 1941–1945*. New York: E. P. Dutton, 1964. pp. 649–665.

1105.   Whittier, Henry S., Jr. "Soviet Special Operations—Partisan Warfare: Implications for Today," *Military Review* 59 (January 1979), 48–58.

1106.   Yeremeyev, L. "Scorched Earth under the Enemy's Feet." *Soviet Military Review*, no. 4 (April 1975), 15–17.

1107.   Zawodny, Janusz K. "Soviet Partisans." *Soviet Studies* 17 (January 1966), 368–377.

1108.   Zvi Bar-On, A. "The Jews in the Soviet Partisan Movement." *Yad Vashem Studies* 4 (1964), 176.

DOCUMENTS, PAPERS, AND REPORTS

1109.   Blumentritt, Guenther. "War in the Rear Communications Zone." Unpublished paper, Foreign Military Studies Program, Historical Division, Headquarters, U.S. Army, Europe, 1947. 10p.

1110.   Drum, Karl. *Airpower and Russian Partisan Warfare*. USAF Historical Studies. Maxwell AFB, Ala.: Research Studies Institute, Air University, 1962. 63p.

1111.   Gordon, Gary H. "Soviet Partisan Warfare, 1941–1944: The German Perspective." PhD dissertation, University of Iowa, 1972.

1112.   Hoehne, Gustav. "Haunted Forests: Enemy Partisans behind the Fronts." Unpublished paper, Foreign Military Studies Program, Historical Division, Headquarters, U.S. Army, Europe, 1953. 14p.

1113.   Howell, Edgar M. *The Soviet Partisan Movement, 1941–1944*. DA Pam 20-244. Washington, D.C.: Department of the Army, 1956. 217p.

1114.   Pronin, Alexander. "Guerrilla Warfare in the German-Occupied Soviet Territories, 1941–1944." PhD dissertation, Georgetown University, 1965.

1115.   United States. Department of the Army. Historical Division. *Rear Area Security in Russia: The Soviet Second Front behind German Lines.* DA Pam 20-240. Washington, D.C., 1951. 39p.

1116.   United States. Office of Strategic Services. Research and Analysis Branch. *Germany and Its Occupied Territories during World War II.* Part 4 of *O.S.S./State Department Intelligence and Research Reports.* 22 reels, 35mm microfilm. Washington, D.C.: University Publications of America, 1976–1977.

1117.   Von Bechtolsheim, Gustav. "Protection of Lines of Communication in the East, September 1941–February 1943." Unpublished paper, Foreign Military Studies Program, Historical Division, Headquarters, U.S. Army, Europe, 1947. 7p.

1118.   Von Greiffenberg, Hans. "Small Unit Tactics—Partisan Warfare." Unpublished paper, Foreign Military Studies Program, Historical Division, Headquarters, U.S. Army, Europe, 1952. 35p.
    Reprinted in part 10 of William S. Detwiler, ed., *World War II German Military Studies,* 24 vols. (New York: Garland, 1980).

Further References

See also sections 2:A and 2:C:1, and *Intelligence, Propaganda and Psychological Warfare, Resistance Movements and Secret Operations, 1939–1945,* vol. 1 of the author's *The Secret Wars,* 3 vols. (Santa Barbara, Calif.: ABC-Clio, 1980–1981), pp. 108–112, 144–149.

e. STRATEGY AND TACTICS

During the early phases of the Great Patriotic War, Soviet strategists sought to design troop and partisan movements which would wear down the invader, to prevent his taking any more land than necessary, and to recapture land when possible. Due to a lack of equipment, the Russians depended upon highly centralized control, lengthy preparation, and superior numbers. Special troops and support elements were tightly controlled, as were reserves, for allocation where they were most needed.

Following the 1943 Battle of Kursk, the Soviets moved to push the Germans out of the Motherland, to liberate Eastern Europe, and to crush the Reich as rapidly as possible. During these great offensives, the Soviets designed their tactics and techniques primarily to overcome the strong defensive positions which the Wehrmacht established. As Soviet commanders gained experience in offensive tactics, they developed greater flexibility, and on numerous occasions carried out complex operations which involved concentrating or regrouping large forces with speed and efficiency.

Despite increased leadership ability and tactical sufficiency, as well as the introduction of large amounts of artillery and tanks, Red Army soldiers continued to suffer as commanders wastefully employed mass and human wave tactics even through the Battle of Berlin.

BOOKS

1119.   Armstrong, Anne. *Unconditional Surrender: The Impact of the Casablanca Policy upon World War II.* New Brunswick, N.J.: Rutgers University Press, 1961. 304p.

1120.   Bazilevich, Konstantin V. *The Russian Art of War.* London: Soviet News, 1945. 44p.

1121.   Burne, Alfred H. *Strategy as Exemplified in the Second World War: A Strategical Examination of the Land Operations.* Lees Knowles Lectures, 1946. Cambridge: At the University Press, 1946. 89p.

1122.   Chandler, David G. *Atlas of Military Strategy.* New York: Macmillan, 1980.

1123.   Mastny, Vojtech. *Russia's Road to the Cold War: Diplomacy, Warfare, and the Politics of Communism, 1941–1945.* New York: Columbia University Press, 1979. 409p.

1124.   *Strategy and Tactics of the Soviet-German War.* London: Hutchinson, 1943. 148p.

ARTICLES

1125.   Ambrose, Stephen E. "Allied Strategy of World War II." *Naval War College Review,* 22 (May 1970), 62–70.

1126.   _____. "The Grand Strategy of World War II." *Naval War College Review* 22 (April 1970), 20–28.

1127.   Andrew, G. S. "To Fit the Situation: A Description of Red Army Tactical Doctrine." *Infantry Journal* 60 (March 1947), 47–49.

1128.   Antsiz, B. "Wartime Experience in Sustaining Offensive Operations Reviewed: Translated from *Voyenno Istoricheskiy Zhurnal,* January 1979." *Translations on USSR Military Affairs,* no. 1414 (March 1, 1979), 89–98.

1129.   Batov, Pavel. "Wartime Experiences of Army River-Crossing Operations Reviewed: Translated from *Voyenno Istoricheskiy Zhurnal,* January 1978." *Translations on USSR Military Affairs,* no. 1349 (May 2, 1978), 3–7.

1130.   Edson, C. A. "German Tactics in Russia." *Command and General Staff School Quarterly* 22 (April 1942), 5–12.

1131.   Erickson, John. "Russians on Soviet Strategy." *Problems of Communism* 15 (July 1966), 59–62.

1132.   Fuqua, Stephen O. "The Geographical Factor in Russian Strategy." *Newsweek* 18 (July 18, 1941), 21.

1133.   Gerasimov, Ivan A. "Rapid Preparation of Operations in World War II Described: Translated from *Voyenno Istoricheskiy Zhurnal,* August 1978." *Translations on USSR Military Affairs,* no. 1391 (October 30, 1978), 125–134.

1134.   Grechko, Andrei A. "The Science and Art of Securing Victory—Soviet Military Science and the Art of Warfare during the Great Patriotic War." *Soviet Military Review,* no. 5 (May 1975), 2–9.

1135.   Hinterhoff, Eugene. "The Evolution of Soviet Strategy and of Army Forces." *NATO's Fifteen Nations* 7 (June-July 1962), 110–113.

1136.   "How Infantry-Artillery Cooperation is Secured in the Red Army." *Field Artillery Journal* 31 (October 1941), 790–794.

1137.   Ionin, G. "The Development of Defensive Tactics." *Soviet Military Review,* no. 1 (January 1980), 34–35.

1138.   [Kennan, George]. "Policy and Strategy in the War in Russia: Winter Interlude." By "X," pseud. *Foreign Affairs* 20 (July 1942), 607–634.

1139.   _____ . "Russia and Germany: Political and Military Reflections." By "X," pseud. *Foreign Affairs* 20 (January 1942), 303–323.

1140.   Kizev, G. "Tankmen in the Enemy's Rear." *Soviet Military Review,* no. 11 (November 1969), 44–46.

1141.   Korzun, L. "Wartime Operations—Troop Control during Regrouping: Translated from *Voyenno Istoricheskiy Zhurnal,* January 1980." *Translations on USSR Military Affairs,* no. 1511 (April 21, 1980), 13–21.

1142.   Kozhevnikov, M. "Air Force and Infantry Operations in World War II: Translated from *Voyenno Istoricheskiy Zhurnal,* February 1979." *Translations on USSR Military Affairs,* no. 1441 (May 24, 1979), 21–29.

1143.   Luchinskiy, A. "Wartime Operations—Commanders Preparations for an Offensive: Translated from *Voyenno Istoricheskiy Zhurnal*,
July 1980." *Translations on USSR Military Affairs*, no. 1544 (November 14,
1980), 20–29.

1144.   Lukas, John A. "Political Expediency and Soviet Russian
Military Operations." *Journal of Central European Affairs* 8 (January
1949), 390–411.

1145.   Mackintosh, Malcolm. "The Development of Soviet Military
Doctrine since 1918." In Michael Howard, ed., *The Theory and Practice of
War.* London: Cassell, 1965. pp. 78–95.

1146.   Martell, Paul. "The Soviet Concept of Waging Major Operations in World War II." *History, Numbers and War* 1 (Spring 1977), 24–33.

1147.   Mastny, Vojtech. "Soviet War Aims at the Moscow and Teheran Conferences of 1943." *Journal of Modern History* 47 (September
1975), 481–504.

1148.   ———. "Stalin and the Prospects of a Separate Peace in
World War II." *American Historical Review* 77 (December 1972), 1365–
1388.

1149.   Matsulenko, V. "Cutting of a Strategic Front." *Soviet Military
Review*, no. 10 (October 1969), 45–46.

1150.   ———. "Encirclement." *Soviet Military Review*, no. 9 (September 1969), 48–49.

1151.   ———. "Methods of Strategic Offensive." *Soviet Military
Review*, no. 12 (December 1969), 45–46.

1152.   "Night Combat." *Military Review* 23 (November 1943), 89–90.

1153.   Ostroumov, N. "Wartime Operations—Aviation and Ground
Forces Cooperation: Translated from *Voyenno Istoricheskiy Zhurnal*, August 1980." *Translations on USSR Military Affairs*, no. 1549 (December 8,
1980), 37–46.

1154.   Radziyevsky, A. "The Art of Gaining Victory." *Soviet Military
Review*, no. 1 (January 1978), 23–26.

1155.   ———. "Division Breakthrough Operations in World War
II Discussed: Translated from *Voyenno Istoricheskiy Zhurnal*, February
1979." *Translations on USSR Military Affairs*, no. 1434 (May 9, 1979),
10–18.

1156.   "Russian and German Tactics in World War II." *Military Review* 29 (September 1949), 100–102.

1157.   Savelyev, V. "River Crossing on the Move." *Soviet Military Review*, no. 7 (July 1970), 6–17.

1158.   Savitskiy, E. "Cooperation between Fighter Planes and Tanks." *Military Review* 26 (August 1946), 89–91.

1159.   Sidorenko, A. A. "Development of the Tactics of Offensive Battle." *Soviet Military Review*, no. 10 (October 1979), 20–22.

1160.   Simonyan, R. "Wartime Operations—Preoffensive Intelligence Work: Translated from *Voyenno Istoricheskiy Zhurnal*, November 1980." *Translations on USSR Military Affairs*, no. 1565 (February 5, 1981), 19–25.

1161.   Sokolov, A. "An Assault Crossing." *Soviet Military Review*, no. 12 (December 1979), 40–42.

1162.   Soskov, A. "Wartime Operations—Methods of Breaching Minefields: Translated from *Voyenno Istoricheskiy Zhurnal*, April 1980." *Translations on USSR Military Affairs*, no. 1525 (July 24, 1980), 12–20.

1163.   "Soviet Tactical Tendencies." *Military Review* 31 (October 1951), 73–81.

1164.   United States. War Department. General Staff. G-2. "Winter Fighting in Russia." *Tactical and Technical Trends* 12 (1942), 20–27.

1165.   Vassiliev, Aleksandr. "Soviet Breakthrough Methods." *Infantry Journal* 54 (January 1944), 52–53.

1166.   Veraksa, Ye. "Cooperation of Aviation with Land Forces in World War II." *Soviet Military Review*, no. 10 (October 1976), 54–56.

1167.   Vorob'yev, I. "Fire and Maneuver Tactics Discussed: Translated from *Krasnaya Zvezda*, June 5, 1979." *Translations on USSR Military Affairs*, no. 1458 (August 23, 1979), 54–58.

1168.   _____. "Fire, Assault, Maneuver." In William F. Scott, ed., *Selected Soviet Military Writings, 1970–1975: A Soviet View*. Soviet Military Thought Series, no. 11. Washington, D.C.: U.S. Government Printing Office, 1977. pp. 219–224.

1169.   Werner, Max. "For a Quick Victory: The Secret of Russian Resistance." *New Republic* 105 (August 18, 1941), 210–213.

1170.   "When the Red Army Attacks a City." *Infantry Journal* 56 (March 1945), 52–53.

1171.   Young, W. R. "Russian Strategy and Tactics." *Fighting Forces* 21 (October 1944), 174–179.

1172.   Zakharov, M. "Triumph of Soviet Military Strategy during the War." *Soviet Military Review,* no. 4 (April 1970), 10–13.

1173.   Zhadov, A. "Wartime Experiences on the Penetration of Enemy Defenses Reviewed: Translated from *Voyenno Istoricheskiy Zhurnal,* January 1978." *Translations on USSR Military Affairs,* no. 1349 (May 2, 1978), 1–3.

1174.   Zhilin, P. A. "Policy and Strategy of the Soviet Union in the Second World War." *International Review of Military History,* no. 44 (1979), 24–42.

DOCUMENTS, PAPERS, AND REPORTS

1175.   Germany. Wehrmacht Oberkommando. *Combat Tactics of the Red Army.* Translated from the German. Fort Monroe, Va: Intelligence Section, U. S. Army Field Forces, 1949. 65p.

1176.   Popel, N. N. *Troop Control during the Great Patriotic War.* Translated from the Russian. JPRS-64920. Arlington, Va.: Joint Publications Research Service, 1975. 146p.

1177.   United States. Department of the Army. Historical Section. *Russian Combat Methods in World War II: Historical Study.* DA Pam. Washington, D.C., 1950. 116p.

Further References

See also sections 2:A, 2:C:2:a, and 4:B. Works on strategy and tactics in operations are in 2:C:3.

f. REAR SERVICES: LOGISTICS AND COMMUNICATIONS

This section details Soviet organization and use of supply and communication in support of field operations. References consider such matters as motor transport, artillery and tank repair, the work of engineers, and the importance of radio contact. Note that all of the sources except one are translations from Russian-language publications.

ARTICLES

1178.   Aganov, Sergei K. "Service Chiefs on Lessons Learned in the Great Patriotic War—Aganov on Engineer Troops: Translated from *Voyenno Istoricheskiy Zhurnal,* November 1977." *Translations on USSR Military Affairs,* no. 1327 (January 27, 1978), 92–97.

1179.   Belov, Andrey I. "Service Chiefs on Lessons Learned in the Great Patriotic War—Belov on Signal Troops: Translated from *Voyenno Istoricheskiy Zhurnal*, November 1977." *Translations on USSR Military Affairs*, no. 1327 (January 27, 1978), 97–103.

1180.   Bulychev, I. "Wartime Operations—Front Communications in the Vistula-Oder Operation: Translated from *Voyenno Istoricheskiy Zhurnal*, February 1980." *Translations on USSR Military Affairs*, no. 1516 (May 30, 1980), 39–45.

1181.   Kiselov, A. "Wartime Operations of Artillery Repair Units Described: Translated from *Voyenno Istoricheskiy Zhurnal*, October 1979." *Translations on USSR Military Affairs*, no. 1487 (January 7, 1980), 72–80.

1182.   Klevtsov, V. "Wartime Combat Equipment—Supply and Effectiveness: Translated from *Voyenno Istoricheskiy Zhurnal*, December 1979." *Translations on USSR Military Affairs*, no. 1508 (March 28, 1980), 29–38.

1183.   Kovalev, S. F. "Capabilities of Motor Transport [Troops] Personnel: Translated from *Za Rulem*, January 1978." *Translations on USSR Military Affairs*, no. 1329 (February 10, 1978), 78–80.

1184.   Kuybyshev, V. V. "Wartime Operations—Engineer Support of Ground Attacks: Translated from *Voyenno Istoricheskiy Zhurnal*, August 1980." *Translations on USSR Military Affairs*, no. 1549 (December 8, 1980), 47–56.

1185.   Leoshenya, Ye., et al. "Wartime Order on the Organization and Tasks of the Engineering Service: Translated from *Voyenno Istoricheskiy Zhurnal*, December 1978." *Translations on USSR Military Affairs*, no. 1425 (April 3, 1979), 1–4.

1186.   Lipatov, S. "Tank Repair Operations in World War II Discussed: Translated from *Voyenno Istoricheskiy Zhurnal*, February 1979." *Translations on USSR Military Affairs*, no. 1439 (May 9, 1979), 28–35.

1187.   Odintsov, V. "Wartime Operations—Logistical Support during Troop Regrouping: Translated from *Voyenno Istoricheskiy Zhurnal*, April 1980." *Translations on USSR Military Affairs*, no. 1525 (July 24, 1980), 31–40.

1188.   Peresypkin, I. T. "Peresypkin on Communications in Wartime Front and Army Operations: Translated from *Voyenno Istoricheskiy Zhurnal*, January 1978." *Translations on USSR Military Affairs*, no. 1334 (March 2, 1978), 1–15.

1189.   Petukhov, D. "Signal Communication in the War Years." *Soviet Military Review*, no. 9 (September 1973), 40–41.

1190.   "Russian Armored Trains." *Infantry Journal* 52 (February 1943), 77–78.

1191.   Shcherbakov, B. "Wartime Logistical Support of the 4th Tank Army Described: Translated from *Voyenno Istoricheskiy Zhurnal,* June 1979." *Translations on USSR Military Affairs,* no. 1466 (October 2, 1979), 11–20.

1192.   Skryabin, S. "Early Development of Soviet Rear Services Described: Translated from *Voyenno Istoricheskiy Zhurnal,* July 1979." *Translations on USSR Military Affairs,* no. 1476 (November 28, 1979), 68–76.

1193.   Taran, I. "Wartime Communications in a Tank Army Described: Translated from *Voyenno Istoricheskiy Zhurnal,* February 1979." *Translations on USSR Military Affairs,* no. 1434 (May 9, 1979), 48–56.

1194.   Volkotrubenko, I. "Wartime Operations—Supplying Artillery Weapons and Ammunition: Translated from *Voyenno Istoricheskiy Zhurnal,* May 1980." *Translations on USSR Military Affairs,* no. 1532 (September 10, 1980), 81–88.

DOCUMENTS, PAPERS, AND REPORTS

1195.   Peresypkin, I. T. *Communications during the Great Patriotic War.* Translated from the Russian. JPRS-63074. Arlington, Va.: Joint Publications Research Service, 1974. 65p.

Further References

See also sections 2:A, 2:C:2:a, and 4:D.

3. Specific Campaigns and Battles

Citations in this section detail the Red Army's many campaigns during the Great Patriotic War. Among them are the famous battles fought at Stalingrad, Kursk, and Berlin, and general campaigns like those in Byelorussia, throughout Eastern Europe, and Manchuria.

Each subsection has a general introduction. When taken together, they form a catalog of immense and dreadful combat.

a. OPERATION BARBAROSSA: THE GERMAN INVASION, SUMMER-FALL 1941

Out of his hatred for communism and desire for territory, Hitler ordered the invasion of the Soviet Union, which began early on the morning of June 22, 1941. More than 180 Wehrmacht divisions poured into Russia, meeting an underestimated but poorly led 158 Red infantry divisions.

Although evidence suggests that Stalin knew that Barbarossa was coming, Soviet units were everywhere surprised and, during the next few weeks, cut to pieces. Added to Red worries was a renewal of hostilities with Finland, which began a "Continuation War" on the side of the Germans.

After the initial blows, Soviet resistance began to stiffen. Under siege, Leningrad held in the north. Wehrmacht efforts to capture Moscow progressed, but delays in the south and the coming of winter brought slowdowns. Kiev was valiantly defended, slowing the Germans for two critical months. Although Odessa was lost, the Crimea remained in Russian hands. The stage was set for the first of several important battles, the winter Moscow offensives.

BOOKS

1196.   Bethell, Nicholas W. *Russia Besieged*. World War II Series. Alexandria, Va.: Time-Life Books, 1977. 208p.

1197.   Cecil, Robert. *Hitler's Decision to Invade Russia, 1941*. London: Davis Poynter, 1975. 192p.

1198.   Critchley, Julian. *Warning and Response: A Study of Surprise Attack in the Twentieth Century and an Analysis of Its Lessons for the Future*. New York: Crane, Russak, 1978. 123p.

1199.   Erickson, John. *The Road to Stalingrad: Stalin's War with Germany*. New York: Harper & Row, 1975. 595p.

1200.   Keegan, John. *Barbarossa: Invasion of Russia, 1941*. Ballantine's Illustrated History of World War II. New York: Ballantine Books, 1971. 160p.

1201.   Petrov, Vladimir. *"June 22, 1941": Soviet Historians and the German Invasion, Including a Complete Translation of Aleksandr M. Nekrich's, "1941, 22 Iyunia."* Columbia: University of South Carolina Press, 1968. 322p.

1202.   Smirnov, Sergei S. *Heroes of Brest Fortress*. Moscow: Foreign Language Publishing House, 1957. 211p.

1203.   Whaley, Barton. *Codeword BARBAROSSA*. Cambridge, Mass.: M.I.T. Press, 1973. 376p.

ARTICLES

1204.   Ainsztein, Reuben. "Stalin and June 22, 1941: Some New Soviet Views." *International Affairs* (London) 42 (October 1966), 662–672.

1205.   Benson, Oliver E. "Hitler's Russian Gamble." *Current History*, ns 1 (September 1941), 16–25.

1206.   Ben-Zvi, A. "The Study of Surprise Attacks." *British Journal of International Studies* 5 (July 1979), 129–149.

1207.   Brower, Daniel R. "The Soviet Union and the German Invasion of 1941: A New Soviet View." *Journal of Modern History* 41 (Fall 1969), 327–334.

1208.   Chaney, Otto P. "Was It a Surprise?" *Military Review* 49 (April 1969), 56–57.

1209.   Erickson, John. "The Soviet Response to Surprise Attack: Three Directives, 22 June 1941." *Soviet Studies* 23 (April 1972), 519–553.

1210.   "Fierce Blows and Foggy Claims Mark Battle of Soviet Steppes." *Newsweek* 18 (July 21, 1941), 17–20.

1211.   Fuqua, Stephen O. "German Drives and the Russian Defenses." *Newsweek* 18 (July 7, 1941), 21.

1212.   _____ . "The Stand of the Red Army." *Newsweek* 18 (July 24, 1941), 21.

1213.   _____ . "Why the Germans Shifted to the Ukraine." *Newsweek* 18 (August 25, 1941), 21.

1214.   "Fury on Russian Front Mounts as Germans Reach Stalin Line." *Newsweek* 18 (July 14, 1941), 19–22.

1215.   "Fury on Russian Front Mounts as Soviet Morale Slows Nazis." *Newsweek* 18 (August 11, 1941), 21–22.

1216.   Garthoff, Raymond L. "The Soviet Trial by Arms, June–December 1941." *Military Review* 23 (June 1953), 23–31.

1217.   "German Smash into the Ukraine Perils the Position of the Russians." *Newsweek* 18 (September 29, 1941), 19–22.

1218.   "Germany vs. Russia." *Time* 37 (June 30, 1941), 21–24.

1219.   "The Greatest Land War in History Mixes Propaganda with Blitz." *Newsweek* 18 (July 7, 1941), 17–20.

1220.   Jordan, Philip. "When Tank Meets Tank on the Plains of Russia." *New York Times Magazine* (October 19, 1941), 9.

1221.   Kirkpatrick, Lyman B., Jr. "Barbarossa." *Captains without Eyes: Intelligence Failures in World War II*. New York: Macmillan, 1969. Chpt. 1.

1222.   Leontyev, A. "U.S.S.R. Army Paper Sees Historical Lessons of German Invasion: Translated from *Krasnaya Zvezda,* June 22, 1978." *Translations on USSR Military Affairs,* no. 1362 (July 12, 1978), 42–46.

1223.   "The Lessons of Barbarossa." *Military Review* 53 (July 1953), 104–109.

1224.   Liddell-Hart, Basil H. "Was Russia Close to Defeat?" *Military Review* 30 (July 1950), 11–15.

1225.   _____ . "Why Hitler Invaded Russia—and Failed." *Marine Corps Gazette* 40 (December 1956), 22–26.

1226.   Lukas, John A. "The Story behind Hitler's Biggest Blunder." *New York Times Magazine* (June 17, 1951), 10–11.

1227.   Lukin, M. "Army Commander Describes the Loss of Smolansk: Translated from *Voyenno Istoricheskiy Zhurnal,* July 1979." *Translations on USSR Military Affairs,* no. 1476 (November 28, 1979), 48–67.   Taken by German troops on August 6, 1941, after a month-long battle during which Marshal Timoshenko's western sector fought well. The Soviets introduced the new T-34 tank during the same battle.

1228.   Luther, Craig. "German Armoured Operations in the Ukraine, 1941: The Encirclement Battle of Uman." *Army Quarterly* 108 (October 1978), 454–469.   This German victory led to the capture of Kiev.

1229.   Madej, V. "The Smolensk Campaign." *Strategy and Tactics,* no. 57 (May-June 1976), *passim.*

1230.   Markhoff, Alexander. "How Russia Almost Lost the War." *Saturday Evening Post* 222 (May 17, 1950), 31.

1231.   "Mars Gone Mad." *Newsweek* 18 (August 4, 1941), 17–18.

1232.   Martell, Paul. "The Advance of the German 1st Panzer Group in the Ukraine, June 1941." *History, Numbers and War* 1 (Spring 1977), 115–125.

1233.   Matsulenko, V. "The Initial Period of the War." *Soviet Military Review,* no. 2 (February 1976), 48–50.

1234.   Moats, Alice L. "Russians Are Like That: How Moscow Took It." *Collier's* 108 (July 26, 1941), 16.

1235.   "One Day That Shook the World: The Russo-German War." *New Republic* 104 (June 30, 1941), 871–873.

1236.   Pruszynski, Ksawery. "On the Steppes." *Dublin Review* 213 (October 1943), 107–115.

1237.   "The Red Army Battles to the Death for the Survival of the U.S.S.R." *Life* 11 (July 14, 1941), 13–19.

1238.   Reinhardt, Hellmuth. "Encirclement at Yukhnov: A Soviet Airborne Operation in World War II." *Military Review* 43 (May 1963), 61–75.

1239.   "Russians and Nazis Meet on the Long Roads of Russia." *Life* 11 (September 22, 1941), 32–34.

1240.   Sas, Anthony. "The German-Soviet Conflict Thirty Years After: The Invasion of Russia." *Military Review* 51 (June 1971), 38–46.

1241.   Schuman, Frederick L. "The Nazi Road to War." *Current History* 25 (August 1953), 124–125.

1242.   Sella, Amnon. "Barbarossa: Surprise Attack and Communication." *Journal of Contemporary History* 13 (July 1978), 555–583.

1243.   Shevchuk, V. "Wartime Operations—The Battle of Smolensk: Translated from *Voyenno Istoricheskiy Zhurnal,* December 1979." *Translations on USSR Military Affairs,* no. 1508 (March 28, 1980), 13–19.

1244.   Soloveytchik, George. "Reflections on the Russian War." *19th Century* 130 (September 1941), 156–160.

1245.   Trevor-Roper, Hugh R. "The Blitz That Failed." *New York Times Magazine* (June 18, 1961), 8–9.

1246.   _____ . "Hitler's Gamble." *Atlantic* 194 (September 1954), 39–44.

1247.   Werner, Max. "How Much Has Russia Lost?" *New Republic* 105 (October 6, 1941), 426–427.

1248.   White, William W. "War Overtakes Russia." *Current History,* ns 1 (September 1941), 26–29.

1249.   "World Rocked by War's Turn in Hitler's Attack on Russia." *Newsweek* 17 (June 30, 1941), 11–14.

DOCUMENTS, PAPERS, AND REPORTS

1250.   Bergen, Hans. "The Encirclement and Annihilation of the Russian 32nd Cossack Division, 6–7 August 1941." Unpublished paper, Foreign Military Studies Program, Historical Division, Headquarters, U.S. Army, Europe, 1947. 25p.

1251.   _____ . "The Part Played by the 187th Infantry Regiment in the 87th Infantry Division's Attack at the Beginning of the Russian Campaign on 23 June 1941." Unpublished paper, Foreign Military Studies Program, Historical Division, Headquarters, U.S. Army, Europe, 1947. 29p.

1252.   Blau, George E. *The German Campaign in Russia: Planning and Operations, 1940–1942.* DA Pam. Washington, D.C.: Department of the Army, 1955. 197p.

1253.   Blumentritt, Guenther. "'Impossible Situations,' 1941." Unpublished paper, Foreign Military Studies Program, Historical Division, Headquarters, U.S. Army, Europe, 1947. 11p.

1254.   Cuno, Curt. "German Preparations for the Attack Against Russia." Unpublished paper, Foreign Military Studies Program, Historical Division, Headquarters, U.S. Army, Europe, 1947. 13p.

1255.   Dupuy, Trevor N. "Breakthrough of the German 1st Panzer Group in the Ukraine, June 1941." In Trevor N. Dupuy et al., *A Study of Breakthrough Operations.* DNA-4124F. Dun Loring, Va.: Historical Evaluation and Research Organization, 1976. Chpt. 3.

1256.   Fraley, James R. "Adolf Hitler's Decision to Invade the Soviet Union." MA thesis, North Texas State University, 1975.

1257.   Koehler, Wilhelm. "Engagements Fought by the 488th Infantry Regiment at the Stryanitsa and Desna Rivers, September 1941." Unpublished paper, Foreign Military Studies Program, Historical Division, Headquarters, U.S. Army, Europe, 1947. 29p.

1258.   Rendulic, Lothar. "Command in Critical Situations." Unpublished paper, Foreign Military Studies Program, Historical Division, Headquarters, U.S. Army, Europe, 1947. 11p.   Fighting for Kozel'sk, September–October 1941.

1259.   _____ . "Russian Command: The 13th Russian Cavalry Division in Action at Kozel'sk." Unpublished paper, Foreign Military Studies Program, Historical Division, Headquarters, U.S. Army, Europe, 1947. 11p.

1260.   Wagner, Paul. "Engagements Fought by the 16th Panzer Division along the Lower Bug River, August 1941." Unpublished paper, Foreign Military Studies Program, Historical Division, Headquarters, U.S. Army, Europe, 1947. 21p.

1261.   Whaley, Barton. "Operation Barbarossa: A Case Study of Soviet Strategic Information Processing before the German Invasion." PhD dissertation, Massachusetts Institute of Technology, 1969.

Further References

See also sections 2:A and 2:C:1.

b. THE RUSSO-GERMAN MOSCOW OFFENSIVES, 1941–1942

Once Kiev was encircled in the south, the German central army group moved on Moscow. Two salients were moved north and south of the capital and came dangerously near to meeting. Soviet officials and foreign diplomats daily left the city as its fall appeared inevitable, although Stalin and a few others stayed on.

German troops were 60 miles away in October, but within 25 miles of the city by December. Wehrmacht soldiers could see the towers of St. Basil's cathedral. And then the winter.

In late November and early December of 1941, winter weather such as few could remember seized the north. Roads became impassable, and supplies from the south not lost to partisan raiders were cut off as transport broke down. Lacking winter uniforms, many Axis soldiers perished as temperatures fell. When lubricating oil froze, the cylinders of tank engines cracked. By December 7, ironically the same day Japanese aircraft were attacking Pearl Harbor, the Germans were forced to the defensive and began to dig in.

Sensing that the Wehrmacht could not cope with the weather, and believing that the Red Army had inflicted far more casualties than it had, Stalin ordered a counteroffensive along the line from Moscow south. The push relieved much of the pressure on the capital and resulted in the recapture by spring of Rostov. Many lives and much equipment were lost by the Red Army. Leningrad was not relieved nor was the siege of Sevastopol lifted. With the coming of warm weather and reinforcements, the Germans were prepared to open their second summer offensive.

BOOKS

1262.   Beloborodov, Afonasiy P. *They Did Not Pass*. Translated from the Russian. Moscow: Progress Publishers, 1970.

1263.   Frenkel, Nikolai. *The Defense of Moscow*. Translated from the Russian. Moscow: Foreign Language Publishing House, 1944. 39p.

1264.   Jukes, Geoffrey. *The Defense of Moscow*. Ballantine's Illustrated History of World War II. New York: Ballantine Books, 1970. 160p.

1265.   Seaton, Albert. *The Battle for Moscow, 1941–1942*. New York: Stein & Day, 1971. 320p.

1266.   Servuk, Vladimir. *Moscow-Stalingrad: Recollections, Stories, Reports.* Translated from the Russian. Moscow: Progress Publishers, 1974.

1267.   Seth, Ronald S. *Operation Barbarossa: The Battle for Moscow.* London: Blond, 1964. 191p.

1268.   Turney, Alfred W. *Disaster at Moscow:* [Fedor] *von Vock's Campaign, 1941–1942.* Albuquerque: University of New Mexico Press, 1970. 228p.

1269.   Werth, Alexander. *Moscow War Diary.* New York: Alfred A. Knopf, 1942. 297p.

ARTICLES

1270.   Andronikov, N. G. "The Soviet Army's Victory at Moscow." *International Review of Military History,* no. 44 (1979), 98–108.

1271.   Assman, Kurt. "The Battle for Moscow: Turning Point of the War." *Foreign Affairs* 28 (January 1950), 309–326.

1272.   Blumentritt, Guenther. "The Attack on Moscow." *An Cosantoir* 12 (August 1952), 360–363.

1273.   ———. "Moscow." In Seymour Freidin and William Richardson, eds., *The Fatal Decisions.* New York: William Sloane, 1956. pp. 29–86.

1274.   Cherniavsky, Michael. "Corporal Hitler, General Winter, and the Russian Peasant." *Yale Review* 57 (June 1962), 547–558.

1275.   "Death on the Approaches." *Time* 38 (December 8, 1941), 24–26.

1276.   "Fagged and Frozen Nazi Units Strain to Hang on in Russia." *Newsweek* 19 (January 5, 1942), 16.

1277.   Fay, Sydney B. "Hitler's Failure in Russia." *Current History,* ns 1 (February 1942), 527–531.

1278.   "Flamethrower Operations: Translated from *Krasnaya Zvezda,* February 16, 1977." *Review of the Soviet Ground Forces* 1 (August 1977), 26.

1279.   Fuqua, Stephen O. "All Roads Lead to Moscow." *Newsweek* 18 (October 13, 1941), 27.

1280.   ———. "The German Retreat Is Not a Rout." *Newsweek* 19 (January 26, 1942), 19.

1281.   "The German Army Heads for Moscow." *Life* 11 (July 28, 1941), 17–20.

1282.   "The German XLVII Panzer Corps from Orel to Moscow, 13 November–7 December 1941." *History, Numbers and War* 2 (Fall 1978), 142–157.

1283.   Gwynn, Charles W. "Marshal Zhukov's Offensive." *Fortnightly* 159 (February-March 1943), 111–114, 185–188.

1284.   Hofman, Rudolf. "The Battle for Moscow, 1941." In Hans A. Jacobsen and Juergen Rohwer, eds., *Decisive Battles of World War II: The German View*. New York: G. P. Putnam, 1965. pp. 137–180.

1285.   Isayev, F. "Participation of Soviet Far East Troops in World War II Described: Translated from *Voyenno Istoricheskiy Zhurnal*, August 1979." *Translations on USSR Military Affairs*, no. 1472 (October 31, 1979), 77–83.

1286.   Jordan, Philip. "Moscow Holds On." *Life* 11 (December 15, 1941), 18.

1287.   Kerr, Walter B. "The Battle of Moscow." *The Russian Army: Its Men, Its Leaders, Its Battles*. New York: Alfred A. Knopf, 1944. pp. 31–78.

1288.   Krylov, Ivan N. "In the Mozhaisk Direction." *Soviet Military Review*, no. 11 (November 1971), 39–41.

1289.   Kukiel, M. "Notes on Two Moscow Campaigns." *Army Quarterly* 45 (November 1942) 79–85; (February 1943), 172–179.

1290.   Liddell-Hart, Basil H. "How Hitler Failed at Moscow." *Marine Corps Gazette* 41 (March 1957), 28–30.

1291.   Mikhaylenko, I. "Wartime Air Defense of Moscow: Translated from *Voyenno Istoricheskiy Zhurnal*, December 1977." *Translations on USSR Military Affairs*, no. 1329 (February 10, 1978), 14–17.

1292.   "Morale of Nazi Army Shaken by a Solid Month of Retreat." *Newsweek* 19 (January 19, 1942), 19–21.

1293.   "Moscow, 1812 and 1941: A Comparison." *Military Review* 33 (June 1953), 87–92.

1294.   "Muscovites Take Up Their Guns as Nazi Horde Approaches the Russian Capital." *Life* 11 (October 27, 1941), 27–33.

1295.   "The Nazi Ring Around Moscow." *Scholastic* 39 (December 8, 1941), 5.

1296.   "The Nazi Showdown Drive on the Reds Sets the Stage for a New War Crisis." *Newsweek* 18 (October 20, 1941), 23–27.

1297.   Nevzorov, B. "Impregnable Barrier." *Soviet Military Review*, no. 12 (December 1975), 51–53.

1298.   Panov, B. V. "Sharp Turn." *Soviet Military Review*, no 12 (December 1971), 34–37.   The Russian Moscow counteroffensive.

1299.   "Red Victory at Moscow Gates Turns into a Broad Offensive." *Newsweek* 18 (December 22, 1941), 31.

1300.   "Reds Step Up Counterthrusts in Face of New Nazi Pressure." *Newsweek* 18 (October 13, 1941), 21–23.

1301.   Reynolds, Quentin. "City of Courage." *Collier's* 108 (November 8, 1941), 13.

1302.   "The Rout at Rostov." *Newsweek* 18 (December 8, 1941), 28–29.

1303.   Rowan-Robinson, Henry. "The Battle for Moscow." *Fighting Forces* 18 (December 1941), 267–270.

1304.   "Russian Courage and the Cold Rout the Nazis." *Life* 12 (January 12, 1942), 19–25.

1305.   "Russians Hurl Gigantic Tanks at the Stiffened German Lines." *Newsweek* 19 (February 16, 1942), 25.

1306.   "Russians Take Offensive." *Life* 13 (December 7, 1942), 38–39.

1307.   "Russia's Ally: Winter." *Newsweek* 18 (November 24, 1941), 26–27.

1308.   Rzheshevsky, Oleg. "Dawn of the Great Victory." *Soviet Military Review*, no. 11 (November 1976), 14–16.

1309.   Salisbury, Harrison E. "Moscow." In Noble Frankland and Christopher Dowling, eds., *Decisive Battles of the 20th Century*. New York: David McKay, 1976. pp. 127–140.

1310.   Schultz-Naumann, Joachim. "The Demyansk Pocket, March-April 1942." *Military Review* 37 (December 1957), 77–84.

1311.   "Seas of Mud on Wintry Steppes Harass Armies in the Russian War." *Newsweek* 18 (October 6, 1941), 18–23.

1312.   Simonov, Konstantin M. "History of a Film Interview." *Soviet Literature,* no. 5 (May 1979), 115–131.

1313.   Stepanov, F. "The Offensive Spirit." *Soviet Military Review,* no. 6 (June 1972), 39–41.

1314.   Stolfi, Russell. "Chance in History: The Russian Winter of 1941–1942." *Historian* 62 (June 1980), 214–228.

1315.   Vasilevskiy, Aleksandr M. "The Battle of Moscow." *Soviet Military Review,* no. 11 (November 1976), 10–13.

1316.   "Victory of the Soviet Army in the Battle of Moscow." *History Today* 9 (February 1959), 139–140.

1317.   Wagner, Friedrich. "Howitzers Against Soviet Tanks." *Field Artillery Journal* 32 (August 1942), 605–606.

1318.   Werner, Max. "Fighting for Moscow." *New Republic* 105 (October 20, 1941), 497–498.

1319.   ———. "Germany's Winter War." *New Republic* 106 (February 9, 1942), 194–195.

1320.   ———. "Moscow and Pearl Harbor." *New Republic* 105 (December 29, 1941), 883–884.

1321.   ———. "Moscow and Rostov." *New Republic* 105 (December 15, 1941), 821–822.

1322.   White, Margaret B. "A Trip to the Front." *Life* 11 (November 17, 1941), 33–39.

1323.   White, William W. "Axis Armies in Retreat." *Current History,* ns 1 (February 1942), 523–526.

1324.   "Winter and Mud Fail to Stem Battle Fury on the Russian Front." *Newsweek* 18 (November 3, 1941), 19–21.

1325.   "The Winter Battle of Rzhev." *Military Review* 24 (June 1949), 80–84.

1326.   "Winter Fighting in Russia, 1942." *Tactical and Technical Trends* 12 (1942), 20–27.

DOCUMENTS, PAPERS, AND REPORTS

1327.   DePrie, Michael C. "Moscow—The Principle and the Objective." MA thesis, U.S. Army Command and General Staff College, 1977. 145p.

1328.   Dessloch, Otto. "The Winter Battles of Rzhev, Vyazma, and Yuknov, 1941–1942." Unpublished paper, Foreign Military Studies Program, Historical Division, Headquarters, U.S. Army, Europe, 1947. 20p.

1329.   Hoehne, Gustav. "In Snow and Mud: 31 Days of Attack under Seydlitz during Early Spring of 1942." Unpublished paper, Foreign Military Studies Program, Historical Division, Headquarters, U.S. Army, Europe, 1953. 14p.

1330.   Poppe, Walter F. "Campaign of the 255th Infantry Division East and South of Temkino, December 1941–April 1942." Unpublished paper, Foreign Military Studies Program, Historical Division, Headquarters, U.S. Army, Europe, 1947. 21p.

1331.   Schellert, Otto. "Winter Fighting of the 253rd Infantry Division in the Rzhev Area, October 1941–March 1942." Unpublished paper, Foreign Military Studies Program, Historical Division, Headquarters, U.S. Army, Europe, 1947. 27p.

1332.   Turney, Alfred W. "Field Marshal Fedor von Bock and the German Campaigns in Russia, 1941–1942." PhD dissertation, University of New Mexico, 1969.

1333.   Von Greiffenberg, Hans. "The Battle of Moscow, 1941–1942." Unpublished paper, Foreign Military Studies Program, Historical Division, Headquarters, U.S. Army, Europe, 1948. 271p.
    Reprinted in part 10 of Donald S. Detwiler, ed., *World War II German Military Studies,* 24 vols. (New York: Garland, 1980).

1334.   Von Unruh, Walter. "War Experiences in Russia [December 1941]." Unpublished paper, Foreign Military Studies Program, Historical Division, Headquarters, U.S. Army, Europe, 1947. 80p.

Further References

See also the general citations in sections 2:A and 2:C:1.

c. To Stalingrad and German Disaster, 1942–1943

The second German summer offensive opened in late May 1942 and met with rapid successes similar to those of the year before. Rostov fell in July, as Wehrmacht forces swept into the Caucasus. The main point to this year's effort was, however, to capture Stalingrad on the Volga River.

The taking of this city, named for the Russian dictator then but now called Volgograd, was important to German war aims for three basic reasons. First, its capture would open the door to occupation of the southern terminus of river and rail traffic in Astrakhan, cutting the flow of oil and other supplies northward. Second, the city was an important industrial center, control of which would deny the Russians much needed equipment. Finally, its taking would lead to control of the entire Caucasus and take from the Russians the most likely staging area for a 1942–1943 winter offensive. This would be the Gettysburg-type high-water mark of the German invasion; for Hitler's legions to be successful, the city had to fall. The front was, by now, 2,100 miles long.

A German pincers move was made on Stalingrad in August, but determined Russian resistance held those prongs apart. Repeated German efforts were made to no avail, and the invaders failed to reach the city's outskirts until September. Throughout this time, the Volga River town was constantly bombarded by air and artillery and reduced almost entirely to rubble.

Recognizing the vital importance of the city as well as the propaganda value of the loss of a place bearing his name, Stalin ordered the city to hold out at all costs. Under the able leadership of General Vasiliy Chuikov, with Nikita Khrushchev in the background offering advice, the Russian garrison battled the Germans for every square foot. Losses were enormous on both sides, and contemporary reporters compared the fighting with the 1916 Battle of Verdun. Despite the horror, the Russian defenders held and prepared for the planned counterattack.

The hammer fell on the Germans on November 19, when, again in snow, Russian forces began a counterstroke north and south of the Wehrmacht 6th Army salient, closing the pincers on General Friedrich von Paulus's weary men. A determined German effort to break through to the encircled defenders came close, but determined Red Army fighters checked it just 30 miles short. By mid-December, no real relief hope existed for thousands of men.

Von Paulus appealed to Hitler for permission to surrender, but was denied. Soon the Soviets began to attack the defenders again in a final and successful effort to destroy the 6th Army. By the end of January 1943, von Paulus's command was finished.

Hitler's bloody effort to hold on to the last man was a reality, but a costly failure. Almost one quarter million German soldiers were lost in the Stalingrad campaign and morale on both sides reflected the feat of arms. The Russians obtained a dramatic and decisive victory, often referred to as the turning point in the Eastern theater.

BOOKS

1335.   Agapov, Boris N. *After the Battle: Stalingrad Sketches and Notes of a Guerrilla Fighter.* Translated from the Russian. London: Hutchinson, 1943. 78p.

1336.   Chuikov, Vasiliy I. *The Battle for Stalingrad.* Translated from the Russian. New York: Holt, Rinehart & Winston, 1964. 364p.

1337.   Craig, William. *Enemy at the Gates: The Battle for Stalingrad.* New York: Reader's Digest Press, 1973. 462p.

1338.   Dibold, Hans. *Doctor at Stalingrad.* Translated from the German. London: Hutchinson, 1958. 190p.

1339.   Goerlitz, Walter. *Paulus and Stalingrad.* Translated from the German. Westport, Conn.: Greenwood Press, 1974. 301p.

1340.   Jukes, Geoffrey. *Stalingrad: The Turning Point.* Ballantine's Illustrated History of World War II. New York: Ballantine Books, 1968. 160p.

1341.   Kerr, Walter B. *The Secret of Stalingrad.* Garden City, N.Y.: Doubleday, 1978. 274p.

1342.   Kluge, Alexander. *The Battle.* Translated from the German. New York: William Morrow, 1962. 127p.

1343.   *Last Letters from Stalingrad.* Translated from the German. Washington, D.C.: Ryerson Press, 1955. 60p.

1344.   Malaparte, Curzio, pseud. *The Volga Rises in Europe.* Translated from the Italian. London: Redman, 1957. 281p.

1345.   Sammis, Edward K. *Last Stand at Stalingrad: The Battle That Saved the World.* New York: Macmillan, 1966. 96p.

1346.   Schroeter, Heinz. *Stalingrad.* Translated from the German. New York: E. P. Dutton, 1958. 263p.

1347.   Seth, Ronald S. *Stalingrad—Point of Return: The Story of the Battle, August 1942–February 1943.* New York: Coward-McCann, 1959. 254p.

1348.   *Stalingrad: An Eye-Witness Account by Soviet Correspondents and Red Army Commanders.* London: Hutchinson, 1943. 118p.

1349.   Weinert, Erich. *Stalingrad Diary.* Translated from the German. London: I.N.G. Publications, 1944. 48p.

1350.   Werth, Alexander. *The Year of Stalingrad.* New York: Alfred A. Knopf, 1947. 480p.

1351.   Zhilin, P. A. *They Sealed Their Own Doom.* Translated from the Russian. Moscow: Progress Publishers, 1970.

1352.   Zieser, Benno. *The Road to Stalingrad.* Translated from the German. New York: Ballantine Books, 1956. 152p.

ARTICLES

1353.   "Artillery Support of Cavalry and Motorized Infantry at Stalingrad." *Cavalry Journal* 52 (November 1943), 33.

1354.   Balashov, P. "Colonel Gorokhov's Bridgehead." *Soviet Military Review,* no. 10 (October 1972), 52-53.

1355.   Baldwin, Hanson W. "The Battle That Turned the Nazi Tide." *New York Times Magazine* (April 14, 1963), 23-24.

1356.   _____ . "Stalingrad." *Battles Lost and Won: The Great Campaigns of World War II.* New York: Harper & Row, 1966. Chpt. 5.

1357.   Batov, Pavel. "Counteroffensive." *Soviet Military Review,* no. 11 (November 1972), 45-48.

1358.   Bell, J. Bowyer. "Stalingrad." *Besieged: Seven Cities under Siege.* Philadelphia, Pa.: Chilton Books, 1966. Chpt. 4.

1359.   Brown, Ronald J. "Manstein's Winter Miracle, January–April 1943." *Armor* 85 (November-December 1976), 18-21.

1360.   Chuikov, Vasiliy I. "Stalingrad: Front-Line City." *Soviet Military Review,* no. 10 (October 1972), 48-51.

1361.   "City of Steel." *Newsweek* 20 (September 21, 1942), 25-26.

1362.   Corotneff, Nicholas. "Encirclement at Stalingrad." *Cavalry Journal* 52 (July 1943), 36-39.

1363.   "Essen," pseud. "Artillery in the Defense of Stalingrad." *Journal of the Royal Artillery* 70 (October 1943), 297-302.

1364.   _____ . "Artillery in Defense of Stalingrad." *Field Artillery Journal* 34 (June 1944), 343-345.

1365.   Fenyo, Mario. "The Allied Axis Armies and Stalingrad." *Military Affairs* 29 (Summer 1965), 56-72.

1366.   "Flaming Stalingrad." *Newsweek* 20 (September 28, 1942), 22.

1367.   "For Stalin's City." *Time* 40 (September 21, 1942), 23.

1368.   Fuqua, Stephen O. "The Pattern of the Russian Withdrawal." *Newsweek* 20 (August 3, 1942), 18.

1369.   _____ . "Stalingrad, a Lesson in Fighting." *Newsweek* 20 (September 21, 1942), 20.

1370.   "The German Tide Laps at the Caucasus Wall." *Life* 13 (September 7, 1942), 34–36.

1371.   Goerlitz, Walter. "The Battle for Stalingrad, 1942." In Hans A. Jacobsen and Juergen Rohwer, eds., *Decisive Battles of World War II: The German View.* New York: G. P. Putnam, 1965. pp. 219–253.

1372.   Hale, O. J. "The Fuehrer and the Field Marshal." *Virginia Quarterly Review* 26 (Autumn 1950), 492–511.   Hitler's refusal to allow Paulus to break out of Stalingrad.

1373.   "Hell at Stalingrad." *Newsweek* 20 (September 7, 1942), 23.

1374.   Henzel, H. W. "The Stalingrad Offensive." *Marine Corps Gazette* 35 (August 1951), 46–53; (September 1951), 46–57.

1375.   "Impregnable City." *Infantry Journal* 52 (June 1943), 42–47.

1376.   Kane, Steve. "Velikiye Luki: A Miniature Stalingrad." *World War II Journal* 2 (July-August 1975), 4–6.

1377.   Kerr, Walter B. "Battles for Stalingrad." *The Russian Army: Its Men, Its Leaders, Its Battles.* New York: Alfred A. Knopf, 1944. pp. 182–226.

1378.   Lanza, Conrad H. "The Autumn 1942 Campaign in Russia." *Field Artillery Journal* 33 (March 1943), 186–194.

1379.   Mackintosh, Malcolm. "Stalingrad." In Noble Frankland and Christopher Dowling, eds., *Decisive Battles of the 20th Century.* New York: David McKay, 1976. pp. 208–221.

1380.   "The Mighty German Army Wallows in Defeat." *Life* 14 (February 22, 1943), 26–27.

1381.   Mitchell, Donald W. "After Stalingrad." *Nation* 155 (October 10, 1942), 339–340.

1382.   _____ . "The Russian Miracle." *Nation* 156 (March 6, 1943), 335–336.

1383.   "More Than Oil at Stake on the Don." *Business Week* (August 1, 1942), 32.

1384.   Oechsner, F. C. "The Bloodiest Front in History." *Saturday Evening Post* 215 (September 19, 1942), 22.

1385.   Parkam, Dave. "Battle for Stalingrad: The Struggle for the City, September–November 1942." *Strategy and Tactics*, no. 79 (March-April 1980), 25–34.

1386.   Parry, Albert. "Stalingrad: Triumph of Infantry." *Russian Cavalcade: A Military Record*. New York: Washburn, 1944. pp. 299–319.

1387.   Pickert, Wolfgang. "The Stalingrad Airlift: An Eyewitness Commentary." *Aerospace Historian* 17 (December 1971), 183–185.

1388.   Plotnikov, Yu. V. "The Exploit at Stalingrad." *International Review of Military History*, no. 44 (1979), 109–118.

1389.   "The Push to the Volga." *Newsweek* 20 (July 27, 1942), 20–23.

1390.   Rakovsky, L. "Volgograd—A Hero City." *Soviet Military Review*, no. 2 (February 1976), 8–10.

1391.   "The Red Army Fights for Mother Russia." *Life* 13 (October 5, 1942), 29–34.

1392.   "The Red Army Strikes Back." *Life* 14 (January 4, 1943), 11–15.

1393.   Roluti, Francesco. "The Italian Army and the War in Russia." *Military Review* 28 (September 1948), 82–88.

1394.   "Russians Make It a Second Verdun." *Life* 13 (October 5, 1942), 36–37.

1395.   "Russia's Dark Hour." *Newsweek* 20 (August 10, 1942), 23–25.

1396.   "Russia's Miracle of the War Enters Third Month of Unconquerable Siege." *Life* 13 (November 2, 1942), 32–33.

1397.   Schuman, Frederick L. "Russia Revisited." *Nation* 183 (July 28, 1956), 80–81.

1398.   Selle, Herbert. "The German Debacle at Stalingrad." *Military Review* 37 (September-October 1957), 3–13, 37–47.

1399.   Smith, Truman. "Stalingrad or Bust." *Infantry Journal* 59 (August 1946), 14–19.

1400.   Snow, Edgar. "Unyielding Shoulder on the Volga." *Survey Graphic* 33 (February 1944), 67–69.

1401.   _____ . "Victory on the Steppe." *Saturday Evening Post* 215 (March 6, 1943), 16–17.

1402.   "Stalin Strikes." *Newsweek* 20 (December 7, 1942), 23–26.

1403.   "Stalingrad Halt: Nazis' Frontal Assault Ceases in Siege Comparable to Verdun." *Newsweek* 20 (November 19, 1942), 25–27.

1404.   "The Stalingrad Story." *Time* 42 (December 27, 1943), 32.

1405.   "Stalingrad's Story." *Newsweek* 21 (February 22, 1943), 22–23.

1406.   "Stand in Stalingrad." *Newsweek* 20 (October 12, 1942), 24–25.

1407.   "Stubborn Defense." *Soviet Military Review*, no. 1 (January 1968), 41–43.

1408.   Sulzberger, Cyrus L. "The Russian Battlefront." *Life* 13 (July 29, 1942), 78–80.

1409.   "Turnabout in Russia." *Fortune* 26 (December 1942), 102–105.

1410.   United States. War Department. General Staff. G-2. "A Visit to the Don-Stalingrad Front." *Military Reports on the United Nations* 4 (March 1943), 47–60.

1411.   Vagts, Alfred. "Stalingrad: City into Fortress." *Infantry Journal* 52 (January 1943), 44–45.

1412.   "The Valiant Red Stand." *Newsweek* 20 (October 5, 1942), 17–18.

1413.   Vasilevskiy, Aleksandr M. "Counteroffensive Against Manstein." *Soviet Military Review*, no. 1 (January 1968), 44–48. Kotelnikovskiy, December 12–29, 1942.

1414.   Vasilyev, N. "Tanks Destroy [Luftwaffe] Airfields [December 24, 1942.]." *Soviet Military Review*, no. 3 (March 1969), 43–44.

1415.   Voronov, Nikolai N. "'Operation Koltso' [January 10–February 2, 1943]." *Soviet Military Review*, no. 2 (February 1968), 52–56.

1416.   "War on the Volga: The Heroic Stalingrad Defense." *Newsweek* 20 (September 14, 1942), 22–24.

1417.   Weinert, Erich. "Russian Against German." *Atlantic* 173 (March 1944), 51–56.

1418.   Werner, Max. "Russian Offensive, German Crisis." *New Republic* 108 (January 25, 1943), 105–107.

1419.   Werth, Alexander. "Red Run the Tide of the Volga." *Saturday Review of Literature* 47 (March 14, 1964), 29.

1420.   "Where Hitler Was Halted." *Time* 91 (February 2, 1968), 27.

1421.   White, William W. "Russia Foils the Nazi Offensive." *Current History,* ns 2 (May 1942), 186–187.

1422.   _____ . "Russia Loses Ground." *Current History,* ns 3 (September 1942), 16–19.

1423.   _____ . "The Russian Bulwark." *Current History,* ns 2 (June 1942), 247–249.

1424.   _____ . "Russian Successes." *Current History,* ns 2 (March 1942), 23–25.

1425.   _____ . "Russia's Fight for Time." *Current History,* ns 3 (October 1942), 94–96.

1426.   _____ . "The Stalingrad Epic." *Current History,* ns 3 (November 1942), 183–187.

1427.   Woods, Thomas G. "A True Mobile Defense: The 11th Panzer Division at Chir River, 7–20 December 1942." *Armor* 77 (September-October 1968), 15–17.

1428.   "The Word is Stalingrad." *Time* 40 (October 19, 1942), 24.

1429.   "Wounded Hedgehogs." *Newsweek* 21 (January 25, 1943), 19–20.

1430.   Zeitzler, Kurt. "Stalingrad." In Seymour Freidin and William Richardson, eds., *The Fatal Decisions.* New York: William Sloane, 1956. pp. 125–189.

1431.   Zhukov, Georgiy K. "Stalingrad on the Defensive." *Soviet Military Review,* no. 9 (September 1972), 38–41.

1432.   Zvenzlovsky, A. "Victory on the Upper Don." *Soviet Military Review,* no. 3 (March 1973), 57–59.

DOCUMENTS, PAPERS, AND REPORTS

1433.   Dupuy, Trevor N. "Breakthrough Operation of the Soviet 2d Assault Army, Volkhov Army Group, 12–18 January 1943." In Trevor N. Dupuy et al., *A Study of Breakthrough Operations.* DNA-4124F. Dun Loring, Va.: Historical Evaluation and Research Organization, 1976. Chpt. 5.

Further References

See also the general citations in sections 2:A and 2:C:1.

d. LENINGRAD AND THE NORTHERN WAR (FINLAND, NORWAY, DENMARK), 1941–1945

The war in the north can be categorized into two major campaigns: the defensive, from 1941 to 1944, and the offensive, from 1944 to 1945.

By September 1, 1941, German forces were close enough to begin an artillery bombardment of Leningrad. Two weeks later, the city was completely surrounded and forced to undergo a siege which lasted nine hundred days. Civilians and army personnel alike moved, despite widespread suffering and starvation, to keep the Germans out of the city. On Christmas Day, as a part of the Moscow counteroffensive, Red Army soldiers were able to open a limited supply line to the city.

Leningraders had little hope until January 1944, when Soviet fronts opened an offensive against the Germans in the area and by the end of the month had forced them to retreat. Railroads and other supply routes into the city were reopened and citizens, who had been dying of cold, hunger, and disease at the rate of 20,000 per day, rejoiced in their deliverance.

Finland, which had joined the war on the side of the Germans in June 1941, was attacked along the Mannerheim line in late June 1944. By the end of August, Finland was out of the war.

German troops which escaped capture in Finland and Byelorussia retreated into other Baltic states and eastern Norway. In the months that followed, these were either defeated or bottled up to await surrender at war's end. Soviet airborne troops participated in the liberation of Denmark in 1945.

BOOKS

1434.　　Fadeev, Aleksandr A. *Leningrad in the Days of the Blockade.* Translated from the Russian. London: Hutchinson, 1946. 104p.
　　Reprinted by Greenwood Press (Westport, Conn.) in 1971.

1435.　　Gouré, Leon. *The Siege of Leningrad.* Stanford, Calif.: Stanford University Press, 1962. 363p.

1436.　　*Heroic Leningrad.* Moscow: Foreign Language Publishing House, 1945. 152p.

1437.　　*The Last Finnish War, 1941–1944.* Washington, D.C.: University Press of America, 1978. 240p.

1438.　　Lundin, Charles L. *Finland in the Second World War.* Bloomington: Indiana University Press, 1957. 303p.

1439.   Pavlov, Dmitri. *Leningrad, 1941: The Blockade.* Translated from the Russian. Chicago, Ill.: University of Chicago Press, 1965. 186p.

1440.   Salisbury, Harrison E. *The 900 Days: The Siege of Leningrad.* New York: Harper & Row, 1969. 635p.

1441.   Skomorovsky, Boris A. *The Siege of Leningrad: The Saga of the Greatest Siege of All Time.* New York: E. P. Dutton, 1944. 196p.

1442.   Tikhonov, Nikolai S., et al. *The Defence of Leningrad: Eye-Witness Accounts of the Siege.* London: Hutchinson, 1943. 136p.

1443.   Vardys, V. Stanley, and Romuald J. Misiunas, eds. *The Baltic States in Peace and War, 1917–1945.* University Park: Pennsylvania State University Press, 1978. 240p.

1444.   Werth, Alexander. *Leningrad.* London: Harnish Hamilton, 1944. 189p.

1445.   Wykes, Alan. *The Siege of Leningrad: Epic of Survival.* Ballantine's Illustrated History of World War II. New York: Ballantine Books, 1970. 160p.

ARTICLES

1446.   Alferov, S., ed. "Text of the Documents for the 1944 Leningrad-Novgorod Operations: Translated from *Voyenno Istoricheskiy Zhurnal,* January 1979." *Translations on USSR Military Affairs,* no. 1414 (March 1, 1979), 119–124.

1447.   Asprey, Robert B. "The Fight in the North." *Marine Corps Gazette* 39 (April 1955), 38–45.

1448.   Bergolts, Olga. "A Walk along the Neva: The Siege of Leningrad." *Atlantic* 205 (June 1960), 50–56.

1449.   Buckner, Alex. "Attack in the Tundra." *Military Review* 36 (April 1956), 98–109.   The fighting around Murmansk.

1450.   "The Conditions of Fighting in the Leningrad Sector." *Command and General Staff School Quarterly* 21 (January 1942), 69–70.

1451.   Dau, Mary. "The Soviet Union and the Liberation of Denmark." *Survey,* no. 76 (1970), 64–81.

1452.   Dittmar, Kurt. "'Motti': War in the Far North." *Marine Corps Gazette* 41 (February 1957), 34–52.

1453.   Dobrovol'skiy, Pavel. "Directives for World War II Operations at Leningrad: Translated from *Voyenno Istoricheskiy Zhurnal*, January 1978." *Translations on USSR Military Affairs*, no. 1344 (April 7, 1978), 32–38.

1454.   Fay, Sydney B. "Russo-Finnish Relations: No Satisfactory Armistice Terms Have Yet Been Reached." *Current History*, ns 6 (May 1944), 385–390.

1455.   "Finland-Soviet Union: Armistice Text." *American Journal of International Law* 39 (April 1945), 85–88.

1456.   Grushevoy, K. "The Liberation of Northern Norway." *Soviet Military Review*, no. 10 (October 1969), 47–49.

1457.   Korbrin, Nikolai. "'Operation Iskra.'" *Soviet Military Review*, no. 2 (February 1978), 9–11.   Raising the Leningrad siege in 1944.

1458.   Korenevskiy, M. "Operational Camouflage in Leningrad Battle Described: Translated from *Krasnaya Zvezda*, August 28, 1979." *Translations on USSR Military Affairs*, no. 1491 (January 23, 1980), 62–68.

1459.   Kozlov, L. "Liberation of the Baltic Region." *Soviet Military Review*, no. 11 (November 1974), 49–51.

1460.   Krypton, Constantine. "The Siege of Leningrad." *Russian Review* 13 (October 1954), 255–265.

1461.   Kurov, N. "Victory beyond the Polar Circle." *Soviet Military Review*, no. 11 (November 1974), 52–54.

1462.   "Lettish Rifles." *Soviet Military Review*, no. 7 (July 1970), 42–43.   Latvia.

1463.   Matsulenko, V. "Breakthrough of Enemy Defenses." *Soviet Military Review*, no. 1 (January 1974), 54–56.

1464.   "Nazis Striking at Leningrad to Cut Off Main Red Supplies and the Red Air Might." *Newsweek* 18 (September 15, 1941), 20–23.

1465.   Orlov, A. "Blow in the North." *Soviet Military Review*, no. 10 (October 1974), 43–45.

1466.   Petukhov, D. "Two Blows." *Soviet Military Review*, no. 5 (May 1974), 48–50.   To relieve Leningrad and attack Finland, 1944.

1467.   Quarrie, Bruce. "Soviet Heavy Tanks at Leningrad." *Airfix Magazine Annual for Military Modellers*. New York: Arbor House, 1978. Chpt. 4.

1468.   Raus, E. "The Gateway to Leningrad." *Military Review* 34 (September 1954), 99–109.

1469.   "Reds Dig in at Leningrad and Hit Back Swiftly at Gomel." *Newsweek* 18 (September 1, 1941), 15–18.

1470.   "The Release of Leningrad." *Newsweek* 23 (January 31, 1944), 22–23.

1471.   "The Relief of Leningrad." *Illustrated London News* 204 (January 29, 1944), 122–123.

1472.   Riste, Olav. "The Great Powers and the Northern Cap, 1940–1945." *Cooperation and Conflict* 7 (Spring 1972), 1–12.

1473.   Salisbury, Harrison E. "The 900 Days." *Reader's Digest* 94 (March 1969), 201–207; (April 1969), 243–256.

1474.   "Ski Patrols of the Soviet Army." *Tactical and Technical Trends* 16 (1943), 17–22.

1475.   Sorokin, Mikhail I. "Leningrad Military District Commander on Combat Traditions: Translated from *Krasnaya Zvezda*, March 19, 1978." *Translations on USSR Military Affairs*, no. 1365 (July 19, 1978), 18–22.

1476.   _____. "Leningrad Military District Commander on Combat Traditions and Training: Translated from *Kommunist Vooruzhennykh Sil*, October 1977." *Translations on USSR Military Affairs*, no. 1321 (January 9, 1978), 1–11.

1477.   "Soviet Efforts in the Liberation of Norway in World War II Recalled: Translated from *Voyenno Istoricheskiy Zhurnal*, October 1979." *Translations on USSR Military Affairs*, no. 1487 (January 7, 1980), 34–50.

1478.   Stesarev, Pavel. "The Struggle for Lines of Communication in Winter." *Military Review* 23 (July 1943), 83–85.

1479.   Varstavski, T. "Soviet Motor Maintenance on Winter Marches." *Field Artillery Journal* 33 (March 1943), 183.

1480.   Werth, Alexander. "The Spirit That Spurs Russia On." *New York Times Magazine* (October 17, 1943), 5–7.

1481.   Zheltov, A. "Wartime Operations—Karelain Front Activities, 1941–1942: Translated from *Voyenno Istoricheskiy Zhurnal*, January 1980." *Translations on USSR Military Affairs*, no. 1511 (April 21, 1980), 58–68.

1482. _____ . "Wartime Operations—Soviet Arctic Karelia: Translated from *Voyenno Istoricheskiy Zhurnal*, December 1979." *Translations on USSR Military Affairs*, no. 1508 (March 28, 1980), 37–49.

1483.   Zvenzlovsky, A. "The Liquidation of the 'Northern Wall.'" *Soviet Military Review*, no. 1 (January 1969), 42–46.

DOCUMENTS, PAPERS, AND REPORTS

1484.   Brennecke, Kurt, et al. "Army Group North, Advance to Leningrad, 1941." Unpublished paper, Foreign Military Studies Program, Historical Division, Headquarters, U.S. Army, Europe, 1948. 607p.

1485.   Erfurth, Waldemar. "The Last Finnish War, 1941–1944." Unpublished paper, Foreign Military Studies Program, Historical Division, Headquarters, U.S. Army, Europe, 1949. 370p.

1486.   Grasser, Alfred. "Fighting during the Retreat of XXVI Corps to Pskov, February 1944." Unpublished paper, Foreign Military Studies Program, Historical Division, Headquarters, U.S. Army, Europe, 1947. 7p.

1487.   Gundelach, Herbert. "21st Infantry Division, Defensive Combat, Disengagement, and Withdrawal from Volkhov to Pskov, January–February 1944." Unpublished paper, Foreign Military Studies Program, Historical Division, Headquarters, U.S. Army, Europe, 1947. 14p.

1488.   Mueller-Hillebrand, Burkhart, et al. "The Retrograde Defense of Army Group North in 1944." Unpublished paper, Foreign Military Studies Program, Historical Division, Headquarters, U.S. Army, Europe, 1950. 432p.

1489.   United States. Department of the Army. Historical Division. *Warfare in the Far North: Historical Study*. DA Pam 20-292. Washington, D.C., 1951. 24p.

1490.   Ziemke, Earl F. *The German Northern Theater of Operations, 1940–1945*. DA Pam 20–271. Washington, D.C.: Department of the Army. 1959. 342p.

Further References

See also the general citations in sections 2:A and 2:C:1.

e. The Southern Region, 1941–1944

The initial phase of Operation Barbarossa in 1941 featured a move on Kiev in the southern sector of the U.S.S.R. Soviet resistance slowed the Wehrmacht advance, but Von Rundstedt's victories in the battles at Uman and Gomel opened the way for the capture of Kiev by the close of September. That month the Germans attacked the Crimea, but again Russian defenses held for awhile. Kerch and Sevastopol were saved, but by the end of the 1941 campaign, both Odessa and Rostov were in the possession of the invader. Rostov was recaptured by the Red Army during the Soviet winter counteroffensive of early 1942.

The second German summer offensive opened in late May 1942, when Wehrmacht forces captured the important Ukrainian city of Kharkov and again took possession of Rostov. At this point, some Axis troops swept into the Caucasus, while others paused to polish off Sevastopol, which finally fell on July 2 after a ten-month siege. All organized resistance ceased in the Crimea a few days later. The most important objective of the summer campaign was, however, the city of Stalingrad (see section 2:C:3:d).

The Soviet counteroffensive which began at Stalingrad on November 19 was also aimed all along the eastern front. Once again Rostov came to the Russians. Wehrmacht troops were forced to evacuate the Stalingrad, Grozny, and Vyaxma-Rzhev salients. By July 1943, Red soldiers could be proud of gains made all along the line.

The main German objective in the summer campaign of 1943 was the reduction of the Kursk salient, near Orel. The battle, often considered more important than Stalingrad, is covered in section 2:C:3:f. It is sufficient to say here that the Germans suffered a disaster at Kursk.

Following the Wehrmacht debacle, the Red Army undertook its first successful summer offensive—conducted brilliantly—and Soviet troops soon recaptured Taganrob, Smolensk, Kharkov, and Orel and dashed any German hopes of mounting further offensive action.

Following the liberation of Gomel in late November, the Soviets prepared to assault Kiev, hoping to take large numbers of German troops. Alerted, the Wehrmacht was withdrawn to stronger positions along the Dneiper and the city fell in a single day. Once again the Russians moved to trap Hitler's men, this time on the Dneiper bend, and this time with more success.

Meanwhile, farther south, the German bridgehead on the Kuban was eliminated in October 1943, ending any threat to the Caucasus.

Soviet forces went on the offensive in the Crimea in April 1944 and, in a tornado of action, cleared the Wehrmacht from the peninsula within a month. Sevastopol, assaulted on May 7, fell two days later with a dozen German and Rumanian divisions annihilated.

On June 23, four Soviet army groups, or fronts, opened a major offensive along a 300-mile sector, and a month and a half later in the south a large assault began, on July 14. Within two weeks, Red Army soldiers were in Lvov, preparing to sweep into the Balkans.

Books

1491.   Brezhnev, Leonid I. *How It Was: The War and Post-War Reconstruction in the Soviet Union.* Translated from the Russian. London and New York: Pergamon Press, 1979. 115p.   The current Soviet president participated in the 1943 Battle of Novorossiisk.

1492.   Grechko, Andrei A. *The Battle for the Caucasus.* Translated from the Russian. Moscow: Progress Publishers, 1971. 366p.

1493.   Kamenetsky, Igor. *Hitler's Occupation of the Ukraine, 1941–1944: A Study of Totalitarian Imperialism.* Milwaukee, Wis.: Marquette University Press, 1956. 101p.

1494.   *Kharkov.* Translated from the Russian. Moscow: Foreign Language Publishing House, 1943. 27p.

1495.   Krylov, Nikolai I. *Glory Eternal: The Defense of Odessa, 1941.* Translated from the Russian. Moscow: Progress Publishers, 1972. 293p.

1496.   *Sevastopol, November 1941–July 1942: A Collection of Articles.* London: Hutchinson, 1943. 76p.

1497.   Voitekhov, Boris I. *The Last Days of Sevastopol.* Translated from the Russian. London: Cassell, 1943. 150p.

Articles

1498.   Balev, B. "Seaborne Landing at Novorossiisk." *Soviet Military Review,* no. 7 (July 1972), 40–42.

1499.   "Battles along the Dneiper." *Cavalry Journal* 53 (March 1944), 54–59.

1500.   Besschyotov, Ye. "Beachhead." *Soviet Military Review,* no. 9 (September 1978), 36–37.   Novorossiisk.

1501.   Brezhnev, Leonid I. "Little Land." *Soviet Literature,* no. 6 (June 1968), 3–44.   Novorossiisk.

1502.   Brown, Ronald J. "Assault on the Crimea." *Marine Corps Gazette* 62 (February 1978), 43–47.

1503.   Budrin, K. "Night Battle for a Populated Point." *Military Review* 22 (October 1942), 89–90.

1504.   Cassidy, Henry C. "Artillery at Orel." *Field Artillery Journal* 33 (November 1943), 813.

1505.   "The Caucasian Wall." *Newsweek* 20 (August 24, 1942), 25–27.

1506.   Chedleyev, N. "Defending Communications." *Soviet Military Review,* no. 1 (January 1977), 55–57.

1507.   "Combat at Kharkov." *Newsweek* 19 (June 1, 1942), 24–26.

1508.   "The Crucial Ukraine." *Newsweek* 23 (January 17, 1944), 21–23.

1509.   Decker, Edward T. "Retreat and Counterstroke." *Armor* 72 (January-February 1963), 8–12.   German Army Group Don's 1943 activities.

1510.   "Duel on the Donets." *Newsweek* 21 (March 29, 1943), 22–23.

1511.   "Fall of a City." *Time* 40 (July 13, 1942), 21.   Sevastopol.

1512.   "The Fall of Kiev: Nazis Take Ukraine Capital." *Life* 11 (November 3, 1941), 36–37.

1513.   "The Feats of Fathers Are the Legacy of Their Sons: Translated from *Krasnaya Zvezda,* April 17, 1977." *Review of the Soviet Ground Forces* 1 (August 1977), 47–48.   The Soviet marine landing at Nikolayev on the Black Sea coast, March 26, 1944.

1514.   Frolov, B. "Battle for the Dneiper." *Soviet Military Review,* no. 10 (October 1978), 46–49.

1515.   Fuqua, Stephen O. "The Central Front after Rzhev." *Newsweek* 21 (March 15, 1943), 24.

1516.   ———. "Hitler's Headache in the Caucasus." *Newsweek* 21 (January 18, 1943), 22.

1517.   ———. "Kharkov and the Second Front." *Newsweek* 19 (June 8, 1942), 26.

1518.   Galitsan, A. "A Cutting Blow." *Soviet Military Review,* no. 3 (March 1974), 51–53.   March–April 1944 exploits of the 2d Ukrainian Front.

1519.   Garthoff, Raymond L. "Soviet Employment of Seapower and Amphibious Operations." *Soviet Military Doctrine*. Glencoe, Ill.: Free Press, 1953. pp. 361–374.

1520.   "The Great Retreat." *Newsweek* 22 (October 4, 1943), 23–25.

1521.   "The Greatest Gun." *Field Artillery Journal* 42 (May–June 1974), 30–38; (July–August 1974), 46–48; (September–October 1974), 4; (November–December 1974), 63; 43 (March–April 1975), 5; (September–October 1975), 3–4.   The German 800mm "Gustav" employed against the defenders of Sevastopol.

1522.   Gusev, Vladimir. "Kiev: A Hero-City." *Soviet Military Review*, no. 11 (November 1975), 9–11.

1523.   "Gustav." In Bernard Fitzsimons, ed., *Illustrated Encyclopedia of 20th Century Weapons and Warfare*. 24 vols. New York: Columbia House, 1978. XI: 1178–1179.

1524.   Gwynn, Charles. "The Dneiper Battles." *Fortnightly* 160 (December 1943), 397–400.

1525.   _____ . "The Russian Outlook." *Fortnightly* 157 (April 1942), 319–322.

1526.   _____ . "Sevastopol and After." *Fortnightly* 161 (June 1944), 371–377.

1527.   Ivanov, S. "The Crimean Landing." *Soviet Military Review*, no. 11 (November 1973), 57–59.

1528.   Jentz, Thomas. "Tigers at the Front." *World War II Journal* 2 (September–October 1975), 20–21.   Rostov, 1943.

1529.   Khamadan, Alexander. "Inside Besieged Odessa." *Life* 11 (October 20, 1941), 14.

1530.   "Kharkov Tally." *Newsweek* 19 (June 8, 1942), 22–25.

1531.   "Kharkov's Story." *Newsweek* 21 (March 8, 1943), 22–23.

1532.   Kirsanov, V. "On the Road to Odessa." *Cavalry Journal* 53 (July 1944), 48–52.

1533.   Konev, Ivan. "The Korsun-Shevchenkousky Pocket." *Soviet Military Review*, no. 2 (February 1974), 46–49.   Following the encirclement of six German divisions in January 1944, the Soviets were able to contain only 30,000 in the Ukrainian city due to a daring and costly breakout.

1534. _____ . "The Rush to the Dneiper." *Soviet Military Review,* no. 8 (August 1973), 50–52.

1535. Kotov, Mikhail. "Immortal Exploit." *Soviet Literature,* no. 7 (July 1978), 136–143.   The 1943 battle of Novorossiisk.

1536. Kozlov, L. "Repulsing a Counterstroke." *Soviet Military Review,* no. 12 (December 1973), 42–44.   The November–December 1943 German attack on Kiev.

1537. Kurov, N. "Liberation of the Crimea [April–May 1944]." *Soviet Military Review,* no. 4 (April 1974), 47–49.

1538. Lanza, Conrad H. "Kharkov." *Field Artillery Journal* 32 (August 1942), 602–603.   This large eastern Ukraine city was captured by the Germans in May 1942 and liberated by the Soviets in early 1943.

1539. _____ . "Recent Events in Russia: Kerch." *Field Artillery Journal* 32 (August 1942), 601–602.   The Germans captured this area of the Crimea in May 1942.

1540. Larichev, N. "Liberation of the Crimea." *Soviet Military Review,* no. 4 (April 1979), 40–41.

1541. Lashchenko, P. "Battle by Battle." *Soviet Military Review,* no. 9 (September 1973), 53–55; no. 10 (October 1973), 56–59; no. 11 (November 1973), 60–62, no. 12 (December 1973), 56–58.   How the Soviets forced the Dneiper in 1943.

1542. Lederry, E. "Operations of Marshal von Manstein in Southern Russia, December 1942–March 1943." *Military Review* 37 (January 1958), 98–101.

1543. Marolda, Edward J. "The Failure of the German World War II Strategy in the Black Sea." *Naval War College Review* 28 (Summer 1975), 39–54.

1544. Mazunin, N. "The Defense of Naval Bases." *Soviet Military Review,* no. 5 (May 1974), 51–53.

1545. Mitchell, Donald W. "The Red Army's Offensive." *Nation* 157 (September 4, 1943), 265–266.

1546. Moskalenko, Kirill S. "The Battle for the Dneiper (September 1943)." *Soviet Military Review,* no. 9 (September 1968), 34–40.

1547. "Nazi Rollback: Red Blitz on in the Ukraine." *Newsweek* 22 (August 23, 1943), 27–28.

1548.   Nikolayev, G. "City of Courage and Glory." *Soviet Military Review,* no. 12 (December 1976), 9–11.   Novorossiisk.

1549.   "Onslaught on the Crimea." *Newsweek* 19 (June 15, 1942), 20–21.

1550.   Panin, M. "The Korsun-Shevchenko Operation Discussed: Translated from *Voyenno Istoricheskiy Zhurnal,* February 1979." *Translations on USSR Military Affairs,* no. 1434 (May 9, 1979), 36–41.

1551.   Patrick, Stephen B. "Kharkov: The Soviet Spring Offensive." *Strategy and Tactics,* no. 68 (May-June 1978), 4–13.

1552.   Pechenenko, S. "Dneiper Assault Crossing in World War II Discussed: Translated from *Voyenno Istoricheskiy Zhurnal,* November 1979." *Translations on USSR Military Affairs,* no. 1500 (February 28, 1980), 42–50.

1553.   Pirich, Hermann. "The Struggle for Kharkov and the Dneiper, February–March 1943." *Military Review* 23 (December 1943), 86–89.

1554.   "The Push in the Ukraine." *Newsweek* 21 (January 4, 1943), 24.

1555.   "The Red Gamble." *Newsweek* 21 (March 22, 1943), 18–19.

1556.   "The Red Stalemate." *Newsweek* 21 (April 12, 1943), 22–23.

1557.   "Red's Second Try." *Newsweek* 21 (February 1, 1943), 19–20.

1558.   "The Relief of Sevastopol." *Newsweek* 23 (April 24, 1944), 22–24.

1559.   "The Russian Rat Trap: Encircled Germans at the Dneiper." *Newsweek* 23 (February 28, 1944), 24–25.

1560.   "The Russian Summer Offensive." *Cavalry Journal* 52 (November 1943), 22–23.

1561.   "The Russians Surge Ahead in Europe." *Newsweek* 23 (April 3, 1944), 25–26.

1562.   "Sevastopol: Defied Germans for 8 Months, Retaken in 3 Weeks." *Illustrated London News* 204 (May 20, 1944), 572–573.

1563.   "Sevastopol's Stand." *Newsweek* 20 (July 6, 1942), 22–23.

1564.   "Sevastopol's Story." *Newsweek* 21 (May 17, 1943), 72.

1565.   Shutov, Z. "Battle for the Dneiper." *Soviet Military Review,* no. 9 (September 1973), 48–51.

1566.   _____ . "Infantry-Artillery Cooperation during Water Crossings Discussed: Translated from *Voyenno Istoricheskiy Zhurnal,* June 1979." *Translations on USSR Military Affairs,* no. 1466 (October 2, 1979), 21–28.

1567.   "The Slaughter at Sevastopol." *Newsweek* 19 (June 29, 1942), 25–26.

1568.   Spiridonov, A. "End of the Battle for the Caucasus." *Soviet Military Review,* no. 10 (October 1973), 49–51.

1569.   "Spring in Russia." *Newsweek* 19 (March 30, 1942), 20–21.

1570.   "Struggle for the Best Black Sea Port Makes War's Bloodiest Battlefield." *Life* 13 (July 6, 1942), 26–27.   Sevastopol.

1571.   Svetlishin, N. "On the Main Line of Advance." *Soviet Military Review,* no. 3 (March 1969), 6–10.   Ukraine, 1944.

1572.   Thompson, Paul W. "Bridgehead on the Irsha: The Attempt of the Germans to Take Malin [1943]." *Infantry Journal* 52 (May 1943), 28–32.

1573.   _____ . "Sevastopol and Verdun." *Infantry Journal* 52 (February 1943), 14–24.

1574.   Turbiville, Graham H., Jr. "Paradrop at the Bukrin Bridgehead: An Account of the Soviet Dneiper Operation." *Military Review* 56 (December 1976), 26–40.

1575.   United States. War Department. General Staff. G-2. "Behind the Red Army Kiev Front." *Military Reports on the United Nations* 17 (April 1944), 26–42.

1576.   _____ . "The German Advance from the North: The Kiev Operation, 1943." *Tactical and Technical Trends* 16 (1943), 50–56.

1577.   _____ . "A German Spearhead in the Kiev Operation: The Advance of the 6th Army." *Tactical and Technical Trends* 11 (1942), 49–60.

1578.   _____ . "German Tactics in the Final Phase at Kharkov, 1942." *Tactical and Technical Trends* 12 (1942), 27–29.

1579.   _____ . "A Visit to the Caucasus Front." *Military Reports on the United Nations* 6 (May 1943), 57–64.

1580.   Valyushkin, G. "Cavalry and Tanks Capture Taganrog." *Cavalry Journal* 52 (November 1943), 2–5.

1581.   Von Manstein, Erich. "The Campaign in the Crimea, 1941– 1942." *Marine Corps Gazette* 40 (May 1956), 32–47.

1582.   _____ . "Defensive Operations in Southern Russia, 1943– 1944." *Marine Corps Gazette* 41 (April 1957), 40–53.

1583.   Vorob'yev, I. "Defense of the Coast." *Soviet Military Review,* no. 8 (August 1972), 10–13.

1584.   _____ . "Joint Actions by Land Forces and the Navy." *Soviet Military Review,* no. 10 (October 1974), 26–28.

1585.   Vorontsov, G. "The Army Forces the Dneiper." *Soviet Military Review,* no. 7 (July 1970), 12–15.

1586.   _____ . "The Art of Troop Control." *Soviet Military Review,* no. 7 (July 1972), 36–39.   Korsun-Shevchenkovsky campaign.

1587.   Washburn, Stanley. "Caucasus Fight Estimated." *Cavalry Journal* 51 (September 1942), 15–16.

1588.   Werner, Max. "Kharkov Is Just the Beginning." *New Republic* 106 (June 1, 1942), 755–756.

1589.   "What Hitler Lost: Vital Oil, Ores Lie behind the Vistula-Carpathian Line." *Business Week* (April 8, 1944), 20–22.

1590.   Yakubovsky, Ivan I. "In Battles in the Right-Bank Ukraine." *Soviet Military Review,* no. 8 (August 1969), 38–42: no. 9 (September 1969), 39–41.

1591.   Zvenzlovsky, A. "Night Assault." *Soviet Military Review,* no. 5 (May 1973), 50–52.   The liberation of Zaporoshe.

1592.   _____ . "Victory in the South." *Soviet Military Review,* no. 11 (November 1969), 36–39.

Documents, Papers, and Reports

1593.   Breith, Hermann. "Breakthrough of 111 Panzer Corps through Deeply Echeloned Russian Defenses, Kharkov, July 1943." Unpublished paper, Foreign Military Studies Program, Historical Division, Headquarters, U.S. Army, Europe, 1947. 19p.

1594.   Buercky, Heinrich. "Advance and Action of the 528th Infantry Regiment from 22 June 1941–January 1942." Unpublished paper,

Foreign Military Studies Program, Historical Division, Headquarters, U.S. Army, Europe, 1947. 36p.   Battles in the Ukraine.

1595.   Francke, Major. "Sixth Army, Russia." Unpublished paper, Foreign Military Studies Program, Historical Division, Headquarters, U.S. Army, Europe, 1950. 74p.   Fighting on the Mius Front, July–August 1942.

1596.   Harteneck, Gustav. "Second Army Gets Out of the Mud." Unpublished paper, Foreign Military Studies Program, Historical Division, Headquarters, U.S. Army, Europe, 1947. 19p.   During the Kiev campaign.

1597.   Luz, Helwig. "The 11th Panzer Division in the Fighting for the Dneiper Bridge Near Gornostaypol, 23–29 August 1941." Unpublished paper, Foreign Military Studies Program, Historical Division, Headquarters, U.S. Army, Europe, 1947. 18p.

1598.   Rendulic, Lothar. "The Command Decision: Rogachev, 1941." Unpublished paper, Foreign Military Studies Program, Historical Division, Headquarters, U.S. Army, Europe, 1947. 31p.

1599.   Schulz, Friedrich, et al. "Battle for the Crimea (Sevastopol)." Unpublished paper, Foreign Military Studies Program, Historical Division, Headquarters, U.S. Army, Europe, 1948. 63p.

1600.   ———. "Reverses on the Southern Wing, 1942–1943." Unpublished paper, Foreign Military Studies Program, Historical Division, Headquarters, U.S. Army, Europe, 1948. 410p.

1601.   Schulz, Paul. "Combat in the Caucasus Woods and Mountains during Autumn 1942." Unpublished paper, Foreign Military Studies Program, Historical Division, Headquarters, U.S. Army, Europe, 1947. 21p.

1602.   Von Gyldenfeldt, Heinz. "The 1942 Offensive." Unpublished paper, Foreign Military Studies Program, Historical Division, Headquarters, U.S. Army, Europe, 1948. 328p.

1603.   Von Roman, Rudolf. "XX Corps in the Defense on the Area Southwest of Orel, Summer 1943." Unpublished paper, Foreign Military Studies Program, Historical Division, Headquarters, U.S. Army, Europe, 1947. 30p.

1604.   Winter, August, et al. "Army Group South, Advance to the Dneiper, 1941." Unpublished paper, Foreign Military Studies Program, Historical Division, Headquarters, U.S. Army, Europe, 1948. 144p.

Further References

See also sections 2:A, 2:C:1, and 2:C:3:a.

f. KURSK, 1943

Following the 1942–1943 Soviet winter counteroffensive, a strong German salient thrust into the Russian lines north of the city of Kursk. Hoping to reverse the Stalingrad disaster and shorten lines of support, German planners elected to return to the attack. Soviet planners thought that a determined assault could open the Moscow-Orel-Kursk communication line.

Throughout May and June, both sides massed men and materiel in the area. Russian aircraft and partisans ranged far behind German lines attempting as much mischief as possible. In Operation Citadel, the Germans struck first on July 5. Pincers moved on the city from north and south—but the Russians knew they were coming. Effective intelligence work allowed Marshal Zhukov to dig in the men of the Central and Voronezh fronts and within a week the German tide was turned.

On July 12, the Soviets opened a counteroffensive, with the western and Bryansk fronts moving first against Orel. The move was a big success. In the south, German armor made progress against the Voronezh Front, and by July 13, large numbers of Soviet soldiers were trapped between a pair of panzer corps. And then in the evening of the thirteenth, as Anglo-American forces moved into Sicily, Hitler called Citadel off.

For most of the next three weeks, the fighting in the south of Kursk tipped back and forth. During this period, the Germans began work on a new defensive line across the base of the Orel salient. After the first of August, they began moving behind it, and by August 17 the retreat was complete and the battle finished.

Kursk was the largest land battle in history, with more than two million men involved. It also featured some of the largest contests between tanks and aircraft. When it was over, many were convinced that the end of the war on the eastern front was only a matter of time.

BOOKS

1605.   Caidin, Martin. *The Tigers Are Burning.* New York: Hawthorn Books, 1974. 243p.

1606.   Chant, Christopher, and Keith Ward. *Kursk.* Warren, Mich.: Squadron/Signal Publications, 1975. 48p.

1607.   Jukes, Geoffrey. *Kursk, the Clash of Armor.* Ballantine's Illustrated History of World War II. New York: Ballantine Books, 1969. 160p.

1608.   Konev, Ivan, et al. *The Battle of Kursk.* Translated from the Russian. Moscow: Progress Publishers, 1974. 350p.

1609.   O'Neill, Herbert C. *Foothold in Europe: The Campaigns in Sicily, Italy, the Far East and Russia, between July 1943 and May 1944.* By "Strategicus," pseud. London: Faber & Faber, 1945. 242p.

1610.   *Orel, the July Battle, 1943.* Translated from the Russian. Moscow: Foreign Language Publishing House, 1943. 92p.

1611.   Solovyov, Boris. *The Battle of Kursk.* Translated from the Russian. Moscow: Novosti Press Agency Publishing House, 1973. 40p.

ARTICLES

1612.   Christyakov, I. "The Victory at Kursk: An Interview." *Soviet Military Review,* no. 7 (July 1978), 42–45.

1613.   "A Clash of 1,500 Tanks at Prokhorovka." *Soviet Military Review,* no. 6 (June 1973), 1–67.

1614.   Dmitrin, N. "On the Kursk Bulge." *Soviet Military Review,* no. 7 (July 1979), 15–16.

1615.   Erickson, John. "Kursk." In Noble Frankland and Christopher Dowling, eds., *Decisive Battles of the 20th Century.* New York: David McKay, 1976. pp. 222–238.

1616.   "The German Failure in the Orel-Belgorod Front." *Illustrated London News* 203 (August 7, 1943), 142–143.

1617.   Gwynn, Charles W. "The Kursk Offensive." *Fortnightly* 160 (August 1943), 113–116.

1618.   Holder, L. D. "Kursk: The Breaking of the Panzer Corps." *Armor* 84 (January-February 1975), 12–17.

1619.   "How the Russians Took Orel." *Life* 15 (August 16, 1943), 21–27.

1620.   Jessup, John E., Jr. "Battle of Kursk." In Thomas Parrish, ed., *The Simon and Schuster Encyclopedia of World War II.* New York: Simon & Schuster, 1978. pp. 350–352.

1621.   Koltunov, G. A. "Kursk: The Clash of Armor." In Bernard Fitzsimons, ed., *Tanks and Weapons of World War II.* New York: Beekman House, 1973. pp. 81–97.

1622.   "The Kursk Battle—30 Years." *Soviet Military Review,* no. 6 (June 1973), 2–39.

1623.   "Legend Dispelled: Triumphs at Orel and Belgorod." *Newsweek* 22 (August 16, 1943), 23.

1624.   Levidov, Colonel. "Artillery Counterpreparation." *Field Artillery Journal* 33 (November 1943), 811–812.

1625.   Mitchell, Donald W. "Germany's Swan Song." *Current History,* ns 5 (October 1943), 103–107.

1626.   Nikitin, V. "Fuel Supply Operations during the Kursk Counteroffensive Described: Translated from *Voyenno Istoricheskiy Zhurnal,* August 1979." *Translations on USSR Military Affairs,* no. 1472 (October 31, 1979), 31–38.

1627.   Orlov, A. "The Turning Point." *Soviet Military Review,* no. 5 (May 1978), 42–44.

1628.   Panchenko, A. "The Enemy Retreats." *Soviet Military Review,* no. 3 (March 1969), 40–42.

1629.   Parrish, Michael. "The Battle of Kursk." *Army Quarterly* 99 (October 1969), 39–51.

1630.   Ratley, Lonnie O., 3d. "Air Power at Kursk: The Confrontation of Aircraft and Tanks—A Lesson for Today." *Journal of the Royal United Services Institute for Defence Studies* 122 (June 1977), 25–29.

1631.   Rocafort, Colonel. "Two German-Russian Tank Battles." *Military Review* 30 (June 1950), 100–107.

1632.   Rokossovskiy, Konstantin. "The Kursk Battle, July 5–August 23, 1943." *Soviet Military Review,* no 7 (July 1968), 2–7; no. 8 (August 1968), 30–36.

1633.   Shutov, Z. "In the Enemy Rear." *Soviet Military Review,* no. 12 (December 1973), 45–47.

1634.   Sidorov, V. "Wartime Use of Engineer Obstacles Described: Translated from *Voyenno Istoricheskiy Zhurnal,* September 1979." *Translations on USSR Military Affairs,* no. 1483 (December 20, 1979), 98–105.

1635.   "Skinning Tigers: Huge Tanks Ripped by Reds as Nazis Launch '43 Drive." *Newsweek* 22 (July 19, 1943), 26–27.

1636.   Solovyov, Boris G. "The Battle of Kursk." *International Review of Military History,* no. 44 (1979), 119–127.

1637.   Stesarev, Pavel. "Self-Propelled Artillery vs. Tanks." *Field Artillery Journal* 34 (November 1944), 787–788.

1638.   Sukovsky, K. O. "The Tank Battle of Prokhorovka." *Cavalry Journal* 52 (November 1943), 31–33.

1639.   Tannenbaum, Rudolf. "The Battle for Kursk: I Fought at Prokhorovka." *World War II Enthusiast, 1939–1945* 2 (January–February 1975), 8–10; (March–April 1975), 62–64.

1640.   Vasilevskiy, Aleksandr M. "An Epoch-Making Victory." *Soviet Military Review*, no. 4 (April 1975), 2–5.

1641.   Von Manstein, Erich. "Operation Citadel." *Marine Corps Gazette* 40 (August 1956), 44–47.

1642.   Vysokoostrovsky, L. "Artillery vs. Tiger and Ferdinand." *Field Artillery Journal* 33 (November 1943), 810–811.

1643.   Zhukov, Georgiy K. "The Battle of Kursk, 1943." *Military Review* 49 (August 1969), 82–96.

DOCUMENTS, PAPERS, AND REPORTS

1644.   "The Attack of the XLVIII Panzer Corps on the 6th Guards Army of the Voronezh Army Group at Kursk, 5–12 July 1943." *Historical Evaluation of Barrier Effectiveness.* DAAG 39-74-C-0033. Dun Loring, Va.: Historical Evaluation and Research Organization, 1974. Chpt. 3.

1645.   Busse, Theodor, et al. "The Zitadelle Offensive, 1943." Unpublished paper, Foreign Military Studies Program, Historical Division, Headquarters, U.S. Army, Europe, 1947. 209p.   Reprinted in part 10 of Donald S. Detwiler, ed., *World War II German Military Studies,* 24 vols. (New York: Garland, 1980).

1646.   Dupuy, Trevor N. "Belgorod-Kharkov: Soviet Offensive from the Kursk Salient, August 1943." In Trevor N. Dupuy et al., *A Study of Breakthrough Operations.* DNA-4124F. Dun Loring, Va.: Historical Evaluation and Research Organization, 1976. Chpt. 7.

1647.   _____ . "Daily Scenario of the Attack of the German XLVIII Panzer Corps in the Battle of Kursk, 4–15 July 1943." In Trevor N. Dupuy et al., *A Study of Breakthrough Operations.* DNA-4124F. Dun Loring, Va.: Historical Evaluation and Research Organization, 1976. Chpt. 2.

1648.   _____ . "Operation Citadel: The Offensive of the German XLVIII Panzer Corps in the Southern Region of the Kursk Bulge, 4–15 July 1943." In Trevor N. Dupuy et al., *A Study of Breakthrough Operations.* DNA-4124F. Dun Loring, Va.: Historical Evaluation and Research Organization, 1976. Chpt. 6.

1649.   Thach, Joseph E., Jr. "The Battle of Kursk, July 1943: Decisive Turning Point on the Eastern Front." PhD dissertation, George Washington University, 1969.

Further References

See also the general citations in section 2:A, 2C:1, and 2:D:4.

g. BYELORUSSIA OFFENSIVE, 1944

With their tremendous losses in Russia to spring 1944, the Germans' only hope seemed to be to retreat into a shorter front and construct strong defensive positions. Unfortunately for the men of the Wehrmacht, Hitler's territorial obsessions would not permit retrograde movements, and by May 1944, their lines were overextended across 1,400 miles with few reserves.

On June 23, the axe fell. Under Marshal Zhukov, the 1st, 2d, and 3d Byelorussian fronts fell on German Army Group Centre. Assisted by partisans and artillery (almost 400 pieces per mile), the Soviet soldiers hit a 350-mile front and split it apart. By the end of July, Minsk, Vilnyus, and Brest Litovsk were in Russian hands and 25 of 33 Wehrmacht divisions were trapped. At the close of the following month, Zhukov's offensive had reached Riga in the north and Warsaw in the south, with Russian troops poised on the borders of East Prussia. In two months, the Soviets had repeated the same sorts of gains the Germans had enjoyed earlier in the war. Advancing 450 miles, the Red Army had outstripped its supply capability and was forced to come to a temporary halt in this arena.

BOOKS

1650.   Grossman, Vasiliy S. *With the Red Army in Poland and Byelorussia.* Translated from the Russian. London: Hutchinson, 1945. 52p. Activities of the 1st Byelorussian Front, June–July 1944.

ARTICLES

1651.   Batov, Pavel I. "The Blow in Byelorussia: An Interview." *Soviet Military Review,* no. 6 (June 1979), 16–18.

1652.   Boldyrev, P. "The Bobruisk Operation." *Military Review* 24 (March 1945), 105–108.

1653.   FitzGerald, Charles G. "Operation Bagration.'" *Military Review* 44 (May 1964), 59–72.

1654.   Gackenholtz, Hermann. "The Collapse of Army Group Centre in 1944." In Hans A. Jacobsen and Juergen Rohwer, eds., *Decisive Battles of World War II: The German View*. New York: G. P. Putnam, 1965. pp. 355–383.

1655.   Gwynn, Charles W. "The Battle of the Kiev Salient." *Fortnightly* 161 (February 1944), 113–114.

1656.   Izosimov, A. "Documentary Material on the Belorrussian Campaign: Translated from *Voyenno Istoricheskiy Zhurnal*, June 1979." *Translations on USSR Military Affairs*, no. 1466 (October 2, 1979), 45–52.

1657.   Kobrin, Nikolai. "Tank Army in Defense." *Soviet Military Review*, no. 7 (July 1974), 60–62.

1658.   Martell, Paul. "Strategic Surprise in the 1944 Soviet Summer-Fall Campaign: A Case Study." *History, Numbers and War* 2 (Fall 1978), 118–128.

1659.   Nofi, Albert A. "The Destruction of Army Group Centre: The Soviet Summer Offensive, 1944." *Strategy and Tactics*, no. 36 (January 1973), 5–16.

1660.   Novikov, A. "Attack Aircraft vs. Tanks." *Soviet Military Review*, no. 2 (February 1968), 40–43.

1661.   Ogaryov, P. "A Division [63rd Infantry] Breaking Through Enemy Defenses." *Soviet Military Review*, no. 1 (January 1979), 45–46.

1662.   "Red Pincers." *Newsweek* 24 (October 30, 1944), 37–38.

1663.   Rokossovskiy, Konstantin. "'Operation Bagration.'" *Soviet Military Review*, no. 6 (June 1969), 46–49; no. 7 (July 1969), 44–47.

1664.   "Rout à la Napoleon." *Newsweek* 24 (July 10, 1944), 28–29.

1665.   Rudenko, S. I. "The Belorussian Air Offensive." *Aerospace Historian* 20 (March 1973), 17–26.

1666.   Saulin, D. "The Battle of Orsha." *Military Review* 25 (May 1945), 121–124.

1667.   Shishkin, S. "The Vitebsk Operation." *Military Review* 25 (July 1945), 93–97.

1668.   Vasilevskiy, Aleksandr M. "Operation Bagration." *Soviet Military Review*, no. 6 (June 1974), 2–55.

1669.   Yelshin, N. "[Brest] Fortress on the Bug." *Soviet Military Review*, no. 6 (June 1976), 39–41.

1670.   Young, W. R. "The Minsk Operation: A Preliminary Study." *Journal of the Royal United Service Institution* 90 (February 1945), 93–97.

1671.   Zaytsev, Mikhail M. "Historical Data on the Belorussian Military District: Translated from *Voyenno Istoricheskiy Zhurnal*, November 1978." *Translations on USSR Military Affairs*, no. 1408 (January 24, 1979), 32–37.

DOCUMENTS, PAPERS, AND REPORTS

1672.   Von der Groeben, Peter. "The Collapse of Army Group Centre, 1944." Unpublished paper, Foreign Military Studies Program, Historical Division, Headquarters, U.S. Army, Europe, 1947. 79p.   Reprinted in part 10 of Donald S. Detwiler, ed., *World War II German Military Studies*, 24 vols. (New York: Garland, 1980).

Further References

See also the general citations in sections 2:A and 2:C:1.

h. THE THRUST INTO EASTERN EUROPE, 1944–1945

Once the German invader was cleared from Russia proper, Red Army troops sped on to liberate or assist in the liberation of Eastern Europe. The majority of the literature on this thrust concentrates on four areas: Poland, Czechoslovakia, Yugoslavia, and Rumania-Hungary-Bulgaria.

(1). Poland

As noted in the previous section, Soviet troops were in prewar Poland by early July 1944. By the end of the month, one army group was across the Vistula approaching Warsaw. At this point, the Byelorussia offensive ended to allow the Russians to resupply and bring up new equipment and men.

It was at this point that one of the most bitterly controversial episodes of World War II occurred. By the end of July, Soviet propaganda was calling upon the Poles to rise against the Germans. Assuming that they would be assisting Russian arms now crossing the Vistula, the Polish Home Army under General Bor-Komorowski attacked throughout Warsaw on August 1. Within three days, the Poles all but controlled the city. Claiming the 2d Tank Army was halted at Praga (but failing to explain other advances across the Vistula south of the city), the Soviets did not move to assist General Bor. The Russians, usually blamed for wanting to wash their hands of the local non-Communist leadership, watched as throughout August and September the SS smashed the Polish revolt and razed the city.

Despite the ill effects of the Warsaw Uprising, the Soviet advance into Poland was continued. In January 1945, the Red Army took Warsaw and found it 85 percent destroyed, with half its prewar population dead.

Elsewhere that month, the 1st Byelorussian and 1st Ukrainian fronts launched an offensive on a wide front stretching from Jasto to Warsaw. In one of the fastest, largest, and most costly advances of the conflict, Marshal Zhukov's forces reached the Oder River by month's end. Pockets of German resistance were bypassed and mopped up later; by February, over 1.5 million men were ready to move into Germany.

BOOKS

1673.   Bor-Komorowski, Tadeusz. *The Secret Army*. London: Gollancz, 1950. 407p.

1674.   Bruce, George. *The Warsaw Uprising, 1 August –2 October 1944*. London: Hart-Davis, 1972. 224p.

1675.   Bytniewska, Irena. *Silent Is the Vistula: The Story of the Warsaw Uprising*. Translated from the Polish. New York: Longmans, Green, 1946. 275p.

1676.   Ciechanowski, Jan M. *Defeat in Victory*. Garden City, N.Y.: Doubleday, 1947. 397p.

1677.   _____ . *The Warsaw Rising of 1944*. London and New York: Cambridge University Press, 1974. 332p.

1678.   Deschner, Guenther. *Warsaw Rising*. Ballantine's Illustrated History of the Violent Century: Politics in Action, no. 5. New York: Ballantine Books, 1972. 160p.

1679.   Friedman, Philip, ed. *Martyrs and Fighters: The Epic of the Warsaw Ghetto*. New York: Praeger, 1954. 324p.

1680.   Korbonski, Stefan. *Fighting Warsaw*. New York: Funk and Wagnalls, 1968. 495p.

1681.   Kurzman, Dan. *The Bravest Battle: The 28 Days of the Warsaw Ghetto*. New York: G. P. Putnam, 1976. 386p.

1682.   Orme, Alexandra. *Comes the Comrade*. New York: William Morrow, 1950. 376p.

1683.   Polonsky, Antony, and Boleslaw Drukier, eds. *The Beginnings of Communist Rule in Poland, 1944–1945*. London: Routledge & Kegan Paul, 1980. 464p.

1684.   Saluski, Zbigniew. *Poles on the Fronts of the Second World War.* Translated from the Polish. Warsaw: Interpress Publishers, 1969. 94p.

1685.   Starr, Richard F. *Poland, 1944–1962: The Sovietization of a Captive People.* Baton Rouge: Louisiana State University Press, 1962. 300p.

1686.   Tushnet, Leonard. *To Die with Honor.* New York: Citadel Press, 1965. 128p.

1687.   Umiastowski, Roman, with Joanna M. Aldridge. *Poland, Russia, and Great Britain, 1941–1945: A Study of Evidence.* London: Hollis & Carter, 1946. 544p.

1688.   Wdowinski, David. *And We Are Not Saved.* New York: Philosophical Library, 1963. 124p.

1689.   Zagorski, Waclaw. *Seventy Days.* Translated from the Polish. London: Muller, 1957. 267p.

ARTICLES

1690.   Davies, Norman. "The Soviet Command and the Battle of Warsaw." *Soviet Studies* 23 (April 1972), 573–585.

1691.   Kleczkowski, Stefan. "Warsaw Rising, August 1944." *Contemporary Review* 211 (August 1967), 82–84.

1692.   Konev, Ivan. "From the Vistula to the Oder." *Soviet Military Review,* no. 2 (February 1970), 44–48.

1693.   Kozlowski, E. "The Polish War Effort on World War II Fronts and Poland's Contribution to the Victory over Fascism." *Polish World Affairs* 1 (1975), 37–52.

1694.   Levin, Nora. "The Warsaw Ghetto Uprising." *The Holocaust: The Destruction of European Jewry, 1933–1945.* New York: Crowell, 1968. pp. 317–361.

1695.   Lukas, Richard C. "The Big Three and the Warsaw Uprising." *Military Affairs* 34 (October 1975), 129–136.

1696.   "Lvov-Sandomir Operational Documents: Translated from *Voyenno Istoricheskiy Zhurnal,* July 1979." *Translations on USSR Military Affairs,* no. 1476 (November 28, 1979), 77–84.

1697.   Margolin, Julius. "When the Red Army Liberated Pinsk." *Commentary* 14 (December 1952), 517–528.

1698.   Mitchell, David. "The Complex Tragedy of the Warsaw Uprising." *Mankind* 5 (December 1975), 34.

1699.   Panov, B. V. "The Lvov-Sandomir Operation." *Soviet Military Review*, no. 5 (May 1968), 45–48.   July 13–August 29, 1944.

1700.   Poland. "Polish Statement on Russian Advances." *Current History*, ns 6 (February 1944), 158–159.

1701.   Strong, A. L. "Bor's Uprising." *Atlantic* 176 (December 1945), 80–85.

1702.   Szkoda, W. E. "Soviet Tactics Against the Polish Resistance in World War II." *Military Review* 44 (September 1964), 88–93.

1703.   Taub, Walter. "The Warsaw Tragedy." *Collier's* 115 (March 17, 1945), 17.

1704.   Tsygankov, P. "Wartime Operations—Breaching Prepared Enemy Defense: Translated from *Voyenno Istoricheskiy Zhurnal*, June 1980." *Translations on USSR Military Affairs*, no. 1536 (September 26, 1980), 39–47.   The 128th Guards Rifle Regiment in Poland, January 1945.

1705.   Zvenzlovsky, A. "The Lvov-Sandomir Operation, 1944." *Soviet Military Review*, no. 8 (August 1974), 50–52.

DOCUMENTS, PAPERS, AND REPORTS

1706.   Ciechanowski, Jan M. "The Political and Ideological Background of the Warsaw Rising, 1944." PhD dissertation, University of London, 1968.

1707.   Instytut Historyczmy imienia Generala Sikorskiego [London]. *Documents on Polish-Soviet Relations, 1939–1945*. 2 vols. London: Heinemann, 1961–1967.

1708.   United States. Congress. Senate. Committee on the Judiciary. Subcommittee to Investigate the Administration of the Internal Security Act and Other Internal Security Laws. *The Warsaw Insurrection: The Communist Version vs. the Facts*. 91st Cong., 1st sess. Washington, D.C.: U.S. Government Printing Office, 1969. 18p.

Further References

See also the general citations in sections 2:A and 2:C:1.

(2). Czechoslovakia

Insurgents, supported by the Soviets, unsuccessfully rose in Slovakia in the fall of 1944. Like the Poles, citizens of the state virtually destroyed by the Munich Accords in 1938, would have to wait for the new year.

At the close of the first week in March 1945, units of the 2d and 4th Ukrainian fronts had overrun much of Slovakia. By March 6, they were well into Moravia and had raised hopes so high that Czech partisans all over the country began an uprising. The position of the German defenders was hopeless.

With the fall of Berlin, Czechoslovakia was surrounded. On the western side, the U.S. Third Army, under General George Patton, blocked escape. On the north, south, and eastern approaches, the Russians were ready to step off.

The Soviet assault came on May 8. Troops of the 1st, 2d, 3d, and 4th Ukrainian fronts bore in with overwhelming power. Prague was liberated the following day, and on May 11, U.S. and Soviet troops met along a line extending from Linz to Karlovy Vary. Completely cut off, the Germans surrendered. The war in Europe was over.

BOOKS

1709.   Nemec, Frantisek, and Vladimir Moudry. *The Soviet Seizure of Subcarpathian Ruthenia.* Toronto, Ont.: W. B. Anderson, 1955. 375p.

ARTICLES

1710.   "Anniversary of the Liberation of Czechoslovakia." *Department of State Bulletin* 20 (May 22, 1949), 665–667.

1711.   Galitsan, A. "The Liberation of Czechoslovakia." *Soviet Military Review,* no. 4 (April 1980), 20–22.

1712.   Kliment, Charles K. "The Last Tank Battle of World War II." *Military Journal* 1 (May-June 1977), 12–16.   German Army Group "Mitte" vs. the 4th Ukrainian Front, Moravia, May 7, 1945.

1713.   Konev, Ivan. "The Prague Operation." *Soviet Military Review,* no. 5 (May 1975), 46–49.

1714.   Lelyushenko, D. "The Prague Operation." *Soviet Military Review,* no. 5 (May 1970), 46–49.

1715.   Matronov, P. "Sources of Soviet-Czech Combat Cooperation Traced: Translated from *Voyenno Istoricheskiy Zhurnal,* October 1979." *Translations on USSR Military Affairs,* no. 1487 (January 7, 1980), 51–56.

1716.   Sandalov, L. "In the Final Battles." *Soviet Military Review,* no. 5 (May 1970), 50–51.

1717.   Shtemenko, Sergei M. "Across the Carpathians into Slovakia." *Soviet Military Review,* no. 10 (October 1974), 8–11.

1718.   Tolubko, Vladimir F. "Wartime Operations—Liberation of Czechoslovakia: Translated from *Voyenno Istoricheskiy Zhurnal,* May 1980." *Translations on USSR Military Affairs,* no. 1532 (September 10, 1980), 33–41.

1719.   Toma, P. A. "Soviet Strategy in the Slovak Uprising of 1944." *Journal of Central European Affairs* 19 (October 1959), 290–298.

DOCUMENTS, PAPERS, AND REPORTS

1720.   Elias, Andrew. "The Slovak Uprising of 1944." PhD dissertation, New York University, 1963.

Further References

See also the general citations in sections 2:A and 2:C:1.

(3). Yugoslavia

From the earliest days of their involvement in the war, the Yugoslavs fought the German invader. By late 1944 and early 1945, partisan armies under Tito were proving themselves more than a match for the Germans.

Yugoslavia appears to be the only Eastern European nation other than Albania which, in combat with the Germans, was able to carry the war without much in the way of direct Soviet manpower involvement. In October 1944, the 3d Ukrainian Front did aid Tito in driving the Wehrmacht out of Belgrade, but for the most part, Soviet assistance consisted of arms and advisors.

In the short run, this was not at all bad for the Russians, as it allowed them to concentrate their forces farther north. In the long run, Tito's success laid the groundwork for his independent postwar political course.

BOOKS

1721.   Clissold, Stephen. *Yugoslavia and the Soviet Union, 1939–1973: A Documentary Survey.* New York: Published for the Royal Institute of International Affairs by Oxford University Press, 1975. 318p.

1722.   Djilas, Milovan. *Wartime.* Translated. New York: Harcourt Brace Jovanovich, 1977. 470p.

1723.   Donlagic, Ahmet, et al. *Yugoslavia in the Second World War.* Translated. Belgrade, Yugoslavia: Medunarodna Stampa, 1967. 244p.

1724.   *The Liberation Struggle of the Yugoslav Peoples, 1941–1945.* Translated. Belgrade, Yugoslavia, 1961. 146p.

1725.   Moraca, Pero, and Viktor Kucan. *The War and Revolution of the Peoples of Yugoslavia, 1941–1945*. Translated. New York: Vanoris, 1964. 206p.

1726.   Roberts, Walter R. *Tito, Mihailovic, and the Allies, 1941–1945*. New Brunswick, N.J.: Rutgers University Press, 1973. 406p.

1727.   Tomasevich, Jozo. *War and Revolution in Yugoslavia, 1941–1945*. 3 vols. Stanford, Calif.: Stanford University Press, 1975.

1728.   United Committee of South-Slavs in London. *The Epic of Yugoslavia, 1941–1945*. London, 1945. 96p.

1729.   Yugoslav Peoples' Army. Military-Historical Institute. *Historical Atlas of the Liberation War of the Peoples of Yugoslavia, 1941–1945*. Belgrade, Yugoslavia, n.d. 120p.

ARTICLES

1730.   Andreyev, N. "The Soviet Wartime Role in Yugoslavia Discussed: Translated from *Kommunist Vooruzhennykh Sil*, October 1979." *Translations on USSR Military Affairs*, no. 1501 (March 5, 1980), 60–71.

1731.   Anic, Nikola. "Wartime Operations—Yugoslav Art of Warfare: Translated from *Voyenno Istoricheskiy Zhurnal*, November 1980." *Translations on USSR Military Affairs*, no. 1565 (February 5, 1981), 50–54.

1732.   Antosyak, A. "Soviet-Yugoslav Combat Cooperation in World War II Reviewed: Translated from *Voyenno Istoricheskiy Zhurnal*, May 1978." *Translations on USSR Military Affairs*, no. 1373 (August 29, 1978), 8–19.

1733.   Bosnitch, Sava D. "The Significance of the Soviet Military Intervention in Yugoslavia, 1944–1945." *Review (Jugoslav Affairs)*, no. 8 (August 1969), 695–710.

1734.   Djilas, Milovan. "Wartime: Memories of Yugoslavia." *Dissent* 24 (Spring 1977), 174–180.

1735.   Galitsan, A. "The Liberation of Belgrade." *Soviet Military Review*, no. 9 (September 1979), 42–44.

1736.   Hoffman, George W., and Fred W. Neal. "World War II." *Yugoslavia and the New Communism*. New York: 20th Century Fund, 1962. pp. 69–81.

1737.   "In the Battle of Belgrade, 1944." *Soviet Military Review*, no. 10 (October 1975), 36–37.

1738.   "Russian Soldiers: [David] Fredenthal's Sketches Show the Soviet Army in Yugoslavia." *Life* 18 (February 5, 1945), 83–89.

1739.   Zalar, Charles. "National Liberation War, 1941–1945." In U.S. Congress, Senate, Committee on the Judiciary, Subcommittee to Investigate the Administration of the Internal Security Act and Other Internal Security Laws, *Yugoslav Communism: A Critical Study.* 87th Cong., 1st sess. Washington, D.C.: U.S. Government Printing Office, 1961. pp. 55–116.

Documents, Papers, and Reports

1740.   Biryuzov, S. S. *The Liberation of Belgrade, October 1944.* Translated from the Russian. Alexandria, Va.: Joint Publication Research Service, 1963. 24p.

Further References

See also the general citations in sections 2:A and 2:C:1.

(4). Rumania-Hungary-Bulgaria

Rumania, Bulgaria, and Hungary were all German allies during the years of German victories. All were to feel Soviet wrath in the fall of 1944.

At the end of August 1944, the 2d and 3d Ukrainian fronts were on the Danube River. Most of these troops moved west then north and by September 24 Rumania had been overrun. A smaller group from the 3d Ukrainian Front crossed the Danube during the same period and moved south into Bulgaria. By early October, both Axis nations were in Russian hands and switching allegiances.

The battle for Hungary took a little longer. In October, Marshal Malinovskiy's men, assisted by the 4th Ukrainian Front, bit off a chunk of Hungary. The offensive continued throughout November and December and into January 1945. By early February, Hungary was liberated from the Czech border to Lake Balaton. All that remained was Budapest.

German General Johannes Friessner was successful in repulsing early Soviet assaults on Budapest, but could not prevent its encirclement. Hitler ordered the city defended to the last man and a siege not unlike that of Leningrad began. The battle continued amongst the rubble until February 10, 1945. The following day, 16,000 German soldiers tried to break out, but only a couple of hundred made it. The following day the 33,000 remaining defenders surrendered.

The success at Budapest aided the Soviets to quickly take Vienna and Berlin in April, as precious German reserves were squandered in the vain attempt to hold the lost city.

BOOKS

1741.   Anescu, Vasile, Eugen Banat, and Ian Cupsa. *Participation of the Romanian Army in the Anti-Hitlerite War.* Translated from the Rumanian. Bucharest, Rumania: Military Publishing House, 1966. 108p.

1742.   Bantea, Eugen, et al. *Romania in the War Against Hitler's Army, August 1944–May 1945.* Translated from the Rumanian. Bucharest, Rumania: Meridiane Publishing House, 1970. 292p.

1743.   Galantai, Mari. *The Changing of the Guard: The Siege of Budapest, 1944–1945.* London: Pall Mall Press, 1961. 224p.

1744.   Kertesz, Stephen D. *Diplomacy in a Whirlpool: Hungary between Nazi Germany and Soviet Russia.* Notre Dame, Ind.: Notre Dame University Press, 1953. 273p.

1745.   Miller, Marshall L. *Bulgaria during the Second World War.* Stanford, Calif.: Stanford University Press, 1975. 290p.

ARTICLES

1746.   "Events of the Iasi-Kishinev Operation Recounted: Translated from *Voyenno Istoricheskiy Zhurnal,* August 1979." *Translations on USSR Military Affairs,* no. 1472 (October 31, 1979), 60–66.

1747.   Kobrin, Nikolai. "The Jassy-Kishinev Operation." *Soviet Military Review,* no. 8 (August 1979), 40–42.   Fighting in Rumania, 1944.

1748.   Pethö, Tibor. "Hungary in the Second World War." *Hungarian Quarterly* 1 (Spring 1960), 193–200.

1749.   Shutov, Z. "The Jassey-Kishinev Operation." *Soviet Military Review,* no. 9 (September 1974), 56–58.

1750.   Tolubko, Vladimir F. "Artillery of the 2d Ukrainian Front in the Iasi-Kishinev Operation, August 1944: Translated from *Voyenno Istoricheskiy Zhurnal,* August 1979." *Translations on USSR Military Affairs,* no. 1472 (October 31, 1979), 39–46.

1751.   Vorontsov, G. "The Army Repulses a Counterblow." *Soviet Military Review,* no. 4 (April 1971), 44–47.   During the Battle of Budapest.

1752.   Wagner, Hans O. "Action at Facuti." *Armor* 85 (July–August 1976), 36–38.   The Battle of Targul Frumos, Rumania, 1944.

Documents, Papers, and Reports

1753.   Felzmann, Maximilian. "The Last Russian Offensive, 1945: XXVIII Corps Sector." Unpublished paper, Foreign Military Studies Program, Historical Division, Headquarters, U.S. Army, Europe, 1947. 49p.

Further References

See also the general references in sections 2:A and 2:C:1.

i. Berlin and Germany, 1945

The main objective of the final Soviet offensive of January through May 1945 was, of course, the destruction of Germany and the capture of its capital. The offensive was very costly to the Russians, as everywhere the Wehrmacht put up determined last-ditch defenses.

On January 12, the Russians began a drive on the northern front, moving into East Prussia. At the end of the following month, they swung north in an effort to push the Germans retreating before them into the Baltic. The last winter offensive ended on March 20, with Soviet soldiers on the Baltic and strung out all along the Oder River.

As the northern advance slowed, Soviet fronts farther south began to move. By April 16, most of the Balkans were cleared and Vienna was in the bag. On that day, Marshal Zhukov's troops began to move forward along 200 miles of the Oder, with the 1st Byelorussian Front aimed at Berlin. Within ten days, the German capital was surrounded, and on April 26, elements of the U.S. 1st Army met elements of the 1st Ukrainian Front at Torgau on the Elbe River.

What Cornelius Ryan called "The Last Battle," according to the Soviets, began with a great artillery bombardment on April 16. A week later, the 1st Byelorussian and 1st Ukrainian fronts encircled the city and began to move in on it. Fierce house-to-house fighting somewhat reminiscent of Stalingrad ensued, with both sides taking heavy losses. On April 30, the Reichstag was captured and Hitler committed suicide. Still the fighting raged on. At 3 p.m. on May 2, General Helmuth Weidling surrendered the city and its remaining survivors. The final capitulation came on May 8.

Berlin was a very expensive battle, as General Eisenhower earlier pointed out. The Soviets suggest that the Germans suffered a million casualties while putting their own losses at 304,000 men.

Books

1754.   Ambrose, Stephen E. *Eisenhower and Berlin, 1945: The Decision to Halt at the Elbe.* New York: W. W. Norton, 1967. 119p.

1755.   Bongartz, Heinz. *Flight in Winter: Russia Conquers, January to May 1945*. New York: Pantheon Books, 1951. 318p.

1756.   Chuikov, Vasiliy I. *The Fall of Berlin*. Translated from the Russian. New York: Holt, Rinehart & Winston, 1968. 261p.

1757.   Doenitz, Karl. *Memoirs: Ten Years and Twenty Days*. Translated from the German. Cleveland, Ohio: World Publishing, 1959. 500p.

1758.   Essame, Hubert. *The Battle for Germany*. New York: Scribners, 1969. 228p.

1759.   Gavin, James M. *On to Berlin: Battles of an Airborne Commander, 1943–1946*. New York: Viking Press, 1978. 336p.

1760.   Kuby, Erich. *The Russians and Berlin, 1945*. Translated from the German. London: Heinemann, 1968. 372p.

1761.   Ryan, Cornelius. *The Last Battle*. New York: Simon & Schuster, 1966. 571p.

1762.   Shtemenko, Sergei M. *The Last Six Months: Russia's Final Battles with Hitler's Army in World War II*. Translated from the Russian. Garden City, N.Y.: Doubleday, 1977. 436p.

1763.   Slater, Lisa A. *The Rape of Berlin*. Brooklyn, N.Y.: Pageant-Poseidon, 1972. 91p.

1764.   Smith, Jean E. *The Defense of Berlin*. Baltimore, Md.: Johns Hopkins Press, 1963. 431p.

1765.   Steinert, Marlis G. *Capitulation, 1945: The Story of the Doenitz Regime*. Translated from the German. London: Constable, 1969. 326p.

1766.   Strawson, John. *The Battle for Berlin*. New York: Scribners, 1974. 182p.

1767.   Toland, John. *The Last 100 Days*. New York: Random House, 1966. 622p.

1768.   Troyanovsky, Pavel. *Last Days of Berlin*. Translated from the Russian. London: Soviet News, 1945. 48p.

1769.   Tully, Andrew. *Berlin: Story of a Battle, April–May 1945*. New York: Simon & Schuster, 1963. 304p.

1770.   *What We Saw in Germany: With the Red Army to Berlin, by 13 Leading Soviet War Correspondents*. Translated from the Russian. London: Soviet News, 1945. 63p.

1771.   Whiting, Charles. *The End of the War: Europe, April 15 –May 23, 1945.* New York: Stein & Day, 1973. 178p.

1772.   Ziemke, Earl F. *The Battle for Berlin: End of the Third Reich.* Ballantine's Illustrated History of World War II. New York: Ballantine Books, 1968. 160p.

ARTICLES

1773.   Alekseyev, Nikolai N. "Wartime Operations—Results of the East Prussian Operation: Translated from *Voyenno Istoricheskiy Zhurnal,* February 1980." *Translations on USSR Military Affairs,* no. 1516 (May 30, 1980), 67–69.

1774.   Alferov, S. "Wartime Operations—Vistula-Oder Operations Reviewed: Translated from *Voyenno Istoricheskiy Zhurnal,* February 1980." *Translations on USSR Military Affairs,* no. 1516 (May 30, 1980), 64–66.

1775.   Chatterton-Hill, Georges. "The Last Days of Berlin." *Contemporary Review* 169 (May-June 1945), 280–284, 335–339.

1776.   Chuikov, Vasiliy I. "Capitulation of Nazi Germany." *Atlas* 11 (May 1966), 277–281.

1777.   "Collapse of the Reich." *Newsweek* 25 (May 7, 1945), 31–40.

1778.   "Doom and Triumph." *Time* 45 (April 30, 1945), 29–30.

1779.   "Doomsday Strikes for the Nazis with Berlin Dying, Nation Split." *Newsweek* 25 (April 30, 1945), 25–26.

1780.   "Economic Target: The Russian Army Rolls Ahead Liberating a Rich Industrial Area." *Business Week* (January 27, 1945), 113–114.

1781.   Fayzulin, A. "Documentary Material on the Meeting at the Elbe in 1945: Translated from *Voyenno Istoricheskiy Zhurnal,* April 1979." *Translations on USSR Military Affairs,* no. 1446 (June 13, 1979), 33–36.

1782.   Fleischer, Jack, and Seymour Freidin. "The Last Days of Berlin." *Collier's* 116 (August 25, 1945), 14–15; (September 1, 1945), 14.

1783.   Flynn, John T. "Why the Americans Did Not Take Berlin." *Reader's Digest* 53 (August 1948), 31–34.

1784.   "The Headlong Red Drive into the Reich." *Newsweek* 25 (February 5, 1945), 25–27.

1785.   "How Berlin Got behind the [Iron] Curtain." *Time* 78 (September 29, 1961), 18–19.

1786. "Is the World's Greatest Battle ahead as Russian Armies Crash the Reich?" *Newsweek* 25 (January 29, 1945), 26–27.

1787. Kane, Steve. "Last Gasp of the Waffen SS: Operations in Hungary and Austria, December 1944–May 1945." *World War II Enthusiast, 1939–1945* 2 (March-April 1975), 42–48.

1788. Kecskemeti, Paul. "Germany, 1945." *Strategic Surrender: The Politics of Victory and Defeat.* New York: Atheneum, 1964. Chpt. 3.

1789. Kiselov, A. "Wartime Operations—The Berlin Operation: Translated from *Voyenno Istoricheskiy Zhurnal,* May 1980." *Translations on USSR Military Affairs,* no. 1532 (September 10, 1980), 76–81.

1790. Konev, Ivan. "From the Vistula to the Oder." *Soviet Military Review,* no. 2 (February 1970), 44–48.

1791. _____ . "Toasting the Americans." *Atlas* 11 (May 1966), 284–288. Russian and U.S. troops meet on the Elbe in 1945.

1792. Kozlov, L. "From the Vistula to the Oder." *Soviet Military Review,* no. 1 (January 1980), 38–41.

1793. Krivitsky, Aleksandr I. "Handshake on the Elbe." *Soviet Literature,* no. 4 (April 1980), 110–120.

1794. Krupchenko, I. Ye. "The Battle for Berlin." *International Review of Military History,* no. 44 (1979), 128–138.

1795. Kurnatsishvili, V. "Banner of Victory." *Soviet Military Review,* no. 4 (April 1973), 8–10. Capture of the Reichstag on April 30, 1945.

1796. Lazutkin, S. "Wartime Operations—Infantry Regiment Battle Described: Translated from *Voyenno Istoricheskiy Zhurnal,* January 1980." *Translations on USSR Military Affairs,* no. 1511 (April 21, 1980), 39–44. The 243d Rifle Regiment in the Battle for Oppelin, January 23–29, 1945.

1797. Malkov, D. "In Eastern Pomerania." *Soviet Military Review,* no. 5 (May 1971), 42–44.

1798. "Masterpiece of Madness." *Time* 45 (May 7, 1945), 40.

1799. Menshikov, G. "Artillery in [Berlin] Street Fighting." *Field Artillery Journal* 36 (August 1946), 471–472.

1800. Murphy, Robert D. "The Story of How Berlin Became the World's No. 1 Danger Spot." *U.S. News and World Report* 52 (April 9, 1962), 72–75.

1801.   "On to Berlin: The Huge Russian Offensive." *Life* 18 (February 5, 1945), 30–31.

1802.   Patrick, Stephen B. "The Battle for Germany: The Destruction of the Reich, December 1944–May 1945." *Strategy and Tactics,* no. 50 (May-June 1975), 4–16.

1803.   Plotnikov, Yu. V. "Assault on a Fort." *Soviet Military Review,* no. 3 (March 1972), 44–45.   Battle of Koenigsberg.

1804.   Polevoi, Boris N. "Most Memorable Moments." *Soviet Literature,* no. 2 (February 1980), 3–23.   Battle for Berlin.

1805.   Prokofyev, N. "The Storming of Königsberg." *Soviet Military Review,* no. 4 (April 1969), 42–44.

1806.   Ramanichev, N. M. "Preparations for the Berlin Operation in World War II Described: Translated from *Voyenno Istoricheskiy Zhurnal,* August 1979." *Translations on USSR Military Affairs,* no. 1472 (October 31, 1979), 9–19.

1807.   "River of Destiny: Can the Oder Stave Off the Relentless Reds?" *Newsweek* 25 (February 19, 1945), 29–30.

1808.   Rosly, I. "At the Walls of the 'Fuehrer Bunker.'" *Soviet Military Review,* no. 4 (April 1970), 28–29.

1809.   "The Russians Drive on Hitler's Berlin." *Life* 18 (February 12, 1945), 23–29.

1810.   "Total Death." *Newsweek* 25 (May 7, 1945), 36–37.

1811.   Vasilevskiy, Aleksandr M. "Collapse of the Citadel of German Militarism." *Soviet Military Review,* no. 1 (January 1970), 2–7.

1812.   Von Hopffgarten, Hans-Joachim. "The Battle for the Lebus and Goritz Bridgeheads on the Oder." *Military Review,* 35 (March 1956), 98–107.

1813.   Zhukov, Georgiy K. "The Berlin Operation." *Soviet Military Review,* no. 4 (April 1970), 14–19.

1814.   _____ . "On the Berlin Front." *Atlas* 11 (May 1966), 281–284.

1815.   Ziemke, Earl F. "The Soviets' Lost Opportunity: Berlin in February 1945." *Military Review* 49 (June 1969), 45–53.

1816.   _____ . "Zero Year: The World in 1945." *Air University Review* 31 (November-December 1979), 98–101.

1817.   Zinchenko, F. "Wartime Operations—Capture of the Reichstag Described: Translated from *Voyenno Istoricheskiy Zhurnal,* April 1980." *Translations on USSR Military Affairs,* no. 1525 (July 24, 1980), 57–67.

1818.   Zvenzlovsky, A. "The Berlin Operation." *Soviet Military Review,* no. 4 (April 1980), 17–19.

1819.   _____ . "Breakthrough to the Oder, 1945." *Soviet Military Review,* no. 1 (January 1975), 7–9.

DOCUMENTS, PAPERS, AND REPORTS

1820.   Schramm, Percy E. "The German Wehrmacht in the Last Days of the War, 1 January–7 May 1945." Unpublished paper, Foreign Military Studies Program, Historical Division, Headquarters, U.S. Army, Europe, 1948. 674p.

1821.   Willemer, Wilhelm. "The German Defense of Berlin, 1945." Unpublished paper, Foreign Military Studies Program, Historical Division, Headquarters, U.S. Army, Europe, 1953. 115p.

Further References

See also the general citations in sections 2:A and 2:C:1.

j. WAR IN THE FAR EAST, 1945

In April 1941, the U.S.S.R. and Japan concluded a neutrality pact designed to put an end to the pre-Barbarossa border clashes between the two countries in Mongolia and Manchuria.

Throughout the period of defense, Soviet leaders feared that the Japanese would enter the war on the side of the Germans. The collapse of Germany permitted Stalin to denounce the pact almost four years to the day after it was signed. On August 9, 1945, the U.S.S.R. declared war on Japan and began an invasion of Manchuria.

All went according to Russian plans developed in the interval following the German surrender. Three Russian fronts, with air and naval support, succeeded in crushing all Japanese opposition in a blitzkrieg lasting less than two months. In addition to Manchuria, North China, Korea, and the southern part of Sakhalin Island and the Kurile Islands were liberated. The contrast between this smoothly oiled offensive and the bewildered defense put up in June–July 1941 demonstrated to the world how much the Soviets had learned about war in four short, horrible years.

BOOKS

1822.   Allen, Louis. *The End of the War in Asia.* New York: Hart-Davis, 1976. 306p.

1823.   Bateson, Charles. *The War with Japan: A Concise History.* East Lansing: Michigan State University Press, 1968. 417p.

1824.   Bergamini, David. *Japan's Imperial Conspiracy.* New York: William Morrow, 1971. 1,239p.

1825.   Collier, Basil. *The War in the Far East, 1941–1945.* New York: William Morrow, 1969. 530p.

1826.   Lensen, George A. *The Strange Neutrality: Soviet-Japanese Relations during the Second World War, 1941–1945.* Tallahassee, Fla.: Diplomatic Press, 1972. 332p.

1827.   Toland, John. *The Rising Sun: The Decline and Fall of the Japanese Empire, 1936–1945.* New York: Random House, 1970. 954p.

ARTICLES

1828.   Achkasov, V. I. "Victory in the Far East." *International Review of Military History,* no. 44 (1979), 139–147.

1829.   Andronov, I. "The 25th Anniversary of V-J Day." *New Times* (Moscow), no. 35 (1970), 26–29.

1830.   Betit, Eugene D. "The Soviet Manchurian Campaign, August 1945: Prototype for the Soviet Offensive." *Military Review* 56 (May 1976), 65–73.

1831.   Ekman, Michael E. "The 1945 Soviet Manchurian Campaign: A Model for Sino-Soviet War." *Naval War College Review* 27 (July-August 1974), 81–89.

1832.   Frank, W. F. "Soviet Operations in the War with Japan, August 1945." *U.S. Naval Institute Proceedings* 92 (May 1966), 50–63.

1833.   Garthoff, Raymond L. "Marshal [Rodion] Malinovsky's Manchurian Campaign." *Military Review* 46 (October 1966), 50–61.

1834.   Gorelov, G. "Rout of the Kwantung Army." *Soviet Military Review,* no. 8 (August 1970), 36–37.

1835.   Grayson, Benson L. "Soviet Military Operations in the Far East, 1945." *Military Engineer* 50 (January-February 1958), 41–45.

1836.   Grey, Arthur L., Jr. "38th Parallel." *Foreign Affairs* 29 (April 1951), 482–487.

1837.   Hagerty, James J. "The Soviet Share in the War Against Japan." *Institute for the Study of the U.S.S.R. Bulletin* 17 (September 1970), 5–15.

1838.   Ivanov, S. "Victory in the Far East, August 1945." *Soviet Military Review,* no. 8 (August 1975), 2–5.

1839.   Kalashnikov, K. "Wartime Operations—The Manchurian Campaign: Translated from *Voyenno Istoricheskiy Zhurnal,* August 1980." *Translations on USSR Military Affairs,* no. 1549 (December 8, 1980), 57–68.

1840.   Khrenov, A. "Wartime Operations—Engineer Operations in the Far East: Translated from *Znamya,* August 1980." *Translations on USSR Military Affairs,* no. 1545 (November 20, 1980), 81–97.

1841.   Loskutov, Yu. "Wartime Operations—Manchurian Campaign Preparations: Translated from *Voyenno Istoricheskiy Zhurnal,* February 1980." *Translations on USSR Military Affairs,* no. 1516 (May 30, 1980), 46–54.

1842.   MacCaskill, Douglas C. "The Soviet Union's Second Front: Manchuria." *Marine Corps Gazette* 59 (January 1975), 18–26.

1843.   May, Ernest R. "The United States, the Soviet Union, and the Far Eastern War, 1941–1945." *Pacific Historical Review* 24 (May 1955), 153–174.

1844.   Morton, Louis. "Soviet Intervention in the War with Japan." *Foreign Affairs* 40 (July 1962), 653–662.

1845.   Plotnikov, G. "The Far East: Liberation Mission." *Soviet Military Review,* no. 9 (September 1978), 2–5.

1846.   _____ . "Wartime Operations—The Defeat of Japan: Translated from *Kommunist Vooruzhennykh Sil,* September 1980." *Translations on USSR Military Affairs,* no. 1555 (January 7, 1981), 24–31.

1847.   "The Russian Stroke: Whirlwind in Manchuria." *Newsweek* 26 (August 20, 1945), 26–27.

1848.   Sapozhnikov, G. "The Soviet Union's Role in the War Against Japan—The Liberating Mission of the U.S.S.R. in the Far East in the Second World War: Translated from *Voyenno Istoricheskiy Zhurnal,* July-August 1965." *Current Digest of the Soviet Press* 17 (November 10, 1965), 15–20.

1849.   Sidorov, A. "Wartime Operations—The Route of Japanese Militarism: Translated from *Voyenno Istoricheskiy Zhurnal*, August 1980." *Translations on USSR Military Affairs*, no. 1549 (December 8, 1980), 10–16.

1850.   Sologub, V. "Wartime Operations—Sakhalin Amphibious Operation: Translated from *Voyenno Istoricheskiy Zhurnal*, February 1980." *Translations on USSR Military Affairs*, no. 1516 (April 1, 1980), 70–76.

1851.   Stadkovskiy, M. I. "Some Lessons of the Second World War in the Far East." *International Affairs* (Moscow), no. 10 (October 1970), 39–43.

1852.   Tret'yak, Ivan M. "Preparations for World War II Manchurian Operation Described: Translated from *Voyenno Istoricheskiy Zhurnal*, November 1979." *Translations on USSR Military Affairs*, no. 1500 (February 28, 1980), 11–18.

1853.   Union of Soviet Socialist Republics. Ministry of Information. "The U.S.S.R. Declares War on Japan: Text." *Current History*, ns 9 (September 1945), 187–188.

1854.   "The U.S.S.R. Joins the War Against Japan." *Life* 19 (August 20, 1945), 36–37.

1855.   Vasilevskiy, Aleksandr M. "The Campaign in the Far East: Translated from *Voyenno Istoricheskiy Zhurnal*, October 1975." *Translations on USSR Military Affairs* (December 2, 1975), 27.

1856.   _____. "Rout of the Kwantung Army." *Soviet Military Review*, no. 8 (August 1980), supplement, 1–14.

1857.   _____. "Victory in the Far East: Translated from *Voyenno Istoricheskiy Zhurnal*, August–September 1970." *Translations on USSR Military Affairs* (November 4, 1970), 41–42.

1858.   Vigor, Peter H., and Christopher Donnelly. "The Manchurian Campaign and Its Relevance to Modern Strategy." *Conflict* 2 (1980), 157–178.

1859.   Zakharov, M. "Wartime Operations—Soviet Far East Campaign: Translated from *Voyenno Istoricheskiy Zhurnal*, September 1960." *Translations on USSR Military Affairs*, no. 1534 (September 18, 1980), 1–16.

DOCUMENTS, PAPERS, AND REPORTS

1860.   Despres, John H. *Timely Lessons of History: The Manchurian Model for Soviet Strategy.* RAND Report R-1825-NA. Santa Monica, Calif.: RAND Corporation, 1976. 84p.

1861.   Dupuy, Trevor N. "The Soviet Invasion of Manchuria, August 1945: Breakthrough Operations of the 1st Far Eastern Army Group." In Trevor N. Dupuy, et al., *A Study of Breakthrough Operations.* DNA-4124F. Dun Loring, Va.: Historical Evaluation and Research Organization, 1976. Chpt. 10.

1862.   Dzirkals, Lilita. *'Lightning War' in Manchuria: Soviet Military Analysis of the 1945 Far East Campaign.* RAND Paper P-5589. Santa Monica, Calif.: RAND Corporation, 1976. 116p.

1863.   Hagerty, James J., Jr. "The Soviet Share in the War with Japan." PhD dissertation, University of California, Los Angeles, 1966.

1864.   United States. Department of Defense. *The Entry of the Soviet Union into the War Against Japan: Military Plans, 1941–1945.* Washington, D.C., 1955. 107p.

Further References

See also the general citations in sections 2:A and 2:C:1.

4. Lend-Lease and Foreign Cooperation

The March 11, 1941, Lend-Lease Act, passed by the U.S. Congress and called by Winston Churchill "The most unsordid act in the history of any nation," was extended to the Russians following the German invasion. The major objective was to supply aid.

The citations in this section reflect some of the background maneuvering around how and how much aid could be extended to the Soviets and the manner in which it was to be delivered. The amount given was large, though perhaps not decisive, and the major pipeline was the Persian Corridor through Iran.

Additionally, the references here reveal in general form the diplomatic and political arrangements, deals, and meetings between Stalin and the Western allies, and their combined strategy.

BOOKS

1865.   Beitzel, Robert. *The Uneasy Alliance: America, Britain, and Russia, 1941–1943.* New York: Alfred A. Knopf, 1972. 404p.

1866.   Bethell, Nicholas. *The Last Secret: The Delivery of Over Two Millian Russians by Britain and the United States.* New York: Basic Books, 1974. 224p.

1867.   Epstein, Julius. *Operation Keelhaul: The Story of Force Repatriation from 1944 to the Present.* Old Greenwich, Conn.: Devin-Adair, 1973. 255p.

1868.   Fehling, Helmut M. *One Great Prison: The Story behind Russia's Unreleased POW's.* Translated from the German. Boston, Mass.: Beacon Press, 1951. 175p.

1869.   Feis, Herbert. *Churchill, Roosevelt, Stalin: The War They Waged and the Peace They Sought.* Princeton, N.J.: Princeton University Press, 1957. 692p.

1870.   Harriman, William A., and Elie Abel. *Special Envoy to Churchill and Stalin, 1941–1946.* New York: Random House, 1975. 959p.

1871.   Herring, George C., Jr. *Aid to Russia, 1941–1946: Strategy, Diplomacy, and the Origins of the Cold War.* New York: Columbia University Press, 1973. 365p.

1872.   Higgins, Trumbull. *Winston Churchill and the Second Front, 1940–1943.* London and New York: Oxford University Press, 1957. 281p.

1873.   Huxley-Blythe, Peter J. *The East Came West.* Caldwell, Idaho: Caxton Printers, 1964. 225p.

1874.   Jones, Robert H. *The Roads to Moscow: United States Lend-Lease to the Soviet Union.* Norman: University of Oklahoma Press, 1969. 326p.

1875.   Jordan, George A. *From Major Jordan's Diaries.* New York: Harcourt, 1952. 284p.

1876.   Lenczowski, George. *Russia and the West in Iran.* Ithaca, N.Y.: Cornell University Press, 1949. 383p.

1877.   McNeill, William H. *America, Britain, and Russia: Their Cooperation and Conflict, 1941–1946.* London and New York: Oxford University Press, 1953.

1878.   Mee, Charles L. *Meeting at Potsdam.* New York: Evans, 1975. 370p.

1879.   Nelson, Daniel J. *Wartime Origins of the Berlin Dilemma: A Study of Alliance Diplomacy.* University: University of Alabama Press, 1976. 380p.

1880.   Pogue, Forrest C. *The European Theater of Operations: The Supreme Command.* United States Army in World War II: European Theater. Washington, D.C.: Office of the Chief of Military History, Department of the Army, 1954. 610p.

1881.   Sharp, Tony. *The Wartime Alliance and the Zonal Division of Germany.* Oxford: At the Clarendon Press, 1975. 220p.

1882.   Stoler, Mark A. *The Politics of the Second Front: American Military Planning and Diplomacy in Coalition Warfare, 1941–1943.* Westport, Conn.: Greenwood Press, 1977. 244p.

1883.   Vail Motter, T. H. *The Persian Corridor and Air to Russia.* United States Army in World War II: The Middle East Theater. Washington, D.C.: Office of the Chief of Military History, Department of the Army, 1952. 544p.

ARTICLES

1884.   Andrews, William R. "The Azerbaijan Incident: The Soviet Union in Iran, 1941–1946." *Military Review* 54 (August 1974), 74–85.

1885.   Baldwin, Hanson W. "Contributions of Britain and the United States to Russia's Campaign."*Foreign Affairs* 22 (January 1944), 209–212.

1886.   Fatemi, Faramarz S. "Anglo-Soviet Intervention, 1941." In *The U.S.S.R. in Iran.* South Brunswick, N.J.: A. S. Barnes, 1980. pp 13–42.

1887.   Herndon, James S., and J. O. Baylen. "Col. Philip R. Faymonville and the Red Army, 1934–1943."*Slavic Review* 34 (September 1975), 483–505.

1888.   Jordan, George A. "We Gave the Reds Everything." *Reader's Digest* 61 (December 1952), 55–61.

1889.   Langer, John D. "The Harriman-Beaverbrook Mission and the Debate Over Unconditional Aid for the Soviet Union, 1941."*Journal of Contemporary History* 14 (July 1979), 463–482.

1890.   Matloff, Maurice. "British-American Plans and Soviet Expectations: August-November 1943." *Strategic Planning for Coalition Warfare, 1943–1944.* United States Army in World War II: The War Department. Washington, D.C.: Office of the Chief of Military History, Department of the Army, 1959. pp. 280–306.

1891.   _____ , and Edwin M. Snell. "British and American Plans and Soviet Expectations." *Strategic Planning for Coalition Warfare, 1941–1942.* United States Army in World War II: The War Department. Washington, D.C.: Office of the Chief of Military History, Department of the Army, 1953. pp. 328–349.

1892.   Morton, Louis. "Military Background of the Yalta Agreements." *Reporter* 12 (April 7, 1956), 19–21.

1893.   Rigge, Simon. "Lifeline to the Russians." *War in the Outposts.* World War II Series. Alexandria, Va.: Time-Life Books, 1980. pp. 76–100.

1894.   Sekistov, V. "Why the Second Front Was Not Opened in 1942." *Soviet Military Review,* no. 8 (August 1972), 50–52.

1895.   Van Alstyne, R. W. "The United States and Russia in World War II." *Current History,* ns 19 (November-December 1950), 257–260, 334–339.

1896.   Zorin, L. "Lend-Lease Operations in Iran during World War II Described: Translated from *Voyenno Istoricheskiy Zhurnal,* December 1977." *Translations on USSR Military Affairs,* no. 1335 (March 7, 1978), 24–33.

DOCUMENTS, PAPERS, AND REPORTS

1897.   Nelson, Daniel J. "The Allied Creation of the Postwar Status of Berlin: A Study in Wartime Alliance Diplomacy." PhD dissertation, Columbia University, 1970.

Further References

See also the general references in sections 2:A and 2:C:1.

D. Armaments and Accoutrements

These five subsections provide citations on the various artillery pieces, small arms, tanks and self-propelled cannons, uniforms, medals, and insignia in use by units of the Red Army during World War II. One might call this part our World War II "hardware" section.

1. General Works

The references in this section are overviews of the weapons, uniforms, and orders available in Soviet forces during World War II. The overviews complement the specific subsections.

BOOKS

1898.   Barnes, Gladeon M. *Weapons of World War II.* Princeton, N.J.: Van Nostrand, 1947. 317p.

1899.   Dupuy, Trevor N. *The Evolution of Weapons and Warfare.* Indianapolis, Ind.: Bobbs-Merrill, 1980. 365p.

1900.   Kershaw, Andrew, ed. *Weapons and Uniforms of the U.S.S.R.* Purnell's History of the Second World War Special. London: Phoebus Books, 1975. 64p.

1901.   Kirk, John, and Robert Young. *Great Weapons of World War II*. New York: Walker, 1961. 347p.

1902.   Weeks, John. *Airborne Equipment: A History of Its Development*. New York: Hippocrene Books, 1976. 191p.

1903.   Wilkinson, Frederick J. *A Source Book of World War II Weapons and Uniforms*. London: Ward-Lock, 1980. 128p.

ARTICLES

1904.   Shevchenko, N. "The Weapons of Victory." *Soviet Military Review*, no. 8 (August 1980), 40–42.

1905.   "The Soviet Army's New Weapons." *Life* 8 (April 1, 1940), 34–35.

1906.   "Weapons of World War II: Tanks and Anti-Aircraft Guns." *World War II Magazine* 2 (December 1972), 61–66.

DOCUMENTS, PAPERS, AND REPORTS

1907.   United States. War Department. General Staff. G-2. *Soviet Weapons*. 3 pts. Washington, D.C., 1944.

Further References

See also sections 1:D and E, and 4:F.

2. Artillery

Artillery has been an important branch of every army since before Napoleon's time. It was not until World War II, however, that the Soviets were forced, due to the tremendous losses of Barbarossa, to incorporate new innovations. By the time of Kursk and Byelorussia, Stalin could truly call his artillery the Red Army's "God of War."

Major pieces in use by Soviet forces included the following:
1) the 120mm Type 38 mortar, which could throw a 35½-pound shell 6,600 yards
2) the 122mm Type 31/37 howitzer, which could lob a 55-pound shell 22,000 yards
3) the 76.2mm Type 39 howitzer, which could fire a 13¾-pound shell 14,766 yards
4) the 45mm Type 32 antitank gun, which could fire a 3¼-pound antitank round 9,850 yards or a high-explosive 4¾-pound shell 5,200 yards

5) the 82mm Katyusha rocket mortar, often seen in large launcher assemblies of 32 to 48 rails mounted on tanks and trucks, which could send solid-fueled, fin-stabilized projectiles 6,500 yards in nonprecision area fire.

BOOKS

1908.   Chamberlain, Peter, and Terry J. Gander. *Anti-Aircraft Guns.* World War II Fact Files. New York: Arco, 1976. 64p.

1909.   _____ . *Heavy Artillery.* World War II Fact Files, New York: Arco, 1975. 64p.

1910.   _____ . *Infantry, Mountain and Airborne Guns.* World War II Fact Files. New York: Arco, 1976. 64p.

1911.   _____ . *Light- and Medium-Field Artillery.* World War II Fact Files. New York: Arco, 1976. 64p.

1912.   _____ . *Mortars and Rockets.* World War II Fact Files. New York: Arco, 1976. 64p.

1913.   _____ , and John Milson. *Self-Propelled Anti-Tank and Anti-Aircraft Guns.* World War II Fact Files. New York: Arco, 1976. 64p.

1914.   *Guns:Allied and Enemy.* London: Hutchinson, 1943. 64p.

1915.   Hogg, Ian V. *Artillery in Color, 1923–1963.* New York: Arco, 1980. 64p.

1916.   _____ . *Barrage: The Guns in Action.* Ballantine's Illustrated History of World War II, Weapons Book, no. 18. New York: Ballantine Books, 1970. 160p.

1917.   _____ . *The Guns: 1939/1945.* Ballantine's Illustrated History of World War II. New York: Ballantine Books, 1970. 159p.

1918.   _____ . *The Guns of World War II.* London: Macdonald and Janes, 1976. 152p.

1919.   _____ , and John Batchelor. *Artillery.* New York: Scribners, 1972. 158p.

1920.   _____ . *A History of Artillery.* London and New York: Hamlyn, 1974. 240p.

1921.   Hogg, Oliver F. G. *Artillery: Its Origins, Heydey and Decline.* Hamden, Conn.: Archon Books, 1970. 330p.

1922.   Jobé, Joseph, ed. *Guns: An Illustrated History of Artillery.* Greenwich, Conn.: New York Graphic Society, 1971. 216p.

1923.   Prochko, I. S. *Artillery, God of War.* London: Soviet News, 1945. 63p.

1924.   Rogers, Hugh C. B. *A History of Artillery.* Secaucus, N.J.: Citadel Books, 1975. 230p.

ARTICLES

1925.   Alexeyev, I. I. "Antitank Artillery of the Red Army." *Field Artillery Journal* 32 (August 1942), 604–605.

1926.   Botin, V. "Development of Recoilless Guns Discussed: Translated from *Voyenngye Znaniya,* December 1978." *Translations on USSR Military Affairs,* no. 1418 (March 13, 1979), 84–90.

1927.   Hofmann, Kurt. "An Analysis of Soviet Artillery Development." *International Defense Review* 10 (December 1977), 1057–1061.

1928.   Hogg, Ian V. "The Guns." In Bernard Fitzsimons, ed., *Tanks and Weapons of World War II.* New York: Beekman House, 1973. pp. 12–29.

1929.   Hull, Andrew W. "Evolution of Soviet Self-Propelled Artillery." *Field Artillery Journal* 46 (March-April 1978), 8–12.

1930.   Kamarck, Andrew. "Rebirth of the War Rocket." *Field Artillery Journal* 33 (July 1943), 506–509.

1931.   Khainatskiy, G. "Heavy [203mm] Self-Propelled Guns in Tank Battles." *Field Artillery Journal* 36 (January 1946), 24–25.

1932.   Kharitonov, N. "The Legendary Katyusha." *Soviet Military Review,* no. 4 (April 1975), 24–25.

1933.   "Multiple Rocket Launchers—Development Reviewed: Translated from *Truppenpraxis,* February 1980." *Translations on USSR Military Affairs,* no. 1509 (April 1, 1980), 30–43.

1934.   Parry, Albert. "The Soviets' First Rocket Gun." *Military Review* 41 (October 1961), 56–64.

1935.   Rice, Kevin J. "The Light Antitank Weapon of World War II." *World War II Journal* 3 (March-April 1976), 22–23.

1936.   Roland, Paul. "Soviet Self-Propelled Artillery, 1921–1945." *Military Journal* 1 (January-February 1977), 5–11.

1937.   Ryabchikov, V. "The First Rocket Battery." *Soviet Military Review,* no. 11 (November 1978), 13–14.

1938.   "Soviet Artillery." In Bernard Fitzsimons, ed., *Illustrated Encyclopedia of 20th Century Weapons and Warfare.* New York: Columbia House, 1978. XII: 1327–1350.

1939.   United States. War Department. General Staff. G-2. "Soviet Medium and Heavy Field Artillery." *Military Reports on the United Nations* 19 (June 1944), 7–13.

1940.   Zaloga, Steve. "Soviet Rocket Artillery, 1917–1945." *Military Journal* 1 (March-April 1977), 4–7; (July-August 1977), 5–11.

DOCUMENTS, PAPERS, AND REPORTS

1941.   Graewe, Ernst. "Rocket Projectors on the Eastern Front." Unpublished paper, Foreign Military Studies Program, Historical Division, Headquarters, U.S. Army, Europe, 1947. 11p.

Further References

See also sections 2:A, 2:C:1, 2:C:2:b:(2), 4:C:2, and 4:F:2.

3. Small Arms

The small arms employed by Red infantrymen during the war included machine guns, submachine guns, rifles, pistols and revolvers, and grenades. Firing projectiles were simple in construction and relatively simple to maintain. For the most part, ammunition was standardized at 7.62mm.

Among the more important small arms in Soviet service were:
1) the 12.7mm 1938 heavy machine gun, the first of its kind produced in large quantity, which featured a rate of fire of 540–600 rpm.
2) the 7.62 1930 rifle, which carried 5 rounds in the magazine
3) the Tokarev TT 7.62mm automatic pistol, with 8 rounds available
4) the PPSH 7.62mm submachine gun, which carried 71 rounds in a drum magazine
5) a standard "stick" type hand grenade.

BOOKS

1942.   Barker, Arthur J., and John Walter. *Russian Infantry Weapons of World War II.* New York: Arco, 1971. 80p.

1943.   Burrell, Brian. *Combat Weapons: Handguns and Shoulder Arms of World War II.* Bourne, Eng.: Spurbooks, 1974. 112p.

1944.   Chamberlain, Peter, and Terry J. Gander. *Allied Pistols, Rifles, and Grenades.* World War II Fact Files. New York: Arco, 1976. 64p.

1945.   _____ . *Anti-Tank Weapons.* World War II Fact Files. New York: Arco, 1974. 64p.

1946.   _____ . *Sub-Machine Guns and Automatic Rifles.* World War II Fact Files. New York: Arco, 1977. 64p.

1947.   Ellis, John A. *The Social History of the Machine Gun.* New York: Pantheon, 1976. 186p.

1948.   Hobart, Frank W. A. *Pictorial History of the Sub-Machine Gun.* New York: Scribners, 1975. 224p.

1949.   Hogg, Ian V. *The Encyclopedia of Infantry Weapons of World War II.* London: Bison Books, 1977. 192p.

1950.   _____ . *Military Pistols and Revolvers: The Handguns of the Two World Wars.* New York: Arco, 1970. 79p.

1951.   _____ , and John H. Batchelor. *The Machine Gun.* Purnell's History of the Second World War Special. London: Phoebus Books, 1976. 64p.

1952.   _____ , and John Weeks. *Military Small Arms of the 20th Century: A Comprehensive Illustrated Encyclopedia of the World's Small-Calibre Firearms, 1900–1977.* London: Leventhal, 1977. 284p.

1953.   Johnson, Melvin M. *Rifles and Machine Guns: A Modern Handbook of Infantry and Aircraft Arms.* New York: William Morrow, 1944. 390p.

1954.   _____ , and Charles T. Haven. *Automatic Weapons of the World.* New York: William Morrow, 1945. 644p.

ARTICLES

1955.   "Degtyarev." In Bernard Fitzimons, ed., *Illustrated Encyclopedia of 20th Century Weapons and Warfare.* 24 vols. New York: Columbia House, 1978. VII: 715–717.

1956.   "Federov." In Bernard Fitzsimons, ed., *Illustrated Encyclopedia of 20th Century Weapons and Warfare.* 24 vols. New York: Columbia House, 1978. IX: 925.

1957.   "Goryunov." In Bernard Fitzsimons, ed., *Illustrated Encyclopedia of 20th Century Weapons and Warfare.* 24 vols. New York: Columbia House, 1978. XI: 1154–1156.

1958.   "Infantry Firepower." In Bernard Fitzsimons, ed., *Tanks and Weapons of World War II.* New York: Beekman House, 1973. pp. 30–40.

1959.   "PM." In Bernard Fitzsimons, ed., *Illustrated Encyclopedia of 20th Century Weapons and Warfare*. 24 vols. New York: Columbia House, 1978. XX: 2130–2131.

1960.   "Shpagin." In Bernard Fitzsimons, ed., *Illustrated Encyclopedia of 20th Century Weapons and Warfare*. 24 vols. New York: Columbia House, 1978. XXI: 2322.

1961.   "Simonov." In Bernard Fitzsimons, ed., *Illustrated Encyclopedia of 20th Century Weapons and Warfare*. 24 vols. New York: Columbia House, 1978. XXI: 2330–2331.

1962.   Underhill, Garrett. "The Red Army's Small Arms." *Infantry Journal* 56 (May 1945), 44–49.

Further References

See also section 4:F:3.

4. Tanks

Prior to the invasion of Russia in June 1941, one of the Soviet armaments most underestimated by the Germans was tanks. By the time of the Moscow offensives, Wehrmacht panzers were encountering new and superior Russian armor, which quickly made Hitler's machines obsolete. In the beginning, the new Russian models were few and were employed primarily to support infantry, thereby allowing the Nazis to hold their own with superior tactics. By 1943, despite the slow introduction of newer and heavier German types, Soviet tanks on the eastern front took the upper hand and retained it.

Some of the most important Red tanks and SPs employed during the war were:
1) the 43½-ton KV-1, first Soviet heavy tank, with one 76.2mm cannon and three 7.62mm machine guns
2) the 52-ton KV-2, unsuccessful assault gun version of the KV-1, with one 152mm cannon and three 7.62mm machine guns
3) the 26⅓-ton T-34, which, with one 76.2mm cannon and two 7.62mm machine guns, well-sloped armor, wide tracks, and high speed, outclassed many German tanks and was perhaps the most outstanding armored vehicle of the war
4) the 45¼–45½-ton JS (Joseph Stalin) 1-4 series of heavy tanks, which progressed through cannons of 85mm and 122mm
5) the 46-ton JSU-152 SP gun, based on the JS-1 tank, with one 152mm cannon

6) the 30.9-ton SU-122 SP gun, with one 122mm gun, which employed the tank hull of the T-34.

BOOKS

1963.   Bishop, Denis. *Vehicles at War.* South Brunswick, N.J.: A. S. Barnes, 1979. 222p.

1964.   Bradford, George, and Len Morgan. *Fifty Famous Tanks.* New York: Arco, 1967. 96p.

1965.   Brereton, J. M., and Uwe Feist. *Russian Tanks.* Fallbrook, Calif.: Aero Publishers, 1978. 80p.

1966.   Chamberlain, Peter. *Allied Combat Tanks.* World War II Fact Files. New York: Arco, 1978. 64p.

1967.   _____ , and Chris Ellis. *Pictorial History of Tanks of the World, 1915–1945.* Harrisburg, Pa.: Stackpole Books, 1972. 256p.

1968.   _____ . *Soviet Combat Tanks, 1939–1945.* Edgware, Eng.: Almark, 1970. 64p.

1969.   Ellis, Chris. *Military Transport of World War II.* New York: Macmillan, 1971. 177p.

1970.   _____ , and Peter Chamberlain. *The Great Tanks.* London and New York: Hamlyn, 1975. 176p.

1971.   Grove, Eric. *Russian Armour, 1941–1943.* London: Almark, 1977. 72p.

1972.   _____ . *World War II Tanks.* London: Orbis Books, 1976. 143p.

1973.   Halle, Armin. *Tanks: An Illustrated History of Fighting Vehicles.* Greenwich, Conn.: New York Graphic Society, 1971. 175p.

1974.   Hogg, Ian V., and John Batchelor. *The Tank Story.* London: Phoebus Books, 1977. 160p.

1975.   Icks, Robert J. *Tanks and Armored Vehicles, 1900–1945.* 2d ed. Old Greenwich, Conn.: WE, Inc., 1970. 264p.

1976.   Macksey, Kenneth J. *Tank Force: Allied Armor in World War II.* Ballantine's Illustrated History of World War II: Weapons Book, no. 15. New York: Ballantine Books, 1970. 160p.

1977.   _____ , and John Batchelor. *Tank: A History of the Armored Fighting Vehicle.* New York: Ballantine Books, 1971. 160p.

1978.   MacLeod, Ross G., and Clarke E. M. Campbell. *The Business of Tanks, 1933–1945*. New York: Hippocrene Books, 1977. 338p.

1979.   Milsom, John. *Russian Tanks, 1900–1970: The Complete Illustrated History of Soviet Armored Theory and Design*. Harrisburg, Pa.: Stackpole Books, 1971. 192p.

1980.   _____ , and Steve Zaloga. *Russian Tanks of World War II*. Airfax Magazine Guide, no. 22. London: Stephens, 1977. 64p.

1981.   Morris, Eric. *Tanks*. London: Octopus Books, 1975. 144p.

1982.   Ogorkiewicz, Richard M. *Armor: A History of Mechanized Forces*. New York: Praeger, 1960. 475p.   Reprinted by Arco in 1971 under the title *Armored Forces: A History of Armored Forces and Their Vehicles*.

1983.   _____ . *The Design and Development of Fighting Vehicles*. Garden City, N.Y.: Doubleday, 1968. 208p.

1984.   Orgill, Douglas. *T-34: Russian Armor*. Ballantine's Illustrated History of World War II, Weapons Book, no. 21. New York: Ballantine Books, 1971. 159p.

1985.   _____ . *The Tank: Studies in the Development and Use of the Weapon*. London: Heinemann, 1970. 280p.

1986.   Pugh, Stevenson, ed. *Armor in Profile*. 5 vols. Garden City, N.Y.: Doubleday, 1968–1972.   Bound pamphlets; those of interest here include no. 17, *Russian KV and JS*; no. 37, *Russian BT Series*; and no. 47, *Russian T-34/76, T-34/86*.

1987.   Rogers, Hugh C. B. *Tanks in Battle*. London: Seeley Service, 1965. 240p.

1988.   Steuard, James G., ed. *The Best Articles and Illustrations from Volume One of AFV-G2: An Anthology*. La Puente, Calif.: Baron Publishing, 1972. 102p.

1989.   *Tank Data*. Aberdeen Proving Ground Series. Old Greenwich, Conn.: WE, Inc. [196?]. 241p.

1990.   Vanderveen, Bart H., ed. *The Observer's Fighting Vehicles Directory: World War II*. Rev. ed. London: Warne, 1972. 370p.

1991.   _____ . *Tanks and Transport Vehicles: World War II*. London: Warne, 1974. 64p.

1992.   White, Brian T. *Tanks and Other Armored Fighting Vehicles, 1942–1946*. New York: Macmillan, 1976. 171p.

1993.   _____ . *Tanks and Other Armored Fighting Vehicles of the Blitzkrieg Era, 1939–1941.* New York: Macmillan, 1971. 152p.

ARTICLES

1994.   Arnoldt, Robert P. "The Nemesis of the Panzer Armies." *Armor* 86 (September-October 1976), 44–47.   The T-34.

1995.   Carey, M. L. "Armor: Past, Present and Future." *Armor* 65 (March-April 1956), 34–41.

1996.   Gibb, Charles. "Armored Fighting Vehicles of the War." *Engineer* 181 (January 4, 1946), 5–8.

1997.   Hawkins, Hamilton S. "Evaluation of [Soviet] Armor." *Cavalry Journal* 52 (November 1943), 35–37.

1998.   "History of Soviet Tank Development." *Soviet Military Translations,* no. 317 (September 1966), 9.

1999.   "Josef Stalin." In Bernard Fitzsimons, ed., *Illustrated Encyclopedia of 20th Century Weapons and Warfare.* 24 vols. New York: Columbia House, 1978. XIV: 1505–1506.

2000.   "Klimenti Voroshelov." In Bernard Fitzsimons, ed., *Illustrated Encyclopedia of 20th Century Weapons and Warfare.* 24 vols. New York: Columbia House, 1978. XV: 1640.

2001.   Kotin, Zh. Ya. "Tank Development: Translated from *Trud,* October 21, 1977." *Translations on USSR Military Affairs,* no. 1329 (February 10, 1978), 63–67.

2002.   Macksey, Kenneth J. "The Tanks." In Bernard Fitzsimons, ed., *Tanks and Weapons of World War II.* New York: Beekman House, 1973. pp. 41–53.

2003.   Patrick, Stephen B. "Tank: A Weapons System Survey." *Strategy and Tactics,* no. 44 (March-April 1974), *passim.*

2004.   Rigg, Robert B. "Pictorial History of Armor." *Armor* 68 (September-October 1959), 42–53.

2005.   "Russian Realism and Careful Design Make the T-34 a Bargain Basement Tank." *Product Engineering* 22 (February 1951), 124–129.

2006.   Stark, Warner. "Tanks." In Thomas Parrish, ed., *Simon and Schuster Encyclopedia of World War II.* New York: Simon & Schuster, 1978. pp. 615–621.

2007.   Starry, Donn A. "Tank Design: Ours and Theirs." *Armor* 84 (November-December 1975), 5–7.

2008.   Steiger, A. J. "Forging the Weapons of Red Victory." *Travel* 84 (March 1945), 25–29.

2009.   "The Story of Soviet Armor." *Armored Cavalry Journal* 59 (March 1950), 40–46; (June 1950), 14–21.

2010.   "T-34." In Bernard Fitzsimons, ed., *Illustrated Encyclopedia of 20th Century Weapons and Warfare.* 24 vols. New York: Columbia House, 1978. XXII: 2447–2448.

2011.   United States. War Department. General Staff. G-2. "Russian Tank Camouflage in Winter." *Tactical and Technical Trends* 17 (1943), 32–36.

2012.   Williams, Larry W., and Joseph E. Backofen, Jr. "Origins of Soviet Tank Guns." *Armor* 87 (March-April 1978), 48–51.

2013.   Yelshin, N. "Fire, Maneuvre, Protection: Soviet Tanks, 1941–1945." *Soviet Military Review,* no. 8 (August 1978), 28–30.

Further References

See also sections 2:A, 2:C:1, 2:C:2:b:(1), and 4:F:4.

5. Uniforms, Medals, and Insignia

Like other armies, the Red Army in World War II came to employ a fairly standardized uniform for its regular officers and men. Epaulets and chevrons of various sizes and colors were mixed with various badges to denote rank and unit. Steel helmets and high boots were worn.

From the beginning of the conflict, Stalin called upon the patriotic sentiment of the Russian people and appealed not to communism but to nationalism. To that end, many of the medals and orders were based on a nationalist motif. The Orders of Suvorov and Kutuzov reminded Soviet servicemen of pre-Bolshevik military prowess. Outstanding acts of bravery often won a soldier the title of "Hero of the Soviet Union," while units which displayed particular battle efficiency were named "Guards" units.

Books

2014.   Mollow, Andrew. *Army Uniforms of World War II.* New York: Macmillan, 1974. 183p.

2015.   _____ . *Naval, Marine, and Air Force Uniforms of World War II.* London: Blandford Press, 1975. 231p.   Our interest here is in the Soviet Naval Infantry and Marines.

2016.   Rosignoli, Guido. *Army Badges and Insignia of World War II.* New York: Macmillan, 1975. 228p.

2017.   Schick, I. T., ed. *Battledress: The Uniforms of the World's Great Armies, 1700 to the Present.* Boston, Mass.: Little, Brown, 1978. 256p.

2018.   *Soviet Army Uniforms and Insignia, 1945–1975.* New York: Hippocrene Books, 1977. 91p.

2019.   Windrow, Martin. *Tank and AFV Crew Uniforms since 1916.* Carrollton, Tex.: Squadron/Signal Publications, 1979. 104p.

2020.   _____ . *World War II Combat Uniforms and Insignia.* Warren, Mich.: Squadron/Signal Publications, 1977. 104p.

ARTICLES

2021.   "The First Soviet Order." *Soviet Military Review,* no. 8 (August 1974), 47.   Order of the Red Banner.

2022.   "The Highest Distinction." *Soviet Military Review,* no. 4 (April 1974), 50–51.   Hero of the Soviet Union.

2023.   Lebedev, V. "Decorations for Valor and Combat Service Described: Translated from *Voyenno Istoricheskiy Zhurnal,* October 1978." *Translations on USSR Military Affairs,* no. 1404 (December 21, 1978), 99–103.

2024.   Petrov, Vladimir. "Order of the Red Banner—History, Criteria: Translated from *Krasnaya Zvezda,* September 16, 1978." *Translations on USSR Military Affairs,* no. 1403 (December 18, 1978), 22–28.

2025.   "The Order of Victory." *Soviet Military Review,* no. 4 (April 1975), 64.

2026.   Rybkin, V. "Combat Traditions for Flags of Guards Units Described: Translated from *Voyenno Istoricheskiy Zhurnal,* July 1979." *Translations on USSR Military Affairs,* no. 1476 (November 28, 1979), 85–92.

2027.   Savichev, N. "History of the Order of Victory: Translated from *Agitator Armii I Flota,* September 1978." *Translations on USSR Military Affairs,* no. 1392 (November 2, 1978), 64–66.

2028.   "The Soviet Guards." *Review of the Soviet Ground Forces* 1 (August 1977), 54–58.

2029.   "Uniforms [and] Medals of the Second World War." In Bernard Fitzsimons, ed., *Heraldry and Regalia of War.* New York: Beekman House, 1973. pp. 108–125, 129–134.

DOCUMENTS, PAPERS, AND REPORTS

2030.   Great Britain. War Office. *New Notes on the Red Army: Uniforms and Insignia*. London: H.M. Stationery Office, 1944. 41p.

Further References

See also section 4:F:6.

3 / The Soviet Economy and Defense Establishment

Introduction

The citations in the subsections below provide information on the organization of the Soviet defense establishment, the Soviet High Command, military intelligence, political indoctrination and security in the armed forces, military policy and doctrine, theory and strategy, defense expenditures, and weapons procurement.

A. The Soviet Defense Establishment

1. Organization

Immediate control of the Soviet military is exercised by the minister of defense. Within the Russian government, the defense chief is a member of the Council of Ministers, appointed by and technically answerable to the Supreme Soviet or its Presidium. In practice, the minister of defense is responsible to the Central Committee of the Communist Party (CPSU) and its Politburo.

The current minister of defense, Marshal of the Soviet Union (MSU) Dimitriy F. Ustinov, is a member of the Politburo, as was his predecessor, MSU A. A. Grechko. Politburo control is streamlined by the presence of the Defense Council, successor organization to the World War II State Defense Committee, chaired by the general secretary of the CPSU. In 1976, General Secretary and President Leonid Brezhnev was awarded the rank of MSU—Russia's highest—which indicates to Western analysts that ultimate operational and policymaking control of the armed forces was being vested in the Defense Council.

The Ministry of Defense, which MSU Ustinov heads, has a broad spectrum of activities involving both administrative and operational functions. It controls and directs the armed forces General Staff or High Command, the Warsaw Pact Headquarters, the five major armed forces components—Ground, Navy, Air, Air Defense, and Strategic

Rocket Forces—and sixteen military districts, ten air defense districts, four naval fleets, and four groups of forces.

MSU Ustinov controls the armed forces through his various deputies. Together these men form the High Command, subject of section 3:A:1:b.

The citations in this section provide general information on the overall organization of the Soviet armed forces.

a. GENERAL WORKS

BOOKS

2031.   Deitchman, Seymour J. *New Technology and Military Power: General Purpose Military Forces for the 1980's and Beyond.* Boulder, Colo.: Westview Press, 1979. 350p.

2032.   Grechko, Andrei A. *The Armed Forces of the Soviet State: A Soviet View.* Soviet Military Thought Series, no. 12. Washington, D.C.: U.S. Government Printing Office, 1978. 349p.

2033.   Ryabov, V. *The Soviet Armed Forces, Yesterday and Today.* Moscow: Progress Publishers, 1976. 164p.

2034.   Scott, Harriett F., and William F. *The Armed Forces of the U.S.S.R.* Boulder, Colo.: Westview Press, 1978. 400p.

2035.   _____ . *The Armed Forces of the U.S.S.R.* 2d ed., rev. Boulder, Colo.: Westview Press, 1981. 439p.

2036.   *Soviet Military Organization: A Compilation of Articles from the Army Information Digest.* Fort Slocum, N. Y.: Armed Forces Information School, 1951. 64p.

2037.   Whetten, Lawrence L., ed. *The Future of Soviet Military Power.* New York: Crane, Russak, 1976. 190p.

ARTICLES

2038.   Anemaet, J. "Modern Types of Battle Organization: Russia." *NATO's Fifteen Nations* 11 (April-June 1966), 90–94.

2039.   "The Armed Forces of the U.S.S.R. in the Post-War Period." *Soviet Military Translations*, no. 134 (April 1964), 28–37.

2040.   Asprey, Robert B. "Soviet Military Problems: An Informed Assessment." *Marine Corps Gazette* 46 (June 1962), 22–26.

2041.   Brown, Harold. "Soviet Union Armed Forces: Excerpt from Report, January 25, 1979." *Congressional Digest* 58 (November 1979), 264–266.

2042.   Canby, Steven L. "General Purpose Forces." *International Security Review* 5 (Fall 1980), 317–346.

2043.   Copley, Gregory. "The State of the Soviets." *Defense and Foreign Affairs Digest* 6 (1976), 6–9.

2044.   Debalyuk, A. "General Debalyuk on Tasks and Capabilities of the Armed Forces: Translated from *Kommunist Belorussii,* February 1978." *Translations on USSR Military Affairs,* no. 1353 (May 22, 1978), 35–41.

2045.   "The Development of Soviet Military Power in the Past Twenty Years." *NATO's Fifteen Nations* 16 (April-May 1971), 36–42.

2046.   Donnelly, Christopher N. "The Structure of the Soviet Armed Forces." *NATO's Fifteen Nations* 25 (April-May 1980), 94–96.

2047.   Erickson, John. "The Soviet Military Effort in the 1970's: Perspectives and Priorities." In Royal United Services Institute for Defence Studies, ed., *R.U.S.I. and Brassey's Defence Yearbook, 1976–1977.* Boulder, Colo.: Westview Press, 1976. pp. 84–109.

2048.   ———. "Soviet Military Power." *Strategic Review* 1 (Spring 1973), 1–127.

2049.   Garthoff, Raymond L. "The [Soviet] Military Establishment." *Eastern Europe* 14 (September 1965), 2–16.

2050.   ———. "The Organization and Posture of the Armed Forces." *Soviet Strategy in the Nuclear Age.* New York: Praeger, 1958. pp. 41–60.

2051.   ———. "The Organization of the Armed Forces of the U.S.S.R." *U.S. Army Combat Forces Journal* 39 (April 1953), 36–39.

2052.   Heinl, Robert D., Jr. "The Soviet Military Machine: Morale, Muscles, and Megatons." *Sea Power* 19 (May 1976), 31–34.

2053.   Hilton, Richard. "The Soviet Armed Forces." *Journal of the Royal United Services Institution* 94 (November 1949), 552–566.

2054.   International Institute for Strategic Studies. "The Soviet Union." *Air Force Magazine* 57 (December 1974), 47–49; 58 (December 1975), 49–51; 59 (December 1976), 47–49; 60 (December 1977), 68–70; 61 (December 1978), 68–70; 62 (December 1979), 68–70; 63 (December 1980), 68–70.

2055.   Kir'yan, M. M. "The Superiority of the Soviet Military Organization." In William F. Scott, ed., *Selected Soviet Military Writings, 1970–1975: A Soviet View.* Soviet Military Thought Series, no. 11. Washington, D.C.: U.S. Government Printing Office, 1977. pp. 141–147.

2056.   Kozicharow, E. "Across the Board Gains in Soviet Forces Detailed." *Aviation Week and Space Technology* 107 (August 29, 1977), 17–18.

2057.   Krauss, Paul H., and Robert W. Coonrod. "Armed Forces." In George B. deHuszar, ed., *Soviet Power and Policy*. New York: Crowell, 1955. pp. 268–302.

2058.   Krylov, Nikolai I. "Guarding Socialism's Gains." *New Times* (Moscow), no. 8 (February 28, 1968), 3–5.

2059.   Lee, William T. "The Soviet Defense Establishment in the '80's." *Air Force Magazine* 63 (March 1980), 100–108.

2060.   Legvold, Robert. "The Nature of Soviet Power." *Foreign Affairs* 56 (October 1977), 49–71.

2061.   Levin, Bob. "Sizing Up the Soviets' Might." *Newsweek* 96 (October 27, 1980), 56–57.

2062.   London, Kurt. "Soviet Strengths and Weaknesses." In David M. Abshire and Richard V. Allen, eds., *National Security*. New York: Praeger, 1963. pp. 41–74.

2063.   Long, J. F. L. "Soviet Armed Forces in the 1970's." *Royal Air Forces Quarterly* 9 (Spring 1969), 33–38.

2064.   McDonnell, John A. "The Organization of Soviet Defense and Military Policy Making." In Michael MccGwire and John McDonnell, eds., *Soviet Naval Influence: Domestic and Foreign Dimensions*. New York: Praeger, 1977. pp. 61–106.

2065.   Mackintosh, Malcolm. "The Soviet Military." *Problems of Communism* 22 (September 1973), 1–26.

2066.   Mahoney, Shane E. "Posture and Purpose of the Soviet Military." *Problems of Communism* 28 (January-February 1979), 55–58.

2067.   Manning, Stephen O., 3d. "The Soviet Armed Forces." *Airman* 21 (January 1977), 2–7; (February 1977), 42–48; (March 1977), 11–15.

2068.   Martin, Robert P. "How Strong Is Russia?" *U.S. News and World Report* 88 (February 11, 1980), 17–21.

2069.   "Moscow's Military Machine." *Time* 115 (June 23, 1980), 30–31.

2070.   Murphy, Charles J. V. "Khrushchev's Paper Bear." *Fortune* 70 (December 1964), 114–115.

2071.   O'Ballance, Edgar. "A New Look at Soviet Military Forces." *Military Review* 41 (April 1961), 71–81.

2072.   "The Organization of the Soviet Armed Forces." *Air Force Magazine* 61 (March 1978), 89–91; 62 (March 1979), 95–97.

2073.   Panov, B. V. "The Postwar Development of the Soviet Armed Forces." *International Review of Military History*, no. 44 (1979), 233–242.

2074.   Pavlovskiy, Ivan G. "Pavlovskiy on Armed Forces Accomplishments and Combat Readiness: Translated from *Kommunist Vooruzhennykh Sil*, December 1977." *Translations on USSR Military Affairs*, no. 1331 (February 16, 1978), 66–75.

2075.   Schneider, William, Jr. "Soviet General Purpose Forces." *Orbis* 21 (Spring 1977), 95–106.

2076.   _____ . "Soviet General Purpose Forces." *Military Review* 50 (January 1978), 25–34.

2077.   Scott, Harriet F. "Insights into the Soviet Military." *Problems of Communism* 26 (January-February 1977), 70–72.

2078.   Smith, W. Y. "The Soviet Armed Forces." *Air Force Policy Letter for Commanders*, no. 8 (August 1978), 12–23.

2079.   "The Soviet Armed Forces." *Military Review* 30 (August 1950), 73–79.

2080.   "The Soviet Armed Forces." *Soviet Military Review*, no. 10 (October 1965), 30–55.

2081.   "Soviet Armed Forces: Facts and Figures." *Air Force Magazine* 58 (March 1975), 76–77; 59 (March 1976), 108–109; 60 (March 1977), 109–110.

2082.   "Soviet Military Organization." *Canadian Army Journal* 5 (April 1951), 40–57; (May 1951); 5–6; (June 1951), 27–37; (July 1951), 5–17; (August 1951), 15–22; (September 1951), 43–49.

2083.   "The Soviet Military Organization: Its Heritage and Development." *Army Information Digest* 5 (October 1950), 2–20; (November 1950), 53–64; (December 1950), 33–42; 6 (January 1951), 17–28; (February 1951), 57–64; (March 1951), 58–64.

2084.   Sulimov, Ye. "Principles of the Development of the Soviet Armed Forces." *Soviet Military Review*, no. 3 (March 1973), 12–14.

2085.   Thomson, I. W. "The U.S.S.R.'s Large Conventional Forces." *Royal Air Forces Quarterly* 13 (Spring 1973), 45–50.

2086. Vigor, Peter H. "The Size and Quality of the Soviet Armed Forces and Soviet Military Policy." *NATO's Fifteen Nations* 22 (October-November 1977), 24–26.

2087. _____ . "Soviet Military Developments, 1976." *Strategic Review* 5 (Spring 1977), 74–82.

2088. Viktorov, G. M., and Will W. Groves, Jr. "The Armed Forces of the U.S.S.R." *Infantry* 52 (September-October 1962), 63–66.

2089. Wolfe, Thomas W. "The Soviet Military since Khrushchev." *Current History* 57 (October 1969), 220–227.

2090. Zubarev, V. "The Highest Principle." *Soviet Military Review*, no. 11 (November 1968), 6–11.

DOCUMENTS, PAPERS, AND REPORTS

2091. Holloway, David. *Technology, Management and the Soviet Military Establishment.* Adelphi Papers, no. 76. London: Institute for Strategic Studies, 1971. 44p.

2092. Marshall, Andrew. *Sources of Soviet Power: The Military Potential in the 1980's.* Adelphi Papers, no. 152. London: International Institute for Strategic Studies, 1979. 25p.

2093. United States. Air Force. Headquarters. *Military Forces Handbook: Military Forces of the U.S.S.R. and Peoples Republic of China.* Washington, D.C., 1978.

2094. United States. Congress. Senate. Committee on Government Operations. Subcommittee on National Policy Machinery. *National Policy Machinery in the Soviet Union: Report.* 85th Cong., 2d sess. Washington, D.C.: U.S. Government Printing Office, 1960. 70p.

2095. United States. Department of the Army. *Soviet Military Power.* Washington, D.C., 1959. 186p.

2096. _____ . Office of the Assistant Chief of Staff for Intelligence. *Understanding Soviet Military Developments: Background Material for Addressing Soviet Military Developments.* AST 11005-100-77. Washington, D.C., 1977. 90p.

2097. United States. Department of Defense. Defense Intelligence Agency. *Handbook on the Soviet Armed Forces.* DDB-2680-40-78. Washington, D.C.: U.S. Government Printing Office, 1978. Unpaged.

2098. Whiting, Kenneth R. *The Development of the Soviet Armed Forces, 1917–1972.* Air University Documentary Research Study AU-201-72-IPD. Maxwell AFB, Ala.: Directorate of Documentary Research, Air University Institute for Professional Development, 1972. 102p.

2099. Zemskov, V. I. *Types of Armed Forces and Combat Arms.* Translated from the Russian. JPRS-66305. Arlington, Va.: Joint Publication Research Service, 1975. 40p.

Further References

See also section 3:A:2.

b. THE SOVIET HIGH COMMAND

The Russian minister of defense, MSU Ustinov, exercises control of the Soviet armed forces through his various deputies. These men form the High Command, which currently consists of the minister of defense, three first deputy ministers, eleven deputy ministers, and the chief of the Main Political Directorate. The first deputy ministers and the deputy ministers are responsible to Ustinov for policymaking, planning, coordination, and the control of the services. Relationships within the Ministry of Defense vary in the degree of authority delegated among the deputies and also in established mechanisms for coordination.

The chief of the General Staff is a first deputy minister responsible for overall planning and coordination and for the implementation of all orders emanating from the minister of defense. In the operational chain of command, he is between Ustinov and theater force commanders.

Organizationally, the General Staff is composed of the chief, an assistant to him for naval affairs, an executive officer, two first deputy chiefs, five deputy chiefs, and numerous chiefs of directorates (some of whom may be deputy chiefs). One of the first deputy chiefs is also first deputy commander and chief of staff of the Warsaw Pact Forces. Through its directorates, the General Staff effectively constitutes the nerve center of the Soviet armed forces, directing all military activities concerned with intelligence, operations, organization, conscription, mobilization, reserve affairs, communications, cryptography, foreign military assistance, external relations, military science, and possibly some planning aspects of military transportation and research and development. In addition, the General Staff exercises administrative and political control over its own personnel and supervises the Academy of the General Staff.

BOOKS

2100.	Institut zur Erforschung der U.S.S.R. [Munich]. *Party and Government Officials of the Soviet Union, 1917–1967.* Metuchen, N.J.: Scarecrow Press, 1969. 214p.

2101.	_____ . *Prominent Personalities in the U.S.S.R.: A Biographic Directory.* Metuchen, N.J.: Scarecrow Press, 1968. 1,189p.

2102.	_____ . *The Soviet Diplomatic Corps, 1917–1969.* Metuchen, N.J.: Scarecrow Press, 1970. 240p.

2103.	_____ . *Who Was Who in the Soviet Union.* Metuchen, N. J.: Scarecrow Press, 1972. 687p.

2104.	Lewytzkyj, Borys, ed. *Who's Who in the Socialist Countries.* New York: K. G. Saur, 1978. 748p.

ARTICLES

2105.	Bialer, Seweryn. "The Men Who Run Russia's Armed Forces." *New York Times Magazine* (February 21, 1965), 14–15, 53–54.

2106.	Erickson, John. "Soviet Command and Control." *Military Review* 52 (January 1972), 41–50.

2107.	_____ . "Towards a 'New' Soviet High Command: 'Rejuvenation' Reviewed, 1959–1969." *Journal of the Royal United Service Institution* 114 (September 1969), 37–44.

2108.	Galay, Nikolai. "Changes among the Leaders of the Soviet Armed Forces." *Institute for the Study of the USSR Bulletin* 10 (June 1963), 36–40.

2109.	_____ . "The New Marshals." *Institute for the Study of the USSR Bulletin* 2 (March 1955), 7–12.

2110.	_____ . "The Significance of the Reestablishment of the Supreme Command of the Soviet Armed Forces." *Institute for the Study of the USSR Bulletin* 11 (July 1964), 19–27.

2111.	Garthoff, Raymond L. "The High Command and General Staff." In Basil H. Liddel-Hart, ed., *The Soviet Army.* London: Weidenfeld & Nicolson, 1956. pp. 255–263.

2112.	Ghebhardt, Alexander O., and William Schneider, Jr. "The Soviet High Command: Recent Changes and Policy Implications." *Military Review* 53 (May 1973), 3–14.

2113.   Kruzhin, Petr. "New Appointments in the Soviet Armed Forces." *Institute for the Study of the USSR Bulletin* 14 (July 1967), 35–44.

2114.   Kurochkin, Pavel A. "Unity of Command in the Soviet Armed Forces." *Soviet Military Review*, no. 7 (July 1965), 16–18.

2115.   Parrish, Michael. "The New Soviet High Command." *Military Review* 49 (February 1969), 22–27.

2116.   Scott, Harriet F. "The Soviet High Command." *Air Force Magazine* 60 (March 1977), 52–56.

2117.   _____ . "Top Leaders of the Soviet Armed Forces." *Air Force Magazine* 62 (March 1979), 94.

2118.   "The Structure of the High Command." *Army Information Digest* 6 (March 1951), 59–64.

2119.   Wolfe, Thomas W. "The Soviet General Staff." *Problems of Communism* 28 (January-February 1979), 51–54.

DOCUMENTS, PAPERS, AND REPORTS

2120.   Jones, Ellen. *The Soviet Ministry of Defense and Military Management.* DDB-2610-22-79. Washington, D.C.: Defense Intelligence Agency, Department of Defense, 1979.

2121.   Spahr, William J. "The Soviet Military High Command, 1957–1967: Political Socialization, Professionalization, and Modernization." PhD dissertation, George Washington University, 1972.

2122.   United States. Central Intelligence Agency. Office of Political Research. *Appearances of Soviet Leaders.* Washington, D.C.: Document Expediting Project, Exchange and Gift Division, Library of Congress, 1972–. v. 1–.

2123.   _____ . *Directory of Soviet Officials.* Washington, D.C.: Document Expediting Project, Exchange and Gift Division, Library of Congress, 1973–. v. 1–.

2124.   _____ . *Directory of USSR Ministry of Defense Officials.* Washington, D.C.: Document Expediting Project, Exchange and Gift Division, Library of Congress, 1972–. v. 1–.

2125.   _____ . *Directory of USSR Ministry of Foreign Affairs Officials.* Washington, D. C.: Document Expediting Project, Exchange and Gift Division, Library of Congress, 1974–. v. 1–.

Further References

For additional biographical information, consult section 1:G.

c. MILITARY INTELLIGENCE AND RECONNAISSANCE

The Main Intelligence Directorate or GRU, functioning under control of the General Staff of the Armed Forces, provides intelligence on military related activities around the world. According to John Barron, the GRU has in the past often been subordinate to the Committee for State Security or KGB.

The principal manner of gaining information directly related to the tactical requirements of the Soviet Army is reconnaissance, the combat-intelligence gathering which might be known in the United States as scouting.

The citations in this subsection detail the work of the GRU and KGB in military intelligence and provide examples, mostly from Russian sources in translation, of Red Army reconnaissance.

BOOKS

2126.　　Chuyev, Yu. V., and Yu. B. Mikhaylov. *Forecasting in Military Affairs: A Soviet View.* Translated from the Russian. Soviet Military Thought Series, no. 16. Washington, D.C.: U.S. Government Printing Office, 1980. 230p.

2127.　　Pen'kovskiy, Oleg V. *The Penkovskiy Papers.* Translated from the Russian. Garden City, N.Y.: Doubleday, 1965. 411p.

ARTICLES

2128.　　Barron, John. "The G.R.U.: Soviet Military Intelligence." *K.G.B.: The Secret Work of Soviet Secret Agents.* New York: Reader's Digest Press, 1973. pp. 343–345.

2129.　　"The Basic Task of Scouts." *Soviet Military Translations,* no. 151 (July 1964), 8–12.

2130.　　Baxter, William P. "What Ivan Knows about Us." *Army* 30 (May 1980), 33–35.

2131.　　Bell, Raymond E., Jr., and E. Joe Shimek, 3d. "Soviet Reconnaissance." *Armor* 76 (January-February 1967), 36–38.

2132.　　Bezvershenko, V. "Reconnaissance in Mountainous and Wooded Country." *Soviet Military Review,* no. 7 (July 1979), 24–25.

2133.　　Chikin, V. "Army-Level Combat Intelligence Operations Described: Translated from *Voyenno Istoricheskiy Zhurnal,* October 1979." *Translations on USSR Military Affairs,* no. 1487 (January 7, 1980), 62–71.

2134.   Dziak, John J. "Soviet Intelligence and Security Services in the Eighties: The Paramilitary Dimension." *Orbis* 24 (Winter 1981), 771–786.

2135.   Galeyev, R. "The Need for Constant Combat Intelligence Discussed: Translated from *Krasnaya Zvezda*, May 27, 1978." *Translations on USSR Military Affairs*, no. 1370 (August 17, 1978), 73–77.

2136.   Garthoff, Raymond L. "The Soviet Intelligence Services." In Basil H. Liddell-Hart, ed., *The Red Army*. New York: Harcourt, 1956. pp. 265–274.

2137.   Grayson, Benson L. "Security Control in the Soviet Army." *Antiaircraft Journal* 97 (July-August 1954), 15–17.

2138.   Gredasov, P. "Combat Intelligence Procedures Described: Translated from *Krasnaya Zvezda*, August 2, 1979." *Translations on USSR Military Affairs*, no. 1488 (January 11, 1980), 3–7.

2139.   _____ . "Tactical Reconnaissance." *Soviet Military Review*, no. 3 (March 1980), 34–35.

2140.   Ionov, G. "Reconnaissance in Force." *Soviet Military Review*, no. 1 (January 1967), 14–18.

2141.   Ivanov, N. "Reconnaissance in Mountains: Translated from *Znamenosets*, September 1980." *Translations on USSR Military Affairs*, no. 1553 (December 29, 1980), 109–113.

2142.   Ivanov, S. "Reconnaissance and Intelligence in Contemporary Warfare." *Soviet Military Review*, no. 11 (November 1966), 20–23.

2143.   Korzun, L. "Independent Operations." *Soviet Military Review*, no. 4 (April 1980), 26–28.

2144.   Kulishev, O. "Ground Forces—Improving Battlefield Reconnaissance: Translated from *Voyenno Istoricheskiy Zhurnal*, June 1980." *Translations on USSR Military Affairs*, no. 1536 (September 26, 1980), 59–66.

2145.   McMaster, Arthur W., 3d. "Soviet Reconnaissance in the Seventies." *Military Review* 57 (September 1977), 64–71.

2146.   Medlev, L. "Engineer Reconnaissance from Aboard a Helicopter: Translated from *Voennyi Vestnik*, May 1978." *Review of the Soviet Ground Forces* 3 (May 1980), 14–16.

2147.   Popov, A. "Reconnaissance in Strength." *Soviet Military Review*, no. 3 (March 1979), 39–41.

2148.   Simonyan, R. "Combat Intelligence in Wartime Front Operations: Translated from *Voyenno Istoricheskiy Zhurnal,* December 1977." *Translations on USSR Military Affairs,* no. 1329 (February 10, 1978), 1–3.

DOCUMENTS, PAPERS, AND REPORTS

2149.   United States. Department of Defense. Defense Intelligence Agency. "Militarized Security Forces." *Handbook on the Soviet Armed Forces.* DDB-2680-40-78. Washington, D.C.: U.S. Government Printing Office, 1978. pp. 13/1–6.

2150.   ———. *Soviet Tactical Intelligence and Reconnaissance.* DDI 1100-148-77. Washington, D.C., 1977.

2151.   United States. Department of the Army. "Intelligence Indicators." *Opposing Forces: Europe.* FM 30-102. Washington, D.C.: U.S. Government Printing Office, 1977. pp. 2/26–2/32.

2152.   ———. "Reconnaissance-Signal Intelligence and Radio-electronic Warfare." *Opposing Forces: Europe.* FM 30-102. Washington, D.C.: U.S. Government Printing Office, 1977. pp. 14/1–14/7.

2153.   Zickel, Raymond E. *Soviet Combat Intelligence and Reconnaissance.* New York: U.S. Army Institute for Advanced Russian and East European Studies, 1973. 41p.

2. The Communist Party and the Military

a. GENERAL WORKS

Among the most important of the administrative, technical, and support elements which assist the minister of defense in nonoperational activities is the Main Political Directorate, sometimes called the Main Political Administration. This unit is the principal instrument used by the Central Committee of the Communist Party to maintain political control over the armed forces, including rigid adherence to Party policies and directives.

The directorate consists of a chief, a first deputy chief, seven deputy chiefs who head major directorates concerned with political agitation and propaganda, party organization, and the administration of political affairs in the five major force components, and five deputy chiefs with unknown portfolios. An additional directorate handles personnel administration for the Political Directorate, and two separate departments exist for Communist Youth League (Komsomol) affairs and military-sociological research.

The Central Committee appoints members of the Main Political Directorate to serve on the Bureau, the directorate's executive body, which is responsible for the overall implementation of Party policies in the armed forces. All Bureau actions are based on Central Committee directives and Secretariat instructions. Its decisions are embodied in decrees and orders issued by the chief of the Main Political Directorate. The most important of these require the signature of both that leader and the minister of defense, as well as Central Committee approval.

The citations below treat the relationship between the Party and the military in general and show the unique political control exercised in Russia over the military.

BOOKS

2154.   Avtorkhanov, Abdurakhman. *The Communist Party Apparatus.* Chicago, Ill.: Regnery, 1966. 422p.

2155.   Barry, Donald D., and Carol B. *Contemporary Soviet Politics: An Introduction.* Englewood Cliffs, N. J.: Prentice-Hall, 1978. 406p.

2156.   Brzezinski, Zbigniew K., ed. *Political Controls in the Soviet Army.* New York: Praeger, 1954. 93p.

2157.   Colton, Timothy J. *Commissars, Commanders, and Civilian Authority: The Structure of Soviet Military Politics.* Cambridge, Mass.: Harvard University Press, 1979. 376p.

2158.   Conquest, Robert. *Power and Policy in the U.S.S.R.: A Study of Soviet Dynastics.* New York: St. Martin's Press, 1961. 485p.

2159.   _____ . *The Soviet Political System.* New York: Praeger, 1968. 144p.

2160.   Deane, Michael J. *Political Control of the Soviet Armed Forces.* New York: Crane, Russak, 1977. 297p.

2161.   Hazard, John N. *The Soviet System of Government.* 5th ed. Chicago, Ill.: University of Chicago Press, 1980. 288p.

2162.   Hendel, Samuel, ed. *The Soviet Crucible: Soviet Government in Theory and Practice.* Princeton, N.J.: Van Nostrand, 1959. 594p.

2163.   Hough, Jerry F. *How the Soviet Union Is Governed.* Cambridge, Mass.: Harvard University Press, 1979. 696p.

2164.   Kelleher, Catherine, ed. *Political-Military Systems: Comparative Perspectives.* Sage Research Progress Series on War, Revolution, and Peacekeeping, v. 4. Beverly Hills, Calif.: Sage, 1974. 306p.

2165.   Kelly, Donald R., ed. *Soviet Politics in the Brezhnev Era.* New York: Praeger, 1980. 269p.

2166.   Kolkowicz, Roman. *The Soviet Military and the Communist Party.* Princeton, N.J.: Princeton University Press, 1967. 429p.

2167.   Morton, Henry W., ed. *Soviet Politics and Society in the 1970's.* New York: Free Press, 1974. 401p.

2168.   Perlmutter, Amos, ed. *Political Influence of the Military: A Comparative Reader.* New Haven, Conn.: Yale University Press, 1980. 508p.

2169.   Reshetar, John S., Jr. *The Soviet Polity: Government and Politics in the U.S.S.R.* 2d ed. New York: Harper & Row, 1978. 413p.

2170.   Schuman, Frederick L. *Government in the Soviet Union.* 2d ed. New York: Crowell, 1967. 226p.

2171.   Warner, Edward L. *The Military in Contemporary Soviet Politics: An Institutional Analysis.* New York: Praeger, 1977. 374p.

2172.   Werth, Alexander. *Russia: The Post-War Years.* New York: Taplinger, 1971. 446p.

2173.   Wesson, Robert G. *Communism and Communist Systems.* Englewood Cliffs, N.J.: Prentice-Hall, 1978. 227p.

ARTICLES

2174.   Abbott, Steve. "The Soviet Army: Who Gives the Orders?" *Soldiers* 35 (October 1980), 26–27.

2175.   Artemiev, Vyacheslav P. "The Communist Party and the Soviet Armed Forces." *Military Review* 44 (February 1964), 29–37.

2176.   Avtorkhanov, Abdurakhman. "The Soviet Triangular Dictatorship: Party, Police, and Army—Formation and Situation." *Ukrainian Quarterly* (Summer 1978), 135–153.

2177.   Beck, Carl, and Karen E. Rawlings. "The Military as a Channel of Entry into Positions of Political Leadership in Communist Party States." *Armed Forces and Society* 3 (Winter 1977), 199–218.

2178.   Brzezinski, Zbigniew. "Party Controls in the Soviet Army." *Journal of Politics* 14 (November 1952), 565–591.

2179.   Caron, Gerald C. "Soviet Military-Civil Relations: Conflict and Collaboration among Comrades." *Naval War College Review* 24 (December 1971), 65–93.

2180.   Colton, Timothy J. "Civil-Military Relations in the Soviet Union: The Developmental Perspective." *Studies in Comparative Communism* 11 (Autumn 1978), 213–224.

2181.   _____ . "The Impact of the Military on Soviet Society." In Seweryn Bialer, ed., *The Domestic Context of Soviet Foreign Policy.* Boulder, Colo.: Westview Press, 1980. Chpt. 5.

2182. _____ . "Civil-Military Relations in Soviet Politics." *Current History* 67 (October 1974), 160–163.

2183. Drachkovitch, Milorad M. "The Selling of the Soviet Pentagon." *National Review* 23 (June 29, 1971), 694–696.

2184. Eitner, Hans-Juergen. "Soviet Marshals and the Khrushchev Regime." *Military Review* 40 (April 1960), 101–108.

2185. Erickson, John. "The Army, the Party, and the People: U.S.S.R." *Journal of the Royal United Service Institution* 115 (December 1970), 27–31, 45–47.

2186. _____ . "The Soviet Military, Soviet Policy, and Soviet Politics." *Strategic Review* 1 (Fall 1973), 23–36.

2187. _____ . "Zhukov, Khrushchev and the Red Army." *Marine Corps Gazette* 42 (November 1958), 48–51.

2188. Ermarth, Fritz. "Soviet Military Politics." *Military Review* 48 (January 1968), 32–36.

2189. "The Fight Inside Russia." *U.S. News and World Report* 35 (July 17, 1953), 15–18.

2190. Galay, Nikolay. "The Role of the Soviet Army in the Crisis of the Collective Leadership." *Institute for the Study of the USSR Bulletin* 3 (August 1957), 13–20.

2191. _____ . "Military Representation in the Higher Party Echelons." *Institute for the Study of the USSR Bulletin* 2 (March 1956), 3–11.

2192. _____ . "The Soviet Army and Domestic Policy." *Institute for the Study of the USSR Bulletin* 6 (October 1960), 3–15.

2193. Garthoff, Raymond L. "The Marshals and the Party: Soviet Civil-Military Relations in the Post-War Period." In Harry L. Coles, ed., *Total War and Cold War: Problems in Civilian Control of the Military.* Columbus: Ohio State University Press, 1962. pp. 241–266.

2194. _____ . "The Military as a Social Force." In Cyril E. Black, ed., *The Transformation of Russian Society: Aspects of Social Change since 1861.* Cambridge, Mass.: Harvard University Press, 1960. pp. 323–338.

2195. _____ . "The Role of the Military in Recent Soviet Politics." *Russian Review* 16 (April 1957), 15–25.   Reprinted in Garthoff, *Soviet Strategy in the Nuclear Age* (New York: Praeger, 1958), pp. 18–40.

2196. Gouré, Leon. "The Political Position of the Soviet Army since Stalin." *New Leader* (June 9, 1958), 7–11.

2197.   Grechko, Andrei A. "The Party, the People, the Army Are One." *Soviet Military Review,* no. 5 (May 1971), 2–5.

2198.   Herspring, Dale R. "The C.P.S.U. and the Military." *Problems of Communism* 25 (March 1976), 71–75.

2199.   Holloway, David. "The Role of the Military in Soviet Politics." In Royal United Service Institution, eds., *The Soviet Union in Europe and the Near East: Her Capabilities and Intentions.* London, 1970. p. 12.

2200.   "How the New Men Run Russia." *Business Week* (July 23, 1966), 138–144.

2201.   Jacobs, Walter D. "The Red Army's Role in Building Communism." *Military Review* 41 (September 1961), 10–19.

2202.   Jones, Christopher D. "The 'Revolution in Military Affairs' and Party-Military Relations, 1965–1970." *Survey* 20 (Winter 1974), 84–100.

2203.   Kime, Steve F. "How the Soviet Union Is Ruled." *Air Force Magazine* 63 (March 1980), 54–60.

2204.   Kolkowicz, Roman. "Generals and Politicians: An Uneasy Truce." *Problems of Communism* 17 (May 1968), 71–76.

2205.   _____ . "Interest Groups in Soviet Politics: The Case of the Military." In Dale R. Herspring and Ivan Volgyes, eds., *Civil-Military Relations in Communist Systems.* Boulder, Colo.: Westview Press, 1978. Chpt. 1.

2206.   Kozlov, N. "The Party and the Army: Translated from *Kommunist,* March 1978." *Translations from Kommunist,* no. 4 (April 28, 1978), 153–158.

2207.   Kux, Ernst. "The Red Army and Khrushchev." *Swiss Review of World Affairs* 14 (July 1964), 11–13.

2208.   Nor-Mesek, Nikolay. "The Influence of Military Officers in Soviet Politics Discussed: Translated from *Frankfurter Allgemeine,* June 20, 1979." *Translations on USSR Military Affairs,* no. 1457 (August 21, 1979), 86–91.

2209.   Odom, William E. "The Party-Military Connection: A Critique." In Dale R. Herspring and Ivan Volgyes, eds., *Civil-Military Relations in Communist Systems.* Boulder, Colo.: Westview Press, 1978. pp. 27–52.

2210.   _____ . "Who Controls Whom in Moscow?" *Foreign Policy,* no. 19 (Summer 1975), 109–123.

2211. "Party Leadership Is the Source of Soviet Army and Navy Power." *Soviet Military Translations*, no. 193a (October 1965), 33–47.

2212. Pierre, André. "The Army and the Party in the Soviet Union." *Military Review* 35 (September 1955), 92–97.

2213. Pipes, Richard. "Militarism and the Soviet State." *Daedalus* 109 (Fall 1980), 1–12.

2214. Plekhov, A. "The Role of the Military in the Soviet Political System Discussed: Translated from *Kommunist Vooruzhennykh Sil*, May 1978." *Translations on USSR Military Affairs*, no. 1373 (August 29, 1978), 38–48.

2215. Ploss, Sidney I. "Politics in the Kremlin." *Problems of Communism* 19 (May-June 1970), 1–14.

2216. "The Politics of the Red Army." *Fortune* 47 (May 1953), 90.

2217. Raymond, Ellsworth. "Russia's Garrison State." *American Legion Magazine* 99 (November 1975), 18.

2218. "Red Army Marshals Wield New Power in Moscow." *Business Week* (January 16, 1954), 136–138.

2219. Seton-Watson, Hugh. "Russia: Army and Autocracy." In Michael Howard, ed., *Soldiers and Governments: Nine Studies in Civil-Military Relations*. Bloomington: Indiana University Press, 1959. pp. 49–115.

2220. Tanin, Ye. "The Army and the Supreme Soviet." *Institute for the Study of the USSR Bulletin* 1 (April 1954), 23–26.

2221. Ustinov, Dimitriy F. "U.S.S.R. Defense Minister on C.P.S.U. Role in Building the Armed Forces: Translated from *Voprosy Istorii Kpss*, January 1979." *Translations on USSR Military Affairs*, no. 1422 (March 23, 1979), 1–27.

2222. Volkov, Leon. "Malenkov and the Red Army." *Newsweek* 41 (May 25, 1953), 43.

2223. Wesson, Robert G. "The Military in Soviet Society." *Russian Review* 30 (April 1971), 139–145.

2224. Whiting, Kenneth R. "The Debate between Khrushchev and His Marshals." *Air University Quarterly Review* 16 (March-April 1965), 68–79.

2225. Wolfe, Thomas W. "Are the Generals Taking Over?" *Problems of Communism* 18 (July-October 1969), 106–110.

2226.   Zorza, Victor. "Khrushchev's Losing Fight with His Marshals." *Life* 57 (November 6, 1964), 43, 79, 85.

DOCUMENTS, PAPERS, AND REPORTS

2227.   Davis, Paul D. "A Study of the U.S.S.R. Governmental Structure, with Particular Reference to the Soviet Military Establishment." MA thesis, George Washington University, 1962.

2228.   Duevel, Christian. *Disarray among the Soviet Marshals.* New York: Radio Liberty Committee, 1969. 13p.

2229.   Erickson, John. *The Soviet Military, Soviet Policy, and Soviet Politics.* USSI Report 73-3. Washington, D.C.: United States Strategic Institute, 1973. 20p.

2230.   Galay, Nikolay. *The Role of the Soviet Army in Khrushchev's Overthrow.* Reference paper, no. 16. Munich, W. Ger.: Institute for the Study of the U.S.S.R., 1965. 20p.

2231.   Kolkowicz, Roman. *Conflicts in Soviet Party-Military Relations, 1962–1963.* RAND Memorandum RM-3760-PR. Santa Monica, Calif.: RAND Corporation, 1963.

2232.   _____ . *Political Controls in the Red Army: Professional Autonomy vs. Political Integration.* RAND Paper P, 3402. Santa Monica, Calif.: RAND Corporation, 1966. 30p.

2233.   _____ . "The Political Role of the Soviet Military." PhD dissertation, University of Chicago, 1965.

2234.   McConnell, James M. *Military-Political and Military-Strategic Leadership in the U.S.S.R: A Working Paper.* Arlington, Va.: Center for Naval Analysis, Department of the Navy, 1975.

2235.   Nemzer, Louis. *Conflicting Patterns of Civil-Military Relations in the U.S.S.R.* RAC-TP-142. McLean, Va.: Research Analysis Corporation, 1964.

2236.   *Soviet Dynamics —Political, Economic, Military: The Findings of a Trilogy of Panel Studies by Recognized Experts.* Pittsburgh, Pa.: World Affairs Council of Pittsburgh, 1978. 97p.

2237.   United States. Central Intelligence Agency. National Foreign Assessment Center. *Political Control of the Soviet Armed Forces: A Research Paper.* SR-80-10058-U. Langley, Va.: Office of Public Information, Central Intelligence Agency, 1980. 11p.

2238.   United States. Department of Defense. Defense Intelligence Agency. *Political Control of the Soviet Armed Forces: The Committee of Peoples Control.* DIA-DDB-2600-1279-78. Washington, D.C., 1978.

2239. _____ . *U.S.S.R.: The Unity and Integration of Soviet Political and Industrial Leadership.* DIA-DDI-2250-12-77. Washington, D.C., 1977. 65p.

2240.   Warner, Edward L. "The Military in Contemporary Soviet Politics: An Institutional Analysis." PhD dissertation, Princeton University, 1975.

b. POLITICAL INDOCTRINATION AND SECURITY
IN THE SOVIET ARMED FORCES

The political apparatus in the Main Political Directorate extends down through, and is an integral part of, all headquarters throughout Soviet military forces to company level. It trains, administers, and directs the political officers responsible for the indoctrination of all personnel, morale-building programs, assurance of political reliability, and the disciplinary and administrative control of members of the CPSU and Komsomol.

During the early history of the Red Army and again around the time of Stalin's purges, political officers often played important—if ignorant—roles in operational details. Today the commissars work only to teach and check their men. Soviet soldiers receive heavy doses of indoctrination, complete with hefty manuals, guidebooks for discussion leaders, and audio-visual support. Even if a man is completely loyal, he must endure long sessions, as political officers' reports influence the upward mobility of officers and enlisted personnel not only in the Red Army but throughout the Soviet military.

The citations in this section provide some information on what the Russians call "Party-political work" in the armed forces.

ARTICLES

2241.   Artemiev, Vyacheslav P. "Coercion and Fear in the Soviet Armed Forces." *Military Review* 49 (November 1969), 51–55.

2242. _____ . "Party Political Work in the Soviet Armed Forces." *Military Review* 44 (March 1964), 62–68.

2243.   Burney, John C. "The Soviet Political Officer—Asset or Liability?" *Marine Corps Gazette* 50 (April 1966), 49–52.

2244.   Danowitz, Edward F. "Party Control of the Soviet Army." *Marine Corps Gazette* 42 (September 1957), 19–22.

2245.   Deane, Michael J. "The Main Political Administration as a Factor in Communist Party Control over the Military in the Soviet Union." *Armed Forces and Society* 3 (Winter 1977), 295–324.

2246.   Dement'yev, V. "Political Training in the Kiev Military District: Translated from *Kommunist Vooruzhennykh Sil,* October 1977." *Translations on USSR Military Affairs,* no. 1320 (January 5, 1978), 64–71.

2247.   "The Development of Party-Political Work in the Troops." *Soviet Military Translations,* no. 22 (August 1960), 12–16.

2248.   Donnelly, Christopher N. "Military-Political Infrastructure." In Ray Bonds, ed., *The Soviet War Machine: An Encyclopedia of Russian Military Equipment and Strategy.* New York: Chartwell Books, 1976. pp. 30–41.

2249.   Fomichev, Pavel. "Political Training in the Odessa Military District: Translated from *Voyenno Istoricheskiy Zhurnal,* September 1978." *Translations on USSR Military Affairs,* no. 1394 (November 14, 1978), 13–22.

2250.   Galay, Nikolay. "Dogmatism and the Soviet Armed Forces." *Institute for the Study of the USSR Bulletin* 5 (November 1958), 3–12.

2251.   Heinlein, Joseph J., Jr. "The Main Political Administration in Today's Soviet Forces." *Military Review* 53 (November 1973), 55–64.

2252.   Henderson, B. A. "Communist Indoctrination Methods." *Military Review* 35 (November 1955), 22–38.

2253.   Hittle, John D. "The Military Commissar—An Enigma." *Marine Corps Gazette* 34 (September 1950), 18–20.

2254.   Kalashinik, M. "Political Education in the Soviet Armed Forces." *Soviet Military Review,* no. 10 (October 1965), 12–16.

2255.   Kalinchuk, L. "The Postwar Years." *Soviet Military Review,* no. 6 (June 1977), 57–59.   Party-political work, 1945–1975.

2256.   Mackintosh, Malcolm. "The Political Administration." In Basil H. Liddell-Hart, ed., *The Soviet Army.* London: Weidenfeld & Nicolson, 1956. pp. 233–238.

2257.   _____ . "Soldiers of the Party." *Military Review* 43 (May 1963), 27–31.

2258.   Malinovskiy, Rodion Y. "The Role of the Soviet Political Officer." *Military Review* 44 (September 1964), 94–98.

2259.   Miller, David C. "The Soviet Armed Forces and Political Pressure." *Military Review* 49 (December 1969), 62–68.

2260.   Moroz, I. M. "Important Sector of Political Educational Work." *Soviet Military Review,* no. 3 (March 1974), 10–12.

2261.   _____ . "Interview: Translated from *Kryl'ya Rodiny,* August 1978." *Translations on USSR Military Affairs,* no. 1388 (October 23, 1978), 7–13.

2262.   Niessel, A. "The Political Basis of the Red Army." In Basil H. Liddell-Hart, ed., *The Soviet Army.* London: Weidenfeld & Nicolson, 1956. pp. 222–227.

2263.   Pigurnov, A. "Party-Political Work in Combat Conditions." *Soviet Military Review,* no. 2 (February 1972), 43–45.

2264.   Rogatin, I. "The Effectiveness of Political Work in the Ground Forces Discussed: Translated from *Krasnaya Zvezda,* May 13, 1979." *Translations on USSR Military Affairs,* no. 1458 (August 23, 1979), 17–21.

2265.   Smirnov, Y. "The Soldier and Politics." *Soviet Military Review,* no. 12 (December 1973), 6–7.

2266.   Smith, R. G. "Political Controls within the Structure of the Soviet Armed Forces—Some Problems?" *Royal Air Forces Quarterly* 16 (Spring 1976), 45–49.

2267.   Solntsev, N. "Indoctrination Guidelines for the Soviet Armed Forces: Translated from *Kommunist Vooruzhennykh Sil,* January 1979." *Translations on USSR Military Affairs,* no. 1438 (May 18, 1979), 1–10.

2268.   "To Strengthen the Ties between Officers and the Masses of the Armed Forces: Translated from *Krasnaya Zvezda,* August 21, 1957." *Current Digest of the Soviet Press* 9 (October 2, 1957), 33–34.

2269.   Wainhouse, E. R. "Motivating Ivan: Indoctrinations in the Soviet Army." *Military Review* 35 (March 1956), 48–54.

2270.   Yepishev, Aleksey A. "The Soviet Army, a School of Ideological Education and Discipline." *Soviet Military Review,* no. 2 (February 1977), 2–6.

2271.   Zabolotskiy, G. "Troop Indoctrination Requirements, Instructions: Translated from *Kommunist Vooruzhennykh Sil,* March 1978." *Translations on USSR Military Affairs,* no. 1355 (May 30, 1978), 13–30.

2272.   Zhuravel, V. "Political Information Classes." *Soviet Military Review,* no. 11 (November 1973), 34–35.

DOCUMENTS, PAPERS, AND REPORTS

2273.   Deane, Michael J. "The Evolution, Responsibilities, and Influence of the Main Political Administration of the Soviet Army and Navy under General A. A. Yepishev, May 1962–March 1973." PhD dissertation, University of Miami (Florida), 1974.

2274.   Dmitriev, I. *Party and Political Organs in the Soviet Army.* New York: East European Fund, 1953. 59p.

2275.   Gambolati, Roland L. *Propaganda and Agitation in the Soviet Military.* New York: U.S. Army Institute for Advanced Russian and East European Studies, 1975. 35p.

2276.   Gouré, Leon. *The Military Indoctrination of Soviet Youth.* Strategy papers, no. 16. New York: National Strategy Information Center, 1973. 75p.

2277.   Union of Soviet Socialist Republics. Ministry of Defense. *The Inculcation of Loyalty to the Military Profession in Officer Schools for the Service Branches.* JPRS-6028. Alexandria, Va.: Joint Publication Research Service, 1961. 61p.

Further References

For additional citations relative to the Communist party and the armed forces, see appropriate biographies (e.g., Khrushchev) in section 1:G:2 and general works on the Soviet ground forces (section 4:A).

3. Military Policy and Doctrine, Theory, and Strategy

Military doctrine is the officially approved Soviet system for viewing the problems of war. It covers the nature and methods of waging future war, as well as the organization and preparation of the military. In Russia, the basic principles of doctrine are determined by the political leadership of the Politburo. *Military strategy* is an elaboration of the forms and methods for conducting and directing war, the problems regarding comprehensive strategic support of combat operations, the training objectives for the armed forces as a whole, and the strategic employment of the individual force components in war. Both the political and military leadership are involved in developing strategy.

Strategy is subordinate to doctrine. Military doctrine is overall policy. Using doctrine as a starting point, Soviet military strategists amplify and investigate concrete problems regarding future war. Military doctrine is subject to change. In light of shifting conditions or new theories, the state may either alter or replace existing doctrine. Several stages have marked the development of Soviet military doctrine since the Great Patriotic War.

From 1945 until Stalin's death in 1953, the Soviets confined their military goals primarily to protecting their western flanks by consolidating control over East European "satellites," which formed a buffer zone between the U.S.S.R. and Western Europe. The Russians lacked any significant atomic weapons during this period. Thus, Soviet doctrine included the possibility of only a conventional war with the Western allies, in which Central Europe would be the primary theater of operations.

With the development between 1953 and 1958 of means for delivery of nuclear weapons, the Soviets sought to integrate new weapons systems into military doctrine. However, doctrine continued to emphasize the capability of the Soviet Army, which most likely would be employed in Europe, treating nuclear weapons more as powerful cousins of conventional armaments and holding to traditional principles of war. During this time, Soviet doctrine became the joint doctrine for the Warsaw Pact, formed in 1955.

From 1958 through the early 1960s, the Soviets reviewed their military doctrine extensively and, with shoving from Nikita Khrushchev, concluded that nuclear weapons would be decisive in a future war. War would inevitably be worldwide and would be thermonuclear from the outset, with conventional forces, especially the Soviet ground forces, taking a secondary role. These aspects of Russian doctrine, along with emphasis upon offensive operations and strategic surprise, were promulgated in open-press writings in the early 1960s.

While maintaining that nuclear weapons would be decisive in a future war, Soviet doctrine in the mid-1960s—after the fall of Khrushchev—began to reflect the need for more balanced theater and strategic forces. Analysts recognized that a theater conflict might begin conventionally but would soon escalate to nuclear war.

In the late 1960s and continuing into the 1970s, the U.S.S.R. modernized its conventional forces and apparently considered the limited use of nuclear weapons. However, no major doctrinal shift is evident. The basic tenets of Soviet military doctrine remain consistent: 1) in a future war, nuclear weapons will be decisive; 2) offensive operations and the element of surprise are paramount; 3) war, including thermonuclear war, can be won; and 4) joint efforts of all forces, including large armies, will be required.

The influence of politics on Soviet military doctrine and theory, strategy and policy is not limited to determining their general nature. The resolution of many concrete problems also depends directly on state policy. The Soviets consistently and energetically have attempted to reconcile strategic capabilities with the demands of their military doctrine. This has never taken the form of shaping doctrine to existing capabilities, but rather, has been restricted to developing strategic force structures and equipment in line with the requirements of relatively static doctrine.

The essence of the approved doctrine is instilled in Soviet citizens throughout their lives through such programs as civil defense training, as well as during premilitary training and active and reserve military service. The overall doctrine requires superiority in personnel, armaments, and training both as a deterrent to war and as a means for winning war should the deterrent fail. It also demands a national organization of human and economic resources to support these requirements.

BOOKS

2278.   Baylis, John, et al. *Contemporary Strategy, Theories and Practice.* New York: Holmes & Meier, 1975. 324p.

2279.   Bidwell, Shelford. *Modern Warfare: A Study of Men, Weapons and Theories.* London: Lane, 1973. 242p.

2280.   Brodie, Bernard. *Strategy in the Missile Age.* Princeton, N.J.: Princeton University Press, 1959. 423p.

2281.   DeHuszar, George B., et al. *Soviet Power and Policy.* New York: T. Y. Crowell, 1955. 598p.

2282.   Dinerstein, Herbert S. *War and the Soviet Union: Nuclear Weapons and the Revolution in Soviet Military and Political Thinking.* New York: Praeger, 1962. 268p.

2283.   Douglass, Joseph D., Jr., and Amoretta Hoeber. *Soviet Strategy for Nuclear War.* Stanford, Calif.: Hoover Institution Press, 1979. 138p.

2284.   Erickson, John, ed. *The Military-Technical Revolution.* New York: Praeger, 1966. 284p.

2285.   Garthoff, Raymond L. *The Soviet Image of Future War.* Washington, D.C.: Public Affairs Press, 1959. 240p.

2286.   _____ . *Soviet Military Doctrine.* Glencoe, Ill.: Free Press, 1953. 587p.

2287.   _____ . *Soviet Military Policy: A Historical Analysis.* New York: Praeger, 1966. 276p.

2288.   Heilbrunn, Otto. *Conventional Warfare in the Nuclear Age.* New York: Praeger, 1965. 164p.

2289.   Heselkorn, Avigdor. *The Evolution of Soviet Security Strategy, 1965–1975.* New York: Crane, Russak, 1978. 139p.

2290.   Hobbs, Richard. *The Myth of Victory: What Is Victory in War?* Boulder, Colo.: Westview Press, 1979. 450p.

2291.   Kintner, William R., and Harriet F. Scott, comps. *The Nuclear Revolution in Soviet Military Affairs.* Norman: University of Oklahoma Press, 1968. 420p.

2292.   Milovidov, A. S., and V. G. Kozlov, eds. *The Philosophical Heritage of V. I. Lenin and the Problems of Contemporary War: A Soviet View.* Soviet Military Thought Series, no. 5. Washington, D.C.: U.S. Government Printing Office, 1974. 292p.

2293.   Modrzhinskaya, Ye. D., et al. *Problems of War and Peace.* Moscow: Progress Publishers, 1972.

2294.   Osgood, Robert E. *Limited War Revisited.* Boulder, Colo.: Westview Press, 1979. 124p.

2295.   Parson, Nels A., Jr. *Missiles and the Revolution in Warfare.* Cambridge, Mass.: Harvard University Press, 1962. 245p.

2296.   Semmel, Bernard. *Marxism and the Science of War.* London and New York: Oxford University Press, 1981. 288p.

2297.   Sokolovskiy, Vasiliy D. *Soviet Military Strategy.* Translated from the Russian and edited, with an analysis and commentary, by Harriet F. Scott. 3d ed. New York: Crane, Russak, 1975. 494p.

2298.   Stoessinger, John G. *Why Nations Go to War.* 2d ed. New York: St. Martin's Press, 1978. 246p.

2299.   Vigor, Peter H. *The Soviet View of War, Peace and Neutrality.* Boston, Mass.: Routledge & Kegan Paul, 1975. 256p.

2300.   Wolfe, Thomas W. *Soviet Strategy at the Crossroads.* Cambridge, Mass.: Harvard University Press, 1964. 342p.

ARTICLES

2301.   Abshire, David M., and Robert D. Crane. "Soviet Strategy in the '60's: An Analysis of the Current Russian Debate over Strategy." *Army* 13 (July 1963), 20–21.

2302.   Arbeiter, Juergen B. "A Transparent Figleaf: The Offensive Nature of Soviet Military Doctrine." *Air University Review* 32 (November-December 1980), 93–98.

2303.   Atkeson, Edward B. "Hemisphere Denial: Geo-Political Imperatives and Soviet Strategy." *Strategic Review* 4 (Spring 1976), 29.

2304.   Atkinson, James D. "The Impact of Soviet Theory on Warfare as a Contribution of Politics." *Military Affairs* 24 (Spring 1960), 1–6.

2305.   Bailey-Cowell, G. M. "Detente in Soviet Strategy." *NATO's Fifteen Nations* 20 (December 1975–January 1976), 86–90.

2306.   Barber, Ransom E. "The Conventional Wisdom on Soviet Strategy—Is It Conventional?" *Forum*, no. 17 (Summer 1973), 21–30.

2307.   Barnett, Frank R. "An Overview of Soviet Strategy." *Naval War College Review* 23 (June 1971), 16–21.

2308.   Barrett, Raymond. "Geography and Soviet Strategic Thinking." *Military Review* 50 (January 1970), 17–25.

2309.   Cade, David J. "Russian Military Strategy: A Fresh Look." *Air University Review* 29 (September-October 1978), 18–27.

2310.   Candlin, A. H. S. "Contrast in Strategies: U.S.A. and U.S.S.R." In James L. Moulton, ed., *Brassey's Annual, 1973*. New York: Praeger, 1973. pp. 232–244.

2311.   "Changing Military Thought in the Soviet Union." *World Today* 13 (December 1957), 517–528.

2312.   Clark, Donald L. "Soviet Strategy for the Seventies." *Air University Review* 22 (January-February 1971), 2–18.

2313.   Crane, Robert D. "Soviet Military Policy during the Era of Ballistic Missile Defense." In Denis Dirscherl, ed., *The New Russia*. Dayton, Ohio: Pflaum Press, 1968. pp. 157–170.

2314.   _____ . "The Structure of Soviet Military Thought." *Studies in Soviet Thought* 7 (Spring 1967), 28–34.

2315.   Douglass, Joseph D., Jr. "Soviet Military Thought." *Air Force Magazine* 59 (March 1976), 88–91.

2316.   Dulacki, Leo J. "Soviet Military Strategy." *Marine Corps Gazette* 47 (August 1963), 18–22.

2317.   Emmott, N. "Air Power, Land Power, and Modern Weapons." *RCAF Staff College Journal* (1958), 68–72.

2318.   Erickson, John. "Detente, Deterrence, and 'Military Superiority': A Soviet Dilemma." *World Today* 21 (August 1965), 337–345.

2319.   _____ . "Detente: Soviet Policy and Purpose." *Strategic Review* 4 (Spring 1976), 37–43.

2320.   _____ . "The 'Military Factor' in Soviet Policy." *International Affairs* (London) 39 (April 1963), 214–226.

2321.   _____ . "Soviet Military Policy in the 1980's." *Current History* 75 (October 1978), 97–99.

2322.   _____ . "Soviet Military Policy: Priorities and Perspectives." *Round Table,* no. 256 (October 1974), 364–379.

2323.   _____ . "The Soviet Military System: Doctrine, Technology, and 'Style.'" In John Erickson and E. J. Feuchtwanger, eds., *Soviet Military Power and Performance.* Hamden, Conn;: Archon Books, 1979. pp. 18–44.

2324.   "Five Keys to Soviet Strategy: A Special Report." *Air Force and Space Digest* 44 (October 1961), 29–32.

2325.   Galay, Nikolay. "Khrushchev's Military Doctrine." *Institute for the Study of the USSR Bulletin* 9 (March 1962), 45–48.

2326.   _____ . "New Trends in Soviet Military Doctrine." *Institute for the Study of the USSR Bulletin* 3 (June 1956), 3–12.

2327.   _____ . "Problems of Atomic Warfare and the Soviet Armed Forces." *Institute for the Study of the USSR Bulletin* 2 (April 1955), 3–10.

2328.   _____ . "The Soviet Approach to the Modern Military Revolution." In John Erickson, ed., *The Military-Technical Revolution.* New York: Praeger, 1966. pp. 20–34.

2329.   _____ . "Soviet Military Thinking since Stalin." *Army* 7 (September 1956), 59–61.

2330.   Gallagher, Matthew P. "The Military Role in Soviet Decision-Making." In Michael MccGwire, Ken Booth, and John McDonnell, eds., *Soviet Naval Policy: Objectives and Constraints.* New York: Praeger, 1975. pp. 40–58.

2331.   Garthoff, Raymond L. "Military Power in Soviet Policy." In John Erickson, ed., *The Military-Technical Revolution.* New York: Praeger, 1966. pp. 239–258.

2332.   _____ . "Military Strategy and Soviet Policy." *Soviet Strategy in the Nuclear Age.* New York: Praeger, 1958. pp. 3–17.

2333. _____ . "Military Theory and Practice." In Milorad M. Drachkovitch, ed., *Fifty Years of Communism in Russia.* State College: Pennsylvania State University Press, 1968. pp. 213–244.

2334. _____ . "Significant Features of Soviet Military Doctrine." *Military Review* 34 (March 1955), 3–13.

2335. _____ . "Soviet Military Doctrine on the Decisive Factors in Modern War." *Military Review* 39 (July 1959), 3–22.

2336. _____ . "Soviet Military Theory." *Military Review* 42 (March 1962), 78–87.

2337. _____ . "War and Peace in Soviet Policy." *Russian Review* 20 (April 1961), 121–133.

2338. Gasteyger, Curt. "Modern Warfare and Soviet Strategy." *Survey,* no. 57 (October 1965), 46–55.

2339. Gerasimov, Ivan A. "Kiev Military District Commander on the Mission of the Armed Forces: Translated from *Pod Znamenem Leninizma,* September 1977." *Translations on USSR Military Affairs,* no. 1322 (January 9, 1978), 7–15.

2340. Gordon, Andrew. "Soviet Strategic Crisis Management." *Strategic Review* 3 (Spring 1975), 30–40.

2341. Gouré, Leon. "Soviet Military Doctrine." *Air Force Magazine* 60 (March 1977), 47–50.

2342. Gray, Colin. "War and Peace: The Soviet View." *Air Force Magazine* 59 (October 1976), 28–31.

2343. Green, Murray. "Soviet Military Strategy." *Air Force* 46 (March 1963), 38–42.

2344. Halperin, Morton. "Soviet Military Strategy." *Contemporary Military Strategy.* Boston, Mass.: Little, Brown, 1966. pp. 56–65.

2345. _____ . "Soviet Military Strategy." *Defense Strategies for the Seventies.* Boston, Mass.: Little, Brown, 1971. Chpt. 5.

2346. Hinterhoff, Eugene. "The Evolution of Soviet Strategy and of the Armed Forces." *NATO's Fifteen Nations* 7 (June-July 1962), 110–113.

2347. Holloway, David. "Strategic Concepts and Soviet Policy." *Survival* 13 (November 1971), 364–369.

2348.   Horelick, Arnold L. "Deterrence and Surprise Attack in Soviet Strategic Thought." *RCAF Staff College Journal* (1960), 12–20.

2349.   _____ . "The Strategic Mind-Set of the Soviet Military." *Problems of Communism* 26 (March-April 1977), 80–85.

2350.   Jacobs, Walter D. "Sokolovskiy's Strategy." *Military Review* 43 (July 1963), 9–19.

2351.   Jacobsen, Carl G. "Deterrence or Water Fighting—The Soviet Case: Soviet Military Posture and Its Relevance to Soviet Concepts of Strategy." *Canadian-American Slavic Studies* 8 (Spring 1975), 18–29.

2352.   Jonas, Anne M. "New Dimensions in Soviet Strategy." *Air Force and Space Digest* 51 (January 1968), 22–27.

2353.   Kime, Steve F. "The Soviet View of War." *Comparative Strategy* 2 (Fall 1980), 205.

2354.   Kincade, W. H. "A Strategy for All Seasons." *Bulletin of the Atomic Scientists* 34 (May 1978), 14–20.

2355.   King, Peter. "Two Eyes for a Tooth: The State of Soviet Strategic Doctrine." *Survey* 24 (Winter 1979), 45–56.

2356.   Kolkowicz, Roman. "Strategic Parity and Beyond: Soviet Perspectives." *World Politics* 23 (April 1971), 431–451.

2357.   Laske, Robert M. "Soviet Strategic Thinking, 1917–1962: Some History Reexamined." *Naval War College Review* 24 (February 1972), 24–34.

2358.   LeCheminant, Pierre. "Soviet Military Doctrine: A Possible Pattern of War." In James L. Moulton, ed., *Brassey's Annual, 1959*. New York: Macmillan, 1959. pp. 210–216.

2359.   Lee, William T. "Soviet Military Policy: Objectives and Capabilities." *Air Force Magazine* 62 (March 1979), 54–59.

2360.   Leontin, L. "The Soviet Concept of National Defense." *Military Review* 34 (January 1955), 89–96.

2361.   Long, J. F. L. "Soviet Policy and the Role of the Military." *Royal Air Forces Quarterly* 4 (Winter 1964), 267–271.

2362.   Mackintosh, Malcolm. "The Development of Soviet Military Doctrine since 1918." In Michael Howard, ed., *The Theory and Practice of War: Essays Presented to Captain Basil H. Liddell-Hart on His Seventieth Birthday.* New York: Praeger, 1966. pp. 78–95.

2363. ———— . "The East-West Military Balance and Soviet Defence Policy." In James L. Moulton, ed., *Brassey's Annual, 1972*. New York: Praeger, 1972. pp. 37–49.

2364. ———— . "The Soviet Defense Debate." *Strategy and Tactics of Soviet Foreign Policy*. London and New York: Oxford University Press, 1963. pp. 88–105.

2365. ———— . "Soviet Military Strategy." In Michael MccGwire, ed., *Soviet Naval Developments: Capabilities and Context*. New York: Praeger, 1973. pp. 57–69.

2366. ———— . "Soviet Strategy in World War III." *Army* 10 (May 1960), 23–32.

2367. ———— . "Soviet Thinking on War." *Strategy and Tactics of Soviet Foreign Policy*. London and New York: Oxford University Press, 1963. pp. 299–315.

2368. Mahoney, Shane E. "Military Decision-Making in the U.S.S.R.: The Empirical Past and Conceptual Present." *Armed Forces and Society* 3 (Winter 1977), 271–294.

2369. Malinovskiy, Rodion Y. "Soviet Defense Policy." *Military Review* 46 (October 1966), 85–90.

2370. ———— . "Soviet Strategy." *Survival* 4 (September-October 1962), 229–232.

2371. "Military Doctrine and Military Strategy." *Soviet Military Translations*, no. 143 (May 1964), 14–24.

2372. Monks, Alfred L. "The Evolution of Soviet Military Thinking." *Military Review* 51 (March 1971), 78–93.

2373. Mulley, Frederick W. "Soviet Strategy and Forces." *Politics of Defense*. New York: Praeger, 1962. pp. 32–49.

2374. Nicholl, A. D. "Geography and Strategy." In George M. Saunders, ed., *The Soviet Navy*. New York: Praeger, 1958. pp. 243–259.

2375. Odom, William E. "Sokolovskiy's Strategy Revisited." *Military Review* 44 (October 1964), 49–53.

2376. "On Soviet Military Doctrine." *Soviet Military Translations*, no. 99 (April 1964), 31–44.

2377. Onacewicz, Wlodzimier. "Soviet Military Strategy in Brief." In Robert D. Crane and Wlodzimier Onacewicz, eds., *Soviet Materials on Military Strategy: Inventory and Analysis for 1963*. Washington, D.C.: Center for Strategic Studies, Georgetown University, 1964. pp. 13–33.

2378.   Pappageorge, John G. "The Development of Soviet Military Policy." *Military Review* 52 (July 1972), 36–43.

2379.   Petersen, Philip A. "Flexibility: A Driving Force in Soviet Strategy." *Air Force Magazine* 63 (March 1980), 94–99.

2380.   _____ . "The Soviet Conceptual Framework for the Application of Military Manpower." *Naval War College Review* 34 (May-June 1981), 15–25.

2381.   Pfaltzgraff, Robert L. "The Role of the Soviet Armed Forces, Soviet Military Strategy, and Force Levels." In Kurt London, ed., *The Soviet Union in World Politics.* Boulder, Colo.: Westview Press, 1980. Chpt. 3.

2382.   Pioro, Tadeusz. "Soviet Military Doctrine." *Marine Corps Gazette* 47 (March 1963), 18.

2383.   Quester, George H. "On the Identification of Real and Pretended Communist Military Doctrine." *Journal of Conflict Resolution* 10 (June 1966), 172–180.

2384.   Richelson, J. T. "Soviet Strategic Doctrine and Limited Nuclear Operations: A Metagame Analysis." *Journal of Conflict Resolution* 23 (June 1979), 326–336.

2385.   Rummel, Rudolph J. "Detente and Reality." *Strategic Review* 4 (Fall 1976), 33–43.

2386.   Scott, William F. "Soviet Military Doctrine and Strategy: Realities and Misunderstandings." *Strategic Review* 3 (Summer 1975), 57–66.

2387.   Shackleton, N. A. "Soviet Strategy in the Cold War: A Reappraisal." *Canadian Army Journal* 18 (Fall 1964), 2–15.

2388.   Sidelnikov, Ivan. "On Soviet Military Doctrine." *Air University Quarterly Review* 13 (Summer 1962), 142–150.

2389.   Sidorov, P. "Foundations of Soviet Military Doctrine." *Military Review* 52 (December 1972), 89–91.

2390.   Smirnov, M. V. "Soviet Military Theory." *Military Review* 42 (March 1962), 78–87.

2391.   Sokol, Anthony E. "The Soviet's War Potential." *Military Review* 33 (December 1953), 44–60.

2392.   Sokolovskiy, Vasiliy D. "Current Military Strategy." *Survival* 8 (August 1968), 266–270.

2393. _____ . "On the Soviet Military Doctrine." *Soviet Military Review*, no. 4 (April 1965), 6–9.

2394. _____ . "Soviet Views of Modern Military Strategy." *Soviet Military Translations*, no. 246 (April 1964), 1–12.

2395. _____ . "On Contemporary Military Strategy." In William R. Kintner and Harriet F. Scott, eds., *The Nuclear War in Soviet Military Affairs*. Norman: University of Oklahoma Press, 1968. pp. 260–277.

2396. _____ , and M. I. Cherednichenko. "The Military Revolution." *Survival* 6 (November-December 1964), 280–283.

2397. "Soviet Attitudes on the Use of Military Power: An Analysis." *Army Information Digest* 15 (June 1960), 32–37.

2398. "The Soviet General Staff Takes Stock: Changes in Military Doctrine." *World Today* 11 (November 1955), 492–502.

2399. Spahr, William J. "The Soviet Military Decisionmaking Process." *Parameters* 2 (Summer 1972), 51–62.

2400. Starr, Richard F. "Current Soviet Military Strategy." *Naval War College Review* 18 (January 1966), 1–23.

2401. Strauz-Hupe, Robert. "The Protracted Conflict." *Air Force* 42 (April 1959), 56–63.

2402. _____ . "Soviet Strategy, 1962–1970." In David M. Abshire and Richard V. Allen, eds., *National Security*. New York: Praeger, 1963. pp. 3–19.

2403. Van den Berk, L. J. M. "Strategic Concepts of the Russian High Command." *NATO's Fifteen Nations* 10 (December 1965–January 1966), 58–60.

2404. Vernon, Graham D. "Soviet Options for War: Nuclear or Conventional?" *Strategic Review* 7 (Winter 1979), 56–66.

2405. Vick, Alan J. "Soviet Military Forces and Strategy Come of Age." *Air University Review* 32 (January-February 1981), 18–26.

2406. Vigor, Peter H. "Doubts and Difficulties Confronting a Would-Be Soviet Attacker." *Journal of the Royal United Service Institution for Defence Studies* 125 (June 1980), 32–38.

2407. _____ . "The Semantics of Deterrence and Defense." In Michael MccGwire, Ken Booth, and John McDonnell, eds., *Soviet Naval Policy: Objectives and Constraints*. New York: Praeger, 1975. pp. 471–478.

2408. _____ . "The Size and Quality of the Soviet Armed Forces and Soviet Military Policy." *NATO's Fifteen Nations* 22 (October-November 1978), 24–26.

2409. _____ . "The Soviet View of War." In Michael MccGwire, ed., *Soviet Naval Developments: Capability and Context.* New York: Praeger, 1973. pp. 16–30.

2410. _____ , and John Erickson. "The Soviet View of the Theory and Practice of War." *Journal of the Royal United Service Institution* 115 (June 1970), 3–11.

2411. Whiting, Kenneth R. "The Past and Present of Soviet Military Doctrine." *Air University Quarterly Review* 11 (Spring 1959), 38–60.

2412. _____ . "Some Soviet Views of American Strategy." *Air University Quarterly Review* 14 (Summer 1963), 114–130.

2413. Wilson, William T. "A New Vitality in Soviet Defense Posture: Variations to Standard Soviet Military Strategy." *Air University Review* 20 (July-August 1969), 78–86.

2414. Wolfe, Thomas W. "The Impact of Khrushchev's Downfall on Soviet Military Policy and Detente." In Eleanor L. Dulles, ed., *Detente: Cold War Strategies in Transition.* New York: Praeger, 1965. pp. 280–303.

2415. _____ . "Military Policy: A Soviet Dilemma." *Current History* 40 (October 1965), 201–207.

2416. _____ . "Problems of Soviet Defense Policy under the New Regime." *Slavic Review* 27 (June 1965), 175–188.

2417. _____ . "Shifts in Soviet Strategic Thought." *Foreign Affairs* 42 (April 1964), 475–486.

2418. _____ . "Some New Developments in the Soviet Military Debate." *Orbis* 8 (Fall 1964), 550–562.

2419. _____ . "Soviet Military Policy after Khrushchev." In Alexander Dallin and Thomas B. Larson, eds., *Soviet Politics after Khrushchev.* Englewood Cliffs, N.J.: Prentice-Hall, 1968. Chpt. 5.

2420. Wolk, Herman S. "Debating Deterrence." *Air University Review* 30 (July-August 1979), 80–81.

2421. Yeuell, Donovan P. "The Shift in Soviet Strategy." *Military Review* 45 (June 1965), 87–92.

2422.   Zavyalov, I. G. "On Soviet Military Doctrine: Translated from *Krasnaya Zvezda,* March 30–31, 1967." In William R. Kintner and Harriet F. Scott, eds., *The Nuclear Revolution in Soviet Military Affairs.* Norman: University of Oklahoma Press, 1968. pp. 374–389.

2423.   Zimmerman, William. "Sokolovskiy and His Critics." *Journal of Conflict Resolution* 8 (September 1964), 322–328.

DOCUMENTS, PAPERS, AND REPORTS

2424.   Atkeson, Edward B. *The Dimensions of Military Strategy.* Military Issues Research Memo. Carlisle Barracks, Pa.: Strategic Studies Institute, U.S. Army War College, 1977. 26p.

2425.   Collins, Edward M. "The Evolution of Soviet Strategy under Khrushchev." PhD dissertation, Georgetown University, 1966.

2426.   Dinerstein, Herbert S. *The Revolution in Soviet Strategic Thinking.* RAND Memorandum RM-1927. Santa Monica, Calif.: RAND Corporation, 1957. 24p.

2427.   Goldhamer, Herbert. *Reality and Belief in Military Affairs: A First Draft.* RAND Report R-2448-NA. Santa Monica, Calif.: RAND Corporation, 1979. 196p.

2428.   Gouré, Leon. *Soviet Commentary on the Doctrine of Limited Nuclear War.* RAND Translation T-82. Santa Monica, Calif.: RAND Corporation, 1958.

2429.   _____ . *Soviet Limited War Doctrine.* RAND Paper P-2744. Santa Monica, Calif.: RAND Corporation, 1963. 15p.

2430.   Green, Murray. *Soviet Military Strategy Brought Up to Date.* Washington, D.C.: Headquarters, U.S. Air Force, 1963. 280p.

2431.   Holst, Johan J. *Comparative U.S. and Soviet Deployments, Doctrines, and Arms Limitations.* Occasional Paper. Chicago, Ill.: Center for Policy Study, University of Chicago, 1971. 60p.

2432.   Institute for Strategic Studies. *Problems of Modern Strategy.* Adelphi Papers, no. 54. 2 vols. London, 1969.

2433.   Jones, Isaac R. *Soviet Military Strategy.* Professional paper. Maxwell AFB, Ala.: Air War College, Air University, 1974. 51p.

2434.   Kolkowicz, Roman. *The Dilemma of Superpower: Soviet Policy and Strategy in Transition.* Arlington, Va.: Institute for Defense Analysis, 1967.

2435.   Lambeth, Benjamin S. *How to Think about Soviet Military Doctrine.* RAND Paper P-5939. Santa Monica, Calif.: RAND Corporation, 1978. 22p.

2436.   Mackintosh, Malcolm. *Contemporary Soviet Military Doctrine.* Oxford, Eng.: St. Anthony's College, 1959. 18p.

2437.   Monks, Alfred L. "Soviet Military Doctrine, 1964 to Armed Forces Day, 1969." PhD dissertation, University of Pennsylvania, 1969.

2438.   Pauker, Guy J. *Military Implications of a Possible World Order Crisis in the 1980's.* RAND Report R-2003-AF. Santa Monica, Calif.: RAND Corporation, 1977. 101p.

2439.   Rehm, Allan S. *An Assessment of Military Operations Research in the U.S.S.R.* Professional paper, no. 116. Arlington, Va.: Center for Naval Analysis, Department of the Navy, 1973. 19p.

2440.   Scott, Harriet F. *The Soviet View of the Character and Features of Modern War.* Technical Note SSC-TN-8260-1. Stanford, Calif.: Stanford Research Institute, 1969.

2441.   _____ , and John Erickson. *Soviet Military Doctrine: Its Formulation and Dissemination.* Stanford, Calif.: Stanford Research Institute, 1971.

2442.   Sonnenfeldt, Helmut, and William G. Hyland. *Soviet Perspectives on Security.* Adelphi papers, no. 150. London: International Institute for Strategic Studies, 1979. 24p.

2443.   Union of Soviet Socialist Republics. Ministry of Defense. *The Development of Soviet Military Theory in the Postwar World.* JPRS-24667. Alexandria, Va.: Joint Publication Research Service, 1964. 18p.

2444.   United States. Air Force. Air War College. *Selected Soviet Writings on Military Power and Strategy.* Translated from the Russian. Maxwell AFB, Ala.: Text Development Division, Air University, 1976. Unpaged.

2445.   Wolfe, Thomas W. *The Communist Outlook on War.* RAND Paper P-3640. Santa Monica, Calif.: RAND Corporation, 1967.

2446.   _____ . *The Impact of Khrushchev's Downfall on Soviet Military Policy.* RAND Paper P-3025. Santa Monica, Calif.: RAND Corporation, 1964. 38p.

2447.   _____ . *The Military Dimension in the Making of Secret Foreign and Defense Policy.* RAND Paper P-6024. Santa Monica, Calif.: RAND Corporation, 1977. 44p.

2448.   _____ . *Military Power and Soviet Policy.* RAND Paper P-5388. Santa Monica, Calif.: RAND Corporation, 1975. 82p.

2449.   _____ . *Problems of Soviet Defense Policy under the New Regime.* RAND Paper P-3098. Santa Monica, Calif.: RAND Corporation, 1965. 27p.

2450.   _____ . *Some Recent Signs of Reaction Against Prevailing Soviet Doctrinal Emphasis on Missiles.* RAND Paper P-2929. Santa Monica, Calif.: RAND Corporation, 1964. 11p.

2451.   _____ . *Soviet Military Trends under the Brezhnev-Kosygin Regime.* RAND Paper P-3556. Santa Monica, Calif.: RAND Corporation, 1967. 29p.

2452.   _____ . *Soviet Military Policy under Khrushchev's Successors.* RAND Paper P-3168. Santa Monica, Calif.: RAND Corporation, 1965. 34p.

2453.   _____ . *The Soviet Military Scene: Institutional and Defense Policy Considerations.* RAND Memorandum RM-4913-PR. Santa Monica, Calif.: RAND Corporation, 1966. 180p.

2454.   _____ . *Soviet Military Theory: An Additional Source of Insight into Its Development.* RAND Paper P-3258. Santa Monica, Calif.: RAND Corporation, 1965. 54p.

2455.   _____ . *Soviet Policy in the Setting of a Changing Power Balance.* RAND Paper P-4055. Santa Monica, Calif.: RAND Corporation, 1969.

2456.   _____ . *Soviet Strategic Thought in Transition.* RAND Paper P-2906. Santa Monica, Calif.: RAND Corporation, 1964. 21p.

2457.   _____ . *Soviet Strategy at the Crossroads.* RAND Memorandum RM-4085-PR. Santa Monica, Calif.: RAND Corporation, 1964. 338p.

2458.   _____ . Trends in Soviet Thinking on Theater Warfare, Conventional Operations and Limited War. RAND Memorandum RM-4305-PR. Santa Monica, Calif.: RAND Corporation, 1964. 105p.

Further References

See also section 4:B for the doctrine and policy of the Soviet ground forces.

B. The Soviet Economy and the Military

1. Defense Expenditures

Soviet military expenditures, while impressive in the 1970s, were tremendously burdensome for the Soviet citizenry. According to Central Intelligence Agency studies, Soviet military spending from 1970 to 1979 exceeded U.S. expenditures by 30 percent. In 1979, the $165 billion that Russians poured into defense was almost 50 percent higher than the $108 billion expended by Americans. Pentagon and CIA analysts estimate that between 11 and 14 percent of the U.S.S.R.'s gross national product went to armed forces activities during the 1970s, as compared to 5 to 8 percent for the United States. This lopsided allotment severely damaged the Russian civilian economy and could force difficult choices on the Kremlin leadership in the near future.

Examples of difficulties within the Soviet economy include agricultural failures, a growing energy problem, labor shortages, and a significant "computer gap"—and some of these problems directly affect the military. U.S. intelligence projects only a 3 percent growth of the Russian economy in the 1980s, compared with gains of 6 percent or more in the 1950s; the rate of capital growth is expected to decline.

Despite these economic worries, it is anticipated that the Soviet weapons industry will continue to work at a brisk pace as the ground forces, together with other services, receive new equipment and add more men.[1]

---

1. See Robert P. Martin, "Special Report: How Strong Is Russia," *U.S. News and World Report* 88 (February 11, 1980), 18–19.

BOOKS

2459.   Holzmann, Franklyn D. *Financial Checks on Soviet Defense Expenditures.* Boston Mass.: D. C. Heath, 1975. 103p.

2460.   Lee, William T. *Estimation of Soviet Defense Expenditures, 1955–1975: An Unconventional Approach.* New York: Praeger, 1977. 358p.

2461.   Menken, Jules. *The Economics of Defence.* London: Ampersand, 1955. 100p.

ARTICLES

2462.   Bartenev, S. "The Economic Base of Defense Potential." *Soviet Military Review,* no. 8 (August 1973), 2–5.

2463.   Becker, Abraham. "The Meaning and Measure of Soviet Military Expenditure." In U.S. Congress. Joint Economic Committee, *Soviet Economy in a Time of Change: A Compendium of Papers.* 96th Cong., 1st sess. 2 vols. Washington, D.C.: U.S. Government Printing Office, 1979. I: 352–368.

2464.   Brownlow, Cecil. "Soviet Military Spending Stressed." *Aviation Week and Space Technology* 96 (February 21, 1972), 14–16.

2465.   Galay, Nikolay. "The Burden of Soviet Military Expenditure." *Institute for the Study of the USSR Bulletin* 8 (March 1961), 29–34.

2466.   _____ . "Soviet Economic Reorganization: The Military Significance." *Institute for the Study of the USSR Bulletin* 4 (June 1957), 21–25.

2467.   Graham, Daniel O. "The Soviet Military Budget Controversy." *Air Force Magazine* 59 (May 1976), 33–37.

2468.   Hansen, Philip. "Analysis of Soviet Defense Expenditures." In Michael MccGwire, Ken Booth, and John McDonnell, eds., *Soviet Naval Policy: Objectives and Constraints.* New York: Praeger, 1975. pp. 123–126.

2469.   Hardt, John P. "Soviet Economic Capabilities and Defense Resources." In Grayson Kirk and Nils H. Wessell, eds., *The Soviet Threat: Myths and Realities.* New York: Praeger, 1978. pp. 122–134.

2470.   Holzmann, Franklyn D. "Is There a Soviet-U.S. Military Spending Gap?" *Challenge* 23 (September-October 1980), 3–9.

2471.   International Institute for Strategic Studies. "Comparative Defense Expenditure, Gross National Product, and Manpower Figures, 1952–1972." *Air Force Magazine* 56 (December 1973), 120–121.

2472.   Krylov, Konstantin K. "The Soviet Military-Economic Establishment." *Military Review* 51 (November 1971), 89–97.

2473.   Lee, William T. "Military Economics in the U.S.S.R." *Air Force Magazine* 59 (March 1976), 48–51.

2474.   _____ . "Soviet Defense Spending: Planned Growth, 1976–1980." *Strategic Review* 5 (Winter 1977), 74–79.

2475.   _____ . "Trends in Soviet Military Spending." *Air Force Magazine* 60 (March 1977), 84–87.

2476.   Leggett, Robert E., and Sheldon T. Rabin. "A Note on the Meaning of the Soviet Defense Budget." *Soviet Studies* 30 (October 1978), 561.

2477.   Reitz, James T. "Military Readiness of the Soviet Economy." *East Europe* 21 (May 1972), 5–10.

2478.   Schaefer, Henry W. "Soviet Power and Intentions: Military-Economic Choices." In U.S. Congress. Joint Economic Committee, *Soviet Economy in a Time of Change: A Compendium of Papers.* 96th Cong., 1st sess. 2 vols. Washington, D.C.: U.S. Government Printing Office, 1979. I, 341–351.

2479.   Sosnovy, Timothy. "The Soviet Military Budget." *Foreign Affairs* 42 (April 1964), 487–494.

2480.   "Soviet Defense Expenditures." *Air Force Magazine* 59 (December 1976), 49–50.

2481.   "Soviet Defense Spending Continues to Exceed U.S." *Aviation Week and Space Technology* 108 (January 23, 1978), 15–16.

2482.   "Soviet Military Spending Found to Top U.S." *Aviation Week and Space Technology* 111 (October 27, 1979), 67.

DOCUMENTS, PAPERS, AND REPORTS

2483.   Alexander, Arthur J.; Abraham S. Becker; and William E. Hoehn, Jr. *The Significance of Divergent U.S.-U.S.S.R. Military Expenditure.* RAND Note RN-1000-AF. Santa Monica, Calif.: RAND Corporation, 1979. 57p.

2484.   Kershaw, Andrew. *The Economic War Potential of the U.S.S.R.* RAND Paper P-182. Santa Monica, Calif.: RAND Corporation, 1950. 12p.

2485.   Kuchinski, John G. "A Quantitative Analysis of Defense Expenditure Patterns in Warsaw Treaty Organization Countries, 1960–1974." MA thesis, U.S. Naval Postgraduate School, 1978. 165p.

2486.   Lee, William T. *Soviet Defense Expenditures in the Era of SALT.* Report 79-1. Washington, D.C.: United States Strategic Institute, 1979.

2487.   ———. *Trends in Soviet Defense Expenditure.* AAC-TR-10001/79. Washington, D.C.: Analytical Assessments Corporation, 1979.

2488.   United States. Arms Control and Disarmament Agency. *World Military Expenditures and Arms Trade, 1963–1973.* Publication, no. 74. Washington, D.C.: U.S. Government Printing Office, 1975. 123p.

2489.   United States. Central Intelligence Agency. National Foreign Assessment Center. *A Dollar Comparison of Soviet and U.S. Defense Activities.* Washington, D.C.: Document Expediting Project, Exchange and Gift Division, Library of Congress, 1976–. v. 1–.

2490. _____ . *Estimated Soviet Defense Spending in Rubles, 1970–75.* Washington, D.C.: Document Expediting Project, Exchange and Gift Division, Library of Congress, 1976. 17p.

2491. _____ . *Estimated Soviet Defense Spending: Trends and Prospects.* Washington, D.C.: Document Expediting Project, Exchange and Gift Division, Library of Congress, 1978–. v. 1–.

2492. _____ . *The Soviet State Budget since 1965: A Research Paper.* SF 77-10529. Washington, D.C.: Document Expediting Project, Exchange and Gift Division, Library of Congress, 1977. 40p.

2493. United States. Congress. House. Permanent Select Committee on Intelligence. *CIA Estimates on Soviet Defense Spending: Hearings.* 96th Cong., 2d sess. Washington, D.C.: U.S. Government Printing Office, 1980. 95p.

2494. United States. Congress. Joint Economic Committee. *The Economic Basis of the Russian Military Challenge to the United States: Hearings.* 91st Cong., 1st sess. Washington, D.C.: U.S. Government Printing Office, 1969. 55p.

2495. _____ . *Economic Performance and the Military Burden in the Soviet Union: Hearings.* 91st Cong., 2d sess. Washington, D.C.: U.S. Government Printing Office, 1970.

2496. _____ . *The Soviet Economy in a New Perspective: A Compendium of Papers.* 94th Cong., 2d sess. Washington, D.C.: U.S. Government Printing Office, 1976. 821p.

2497. _____ . Subcommittee on Economic Statistics. *Comparisons of the United States and Soviet Economies: Supplemental Statements on the Costs and Benefits to the Soviet Union of Its Bloc and Pact System, Prepared by the Central Intelligence Agency.* 81st Cong., 2d sess. Washington, D.C.: U.S. Government Printing Office, 1960. 50p.

2498. _____ . Subcommittee on Priorities and Economy in Government. *Allocation of Resources in the Soviet Union and China, 1977: Hearings.* 95th Cong., 1st sess. 4 pts. Washington, D.C.: U.S. Government Printing Office, 1977.

2499. _____ . *Allocation of Resources in the Soviet Union and China, 1978: Hearings.* 4 pts. 95th Cong., 2d sess. Washington, D.C.: U.S. Government Printing Office, 1978.

2500. Walker, Robert A. "Methodologies for Estimating and Comparing Soviet Defense Expenditures." PhD dissertation, University of Southern California, 1979.

Further References

Limited additional information is found in the next sction, 3:B:2, on weapons procurement.

2. Weapons Procurement

Despite consumer difficulties engendered by high military expenditure, Soviet political leaders continue to procure new and improved weapons just as they have throughout the past three and a half decades. Much of this development is based on steady R & D and an insistence on simple, reliable, and relatively easily manufactured models.

In many cases, older weapons, such as the 7.62mm Goryunov heavy machine gun, remain in service but are undergoing replacement. Some famous weapons like the Kalashnikov AK-47 assault rifle have been modified and upgraded. Progress in tank design has followed a logical progression since the T-34, resulting in the T-54, T-55, T-62, and the latest model, the T-72, while Russian armored personnel carriers (APCs) and infantry fighting vehicles (IFVs) are considered among the world's finest.

Soviet weapons procurement has been great across the board. Since 1964, the land forces have seen an increase in artillery tubes and rocket launchers to 20,000, up nearly double from 11,000. The number of tanks have increased during the same period from 30,000 to 45,000. In the 1977–1979 period, according to U.S. Defense Department figures, the Soviets outbuilt the United States by a yearly margin of 5,000 to 1,000 in combat vehicles (e.g., APCs) and 2,000 to 650 in tanks. Quality has improved rapidly as has reliability, based on the necessity for Soviet defense plants to compete for new weapons contracts.

BOOKS

2501.   Gallagher, Matthew P., and Karl F. Spielmann. *Soviet Decision-Making for Defense: A Critique of U.S. Perspectives on the Arms Race.* New York: Praeger, 1972. 102p.

2502.   Langford, David. *War in 2080: The Future of Military Technology.* New York: William Morrow, 1979. 232p.

2503.   Lomov, Nikolay A., ed. *Scientific-Technical Progress and the Revolution in Military Affairs: A Soviet View.* Translated from the Russian. Soviet Military Thought Series, no. 3. Washington, D.C.: U.S. Government Printing Office, 1974. 279p.

2504.   Pokrovskiy, Georgiy I. *Science and Technology in Contemporary War.* Translated from the Russian. New York: Praeger, 1959. 180p.

2505.   Shabad, Theodore. *Basic Industrial Resources of the U.S.S.R.* New York: Columbia University Press, 1969. 393p.

2506.   Sutton, Anthony C. *National Suicide: Military Aid to the Soviet Union.* New Rochelle, N.Y.: Arlington House, 1973. 283p.   On U.S. technical assistance, e.g., computers, trucks.

2507.   _____ . *Western Technology and Soviet Economic Development, 1917–1965.* 3 vols. Stanford, Calif.: Stanford University Press, 1968– 1973.

ARTICLES

2508.   Agursky, Mikhail, and Hannes Adomeit. "The Soviet Military-Industrial Complex." *Survey* 24 (Spring 1979), 106–124.

2509.   Aleveyev, N. "Scientific and Technological Progress and the Armed Forces." *Soviet Military Review,* no. 2 (February 1979), 2–7.

2510.   Anureyev, I. "Scientific Progress and Defensive Potential." *Soviet Military Review,* no. 2 (February 1976), 13–15.

2511.   Ashley, Eric. "Science and the Soviet Army." In Basil H. Liddell-Hart, ed., *The Soviet Army.* London: Weidenfeld & Nicolson, 1956. pp. 452–460.

2512.   Aspaturian, Vernon V. "The Soviet Military-Industrial Complex—Does It Exist?" *Journal of International Affairs* 26 (1972), 1–28.

2513.   Butz, J. S. "Soviet Union Decentralizes Weapon System Authority." *Aviation Week and Space Technology* 69 (November 17–24, 1958), 50–58, 91–104.

2514.   Cane, J. W. "The Technology of Modern Weapons for Limited Military Use." *Orbis* 22 (Spring 1978), 217–266.

2515.   Cherednichenko, M. I. "Conventional Weapons and the Prospects of Their Development." In N. A. Lomov, ed., *Scientific-Technical Progress and the Revolution in Military Affairs: A Soviet View.* Translated from the Russian. Soviet Military Thought Series, no. 3. Washington, D.C.: U.S. Government Printing Office, 1974. pp. 73–98.

2516.   Deane, Michael J., and Mark E. Miller. "Science and Technology in Soviet Military Planning." *Strategic Review* 5 (Summer 1977), 77–86.

2517.   DeVore, Charles. "Trends in Soviet Military Technology." *Signal* 30 (July 1976), 47–50.

2518.   DeWitt, N. "Soviet Research and Science Reorganized." *Aviation Week and Space Technology* 75 (September 11, 1961), 50–73.

2519.   Foster, John S., Jr. "The U.S.S.R. Is Headed toward Technological Superiority." *Air Force Magazine* 54 (August 1971), 28–35.

2520.   Gallik, Daniel. "The Military Burden and Arms Control." In Holland Hunter, ed., *The Future of the Soviet Economy, 1978–1985.* Boulder, Colo.: Westview Press, 1978. Chpt. 4.

2521.   Gooch, William A. "Soviet Design Philosophy and Armor." *Armor* 81 (September-October 1972), 17–19.

2522.   Head, Richard G. "Technology and the Military Balance: The U.S. and Soviet R & D Systems." *Foreign Affairs* 56 (April 1978), 544–563; 57 (Fall 1978), 207–213.

2523.   Herold, Robert C., and Shane E. Mahoney. "Military Hardware Procurement: Some Comparative Observations on Soviet and American Policy Processes." *Comparative Politics* 6 (July 1974), 571–599.

2524.   Heuer, Jill E. "Soviet Professional, Scientific, and Engineering Manpower." *Air University Review* 30 (July-August 1979), 62–67.

2525.   Hollist, W. L. "Analysis of Arms Processes in the United States and Soviet Union." *International Studies Quarterly* 21 (September 1977), 503–528.

2526.   Holloway, David. "Technological Change and Military Procurement." In Michael MccGwire and John McDonnell, eds., *Soviet Naval Influence: Domestic and Foreign Dimensions.* New York: Praeger, 1977. pp. 123–132.

2527.   ———— . "Technology and Political Decision in Soviet Armaments Policy." *Journal of Peace Research* 11 (Fall 1974), 257–279.

2528.   Hull, Andrew W. "Soviet Long-Range Planning." *Armor* 87 (July-August 1978), 20–23.

2529.   ———— . "R & D within the Soviet Ministry of Defense." *Army Research, Development, and Acquisition* 21 (September-October 1980), 36–37.

2530.   Jahn, Egbert. "The Role of the Armaments Complex in Soviet Society." *Journal of Peace Research* 12 (Fall 1975), 179–194.

2531.   Konoplyov, Vasily. "Military Practice and Scientific Foresight." *Soviet Military Review,* no. 5 (May 1974), 5–7.

2532.   Krylov, Konstantin A. "Soviet Armaments Project Organization." *Military Review* 53 (July 1973), 45–50.

2533.   Lee, William T. "Politico-Military-Industrial Complex of the U.S.S.R." *Journal of International Affairs* 26 (Spring 1972), 73–86.

2534.   Leitenberg, Milton. "The Counterpart of Defense Industry Conversion in the United States: The U.S.S.R. Economy, Defense Industry, and Military Expenditure." *Journal of Peace Research* 16 (March 1979), 263–277.

2535.   Lomov, Nikolay A. "Scientific-Technical Progress and the Revolution in Military Affairs." *Military Review* 54 (July 1974), 33–39.

2536.   McDonnell, John A. "The Defense Industry." In David R. Jones, ed., *Soviet Armed Forces Review Annual, 1977.* Gulf Breeze, Fla.: Academic International Press, 1978. pp. 94–99.

2537.   _____ . "The Soviet Defense Industry as a Pressure Group." In Michael MccGwire, Ken Booth, and John McDonnell, eds., *Soviet Naval Policy: Objectives and Constraints.* New York: Praeger, 1975. pp. 87–122.

2538.   "Military Production in the U.S.S.R." *NATO's Fifteen Nations* 21 (June-July 1976), 46–47.

2539.   Miranovich, G. "Tank Proving Ground Operations Discussed: Translated from *Krasnaya Zvezda,* September 9, 1977." *Translations on USSR Military Affairs,* no. 1327 (January 27, 1978), 10–14.

2540.   "Moscow's Military Machine: The Best of Everything." *Time* 95 (May 4, 1970), 36–40.

2541.   Robinson, Clarence A., Jr. "Soviets Press Technology Gains." *Aviation Week and Space Technology* 104 (February 9, 1976), 12–15.

2542.   Schuster, Edward J. "The Impact of Science and Technology on War." *Social Justice Review* 58 (January 1966), 360–364.

2543.   "Soviets Press Technical Modernization of Military Services." *Aviation Week and Space Technology* 78 (March 11, 1963), 92–95.

2544.   Spielmann, Karl F. "Defense Industrialists in the U.S.S.R." In Dale R. Herspring and Ivan Volgyes, eds., *Civil-Military Relations in the Communist System.* Boulder, Colo.: Westview Press, 1978. Chpt. 5.

2545.   Ulsamer, Edgar. "Russia's Drive to Technical Productivity." *Air Force Magazine* 58 (August 1975), 68–69.

2546.   _____ . "The Soviet Objective: Technological Supremacy." *Air Force Magazine* 57 (June 1974), 22–27.

2547.   ———— . "Technological Initiative: A Priceless Asset." *Air Force Magazine* 58 (June 1975), 26–31.

2548.   ———— . "The U.S.S.R. Lifts the Technological Curtain." *Air Force Magazine* 56 (August 1973), 24–29.

2549.   Volchkov, B. "Soviet Heavy Industry's Defense Role: Translated from *Krasnaya Zvezda*, November 17, 1971." *Current Digest of the Soviet Press* 23 (December 14, 1971), 1–4.

2550.   Vorona, Jack. "The Soviet March toward Technological Superiority." *Defense '80*, no. 3 (March 1980), 1–12.

2551.   Vydrin, I. F. "The Soldier and Combat Equipment." *Soviet Military Review*, no. 7 (July 1968), 8–11.

2552.   Warner, Edward L. "The Bureaucratic Politics of Weapons Procurement." In Michael MccGwire, Ken Booth, and John McDonnell, eds., *Soviet Naval Policy: Objectives and Constraints*. New York: Praeger, 1975. pp. 66–86.

DOCUMENTS, PAPERS, AND REPORTS

2553.   Albritton, Britt L. "Weapons Development as Catalyst in Elite Transformation: The Case of the Soviet Military." PhD dissertation, University of Maryland, 1974.

2554.   Alexander, Arthur J. *Armor Development in the Soviet Union and the United States*. RAND Report R-1860-NA. Santa Monica, Calif.: RAND Corporation, 1976. 142p.

2555.   ———— . *Decision Making in Soviet Weapons Procurement*. Adelphi papers, nos. 147–148. 2 vols. London: International Institute for Strategic Studies, 1979.

2556.   ———— . *The Process of Soviet Weapons Design*. RAND Paper P-6137. Santa Monica, Calif.: RAND Corporation, 1978. 37p.

2557.   ———— . *Weapons Acquisition in the Soviet Union, the United States, and France*. RAND Paper P-4989. Santa Monica, Calif.: RAND Corporation, 1973. 33p.

2558.   Basiuk, Victor. *Technology and World Power*. Headline series, no. 200. New York: Foreign Policy Association, 1970. 63p.

2559.   Georgetown University. Center for Strategic Studies. *The Soviet Military-Technological Challenge*. Special Report Series, no. 6. Washington, D.C., 1967. 98p.

2560.   Holloway, David. *Technology, Management, and the Soviet Military Establishment*. Adelphi papers, no. 76. London: Institute for Strategic Studies, 1971. 44p.

2561.   Kassel, Simon. *The Relationship between Science and the Military in the Soviet Union*. RAND Report R-1457-DDRE/ARPA. Santa Monica, Calif.: RAND Corporation, 1974. 46p.

2562.   Kolkowicz, Roman. *The Impact of Technology on the Soviet Military: A Challenge to Traditional Military Professionalism*. RAND Memorandum RM-4198-PR. Santa Monica, Calif.: RAND Corporation, 1964.

2563.   Shidlovskiy, A. A. *Principles of Pyrotechnics*. Translated from the Russian. Report FTD-HC-23-1704-74. Wright Patterson AFB, Ohio: Foreign Technology Division, U.S. Air Force, 1974. 534p.

2564.   United States. Central Intelligence Agency. National Foreign Assessment Center. *Directory of Soviet Research Organizations*. Washington, D.C.: Document Expediting Project, Exchange and Gift Division, Library of Congress, 1978. 290p.

Further References

Additional information is found in some of the general titles cited in sections 3:A:3 and 3:B:1.

4 / The Soviet Ground Forces, 1946 to the Present

Introduction

THE SOVIET Ground Forces (Sukhoputnyye Voyska) or Soviet Army, the name was changed from Red Army in 1946, has been called "the most powerful land army in the world" by the U.S. Defense Intelligence Agency. With a strength of 1.8 million troops in 167 highly mobile divisions, the army constitutes the largest of the five major components of the Soviet armed forces. Although of secondary status in the Khrushchev era, this component has since about 1967 been the focus of expansion and reemphasis. Traditionally, Imperial Russian and Red armies were characterized by horse-drawn artillery and "hordes" of men whose lives were lost in "human-wave" charges. Today, the Soviet ground forces are highly modernized and well equipped, possessing great firepower and mobility.

In the years immediately following the Great Patriotic War, Stalin employed the threat of overwhelming land power against Europe as a counterpoise to American nuclear power. He also believed that in any future war, theater forces would be employed as they were in World War II. Therefore, for ground forces, mass was all important. Maintaining millions of soldiers proved a heavy burden on the Soviet Union's postwar reconstruction. Upon the demise of Stalin and the emergence of a credible Russian strategic retaliatory capability, the primacy of ground forces gave way to nuclear forces and the size of the Soviet Army was significantly reduced.

Stalin's death released Soviet theoreticians from most of the constraints of his prescribed and adamantly followed World War II doctrine, and they began to discuss more freely the composition and employment of theater-type forces. Consequently, there were many progressive changes in the Soviet armed forces during the late 1950s and early 1960s.

Tank and motorized infantry divisions of the Soviet Army were strengthened with new armor and APCs; new guns, amphibious vehicles, and rocket launchers were introduced, and the number of airborne divisions increased. Organizational changes featured the elimination of the rifle corps, conversion of the mechanized and rifle divisions to either tank or motorized rifle divisions, and the restructuring of existing tank divisions. The Russians also augmented divisional and nondivisional artillery with surface-to-surface guided missiles and rockets and introduced surface-to-air missiles into the theater forces inventory.

The Brezhnev regime has continued to build up the armed forces on the foundations established during the Khrushchev years. Changes have been largely evolutionary in nature, based on new weapons and equipment, with some modification in organizational concepts and operational and tactical doctrine. One major shift has been a return to the traditional reliance on ground forces. Thus, for instance, the addition of some twenty-five divisions since 1964 has increased and highlighted the relative value of the Soviet Army. Factors influencing these developments have been the growing threat from China, the increasing recognition that war without the use of strategic nuclear weapons would be possible, and the acceptance of the possibility that a nuclear war might be limited to tactical nuclear weapons. Recent wars and present conflicts in the Far East and Mideast have reinforced such thinking.

Kremlin leaders view upgrading the Soviet ground forces, in concert with expanding the navy and improving long-range air transport capabilities, as adding a desirable flexibility to Soviet military power on a global basis. Increased availability of helicopters, newer armored vehicles, and various types of missiles have provided the Soviet Army with unprecedented flexibility, mobility, and firepower.

A. General Works

BOOKS

2565.   Adelman, Jonathan R. *The Revolutionary Armies: The Historical Development of the Soviet and Chinese People's Liberation Armies.* Contributions in Political Science, no. 38. Westport, Conn.: Greenwood Press, 1980. 248p.

2566.   Borisov, B. *The Soviet Army.* Translated from the Russian. Moscow: Foreign Language Publishing House, 1960. 131p.

2567.   Ely, Louis B. *Red Army Today.* 3d ed. Harrisburg, Pa.: Stackpole Books, 1953. 272p.

2568.   Gabriel, Richard. *The New Red Legions.* 2 vols. Westport, Conn.: Greenwood Press, 1980.

2569.   Kalashnik, M. K. *Safeguarding Peaceful Labor.* Translated from the Russian. Moscow: Novosti Press Agency Publishing House, 1969. 103p.

2570.   Liddell-Hart, Basil H., ed. *The Red Army.* Gloucester, Mass.: Peter Smith, 1968. 480p.   A reprint of the original 1956 edition.

2571.   Skirdo, M. P. *The People, the Army, the Commander: A Soviet View.* Translated from the Russian. Soviet Military Thought Series, no. 14. Washington, D.C.: U.S. Government Printing Office, 1978. 166p.

2572.   Talmy, Vladimir. *The Soviet Army.* Translated from the Russian. Moscow: Progress Publishers, 1971.

2573.   Von Pivka, Otto. *The Armies of Europe Today.* New York: Beekman House, 1974. 232p.

Further References

Additional book-length general histories of the Soviet Red Army are found in sections 2:B:1 and 2:C:2.

ARTICLES

2574.   Adelman, Jonathan R. "The Soviet and Chinese Armies: Their Post Civil-War Roles." *Survey* 24 (Winter 1979), 57–81.

2575.   "Alarming Soviet Buildup." *Time* 107 (March 8, 1976), 35–36.

2576.   Alvarez del Vayo, Julio. "Soviet Military Strength." *Nation* 176 (January 24, 1953), 66–69.

2577.   Arnold, Joseph C. "The Soviet Army: Blitzing, Brawling Child of Evolution." *Army* 27 (May 1977), 22–26.

2578.   Atkeson, Edward B. "Is the Soviet Army Obsolete?" *Army* 24 (May 1974), 10–16.

2579.   Baker, John D., Jr. "Where the Soviets Are Vulnerable." *Army* 28 (August 1978), 22–27.

2580.   Bates, Martin D. "The Soviet Army in the Sixties." *An Cosantoir* 22 (May 1962), 274–277.

2581.   Bellamy, Christopher. "Seventy Years On: Similarities between the Modern Soviet Army and Its Tsarist Predecessor." *Journal of the Royal United Service Institute for Defence Studies* 124 (September 1979), 29–38.

2582.   Biryuzov, S. S. "The Army of the Soviet People." *Soviet Military Review,* no. 1 (January 1965), 11–16.

2583.   Boldyreff, C. W. "Whither the Red Army?" *World Affairs* 116 (Fall 1953), 78–80.

2584.   Braun, Leopold. "The Myth of the Mighty Red Army." *American Legion Magazine* 51 (October 1951), 11–13.   Reprinted in *The American Legion Reader* (New York: Hawthorn Books, 1953), pp. 161–167.

2585.   Campbell, J. W. "Combat Efficiency and Fire Power." *Army Information Digest* 8 (March 1953), 23–50.

2586.   "A Capsule Assessment of Soviet Army Capabilities." *Military Review* 56 (June 1976), 94–95.

2587.   Cavendish, John. "Know Your Adversary." *Army Quarterly* 75 (October 1957), 118–124.

2588.   Clemens, Walter C., Jr. "The Soviet Militia in the Missile Age." *Orbis* 8 (Spring 1964), 84–105.

2589.   Coleman, H. J. "NATO Warned of Soviet Offensive Power." *Aviation Week and Space Technology* 103 (December 15, 1975), 21–22.

2590.   Currie, J. H. C. "A Background to the Soviet Army." *Army Quarterly* 103 (January 1973), 109–181; (March 1973), 342–349.

2591.   DePourichkevitch, Michel. "The Red Army's New Look." *Military Review* 45 (March 1965), 87–95.

2592.   DePue, B. E. M. "The Soviet Army." *Military Review* 33 (November 1953), 73–87.

2593.   "Does Russia Really Have 160 Divisions?" *Marine Corps Gazette* 47 (December 1963), 44–45.

2594.   Donnelly, Christopher N. "The Ground Forces." In David R. Jones, ed., *Soviet Armed Forces Review Annual, 1977.* Gulf Breeze, Fla.: Academic International Press, 1977. pp. 27–39.

2595.   _____ . "The Ground Forces." In Ray Bonds, ed., *The Soviet War Machine.* Secaucus, N.J.: Chartwell Books, 1976. pp. 154–175.

2596.   Dunin, A. "Postwar Development of the Ground Forces Discussed: Translated from *Voyenno Istoricheskiy Zhurnal,* May 1978." *Translations on USSR Military Affairs,* no. 1373 (August 29, 1978), 20–29.

2597.   Dunnigan, James F. "The Organization of the Soviet Ground Forces." *Strategy and Tactics,* nos. 23–24 (September–October 1970), 14–21, 23.

2598.   Ely, Louis B. "A General Assessment." In Basil H. Liddell-Hart, ed., *The Red Army.* London: Weidenfeld & Nicolson, 1956. pp. 197–213.

2599.   Erickson, John. "The Ground Forces in Soviet Military Policy." *Strategic Review* 6 (Winter 1978), 64–79.

2600.   _____ . "Soviet Ground Forces and the Conventional Mode of Operations." *Journal of the Royal United Service Institute for Defence Studies,* 121 (June 1976), 45–49.

2601.   Fitch, A. R. "A Report on the Soviet Ground Forces." *Canadian Army Journal* 16 (Winter 1962), 36–38.

2602.   Fryklund, Richard. "How Tall Are the Russians?" *National Guardsman* 8 (February 1964), 2–6.

2603.   Garder, Michel. "The Impact on Land Warfare." In John Erickson, ed., *The Military-Technical Revolution.* New York: Praeger, 1966. pp. 142–148.

2604.   Garn, Jake. "Soviet Superiority: A Question for National Debate." *International Security Review* 4 (Spring 1979), 1–25.

2605.   Garthoff, Raymond L. "Army in Being." *Army* 8 (January 1958), 51–56.

2606.   Grudinin, I. A. "What Determines the Strength of the Army?" *Military Review* 40 (August 1960), 104–108.

2607.   Guderian, Heinz. "Can the Russian Army Be Beaten: An Interview." *U.S. News and World Report* 29 (September 8, 1950), 24–26.

2608.   Hemsley, John. "The Soviet Ground Forces." In John Erickson and E. J. Feuchtwanger, eds., *Soviet Military Power and Performance.* Hamden, Conn.: Archon Books, 1979. pp. 47–73.

2609.   "Here's a Look at the New Red Army." *U.S. News and World Report* 44 (June 20, 1958), 62–65.

2610.   Heymont, Irving. "The Challenge of the Soviet Army." *Military Review* 40 (August 1960), 49–55.

2611. ———— . "The Division Slice." *Military Review* 42 (October 1962), 64–67.

2612. ———— . "A New Look for the Soviet Ground Forces." *Military Review* 36 (January 1957), 54–62.

2613. Horner, J. A. "The British, American, and Soviet Field Armies." *Kommando* 2 (March 1951), 10–11; (April 1951), 6–7; (May 1951), 10–12; (June 1951), 20–21.

2614. Kaul, B. M. "The Red Army." *United Service Institute of India Journal* 80 (January-April 1950), 59–71.

2615. Kennedy, William V. "The Red Army." *Ordnance* 43 (September-October 1958), 227–230.

2616. "Key to Survival: Know Your Enemy." *Newsweek* 36 (September 4, 1950), 18–20.

2617. Kozicharow, E. "Across-the-Board Gains in Soviet Forces Detailed." *Aviation Week and Space Technology* 107 (August 29, 1977), 17–18.

2618. Kuzmin, N. "Heading the Defense of the Soviet Republic." *Soviet Military Review,* no. 3 (March 1970), 30–35.

2619. Lesueur, Laurence E. "The Soviet Army." In Overseas Press Club of America, *As We See Russia.* New York: E. P. Dutton, 1948. pp. 234–244.

2620. Liddell-Hart, Basil H. "The Red Army: A Searching Analysis of Russian Men and Tactics." *Ordnance* 34 (July-August 1949), 25–8.

2621. ———— . "The Red War Machine." *Ordnance* 33 (May-June 1949), 386–389.

2622. Loeffke, Bernard. "The Soviet Union: Perspectives of an Army Attaché." *Parameters* 10 (December 1980), 52–56.

2623. Lukens, Walter. "The Soviet Army Today." *Army Information Digest* 8 (April 1963), 22–30.

2624. Mackintosh, Malcolm. "The Soviet Army." *American Mercury* 76 (January 1953), 88–93.

2625. Malone, Daniel K. "The Soviet Ground Forces." *NATO's Fifteen Nations* 25 (October-November 1980), 46–48.

2626. "Marshals at Work: Red Army Day." *Time* 65 (March 7, 1955), 36.

2627.   Martel, Gifford. "The Soviet Army." *Tank* 35 (January 1953), 46–50.

2628.   "Memorandum on the Russian Military Power by a Group of German Generals." *U.N. World* 4 (June 1950), 14–17.

2629.   Mochalov, V. V. "Land Forces, Their Role and Future: Translated from *Krasnaya Zvezda*, January 19, 1967." In William R. Kintner and Harriet F. Scott, eds., *The Nuclear Revolution in Soviet Military Affairs*. Norman: University of Oklahoma Press, 1968. pp. 146–152.

2630.   Moskalenko, Kirill S. "True to Lenin's Behests." *Soviet Military Review*, no. 3 (March 1970), 36–41.

2631.   Nielsen, John. "How Good Is the Soviet Army?" *Newsweek* 95 (February 11, 1980), 46–50.

2632.   O'Ballance, Edgar. "The Soviet Army at the Crossroads." *Journal of the Royal United Service Institution* 99 (July-September 1969), 223–228.

2633.   Palaferri, Silvio. "The Role of the War-Men in the Soviet Union." *NATO's Fifteen Nations* 15 (August-September 1970), 88.

2634.   Pavlovskiy, Ivan G. "The Soviet Land Forces Today: An Interview." *Soviet Military Review*, no. 9 (September 1976), 2–7.

2635.   Petrov, Vladimir. "Commander Ground Forces Reviews Progress, Problems: Translated from *Krasnaya Zvezda*, December 23, 1980." *Translations on USSR Military Affairs*, no. 1575 (March 20, 1981), 1–5.

2636.   Phillips, Thomas. "Their 'New' Look and Ours." *Army* 10 (March 1960), 29–31.

2637.   Ponomaryov, M. "The Army and People Are One." *Soviet Military Review*, no. 6 (June 1965), 11–14.

2638.   "Principal Foreign Armies: The Soviet Army." *Brassey's Annual, 1951*. New York: Macmillan, 1951. pp. 258–270.

2639.   Puzik, V. "The Army of Developed Socialism." *Soviet Military Review*, no. 1 (January 1979), 2–6.

2640.   "The Red Army." *Armies and Weapons*, no. 15 (January 15–March 15, 1975), 27–34.

2641.   "The Red Army's 'New' Look." *Newsweek* 95 (February 11, 1980), 46–47.

2642. "The Role of Ground Forces." In Robert D. Crane, ed., *Soviet Nuclear Strategy: A Critical Appraisal.* Washington, D.C.: Center for Strategic Studies, Georgetown University, 1963. pp. 49–67.

2643. Rosinski, Herbert. "The Red Flood." *Combat Forces Journal* 3 (July 1953), 10–15.

2644. "Russia and the U.S.: How Armies Compare." *U.S. News and World Report* 47 (August 3, 1959), 79.

2645. "The Russian Army, Balance of Power." *Newsweek* 55 (May 30, 1960), 33.

2646. "Russians Display Ground Forces." *Aviation Week and Space Technology* 67 (December 9, 1957), 83.

2647. Salmanov, G. I. "Capabilities of Ground Forces Described: Translated from *Voyennyye Znaniya,* January 1978." *Translations on USSR Military Affairs,* no. 1336 (March 10, 1978), 11–15.

2648. Sers, Jean-François. "Soviet Armed Forces Capabilities: Translated from *Countrepoint,* Autumn 1980." *Translations on USSR Military Affairs,* no. 1551 (December 11, 1980), 14–23.

2649. "Several Aspects of Soviet Military Development in the Postwar Period." *Soviet Military Translations,* no. 193a (August 1965), 1–18.

2650. Shtemenko, Sergei M. "The Land Forces." *Soviet Military Review,* no. 4 (April 1965), 10–13.

2651. _____ . "The Land Forces in Contemporary War and Their Combat Training." *Army* 13 (March 1963), 47–56.

2652. _____ . "Soviet Ground Forces in Modern War." *Survival* 5 (July-August 1963), 180–183.

2653. Smogorzewski, Kazimierz M. "Soviet Strength." *20th Century* 150 (December 1951), 482–489.

2654. Sorokin, A. "Moral Potential of the Soviet Army." *Soviet Military Review,* no. 4 (April 1978), 2–5.

2655. "The Soviet Army." *U.S. News and World Report* 30 (April 6, 1951), 18–19.

2656. "The Soviet Army in the Nuclear Era." *Army Information Digest* 13 (August 1958), 20–31.

2657. "The Steadily Rising Combat Strength of the Soviet Ground Forces, 1970–1980: Translated from *Soldat und Technik,* January 1981." *Translations on USSR Military Affairs,* no. 1573 (March 13, 1981), 10–24.

2658.   Stevenson, Charles S. "A Study of Contrasts: The Soviet Soldier and His Army." *Army Information Digest* 15 (June 1960), 28–31.

2659.   Timorin, A. "Army of Developed Socialism." *Soviet Military Review,* no. 4 (April 1977), 10–11.

2660.   Underhill, Garrett. "Report on the Red Army." *New York Times Magazine* (October 16, 1949), 12.

2661.   United States. Department of Defense. "General Purpose Forces: An Evaluation of U.S., U.S.S.R., P.R.C., and Warsaw Pact Capabilities." *Commander's Digest* 21 (March 23, 1978), 1–20.

2662.   ———. Defense Intelligence Agency. "The Ground Forces." *Handbook of the Soviet Armed Forces.* DDB-2680-40-78. Washington, D.C.: U.S. Government Printing Office, 1978. pp. 8/1–8/28.

2663.   United States. Department of the Army. "The Enemy." *Fire Support in Combined Arms Operations.* FM 6-20C-1. Washington, D.C., 1980. pp. 2/1–2/34.

2664.   ———. "The Front." *Opposing Forces: Europe.* FM 30-102. Washington, D.C., 1977. pp. 13/1–13/14.

2665.   ———. "Targets." *Field Artillery Target Acquisition.* FM 6-121. Washington, D.C., 1980. pp. 10/1–10/13.

2666.   ———. "Theater Forces." *Soviet Russia: Strategic Survey.* DA Pam 20-64. Washington, D.C., 1963. pp. 173–188.

2667.   ———. "Threat Organization and Equipment." *Engineer Combat Operations.* FM 5-100. Washington, D.C., 1978. pp. C/1–C/45.

2668.   Vassiliev, M. F. "Military Trends in the U.S.S.R." *An Cosantoir* 17 (July 1957), 333–339.

2669.   Vasyagin, S. P. "Combat Readiness of Ground Forces Noted: Translated from *Znamenosets,* October 1977." *Translations on USSR Military Affairs,* no. 1323 (January 11, 1978), 32–34.

2670.   Vostokov, Ye. "The Army: A School of High Culture." *Soviet Military Review,* no. 3 (March 1974), 28–29.

2671.   "Where Russia Is Outstripping U.S. in Military Might." *U.S. News and World Report* 80 (February 9, 1976), 20–21.

2672.   Wimberley, Jerry M. "The Soviet Army Today." *Military Review* 37 (March 1958), 14–28.

2673.   Yakubovsky, Ivan I. "Soviet Ground Forces." *Military Review* 47 (December 1967), 85–87.

2674.   Yepishev, Aleksey A. "The Soviet Army's Historic Mission." *Soviet Military Review,* no. 2 (February 1974), 4–6.

2675.   Yukushin, V. Z. "Greater Vigilance for Ground Forces Urged: Translated from *Znamenosets,* February 1978." *Translations on USSR Military Affairs,* no. 1351 (May 12, 1978), 9–12.

DOCUMENTS, PAPERS, AND REPORTS

2676.   Aspin, Les, and Jack F. Kemp. *Realities of Soviet Power: Two Views.* AEI Defense Review, v. 2, no. 3. Washington, D.C.: American Enterprise Institute for Public Policy Research, 1978. 36p.

2677.   BDM Corporation. *Soviet Army Operations.* IAG-13-U-78. McLean, Va., 1978. 365p.

2678.   Buffardi, Louis N. *The Soviet Railroad Troops (Zheleznodorozhniki).* Research Report. New York: U.S. Army Institute for Advanced Russian and East European Studies, 1978. 35p.

2679.   Grechko, Andrei A. *On Guard for Peace and the Building of Communism.* Translated from the Russian. JPRS 54602. Washington, D.C.: Joint Publication Research Service, 1971.

2680.   Record, Jeffrey. *Sizing Up the Soviet Army.* Washington, D.C.: Brookings Institution, 1975. 56p.

2681.   Sulimov, Ye. *Army of All-People's State, U.S.S.R.* JPRS 21183. Washington, D.C.: Joint Publication Research Service, 1963. 8p.

2682.   United States. Department of the Army. *Handbook on the Soviet Army.* Washington, D.C., 1958. 260p.

2683.   _____ . *Handbook on the Soviet and Satellite Armies, Pt. 1: The Soviet Army.* DA Pam 30-50-1. Washington, D.C., 1953. 172p.

Further References

Additional general references on the Soviet Red Army are found in section 2.

B. Mission and Doctrine, Strategy and Tactics

The missions of the Soviet ground forces are deterrence, defense, and offense in the land theaters of military operations. The primary area in which these troops are to be employed is the territory of the U.S.S.R. and of the Warsaw Pact member states. However, large numbers of men have been guarding the China border for two decades, and the 1979–1980 invasion of Afghanistan demonstrates Soviet Army capability to move along other borders. The Soviet Army must neither allow an enemy to invade the socialist countries nor permit an aggressor to subvert the internal security of those states.

The Soviets believe that to achieve final victory they must not only destroy an enemy's means of nuclear attack and disorganize its interior, but also completely defeat the enemy's main forces and occupy its territory. Thus the main tasks of the Soviet Army are to annihilate the enemy's military formations through rapid offensive movements and to gain possession of vital installations and regions.

Soviet military doctrine is based on the assumption that a major war will involve the use of nuclear weapons—though not necessarily strategic nuclear weapons—and that, since the initial stage will be decisive, massive forces will have to be deployed quickly across unprecedented distances. In the European theater, where the Soviet Army is predominant, strategy calls for the rapid defeat of NATO forces and the occupation of Western Europe.

Soviet forces would thrust through holes blasted in enemy lines by massive strikes on his strongpoints and reserve concentrations, with the initial breakthroughs on the scale of a division front. The Russians envision armored spearheads smashing through such prepared gaps and proceeding rapidly into the enemy's communications zone, or operational rear, where they will destroy all reinforcements or reserve formations in a series of meeting engagements. The brief, decisive campaign would be characterized by quickly changing situations requiring flexible command and control systems and highly maneuverable troop units capable of coping with contaminated environments, of exploiting opportunities, of remaining effective with a minimum of logistic support, and able to escape any temporary defensive stands quickly.

The current Soviet concepts of future theater warfare reflect the experiences of the Great Patriotic War. Thus they classify offensive actions into three major types: the breakthrough, the meeting engagement, and the pursuit. The defensive is seen as a temporary expedient only, but drawing upon experiences with the Germans, the Soviets well realize that units must be protected by successive defensive belts.

The citations in this section examine the mission and doctrine, strategy and tactics of the Soviet Army, with numerous references drawn directly from translations of Russian military writings.

BOOKS

2684.   Heilbrunn, Otto. *Conventional Warfare in the Nuclear Age.* New York: Praeger, 1965. 164p.

2685.   Savkin, V. Ye. *The Basic Principles of Operational Art and Tactics: A Soviet View.* Translated from the Russian. Soviet Military Thought Series, no. 4. Washington, D.C.: U.S. Government Printing Office, 1974. 284p.

2686.   Sidorenko, A. A. *The Offensive: A Soviet View.* Translated from the Russian. Soviet Military Thought Series, no. 1. Washington, D.C.: U.S. Government Printing Office, 1973. 228p.

Articles

2687.   Akimov, A. "Pursuit." *Soviet Military Review,* no. 8 (August 1979), 13–15.

2688.   _____ . "Repulsing Counterattacks." *Soviet Military Review,* no. 6 (June 1979), 25–27.

2689.   Arnold, Joseph C. "Current Soviet Tactical Doctrine: A Reflection of the Past." *Military Review* 57 (July 1977), 16–24.

2690.   Baritz, Joseph J. "Soviet Military Theory: Politics and War." *Military Review* 43 (September 1966), 3–10.

2691.   Berezhnov, P. "Fighting in the Depth of Defense." *Soviet Military Review,* no. 11 (November 1966), 24–27.

2692.   Bidwell, Shelford. "The Use of Small Nuclear Weapons in War on Land." *Army Quarterly* 101 (April 1971), 295–306.

2693.   Boman, Truman R. "Current Soviet Tactics." *Military Review* 42 (March 1962), 41–46.

2694.   Bree, Betsey. "Tactics, Training and Equipment." *Review of the Soviet Ground Forces* 3 (May 1980), 10–14.

2695.   Brown, William A. "Soviet Offensive Tactics." *Infantry* 51 (March-April 1961), 4–8.

2696.   Bulatov, A. "Surprising Tactics in Modern Combat." *Soviet Military Review,* no. 3 (March 1965), 14–18.

2697.   Cabaniss, Edward H., 4th. "Soviet Ground Tactics." *Military Review* 59 (December 1979), 37–45.

2698.   Caiger-Watson, R. H. "Soviet Military Doctrine: A Study of the Influence of Von Schlieffen." *Journal of the Royal United Service Institution* 103 (August 1958), 346–355.

2699.   "Capability and Reality in Combat." *Soviet Military Translations,* no. 264 (May 1966), 8.

2700.   Chernyshov, Yu. "A Battalion-Strong Advanced Detachment Defense." *Soviet Military Review,* no. 4 (April 1980), 36–37.

2701.   _____ . "Committing the Second Echelon to Action." *Soviet Military Review,* no. 5 (May 1979), 15–17.

2702.   "The Clearness of Purpose and System in the Conduct of Combat Operations." *Soviet Military Translations,* no. 118 (March 1963), 1–13.

2703.   Colby, Steven. "Soviet Warfighting Concepts." *The Alliance and Europe, Pt. IV: Military Doctrine and Technology.* London: International Institute for Strategic Studies, 1975. Chpt. 2.

2704.   DeCesare, Armand, and Adolf Carlson. "The Soviet Approach." *Infantry* 69 (January-February 1979), 16–19.

2705.   "Dialectics and the Cooperation between Fire and Movement in Armed Combat." *Soviet Military Translations,* no. 203 (September 1965), 13–23.

2706.   Donnelly, Christopher N. "Soviet Tactics for Overcoming NATO Antitank Defenses." *International Defense Review* 12 (July 1979), 1099–1106.

2707.   _____ . "Tactical Problems Facing the Soviet Army: Recent Debates in the Soviet Military Press." *International Defense Review* 11 (September 1978), 1405–1412.

2708.   Erickson, John. "Trends in the Soviet Combined-Arms Concept." *Strategic Review* 5 (Winter 1977), 38–53.

2709.   Fullerton, John. "Re-Equipment and Doctrine of the Soviet Ground Forces." *Defense and Foreign Affairs Digest,* no. 12 (1977), 36–37.

2710.   Garthoff, Raymond L. "Land Power in Soviet Strategy." *Soviet Strategy in the Nuclear Age.* New York: Praeger, 1958. pp. 149–169.

2711.   _____ . "Soviet Strategy: Flexibility, Firepower, Followup." *Army* 10 (August 1959), 38–43.

2712.   _____ . "Surprise and Blitzkrieg in Soviet Eyes." *RCAF Staff College Journal* (1959), 16–29.

2713.   Grudinin, I. A. "Firepower and Manpower in the Soviet Army." *NATO's Fifteen Nations* 15 (August 1960), 66–67.

2714.   Guillaume, Augustin. "The Relationship of Policy and Strategy." In Basil H. Liddell-Hart, ed., *The Soviet Army.* London: Weidenfeld & Nicolson, 1956. pp. 234–241.

2715.   Hawke, Willard W. "A New Look at Soviet Tactics." *Infantry* 53 (January-February 1963), 62–64.

2716.   Hayes, James H. "Patterns, Plain and Fancy." *Military Review* 59 (July 1979), 2–10.

2717.   Ionov, G. "Ambush Operations." *Soviet Military Review*, no. 2 (February 1966), 22–23.

2718.   _____ . "In the Wake of a Crushing Strike." *Soviet Military Review*, no. 8 (August 1965), 14–16.

2719.   Jackson, Charles A. "Soviet Tactics." *Infantry School Quarterly* 45 (October 1953), 60–73.

2720.   Jacobs, Walter D. "The Art of Operations." *Army* 12 (November 1961), 60–64.

2721.   Kashuba, G. "At the Water's Edge: Translated from *Krasnaya Zvezda*, July 13, 1977." *Review of the Soviet Ground Forces* 1 (October 1977), 3–8.

2722.   Khetagurov, G. "Manoeuvrability and Dynamic Capability in Modern Warfare." *Soviet Military Review*, no. 1 (January 1965), 17–19.

2723.   Kokhanov, V. "Antilanding Defense." *Soviet Military Review*, no. 8 (August 1972), 14–17.

2724.   Korzun, L. "Counterattack." *Soviet Military Review*, no. 12 (December 1969), 16–18.

2725.   _____ . "Ground Forces—Postwar Development of Defensive Tactics: Translated from *Voyenno Istoricheskiy Zhurnal*, October 1980." *Translations on USSR Military Affairs*, no. 1557 (January 16, 1981), 88–96.

2726.   _____ . "Fire and Manoeuvre." *Soviet Military Review*, no. 12 (December 1965), 25–26.

2727.   _____ . "Unit Manoeuvres in Combat." *Soviet Military Review*, no. 10 (October 1966), 12–14.

2728.   Kotikov, V. "Attack from March Column." *Soviet Military Review*, no. 5 (May 1980), 24–26.

2729.   "The Kremlin's Reliance on Blitzkrieg." *Far Eastern Economic Review* 90 (October 31, 1975), 33–34.

2730.   Larinov, V. V. "New Means of Fighting and Strategy: Translated from *Krasnaya Zvezda*, April 1964." In William R. Kintner and Harriet F. Scott, eds., *The Nuclear Revolution in Soviet Military Affairs.* Norman: University of Oklahoma Press, 1968. pp. 34–44.

2731.   "L'Heretique," pseud. "The Pattern of Soviet Army Tactics." *Military Review* 40 (June 1960), 102–107.

2732.   Liddell-Hart, Basil H. "If I Were Russia's Chief-of-Staff." *U.N. World* 7 (February 1953), 10–14.

2733.   Loktev, G. "Tactics in Modern Combat Discussed: Translated from *Voyennyye Znaniya*, November 1978." *Translations on USSR Military Affairs,* no. 1415 (March 5, 1979), 1–5.

2734.   Lomakin, M. "Meeting Counterattacks." *Soviet Military Review,* no. 11 (November 1965), 28–30.

2735.   Lomov, Nikolay A. "The Influence of Soviet Military Doctrine on the Development of Military Art." In William R. Kintner and Harriet F. Scott, eds., *The Nuclear Revolution in Soviet Military Affairs.* Norman: University of Oklahoma Press, 1968. pp. 153–170.

2736.   Lukava, G. "The Art of Victory." *Soviet Military Review,* no. 3 (March 1970), 42–44.

2737.   Mackintosh, Malcolm. "Soviet Strategy in World War III." *Army* 10 (May 1960), 23–32.

2738.   Matsulenko, V. "Surprise: How It Is Achieved and Its Role." *Soviet Military Review,* no. 5 (May 1972), 37–39; no. 6 (June 1972), 37–39.

2739.   Matveyev, V. I. "The Effect of New Means of Waging War on Tactics." In Nikolay A. Lomov, ed., *Scientific-Technical Progress and the Revolution in Military Affairs: A Soviet View.* Translated from the Russian. Soviet Military Thought Series, no. 3. Washington, D.C.: U.S. Government Printing Office, 1974. pp. 148–157.

2740.   _____ . "Modern Means of Waging War and Operations-Level Strategy." In Nikolay A. Lomov, ed., *Scientific-Technical Progress and the Revolution in Military Affairs: A Soviet View.* Translated from the Russian. Soviet Military Thought Series, no. 3. Washington, D.C.: U.S. Government Printing Office, 1974. pp. 141–147.

2741.   Miksche, Ferdinand O. "Geography and Strategy." In Basil H. Liddell-Hart, ed., *The Soviet Army.* London: Weidenfeld & Nicolson, 1956. pp. 242–253.

2742.   Miroshnichenko, N. F. "Changes in the Context and Nature of Modern Combat." In William R. Kintner and Harriet F. Scott, eds., *The Nuclear Revolution in Soviet Military Affairs.* Norman: University of Oklahoma Press, 1968. pp. 366–374.

2743.   "Necessity and Chance in Armed Combat." *Soviet Military Translations,* no. 152a (September 1964), 1–12.

2744.   Novgorodov, A. "Infantry, Artillery, Tanks: One Team in Battle." *Soviet Military Review,* no. 1 (January 1966), 20–22.

2745.   Patrick, Stephen B. "Firefight: U.S. vs. Soviet Small Unit Tactics." *Strategy and Tactics,* no. 56 (March-April 1976), *passim.*

2746.   "The Pattern of Soviet Army Tactics." *Military Review* 40 (June 1960), 102–107.

2747.   "Planning and Purpose in Combat." *Soviet Military Translations,* no. 371a (February 1967), 1–10.

2748.   Pontryagin, M. "Security on Flanks, Limiting Points, and Gaps between Units." *Soviet Military Review,* no. 7 (July 1966), 34–35.

2749.   Raymond, Ellsworth L. "What the Russian Generals Are Thinking." *U.N. World* 2 (March 1948), 14–17.

2750.   Reznichenko, Vasiliy G. "The Role of Tactics in Modern War." *Soviet Military Review,* no. 9 (September 1976), 8–11.

2751.   _____ , and A. Sidorenko. "Soviet Tactics on the Nuclear Battlefield." *Military Review* 45 (June 1965), 76–80.

2752.   Riedel, Rudi. "The Offensive Doctrine of the Soviet Army." *Military Review* 42 (November 1962), 61–67.

2753.   Senyuk, V. "Tanks in Coastal Defense." *Soviet Military Review,* no. 7 (July 1969), 19–21.

2754.   Shrader, Cecil L. "The New Blitzkrieg." *Armor* 81 (September-October 1972), 12–16.

2755.   Shutov, Z. "Defense during an Offensive." *Soviet Military Review,* no. 11 (November 1979), 37–40.

2756.   Slyusar, A. "In Different Types of Combat." *Soviet Military Review,* no. 2 (February 1977), 18–21.

2757.   Sobik, Erich. "Command and Control in the Soviet Ground Forces." *NATO's Fifteen Nations* 24 (October-November 1979), 96–98.

2758. _____ . "Soviet Ground Forces Command Principles: Translated from *Truppenpraxis*, August 1980." *Translations on USSR Military Affairs*, no. 1564 (February 2, 1981), 1–22.

2759. Sredin, G. V. "Marxist-Leninist Doctrine on War and the Army." *Soviet Military Review*, no. 1 (January 1978), 18–21.

2760. Steger, George F. "A Dilemma in Studying Soviet Tactics." *Military Review* 56 (June 1976), 76–79.

2761. _____ . "More Dilemmas in Studying Soviet Tactics." *Military Review* 58 (February 1978), 88–96.

2762. Stockell, Charles. "Soviet Military Strategy: The Army View." *Military Review* 53 (October 1973), 72–83.

2763. Szkoda, W. E. "The Red Soldier—Mentality and Tactics: Offensive Tactics." *Armor* 70 (November-December 1961), 42–52.

2764. Tokmakov, A. "Antitank Reserve on Defense." *Soviet Military Review*, no. 8 (August 1977), 18–19.

2765. United States. Department of the Army. "Basic Tactical Doctrine." *Opposing Forces: Europe*. FM 30-102. Washington, D.C., 1977. pp. 2/1–2/25.

2766. Valenets, I. "Assuming the Defensive during an Advance." *Soviet Military Review*, no. 1 (January 1977), 15–18.

2767. Vaselov, L. "Attack in Prebattle Formation." *Soviet Military Review*, no. 7 (July 1977), 13–15.

2768. _____ . "Counterattack in Defense." *Soviet Military Review*, no. 3 (March 1977), 26–28.

2769. Vigor, Peter H. "The Soviet Army Wave Attack Philosophy: The Single-Echelon Option." *International Defense Review* 12 (January 1979), 43–46.

2770. Vorob'yev, I. "Maneuver in Battle." *Soviet Military Review*, no. 11 (November 1972), 36–39.

2771. Voznenko, V. V. "Modern Means of Conducting Military Operations and Military Strategy." In Nikolay A. Lomov, ed., *Scientific-Technical Progress and the Revolution in Military Affairs: A Soviet View*. Translated from the Russian. Soviet Military Thought Series, no. 3. Washington, D.C.: U.S. Government Printing Office, 1974. pp. 134–140.

2772.　　Wolfe, Thomas W. "Trends in Soviet Thinking on Theater Warfare and Limited War." In John Erickson, ed., *The Military-Technical Revolution*. New York: Praeger, 1966. pp. 52–80.

2773.　　Zhukov, V. "Maneuver as the Essence of Tactics." *Soviet Military Review*, no. 6 (June 1977), 11–13.

DOCUMENTS, PAPERS, AND REPORTS

2774.　　Astakhov, N. N., et al. *The Soldier and War*. Translated from the Russian. OACS(I)-K-5111. Washington, D.C.: National Technical Information Service, 1974. Unpaged.

2775.　　Cole, William. *The Soviet Ground Forces: Doctrine and Capabilities (European Theater)*. Research Report. New York: U.S. Army Institute for Advanced Russian and East European Studies, 1974. 27p.

2776.　　Concannon, John F. *The Soviet Concept of the Meeting Engagement*. Research Report. New York: U.S. Army Institute for Advanced Russian and East European Studies, 1976. 48p.

2777.　　Conroy, Bruce. "Tactics of the Soviet Army Regiment." MA thesis, U.S. Army Command and General Staff College, 1979. 144p.

2778.　　Hayes, James H. *Patterns, Plain and Fancy*. RAND Paper P-6278. Santa Monica, Calif.: RAND Corporation, 1979. 15p.

2779.　　Hoeffding, O. *Troop Movements in Soviet Tactical Doctrine*. RAND Report R-878-PR. Santa Monica, Calif.: RAND Corporation, 1971. 40p.

2780.　　Paxson, E. W. *Interactions between Tactics and Technology in Ground Warfare*. RAND Report R-2377-ARPA. Santa Monica, Calif.: RAND Corporation, 1979. 51p.

2781.　　Reznichenko, Vasiliy G. *Tactics*. Translated from the Russian. FTD-MT-67-35. Washington, D.C.: National Technical Information Service, 1967.

2782.　　Sushko, N. Ia., and S. A. Tinshkevich, eds. *Marxism-Leninism on War and the Army*. Soviet Military Translations, no. 272. Alexandria, Va.: Joint Publication Research Service, 1966. 315p.

2783.　　Turchenko, V. V., and M. V. Fedulov. *Defensive Operations during an Offensive*. Translated from the Russian. Report FSTC-HT-23-69-75. Charlottesville, Va.: U.S. Army Foreign Science and Technology Center, 1974. 249p.

2784.   Turner, Frederick C. *Comments on FM 100-5 from a Soviet Point-of-View.* Special Report. Carlisle Barracks, Pa.: Strategic Studies Institute, U.S. Army War College, 1978. 103p.   A comparison of ground doctrines.

2785.   United States. Department of Defense. Defense Intelligence Agency. *Soviet Doctrine and Planning Factors for Ground Operations.* DIA-PC-210/4-1-70. Washington, D.C., 1970. Unpaged.

2786.   _____ . *Soviet Tactics: The Meeting Engagement.* DIA-DDI-1100-143-76. Washington, D.C., 1976. 10p.

2787.   United States. Department of the Army. Intelligence Threat Analysis Division. *Military Operations of the Soviet Union.* USAITAD-14-U-76. Arlington, Va., 1976. 247p.

2788.   Wolfe, Thomas W. *Trends in Soviet Thinking on Theater Warfare, Conventional Operations, and Limited War.* RAND Memorandum RM-4305-PR. Santa Monica, Calif.: RAND Corporation, 1964. 105p.

Further References

Additional citations relative to this section are found in sections 2:C:2:a and 3:A:3 and in parts dealing with training in 4:E.

C. Combat Arms of the Soviet Ground Forces

Within the Ministry of Defense, the commander-in-chief of the Soviet ground forces is a deputy minister equal in status to the commanders of the other armed forces components. His duties are essentially supervision of technical affairs and research and development, direct control of nonoperational training, and supervision of army administrative organs. He *does not* have direct operational control over the troops. General Ivan Pavlovskiy, current ground forces chief, is assisted by a first deputy chief, a chief of the main staff who is also a first deputy commander, several deputies, and an assistant commander.

The lack of operational control authority of the ground forces headquarters establishment is not immediately apparent from its composition, which includes the Main Staff and several technical directorates. The Main Staff, briefly abolished after World War II, apparently fills a traditional role of coordinating, planning, maintaining liaison with the Soviet General Staff on ground forces matters, and acting as a consolidation point for the work of the army directorates. Among the principal directorates of the Soviet Army are the Political Directorate, the Combat Training Directorate, the Personnel Directorate, and the Military Educational Institutions Directorate, all of which have counterparts at Ministry of Defense level. In addition, there are large technical directorates for those troop branches peculiar to the ground forces.

The Soviet ground forces are divided into combat arms, special troops, and services. The combat arms are the firing elements and consist of motorized infantry troops, tank troops, rocket and artillery troops, airborne troops, and air defense troops of the ground forces. It is these combat arms which are referenced in this section.

1. Armor

Soviet armor or tank troops have at their head the chief of tank troops in ground forces headquarters. Usually a marshal of tank troops, he is supported by the Main Directorate of Tank Troops, an intricate organization with all the trappings of an administrative headquarters. This directorate is responsible for research and development in tactics and equipment, monitoring the procurement of weapons systems, even to the extent of undertaking quality control inspections at tank factories, and provides for speciality training of personnel.

Russian armor officers or generals command armored units at all levels. Combined arms formations feature a special staff officer as chief of tank troops, and it is he who commands subordinate armored elements and reports to the combined arms commander.

The role of the tank army, a heavily armored force of tanks and motorized infantry, is to rupture and penetrate enemy defenses and to exploit breakthroughs deep into the enemy's rear areas. This army is a tactical and administrative field force capable of independent operations, although its normal employment is as a component of a front or army group. The size of a tank army and its force composition depends upon its mission, the situation, and the area of operations.

Each front or army group usually contains at least one tank army made up of four to five divisions. Each division is formed around three tank regiments, of three tank battalions of three tank companies each. The personnel strength of a Soviet tank division is considerably less than a comparable U.S. division, with the former having about 11,000 men and the latter 16,500. On the other hand, the ratio of tanks to troops in a Soviet tank division is very high at about 1 to 33, while in a U.S. division the ratio would be approximately 1 to 51. Other components of a tank army would include a motorized infantry division, SCUD, SAM, and artillery brigades, and special combat and support troops such as signal people and engineers. Nevertheless, as the name implies, emphasis in a Soviet armored unit is on the tank and its ability to provide the mobility necessary to promote the overall ground forces doctrine of the offensive.

The citations in this subsection provide information on modern-day Soviet tank troops as viewed by both Soviet and Western writers and analysts.

BOOKS

2789.   Simpkin, Richard. *Brassey's Tank Warfare: An Analysis of Soviet and NATO Tank Philosophy.* New York: Crane, Russak, 1979. 232p.

ARTICLES

2790.   Adams, Charles. "The 'Kantemirovka' Guards Tank Division." *Review of the Soviet Ground Forces* 4 (November 1979), 15–19.

2791.   Averyanov, Z. "In the Advance Party." *Soviet Military Review,* no. 11 (November 1971), 13–15.

2792.   _____ . "Tank Battalion Offensive on the Move." *Soviet Military Review,* no. 12 (December 1971), 10–13.

2793.   Babadzhanyan, Amazasp K. "The Main Strike Force." *Soviet Military Review,* no. 9 (September 1970), 1–4.

2794.   Bogdanov, S. I. "On Guard for Peace and Security: Translated from *Pravda,* September 14, 1952." *Current Digest of the Soviet Press* 4 (October 25, 1952), 21.

2795.   Daignault, David W. "The Threat." *Armor* 84 (November-December 1975), 37–38.

2796.   Davidenko, A. "Ground Forces—Historiography of Soviet Tank Troops: Translated from *Voyenno Istoricheskiy Zhurnal,* October 1980." *Translations on USSR Military Affairs,* no. 1557 (January 16, 1981), 132–137.

2797.   Dawson, Joseph. "Trucks and Tanks: What Is Their Place in Modern Warfare?" *NATO Review* 2 (March 1962), 28–30.

2798.   Ely, Louis B. "Armies of Armor." *Armor* 60 (July-August 1951), 34–42.

2799.   Erickson, John. "Soviet Combined Arms Operations." *Armor* 89 (May-June 1980), 16–21.

2800.   Flemming, Roland. "The Soviet Tank Division." *Review of the Soviet Ground Forces* 4 (November 1979), 1–5.

2801.   Galay, Nikolay. "The Armored Forces: Recent Trends." In Basil H. Liddell-Hart, ed., *The Soviet Army.* London: Weidenfeld & Nicolson, 1956. pp. 312–322.

2802.   _____ . "Tank Forces in the Soviet Army." *Institute for the Study of the USSR Bulletin* 1 (October 1954), 3–15.

2803.   Gavrikov, F. "Mobility and Secrecy." *Soviet Military Review*, no. 11 (November 1969), 19–21.

2804.   Greenhut, Jeffrey. "Soviet Armor Doctrine." *Armor* 86 (January-February 1977), 18–21.

2805.   Grover, Joel M., and John Kerby. "The Myth of the Soviet Driver-Mechanic." *Armor* 87 (March-April 1978), 42–44.

2806.   Hollingsworth, James F., and Allan T. Wood. "The Light Armored Corps: A Strategic Necessity." *Armed Forces Journal International* 117 (January 1980), 20–22.

2807.   Krupchenko, I. Ye. "Tanks in the Offensive." *Soviet Military Review* no. 8 (August 1971), 5–9; no. 9 (September 1971), 40–43.

2808.   Loginov, M. "Rapidity and Onslaught: Tank Battalion Destroys Airborne Troops." *Soviet Military Review*, no. 10 (October 1971), 13–15.

2809.   Losik, O. A. "Soviet Tankmen: An Interview." *Soviet Military Review*, no. 8 (August 1977), 2–3.

2810.   McGuire, James D. "Soviet Army Mobility." *Armor* 70 (January-February 1961), 32–33.

2811.   McMaster, Arthur W., 3d. "Soviet Armor: A Study in Efficiency." *Armor* 87 (January-February 1978), 30–33.

2812.   Malyugin, N. "Tank Battalion on the March." *Soviet Military Review*, no. 11 (November 1969), 34–35.

2813.   Nargele, D. G. "The Soviet Tank Company Is Designed to Be an Effective Part of a Larger Tank Force." *Marine Corps Gazette* 61 (April 1977), 49–54.

2814.   Niessel, A. "Cavalry." In Basil H. Liddell-Hart, ed., *The Soviet Army*. London: Weidenfeld & Nicolson, 1956. pp. 337–343.

2815.   Ogorkiewicz, Richard M. "Armoured Concepts and Trends." *Military Review* 41 (March 1961), 63–69.

2816.   _____ . "Soviet Armored Formations." *Military Review* 35 (March 1956), 83–88.

2817.   _____ . "The Structure and Functions of Armored Divisions, Pt. 1: British and Soviet Organization." *Armor* 67 (January-February 1958), 14–21.

2818.   Paddock, C. "Armoured Formations." *Army Quarterly* 74 (April 1957), 63–68.

2819.   Perrett, Bryan. "Armour and the Russian Officer." *Army Quarterly* 51 (August 1971), 70–79.

2820.   Poluboyarov, Pavel. "The Soviet Armoured Corps." *National Defense* 6 (September 1968), 18–19.

2821.   Pyman, H. E. "Armor in the Land Battle." *Military Review* 34 (March 1955), 86–93.

2822.   Rotmistrov, P. A. "The Main Striking Power of Land Forces." *Soviet Military Review,* no. 9 (September 1965), 11–13.

2823.   _____ . "Modern Armor and Nuclear Weapons." *Current Digest of the Soviet Press* 14 (November 1962), 20–21.

2824.   _____ . "The Postwar Development of Tank Forces." In William F. Scott, ed., *Selected Soviet Military Writings, 1970–1975: A Soviet View.* Translated from the Russian. Soviet Military Thought Series, no. 11. Washington, D.C.: U.S. Government Printing Office, 1977. pp. 251–295.

2825.   Ryabchikov, V. "Overcoming Antitank Defenses." *Soviet Military Review,* no. 5 (May 1971), 15–16.

2826.   Shackleton, N. A. "The Tank Threat." *Canadian Army Journal* 18 (February 1964), 2–12.

2827.   "The Soviet Army Is an Entirely Armored Army." *Military Review* 30 (January 1951), 80–84.

2828.   Trofimov, R. "The Armored Forces of the Future." *Soviet Military Review,* no. 9 (September 1976), 21–23.

2829.   Tychkov, M. "In the Depth of Defenses." *Soviet Military Review,* no. 8 (August 1971), 18–20.

2830.   Underhill, Garrett. "Red Armor." *Marine Corps Gazette* 38 (September 1954), 20–27.

2831.   United States. Department of the Army. "The Enemy in Modern Battle." In *Armored and Mechanized Division Operations.* FM 71-100. Washington, D.C., 1978. pp. 2/1–2/24.

2832.   _____ . "The Tank Army, Battalion, Company, Division [and] Regiment." In *Opposing Forces: Europe.* FM 30-102. Washington, D.C., 1977. pp. 12/1, 6/1, 4/1, 10/1, 8/1.

2833.   ———— . "How the Enemy Attacks." *Armored and Mechanized Brigade Operations.* FM 71-3. Washington, D.C., 1980. pp. 4/6–4/16.

2834.   Vassiliev, M. F. "Ready for Work and War." *An Cosantoir* 16 (January 1956), 30–34.

2835.   ———— . "Soviet Armored Principles." *An Cosantoir* 15 (October 1955), 469–477.

2836.   Vinnikov, V. "Tank Company in Defence." *Soviet Military Review,* no. 7 (July 1968), 16–20.

2837.   Von Senger und Etterlin, Fridolin M. "Trends in the Mechanization of Armies." In Royal United Service Institute for Defence Studies, ed., *R.U.S.I. and Brassey's Defence Yearbook, 1976–1977.* Boulder, Colo.: Westview Press, 1976. pp. 157–194.

2838.   Yevreyev. V. "Tank Crew Operations Described: Translated from *Znamenosets,* September 1977." *Translations on USSR Military Affairs,* no. 1324 (January 13, 1978), 79–81.

2839.   Zyrzanov, A. "Tanks and APC's in Defense." *Soviet Military Review,* no. 4 (April 1972), 20–22.

DOCUMENTS, PAPERS, AND REPORTS

2840.   Boles, John K., 3d. *Soviet Armored Doctrine.* Alexandria, Va.: U.S. Army Military Personnel Center, 1978. 180p.

2841.   Cabaniss, Edward H., 4th. *The Soviet Tank Battalion in the Offensive.* Research Report. New York: U.S. Army Institute for Advanced Russian and East European Studies, 1976. 40p.

2842.   Hemesley, A. E. *Soviet Tank Company Tactics.* DDI-1120-129-76. Washington, D.C.: Defense Intelligence Agency, Department of Defense, 1976. 76p.

2843.   Solomatin, M. *Armored and Mechanized Troops of the Soviet Army.* Translated from the Russian. DA-G2-TR-3022. Washington, D.C.: Department of the Army, 1949. 20p.

2844.   United States. Department of Defense. Defense Intelligence Agency. *Soviet Tank Battalion Tactics.* DDI-1120-10-77. Washington, D.C., 1977. 70p.

Further References

Additional citations relative to this section are in sections 2:C:2:b:(1), 4:B, and 4:E.

2. *Artillery*

One of the most prestigious branches of the Soviet ground forces or, for that matter, within the Ministry of Defense, is artillery, now properly known as Rocket Troops and Artillery. Artillery troops have long held an honorable position in Russian military annals—they were Stalin's "God of War"—and technological advances in missile weaponry in recent decades have enhanced that position. Since missile armaments have also become important to other armed forces components, missile equipment development is probably centered at the Ministry of Defense level. Nonetheless, a chief of rocket troops and artillery is present in Soviet Army headquarters with a large administrative directorate and coordinating staff.

Artillery and various kinds of missile units are found at the front level as well as in combined arms and tank armies, with representation in every Soviet Army division. An artillery division in a front consists of three artillery regiments, each containing three battalions of varying caliber weapons. Chiefs of rocket troops and artillery are part of the special staffs of fronts, armies, divisions, and regiments.

These citations provide information on the important role of artillery and rocket troops in the modern Soviet Army.

ARTICLES

2845.   Archer, Denis. "Russian Artillery in Land Forces." *NATO's Fifteen Nations* 17 (December 1972–January 1973), 72–76.

2846.   "Artillery, Yesterday and Today." *Soviet Military Translations,* no. 13 (August 1960), 8–15.

2847.   "The Big Guns: In Red Army, Still the 'King of Battle.'" *Army* 30 (September 1980), 29–31.

2848.   Daugherty, Darrell W. "Soviet Artillery, Massing Capability." *Field Artillery Journal* 45 (November-December 1977), 31–33.

2849.   Dick, Charles. "The Growing Soviet Artillery Threat." *Journal of the Royal United Service Institute for Defence Studies* 124 (June 1979), 66–73.

2850.   Donnelly, Christopher N. "Modern Soviet Artillery Doctrine and Practice." *NATO's Fifteen Nations* 24 (June-July 1974), 48–50.

2851.   Gordon, Harold J. "The Artillery." In Basil H. Liddell-Hart, ed., *The Soviet Army.* London: Weidenfeld & Nicolson, 1956. pp. 344–367.

2852.   "Ground Troops Missile Operations." *Soviet Military Translations,* no. 112 (December 1962), 22–25.

2853.   Ivanov, V. "Combatting Self-Propelled Artillery." *Field Artillery Journal* 43 (January-February 1975), 54–58.

2854.   Kazakov, K. P. "Soviet Artillery." *Soviet Military Review,* no. 10 (October 1965), 18–20.

2855.   Kizlov, S. "Battery Site." *Soviet Military Review,* no. 11 (November 1966), 30–32.

2856.   Kolesnik, A. "Artillery Battalion in an Amphibious Force." *Soviet Military Review,* no. 8 (August 1969), 25–27.

2857.   Kolpakov, D. "Artillery in Offensive." *Soviet Military Review* no. 12 (December 1968), 20–21.

2858.   Markov, A. "Calling for Fire 'On Oneself.'" *Soviet Military Review,* no. 11 (November 1974), 20–21.

2859.   Niessel, A. "Soviet Artillery Counterpreparation." *Military Review* 36 (August 1956), 73–75.

2860.   Owens, M. T., Jr. "Artillery Is the Real Threat in the Soviet Weapons Arsenal." *Marine Corps Gazette* 61 (July 1977), 35–42.

2861.   Patrick, George R. "Soviet Self-Propelled Artillery Doctrine." *Field Artillery Journal* 46 (July-August 1978), 27–29.

2862.   Peredl'skiy, G. Ye. "Always Combat Ready: An Interview." *Soviet Military Review,* no. 11 (November 1977), 2–3.

2863.   Polishchuk, S. "Artillery Unit Visual Observation: Translated from *Znamenosets,* November 1977." *Translations on USSR Military Affairs,* no. 1329 (February 10, 1978), 68–72.

2864.   Rodin, A. "Artillery Fire at Maximum Range." *Soviet Military Review,* no. 7 (July 1974), 20–21.

2865.   _____ . "Artillery Battalion in the Offensive." *Soviet Military Review,* no. 4 (April 1969), 26–28.

2866.   _____ . "Artillery Battalion on the March." *Soviet Military Review,* no. 8 (August 1967), 30–33.

2867.   _____ . "Guns vs. Tanks." *Soviet Military Review,* no. 2 (February 1970), 24–26.

2868.   _____ . "Roving Artillery Subunits." *Soviet Military Review,* no. 9 (September 1970), 24–26.

2869.   _____ . "Softening-up Fire before Attack." *Soviet Military Review,* no. 8 (August 1966), 26–28.

2870.   _____ . "Visual Estimation of Artillery Firing Data." *Soviet Military Review*, no. 3 (March 1966), 22–24.

2871.   Rogers, Patrick F. "The New Artillery." *Army* 30 (July 1980), 27–33.

2872.   Rudakov, V. "Destruction of Artillery Battles." *Soviet Military Review*, no. 10 (October 1976), 22–23.

2873.   Selyavin, A. "Co-Operation with the Artillery." *Soviet Military Review*, no. 8 (August 1973), 20–21.

2874.   _____ . "Direct Fire." *Soviet Military Review*, no. 11 (November 1975), 18–19.

2875.   Shackleton, N. A. "Soviet Fire Support." *Ordnance* 49 (July-August 1964), 58–61.

2876.   Shaw, I. R. L. "Soviet Artillery." *Journal of the Royal Artillery* 81 (April 1954), 90–97.

2877.   _____ . "Soviet Artillery." *Military Review* 34 (November 1954), 83–89.

2878.   Shtemenko, Sergei M. "The Queen of the Battlefield Yields Her Crown." In William R. Kintner and Harriet F. Scott, eds., *The Nuclear Revolution in Soviet Military Affairs*. Norman: University of Oklahoma Press, 1968. pp. 46–55.

2879.   Sidorenko, A. A. "The Offensive, a Glimpse of Modern Soviet Artillery Tactics." *Field Artillery Journal* 42 (July-August 1974), 32–45.

2880.   Sokolov, D. "Preparation of Artillery for Firing." *Soviet Military Review*, no. 12 (December 1973), 34–35.

2881.   "Soviet Artillery Counterpreparation." *Military Review* 36 (August 1956), 73–79.

2882.   "Soviet Rocket Artillery." *Military Review* 42 (June 1962), 102–104.

2883.   United States. Department of the Army. "Conventional Artillery Operations." *Opposing Forces: Europe*. FM 30-102. Washington, D.C., 1977. pp. 14/8–14/11.

2884.   Varentsov, S. S. "Missiles on the Battlefield." *Survival* 4 (March-April 1962), 89–90.

2885.   Yelshin, N. "The Soviet Artillery." *Soviet Military Review*, no. 6 (June 1975), 59–60.

DOCUMENTS, PAPERS, AND REPORTS

2886.   Khlebnikov, N. *Soviet Army Artillery.* DA-G2-TR-F-6574A. Washington, D.C.: Department of the Army, 1949. 17p.

2887.   Smith, Eddy. "Defeating Soviet Artillery." MA thesis, U.S. Army Command and General Staff College, 1979. 99p.

3. Motorized Infantry and Antitank Defense

Motorized infantry troops generally parallel the infantry and mechanized infantry of other armies, East and West. Because these troops constitute the basic arm of the Soviet ground forces, various agencies under General Pavlovskiy, rather than one special organization like the Main Directorate of tank troops, administer their affairs. These agencies prescribe motorized infantry as well as combined arms tactics and organization, prepare training schedules for units, and administer motorized infantry schools and officer personnel. Logistic support for the motorized infantry troops is provided by the other arms and services.

In the field, unless a theater command is established, the front is the largest field formation. It is a tactical and administrative unit, with size and composition subject to wide variation depending upon the mission. Roughly equivalent to a U.S. army group, a front could be composed of three or more combined arms armies (fifteen to twenty divisions), a tank army, one air army (ground support elements of the Soviet Air Force), and other appropriate combat and support elements. Airborne troops could be attached as required. Forces organic to the front headquarters could include artillery and missile units, communications and intelligence, and rear support units in battalion or larger strength.

The combined arms army is also a tactical and administrative organization; indeed, it is the basic Soviet field army. A typical combined arms army would include four motorized infantry divisions, a tank division, an artillery brigade, missile units, intelligence, signal, and engineer components. By altering the mix of motorized infantry and tank divisions plus artillery or missile support, the army organization has flexibility for offensive or defensive roles and can operate in different geographical areas or under various operational restraints.

The motorized infantry division in the field forces has three motorized infantry regiments, plus one tank and one artillery regiment. Each motorized infantry regiment has three battalions, with each battalion composed of three companies. The personnel strength in a Soviet division is somewhat smaller than that in a comparable U.S. division, with the former having 14,000 men and the latter 16,000. The ratio of tanks to troops is 1 to 53 in a Russian motorized infantry division, as compared to 1 to 74 in an American division.

Another important role falling to Soviet infantry is that of antitank defense, although such antiarmor duties are also shared by Russian tank and artillery units. Defense is provided through the use of the 100mm antitank gun T-12, the 73mm recoiless gun SPG-9, and antitank grenade launcher RPG-7, and antitank missiles, the AT-1 snapper, AT-2 swatter, and AT-3 sagger.

The citations in this subsection look at Soviet motorized infantry troops as well as the ground force's abilities in antitank warfare.

BOOKS

2888.   Biryukov, G., and G. Melnikov. *Antitank Warfare.* Translated from the Russian. Moscow: Progress Publishers, 1972. 156p.

2889.   Goldhamer, Herbert. *The Soviet Soldier: Soviet Military Management at the Troop Level.* New York: Crane, Russak, 1975. 352p.

2890.   Weeks, John. *Men Against Tanks: A History of Antitank Warfare.* London: David & Charles, 1975. 192p.

ARTICLES

2891.   Adams, Charles. "The Guards Proletarian Moscow-Minsk Motorized Rifle Division." *Review of the Soviet Ground Forces* 5 (January 1980), 15–18.

2892.   _____ . "The 'Iron' [Samara-Ul'yanovsk, Berdichev, 'Iron,' Thrice Red Banner, Orders of Suvorov and Bogdan Khmel'nitskiy] Motorized Rifle Division." *Review of the Soviet Ground Forces* 1 (August 1977), 49–52.

2893.   _____ . "The Sivash-Stettin Motorized Rifle Division." *Review of the Soviet Ground Forces* 5 (May 1980), 7–9.

2894.   _____ . "The 'Taman' Motorized Rifle Division." *Review of the Soviet Ground Forces* 2 (April 1978), 55–61.

2895.   Antsiz, B. "Antitank Guided Missiles in Defense." *Soviet Military Review,* no. 5 (May 1975), 18–20.

2896.   Bakanov, R. "Infantry and Tanks." *Soviet Military Review,* no. 8 (August 1969), 22–24.

2897.   Barabash, V. "The Development and Combat Employment of Antitank Equipment during the Postwar Years: Translated from *Voyenno Istoricheskiy Zhurnal,* March 1979." *Translations on USSR Military Affairs,* no. 1441 (May 24, 1979), 29–36.

2898.   Baxter, William P. "Soviet Doctrine Responds to the Antitank Missile Threat." *Army* 30 (August 1980), 29–32.

2899.   Bogatov, N. "Trainees Learn to Combat Armored Vehicles: Translated from *Znamenosets,* September 1980." *Translations on USSR Military Affairs,* no. 1554 (December 31, 1980), 106–111.

2900.   Donnelly, Christopher N. "Soviet Tactics for Overcoming NATO Antitank Defenses." *Infantry* 70 (September 1980), 20–26; (December 1980), 16–23.

2901.   Gavrikov, F. "Tactics of Small Units in Connection with the Revolution in Military Affairs." *Soviet Military Review,* no. 3 (March 1968), 3–6.

2902.   Gordon, Harold J. "The Infantry—Recent Trends." In Basil H. Liddell-Hart, ed., *The Soviet Army.* London: Weidenfeld & Nicolson, 1956. pp. 328–336.

2903.   Halloran, Bernard F. "Soviet Land Mine Warfare." *Military Engineer* 64 (March-April 1972), 115–118.

2904.   Jackson, W. E. "The Red Rifleman Today." *Marine Corps Gazette* 44 (June 1960), 24–26.

2905.   Karber, Phillip A. "Antitank Weapons and the Future of Armor: Soviet Thought and NATO's Procrastination." *Armed Forces Journal International* 114 (November 1976), 20.

2906.   ———. "The Soviet Antitank Debate." *Military Review* 56 (November 1976), 67–76.

2907.   King, D. E. "The Survival of Tanks in Battle." *Journal of the Royal United Service Institute for Defence Studies* 123 (March 1978), 26–31.

2908.   Kiselov, A. "Postwar Development of Antitank Defense Discussed: Translated from *Voyenno Istoricheskiy Zhurnal,* June 1978." *Translations on USSR Military Affairs,* no. 1376 (September 12, 1978), 24–33.

2909.   Kozlov, L. "Antitank Defense." *Soviet Military Review,* no. 7 (July 1975), 54–57.

2910.   Kubitanov, G. "Tank Tactics Against Antitank Missiles Discussed: Translated from *Znamenosets,* May 1979." *Translations on USSR Military Affairs,* no. 1492 (January 31, 1980), 21–27.

2911.   Lovasz, Steven A. "A Soviet Motorized Rifle Company." *Infantry* 65 (November-December 1975), 30–35.

2912.   Marriott, John. "Antitank Warfare." *NATO's Fifteen Nations* 24 (April-May 1979), 60–62.

2913.   Mataxis, Theodore C. "The Soviets Close the Gap." *Infantry School Quarterly* 47 (January 1957), 18–28.

2914.   ———— . "The Soviets Forge Ahead." *Infantry School Quarterly* 48 (April-June 1958), 14–27.

2915.   Nargele, D. G. "The Soviet Motorized Rifle Company Is Part of a Combined Arms." *Marine Corps Gazette* 62 (October 1978), 30–35.

2916.   Ogorkiewicz, Richard M. "Mechanized Infantry." *Military Review* 54 (August 1974), 67–73.

2917.   Parker, F. C. "The Soviet Motorized Rifle Division." *Review of the Soviet Ground Forces* 5 (January 1980), 1–2.

2918.   Parshin, A. "In the Wake of Battle Formations." *Soviet Military Review*, no. 1 (January 1971), 21–23.

2919.   Radevich, P. "Mines vs. Tanks." *Soviet Military Review*, no. 11 (November 1965), 37–38.

2920.   Robinson, Donald J., 2d. "Myths and Realities of Antitank Capabilities." *Marine Corps Gazette* 64 (March 1980), 41–48.

2921.   Selyavin, V. "[Antitank] Artillery Breeches Obstacles." *Soviet Military Review*, no. 8 (August 1975), 28–29.

2922.   Serov, A. "In an Advanced Detachment." *Soviet Military Review*, no. 8 (August 1969), 28–31.

2923.   ———— . "Motorized Infantry Battalion in Advance Guard." *Soviet Military Review*, no. 2 (February 1970), 19–21.

2924.   Shackleton, N. A. "The Motorized Infantry Threat." *Canadian Army Journal* 17 (January 1963), 16–27.

2925.   Sidorenko, A. A. "The Combat Capabilities of Motorized Infantry." *Soviet Military Review*, no. 9 (September 1966), 16–19.

2926.   Sokolov, K. "Antitank Defense." *Soviet Military Review*, no. 5 (May 1978), 18–21.

2927.   Stasenko, N. "Stars on Armor." *Soviet Military Review*, no. 8 (August 1969), 36–37.   The work of an antitank guided missile battery.

2928.   Szkoda, W. E. "Red Soldier—Mentality and Tactics: Antitank Defense." *Armor* 70 (September-October 1961), 24–28.

2929.   Turbiville, Graham H., Jr. "Soviet Infantry Assault Detachments." *Infantry* 65 (September-October 1975), 37–42.

2930.   Underhill, Garrett. "The Red Rifleman: A Closeup." *Life* 35 (July 14, 1953), 190–192.

2931. United States. Department of the Army. "Conventional Antitank Operations." *Opposing Forces: Europe.* FM 30-102. Washington, D.C., 1977. pp. 14/12–14/16.

2932. _____ . "The Motorized Rifle Battalion, Company, Division, Regiment." *Opposing Forces: Europe.* FM 30-102. Washington, D.C., 1977. pp. 5/1, 3/1, 9/1, 7/1.

2933. _____ . "The Threat." *The Infantry Battalion (Infantry Airborne, Air Assault, Ranger).* FM 7-20. Washington, D.C., 1978. pp. 2/1–2/42.

2934. _____ . "The Threat." *Infantry, Airborne, and Air Assault Division Operations.* FM 71-101. Washington, D.C., 1980. pp. 2/1–2/17.

2935. Yevtikhov, V. "Rocket Launcher vs. Tank." *Soviet Military Review,* no. 12 (December 1971), 20–21.

2936. Yezhov, N. "Fighting Against Tanks." *Soviet Military Review,* no. 2 (February 1974), 20–21.

2937. Zherdeyev, A. "The Assault Team." *Soviet Military Review,* no. 11 (November 1977), 18–20.

DOCUMENTS, PAPERS, AND REPORTS

2938. Baisden, Edward D., Jr. *Soviet Small Unit Defensive Tactics.* Research Report. New York: U.S. Army Institute for Advanced Russian and East European Studies, 1976. 45p.

2939. Frasche, Robert M. *The Soviet Motorized Rifle Company.* DDI-1100-77-76. Washington, D. C.: Defense Intelligence Agency, Department of Defense, 1976. 129p.

2940. Kosevich, Richard S. *The BMP-Equipped Motorized Rifle Battalion in the Offensive.* Research Report. New York: U.S. Army Institute for Advanced Russian and East European Studies, 1977. 36p.

2941. Kuhlman, Jimmy F. *The Influence of Antitank Technology on Soviet Offensive Tactics.* Research Report. New York: U.S. Army Institute for Advanced Russian and East European Studies, 1977. 35p.

2942. Loza, D. F., et al. *The Motorized Rifle Battalion in Modern Combat.* Translated from the Russian. FSTC-HT-23-175-73. Washington, D.C.: National Technical Information Service, 1972.

Further References

Additional citations of value are found in sections 4:A and 4:E.

4. Airborne/Airmobile Troops

Although generally considered a branch of the ground forces, operational control of Soviet airborne/airmobile troops is specifically reserved to the minister of defense and the chief of the General Staff.

These Russian troops do not become subordinate to a field command until committed by the minister of defense. This definite separation tends to impart to the administrative agency regulating these troops the status of a distinct component of the armed forces, even if it is nominally subordinate to the commander of Soviet ground forces.

A Soviet airborne division has a nucleus of three airborne regiments, each with three battalions, which are further subdivided into three companies each. Other components include an artillery regiment, an engineer battalion, a signal battalion, and various support companies and battalions. A Russian unit of this size is less than half as large as a similar American division, containing only 7,000 paratroops as opposed to 15,000 for the United States.

Soviet airborne/airmobile forces are trained to operate in a variety of roles, including activity in an enemy's rear, reconnaissance, or special missions. These units can be deployed from aircraft (by landing or paradrop) and from helicopters. Weapons range from small arms up through the BMD combat vehicle and 85mm antitank cannon.

This section examines the role of the airborne in the postwar Soviet ground forces, with emphasis on the new role of helicopter-borne airmobility.

ARTICLES

2943.   Adams, Charles. "The Guards 'Chernigov' Airborne Division." *Review of the Soviet Ground Forces* 5 (March 1980), 13–14.

2944.   Allard, Kenneth. "Soviet Airborne Forces and Preemptive Power Projection." *Parameters* 10 (December 1980), 42–51.

2945.   "Attacking from the Sky: 40th Birthday of Soviet Airborne Troops." *Soviet Military Review,* no. 8 (August 1970), 31–33.

2946.   Backofen, Joseph E., Jr. "A Legacy from Lenin." *Armor* 88 (January-February 1979), 10–12.

2947.   Belov, M. "Air Landing Forces." *Soviet Military Review,* no. 1 (January 1979), 22–23.

2948.   _____ . "Air Mobilization of Modern Armies." *Soviet Military Review,* no. 10 (October 1975), 13–15.

2949.   _____ . "Helicopters and Land Force Tactics." *Soviet Military Review,* no. 12 (December 1976), 22–24.

2950.   _____ . "Helicopters Used by Ground Troops." *Soviet Military Review,* no. 4 (April 1976), 30–31.

2951.   Blake, Peter J. "Soviet Airmobile Tactics." *U.S. Army Aviation Digest* 23 (April 1977), 1–3.

2952.   Bramlett, David A. "Soviet Airmobility: An Overview." *Military Review* 57 (January 1977), 14–25.

2953.   Butz, J. S. "Soviet Army Airmobility." *Army* 12 (September 1961), 86–88.

2954.   Chernyshov, Yu. "A Tactical Airborne Landing." *Soviet Military Review,* no. 5 (May 1980), 27–29.

2955.   Crutcher, Michael. "The Soviet Airborne Division." *Review of the Soviet Ground Forces* 5 (March 1980), 1–4.

2956.   DeMouche, Louis F. "Soviet Airborne Forces." *National Defence* 58 (November-December 1973), 228–230.

2957.   Donnelly, Christopher N. "Operations in the Enemy Rear: Soviet Doctrine and Tactics." *International Defense Review* 13 (January 1980), 35–41.

2958.   Epatko, Basil. "Will the Soviets Recreate an Organic Aviation Arm of the Ground Forces?" *Review of the Soviet Ground Forces* 5 (January 1980), 3–4.

2959.   Filatvov, V. "Capabilities of an Airborne Division Described: Translated from *Krasnaya Zvezda,* January 11, 1978." *Translations on USSR Military Affairs,* no. 1352 (May 15, 1978), 6–9.

2960.   Fullerton, John. "The New Charioteers: Soviet Assault Helicopter Planning." *Defense and Foreign Affairs Digest* 6 (August 1978), 34–35.

2961.   Kukushkin, V. "Accomplishments of Female Paratroopers Described: Translated from *Krasnaya Zvezda,* December 21, 1977." *Translations on USSR Military Affairs,* no. 1342 (March 29, 1978), 40–43.

2962.   Kurochkin, K. "Airborne Troops—Raiding Actions in Enemy Rear: Translated from *Krasnaya Zvezda,* July 17, 1980." *Translations on USSR Military Affairs,* no. 1565 (February 5, 1981), 4–8.

2963.   Livotov, P. "Soviet Airborne Tactics." *Military Review* 44 (October 1964), 29–33.

2964.   Mackintosh, Malcolm. "Soviet Airborne Troops." In Asher Lee, ed., *The Soviet Air and Rocket Forces.* New York: Praeger, 1959. pp. 160–170.

2965.   Margelov, Vasiliy F. "Commander of Airborne Troops on Organizational Development: Translated from *Voyennyye Znaniya*, December 1978." *Translations on USSR Military Affairs*, no. 1417 (March 9, 1979), 35–41.

2966.   ———. "The Airborne Troops." *Soviet Military Review*, no. 2 (February 1966), 20–21.

2967.   ———. "Soviet Airborne Troops: An Interview." *Soviet Military Review*, no. 5 (May 1973), 2–5.

2968.   Myers, Joe B. "Soviet Airmobility." *U.S. Army Aviation Digest* 17 (September 1971), 1–5.

2969.   Oden, Richard, and Frank Steinert. "The Soviet Airborne Troops." *Review of the Soviet Ground Forces* 5 (March 1980), 5–12.

2970.   "Paratroop Operations." *Soviet Military Translations*, no. 112 (December 1962), 26–30.

2971.   "Paratroopers in the Air." *Soviet Military Translations*, no. 74 (November 1961), 22–25.

2972.   Pavlenko, P. "Airborne Troops' Tactics—Postwar Developments: Translated from *Voyenno Istoricheskiy Zhurnal*, January 1980." *Translations on USSR Military Affairs*, no. 1511 (April 21, 1980), 31–38.

2973.   "Reports on Airborne Training: Translated from *Krasnaya Zvezda*, October 19 and December 18, 1980." *Translations on USSR Military Affairs*, no. 1575 (March 20, 1981), 40–45.

2974.   Samoylenko, Ya. "Tactical Airborne Landings." *Soviet Military Review*, no. 2 (February 1969), 12–16.

2975.   Shutov, G., et al. "The Guards 'Svir' Airborne Division." *Review of the Soviet Ground Forces* 1 (October 1977), 55–61.

2976.   Student, Kurt. "The Airborne Forces." In Basil H. Liddell-Hart, ed., *The Soviet Army*. London: Weidenfeld & Nicolson, 1956. pp. 376–384.

2977.   Sukhorukov, D. S. "Airborne Troops—Commander's Views and Activities: Translated from *Sovetskiy Voin*, July 1980." *Translations on USSR Military Affairs*, no. 1537 (October 3, 1980), 39–44.

2978.   ———. "Soviet Paratroopers: An Interview." *Soviet Military Review*, no. 8 (August 1980), 28–33.

2979.   Tolstoy, S. "The Role of the Helicopter in Combat Discussed: Translated from *Pravda*, August 20, 1978." *Translations on USSR Military Affairs*, no. 1389 (October 24, 1978), 45–49.

2980.   Tsvyetkov, Andrei. "A Rifle Company in an Airborne Landing." *Military Review* 41 (November 1961), 46–51.

2981.   Turbiville, Graham H., Jr. "The Attack Helicopter's Growing Role in Russian Combat Doctrine." *Army* 27 (December 1977), 28–33.

2982.   _____ . "Soviet Airborne Forces: Increasingly Powerful Factor in the Equation." *Army* 26 (April 1976), 18–24.

2983.   _____ . "Soviet Airborne Troops." *Military Review* 53 (April 1973), 60–70.

2984.   _____ . "Soviet Airborne Troops." In David R. Jones, ed., *Soviet Armed Forces Review Annual.* Gulf Breeze, Fla.: Academic International Press, 1979. p. 108.

2985.   _____ . "A Soviet View of Heliborne Assault Operations." *Military Review* 55 (October 1975), 3–15.

2986.   United States. Department of the Army. "Airborne Operations." *Opposing Forces: Europe.* FM 30-102. Washington, D.C., 1977. pp. 16/1–16/5.

2987.   _____ . "Air Assault Operations." *Opposing Forces: Europe.* FM 30-102. Washington, D.C., 1977. pp. 14/28–14/30.

2988.   Van Veen, E. "The Soviet Airborne Forces." *NATO's Fifteen Nations* 17 (June-July 1972), 58–63.

2989.   Vasilyev, S. "Communications in a Tactical Airborne Force." *Soviet Military Review,* no. 4 (April 1976), 26–28.

2990.   Vego, Milan. "The Dramatic Impact of Soviet Airborne Operations." *Defense and Foreign Affairs Digest* 8 (September 1980), 31–32.

2991.   Vigor, Peter H. "The 'Forward Reach' of the Soviet Armed Forces: Seaborne and Airborne Landings." In John Erickson and E. J. Feuchtwanger, eds., *Soviet Military Power and Performance.* Hamden, Conn.: Archon Books, 1979. pp. 183–211.

2992.   Wargo, Peter M. "The Evolution of Soviet Airmobility: Impact on the Seventies." *Military Review* 55 (November 1975), 3–13.

2993.   Wolfe, Thomas W. "Russia's Forces Go Mobile." *Interplay of European-American Affairs* 1 (May 1968), 28, 33–37.

2994.   Zimmerman, John S. "Arctic Airborne Operations." *Military Review* 32 (August 1952), 23–30.

DOCUMENTS, PAPERS, AND REPORTS

2995.   Dye, Joseph D. *Soviet BMD-Equipped Airborne Forces.* Research Report. New York: U.S. Army Institute for Advanced Russian and East European Studies, 1978. 54p.

2996.   Minnehan, Thomas J. *The Role of Airmobility in Soviet Military Doctrine.* Research Report. New York: U.S. Army Institute for Advanced Russian and East European Studies, 1975. 31p.

Further References

See also sections 2:C:2:b:(4) and 4:E, as well as the author's *Soviet Air and Strategic Rocket Forces* (Santa Barbara, Calif.: ABC-Clio, 1981), pp. 112–114.

5. Air Defense Troops of the Ground Forces

The air defense troops of the ground forces include antiaircraft personnel organic to combined arms formations, exclusive of the aviation elements of a front. They are administered from Soviet Army headquarters and serve under combined arms command in the field, with a necessarily close coordination with aviation, radiotechnical, and PVO-Strany elements in operational matters.

Throughout the postwar period, the Soviet ground forces have emphasized antiaircraft operations. Perhaps because of Great Patriotic War experiences, nearly every vehicle seemingly bristles with AAA, and special AAA vehicles are deployed. This defensive posture is of great concern in certain Western countries, especially those with helicopter gunships which seem to have become the latest target for the air defense troops of the ground forces.

The citations in this section examine Soviet Army AAA policy and practice.

ARTICLES

2997.   "Air Defense of the Ground Forces: Translated from *Krasnaya Zvezda*, February 6, 1979." *Review of the Soviet Ground Forces* 4 (November 1979), 30–31.

2998.   Alder, Konrad. "Air Defense Suppression in a Central European Theater." *Armada International* 4 (March-April 1980), 62.

2999.   Babiasz, Frank E., and Carl E. Daschke. "Anti-Helicopter Operations." *U.S. Army Aviation Digest* 26 (May 1980), 24–27.

3000.   Belov, M. "How to Fight Helicopters." *Soviet Military Review,* no. 9 (September 1979), 18–19.

3001.   Bogdanov, Y. "Accurate Antiaircraft Fire: An AA Battery Covers a Motorized Infantry Battalion." *Soviet Military Review,* no. 8 (August 1970), 17–20.

3002.   Campbell, E. Gary. "Threat—Volatile: Small Arms and Helicopters Don't Mix." *U.S. Army Aviation Digest* 26 (August 1980), 26–30.

3003.   Crutcher, Michael H. "Soviet Air Defense Tactics." *Review of the Soviet Ground Forces* 5 (May 1980), 5–6.

3004.   Daschke, Carl E. "The Threat: How to Fight Helicopters—Soviet Style." *U.S. Army Aviation Digest* 26 (January 1980), 45–48.

3005.   Dedov, V. "Control of Antiaircraft Artillery Fire Described: Translated from *Voyennyye Znaniya,* December 1977." *Translations on USSR Military Affairs,* no. 1331 (February 16, 1978), 48–51.

3006.   Kiryukhin, M. "An Antiaircraft Ambush." *Soviet Military Review,* no. 7 (July 1978), 26–27.

3007.   "Know the Threat: The ZSU-23-4." *U.S. Army Aviation Digest* 24 (May 1978), 41.

3008.   Levchenko, Arty P. "Ground Forces Air Defense Chief Reviews Training: Translated from *Krasnaya Zvezda,* August 16, 1978." *Translations on USSR Military Affairs,* no. 1398 (November 29, 1978), 23–27.

3009.   Malone, Daniel K. "The Air Defense of Soviet Ground Forces." *Air Force Magazine* 61 (March 1978), 78–83.

3010.   Mikhailov, V. "Covering the Motorized Infantry." *Soviet Military Review,* no. 8 (August 1973), 24–25.

3011.   ———. "Firing at Low-Flying Targets: The Organization of Air Defense in Motorized Infantry and Tank Battalions in Defense." *Soviet Military Review,* no. 10 (October 1970), 18–20.

3012.   Rose, John P. "The Battlefield Threat: Soviet Concepts, Doctrine, and Strategy." *Air Defense Magazine* (July-August 1978), 24–29.

3013.   Sklyarov, I. "Firing Proficiency for AA Machine Gun Elements." *Soviet Military Review,* no. 11 (November 1966), 33–34.

3014.   Stephan, Robert K. "The Indirect Fire Threat." *U.S. Army Aviation Digest* 24 (July 1978), 15–17.

3015.   United States. Department of the Army. "Ground Forces Air Defense Operations." *Opposing Forces: Europe*. FM 30-102. Washington, D.C., 1977. pp. 14/17–14/20.

3016.   Williams, Forrest D. "Threat: SAM/AAA—You Bet Your Life!" *U.S. Army Aviation Digest* 26 (October 1980), 8–11.

3017.   Zhdanovich, B. "Training Results of Ground Forces Air Defense Units Discussed: Translated from *Znamenosets*, November 1978." *Translations on USSR Military Affairs*, no. 1417 (March 9, 1979), 24–28.

DOCUMENTS, PAPERS, AND REPORTS

3018.   Bailey, Glenn A., Jr. *Air Defense of the Soviet Motorized Rifle Battalion in Combat*. Research Report. New York: U.S. Army Institute for Advanced Russian and East European Studies, 1978. 44p.

3019.   Crutcher, Michael H. *Soviet Tactical Air Defense: An Introduction to the Employment of Antiaircraft Unit Weapons for the Defense of Maneuver Forces*. Research Report. New York: U.S. Army Institute for Advanced Russian and East European Studies, 1975. 58p.

Further References

Additional citations of value are found in the author's *Soviet Air and Strategic Rocket Forces* (Santa Barbara, Calif.: ABC-Clio, 1981), pp. 180–182.

6. Naval Infantry and Marine Corps

Soviet naval infantry and marines are charged with amphibious warfare, but, like the U.S. Marine Corps, these groups are under navy, not ground forces, jurisdiction. Naval infantry is administratively subordinate to the Soviet Navy commander of naval infantry in Moscow, but units operate under the fleet commander in their assigned area.

Fleet naval infantry is organized into regiments which report directly to the deputy fleet commander for naval infantry. These regiments are organizationally similar to motorized infantry regiments, with three infantry battalions, a tank battalion, and several specialized companies, such as those for engineers, signal personnel, and reconnaissance, as well as appropriate rocket, air defense, and antitank batteries.

Naval infantry and marine operations are primarily amphibious landings from the sea or across large rivers. Unlike U.S. Marine Corps operations, the second wave of Soviet amphibious assault troops are not normally naval infantrymen, but motorized infantrymen. Thus the

12,000 naval infantry, with a few marines, have been made responsible for opening beaches for the ground troops, who will then carry on the battle.

ARTICLES

3020.   Abashkin, V. "Naval Infantry—Tank Battalion Training: Translated from *Kommunist Vooruzhennykh Sil,* August 1980." *Translations on USSR Military Affairs,* no. 1548 (November 28, 1980), 8–14.

3021.   Beregov, P. "Tanks in an Amphibious Force." *Soviet Military Review,* no. 10 (October 1969), 28–31.

3022.   Cliff, Donald K. "The Paloondral." *Marine Corps Gazette* 56 (January 1972), 18–27.   Formal title of the naval infantry.

3023.   _____ . "Soviet Naval Infantry, a New Capability." *Naval War College Review* 24 (June 1971), 90–101.

3024.   Daly, Robert W. "Russian Combat Landings." *Marine Corps Gazette* 53 (June 1969), 39–42.

3025.   Garthoff, Raymond L. "Soviet Doctrine on Amphibious Operations." *Marine Corps Gazette* 42 (May 1958), 54–60.

3026.   Groenke, Erwin. "The Soviet Naval Infantry: Translated from *Marine Kalender der D.D.R., 1975." Review of the Soviet Ground Forces* 2 (April 1978), 62–71.

3027.   Howe, Jonathan T. "Soviet Beachhead in the Third World." *U.S. Naval Institute Proceedings* 94 (October 1968), 60–67.

3028.   Hull, Andrew W. "Soviet Naval Infantry." *Marine Corps Gazette* 64 (July 1980), 65–70.

3029.   Meehan, John F., 3d. "The Soviet Marine Corps." *Military Review* 52 (October 1972), 84–94.

3030.   Meister, Juergen. "Amphibious Assault—Soviet Style." *Navy* 62 (October 1957), 328–329.

3031.   Nevskiy, N. A. "Soviet Amphibious Teaching." *Marine Corps Gazette* 44 (March 1960), 26.

3032.   Pritchard, Charles G. "Soviet Amphibious Force Projection." In Michael MccGwire and John McDonnell, eds., *Soviet Naval Influence: Domestic and Foreign Dimensions.* New York: Praeger, 1977. pp. 246–277.

3033.   _____ . "They Are Proud to Claim the Title of Soviet Marines." *U.S. Naval Institute Proceedings* 98 (March 1972), 18–30.

3034.   Shutov, G. "Visiting the Marines." *Soviet Military Review,* no. 12 (December 1976), 58–59.

3035.   Stockell, Charles W. "The Soviet Naval Infantry." In Michael MccGwire, ed., *Soviet Naval Developments: Capabilities and Context.* New York: Praeger, 1973. pp. 172–175.

3036.   Takle, E. P. "The Soviet Naval Infantry." *Journal of the Royal United Service Institute for Defence Studies,* 120 (June 1975), 29–31.

3037.   Van Veen, E. "Soviet Naval Infantry—A Coming Weapon?" *NATO's Fifteen Nations* 18 (February-March 1973), 82–86.

3038.   Villar, G. R. "Amphibious Forces in Europe and the Soviet Union." *U.S. Naval Institute Proceedings* 103 (November 1977), 112–117.

3039.   Vyunenko, N. P. "Soviet Amphibious Operations." *Marine Corps Gazette* 49 (March 1965), 29–33.

Further References

See also section 2:C:3:e and the author's *The Soviet Navy, 1941–78: A Guide to Sources in English* (Santa Barbara, Calif.: ABC-Clio, 1980), pp. 169–172.

D. Rear Services and Combat Support: Logistics and Transport, Communications, Medical and Technical Support, and Engineers

In the Soviet system, the chief of rear services, a deputy minister of defense, is responsible for coordinating all logistical matters and participates in the logistical aspects of high-level staff planning.

Supply and service functions common to all military personnel and units, including those pertaining to food, clothing, personal equipment, fuel and lubricants, medical and veterinary services, post exchanges, and transportation, as well as research and development, procurement, storage, issue, and maintenance of common-use items fall under the office of the chief of rear services.

The Soviet ground forces, like other force components, deal directly with specific directorates and commands for special requirements. Despite the high degree of centralization in rear services, deputies in that area have enough flexibility and opportunity for initiative to permit them to adjust logistic support as combat conditions and technical demands vary.

1. Logistics and Transport

The Soviet military has traditionally emphasized the delivery of combat supplies above all else. The order of priority is usually 1) ammunition; 2) petroleum, oil, and lubricants (POL); 3) technical supplies; 4) rations; and 5) nontechnical equipment.

Ammunition and POL priorities are inflexible, even if troops are forced to forage for rations. The Russians supply units involved in the main combat effort at the expense of units involved in secondary efforts.

According to Soviet logistics doctrine, a higher unit is generally responsible for allocating and delivering supplies to a lower unit. This principle appears to be flexible, however, and can be amended as the situation dictates. For example, higher-level ground forces units may bypass one or more echelons in delivery of supplies (e. g., army to regiment or battalion), while an increase in the amount of transportation available at division and regiment levels allows lower units to pick up supplies from higher units when necessary.

Rail is still the primary method of transporting military supplies to areas as far forward as the front. Beyond this, motor transport is most important, and increased motorization is lessening the dependence on rail. Use of air transport to move urgently needed items is growing. In general, Soviet tank and motorized infantry divisions carry sufficient supplies to operate independently of logistical support by high echelons for a limited time.

ARTICLES

3040.   Baxter, William P. "Logistics with a Difference." *Army* 30 (November 1980), 29.

3041.   Borgart, Peter. "The Soviet Transport Air Force: Aircraft and Capabilities." *International Defense Review* 12 (June 1979), 945–950.

3042.   Brehat, Victor. "Air Transport Logistical Capabilities Discussed: Translated from *Defense Nationale*, October 1978." *Translations on USSR Military Affairs*, no. 1399 (December 4, 1978), 61–63.

3043.   Dibbern, Victoria. "Food for the Soviet Soldier." *Army Logistician* 10 (March-April 1978), 18–23.

3044.   Donnelly, Christopher N. "Rear Support for the Soviet Ground Forces." *International Defense Review* 12 (March 1979), 344–350.

3045.   "Examples of Combat Support Described: Translated from *Krasnaya Zvezda*, July 12, 1979." *Translations on USSR Military Affairs*, no. 1482 (December 13, 1979), 67–69.

3046.   Finayev, A. "Signal Unit Training Described: Translated from *Krasnaya Zvezda*, June 3, 1980." *Translations on USSR Military Affairs*, no. 1540 (October 24, 1980), 80–81.

3047.   Friedman, William S. "Air Transportation, A Key Factor in Soviet Strength." *Pegasus* (April 1951), 4–7.

3048.   Fullerton, John. "Expanding Airlift Capacity." *Defense and Foreign Affairs Digest* 6 (March 1978), 34–35.

3049.   Gavrisheff, Mikhail. "The Third Division (Military Transportation) of the Soviet Armed Forces General Staff." *Military Review* 38 (January 1959), 28–35.

3050.   Golushko, I. "Capabilities of Rear Services Discussed: Translated from *Voyennyye Znaniya*, July 1978." *Translations on USSR Military Affairs*, no. 1384 (October 6, 1978), 1–4.

3051.   _____ . "The Commander's Role in Controlling Logistics." *Soviet Military Review*, no. 9 (September 1978), 12–14.

3052.   Heymont, Irving. "The Soviet Army Logistical System." *Military Review* 37 (January 1958), 9–18.

3053.   Hinrichs, Hans. "The Supply System of the Red Army." In Basil H. Liddell-Hart, ed., *The Soviet Army*. London: Weidenfeld & Nicolson, 1956. pp. 265–294.

3054.   "History and New Tasks of the Fuel Supply Service." *Soviet Military Translations*, no. 238 (October 1965), 5–10.

3055.   Hotze, William R., and Terry L. Schott. "Soviet Logistics: How Good Is It?" *Army Logistician* 8 (March-April 1976), 18–21.

3056.   "An Important Stage in the Development of the Logistical Units of the Soviet Armed Forces." *Soviet Military Translations*, no. 331a (October 1966), 1–8.

3057.   "Improvements in Army Logistical Personnel." *Soviet Military Translations*, no. 266 (February 1966), 6–9.

3058.   "Improving the Organization of Soviet Military Transport." *Soviet Military Translations*, no. 349a (November 1966), 1–6.

3059.   Izgarshev, V. "Operations of Military Transport Aviation Described: Translated from *Pravda*, January 4, 1979." *Translations on USSR Military Affairs*, no. 1419 (March 15, 1979), 85–87.

3060.   Klemin, A. "Tasks and Capabilities of the Central Military Transport Service: Translated from *Krasnaya Zvezda,* March 4, 1978." *Translations on USSR Military Affairs,* no. 1362 (July 12, 1978), 5–8.

3061.   Kryukov, Alexei. "Soviet Railway Troops." *Soviet Military Review,* no. 8 (August 1974), 2–4.

3062.   Kurkotkin, Semen K. "Importance of Logistical Support Discussed: Translated from *Krasnaya Zvezda,* July 3, 1979." *Translations on USSR Military Affairs,* no. 1482 (December 13, 1979), 34–38.

3063.   ———. "Logistics of the Soviet Armed Forces." *Soviet Military Review,* no. 8 (August 1978), 2–6.

3064.   Kushch, I. "Battalion Logistics Control." *Soviet Military Review,* no. 12 (December 1978), 22–24.

3065.   Malyugin, N. "Logistical Support of Combat in a Desert." *Soviet Military Review,* no. 8 (August 1966), 29–30.

3066.   ———. "Problems of Military Transportation." *Soviet Military Review,* no. 3 (March 1976), 25–27.

3067.   Nesterov, N. "Divisional Exchange Point." *Military Review* 24 (June 1944), 73–78.

3068.   Novikov, M. "Combat Logistics Today." *Soviet Military Review,* no. 5 (May 1966), 39–42.

3069.   "Potential Plus Initiative: Notes of an Executive Officer on the Rear Services." *Soviet Military Translations,* no. 41 (December 1960), 8–11.

3070.   Prelle, Karen. "Soviets Cook on the Move." *Army Logistician* 10 (March-April 1978), 22–23.

3071.   "Rear Services Equipment." *Soviet Military Translations,* no. 153a (September 1964), 5–9.

3072.   Safronov, N. M. "The Organization of Rear Troop Support." In Nikolay A. Lomov, ed., *Scientific-Technical Progress and the Revolution in Military Affairs: A Soviet View.* Translated from the Russian. Soviet Military Thought Series, no. 3. Washington, D.C.: U.S. Government Printing Office, 1974. pp. 118–125.

3073.   Scott, William F. "The U.S.S.R's Growing Global Mobility." *Air Force Magazine* 60 (March 1977), 57–61.

3074.   Sysoyev, P. "Logistical Support in Modern Combat Discussed: Translated from *Krasnaya Zvezda,* January 6, 1981." *Translations on USSR Military Affairs,* no. 1575 (March 20, 1981), 60–64.

3075.   "The Trouble with Military Equipment Transport." *Soviet Military Translations,* no. 128 (October 1963), 16–17.

3076.   Turbiville, Graham H., Jr. "Computers Speed Up Soviet Ground Force Logistics." *Army Logistician* 6 (July-August 1974), 28–31.

3077.   _____ . "Soviet Ground Force Logistics." *Army Logistician* 4 (July-August 1972), 18–21.

3078.   _____ . "Soviet Logistic Support for Ground Operations." *Military Review* 56 (July 1976), 29–39.

3079.   Underhill, Garrett. "Soviet Air Transport." *Ordnance* 42 (January-February 1958), 624–628.

3080.   United States. Department of Defense. Defense Intelligence Agency. "Logistics." *Handbook of the Soviet Armed Forces.* DDB-2680-40-78. Washington, D.C.: U.S. Government Printing Office, 1978. pp. 7/1–7/9.

3081.   United States. Department of the Army. "Combat Service Support Operations." *Opposing Forces: Europe.* FM 30-102. Washington, D.C., 1977. pp. 15/1–15/6.

3082.   Veshchikov, P. "Ground Troops Logistical Support in Winter Described: Translated from *Znamenosets,* January 1979." *Translations on USSR Military Affairs,* no. 1438 (May 18, 1979), 61–65.

DOCUMENTS, PAPERS, AND REPORTS

3083.   Corneil, Terry C. *Logistics of the Soviet Army: An Overview.* Research Report. New York: U.S. Army Institute for Advanced Russian and East European Studies, 1979. 40p.

3084.   Trapans, A. *Logistics in Recent Soviet Military Writings.* RAND Memorandum RM-5062-PR. Santa Monica, Calif.: RAND Corporation, 1966. 38p.

Further References

Additional material is found in the general studies cited in section 4:A.

2. Communications

Communications activity in the Soviet Army is known as signal work. Signal troops are organic to all echelons of the ground forces where signal radio or telephone equipment requiring special training for operation and maintenance is used.

Those units whose missions require radar operations, principally in the air defense troops of the ground forces, are served by radiotechnical troops. The central administrative seat for communications personnel is in the headquarters of PVO-Strany, the National Air Defense Forces.

BOOKS

3085.   Raggett, R. J., ed. *Jane's Military Communications*. New York: Watts, 1979–. v. 1–.

ARTICLES

3086.   Belov, Andrey I. "Chief of Signal Troops Discusses the Importance of Field Training: Translated from *Krasnaya Zvezda*, July 14, 1978." *Translations on USSR Military Affairs*, no. 1382 (October 3, 1978), 60–64.

3087.   ———. "Chief of Signal Troops on Present-Day Military Communications: Translated from *Krasnaya Zvezda*, May 6, 1979." *Translations on USSR Military Affairs*, no. 1442 (May 25, 1979), 63–67.

3088.   ———. "Chief of Signal Troops on Tasks and Capabilities: Translated from *Voyennyye Znaniya*, March 1979." *Translations on USSR Military Affairs*, no. 1438 (May 18, 1979), 33–37.

3089.   ———. "Communication and Troop Control." *Soviet Military Review*, no. 4 (April 1980), 22–25.

3090.   ———. "Signal Troops in the Soviet Armed Forces." *Soviet Military Review*, no. 11 (November 1973), 2–4.

3091.   Filimonov, G. "Information about the Signal Troops: Translated from *Agitator Armii I Flota*, April 1978." *Translations on USSR Military Affairs*, no. 1361 (July 7, 1978), 36–39.

3092.   Leonov, A. "The Past and Present of Signal Troops." *Soviet Military Review*, no. 1 (January 1966), 14–16.

3093.   "New Developments in the Communications Field." *Soviet Military Translations*, no. 316 (August 1966), 1–9.

3094.   Obukhov, V. "Establishing Radio Contact." *Soviet Military Review*, no. 12 (December 1973), 22–23.

3095.   Petukhov, D. "Types and Means of Communication." *Soviet Military Review*, no. 11 (November 1973), 5–8.

3096.   Riccardelli, Richard F. "Soviet-Warsaw Pact Alternatives to Radio Communications on the Electronic Battlefield." *Military Intelligence* 5 (January-February 1979), 14–18.

3097.   "The Role of the Signal Specialists in Today's Soviet Army Evaluated." *Soviet Military Translations,* no. 334a (October 1966), 6–10.

3098.   Rossov, Y. "Communication Training Centre." *Soviet Military Review,* no. 9 (September 1973), 30–31.

3099.   Semenchenko, N. "Signal Troop Training Described: Translated from *Izvestiya,* January 19, 1979." *Translations on USSR Military Affairs,* no. 1435 (May 15, 1979), 6–11.

3100.   United States. Department of the Army. "Tactical Communications." *Opposing Forces: Europe.* FM 30-102. Washington, D.C., 1977. pp. 14/46–14/49.

3101.   Vasilyev, S. "Communications in an Offensive." *Soviet Military Review,* no. 9 (September 1975), 18–20.

Further References

See also sections 2:C:2:f and 4:A.

3. Medical and Technical Support

To counter anticipated heavy losses of personnel and equipment in war, the Soviets station their medical support and repair facilities as close to the tactical area as possible without sacrificing security. The increased use of mobile hospitals and equipment repair shops in recent years indicates that the Soviet military hopes to salvage as much of its human and material resources as possible.

The Soviet armed forces medical system is administered at Ministry of Defense level by the chief of the Central Military Medical Directorate, who is subordinate to the chief of rear services. General hospitals in the interior of the U.S.S.R. come under the dual control of the Central Military Medical Directorate and the Ministry of Health. In time of war, the Central Military Medical Directorate establishes specialized hospitals in the interior.

Below the Ministry of Defense level, the military district (of which the U.S.S.R. is divided into sixteen) medical directorate is responsible for the medical services of the entire military district. Additionally, in wartime it administers several front hospitals for screening, special surgery, convalescent care, and evacuation to the interior.

Physicians for the Soviet armed forces come either from civilian life or the Kirov Military Medical Academy in Leningrad. Nurses for military installations are recruited from among civilian nurses. Female civilian nurses may be drafted in wartime.

Repairs to damaged or inoperable equipment are necessary in every army. The Soviets take great pride in their claimed ability to make repairs and adjustments quickly, often in a mobile setting.

The citations in this section detail Russian technical and medical support for their ground forces.

ARTICLES

3102.   Alyoshechkin, Y. "Training in Field Repair." *Soviet Military Review,* no. 6 (June 1975), 28–29.

3103.   Amelchenko, V. "In Reliable Hands." *Soviet Military Review,* no. 10 (October 1969), 7–9.   Armor maintenance.

3104.   Babynin, Ye. "Armored Vehicle Maintenance Procedures Described: Translated from *Krasnaya Zvezda,* May 26, 1978." *Translations on USSR Military Affairs,* no. 1372 (August 23, 1978), 49–52.

3105.   Bezborodko, M. "Tank Maintenance in Conditions of High Humidity." *Soviet Military Review,* no. 10 (October 1965), 34–35.

3106.   "Combat Medics in the Field: Translated from *Krasnaya Zvezda,* July 17, 1979." *Review of the Soviet Ground Forces* 4 (November 1979), 31–32.

3107.   Gruzdev, B. "Tank Maintenance on a March." *Soviet Military Review,* no. 10 (October 1975), 30–31.

3108.   Ivanov, R. "Preparing Tanks for Underwater Driving." *Soviet Military Review,* no. 3 (March 1980), 29–30.

3109.   Komarov, Fedor I. "Medical Care of Servicemen Described: Translated from *Kommunist Vooruzhennykh Sil,* May 1979." *Translations on USSR Military Affairs,* no. 1465 (September 21, 1979), 29–37.

3110.   _____ . "Military Health Care Measures Described: Translated from *Sovetskiy Voin,* October 1978." *Translations on USSR Military Affairs,* no. 1416 (March 7, 1979), 195–200.

3111.   Mashtakov, M. "Field Training of [Armor] Repairmen." *Soviet Military Review,* no. 11 (November 1969), 26–27.

3112.   Pontryagin, M. "Technical Support of a Tank Battalion in the Attack." *Soviet Military Review,* no. 7 (July 1968), 29–31.

3113.   Popov, V. "Preparation of Tanks for Summer Operations: Translated from *Znamenosets,* April 1978." *Translations on USSR Military Affairs,* no. 1361 (July 7, 1978), 26–29.

3114.   Ryazantsev, D. "Armored and Other Vehicle Repairs in Combat." *Soviet Military Review,* no. 12 (December 1977), 39–40.

3115. _____ . "Tank Maintenance." *Soviet Military Review,* no. 12 (December 1974), 40–41.

3116. _____ . "Vehicle Maintenance after Exercises." *Soviet Military Review,* no. 11 (November 1977), 26–27.

3117. Schulz, Heinrich. "Soviet Military Medicine." *Institute for the Study of the USSR Bulletin* 13 (June 1966), 14–20.

3118. Shevchenko, N. "Rehabilitation of Armored Equipment in the Field." *Soviet Military Review,* no. 6 (June 1980), 25–26.

3119. United States. Department of the Army. "Medical Support." *Opposing Forces: Europe.* FM 30-102. Washington, D.C., 1977. pp. 15/7–15/9.

DOCUMENTS, PAPERS, AND REPORTS

3120. Union of Soviet Socialist Republics. Ministry of Defense. *The Maintenance of Tanks.* JPRS 27193. Arlington, Va.: Joint Publications Research Service, 1965. 153p.

3121. United States. Department of Defense. Defense Intelligence Agency. *Medical Support of the Soviet Ground Forces.* DDB-1150-18-79. Washington, D.C., 1979. 33p.

Further References

See also the general works in section 4:A and references in 4:D:4.

4. Engineers

In the ground elements of the combined arms field forces, engineer troops serve purely as "combat engineers," a breed of can-doers known in every modern army. The chief of engineer troops in the Ministry of Defense administers engineer personnel, who should not be confused with the logistical people known as engineer-technical troops. Other Soviet troop branches perform civil engineering, sanitation, and mapping functions; they are comparable to the U.S. Engineer Corps. Engineer troops in units at division level or higher are referred to as "engineers"; those on a lower level closer to combat are called "sappers."

BOOKS

3122. Foss, Christopher F., ed. *Jane's Combat Support Equipment.* New York: Watts, 1978.–. v. 1–.

ARTICLES

3123.   Aganov, Sergei K. "Chief of Engineer Troops on History and Tasks: Translated from *Voyennyye Znaniya*, June 1979." *Translations on USSR Military Affairs*, no. 1464 (September 13, 1979), 36–41.

3124.   ———. "Chief of Engineer Troops on Tasks and Capabilities: Translated from *Krasnaya Zvezda*, June 15, 1978." *Translations on USSR Military Affairs*, no. 1378 (September 21, 1978), 46–50.

3125.   Baberdin, V. "Engineer Equipment—Bridging Equipment Described: Translated from *Voyennyye Znaniya*, January 1980." *Translations on USSR Military Affairs*, no. 1505 (March 20, 1980), 62–66.

3126.   Balagurov, A. "Engineers Pave the Way." *Soviet Military Review*, no. 3 (March 1966), 28–29.

3127.   Bystrov, V. "Engineer Support of a March in Mountains." *Soviet Military Review*, no. 2 (February 1966), 28–29.

3128.   Darn, Helmuth. "Engineer and Technical Forces." In Basil H. Liddell-Hart, ed., *The Soviet Army*. London: Weidenfeld & Nicolson, 1956. pp. 367–376.

3129.   Davidson-Huston, John. "A Russian Soldier." *Royal Engineers' Journal* 68 (March 1954), 49–53.

3130.   Deaton, James E. "Engineer Capabilities of the Soviet and Warsaw Pact Armies." *Military Engineer* 71 (November-December 1979), 416–423.

3131.   Donnelly, Christopher N. "Combat Engineers of the Soviet Army." *International Defense Review* 11 (February 1978), 193–200.

3132.   Draper, Stephen E. "Challenges to Engineer Doctrine." *Engineer* 9 (Fall 1979), 9–14.

3133.   "Engineer Equipment in Modern Battle." *Soviet Military Translations*, no. 216 (December 1965), 15–19.

3134.   "Engineer Support to Water Crossings." *International Defense Review* 11 (February 1978), 201–203.

3135.   "Foreign Combat Engineer Technology: The Soviets. *Army Research, Development, and Acquisition* 20 (July-August 1979), 22–23.

3136.   "Future Engineers." *Soviet Military Translations*, no. 152a (September 1964), 38–44.

3137.   Goshko, P. "Pontoon Regiment Training Described: Translated from *Krasnaya Zvezda*, August 23, 1979." *Translations on USSR Military Affairs*, no. 1491 (January 23, 1980), 58–60.

3138.   Karabievsky, B. "Engineer Reconnaissance of Roads." *Soviet Military Review*, no. 7 (July 1966), 26–27.

3139.   Karin, V. "Bridge-Building Training of a Combat Engineer Platoon: Translated from *Znamenosets*, January 1978." *Translations on USSR Military Affairs*, no. 1344 (April 7, 1978), 115–119.

3140.   Kazmin, L. "Combat Engineers Ensure Tank Crossings." *Soviet Military Review*, no. 5 (May 1968), 29–31.

3141.   Kharchenko, V. "Soviet Army Engineers." *Soviet Military Review*, no. 12 (December 1965), 12–14.

3142.   Kirdeyev, V. "Operations of Combat Area Obstacle-Clearing Parties: Translated from *Znamenosets*, March 1978." *Translations on USSR Military Affairs*, no. 1358 (June 21, 1978), 5–8.

3143.   Parr, Arthur J., Jr. "Soviet Combat Engineers." *Engineer* 8 (Winter 1978–1979), 6–11.

3144.   ———. "Soviet Engineer Equipment." *Engineer* 9 (Fall 1979), 34.

3145.   Polyakov, Alexi. "Special Troops—Pontoon Battalion Training: Translated from *Krasnaya Zvezda*, September 14, 1979." *Translations on USSR Military Affairs*, no. 1499 (February 26, 1980), 49–51.

3146.   Savranchuk, P. "Pontoon Bridge Company Training Procedures Described: Translated from *Znamenosets*, September 1977." *Translations on USSR Military Affairs*, no. 1324 (January 13, 1978), 82–85.

3147.   "Studies on Engineering Support of Combined Arms Combat." *Soviet Military Translations*, no. 277 (June 1966), 1–40.

3148.   "The Training of Military Engineers." *Soviet Military Translations*, no. 255 (May 1966), 1–7.

3149.   United States. Department of the Army. "Engineer Support." *Opposing Forces: Europe*. FM 30-102. Washington, D.C., 1977. pp. 14/41–14/45.

3150.   Zamyatin, G. "Tasks and Capabilities of Engineering Officers Discussed: Translated from *Krasnaya Zvezda*, June 2, 1978." *Translations on USSR Military Affairs*, no. 1379 (September 25, 1978), 1–6.

DOCUMENTS, PAPERS, AND REPORTS

3151.   Parr, Arthur J., Jr. *Soviet Combat Engineer Support.* Research
Report. New York: U.S. Army Institute for Advanced Russian and East
European Studies, 1978. 65p.

3152.   United States. Department of the Army. Training and Doctrine Command. *TRADOC Threat Monograph: A Comparison of Selected
NATO and Warsaw Pact Engineer Organizations and Equipment.* Fort Monroe, Va., 1977. 64p.

Further References

A limited number of follow-up citations are found in section 4:A.

E. Personnel, Training, and Exercises

The Soviet ground forces devote much time and effort to tactical and
military-technical training in field exercises. Soviet military literature,
as reflected in the Joint Publication Research Service's *Translations on
USSR Military Affairs,* the *Soviet Military Review,* and other sources,
frequently reiterates that training and employing troops, units, arms,
and equipment in varying environments will insure success in
combat—and commanders insist that training be conducted under
conditions as closely approximating actual combat as possible. This
realism in training extends from small-scale to giant exercises and
maneuvers, which are coordinated by the combat training directorates
in ground forces headquarters and in the Ministry of Defense.

Military training in the U.S.S.R. includes civilian premilitary training, in-service training, and reserve training. The first is aimed at
young people and is designed to influence both those in school and
those on the job.

In-service training begins when a recruit or draftee arrives at a
tactical unit and normally continues throughout his/her tour of service.
Designed to bring all military personnel to a peak of combat effectiveness, the training programs are usually identical from year to year.
Their major elements are tactical training, firing, physical education,
and political indoctrination. Field training is constant and rigorous.

A system of military high schools and colleges, command and staff
schools, and an academy of the general staff provides career military
personnel with professional, formal academic training. Qualified con-
scripts receive a less formal education for noncommissioned officer
(NCO) positions.

Reservists prepare for military service while attending civilian schools and universities or while working in the national economy. Refresher training through drills, classes, and active duty callups continues until individuals pass out of the reserves at age fifty.

The citations in this subsection deal with the many varied aspects of Soviet Army personnel and their training. To avoid repetition, individual introductions were omitted from some subsections of 4:E:2.

1. Personnel

a. GENERAL WORKS

ARTICLES

3153.   Abbott, Steve. "The Life of a Soviet Soldier." *Soldiers* 35 (July 1980), 6–10.

3154.   Altunin, P. "Living Conditions in the Far North Described: Translated from *Krasnaya Zvezda,* July 26, 1978." *Translations on USSR Military Affairs,* no. 1382 (October 3, 1978), 104–108.

3155.   Berman, Harold J. "The Soviet Soldier." *Russians in Focus.* Boston, Mass.: Little, Brown, 1953. pp. 3–17.

3156.   Bree, Betsey. "The Soviet Soldier." *Review of the Soviet Ground Forces* 5 (May 1980), 18–20.

3157.   "The Combat Value of the Soviet Soldier." *Military Review* 41 (April 1961), 92–96.

3158.   Davidson, J. V. "A Soviet Soldier." *Military Review* 37 (July 1954), 83–86.

3159.   DeWitt, William W. "The Soviet Soldier." *Armor* 73 (January-February 1964), 9–12.

3160.   Donnelly, Christopher N. "The Soviet Soldier: Behavior, Performance, Effectiveness." In John Erickson and E. J. Feuchtwanger, eds., *Soviet Military Power and Performance.* Hamden, Conn.: Archon Books, 1979. pp. 101–128.

3161.   Dutov, V. "Improvements in Troop Living Conditions Described: Translated from *Kommunist Vooruzhennykh Sil,* May 1978." *Translations on USSR Military Affairs,* no. 1373 (August 29, 1978), 71–79.

3162.   Freidin, Seymour, and William Richardson. "The Russian Soldier: How Good Is He?" *Collier's* 131 (January 31, 1953), 18–20.

3163.   Galay, Nikolay. "The New Generation in the Soviet Armed Forces." *Military Review* 45 (July 1965), 77–83; 46 (August 1966), 56–64.

3164.   _____ . "The Significance of the New Regulations Governing Soviet Garrison Troops." *Institute for the Study of the USSR Bulletin* 10 (December 1963), 25–29.

3165.   Jordan, W. F. "I Know the Russian Soldier." *Infantry School Quarterly* 43 (October 1953), 53–58.

3166.   Kurkotkin, Semen K. "Chief of Rear Services on Improving Living Conditions: Translated from *Znamenosets,* March 1978." *Translations on USSR Military Affairs,* no. 1359 (June 26, 1978), 28–35.

3167.   _____ . "Chief of Rear Services on Living Conditions: Translated from *Krasnaya Zvezda,* March 5, 1980." *Translations on USSR Military Affairs,* no. 1523 (July 9, 1980), 5–8.

3168.   Levin, Bjorn, and Hakan Larson. "Swedish Reporters Examine Life in a Soviet Army Camp: Translated from *Suomen Kuvalehti,* December 9, 1977." *Translations on USSR Military Affairs,* no. 1347 (April 19, 1978), 96–100.

3169.   Liberti, Joseph C. "The Soviet Soldier." *Infantry* 66 (January-February 1976), 37–41.

3170.   "Life in the Soviet Army." *Time* 95 (May 4, 1970), 46.

3171.   Mackintosh, Malcolm. "The Soviet Soldiers' Condition of Service." In Basil H. Liddell-Hart, ed., *The Soviet Army.* London: Weidenfeld & Nicolson, 1956. pp. 403–410.

3172.   Meehan, Dallace. "Ethnic Minorities in the Soviet Military: Implications for the Decades Ahead." *Air University Review* 31 (May-June 1980), 63–73.

3173.   "Meet Ivan—Soviet Soldier." *Army Information Digest* 23 (October 1968), 10–13.

3174.   Mozokina, L. "Soviet Women." *Soviet Military Review,* no. 2 (February 1980), 46–47.

3175.   Ogarkov, Nikolay V. "Chief-of-Staff Ogarkov Writes on Military Service: Translated from *Pravda,* February 19, 1978." *Translations on USSR Military Affairs,* no. 1336 (March 10, 1978), 87–93.

3176.   O'Hara, Michael J. "The Soviet Soldier: How Terrible Is Ivan?" *Marine Corps Gazette* 64 (April 1980), 61–66.

3177.   "Peace Is No Soft Spot for the Red Army Man." *Newsweek* 26 (November 19, 1945), 46–48.

3178.   Richardson, William. "Ivan Is Joe in a Different Uniform." *New York Times Magazine* (May 27, 1945), 9.

3179.   Rogers, Jim. "Soviet Women." *Soldiers* 33 (March 1978), 13.

3180.   "The Russian Soldier." *Infantry* 50 (February-March 1960), 4–9.

3181.   Schlieper, Fritz. "Life in the Soviet Forces." *Military Review* 42 (June 1962), 74–86.

3182.   Scott, Harriet F. "The Military Profession in the U.S.S.R." *Air Force Magazine* 59 (March 1976), 76–81.

3183.   "The Selective Distribution and Training of Military Personnel." *Soviet Military Translations,* no. 337 (October 1966), 56–64.

3184.   Sheehan, Regis P. "The Soviet Soldier: A Spartan in the Age of Aquarius." *Marine Corps Gazette* 62 (October 1978), 36–40.

3185.   "The Soviet Soldier." *Atlantic* 190 (September 1952), 4.

3186.   United States. Department of the Army. "The Soldier." *Opposing Forces: Europe.* FM 30-102. Washington, D.C., 1977. pp. 1/1–1/4.

3187.   Wilmeth, James D. "The Russians Are Not 40 Feet Tall." *Military Review* 34 (October 1954), 3–8.

DOCUMENTS, PAPERS, AND REPORTS

3188.   United States. Department of Defense. Defense Intelligence Agency. *Women in the Soviet Armed Forces.* DDI-1100-109-76. Washington, D.C., 1976.

3189.   United States. Department of the Army. Infantry School. *Actions of Soviet Servicemen in Action.* Fort Benning, Ga., 1976. 19p.

Further References

Additional material is found in section 4:A.

b. CONSCRIPTION AND RESERVES

According to manpower studies, there are some 60 million males between the ages of fifteen and forty-nine in the Soviet Union, about 80 percent of whom are fit for military service. Each year some 2 to 2.5

million young men reach military registration age and at the very least, one-half will be inducted when they become eighteen. The remainder, who receive deferrments, may serve later unless physically unfit. If deferred beyond their twenty-seventh birthday, men remain in the reserves, subject to periodic refresher training. Thus, all qualified Soviet male citizens remain in the armed forces until they reach their fiftieth birthday.

The Soviets in 1967 passed the Law on Universal Military Service, which provides for the mandatory conscription of 18-year-old males in semi-annual increments. Those not drafted or declared unfit are immediately entered in the reserves.

The Russian reserve system ensures that all citizens fit for military service have a definite reserve commitment when not on active duty. The program is so administered that "draft dodging" is all but impossible, as military service booklets, issued to all, are required for residence and work permits. There are no reserve units as such; when not on active duty, reservists work in the civilian sector. When called to active duty, reservists receive assignments based on their civilian occupational specialties.

ARTICLES

3190.   Artemiev, Vyacheslav P. "Soviet Military Service Obligations." *Infantry* 58 (September-October 1968), 38–43.

3191.   _____ . "Soviet Mobilization Doctrine." *Military Review* 46 (June 1966), 63–69.

3192.   Barry, James A., Jr. "Military Training of Soviet Youth." *Military Review* 53 (February 1973), 92–103.

3193.   Erickson, John. "Soviet Military Manpower Policies." *Armed Forces and Society* 1 (November 1974), 29–47.

3194.   Foot, Michael R. D. "Conscript Systems: U.S.S.R." *Men in Uniform.* Studies in International Security, no. 3. New York: Praeger, 1961. pp. 51–60.

3195.   Gist, David M. "The Militarization of Soviet Youth." *Naval War College Review* 30 (Summer 1977), 115–133.

3196.   Grechko, Andrei A. "National Service in the U.S.S.R." *Survival* 9 (December 1967), 398–399.

3197.   _____ . "The New Soviet Military Service Law." *Military Review* 48 (February 1968), 73–77.

3198.   Grkovic, George. "Soviet Universal Military Service." *U.S. Naval Institute Proceedings* 95 (April 1969), 54–63.

3199.   Heiman, Leo. "The Russian Reserve Force." *National Guardsman* 20 (November 1966), 22–26.

3200.   Jukes, Geoffrey. "Changes in Soviet Conscription Law." *Australian Outlook* 22 (August 1968), 204–217.

3201.   "The Proper Preparation of Draftees." *Soviet Military Translations,* no. 294 (July 1966), 58–62.

3202.   Pruck, Erich. "The Soviet Compulsory Service Law." *Military Review* 40 (April 1960), 92–100.

3203.   Puzik, V. "Laws Governing the Development of the Socialist Army." *Soviet Military Review,* no. 9 (September 1980), 16–18.

3204.   Scott, Harriet F. "Universal Military Training in the U.S.S.R." *Air Force Magazine* 61 (March 1978), 84–88.

3205.   Smith, David A. "Soviet Military Manpower." *Air Force Magazine* 60 (March 1977), 78–81.

3206.   Underhill, Garrett. "Citizen-Soldiers: Soviet Style." *National Guardsman* 8 (July 1954), 2–4; (August 1954), 2–4.

3207.   Union of Soviet Socialist Republics. Ministry of Defense. "Draft Regulations—Procedures and Draftee Privileges: Translated from *Krasnaya Zvezda,* June 11, 1980." *Translations on USSR Military Affairs,* no. 1539 (October 15, 1980), 33–35.

3208.   ————. "Regulations for Draftees: Translated from *Sovetskiiy Voin,* May-June, 1980." *Translations on USSR Military Affairs,* no. 1554 (December 31, 1980), 21–25.

Further References

See also sections 4:A and 4:E:1:a.

c. OFFICERS

Officers for the Soviet ground forces, and other armed forces components, come into the service from several sources, including the 143 military colleges, ROTC-type programs in civilian universities, and the lower ranks. The Russian military has about .5 million active duty officers, nearly 90 percent of whom are members of the CPSU. Of these, 3,000 to 5,000 are general officers or admirals, about 7 percent of whom are members of the CPSU Central Committee.

A Soviet Army officer usually rotates through a number of assignments, both field and staff. Some officers then attend advanced institutes. Promotions depend on academic training, service experience, duty assignment, job performance, time-in-grade, and political reliability.

Officers remain on active duty until reaching the statutory age for retirement, which varies according to grade. Officers who reach these respective age limits without promotion are transferred to the reserves unless granted a five-year exception.

Soviet military ranks above enlisted include, from bottom to top, warrant (*praporshchik*), junior lieutenant, lieutenant, senior lieutenant, captain, major, lieutenant colonel, colonel, major general, lieutenant general, colonel general, general, chief marshal (of a specific arm), marshal of the Soviet Union.

BOOKS

3209.   Babenko, I. *Soviet Officers*. Translated from the Russian. Moscow: Progress Publishers, 1976. 133p.

3210.   Kozlov, S. N., ed. *The Officer's Handbook: A Soviet View*. Translated from the Russian. Soviet Military Thought Series, no. 13. Washington, D.C.: U.S. Government Printing Office, 1977. 358p.

ARTICLES

3211.   Boman, Truman R. "Operational Efficiency of Soviet Staffs." *Military Review* 49 (March 1969), 21–29.

3212.   "The Commander and His Staff." *Soviet Military Translations*, no. 147 (July 1964), 22–28.

3213.   Drozdov, V. "The Soviet Officer Corps." *Soviet Military Review*, no. 1 (January 1977), 5–9; no. 2 (February 1977), 7–9.

3214.   Ely, Louis B. "The Officer Corps." In Basil H. Liddell-Hart, ed., *The Soviet Army*. London: Weidenfeld & Nicolson, 1956. pp. 345–402.

3215.   Engel, Leonard. "The Red Officer Corps." *Infantry Journal* 52 (June 1943), 18–24.

3216.   Erickson, John. "New Warrant Officers for the Soviet Armed Forces." *Military Review* 53 (December 1975), 70–77.

3217.   Garthoff, Raymond L. "The High Command and General Staff." In Basil H. Liddell-Hart, ed., *The Soviet Army*. London: Weidenfeld & Nicolson, 1956. pp. 244–253.

3218.   Grant, Phillip S. "The Soviet Officer Corps." *Infantry* 49 (July 1959), 42–47.

3219.   Hittle, John D. "Soviet Command and Staff Methods." *U.S. Army Combat Forces Journal* 1 (July 1951), 36–40.

3220.   Kovalyov, V. "Soviet Officers." *Soviet Military Review,* no. 5 (May 1979), 34–36.

3221.   Kruzhin, Petr. "The Restoration of the High Command of the Soviet Land Forces." *Institute for the Study of the USSR Bulletin* 15 (February 1968), 20–27.

3222.   Levedev, V. "The Younger Generation Takes Over." *Soviet Military Review,* no. 3 (March 1970), 62–64.

3223.   Pruck, Erich. "Officer Training in the Soviet Army." *Military Review* 44 (July 1964), 61–66.

3224.   "The Red Army Club." *Life* 23 (December 1, 1947), 83–84.

3225.   Shtemenko, Sergei M. "Staff: Organization and Training." *Military Review* 44 (June 1964), 68–74.

3226.   "The Soviet Union's Officer Corps." *Military Review* 31 (June 1951), 106–107.

3227.   Sterling, A. C. "The Red Army Officer." *The Pointer* 30 (January 16, 1953), 5.

3228.   Tanin, Ye. "The Red Army High Command." *Institute for the Study of the USSR Bulletin* 1 (May 1954), 25–26.

3229.   Veselov, L. "The Commander and His Staff." *Soviet Military Review,* no. 9 (September 1977), 11–13.

Further References

Additional materials relative to this part are in sections 1:G, 2:C:2:c, 4:A, and 4:E:2:f.

2. *Training*

Soviet ground forces training is characterized by repetition. All soldiers undergo individual training each year of their military service, regardless of rank. The avowed aim of such repetitive training is the development of instinctive reflexes to cope with any situation. There is no room for initiative; obedience becomes an end-all. Soviet training concentrates on field exercises under realistic conditions, complete with live bullets and even diluted poison gas. As Herbert Goldhamer put it in 1975: "Training so permeates the hour-to-hour and day-to-day activities of the Soviet forces that the distinction between operational and training activity becomes blurred."[1]

Soviet leaders believe that physical conditioning and proper mental development is necessary for effective combat action. To achieve the former, exercise, diet, calisthenics, and organized sport are widely employed. For attitudinal development, Soviet soldiers undergo political training and discussions on a rigorous schedule of at least five to nine hours per week. Political officers are organic to all units down to company level and are charged with instilling desired attitudes in soldiers. "Soviet military training is all the more onerous, all the more demanding," Goldhamer continues, "because it embraces not only military skills, but also a wide range of ideological, political, moral and character traits and attitudes."[2] Above all, Soviet military training fosters professionalism. Self-improvement is a constant requirement for all career personnel who desire to remain on active duty.

Problems of Soviet training include uneven academic training caused by incompetent teachers, the quashing of young leaders' initiative by overbearing superiors, and the demands of performance parameters which encourage faculties to inflate grades and pad exercise results in the interest of making the organization look good. Soviet shortcomings in training are not unlike those found elsewhere in the world. There is no doubt, however, that the Soviet ground forces are among the world's most professional and well-trained armies.

a. GENERAL WORKS

BOOKS

3230.   Danchenko, A. M., and I. F. Vydrin. *Military Pedagogy: A Soviet View.* Translated from the Russian. Soviet Military Thought Series, no. 7. Washington, D.C.: U.S. Government Printing Office, 1976. 363p.

3231.   Ruban, M. *The Soviet School of Courage and Warcraft: The Main Principles of Training Soldiers in the Soviet Armed Forces.* Translated from the Russian. Moscow: Progress Publishers, 1976. 179p.

ARTICLES

3232.   Agal'tsov, F. A. "Fewer Excuses, Higher Combat Readiness." *Soviet Military Translations,* no. 39 (November 1960), 5–10.

----

1. Quoted in John Nielsen et al., "The Red Army's New Look," *Newsweek* 95 (February 11, 1980), p. 47.
2. *Ibid.*

3233.   Aidarov, V. "The Making of an Officer." *Soviet Military Review,* no. 1 (January 1971), 37–40.

3234.   Averin, A. "Basic Military Training—Tasks and Problems: Translated from *Voyennyye Znaniya,* August 1980." *Translations on USSR Military Affairs,* no. 1543 (November 12, 1980), 33–38.

3235.   Bazhora, O. "Preparedness for Combat." *Soviet Military Review,* no. 3 (March 1974), 26–27.

3236.   Biryuzov, S. S. "Training Battalion Officers in Method." *Soviet Military Review,* no. 8 (August 1977), 20–21.

3237.   _____. "Training the Soviet Forces." *Survival* 6 (July-August 1964), 188–192.

3238.   Bjelajac, Stavko N., and Thomas W. Adams. "Preparing the Soviet Soldier for War." *Military Review* 45 (July 1965), 77–83.

3239.   "Combat Training in the Far East Military District Described: Translated from *Znamenosets,* December 1977." *Translations on USSR Military Affairs,* no. 1343 (April 7, 1978), 43–64.

3240.   "The Combat Training Plan." *Soviet Military Translations,* no. 301 (August 1966), 10–13.

3241.   Dean, Richard L. "Training and Indoctrination of the Soviet Soldier." *Field Artillery Journal* 47 (November-December 1979), 8–12.

3242.   "The Demands of Modern War for the Education of Troops." *Soviet Military Translations,* no. 323 (September 1966), 1–6.

3243.   Demidkov, G. "Command Training of NCO's Discussed: Translated from *Znamenosets,* September 1977." *Translations on USSR Military Affairs,* no. 1320 (January 5, 1978), 9–15.

3244.   "Doctrine and Training." *Soviet Military Translations,* no. 99 (September 1962), 2–62.

3245.   Erickson, John. "The Training of the Soviet Soldier: A Review of Recent Theory and Practice." *Journal of the Royal United Service Institute for Defence Studies* 116 (December 1971), 45–48.

3246.   "The Experiences Gained in World War II Should Be Studied for Present Training of Personnel." *Soviet Military Translations,* no. 271 (May 1966), 13–22.

3247.   "Experience, Tradition, and New Weapons." *Soviet Military Translations,* no. 153a (September 1964), 10–14.

3248.   "Fundamentals of Troop Field Training." *Soviet Military Translations*, no. 257 (May 1966), 12–16.

3249.   Gorchakov, V. "Officer Training in the Central Asian Military District: Translated from *Krasnaya Zvezda*, September 13, 1978." *Translations on USSR Military Affairs*, no. 1403 (December 18, 1978), 6–11.

3250.   Gorodov, P. "A Scientific Approach to Servicemens' Education." *Soviet Military Review*, no. 6 (June 1977), 24–25.

3251.   Grechikhin, A. "Basics of Fire Control Training." *Soviet Military Review*, no. 2 (February 1973), 13–16.

3252.   "Ground Forces—Training and Related Activities: Translated from *Krasnaya Zvezda*." *Translations on USSR Military Affairs*, no. 1554 (December 31, 1980), 65–76.

3253.   "Ground Forces—Training and Related Activities: Translated from *Krasnaya Zvezda*." *Translations on USSR Military Affairs*, no. 1571 (February 26, 1981), 10–28.

3254.   Gudymenko, Yu. "Helicopter Ground Support Training Described: Translated from *Aviatsiya I Kosmonavtika*, May 1978." *Translations on USSR Military Affairs*, no. 1364 (July 18, 1978), 44–49.

3255.   Head, Richard G. "Russian Military Education." *Military Review* 59 (February 1979), 14–16.

3256.   ———. "Soviet Military Education." *Air University Review* 30 (November-December 1978), 45–57.

3257.   "The Importance of Drill Training." *Soviet Military Translations*, no. 332a (November 1966), 27–31.

3258.   "Importance of Motor Vehicle Driver Training Stressed: Translated from *Krasnaya Zvezda*, September 6, 1977." *Translations on USSR Military Affairs*, no. 1328 (February 2, 1978), 28–31.

3259.   "Improve Protection of Troops." *Soviet Military Translations*, no. 332a (October 1966), 1–6.

3260.   "Improving Methods of Combat Training." *Soviet Military Translations*, no. 263 (May 1966), 32–35.

3261.   "Improving the Performance of Duty by Troops." *Soviet Military Translations*, no. 291 (January 1966), 9–16.

3262.   "In the Interest of Combat Readiness." *Soviet Military Translations*, no. 25 (September 1960), 28–30.

3263.   "Information for Draftees." *Soviet Military Translations,* no. 241 (April 1966), 44–47.

3264.   Koshevoi, P. K. "The Importance of Methodology to the Soviet Army Officer." *Soviet Military Translations,* no. 367 (January 1967), 1–8.

3265.   Krainev, Y. "For Better Field Training." *Soviet Military Review,* no. 1 (January 1973), 28–29.

3266.   Maksimov, K. "Troop Training in Central Group of Forces Described: Translated from *Znamenosets,* May 1978." *Translations on USSR Military Affairs,* no. 1372 (August 24, 1978), 1–7.

3267.   Malinovskiy, Rodion Y. "New Frontiers in Soviet Military Education." *Military Review* 47 (February 1967), 30–36.

3268.   _____ . "Of the Political, Professional, and Moral Qualities of Military Personnel." *Soviet Military Review,* no. 12 (December 1965), 3–7.

3269.   Malyshev, A. "New Weapons-Firing Training Method Described: Translated from *Znamenosets,* November 1977." *Translations on USSR Military Affairs,* no. 1320 (January 5, 1978), 28–33.

3270.   Matveyev, V. I. "Modern Demands on the Combat Training of Troops." In Nikolay A. Lomov, ed., *Scientific-Technical Progress and the Revolution in Military Affairs: A Soviet View.* Translated from the Russian. Soviet Military Thought Series, no. 3. Washington, D.C.: U.S. Government Printing Office, 1974. pp. 157–163.

3271.   Mayorov, Aleksandr M. "Baltic Military District Commander on Troop Capabilities, Training: Translated from *Kommunist Estonii,* January 1978." *Translations on USSR Military Affairs,* no. 1343 (April 7, 1978), 87–93.

3272.   _____ . "Combat Training—Baltic Military District Commander on Methods: Translated from *Kommunist Vooruzhennykh Sil,* February 1980." *Translations on USSR Military Affairs,* no. 1520 (June 24, 1980), 62–71.

3273.   "Methodology in Military Affairs." *Soviet Military Translations,* no. 376a (March 1967), 1–10.

3274.   Mikhaylenko, Yu. "Combined Arms School Training Described: Translated from *Krasnaya Zvezda,* March 21, 1980." *Translations on USSR Military Affairs,* no. 1524 (July 15, 1980), 25–29.

3275. "Military Library Facilities Discussed: Translated from *Krasnaya Zvezda,* June 24, 1978." *Translations on USSR Military Affairs,* no. 1382 (October 3, 1978), 15–18.

3276. "Military Training and Service." *Army Information Digest* 6 (January 1951), 17–28.

3277. Moroz, I. M. "Interview: Translated from *Kryl'ya Rodiny,* August 1978." *Translations on USSR Military Affairs,* no. 1388 (October 23, 1978), 7–13.

3278. "A New Man Is Trained." *Soviet Military Translations,* no. 237 (March 1966), 34–35.

3279. Odom, William E. "The Soviet Military-Educational Complex." In Dale R. Herspring and Ivan Volgyes, eds., *Civil-Military Relations in the Communist System.* Boulder, Colo.: Westview Press, 1978. Chpt. 4.

3280. _____. "Soviet Training Economics." *Military Review* 47 (September 1967), 81–85.

3281. Osyko, V. "Motor Vehicle Operator Training—Methods, Importance: Translated from *Krasnaya Zvezda,* February 14, 1978." *Translations on USSR Military Affairs,* no. 1352 (May 15, 1978), 55–59.

3282. Overchuk, A. "Combat Training in the Transcaucasian Military District: Translated from *Krasnaya Zvezda,* October 19, 1977." *Translations on USSR Military Affairs,* no. 1328 (February 2, 1978), 98–103.

3283. Pakhomov, Yu. "Training Activities in the Far East Military District: Translated from *Sovetskiy Voin,* March 1978." *Translations on USSR Military Affairs,* no. 1352 (May 15, 1978), 121–130.

3284. Pavlovskiy, Ivan G. "Fighting Experience and Combat Training." *Soviet Military Review,* no. 5 (May 1972), 2–5.

3285. "Problems of Training Officer Cadres." *Soviet Military Translations,* no. 120 (April 1963), 5–8.

3286. "Programmed Training." *Soviet Military Translations,* no. 194a (August 1965), 26–36.

3287. Prokhorenko, G. "Motor Vehicle Operator Training— Methods and Facilities: Translated from *Krasnaya Zvezda,* December 8, 1977." *Translations on USSR Military Affairs,* no. 1344 (April 7, 1978), 10–13.

3288. "The Real and Prearranged Realism in Combat Training." *Soviet Military Translations,* no. 29 (September 1960), 14–19.

3289.   Repin, I. P. "Development of Warrant Officers as Junior Commanders Discussed: Translated from *Znamenosets,* September 1977." *Translations on USSR Military Affairs,* no. 1320 (January 5, 1978), 1–6.

3290.   "The Revolution in Military Affairs and the Training of Soviet Soldiers." *Soviet Military Translations,* no. 194a (August 1965), 1–14.

3291.   Rosen, S. M. "Basic Military Training in Soviet Schools." *School and Society* 98 (November 1970), 421–423.

3292.   Rumyantsev, N. "Military Education." *Soviet Military Review,* no. 11 (November 1980), 39–40.

3293.   Salmanov, G. I. "Importance of Fire Training for Ground Forces Stressed: Translated from *Znamenosets,* December 1978." *Translations on USSR Military Affairs,* no. 1421 (March 20, 1979), 29–34.

3294.   "The Scientific Solution to Problems in Pedagogy and Psychology." *Soviet Military Translations,* no. 70 (November 1961), 41–43.

3295.   Scott, Frank H. "Training the Soviet Soldier." *Canadian Army Journal* 16 (April 1962), 90–92.

3296.   ———. "Training the Soviet Soldier." *Infantry* 52 (January-February 1962), 14–15.

3297.   Shinkaryov, G. "Fire (Control) Training." *Soviet Military Review,* no. 2 (February 1973), 20–21.

3298.   Sil'chenko, N. "Commander of Urals Military District on Training Results: Translated from *Izvestiya,* October 17, 1978." *Translations on USSR Military Affairs,* no. 1411 (February 8, 1979), 48–51.

3299.   Simchenkov, P. "Field Training Standards." *Soviet Military Review,* no. 7 (July 1973), 11–13.

3300.   Sobik, Erich. "The Training of Soviet Ground Troops— Methods and Results: Translated from *Truppenpraxis,* September 1978." *Translations on USSR Military Affairs,* no. 1395 (November 21, 1978), 1–17.

3301.   "Soviet Staff Training." *Military Review* 30 (July 1950), 80–82.

3302.   "Soviet Style Military Service and Training." *Reserve Officer* 28 (October 1952), 6–8, 20–22.

3303.   "Study Combat Experience Assiduously and Use It Creatively." *Soviet Military Translations,* no. 271 (May 1966), 4–12.

3304.   "Summarized Plan Found Beneficial in Instructing Army Units." *Soviet Military Translations,* no. 294 (July 1966), 32–36.

3305.   Tikhonenkov, N. "Physical Training in Ground Forces Combat Units Described: Translated from *Krasnaya Zvezda,* December 7, 1977." *Translations on USSR Military Affairs,* no. 1344 (April 7, 1978), 8–10.

3306.   Touzakov, Ye. "Need for Incorporating Wartime Experience into Troop Training Stressed: Translated from *Voyenno Istoricheskiy Zhurnal,* September 1978." *Translations on USSR Military Affairs,* no. 1394 (November 14, 1978), 23–31.

3307.   "Training for Modern War." *Soviet Military Translations,* no. 152a (September 1964), 13–18.

3308.   Tret'yak, Ivan M. "Far East Military District Commander on Training Results: Translated from *Kommunist Vooruzhennykh Sil,* October 1978." *Translations on USSR Military Affairs,* no. 1402 (December 13, 1978), 85–93.

3309.   Tyagunov, M. "Guard Duty Training in the Carpathian Military District: Translated from *Krasnaya Zvezda,* February 11, 1978." *Translations on USSR Military Affairs,* no. 1352 (May 15, 1978), 48–52.

3310.   Union of Soviet Socialist Republics. Ministry of Defense. "Conference Report—Educational Role of the Armed Forces: Translated from *Kommunist Vooruzhennykh Sil,* July 1980." *Translations on USSR Military Affairs,* no. 1542 (October 30, 1980), 1–80.

3311.   Ushakov, L. "Dissemination of Military and Technical Knowledge." *Soviet Military Review,* no. 5 (May 1977), 28–29.

3312.   Vassiliev, M. F. "Soviet Recruit Training." *An Cosantoir* 17 (August 1957), 431–436.

3313.   Vasyagin, S. P. "Ground Forces Training Methods, Results Reviewed: Translated from *Kommunist Vooruzhennykh Sil,* February 1980." *Translations on USSR Military Affairs,* no. 1520 (June 24, 1980), 127–138.

3314.   Vinnikov, V. "Method Training for Officers." *Soviet Military Review,* no. 5 (May 1965), 40–41.

3315.   Yezhov, N. "Training for Combat through Smoke and Fire Described: Translated from *Znamenosets,* April 1978." *Translations on USSR Military Affairs,* no. 1367 (July 25, 1978), 48–54.

3316.   Zaytsev, Mikhail M. "Commander of Belorussian Military District on Troop Training Methods: Translated from *Kommunist Voo-*

ruzhennykh Sil, May 1978." *Translations on USSR Military Affairs,* no. 1373 (August 29, 1978), 49–58.

3317.   Zyrzanov, A. "The Organization of a March." *Soviet Military Review,* no. 6 (June 1976), 18–19.

DOCUMENTS, PAPERS, AND REPORTS

3318.   Chomko, Gene N. *Comparative Analysis of Physical Training in the U.S. and Soviet Armies and Its Import.* Oberammergau, W. Ger.: U.S. Army Institute for Advanced Russian Studies, 1962. 489p.

3319.   Glantz, David M., and David J. Sisson. *Survey of Self-Criticism in Selected Soviet Military Journals.* Research Report. New York: U.S. Army Institute for Advanced Russian and East European Studies, 1977. 110p.

3320.   Union of Soviet Socialist Republics. Ministry of Defense. *Military Education.* JPRS 763-D. Arlington, Va.: Joint Publications Research Service, 1959. 6p.

3321.   United States. Department of Defense. Defense Intelligence Agency. *Physical Training of the Soviet Soldier.* DDB-2680-48-78. Washington, D.C., 1978. 36p.

3322.   _____ . *The Soviet Ground Forces: Training Program.* DDB-1100-200-78. Washington, D.C., 1978. 20p.

Further References

See also sections 4:A, 4:E:1, and 4:E:2.

b. DISCIPLINE AND LEADERSHIP/MILITARY LAW AND JUSTICE

With support from the party-political apparatus, leadership and discipline in the Soviet ground forces is primarily accomplished through the chain of command.

In addition to training, political discussion, and such KP-type duties as are found in every army, the Russian soldier is subject to strict military law. Infractions, especially those of a serious nature, are handled through the military justice service. This service functions at every level down to division, but retains a high degree of independence from local control, answering primarily to the next higher echelon of the justice service rather than to the local command. Special military judges and lawyers are available to handle cases, with tribunals hearing many court-martial cases.

BOOKS

3323.   Berman, Harold J., and Miroslav Kerner. *Soviet Military Law and Administration.* Cambridge, Mass.: Harvard University Press, 1955. 208p.

3324.   _____ , eds. *Documents on Soviet Military Law and Administration.* Cambridge, Mass.: Harvard University Press, 1955. 164p.

ARTICLES

3325.   Alexandrov, L. "Obeying the Laws of Army Life." *Soviet Military Review,* no. 11 (November 1974), 26–27.

3326.   Altukhov, P. "Troop Control—Postwar Development for Combined Arms Combat: Translated from *Voyenno Istoricheskiy Zhurnal,* November 1979." *Translations on USSR Military Affairs,* no. 1500 (February 28, 1980), 33–41.

3327.   Artemiev, Vyacheslav P. "Crime and Punishment in the Soviet Armed Forces." *Military Review* 42 (November 1962), 68–74.

3328.   Babenko, I. "The Regulations and Military Service." *Soviet Military Review,* no. 7 (July 1970), 28–31.

3329.   Bashuyev, J. "History and Tasks of Military Tribunals Reviewed: Translated from *Kommunist Vooruzhennykh Sil,* December 1978." *Translations on USSR Military Affairs,* no. 1417 (March 9, 1979), 56–63.

3330.   Baxter, William P. "The 'Scientific' Soviet Commander." *Army* 30 (June 1980), 39–40.

3331.   Berman, Harold J. "Soviet Military Crimes." *Military Review* 32 (July 1952), 3–15.

3332.   _____ . "Soviet Military Discipline." *Military Review* 32 (June 1952), 19–29.

3333.   Bobhov, B. "Operations of 'Comrades Courts' Described: Translated from *Znamenosets,* November 1977." *Translations on USSR Military Affairs,* no. 1324 (January 13, 1978), 89–92.

3334.   "The Decision Theory of Command." *Soviet Military Translations,* no. 260 (May 1966), 1–9.

3335.   Filatvov, V. "Military Discipline—Court Martial Described: Translated from *Krasnaya Zvezda,* April 26, 1980." *Translations on USSR Military Affairs,* no. 1534 (September 18, 1980), 24–28.

3336.   Gabriel, Richard A. "Combat Cohesion in Soviet and American Military Units." *Parameters* 8 (December 1978), 16–27.

3337.   Galay, Nikolay. "Principles of Command in the Soviet Armed Forces." *Institute for the Study of the USSR Bulletin* 2 (June 1955), 11–15.

3338.   Gavrikov, F. "A Commander Takes Decisions and Organizes Battle." *Soviet Military Review,* no. 2 (February 1967), 26–30.

3339.   Gaynor, James K. "Soviet Military Law." *Judge Advocate General's Bulletin,* no. 17 (June 1954), 19–21.

3340.   Gornyy, Artem G. "Legal Education—Chief Judge Advocate Interviewed: Translated from *Kommunist Vooruzhennykh Sil,* January 1980." *Translations on USSR Military Affairs,* no. 1520 (June 24, 1980), 14–22.

3341.   Grinkevich, D. "Command and Control in Response to Contemporary Requirements." *Soviet Press Selected Translations,* no. 77-11 (November 1977), 289–296.

3342.   Gushchin, V. "Military Discipline—Improvement Methods Discussed: Translated from *Kommunist Vooruzhennykh Sil,* April 1980." *Translations on USSR Military Affairs,* no. 1526 (July 31, 1980), 53–61.

3343.   "Important Means of Strengthening Military Discipline." *Soviet Military Translations,* no. 18 (August 1960), 6–13.

3344.   "Indoctrination Guide on Military Discipline: Translated from *Kommunist Vooruzhennykh Sil,* October 1978." *Translations on USSR Military Affairs,* no. 1400 (December 12, 1978), 87–101.

3345.   Isachenko, S. "One-Man Command: Major Principle of Military Leadership." *Soviet Military Review,* no. 11 (November 1970), 2–5.

3346.   Ivanov, V. "Leadership of Military Operations in Theaters of Military Operations Based on the Experience of World War II: Translated from *Voyennaya Mysl,'* April 1967." *Foreign Broadcast Information Service Daily Report: U.S.S.R.,* no. 1135/67 (November 24, 1967), 71.

3347.   Jones, Gilbert E., Jr. "Military Police in the Soviet Armed Forces." *Military Review* 51 (January 1971), 86–92.

3348.   Khobotov, V. "Guide for Indoctrination on the Role of the Commander: Translated from *Kommunist Vooruzhennykh Sil,* November 1978." *Translations on USSR Military Affairs,* no. 1426 (March 16, 1978), 75–92.

3349.   Korzun, L. "The Commander's Initiative and Creative Work." *Soviet Military Review,* no. 2 (February 1965), 20–23.

3350.   Kryazhev, G. "Military Prosecutors Discuss Legal Education: Translated from *Krasnaya Zvezda*, December 14, 1977." *Translations on USSR Military Affairs*, no. 1321 (January 9, 1978), 82–83.

3351.   Lisenko, V. "Officer's Initiative in Combat." *Soviet Military Review*, no. 5 (May 1966), 47–48.

3352.   Melnichuk, N. "The Platoon Commander and His Men." *Soviet Military Review*, no. 5 (May 1966), 54.

3353.   "Military Tribunals: Text of Revised Statute." *Translations on USSR Military Affairs*, no. 1531 (September 2, 1980), 77–86.

3354.   Minayev, N. "Effectiveness of Discipline in a Tank Regiment Discussed: Translated from *Krasnaya Zvezda*, November 24, 1977." *Translations on USSR Military Affairs*, no. 1334 (March 2, 1978), 98–102.

3355.   Mironyuk, V. "Troop Control Emphasized in Transcaucasus Military District: Translated from *Kommunist Vooruzhennykh Sil*, December 1977." *Translations on USSR Military Affairs*, no. 1331 (February 16, 1978), 76–85.

3356.   "Modern Combat and One-Man Command." *Soviet Military Translations*, no. 152a (September 1964), 45–53.

3357.   Morsin, Yu. "The Daily Life of Junior Commanders." *Soviet Military Review*, no. 9 (September 1966), 56.

3358.   Myer, Allan A. "The Structure of Discipline in the Soviet Army." *Military Review* 55 (November 1975), 77–90.

3359.   Noskov, I. "The Commander Sets the Example." *Soviet Military Review*, no. 4 (April 1966), 18–20.

3360.   "Officer Responsibilities." *Soviet Military Translations*, no. 316 (August 1966), 14–18.

3361.   Petrukhin, V. "Loyalty to Combat Traditions." *Soviet Military Review*, no. 8 (August 1969), 16–18.

3362.   Reznichenko, Vasiliy G. "Modern Weapons and Troop Control." *Soviet Military Review*, no. 12 (December 1978), 10–13.

3363.   _____ . "Troop Control in Modern Combat Discussed: Translated from *Krasnaya Zvezda*, December 13, 1977." *Translations on USSR Military Affairs*, no. 1329 (February 10, 1978), 51–56.

3364.   "The Russian Soldier and Leadership." *Marine Corps Gazette* 46 (September 1962), 18.

3365. "The Scientific Approach to Troop Management." *Soviet Military Translations,* no. 295 (July 1966), 34–44.

3366. Simchenkov, P. "Officer's Tactical Skill." *Soviet Military Review,* no. 1 (January 1977), 13–14.

3367. _____ . "Troop Control in Combat." *Soviet Military Review,* no. 1 (January 1976), 14–15.

3368. Skrylnik, A. "Discipline in the Armed Forces." *Soviet Military Review,* no. 9 (September 1974), 28–29.

3369. Sobik, Erich. "Command and Control in the Soviet Ground Forces." *NATO's Fifteen Nations* 24 (October-November 1979), 96–98.

3370. "The Soviet Soldier and His Leaders." *Canadian Army Journal* 5 (June 1951), 27–37.

3371. Tatarchenko, A. Ye., and A. K. Zaporozhchenko. "Troop Control under the Conditions of Modern War." In Nikolay A. Lomov, ed., *Scientific-Technical Progress and the Revolution in Military Affairs: A Soviet View.* Translated from the Russian. Soviet Military Thought Series, no. 3. Washington, D.C.: U.S. Government Printing Office, 1974. pp. 164–186.

3372. Theltoukhov, A. "Squad Leader Training in a Motorized Infantry Platoon: Translated from *Znamenosets,* September 1978." *Translations on USSR Military Affairs,* no. 1402 (December 13, 1978), 103–108.

3373. Titov, S. "Discipline in the Soviet Army." *Soviet Military Review,* no. 8 (August 1970), 6–9.

3374. Yakubovsky, Ivan I. "The Commander's Responsibility." *Military Review* 45 (December 1965), 68–70.

3375. Yakushin, Vladimir Z. "Ground Forces Chief on the Need for Strong Discipline: Translated from *Kommunist Vooruzhennykh Sil,* June 1978." *Translations on USSR Military Affairs,* no. 1382 (October 3, 1978), 1–10.

3376. _____ . "Organizing Troop Control in Combat Discussed: Translated from *Krasnaya Zvezda,* December 10, 1978." *Translations on USSR Military Affairs,* no. 1423 (March 26, 1979), 30–34.

3377. Zashchevko, G. "Concerning the Delegation of Responsibilities to Young Officers." *Soviet Military Translations,* no. 343a (October 1966), 6–14.

DOCUMENTS, PAPERS, AND REPORTS

3378.   Bryson, Edward B. "Corps Rear Area Security: Analysis of Threat, Doctrine, and Force Options." MA thesis, U.S. Army Command and General Staff College, 1976. 171p.

3379.   Leites, N. *What Soviet Commanders Fear from Their Own Forces.* RAND Paper P-5958. Santa Monica, Calif.: RAND Corporation, 1978. 94p.

3380.   Myer, Allan A. *The Structure of Discipline in the Soviet Army.* Research Report. New York: U.S. Army Institute for Advanced Russian and East European Studies, 1975. 37p.

3381.   Union of Soviet Socialist Republics. Ministry of Defense. *Foundations of Soviet Military Law.* JPRS 19814. Arlington, Va.: Joint Publication Research Service, 1963. 144p.

3382.   Zorin, P. *Soviet Military Tribunals.* Research Program on the U.S.S.R., no. 50. New York: East European Fund, 1954. 30p.

Further References

See also sections 3:A:2, 4:A, 4:E:1, and the other parts of this subsection.

c. MILITARY PSYCHOLOGY AND MORALE

Morale-building and military psychology are important to officers of the Soviet Army charged with keeping soldiers happy and ready to fight. Much of this responsibility falls to political officers, who work with commanders to explain Soviet domestic and foreign policies, strengthen discipline, and instill patriotism—all of which are employed to foster the will to fight.

Literature in English, original or translation, on Soviet military psychology and morale is limited, and most of it dates from the 1960s or early 1970s.

BOOKS

3383.   Shelyag, V. V., ed. *Military Psychology: A Soviet View.* Translated from the Russian. Soviet Military Thought Series, no. 8. Washington, D.C.: U.S. Government Printing Office, 1976. 408p.

ARTICLES

3384.   Allred, Kenny. "Military Motivation in Peacetime." *Military Intelligence* 6 (October-December 1980), 56.

3385.   Azama, Rodney S. "The Psychology of the Soviet Army Commander." *Military Review* 57 (September 1977), 32–40.

3386.   Bazanov, A. "Psychological Training of Soldiers." *Soviet Military Review*, no. 8 (August 1966), 15–17.

3387.   Gabriel, Richard A. "The Morale of the Soviet Army: Some Implications for Combat Efficiency." *Military Review* 58 (October 1978), 27–39.

3388.   Krayniy, L. "Outline for Troop Indoctrination on Combat Tradition: Translated from *Kommunist Vooruzhennykh Sil,* July 1979." *Translations on USSR Military Affairs,* no. 1474 (November 16, 1979), 41–48.

3389.   "Military Psychology and Its Practical Application." *Soviet Military Translations,* no. 152a (September 1964), 13–18.

3390.   Milovidov, A. S. "The Fighting Man's Moral Character." *Soviet Military Review,* no. 4 (April 1969), 2–5.

3391.   "Moral and Psychological Training of the Soldiers under Current Conditions." *Soviet Military Translations,* no. 194a (August 1965), 38–51.

3392.   "The Morale Factor and Ways of Forming It." *Soviet Military Translations,* no. 274 (June 1966), 7–19.

3393.   "On the Subject of Military Psychology." *Soviet Military Translations,* no. 284 (June 1966), 20–29.

3394.   Ponomarev, Vadim A., et al. "Command Training—Psychological Factors Discussed: Translated from *Sovetskiy Voin,* October 1980." *Translations on USSR Military Affairs,* no. 1554 (December 31, 1980), 25–31.

3395.   "Psychological Training of Servicemen in the Course of Their Services." *Soviet Military Translations,* no. 240 (April 1966), 44–52.

3396.   "The Psychological Training of the Soldier: What It Must Consist Of." *Soviet Military Translations,* no. 102 (October 1962), 23–28.

3397.   "The Psychology of the Soldier in Modern Combat." *Soviet Military Translations,* no. 113 (December 1962), 1–3.

3398.   Rzheshevskiy, D. "The Army's Morale." *Soviet Military Review,* no. 12 (December 1965), 8–11.

DOCUMENTS, PAPERS, AND REPORTS

3399.   Milovidov, A. S. *The Revolution in Military Affairs and the Spiritual Strength of Troops.* JPRS 33093. Arlington, Va.: Joint Publication Research Service, 1966. 11p.

3400.   Vinogradov, V. *Heroic Traditions Live and Multiply.* FTD-ID(RS)T-1263-79. Wright Patterson AFB, Ohio: Foreign Technology Division, U.S. Air Force, 1979. 12p.

Further References

See also sections 3:A:2, 4:A, and 4:E:a and b.

d. TRAINING BY COMBAT ARM

As noted before, realism is key in Soviet Army training, and it extends to every combat arm, regardless of the size of the exercise or maneuver.

The references in this subsection deal with training in the airborne/airmobile troops, artillery, armor, and motorized infantry. Many are drawn directly from Soviet writers via translation.

(1). Airborne/Airmobile Troops

ARTICLES

3401.   "Airborne Troops—Combat Training Activities: Translated from *Krasnaya Zvezda,* April 4 and July 15, 1980." *Translations on USSR Military Affairs,* no. 1533 (September 12, 1980), 75–103.

3402.   "Airborne Units—Training and Related Activities: Translated from *Krasnaya Zvezda.*" *Translations on USSR Military Affairs,* no. 1505 (March 20, 1980), 95–103.

3403.   Bazarny, F. "Preparation for Parachute Jumping." *Soviet Military Review,* no. 5 (May 1973), 10–11.

3404.   Denisevich, N. "The Training of an Airborne Battalion Commander Described: Translated from *Krasnaya Zvezda,* December 23, 1978." *Translations on USSR Military Affairs,* no. 1426 (April 5, 1979), 1–3.

3405.   Dontsov, I. "Soviet Airborne Tactics." *Military Review* 44 (October 1964), 29–33.

3406. Golovnev, L. "Shortcomings Noted in Airborne Troops Training: Translated from *Krasnaya Zvezda*, August 18, 1978." *Translations on USSR Military Affairs*, no. 1398 (November 29, 1978), 31–33.

3407. Goryunov, V. "Heliborne Motorized Infantry Exercise Described: Translated from *Znamenosets*, January 1979." *Translations on USSR Military Affairs*, no. 1438 (May 18, 1979), 52–54.

3408. Gukasov, G. "Troop Carrier Aircraft in Airborne Exercise: Translated from *Izvestia*, January 26, 1978." *Translations on USSR Military Affairs*, no. 1344 (April 7, 1978), 164–168.

3409. Ivanov, G. "Helicopter Motorized Infantry Landing Exercise: Translated from *Krasnaya Zvezda*, August 2, 1978." *Translations on USSR Military Affairs*, no. 1407 (December 19, 1978), 9–12.

3410. Kostylev, V. "Small Unit Airborne Tactical Training Examined: Translated from *Znamenosets*, August 1978." *Translations on USSR Military Affairs*, no. 1390 (October 26, 1978), 70–76.

3411. Kuts, S. "Helicopter Regiment Training Results Described: Translated from *Krasnaya Zvezda*, November 15, 1977." *Translations on USSR Military Affairs*, no. 1334 (March 2, 1978), 55–58.

3412. Kuvitanov, G. "Airborne Battalion Training Exercise Described: Translated from *Pravda*, December 4, 1979." *Translations on USSR Military Affairs*, no. 1489 (January 16, 1980), 45–49.

3413. Malinovskiy, V. "Parachutists Instructed on Proper Landing Techniques: Translated from *Kryl'ya Rodiny*, August 1979." *Translations on USSR Military Affairs*, no. 1477 (November 29, 1979), 44–46.

3414. Mishanin, S. "Paratrooper Company Training Problems Noted: Translated from *Krasnaya Zvezda*, March 26, 1980." *Translations on USSR Military Affairs*, no. 1524 (July 16, 1980), 42–45.

3415. Oleynik, A. "First Airborne Jump Experience Described: Translated from *Krasnaya Zvezda*, June 20, 1978." *Translations on USSR Military Affairs*, no. 1380 (September 27, 1978), 14–17.

3416. ———. "Transport Aircraft Crew Training for Paradrop Described: Translated from *Krasnaya Zvezda*, May 30, 1978." *Translations on USSR Military Affairs*, no. 1370 (August 17, 1978), 86–89.

3417. Pashikin, K. "Training of Airborne Officers Described: Translated from *Voyennyye Znaniya*, March 1978." *Translations on USSR Military Affairs*, no. 1352 (May 15, 1978), 93–97.

3418. "Psychological Conditioning of Soviet Paratroops." *Soviet Military Translations*, no. 357a (December 1966), 1–14.

3419.   Salikhov, R. "Ambush Training Exercise for an Airborne Platoon: Translated from *Znamenosets,* November 1977." *Translations on USSR Military Affairs,* no. 1320 (January 5, 1978), 18–22.

3420.   Sin'kevich, V. "Transport Aircraft Air Drop Mission Described: Translated from *Krasnaya Zvezda,* January 25, 1978." *Translations on USSR Military Affairs,* no. 1347 (April 19, 1978), 38–40.

3421.   "Soviets Demonstrate Vertical Envelopment Capability with An-22 Heavy Transport." *Aviation Week and Space Technology* 87 (August 14, 1967), 52–55.

3422.   "To Improve the Combat Skill of Airborne Forces." *Soviet Military Translations,* no. 25 (September 1960), 21–24.

3423.   Tychkov, M. "Airborne Force Captures Crossing." *Soviet Military Review,* no. 3 (March 1973), 18–19.

DOCUMENTS, PAPERS, AND REPORTS

3424.   Epatko, Basil. *Training Soviet Military Flight Personnel.* DDB-1300-153-79. Washington, D.C.: Defense Intelligence Agency, Department of Defense, 1979.

Further References

See also section 4:C:4.

(2). Artillery

ARTICLES

3425.   Bandeyev, V. "Artillery Gun Crew Training Described: Translated from *Znamenosets,* November 1978." *Translations on USSR Military Affairs,* no. 1417 (March 9, 1979), 21–23.

3426.   Bozhko, V. "Artillery Battery Training: Translated from *Krasnaya Zvezda,* June 23, 1979." *Translations on USSR Military Affairs,* no. 1459 (August 28, 1979), 19–20.

3427.   Bud'ko, A. "Mobile Missile Crew Training Described: Translated from *Znamenosets,* November 1978." *Translations on USSR Military Affairs,* no. 1417 (March 9, 1979), 18–21.

3428.   Chaplyuk, S. "Artillery Gun Crew Chief Describes Firing Procedures: Translated from *Znamenosets,* July 1978." *Translations on USSR Military Affairs,* no. 1391 (October 30, 1978), 51–60.

3429.   Davidenko, V. "Tactical Exercises with Field Firing." *Soviet Military Review,* no. 2 (February 1974), 17–19.

3430.   Golovnev, L. "Combat Training in Self-Propelled Artillery Battery Described: Translated from *Krasnaya Zvezda*, September 1, 1977." *Translations on USSR Military Affairs*, no. 1328 (February 2, 1978), 4–7.

3431.   Kholodul'kin, V. "Artillery Regiment Training Activities: Translated from *Krasnaya Zvezda*, December 20, 1977." *Translations on USSR Military Affairs*, no. 1343 (April 7, 1978), 36–38.

3432.   Khryashchov, A. "Army Artillery Competitions." *Soviet Military Review*, no. 3 (March 1973), 20–21.

3433.   Lavreichuk, V. "The Training of AA Gunners." *Soviet Military Review*, no. 3 (March 1977), 21–22.

3434.   "Missile Crew Field Training." *Soviet Military Translations*, no. 130 (November 1963), 15–19.

3435.   Nagornyy, V. "Self-Propelled Howitzer Battalion Training Described: Translated from *Krasnaya Zvezda*, November 19, 1978." *Translations on USSR Military Affairs*, no. 1419 (March 15, 1979), 56–60.

3436.   Peredl'skiy, G. Ye. "Basic Directions in the Training of Artillery and Missilemen." *Field Artillery Journal* 42 (November-December 1974), 6–11.

3437.   Petrov, Aleksandr. "Training Activities in [a] Tactical Missile Battery: Translated from *Krasnaya Zvezda*, May 21, 1978." *Translations on USSR Military Affairs*, no. 1372 (August 24, 1978), 42–45.

3438.   Saranchev, V. "Artillery Battalion Training Described: Translated from *Krasnaya Zvezda*, April 17, 1980." *Translations on USSR Military Affairs*, no. 1533 (September 12, 1980), 147–149.

3439.   Skinkevich, A. "Self-Propelled Artillery Unit Training Exercise Described: Translated from *Krasnaya Zvezda*, October 22, 1978." *Translations on USSR Military Affairs*, no. 1412 (February 23, 1979), 29–32.

3440.   "Soviet Crews Simulate [SS-lc] Scud Firing." *Aviation Week and Space Technology* 92 (April 20, 1970), 54–55.

3441.   "Tactical Training with Field Firing." *Soviet Military Translations*, no. 36 (January 1961), 11–15.

3442.   "To Fight a Battle Is Difficult: Notes on Artillery Combat Training." *Soviet Military Translations*, no. 41 (December 1960), 11–17.

3443.   "Training Activities in Artillery Units: Translated from *Krasnaya Zvezda*," *Translations on USSR Military Affairs*, no. 1400 (December

12, 1978), 24–30; no. 1423 (March 26, 1979), 35–44; no. 1428 (April 13, 1979), 16–20.

3444.   Tsvetkov, I. "Teamwork in an Artillery Battalion." *Soviet Military Review,* no. 4 (April 1972), 24–25.

3445.   Vasilenko, S. "Training Activities in an Artillery Battalion: Translated from *Krasnaya Zvezda,* November 19, 1977." *Translations on USSR Military Affairs,* no. 1332 (February 22, 1978), 81–83.

3446.   Vishnevsky, Y. "Training of AA Gunners to Fight Tanks." *Soviet Military Review,* no. 10 (October 1972), 18–19.

3447.   Yelshin, N. "Duties of a Battery Executive." *Soviet Military Review,* no. 12 (December 1966), 34–36.

3448.   Zakharenko, A. "Field Artillery Battalion Training Results: Translated from *Krasnaya Zvezda,* October 13, 1977." *Translations on USSR Military Affairs,* no. 1328 (February 2, 1978), 83–85.

3449.   Zuykov, N. "Howitzer Crew Antitank Firing Training Described: Translated from *Znamenosets,* June 1979." *Translations on USSR Military Affairs,* no. 1482 (December 13, 1979), 1–5.

Documents, Papers, and Reports

3450.   Buckner, Richard A. *Tactics and Training of the Firing Battery in the Soviet Field Artillery.* Research Report. New York: U.S. Army Institute for Advanced Russian and East European Studies, 1976. 39p.

Further References

See also 4:C:2 and 3.

(3). Armor

Articles

3451.   Babynin, Ye. "Tank Company Firing Training Described: Translated from *Krasnaya Zvezda,* February 3, 1978." *Translations on USSR Military Affairs,* no. 1352 (May 15, 1978), 26–29.

3452.   Bakanov, R. "A Tank Company in Attack." *Soviet Military Review,* no. 3 (March 1965), 21–24.

3453.   Bogdanovskiy, V. "Tank Battalion Training Results Analyzed: Translated from *Krasnaya Zvezda,* July 9, 1978." *Translations on USSR Military Affairs,* no. 1381 (October 2, 1978), 9–12.

3454.   "The Combat Skill of Tankmen." *Soviet Military Translations,* no. 332a (October 1966), 7–14.

3455.   "Combat Training of Small Tank Units Described: Translated from *Znamenosets,* June 1978." *Translations on USSR Military Affairs,* no. 1386 (October 16, 1978), 5–16.

3456.   Danilov, A. "Tank Regiment Training Activities Described: Translated from *Sovetskiy Voin,* June 1979." *Translations on USSR Military Affairs,* no. 1463 (September 12, 1979), 61–68.

3457.   Dement'yev, A. "Unit Staff and Combat Training." *Soviet Military Review,* no. 12 (December 1966), 22–24.

3458.   Fabritskiy, M. "Tank Gunnery Training Described: Translated from *Krasnaya Zvezda,* June 7, 1978." *Translations on USSR Military Affairs,* no. 1379 (September 25, 1978), 16–19.

3459.   Glebov, I. "Tankborne Operations." *Soviet Military Review,* no. 8 (August 1966), 23–25.

3460.   Golokolenko, I. "Tank Platoon Training." *Soviet Military Review,* no. 4 (April 1966), 31–33.

3461.   Grigorevskiy, I. "Tank Trainers." *Soviet Military Review,* no. 1 (January 1965), 18–19.

3462.   Gruzdev, B. "High-Speed Tank Driving." *Soviet Military Review,* no. 6 (June 1972), 17–19.

3463.   Khorunzhiy, A. "Tank Company Training Described: Translated from *Krasnaya Zvezda,* October 23, 1977." *Translations on USSR Military Affairs,* no. 1327 (January 27, 1978), 46–49.

3464.   _____. "Tank Regiment Officer Training Described: Translated from *Krasnaya Zvezda,* September 18, 1977." *Translations on USSR Military Affairs,* no. 1328 (February 2, 1978), 59–62.

3465.   Kokhanov, V. "Pursuit." *Soviet Military Review,* no. 6 (June 1975), 16–17.

3466.   Kokorev, V. "Infantry Combat Vehicle Driver Training Described: Translated from *Znamenosets,* July 1978." *Translations on USSR Military Affairs,* no. 1386 (October 16, 1978), 45–48.

3467.   Kononov, I. "Training in Firing from Weapons Posts of Combat Vehicles Described: Translated from *Znamenosets,* February 1979." *Translations on USSR Military Affairs,* no. 1449 (June 25, 1979), 30–36.

3468.   Kovalev, V. "Tank Crew Gunnery Training Described: Translated from *Znamenosets,* September 1977." *Translations on USSR Military Affairs,* no. 1324 (January 13, 1978), 70–73.

3469.   Kozhevnikov, V. "High-Speed Tank Driving Training: Translated from *Znamenosets,* March 1978." *Translations on USSR Military Affairs,* no. 1358 (June 21, 1978), 1–5.

3470.   Laverty, Wayne B. "The Soviet Tanker." *Armor* 72 (November-December 1963), 28–31.

3471.   Lisovskiy, V. "Training Methods in a Tank Division Described: Translated from *Krasnaya Zvezda,* March 31, 1978." *Translations on USSR Military Affairs,* no. 1366 (July 20, 1978), 38–42.

3472.   Loginov, M. "Tanks Firing on the Move." *Soviet Military Review,* no. 6 (June 1971), 15–18.

3473.   ———— . "A Tank Battalion in Advance Guard." *Soviet Military Review,* no. 1 (January 1971), 18–20.

3474.   Malygin, M. "Tank Company Training Deficiencies Discussed: Translated from *Krasnaya Zvezda,* September 8, 1977." *Translations on USSR Military Affairs,* no. 1327 (January 27, 1978), 7–9.

3475.   Mattingly, R. E. "Defeating Soviet Armor: A Perspective." *Marine Corps Gazette* 59 (April 1975), 35–39.

3476.   Miller, Crosby. "The Soviet Armored Division in the Mobile Defense." *Military Review* 35 (June 1955), 21–25.

3477.   Moroz, V. "Training Shortcomings in a Tank Regiment Described: Translated from *Krasnaya Zvezda,* June 24, 1978." *Translations on USSR Military Affairs,* no. 1382 (October 3, 1978), 11–14.

3478.   Munzel, Oskar. "Soviet Armor Tactics." *Armor* 61 (January-February 1952), 22–23.

3479.   Nesterov, V. "Fire Training for a Combat Infantry Vehicle Crew: Translated from *Znamenosets,* March 1978." *Translations on USSR Military Affairs,* no. 1366 (July 20, 1978), 93–101.

3480.   Ogorkiewicz, Richard M. "The Structure and Function of Armored Divisions." *Armor* 67 (January-February 1958), 14–21.

3481.   Panasenko, P. "Tank Unit Combat Training Described: Translated from *Gudok,* October 19, 1978." *Translations on USSR Military Affairs,* no. 1400 (December 12, 1978), 120–122.

3482.   Pechinin, M. "Training of New Tank Personnel Described: Translated from *Znamenosets*, August 1978." *Translations on USSR Military Affairs*, no. 1390 (October 26, 1978), 66–69.

3483.   Petrov, Vladimir. "Tank Subunit Combat Training: Translated from *Sovetskaya Moldaviya*, January 20, 1978." *Translations on USSR Military Affairs*, no. 1336 (March 10, 1978), 110–113.

3484.   Pimenov, A. "Good Results on Paper: Translated from *Krasnaya Zvezda*, March 25, 1977." *Review of the Soviet Ground Forces* 1 (August 1977), 13–17.

3485.   _____ . "Tank Battalion Combat Training Activities: Translated from *Krasnaya Zvezda*, December 4, 1977." *Translations on USSR Military Affairs*, no. 1342 (March 29, 1978), 1–4.

3486.   Pirozhkov, A. "Small Tank Unit Offensive Training Described: Translated from *Znamenosets*, January 1978." *Translations on USSR Military Affairs*, no. 1344 (April 7, 1978), 103–108.

3487.   Ryazantsev, D. "Cadets Train in IFV [Infantry Fighting Vehicle] Driving." *Soviet Military Review*, no. 12 (December 1978), 14–15.

3488.   Savchuk, G. "Tank Company Firing Training Described: Translated from *Krasnaya Zvezda*, March 25, 1978." *Translations on USSR Military Affairs*, no. 1371 (August 21, 1978), 48–51.

3489.   Shipitsyn, E. "Physical Training of Tank Crews Described: Translated from *Krasnaya Zvezda*, February 10, 1978." *Translations on USSR MIlitary Affairs*, no. 1352 (May 15, 1978), 46–48.

3490.   Smith, R. G. "The Soviet Armored Threat and NATO Antitank Capabilities." *Army Quarterly* 109 (April 1979), 153–161.

3491.   Stefanovskiy, G. "Combat Training—Tank Regiments Compete: Translated from *Kommunist Vooruzhennykh Sil*, September 1980." *Translations on USSR Military Affairs*, no. 1555 (January 7, 1981), 18–23.

3492.   Svetikov, V. "Flamethrower Tank Platoon Training: Translated from *Krasnaya Zvezda*, May 26, 1979." *Translations on USSR Military Affairs*, no. 1459 (August 28, 1979), 17–19.

3493.   "Tank Unit Training Activities: Translated from *Krasnaya Zvezda*." *Translations on USSR Military Affairs*, no. 1399 (December 4, 1978), 16–23; no. 1400 (December 12, 1978), 31–40; no. 1416 (March 7, 1979), 51–63; no. 1419 (March 15, 1979), 18–25; no. 1423 (March 26, 1979), 19–27; no. 1426 (April 5, 1979), 98–107; no. 1448 (June 21, 1979), 21–27; no. 1450 (July 3, 1979), 1–8; no. 1484 (December 27,

1979), 52–63; no. 1489 (January 16, 1980), 10–22; no. 1493 (February 4, 1980), 46–51; no. 1503 (March 11, 1980), 1–12; no. 1504 (March 14, 1980), 42–47; no. 1518 (June 11, 1980), 1–10; no. 1521 (July 1, 1980), 31–45; no. 1557 (January 16, 1981), 9–21; no. 1570 (February 24, 1981), 19–34.

3494.   "Training Methods in Tank Battalions: Translated from *Krasnaya Zvezda,* April 11 and 27, 1978." *Translations on USSR Military Affairs,* no. 1364 (July 18, 1978), 70–76.

3495.   Turzenok, V. "A Tank Company in Attack." *Soviet Military Review,* no. 11 (November 1966), 28–29.

3496.   Yakubovskiy, A. "Tank Company Combat Training Examined: Translated from *Krasnaya Zvezda,* July 16, 1978." *Translations on USSR Military Affairs,* no. 1382 (October 3, 1978), 64–68.

3497.   Yezhov, N. "Firing Training for Swimming Tanks Described: Translated from *Znamenosets,* August 1979." *Translations on USSR Military Affairs,* no. 1488 (January 11, 1980), 43–48.

3498.   Zakharenko, A. "Command Training of Tank Regiment Officers Described: Translated from *Krasnaya Zvezda,* April 4, 1979." *Translations on USSR Military Affairs,* no. 1453 (August 10, 1979), 10–15.

3499.   _____ . "Training Activities in an Outstanding Tank Regiment Discussed: Translated from *Krasnaya Zvezda,* November 11, 1977." *Translations on USSR Military Affairs,* no. 1331 (February 16, 1978), 6–9.

3500.   Zeynalov, A. "Training for Use of Flame-Throwing Tank Described: Translated from *Znamenosets,* September 1978." *Translations on USSR Military Affairs,* no. 1402 (December 13, 1978), 94–97.

3501.   Zyzanov, A. "Tank Maneuvers." *Soviet Military Review,* no. 12 (December 1974), 13–15.

Further References

See also sections 4:E:A, 4:E:C: 1 and 3, and 4:F:4.

(4). Motorized Infantry

ARTICLES

3502.   "Battle Formations for the Motorized Infantry Company." *Soviet Military Review,* no. 12 (December 1966), 37–39.

3503. Beshlyaga, A. "Shoulder-to-Shoulder with Motorized Infantry." *Soviet Military Review,* no. 12 (December 1966), 28–31.

3504. Bezyukevich, A. "Firing Training in a Motorized Infantry Battalion Described: Translated from *Krasnaya Zvezda,* March 24, 1978." *Translations on USSR Military Affairs,* no. 1366 (July 20, 1978), 28–32.

3505. Chernenko, P. "Shortcomings Noted in Combat Training: Translated from *Krasnaya Zvezda,* October 22, 1977." *Translations on USSR Military Affairs,* no. 1327 (January 27, 1978), 42–45.

3506. Ezell, Edward C. "Rifleman Training Systems: Preparing the Infantryman to Fight." *International Defense Review* 13 (May 1980), 707–711.

3507. Filin, V. "Infantry Company Raiding Operations: Translated from *Znamenosets,* March 1979." *Translations on USSR Military Affairs,* no. 1445 (June 11, 1979), 55–58.

3508. Glebov, I. "Motorized Infantry Learn to Attack." *Soviet Military Review,* no. 12 (December 1969), 19–23.

3509. Gunyavyy, I. "Combined Training of Small Motorized Infantry, Tank Unit Described: Translated from *Znamenosets,* January 1978." *Translations on USSR Military Affairs,* no. 1344 (April 7, 1978), 109–112.

3510. Ivanov, N. "Training of 'Taman' Motorized Rifle Division Described: Translated from *Znamenosets,* February 1978." *Translations on USSR Military Affairs,* no. 1351 (May 12, 1978), 12–16.

3511. Karpov, B. "Motorized Infantry Regiment Combat Training Described: Translated from *Krasnaya Zvezda,* June 13, 1978." *Translations on USSR Military Affairs,* no. 1378 (September 21, 1978), 32–35.

3512. Khamrayev, I. "Antitank Grenade Launching Procedures Described: Translated from *Znamenosets,* May 1978." *Translations on USSR Military Affairs,* no. 1374 (September 5, 1978), 27–31.

3513. Khorunzhiy, A. "Motorized Infantry Battalion Firing Training Criticized: Translated from *Krasnaya Zvezda,* February 28, 1978." *Translations on USSR Military Affairs,* no. 1353 (May 22, 1978), 31–35.

3514. Kikeshev, N. "Small Unit Combined Arms Tactical Training: Translated from *Krasnaya Zvezda,* January 10, 1978." *Translations on USSR Military Affairs,* no. 1352 (May 15, 1978), 1–3.

3515. Klochkov, D. "A Motorized Infantry Platoon in Attack." *Soviet Military Review,* no. 3 (March 1966), 16–19.

3516.   Kovalev, L. "Training Methods in a Motorized Rifle Regiment Described: Translated from *Kommunist Vooruzhennykh Sil* July 1979." *Translations on USSR Military Affairs*, no. 1474 (November 16, 1979), 21–30.

3517.   Kuplevakhskiy, V. "Training Activities in a Motorized Infantry Regiment: Translated from *Pravda*, February 22, 1979." *Translations on USSR Military Affairs*, no. 1435 (May 15, 1979), 6–10.

3518.   Kuvitanov, G. "Realistic Combat Training of Motorized Infantrymen Described: Translated from *Znamenosets*, June 1978." *Translations on USSR Military Affairs*, no. 1386 (October 16, 1978), 1–5.

3519.   Lazarev, V. "Commander of a Motorized Rifle Regiment Discusses Training Results: Translated from *Krasnaya Zvezda*, May 28, 1978." *Translations on USSR Military Affairs*, no. 1370 (August 17, 1978), 80–83.

3520.   Lobachev, G. "'Taman' Motorized Infantry Division Training: Translated from *Krasnaya Zvezda*, October 28, 1977." *Translations on USSR Military Affairs*, no. 1328 (February 2, 1978), 116–119.

3521.   Loktev, G. "Motorized Infantry Squadron Offensive Training Described: Translated from *Znamenosets*, June 1979." *Translations on USSR Military Affairs*, no. 1482 (December 13, 1979), 6–11.

3522.   Mulyar, N. "Training Results Contrasted in Motorized Rifle Companies: Translated from *Krasnaya Zvezda*, April 14, 1978." *Translations on USSR Military Affairs*, no. 1368 (August 3, 1978), 13–16.

3523.   Nagornyy, V. "Training Deficiencies Noted in Motorized Infantry Regiment: Translated from *Krasnaya Zvezda*, September 3, 1977." *Translations on USSR Military Affairs*, no. 1328 (February 2, 1978), 14–17.

3524.   Nekrylov, A. "Motorized Rifle Regiment Training Results Described: Translated from *Sovetskiy Voin*, August 1978." *Translations on USSR Military Affairs*, no. 1388 (October 23, 1978), 14–18.

3525.   "New Forms of Training with Modern Weapons." *Soviet Military Translations*, no. 161a (October 1964), 13–18.

3526.   Nikiforov, F. "Motorized Infantry Training in the Far East Military District: Translated from *Krasnaya Zvezda*, December 2, 1977." *Translations on USSR Military Affairs*, no. 1339 (March 20, 1978), 1–3.

3527.   Panchenko, A. "Infantry Against Tanks." *Soviet Military Review*, no. 10 (October 1965), 27–28.

3528.   Pestalov, P. "Motorized Infantry Company Attacks from Marching Formation." *Soviet Military Review,* no. 5 (May 1965), 38–39.

3529.   Prokhorov, S. "Instruction in Machine-Gun Firing." *Soviet Military Review,* no. 2 (February 1972), 19–20.

3530.   _____ . "Well-Aimed-Shot Training." *Soviet Military Review,* no. 6 (June 1965), 30–31.   Marksmanship.

3531.   Shtemenko, Sergei M. "Combat Training of Ground Troops for Modern War." *Army* 13 (March 1963), 47–52.

3532.   Strigotsky, I. "Officer Training in a Battalion." *Soviet Military Review,* no. 4 (April 1972), 22–23.

3533.   Titakov, K. "NCO Tactical Training in a Motorized Rifle Subunit: Translated from *Znamenosets,* November 1977." *Translations on USSR Military Affairs,* no. 1320 (January 5, 1978), 23–27.

3534.   "Training Objectives in an Outstanding Motorized Rifle Regiment: Translated from *Krasnaya Zvezda,* November 30, 1977." *Translations on USSR Military Affairs,* no. 1331 (February 16, 1978), 34–37.

3535.   "Training of Motorized Rifle Units Described: Translated from *Krasnaya Zvezda.*" *Translations on USSR Military Affairs,* no. 1401 (December 13, 1978), 113–121; no. 1413 (February 28, 1979), 76–88; no. 1426 (April 5, 1979), 51–70; no. 1449 (June 25, 1979), 91–102; no. 1460 (August 30, 1979), 31–55; no. 1495 (February 12, 1980), 1–30; no. 1504 (March 14, 1980), 1–22; no. 1521 (July 1, 1980), 46–61; no. 1533 (September 12, 1980), 139, 168–175; no. 1559 (January 22, 1981), 76–83; no. 1572 (March 5, 1981), 9–24.

3536.   Tychkov, M. "Infantry Cooperates with Tanks." *Soviet Military Review,* no. 3 (March 1977), 24–25.

3537.   Verbovikov, G. "Motorized Infantry Battalion Attacks through Woods and Swamps." *Soviet Military Review,* no. 2 (February 1966), 24–27.

3538.   _____ . "Motorized Infantry Company Tactical Experience with Field Firing." *Soviet Military Review,* no. 10 (October 1966), 15–17.

3539.   Viktorov, G. M., and William F. Robinson. "Squad, Platoon and Company Tactics—Soviet Style." *Infantry* 52 (November-December 1962), 33–35.

3540.   Yakovlev, I. "Training to Fight Tanks." *Soviet Military Review,* no. 12 (December 1968), 16–19.

3541.   Zherebyat'yev, V. "Motorized Infantry Regiment Training: Translated from *Krasnaya Zvezda,* October 29, 1977." *Translations on USSR Military Affairs,* no. 1328 (February 2, 1978), 119–122.

3542.   Zhidkov, K. "Battle Drill for a Motorized Infantry Company." *Soviet Military Review,* no. 4 (April 1966), 28–30.

DOCUMENTS, PAPERS, AND REPORTS

3543.   Mironenko, I. *Battalion Tactical Exercise with Combat Firing.* JPRS 1138. Arlington, Va.: Joint Publication Research Service, 1960. 22p.

3544.   Shevchenko, N. *Advice on Mastering Small Arms and Rocket Launchers.* Translated from the Russian. FSTC-HT-23-0462-75. Charlottesville, Va.: U.S. Army Foreign Science and Technology Center, 1975. 146p.

3545.   Yurev, A. A. *Competitive Marksmanship with Rifle and Carbine.* Translated from the Russian. ACSI-H-3205B. Washington, D.C.: Assistant Chief of Staff for Intelligence, Department of the Army, 1957. 308p.

Further References

See also sections 4:E:A, 4:C:3, and 4:E:1 and 2.

e. TRAINING BY TERRAIN OR CONDITION

Men and units of the Soviet ground forces are taught to operate over a variety of terrains, and in all weather and lighting conditions.

   Many citations in this section are translations from Soviet military journals.

(1). Deserts

ARTICLES

3546.   Bezborodko, M. "Tanks in Hot, Dry Climate." *Sviet Military Review,* no. 12 (December 1965), 30–31.

3547.   Divinsky, B. "Air Landing in a Desert." *Soviet Military Review,* no. 8 (August 1974), 18–20.

3548.   Grinyov, V. "An Enveloping Detachment in a Desert." *Soviet Military Review,* no. 1 (January 1980), 16–17.

3549.   Lapygin, N. "Employing Motorized Rifle Subunits in Desert Terrain Discussed: Translated from *Voyenno Istoricheskiy Zhurnal*, May 1979." *Translations on USSR Military Affairs*, no. 1452 (July 20, 1979), 45–53.

3550.   Orekhov, E. "Tanks in Desert Sand Combat." *Soviet Military Review*, no. 4 (April 1965), 26–27.

3551.   Petrov, Yu. "Motorized Infantry Desert-Steppe Training Described: Translated from *Znamenosets*, September 1979." *Translations on USSR Military Affairs*, no. 1495 (February 12, 1980), 59–64.

3552.   Rodin, A. "Fire and Maneuver Support: Operations of an Artillery Battalion in a Desert." *Soviet Military Review*, no. 12 (December 1970), 27–30.

3553.   Shan'gin, V. "Combined Arms—Factors in Desert Combat Discussed: Translated from *Krasnaya Zvezda*, August 14, 1979." *Translations on USSR Military Affairs*, no. 1491 (January 23, 1980), 40–44.

3554.   Turbiville, Graham H., Jr. "Soviet Desert Operations." *Military Review* 54 (June 1974), 24–29.

Further References

See also 4:E:2:a.

(2). Mountains

ARTICLES

3555.   Alenichev, A. "Defense of a Tank Battalion in Mountains." *Soviet Military Review*, no. 7 (July 1975), 20–21.

3556.   Antsiz, B. "Meeting Engagement in Mountains." *Soviet Military Review*, no. 1 (January 1975), 24–25.

3557.   Averyanov, Z. "Defense in Mountains." *Soviet Military Review*, no. 12 (December 1978), 25–26.

3558.   Bukh, B. "Signal Communications in Mountains." *Soviet Military Review*, no. 10 (October 1966), 20–21.

3559.   Bundyukov, A. "Capturing a Pass." *Soviet Military Review*, no. 10 (October 1973), 15–16.

3560.   Chepiga, V. "Infantry Alpine Training Exercise Described: Translated from *Sovetskiy Voin*, August 1978." *Translations on USSR Military Affairs*, no. 1388 (October 23, 1978), 23–29.

3561.   Donnelly, Christopher N. "Soviet Mountain Warfare Operations." *International Defense Review* 13 (June 1980), 823–834.

3562.   Gavrikov, F. "Mountain Warfare." *Soviet Military Review*, no. 6 (June 1965), 27–30.

3563.   Kononov, I. "Paratrooper Tactics under Mountain Conditions Discussed: Translated from *Znamenosets*, May 1978." *Translations on USSR Military Affairs*, no. 1374 (September 5, 1978), 23–26.

3564.   Kudryavtsev, T. "Technical Support of a Soviet Night March in the Mountains." *Soviet Military Review*, no. 2 (February 1969), 36–38.

3565.   Kurkotkin, Semen K. "Mountain Eagles." *Soviet Military Review*, no. 8 (August 1969), 2–5.

3566.   Oleynik, A. "Airborne Company Alpine Training Discussed: Translated from *Krasnaya Zvezda*, October 21, 1977." *Translations on USSR Military Affairs*, no. 1328 (February 2, 1978), 106–109.

3567.   Prokhorov, S. "Firing in Mountains." *Soviet Military Review*, no. 5 (May 1966), 50–51.

3568.   Sevastyanov, A. "Attack in the Mountains." *Soviet Military Review*, no. 1 (January 1967), 19–21.

3569.   Severenchuk, M. "Tank Exercise in Carpathian Mountains Described: Translated from *Znamenosets*, February 1980." *Translations on USSR Military Affairs*, no. 1554 (December 31, 1980), 55–57.

3570.   Shakhbazyan, A. "Small Unit Tactics in a Mountain Defile Described: Translated from *Znamenosets*, May 1978." *Translations on USSR Military Affairs*, no. 1374 (September 5, 1978), 15–22.

3571.   Tarlykov, A. "Ground Forces in the Mountains—Motorized Rifles: Translated from *Znamenosets*, January 1980." *Translations on USSR Military Affairs*, no. 1553 (December 29, 1980), 101–103.

3572.   United States. Department of the Army. "Mountain Operations." *Opposing Forces: Europe*. FM 30-102. Washington, D.C., 1977. pp. 16/24–16/26.

3573.   Veksler, L. "Helicopter Assault Landing in Mountains Described: Translated from *Aviatsiya I Kosmonavtika*, August 1979." *Translations on USSR Military Affairs*, no. 1475 (November 14, 1979), 38–40.

3574.   Vinnikov, V. "Tanks Attack in Mountains." *Soviet Military Review*, no. 9 (September 1965), 20–21.

3575.   Vorob'yev, I. "Peculiarities of Defense in Mountains." *Soviet Military Review*, no. 4 (April 1974), 21–23.

3576.   Yezhov, N. "Tank Exercise in Mountains Described: Translated from *Znamenosets*, April 1980." *Translations on USSR Military Affairs*, no. 1554 (December 31, 1980), 58–61.

3577.   Zabelin, A. "Before a March in Mountains." *Soviet Military Review*, no. 6 (June 1975), 20–22.

3578.   Zyrzanov, A. "Tank Offensive in Mountains." *Soviet Military Review*, no. 10 (October 1973), 12–14.

Further References

See also sections 4:E:2:a and 5:G:2:e.

(3). Swamps/Marshes/Woods

ARTICLES

3579.   Arkhipkin, V. "Attack in Think Wood." *Soviet Military Review*, no. 9 (September 1966), 20–23.

3580.   Bessonov, S. "Reconnaissance in Marshy and Wooded Terrain." *Soviet Military Review*, no. 4 (April 1979), 10–11.

3581.   Gruzdev, B. "Tanks Negotiating Forests and Marshes." *Soviet Military Review*, no. 1 (January 1972), 20–22.

3582.   Ionov, G. "Operations in Marshy and Wooded Country." *Soviet Military Review*, no. 1 (January 1969), 25–29.

3583.   Kudryavtsev, T. "Tank-Driving in Cross-Country Terrain." *Soviet Military Review*, no. 12 (December 1966), 48–49.

3584.   Mutsynov, S. "Combat in a Thick Forest." *Soviet Military Review*, no. 11 (November 1965), 34–35.

3585.   Pearson, R. L. V. "Operations in the Taiga." *Military Review*, 37 (April 1957), 40–52.

3586.   Petrukhin, V. "In the Woods and Marshes." *Soviet Military Review*, no. 2 (February 1971), 21–23.

3587.   Viktorov, G. M. "Soviet Forest Tactics." *Infantry* 53 (March-April 1963), 47–48.

3588.   Von Senger und Etterlin, Fridolin M. "March of an Armored Division during the Muddy Season." *Military Review* 35 (September 1955), 98–107.

3589.   Zapadov, A. "Artillery in Wooded Swamps." *Field Artillery Journal* 35 (June 1945), 365–366.

DOCUMENTS, PAPERS, AND REPORTS

3590.   Kolotushkin, A. *The Armored Carrier Driver's Springtime Terrain Problems.* Translated from the Russian. FSTC-HT-23-0061-74. Charlottesville, Va.: U.S. Army Foreign Science and Technology Center, 1974. 8p.

(4). Rivers

ARTICLES

3591.   Babayev, S. "Tanker Training in Deep Water Fording Operations Described: Translated from *Bakinskiy Rabochiy,* September 5, 1978." *Translations on USSR Military Affairs,* no. 1389 (October 24, 1978), 49–51.

3592.   Betit, Eugene D. "River Crossing: Key to Soviet Offense." *Military Review* 51 (October 1971), 88–96.

3593.   Gruzdev, B. "Underwater Tank Driving." *Soviet Military Review,* no. 5 (May 1974), 18–19.

3594.   Mikhailov, L. "Tank Battalion Forces Water Barrier." *Soviet Military Review,* no. 1 (January 1974), 24–26.

3595.   Nargele, D. G. "Soviet River-Crossing Operations." *Marine Corps Gazette* 64 (July 1980), 60–64.

3596.   Roshchupkin, V. "Tank Deep-Fording Operation Described: Translated from *Krasnaya Zvezda,* September 16, 1977." *Translations on USSR Military Affairs,* no. 1328 (February 2, 1978), 49–52.

3597.   United States. Department of the Army. "Assault River Crossings." *Opposing Forces: Europe.* FM 30-102. Washington, D. C., 1977. pp. 16/6–16/12.

3598.   _____. "Enemy River Defense." *River Crossing Operations.* FM 90-13. Washington, D.C., 1978. pp. 2/5–2/9.

DOCUMENTS, PAPERS, AND REPORTS

3599.   United States. Department of Defense. Defense Intelligence Agency. *Soviet and Warsaw Pact River Crossing: Doctrine and Capabilities.* DDI-1150-13-77. Washington, D.C., 1977. 34p.

Further References

See also 4:E:2 and 4:E:2:d:(3).

(5). Urban

ARTICLES

3600.   Hemesley, A. E. "Soviet Military Operations in Built-up Areas." *Infantry* 67 (November-December 1977), 30–34.

3601.   Lomakin, M. "Fighting for Inhabited Localities." *Soviet Military Review*, no. 5 (May 1966), 43–46.

3602.   Meehan, John F., 3d. "Urban Combat: The Soviet View." *Military Review*, 54 (September 1974), 41–47.

3603.   Scharfen, John C., and Michael J. Deane. "To Fight Russians in Cities, Know Their Tactics." *Marine Corps Gazette* 61 (January 1977), 38–42.

3604.   United States. Department of the Army. "Operations in Fortified and Built-up Areas." *Opposing Forces: Europe*. FM 30-102. Washington, D. C., 1977. pp. 16/13–16/16.

3605.   Vigor, Peter H., and Christopher N. Donnelly. "Fighting in Built-up Areas: A Soviet View." *Journal of the Royal United Service Institute for Defence Studies* 122 (June-September 1977), 39–47, 63–67.

DOCUMENTS, PAPERS, AND REPORTS

3606.   Dzirkals, Lilita, et al. *Military Operations in Built-up Areas: Essays on Some Past, Present, and Future Aspects.* RAND Report R-1871-ARPA. Santa Monica, Calif.: RAND Corporation, 1976. 102p.

3607.   Scharfen, John C., and Michael J. Deane. *Soviet Tactical Doctrine for Urban Warfare.* Report no. SSC-TN-2625-16. Menlo Park, Calif.: Strategic Studies Center, Stanford Research Institute, 1975. 159p.

3608.   Shovkolovich, A. K., et al. *Combat Action of a Motorized Rifle Battalion in a City.* Translated from the Russian. OACS(I)K-1400. Washington, D.C.: National Technical Information Service, 1972.

3609.   United States. Department of Defense. Defense Intelligence Agency. *Soviet Military Operations in Built-up Areas.* DDI-1100-155-77. Washington, D.C., 1977. 32p.

Further References

See also sections 2:C and 4:E:2:a.

(6). Night

ARTICLES

3610.   Antonov, A. "Night Engagement." *Soviet Military Review,* no. 12 (December 1973), 8–11.

3611.   Betit, Eugene D. "Soviet Tactical Doctrine for Night Combat." *Military Review* 55 (August 1975), 21–33.

3612.   _____ . "Soviet Technological Preparation for Night Combat." *Military Review* 55 (March 1975), 89–93.

3613.   _____ . "Soviet Training for Night Warfare." *Military Review* 55 (September 1975), 80–86.

3614.   Dukov, R. "Two Attacks–To Persistently Master the Art of Night Combat: Translated from *Krasnaya Zvezda,* March 23, 1977." *Review of the Soviet Ground Forces* 1 (August 1977), 9–12.

3615.   Gavrikov, F. "Company Attacks at Night." *Soviet Military Review,* no. 11 (November 1965), 26–27.

3616.   Kabirov, R. "Acting Expertly in Darkness." *Soviet Military Review,* no. 1 (January 1972), 28–29.

3617.   Kokhanov, V. "Troop Training." *Soviet Military Review,* no. 12 (December 1973), 12–13.

3618.   Kostrov, Nicolai, et al. "Soviet Night Attacks." *Cavalry Journal* 54 (May 1954), 64–65.

3619.   Krainov, K. "Night Tank Gunnery." *Soviet Military Review,* no. 9 (September 1973), 18–19.

3620.   Kuznetsov, P. "Night Training of Artillery Gun Crews Described: Translated from *Znamenosets,* October 1978." *Translations on USSR Military Affairs,* no. 1418 (March 13, 1974), 5–9.

3621.   Lushev, P. "Commander of Central Asian Military District on Night Training: Translated from *Krasnaya Zvezda,* March 19, 1980." *Translations on USSR Military Affairs,* no. 1524 (July 15, 1980), 16–20.

3622.   McMaster, Arthur W., 3d. "Soviet Night Operations." *U.S. Army Aviation Digest* 22 (January 1976), 2–3.

3623.   Mordas, M. "Infantry Squad Night Defensive Training: Translated from *Znamenosets,* March 1979." *Translations on USSR Military Affairs,* no. 1445 (June 11, 1979), 59–62.

3624.   Petrov, Vladimir. "(Night) Attack in the Desert." *Soviet Military Review,* no. 12 (December 1973), 14–16.

3625.   Sobik, Erich. "Soviet Night Operations." *Military Review* 52 (August 1972), 71–76.

3626.   "Soviet Night Attacks." *Military Review* 30 (January 1951), 86–89.

3627.   Sukhinin, Yu. "Division Attacks by Night." *Soviet Military Review,* no. 6 (June 1979), 16–18.

3628.   Trofimov, R. "Preparation of a Tank Company for Night Defense." *Soviet Military Review,* no. 9 (September 1971), 27–29.

3629.   Tsygankov, P. "Post-war Development of Night Operations: Translated from *Voyenno Istoricheskiy Zhurnal,* October 1978." *Translations on USSR Military Affairs,* no. 1404 (December 21, 1978), 71–81.

3630.   United States. Department of the Army. "Night Operations." *Opposing Forces: Europe.* FM 30-102. Washington, D.C., 1977. pp. 16/22–16/23.

3631.   Vinnikov, V. "Tank Battalion Attacks at Night." *Soviet Military Review,* no. 5 (May 1970), 24–27.

3632.   Yashkin, G. "Night Fighting Training: Translated from *Krasnaya Zvezda,* June 18, 1979." *Translations on USSR Military Affairs,* no. 1458 (August 23, 1979), 59–62.

3633.   Yevdokimov, V. "Night Combat: Translated from *Krasnaya Zvezda,* March 17, 1977." *Review of the Soviet Ground Forces* 1 (August 1977), 3–8.

DOCUMENTS, PAPERS, AND REPORTS

3634.   Betit, Eugene D. *Soviet Tactical Doctrine and Capabilities for Warfare at Night and under Conditions of Limited Visibility.* Research Report. New York: U.S. Army Institute for Advanced Russian and East European Studies, 1974. 63p.

3635.   Fenion, James A. *Capabilities and Limitations of the Soviet Army to Conduct Night Attacks.* Research Report. New York: U.S. Army Institute for Advanced Russian and East European Studies, 1978. 48p.

3636. Flannery, Corbett M. "Night Operations: The Soviet Approach." MA thesis, U.S. Army Command and General Staff College, 1978. 86p.

3637. United States. Department of Defense. Defense Intelligence Agency. *Soviet Ground Forces: Night Operations.* DDI-1100-128-76. Washington, D.C., 1976.

Further References

See also section 4:E:1:a.

(7). Winter

ARTICLES

3638. Baxter, William P. "Soviet Norms for Driving Tanks in Winter." *Military Review* 60 (September 1980), 2–8.

3639. "Cold Weather Combat." *Soviet Military Translations,* no. 245 (April 1966), 42–45.

3640. Dobryakov, I. "Winter Tank Driver Training: Translated from *Znamenosets,* January 1979." *Translations on USSR Military Affairs,* no. 1438 (May 18, 1979), 55–58.

3641. Haynes, R. J. H. "Soviet Techniques in Winter Warfare." *Journal of the Royal United Service Institute for Defence Studies* 119 (June 1974), 59–62.

3642. McGuire, James D. "Soviet Cold Weather Operations." *Armor* 71 (July-August 1962), 26–30.

3643. Sobik, Erich. "Soviet Army Winter Operations." *Military Review* 53 (June 1973), 54–58.

3644. "Soviet Winter Operations." *Infantry* 51 (November-December 1961), 43–44.

3645. United States. Department of the Army. "Extreme Cold Operations." *Opposing Forces: Europe.* FM 30-102. Washington, D.C., 1977. pp. 16/27–16/29.

3646. Voronov, G. "Preparation of a Self-Propelled Howitzer for Winter." *Technology and Armament* 11 (November 1977), 111–115.

3647. Ziyemin'sh, M. "Combat Training under Winter Conditions: Translated from *Krasnaya Zvezda,* February 28, 1980." *Translations on USSR Military Affairs,* no. 1516 (May 30, 1980), 16–20.

DOCUMENTS, PAPERS, AND REPORTS

3648.   Know, John W. *Soviet Doctrine and Capabilities for Winter Operations*. Research Report. New York: U.S. Army Institute for Advanced Russian and East European Studies, 1978. 46p.

f. MILITARY EDUCATIONAL FACILITIES

Formal ground forces officer training takes place in a complex and extensive system of approximately seventy military schools and five academies, with program length ranging from three to five years. Each army branch operates its own officer schools and at least one academy. Combined arms, tank, and artillery schools are the most numerous. The most important step in an officer's military education is attending one of the branch or component academies, of which the Frunze Military Academy, essentially a combined arms branch academy, is the best known. The training of senior officers for command assignments at division or higher level and of staff officers for combined arms armies and higher headquarters takes place at the Academy of the General Staff.

The Soviet ground forces also operates specialized technical schools which instruct NCOs in the various military-technical skills. The duration of the courses ranges from a few weeks to a year. On-the-job NCO training is almost continuous in regimental-sized units, which provide refresher courses, equipment familiarization exercises, etc. Due to the cyclical nature of the Soviet draft system, most NCO training lasts for six months to allow for overlapping resources required by the semiannual conscription. Those below NCO status obtain most of their military training within their operational units.

ARTICLES

3649.   Artemiev, Vyacheslav P. "Soviet Military Educational Institutions." *Military Review* 46 (January 1966), 11–14.

3650.   "Artillerymen Training Facilities." *Soviet Military Review,* no. 8 (August 1968), 18–19.

3651.   Baskahov, V. "Frunze Military Academy." *Soviet Military Review,* no. 9 (September 1966), 7–9.

3652.   Beloborodov, Afanasiy P. "Officer Training." *Soviet Military Review,* no. 6 (June 1965), 18–20.

3653.   "A Brief Description of Frunze Military Academy." *Soviet Military Translations,* no. 218 (December 1965), 53–56.

3654.   "Educating the Soviet Army Officer." *Military Review* 29 (December 1949), 3–8.

3655.   "Foreign Language Training of Soviet Officers." *Soviet Military Translations,* no. 193a (August 1965), 61–64.

3656.   "The General Staff Academy." *Soviet Military Translations,* no. 351a (November 1966), 14–37.

3657.   Head, Richard G. "Russian Military Education." *Military Review* 59 (February 1979), 14–16.

3658.   Hendrix, Gaines D. "Soviet Education and the Military." *Military Review* 58 (December 1978), 19–27.

3659.   "In Military Academies and Schools Teachers Both Train and Educate." *Soviet Military Translations,* no. 333a (October 1966), 13–17.

3660.   "The Inculcation of Cadets with High Moral and Combat Qualities." *Soviet Military Translations,* no. 288 (July 1966), 10–17.

3661.   Jacobs, Walter D. "What Do Soviet Officers Read?" *Military Review* 36 (February 1957), 37–43.

3662.   Kozlov, N. "Development of Soviet Military School System Examined: Translated from *Voyenno Istoricheskiy Zhurnal,* July 1978." *Translations on USSR Military Affairs,* no. 1387 (October 18, 1978), 55–64.

3663.   Krupchenko, I. Ye. "Academy of Armored Troops 50th Anniversary Marked: Translated from *Voyenno Istoricheskiy Zhurnal,* September 1980." *Translations on USSR Military Affairs,* no. 1553 (December 29, 1980), 73–76.

3664.   Makarov, V. "Effectiveness of Officer Schools Discussed: Translated from *Krasnaya Zvezda,* September 14, 1977." *Translations on USSR Military Affairs,* no. 1328 (February 2, 1978), 38–42.

3665.   Maksimov, I. "Higher Tank Command School Training Activities: Translated from *Krasnaya Zvezda,* November 22, 1977." *Translations on USSR Military Affairs,* no. 1332 (February 22, 1978), 92–95.

3666.   Malinovskiy, Rodion Y. "Soviet Military Education." *Military Review* 47 (February 1967), 30–37.

3667.   "Military Science and Academies." *Soviet Military Translations,* no. 146 (June 1964), 21–26.

3668.   Morozov, A. "Commandant of Higher Artillery School Describes Training: Translated from *Kommunist Vooruzhennykh Sil,* June 1979." *Translations on USSR Military Affairs,* no. 1478 (November 29, 1978), 22–30.

3669.   Murphy, Paul J., and Margaret, comps. "Higher Soviet Naval and Related Military Schools." In Paul J. Murphy, ed., *Naval Power in Soviet Policy*. Studies in Communist Affairs, no. 2. Washington, D.C.: U.S. Government Printing Office, 1978. pp. 307–311.

3670.   Mutsynov, S. "Training Facilities at Military Schools." *Soviet Military Review*, no. 11 (November 1976), 26–27.

3671.   Ney, Virgil. "Soviet Military Education: A Source of Communist Power." *Military Review* 39 (December 1959), 3–11.

3672.   "Officers' School of the Soviet Ground Forces." *Soviet Military Translations*, no. 237 (March 1966), 8–18.

3673.   Ovcharenko, I. "Activities at Frunze Military Academy Described: Translated from *Kommunist Vooruzhennykh Sil*, December 1978." *Translations on USSR Military Affairs*, no. 1417 (March 9, 1979), 64–71.

3674.   "Post-Graduate Officer Training." *Soviet Military Translations*, no. 310 (August 1966), 27–31.

3675.   Rakovsky, L. "Commanders of Tomorrow." *Soviet Military Review*, no. 11 (November 1972), 30–33.   Examines the Lenin Tashkent Higher Combined Arms Command School.

3676.   Ryabchikov, V. "The Academy of Armored Troops." *Soviet Military Review*, no. 9 (September 1965), 14–15.

3677.   Scott, Harriet F. "Educating the Soviet Officer Corps." *Air Force Magazine* 58 (March 1975), 57–60.

3678.   "Soviet Military Academies and Their Course of Study." *Soviet Military Translations*, no. 304 (August 1966), 16–19.

3679.   Sychev, A. "Higher Tank School Training Activities: Translated from *Krasnaya Zvezda*, February 3, 1978." *Translations on USSR Military Affairs*, no. 1352 (May 15, 1978), 35–39.

3680.   "Thirty Years of the Military Academy of the General Staff Reviewed." *Soviet Military Translations*, no. 372a (January 1967), 23–27.

3681.   "The Training of Officers." *Soviet Military Translations*, no. 310 (August 1966), 23–26.

3682.   "The Training of the Soviet Army Officer Corps." *Soviet Military Translations*, no. 321 (September 1966), 9–17.

3683.   Tsirlin, A. "The Higher School for Military Engineers." *Soviet Military Review*, no. 12 (December 1965), 15–16.

3684.   Yelshin, N. "Military Academy: A Phase in the Making of a Commander." *Soviet Military Review,* no. 10 (October 1974), 36–37.   The Armored Troops Academy.

DOCUMENTS, PAPERS, AND REPORTS

3685.   United States. Department of Defense. Defense Intelligence Agency. *Soviet Military Schools.* DDB-2680-52-78. Washington, D.C., 1978.

Further References

See also sections 4:A, 4:E:1:a,b,c and 4:E:2:a,b,c.

3. Exercises

The Soviet training cycle usually begins following the annual celebration of the Bolshevik Revolution and is divided into two periods, winter and summer. Training during the winter is usually limited, taking place mainly in garrison. Most garrisons are situated on the outskirts of towns or villages, where the adjoining countryside may be used for field training and marches as well as command post exercises. Summer training usually begins right after the May Day celebration and concentrates much more time in the field out of garrison. Summer training usually culminates in autumn divisional maneuvers, which may be combined with Warsaw Pact exercises.

ARTICLES

3686.   Akimov, A. "Company Tactical Exercise: Methods for Preparation and Execution." *Soviet Military Review,* no. 9 (September 1977), 14–16.

3687.   Bazanov, P. "'Berezina' Exercise Air Operations Described: Translated from *Soviet Military Review,* November 1978." *Translations on USSR Military Affairs,* no. 1413 (February 28, 1979), 182–184.

3688.   "'Berezina' Field Training Exercise: Translated from Various Sources." *Translations on USSR Military Affairs,* no. 1350 (May 8, 1978), 32–83.

3689.   "Clear as a Picture: Russian Tank Maneuvres." *Time* 80 (August 17, 1962), 22.

3690.   "The Combined Operations of the Soviet Union." *Armies and Weapons* (December 1977–January 1978), 24–25.

3691.   Dynin, I. "Airborne Battalion Fulfills Task in 'Neman' Exercise: Translated from *Kryl'ya Rodiny,* October 1979." *Translations on USSR Military Affairs,* no. 1495 (February 12, 1980), 42–47.

3692.   Glebov, I. "Tactical Drills and Exercises." *Soviet Military Review,* no. 4 (April 1966), 25–27.

3693.   Ionov, G. "Exercises According to Plan." *Soviet Military Review,* no. 7 (July 1965), 36–37.

3694.   Izgarshev, V. "Comments on Field Exercise 'The Carpathians': Translated from *Kryl'ya Rodiny,* October 1977." *Translations on USSR Military Affairs,* no. 1323 (January 11, 1978), 47–52.

3695.   _____ . "With Assault Troops on Board—A Combat Report from the 'Berezina' Maneuvers: Translated from *Krasnaya Zvezda,* February 8, 1978." *Review of the Soviet Ground Forces* 2 (April 1978), 7–9.

3696.   Kikeshev, N. "The Lessons of Coordination: Translated from *Krasnaya Zvezda,* January 10, 1978." *Review of the Soviet Ground Forces* 2 (April 1978), 10–12.

3697.   Kuvitanov, G. "Tank Company Tactical Training Exercise Described: Translated from *Znamenosets,* September 1978." *Translations on USSR Military Affairs,* no. 1402 (December 13, 1978), 98–102.

3698.   Meehan, John F., 3d. "Soviet Maneuvers: Summer 1971." *Military Review* 52 (April 1972), 14–21.

3699.   Merimskiy, V. "Effectiveness of Opposed Forces Tactical Exercises Discussed: Translated from *Krasnaya Zvezda,* April 11, 1979." *Translations on USSR Military Affairs,* no. 1455 (August 10, 1979), 58–62.

3700.   "Military Exercises Held in Belorussian Military District: Translated from *Krasnaya Zvezda.*" *Translations on USSR Military Affairs,* no. 1336 (March 10, 1978), 52–60.

3701.   Moroz, V. "Ground Forces Combat Training Exercise Evaluated: Translated from *Krasnaya Zvezda,* February 1, 1978." *Translations on USSR Military Affairs,* no. 1352 (May 15, 1978), 13–17.

3702.   "'Neman' Troop Training Exercise Activities: Translated from Various Sources." *Translations on USSR Military Affairs,* no. 1481 (December 13, 1979), 38–88.

3703.   Oden, Richard. "Exercise 'Neman.'" *Review of the Soviet Ground Forces* 5 (January 1980), 5–11.

3704.　"Reports on the 'Druzhba-'79' Training Exercise: Translated from *Krasnaya Zvezda,* February 4 and 8, 1979." *Translations on USSR Military Affairs,* no. 1428 (April 13, 1979), 21–26.

3705.　Salisbury, Thomas M., 3d. "'KAVKAZ-76.'" *Military Review* 57 (June 1977), 47–55.

3706.　"The 'Shchit-'76' Manoeuvres." *Soviet Military Review,* no. 1 (January 1977), 32–33.

3707.　"Senior Officers Evaluate Training Results in the Central Group of Forces, Transbaykal Military District: Translated from *Krasnaya Zvezda,* September 20, 1978." *Translations on USSR Military Affairs,* no. 1401 (December 13, 1978), 139–144.

3708.　Sergeyev, N. "Instructions for Conducting Tactical Exercises: Translated from *Znamenosets,* September 1977." *Translations on USSR Military Affairs,* no. 1324 (January 13, 1978), 73–78.

3709.　"The 'Sever' Maneuvers." *Soviet Military Review,* no. 10 (October 1976), 17–19.

3710.　Shurgyin, V. "Troop Activities during the 'Berezina' Field Exercise Described: Translated from *Sovetskiy Voin,* April 1978." *Translations on USSR Military Affairs,* no. 1358 (June 21, 1978), 17–27.

3711.　Smith, Desmond. "On Maneuvers with the Red Army." *Nation* 206 (May 20, 1968), 658–662.

3712.　"A Tank and Infantry Training Exercise." *Soviet Military Translations,* no. 200 (September 1965), 1–4.

3713.　Tarleton, Bob. "Combined Arms at Work." *Review of the Soviet Ground Forces* 4 (November 1979), 7–11.

3714.　Turbiville, Graham H., Jr. "Warsaw Pact Amphibious Operations in Northern Europe." *Marine Corps Gazette* 60 (October 1976), 20–27.

3715.　———. "Warsaw Pact Exercise 'Shchit-'72.'" *Military Review* 53 (July 1973), 17–24.

3716.　Verstakov, V. "Self-Propelled Artillery Exercise Described: Translated from *Pravda,* November 19, 1978." *Translations on USSR Military Affairs,* no. 1406 (January 2, 1979), 1–3.

3717.　Vigor, Peter H. "Soviet Military Exercises." *Journal of the Royal United Service Institute for Defence Studies* 116 (September 1971), 23–29.

3718.   "Warsaw Pact Training Exercise Held in Hungary: Translated from *Soldat und Technik,* July 1979." *Translations on USSR Military Affairs,* no. 1462 (September 7, 1979), 77–79.

3719.   Zaytsev, Mikhail M. "Belorussian Commander Cites Success of 'Berezina' Exercise: Translated from *Sovetskaya Belorrussiya,* February 22, 1978." *Translations on USSR Military Affairs,* no. 1341 (March 28, 1978), 15–19.

DOCUMENTS, PAPERS, AND REPORTS

3720.   Dziuban, Stanley. *The Warsaw Pact Maneuvres [1961–1965]: Proof of Readiness or Psychological Warfare?* N-369(R). Arlington, Va.: Institute for Defense Analysis, 1966.

3721.   Stadnyuk, Ivan. *Dneiper War Games in Ukraine and Belorussia.* JPRS 43324. Arlington, Va.: Joint Publication Research Service, 1967. 4p.

3722.   United States. Department of Defense. Defense Intelligence Agency. *Soviet Warsaw Pact Exercises, 1976: "Kavkaz-Sever" and "Shchit-'76."* DDI-1100-159-77. Washington, D.C., 1977.

Further References

See also section 4:E:2.

F. Weapons and Accoutrements

1. General Works

As the result of the defense expenditures and weapons procurement policies noted in section 3:B, the Soviet Army possesses many new and excellent weapons. This arsenal includes four times as much artillery as is possessed by the United States and five times the number of tanks. Soviet arms are among the best in the world, often superior to those in the West. "The days when the Russians had more of everything, but all their equipment was inferior, are over," writes Christopher Foss. The noted editor of *Jane's Armour and Artillery* especially believes that "their tanks, other armoured vehicles and transport perform as well as and usually better than their counterparts in the West."[1]

The citations in this section examine the major weapons of the Soviet ground forces, upon which is centered Russian military doctrine, or-

1. Quoted in John Nielsen et al., "The Red Army's New Look," *Newsweek* 95 (February 11, 1980), p. 46.

ganization, and tactics. "Qualitatively, in a lot of weapons systems, theirs are a hell of a lot better than ours," U.S. Army Chief of Staff General Edward Meyer has admitted, and "we've never said that before."[2]

BOOKS

3723.   Barnaby, Frank, and Ronald Huisken. *Arms Uncontrolled.* Cambridge, Mass.: Published for the Stockholm International Peace Research Institute by Harvard University Press, 1975. 232p.

3724.   Beaumont, Roger A., and Martin Edmonds, ed. *War in the Next Decade.* Lexington: University of Kentucky Press, 1974. 217p.

3725.   Bertram, Christopher, ed. *New Conventional Weapons and East-West Security: Based on a 1977 Conference of the International Institute for Strategic Studies.* New York: Praeger, 1979. 97p.

3726.   Calder, Nigel, ed. *Unless Peace Comes: A Scientific Forecast of New Weapons.* New York: Viking Press, 1968. 243p.

3727.   Dickson, Paul. *The Electronic Battlefield.* Bloomington: Indiana University Press, 1976. 256p.

3728.   Holst, Johan J., and Uwe Nerlich, eds. *Beyond Nuclear Deterrence: New Aims, New Arms.* New York: Crane, Russak, 1977. 314p.

3729.   Kemp, Geoffrey; Robert L. Pfaltzgraff; and Uri Ra'anan, eds. *The Other Arms Race: New Technologies and Non-Nuclear Conflict.* Lexington, Mass.: D. C. Heath, 1975. 281p.

3730.   Langford, David. *War in 2080: The Future of Military Technology.* New York: William Morrow, 1979. 232p.

3731.   Marriott, John, comp. *International Weapons Developments.* San Rafael, Calif.: Presidio Press, 1979. 157p.

3732.   Pretty, Ronald T., ed. *Jane's Weapons Systems.* London: Macdonald and Jane's, 1969–. v. 1–.

3733.   Royal United Service Institute for Defence Studies, eds. *International Weapons Developments: A Survey of Current Developments in Weapons Systems.* 4th ed. New York and London: Pergamon Press, 1980. 203p.

3734.   Stockholm International Peace Research Institute. *Anti-Personnel Weapons.* New York: Crane, Russak, 1978. 299p.

2. *Ibid.,* p. 49.

3735.   Tompkins, John S. *The Weapons of World War III: The Long Road Back from the Bomb.* Garden City, N.Y.: Doubleday, 1966. 340p.

ARTICLES

3736.   Alekseyev, Nikolai N. "Deputy Defense Minister for Armaments Writes on Forces' Equipment: Translated from *Krasnaya Zvezda,* February 15, 1978." *Translations on USSR Military Affairs,* no. 1335 (March 7, 1978), 86–88.

3737.   Aviation Week and Space Technology, Editors of. "Special Report on Electronic Warfare." *Aviation Week and Space Technology* 94 (January 27, 1975), 41–144.

3738.   "Battlefield of the 1990's: It's Not Sci-Fi, It's Real." *U.S. News and World Report* 83 (July 4, 1977), 48–50.

3739.   Daschke, Carl E. "Threat: The Soviet '70's Revisited." *U.S. Army Aviation Digest* 26 (September 1980), 44–48.

3740.   Digby, James. "New Nonnuclear Technology: Implications and Exploitable Opportunities." *Air University Review* 29 (November-December 1977), 46–50.

3741.   Gunston, William. "Army Weapons." In Ray Bonds, ed., *The Soviet War Machine.* New York: Chartwell House, 1976. pp. 176–200.

3742.   Haslam, C. B. "A Comparison: Marine and Russian Weapons." *Marine Corps Gazette* 40 (October 1956), 50–57.

3743.   Hayward, P. H. C. "Arms and Equipment of Land Forces Today and Tomorrow." *NATO's Fifteen Nations* 17 (June-July 1972), 28–42.

3744.   Heiman, Leo. "In the Soviet Arsenal." *Ordnance* 52 (January-February 1968), 366–373.

3745.   Heymont, Irving. "Soviet Ground Weapons." *Ordnance* 43 (May-June 1959), 906–910.

3746.   Hotz, Robert. "New Soviet Weapons Unveiled in Mideast: Weapons Captured during the October 1973 War." *Aviation Week and Space Technology* 102 (March 24, 1975), 14–17.

3747.   Knyaz'kov, V. "Reliability of Combat Materiel Discussed: Translated from *Voyennyye Znaniya,* November 1977." *Translations on USSR Military Affairs,* no. 1326 (January 25, 1978), 36–41.

3748.   Larinov, V. V. "New Weapons and the Direction of War: Translated from *Krasnaya Zvezda,* March 3, 1965." In William R. Kintner and Harriet F. Scott, eds., *The Nuclear Revolution in Soviet Military Affairs.* Norman: University of Oklahoma Press, 1968. pp. 56–65.

3749.   "A Look at Soviet Weapons." *Army Information Digest* 12 (August 1957), 2–14.

3750.   "Mastery of Firepower." *Military Review* 44 (April 1964), 69–72.

3751.   "Modern Weapons and Tactics." *Soviet Military Translations,* no. 130 (November 1963), 25–29.

3752.   "Modern Weapons of the Soviet Army." *Interavia* 21 (May 1966), 590–593.

3753.   "The New-Look Soviet Weapons." *Army Information Digest* 13 (March 1958), 24–33.

3754.   Poe, Bryce, 2d. "Cheap Junk and Other Myths about Soviet Equipment." *Defense '81,* no. 2 (February 1981), 2–9.

3755.   Underhill, Garrett. "Red Army Weapons." *Infantry Journal* 51 (August 1942), 8–19.

3756.   United States. Department of the Army. "Equipment Performance Charts." *Opposing Forces: Europe.* FM 30-102. Washington, D.C., 1977. pp. G/1–G/8.

3757.   _____ . "Identify Opposing Force (OPFOR) Weapons and Equipment." *Special Forces Soldier's Manual.* FM 31-11C-S. Washington, D.C., 1980. pp. 2/241–2/251.

3758.   "Visions of the Next War." *Newsweek* 83 (April 22, 1974), 52–55.

3759.   Watson, Mark S. "Soviet Army Weapons Are Modern." *Army* 8 (January 1958), 57–59.

3760.   "Weapons and Equipment." In Basil H. Liddell-Hart, ed., *The Soviet Army.* London: Weidenfeld & Nicolson, 1956. pp. 286–294.

Further References

See other parts of this subsection and section 2:D:1.

2. Artillery, Rockets, AA- and AT-Missiles

Artillery support and antiaircraft/antitank capability reflect the Soviets' historical interest in what Stalin once called the "God of War." The equipment, including self-propelled units, is modern and relatively easy to operate.

Major artillery field guns and howitzers currently in use include:

1) the 122mm D-30 howitzer, found in artillery regiments of airborne, motorized infantry, and tank divisions, capable of firing its high explosive (HE) shell 16,677 yards

2) the 130mm M-46 field gun of artillery divisions, which can project its HE shell 29,430 yards

3) the 152mm D-20 gun-howitzer of artillery divisions, which can place its HE projectile 20,165 yards downrange

4) the older 152mm D-1 howitzer, now being phased out, which can lob its shell 12,500 meters; still found in the artillery regiments of motorized infantry divisions

5) the 122mm D-74 field gun of artillery divisions, which can loft its 55-lb. HE shell 21,900 meters

6) the largest Soviet artillery piece on a towed mount, the 180mm S-23 gun can fire a conventional or nuclear shell 29,250 meters.

Major antitank (AT) guns and missiles currently in service include:

1) the 100mm T-12 antitank gun, found in the AT battalions of motorized infantry divisions and independent artillery units, can fire an HE or armor-piercing 35-lb. shell 21,000 meters

2) the 85mm D-44 antitank gun, similarly employed as the T-12 above, can put its 21-lb. shell 15,650 meters downrange

3) the obsolete AT-1 snapper AT missile with a maximum range of 2,507 yards

4) the AT-2 swatter, found only in Soviet ground forces, with a 3,500 meter range

5) the AT-3 sagger, widely employed in Warsaw Pact armies, with a range of 3,000 meters

6) the 73mm SPG-9 recoiless gun of the motorized infantry battalion can loft its fin-stabilized, rocket-assisted shell 872 yards

7) the shoulder-fired RPG-7 antitank grenade launcher, found in motorized infantry squads, can put its 85mm rocket-assisted projectile into armor 545 yards downrange.

Surface-to-surface tactical ballistic missiles comprise an integral part of Soviet artillery and can deliver conventional, nuclear, or chemical munitions. Major free (unguided) missiles include:

1) the earlier free rocket over ground (FROG) -3, -4, and -5, transported and fired from a light-tracked chassis derived from the PT-76 tank, with a range of 22 miles

2) the FROG-7, transported and launched from a wheeled vehicle; found in special FROG battalions; range: 310 miles.

Major medium range guided missiles in inventory include:

1) the single-stage SS-1B and SS-1C SCUD, transported on the new MAZ-543 erector-launcher, with ranges between 112 and 174 miles

2) also transported and launched from the MAZ-543, the SS-12 scaleboard has a range of between 435 and 500 miles.

Weapons in use by the air defense troops of the ground forces are varied and include:

1) the self-propelled (SP) 23mm quad ZSU-23-4 AA gun, found in tank and motorized infantry regiments, which can fire 1,000 rpm out to 3,270 yards

2) the SP 57mm twin ZSU-57-2 AA gun, similarly employed, which can fire 120 rpm per barrel to a range of 4,360 yards

3) the portable SA-7 grail missile, found in motorized infantry, airborne, and tank regiments, with a slant range of 3.5 kilometers

4) the vehicle-transported SA-8 Gecko, introduced in 1975, found in motorized infantry and tank regiments, with an estimated range of 30 kilometers for high altitude defense

5) the SA-9 Gaskin, mounted on a modified BRDM-2, also introduced in 1975 and employed like the SA-8, with an estimated range of 7 kilometers for defense against low-flying aircraft.

Multiple rocket launchers have seen honorable service in the Soviet Army since the Great Patriotic War. Current models include:

1) the 122mm BM-21, truck-mounted in 40 tubes, which fires a fin-stabilized rocket between 22,345 and 11,990 yards

2) the 140mm BM-14, truck-mounted in 16 tubes, which fires its fin-stabilized rocket to 10,682 yards

3) the 240mm BM-24, truck-mounted in 12 tubes, which fires its fin-stabilized rocket between 11,118 and 7,167 yards.

Another descendent of the Great Patriotic War, the SP gun comes in several models:

1) the SU-100, equipped with the 100mm gun employed on T-55 tank

2) the 122mm SP howitzer, mobile version of the new D-30

3) the 152mm SP howitzer, mobile version of the D-20, which can be issued to tank or motorized infantry units in lieu of the towed model

4) the ASU-57 air-droppable assault gun, equipped with a 57mm gun, designed specifically for use of airborne troops

5) made possible by the Mi-6 and -10 transport helicopter, the ASU-85 assault gun, with its 85mm cannon, is also intended for airborne use.

BOOKS

3761.   Allward, Maurice, and John W. R. Taylor. *ABC Rockets and Missiles.* New Rochelle, N.Y.: Sportshelf, 1960. 36p.

3762.   Barnaby, Frank, ed. *Tactical Nuclear Weapons: European Perspectives.*

3763.   Bidwell, Shelford, ed. *Brassey's Artillery of the World.* London: Brassey's, 1977. 274p.

3764.   Cox, John. *Overkill: Weapons of the Nuclear Age.* New York: T. Y. Crowell, 1978. 208p.

3765.   Foss, Christopher F. *Artillery of the World.* 2d rev. ed. New York: Scribners, 1980. 210p.

3766.   _____. *Jane's Pocket Book of Towed Artillery.* New York: Macmillan, 1979.

3767.   _____, ed. *Jane's Armor and Artillery.* New York: Franklin Watts, 1979–. v. 1–.

3768.   Gatland, Kenneth W. *Missiles and Rockets.* New York: Macmillan, 1975. 256p.

3769.   Parry, Albert. *Russia's Rockets and Missiles.* Garden City, N.Y.: Doubleday, 1960. 382p.

3770.   Pretty, Ronald T., ed. *Jane's Pocket Book of Missiles.* London: Macdonald and Jane's, 1978. 256p.

3771.   Royal United Service Institute for Defence Studies. *Report of Seminar: Tactical Employment and Comparative Performance of Ground- and Air-Launched Antitank Weapons.* London, 1976.

3772.   Taylor, John W. R. *Rockets and Missiles.* New York: Grosset & Dunlap, 1970. 159p.

3773.   Taylor, Michael J. H., and John W. R. *Missiles of the World.* 3d rev. ed. New York: Scribners, 1980. 160p.

3774.   Van Cleave, William R. *Tactical Nuclear Weapons: An Examination of the Issues.* New York: Crane, Russak, 1978.

ARTICLES

3775.   "ASU." In Bernard Fitzsimons, ed., *The Illustrated Encyclopedia of 20th Century Weapons and Warfare.* 24 vols. New York: Columbia House, 1978. II: 186–187.   Self-propelled artillery.

3776. "AT-1 Sapper." In Bernard Fitzsimons, ed., *The Illustrated Encyclopedia of 20th Century Weapons and Warfare.* 24 vols. New York: Columbia House, 1978. XXII: 2358–2359. Antitank missile.

3777. "Already in Service: The Second Generation of Soviet Antitank Missiles." *International Defense Review* 11 (January 1978), 15–17.

3778. "Artillery Weapons of the Soviet Union since World War II." *International Defense Review* 10 (December 1977), 1059.

3779. "BM/BMD." In Bernard Fitzsimons, ed., *Illustrated Encyclopedia of 20th Century Weapons and Warfare.* 24 vols. New York: Columbia House, 1978. IV: 394–395. Postwar rocket artillery.

3780. Bartlett, Charles M. "Soviet Self-Propelled Cannon Artillery." *Military Review* 58 (June 1978), 54–66.

3781. "The Battlefield Missile Tables." *Defense and Foreign Affairs Digest,* no. 2 (February 1976), 15–17.

3782. "Battlefield Rockets for the Red G.I." *Popular Science* 131 (October 1962), 104–105.

3783. Baxter, William P. "The Soviet 122mm Self-Propelled Howitzer." *Field Artillery Journal* 47 (January-February 1980), 35–37.

3784. Brown, Michael J., et al. "Missile, Missile, Missile." *U.S. Army Aviation Digest* 21 (April 1975), 30–33. The SA-7 Strella.

3785. Burtsev, Yu. "Self-Propelled 122mm Howitzer Described: Translated from *Znamenosets,* June 1979." *Translations on USSR Military Affairs,* no. 1482 (December 13, 1979), 16–20.

3786. Crabb, Merle L. "The Low Altitude SAM Threat." *Marine Corps Gazette* 55 (February 1971), 48–49.

3787. Currie, Malcolm R. "Future Tactical Missiles." *National Defence* 61 (July-August 1976), 32–35.

3788. Daschke, Carl E. "The Threat: The Artillery Threat." *U.S. Army Aviation Digest* 25 (November 1979), 16–20.

3789. Dmitriyev, N. "AA Self-Propelled Gun." *Soviet Military Review,* no. 5 (May 1979), 22–23.

3790. Fein, Paul. "The 122mm Self-Propelled Howitzer M1974." *Review of the Soviet Ground Forces* 5 (January 1980), 29–30.

3791. "FROG." In Bernard Fitzsimons, ed., *The Illustrated Encyclopedia of 20th Century Weapons and Warfare.* 24 vols. New York: Columbia House, 1978. pp. 1038–1039.

3792.   Gatland, Kenneth W. "Soviet Missiles." In Ray Bonds, ed., *The Soviet War Machine.* New York: Chartwell House, 1976. pp. 212–231.

3793.   Geiger, George J. "Russian FROGS." *Ordnance* 49 (May-June 1965), 644–646.

3794.   _____ . "Russia's [SS-1c] SCUD Missile." *Ordnance* 51 (May-June 1967), 610–611.

3795.   _____ . "Soviet Battlefield Rockets." *Infantry* 53 (January-February 1963), 62–64.

3796.   Harvey, David. "Missile Muscle: A Report on Battlefield Missiles." *Defense and Foreign Affairs Digest,* no. 2 (February 1976), 12–14.

3797.   Hofmann, Kurt. "An Analysis of Soviet Artillery Development." *International Defense Review* 10 (December 1977), 1057–1061.

3798.   Jarrett, George B. "Soviet Ordnance." *Ordnance* 37 (March-April 1953), 865–870.

3799.   Kharitonov, N. "Antitank Guided Missiles." *Soviet Military Review,* no. 12 (December 1979), 34–36.

3800.   Knyaz'kov, V. "Portable Antitank Missile, Launcher Described: Translated from *Znamenosets,* November 1979." *Translations on USSR Military Affairs,* no. 1512 (May 2, 1980), 65–69.   SA-9 Gaskin.

3801.   Kolesnik, A. "Fighting Antitank Weapons." *Soviet Military Review,* no. 6 (June 1970), 20–21.

3802.   McGuire, Frank G. "Soviet Troops Get New Missiles." *Missiles and Rockets* 2 (December 1957), 37.

3803.   McGuire, James D. "Sino-Soviet Bloc Antitank Wapons." *Armor* 69 (May-June 1960), 34–40.

3804.   _____ . "Soviet Rocket Weapons." *Army* 11 (August 1960), 45–49.

3805.   Maney, Rhoi M. "Man-Portable Air Defense Systems: A Comparison." *Air Defense Magazine* (October-December 1977), 19–23.

3806.   Marriott, John. "Antitank Missiles." *Army Quarterly* 107 (April 1977), 147–153.

3807.   _____ . "Land-Based Surface-to-Air Weapons." *NATO's Fifteen Nations* 23 (August-September 1978), 32–34.

3808. _____ . "Surface-to-Surface Artillery." *NATO's Fifteen Nations* 19 (December 1974–January 1975), 68–73.

3809. _____ . "Update on Tactical Missiles." *NATO's Fifteen Nations* 22 (June-July 1977), 82–86.

3810. Marsh, Roger. "How Good Is Soviet Ordance?" *Ordnance* 33 (July-August 1951), 75–81.

3811. Mataxis, Theodore C. "The Soviets Forge Ahead." *Infantry* 48 (April 1958), 14–27.

3812. Merritt, Jack N. "Field Artillery of the 1980's." *National Defence* 62 (May-June 1978), 544–548.

3813. "Modern Weapons of the Soviet Army." *Interavia* 21 (May 1966), 590–593.

3814. Mostovenko, V. "Soviet Self-Propelled Gun Mounts." *Soviet Military Review,* no. 5 (May 1968), 42–43.

3815. Ogorkiewicz, Richard M. "Antitank Weapons: A Reappraisal." *Armor* 82 (May-June 1973), 23–27.

3816. _____ . "Self-Propelled Guns: Developments and Trends." *Armor* 60 (November-December 1951), 6–11.

3817. Rametta, Thomas P. "Soviet Doctrine and Capabilities, Direct Fire." *Field Artilleryman* 23 (July 1962), 25–32.

3818. Reinhordt, G. C. "Atomic Weapons and Warfare." In Basil H. Liddell-Hart, ed., *The Soviet Army.* London: Weidenfeld & Nicolson, 1956. pp. 420–438.

3819. "SA-8: The Latest Soviet Mobile SAM System." *International Defense Review* 8 (December 1975), 805–806.

3820. "SA-9 Gaskin at Launch." *Air Defense Magazine* (April-June 1979), 55–56.

3821. "SCUD." In Bernard Fitzsimons, ed., *The Illustrated Encyclopedia of 20th Century Weapons and Warfare.* 24 vols. New York: Columbia House, 1978. XXI: 2285–2286.

3822. "Self-Propelled Howitzer [122mm] Described: Translated from *Voyennyye Znaniya,* December 1979." *Translations on USSR Military Affairs,* no. 1505 (March 20, 1980), 41–45.

3823. Shaw, I. R. L. "Soviet Artillery." *Journal of the Royal Artillery* 81 (April 1954), 90–97.

3824.   Sherman, Robert. "A Manual of Missile Capability." *Air Force Magazine* 60 (February 1977), 35–39.

3825.   Solovyov, N. "Artillery." *Soviet Military Review,* no. 4 (April 1978), 29–31.

3826.   "Soviet Tank Killer: The BRDM-2 Sagger." *Born in Battle. Magazine* (November 1979), *passim.*

3827.   "Soviets Show Details of Various Missiles." *Aviation Week and Space Technology* 85 (November 28, 1966), 58–59.

3828.   "The Soviet Union's Missile Artillery." *Field Artilleryman* 11 (December 1959), 24–27.

3829.   "The Threat: SA-9 Gaskin." *U.S. Army Aviation Digest* 24 (August 1978), 44.

3830.   "The Threat: Soviet 122mm Howitzer." *U.S. Army Aviation Digest* 25 (July 1979), 39.

3831.   "U.S.S.R. Unveils New Antitank Missiles." *Aviation Week and Space Technology* 107 (December 5, 1977), 19.

3832.   United States. Department of the Army. "Antiaircraft Guns/Surface-to-Air Missiles." *Aviator's Recognition Manual.* FM 1-88. Washington, D.C., 1980. pp. 106–136.

3833.   _____ . "Antitank Weapons, Mortars and Artillery, Tactical Artillery Missiles/Multiple Rocket Launchers [and] Antiaircraft Guns." *Opposing Forces: Europe.* FM 30-102. Washington, D.C., 1977. pp. 1/5–1/13.

3834.   _____ . "Artillery." *Aviator's Recognition Manual.* FM 1-88. Washington, D.C., 1980. pp. 218–246.

3835.   Walsh, Alden C. "Soviet Artillery Weapons." *Field Artilleryman* 23 (July 1962), 33–41.

3836.   Williams, Forrest D. "Threat: TAC Nukes and the Irrational Bear." *U.S. Army Aviation Digest* 27 (May 1981), 37–41.

3837.   Williams, Larry W. "Soviet Self-Propelled Artillery." *Armor* 87 (September-October 1978), 18–20.

3838.   Wilson, Peter A. "Battlefield Guided Weapons: The Big Equalizer." *U.S. Naval Institute Proceedings* 101 (February 1975), 18–25.

DOCUMENTS, PAPERS, AND REPORTS

3839.   Clemow, John. *Short-Range Guided Weapons.* London: Temple Press, 1961. 64p.

3840.   Digby, James F. *Precision-Guided Weapons*. Adelphi papers, no. 118. London: International Institute for Strategic Studies, 1975. 20p.

3841.   _____ . *Precision-Guided Munitions: Capabilities and Consequences*. RAND Paper P-5257. Santa Monica, Calif.: RAND Corporation, 1974. 19p.

3842.   Gusev, I. *Tube [Howitzer] Artillery*. Translated from the Russian. FSTC-HT-23-812-74. Charlottesville, Va.: U.S. Army Foreign Science and Technology Center, 1974. 11p.

3843.   *U.S. and Soviet Tank Killers*. Boulder, Colo.: Paladin Press, 1979. 26p.

3844.   Union of Soviet Socialist Republics. Ministry of Defense. *Rocket Weapons of Modern Armies, U.S.S.R.* JPRS 12045. Arlington, Va.: Joint Publication Research Service, 1962. 11p.

3845.   United States. Department of the Army. *Range and Lethality of U.S. and Soviet Antiarmor Weapons*. TRADOC Bulletin, no. 1U. Washington, D.C., 1976.

Further References

See also sections 2:D:2, 4:C:2 and 3, and 4:E:2:d:(2).

3. Small Arms

Soviet individual and light crew-served weapons are unfailingly simple, reliable, and easy to manufacture. For these reasons, specific models often remain in service long after the appearance of improved replacements. Current front line infantry weapons include:

1) the 82mm M1937 mortar, with a range of 3,270 yards
2) the 120mm M1943 mortar, with a range of 6,213 yards, is found in motorized infantry, marine, and airborne regiments
3) the vehicle-towed 160mm M-160 mortar, with a range of 8,720 yards
4) the largest mortar, the 240mm M-240, has a range of 10,573 yards
5) the standard sidearm of the Warsaw Pact is the 9mm Makarov PM pistol with a range of 54.5 yards
6) the 7.62mm Kalashnikov AK and AKM assault rifles, produced in greater number than any other modern small weapon, with an effective range of 436 yards
7) the 7.62 Dragunov SVD snipers rifle, with a range of 1,417 yards

8) the 7.62mm Kalasnikov light machine gun (RPK), developed from the AKM, which can fire 600 rpm to an effective range of 872 yards

9) the general purpose 7.62mm Kalashnikov machine gun, in models PK, PKB, PKS, and PKT, which can be employed as a light- or heavy- machine gun or a tank machine gun, with a range of 1,090 yards and a firing rate of 650 rpm

10) the older 7.62mm Goryunov SGM heavy machine gun, which can fire 600-700 rpm to an effective range of 1,090 yards

11) the standard Communist heavy machine gun, the 12.7mm Degtyarev DShK-38 or DShKM, can be employed in antipersonnel, -vehicular, or -aircraft roles and can fire 540-600 rpm to a range of 1,635 yards

12) the RGD-5 hand grenade, weighing less than a pound, which can be thrown to about 50 yards and which has a fragmentation radius of just under 22 yards.

BOOKS

3846.   Allen, Walter G. B. *Pistols, Rifles, and Machineguns.* London: Musson, 1953. 178p.

3847.   Archer, Denis, ed. *Jane's Infantry Weapons.* London: Macdonald and Jane's, 1975–. v. 1–.

3848.   _____ . *Jane's Pocket Book of Pistols and Sub-Machine Guns.* New York: Macmillan, 1977. 237p.

3849.   _____ . *Jane's Pocket Book of Rifles and Light Machine Guns.* New York: Macmillan, 1977. 231p.

3850.   Barnes, Frank C. *Cartridges of the World.* 3d ed., rev. Chicago, Ill.: Follett, 1972. 378p.

3851.   Boothroyd, Geoffrey. *The Hand Gun.* New York: Crown, 1970. 564p.

3852.   DeHaas, Frank. *Bolt-Action Rifles.* Northfield, Ill.: Digest Books, 1971. 320p.

3853.   Foss, Christopher F., and Terry J. Gander. *Infantry Weapons of the World.* New York: Scribners, 1977. 141p.

3854.   Josserand, Michel H., and Jan A. Stevenson. *Pistols, Revolvers, and Ammunition.* New York: Crown, 1972. 341p.

3855.   Labbett, Peter. *Military Small Arms Ammunition of the World, 1945–1980*. San Rafael, Calif.: Presidio Press, 1980. 160p.

3856.   LaMont, Wyant. *The AK-47 Assault Rifle*. Forest Grove, Oreg.: Normount Technical Publications, 1969. 155p.

3857.   Marsh, Roger. *Weapons: A Pictorial Survey of Russian Small Arms*. 2 vols. Hudson, Ohio, 1950–1952.

3858.   Moyer, Frank A. *Foreign Weapons Handbook*. Boulder, Colo.: Panther Publications, 1970. 326p.

3859.   _____ , and Robert J. Scroggie. *Combat Firing Techniques: The Latest Doctrine on Combat Firing of U.S. and Foreign Assault Rifles, Machine Rifles, Submachine Guns, Light Machine Guns, and Shoulder-Stocked Pistols*. Boulder, Colo.: Paladin Press, 1971. 116p.

3860.   Musgrave, Daniel D., and Thomas G. Nelson. *The World's Assault Rifles and Automatic Carbines*. Washington, D.C.: Goetz, 1967. 547p.

3861.   Myatt, Frederick. *Modern Small Arms: An Illustrated Encyclopedia of Famous Military Firearms*. London: Salamander Books, 1978. 160p.

3862.   Owen, John, ed. *Brassey's Infantry Weapons of the World*. New York: Crane, Russak, 1977–. v. 1–.

3863.   Smith, Walter H.B., and Edward C. Ezell. *Small Arms of the World*. 11th rev. ed. Harrisburg, Pa.: Stackpole Books, 1977. 671p.

3864.   Stebbins, Henry M. *Rifles: A Modern Encyclopedia*. Harrisburg, Pa.: Stackpole Books, 1958. 376p.

3865.   _____ ; Albert J. E. Shay; and Oscar R. Hammond. *Pistols: A Modern Encyclopedia*. Harrisburg, Pa.: Stackpole Books, 1961. 380p.

3866.   Steindeler, R. A. *The Firearms Dictionary*. Harrisburg, Pa.: Stackpole Books, 1970. 288p.

3867.   United States. Department of the Army. Foreign Science and Technology Center. *Small Arms Ammunition Identification Guide*. Rev. ed. Forest Grove, Oreg.: Nourmont Technical Publications, 1971. 151p.

ARTICLES

3868.   "Firepower of the Soviet Army: Infantry-Battalion Weapons." *Canadian Army Journal* 16 (Winter 1962), 47–58.

3869.   "Flame Throwers–Description and Employment: Trans-lated from *Voyennyye Znaniya,* December 1977." *Translations on USSR Military Affairs,* no. 1333 (February 27, 1978), 64–70.

3870.   Helgeson, Thomas C. "Automatic Weapons of the U.S.A., U.S.S.R., England." *Infantry School Quarterly* 46 (January 1956), 105–112.

3871.   Henk, Daniel W. "Assault Rifles." *Infantry* 65 (May-June 1975), 46–50.

3872.   Hobart, Frank W. A. "The Russian RPK." *Ordnance* 56 (July-August 1971), 50–54.

3873.   Johnson, Thomas M. "The AK-47." *Army* 20 (June 1970), 40–45.

3874.   "Kalashnikov." In Bernard Fitzsimons, ed., *The Illustrated Encyclopedia of 20th Century Weapons and Warfare.* 24 vols. New York: Columbia House, 1978. XIV: 1551–1556.

3875.   "The Kalashnikov Sub-Machine Gun." *Soviet Military Review,* no. 2 (February 1966), 36–37.

3876.   Kogan, R. "Kalashnikov AK-47 Described: Translated from *Voyennyye Znaniya,* February 1980." *Translations on USSR Military Affairs,* no. 1520 (June 24, 1980), 211–214.

3877.   Liu, Melinda. "The [Kalashnikov] King of Battle." *Newsweek* 96 (February 11, 1980), 49.

3878.   McGuire, James D. "Soviet Army Mortars." *Infantry* 51 (May-June 1961), 10–12.

3879.   Marsh, Roger. "Russian Small Arms." *American Rifleman* 99 (July 1951), 10–13.

3880.   "RPG." In Bernard Fitzsimons, ed., *The Illustrated Encyclopedia of 20th Century Weapons and Warfare.* 24 vols. New York: Columbia House, 1978. XXI: 2241.   An antitank weapon.

3881.   Simmons, Douglas M., Jr. "Modern Automatic Pistols." *Ordnance* 56 (May-June 1972), 493–495.

3882.   "The Simonov Semi-Automatic Carbine." *Soviet Military Review,* no. 10 (October 1966), 30–31.

3883.   Smirnov, D. "Firing the Sub-Machine Gun with a Burst." *Soviet Military Review,* no. 1 (January 1965), 20–21.

3884.   Smith, Joseph E. "Current Soviet Small Arms." *Infantry* 51 (March-April 1961), 21–26.

3885.   "The Soviet AK-47 Assault Rifle." *Armor* 89 (July-August 1980), 70–71.

3886.   "Stetchkin." In Bernard Fitzsimons, ed., *The Illustrated Encyclopedia of 20th Century Weapons and Warfare.* 24 vols. New York: Columbia House, 1978. XXII: 2398–2400.

3887.   Stewart-Smith, D. G. "Russian Small Arms Reviewed." *Services and Territorial Magazine* 20 (November 1951), 19–21.

3888.   Symington, McKim. "Infantryman's Implements: A Review of Assault Rifle Trends." *Defense and Foreign Affairs Digest,* no. 5 (1977), 50–52.

3889.   United States. Department of the Army. "Identify Opposing Force (OPFOR) Weapons and Equipment." *Soldier's Manual: Infantryman.* FM 7-11B 1/2. Washington, D.C., 1978. pp. 2-11-C-7/1 –2-11-C-7/9.

3890.   _____ . "Small Arms Weapons." *Opposing Forces: Europe.* FM 30-102. Washington, D.C., 1977. pp. 1/4–1/5.

3891.   Weller, Jac. "Russian Small Arms and Tactics." *An Cosantoir* 23 (January-February 1963), 12–21, 105–113.

3892.   _____ . "Russian Small Arms and Tactics." *Marine Corps Gazette* 96 (October-November 1962), 28–33, 64–68.

3893.   _____ . "Soviet Infantry Weapons." *Infantry* 57 (July-August 1967), 6–10.

3894.   White, William H. "The Soviet Assault Rifle [AK-47] vs. the M-16." *Marine Corps Gazette* 57 (January 1973), 8–9.

3895.   Yelshin, N. "A Famous Sub-Machine Gun." *Soviet Military Review,* no. 10 (October 1979), 28–30.

3896.   _____ . "Soviet Small Arms." *Soviet Military Review,* no. 2 (February 1977), 15–17.

3897.   Zaitsev, S. "The Preservation of Weapons." *Soviet Military Review,* no. 2 (February 1977), 24–25.   Care of small arms.

DOCUMENTS, PAPERS, AND REPORTS

3898.   Blangoravov, A. *The Degtyarev DT 7.62mm Tank Machine Gun.* Translated from the Russian. FSTC-HT-23-339-74. Charlottesville, Va.: U.S. Army Foreign Science and Technology Center, 1974. 6p.

3899.   _____ . *The Nagant [Revolver] and the TT [Pistol].* Translated from the Russian. AD/A-000-233/7GA. Charlottesville, Va.: U.S. Army Foreign Science and Technology Center, 1974. 8p.

3900.   Johnson, Harold E. *The Soviet 9mm Stechkin Machine Pistol.* FSTC-CW-07-104-75. Charlottesville, Va.: U.S. Army Foreign Science and Technology Center, 1975. 50p.

3901.   United States. Department of the Army. *Soviet RPG-7 Anti-tank Grenade Launcher.* TRADOC Bulletin, no. 3U. Washington, D.C., 1976.

3902.   _____. Ordnance Department. *Soviet Rifles and Carbines: Identification and Operation.* ORD-17-101. Burbank, Calif.: Inco Military Books, 1973. 53p.   A reprint of the 1954 U.S. government publication.

Further References

See also sections 2:D:3, 4:C:3, and 4:E:2:d:(4).

4. Armor, Armored Personnel Carriers (APCs), and Infantry Fighting Vehicles (IFVs)

Perhaps nowhere in ground forces equipment has there been more worry about a "gap" during the postwar years than in the area of armor. The debate goes on today with both East and West rushing new models in to make certain no advantage is lost. The new T-72 tank is generally considered the world's best, while the BMD, a new APC, which can carry six soldiers and keep pace with the T-72 but which was roughly handled in the Yom Kippur War, is the subject of much controversy in Soviet and Western writings.

Soviet tanks generally have a lower rate of fire and a smaller ammunition magazine for their main guns than have U.S. tanks and show less armor protection. Russian APCs and IFVs are fast, well-armed (including upwards of a 73mm gun and AT missiles), amphibious, and allow infantrymen to fire their rifles and machine guns from within.

The following tanks, APCs, and IFVs are in the inventory of the Soviet ground forces:

1) the T-72, latest tank model, with a crew of 3, a 115mm gun, improved armor and fire control, a range of 310 miles, and a top speed of 50mph
2) the T-62, widely employed in tank and motorized infantry units, with a crew of 4, a 115mm gun, up to 100mm of armor protection, and a range of 310 miles
3) the T-55, standard Communist tank, with a crew of 4, a 100mm gun, 100mm of armor, a 310-mile range, and multiple roles: combat, bridgelaying, mine-clearing, flame-thrower, recovery vehicle, and dozer

4) the T-34/85, of World War II fame, used for training in Russia, but standard in the armies of some twenty nations

5) the PT-76 amphibious light tank, with a crew of 3, a 76mm gun, 11–14mm of armor, and a range of 162 miles, is being phased out in favor of the BMP; its chasis, however, is employed as the body for various missile-launchers and SP guns

6) the airborne amphibious combat vehicle BMD, organic to airborne divisions, tracked and featuring a 73mm gun and one AT-3 sagger

7) the tracked amphibious armored infantry fighting vehicle BMP combines the features of a light tank, an APC, and an AT missile carrier, which carries a crew of 3 with room for 8 passengers (who can fire through gunports), a 73mm gun, one AT-3 sagger, and has a road speed of 37 mph—widely used in Afghanistan

8) the amphibious APC BTR-60P, which carries a crew of 2 plus 14 soldiers, mounts a 12.7 or 7.62mm machine gun in a flat roof, and has a top land speed of 50 mph

9) the amphibious APC BTR-60B, identical to the BTR-60P, except that it features a small turret with a 12.7mm machine gun

10) the amphibious armored reconnaissance vehicle BRDM, a wheeled scout car, which carries a crew of 2 and up to 5 soldiers, a 7.62mm machine gun, and has a road speed of 50 mph

11) the amphibious armored reconnaissance vehicle BRDM-2, a wheeled replacement for the BRDM, with a 14.5mm and a 7.62mm machine gun, a range of 466 miles, and a road speed up to 60 mph.

BOOKS

3903.   Bonds, Ray, ed. *Illustrated Guide to Modern Tanks and Fighting Vehicles.* New York: Arco, 1980. 159p.

3904.   Cary, James. *Tanks and Armor in Modern Warfare.* New York: Franklin Watts, 1966. 267p.

3905.   Foss, Christopher F. *Armoured Fighting Vehicles of the World.* 3d ed. London: Ian Allan, 1977. 200p.

3906.   _____ . *Jane's Pocket Book of Modern Tanks and Armored Fighting Vehicles.*

3907.   _____ . *Jane's World Armoured Fighting Vehicles.* New York: St. Martin's Press, 1977. 437p.

3908.   _____ , ed. *Jane's Armour and Artillery.* New York: Franklin Watts, 1979–. v. 1–.

3909.   Hogg, Ian, and John Weeks. *The Illustrated Encyclopedia of Military Vehicles*. Englewood Cliffs, N.J.: Prentice-Hall, 1980. 320p.

3910.   Humble, Richard. *Tanks*. London: Weidenfeld & Nicolson, 1977. 144p.

3911.   International Defense Review, Editors of. *Battle Tanks: A Special Report*. Geneva, Switzerland: Interavia, 1976. 64p.

3912.   Jarrett, George B. *Combat Tanks*. New York: Meredith, 1969. 92p.

3913.   McGregor, Malcolm. *Armoured Fighting Vehicles*. London: Hugh Evelyn, 1969. 22p.

3914.   Perrett, Bryan. *Fighting Vehicles of the Red Army*. London: Ian Allan, 1969. 104p.

3915.   Scarborough, Gerald. *Modelling Armoured Cars*. London: Stephens, 1977. 64p.

3916.   Schneible, Anthony T., ed. *Combat Vehicles*. Greenwich, Conn.: Defense Marketing Service, 1977. Unpaged.

3917.   Vanderveen, Bart H., ed. *A Source Book of Military Tracked Vehicles*. London: Ward, Lock, 1973. 143p.

3918.   Von Senger und Etterlin, Fridolin M. *The World's Armored Fighting Vehicles*. Translated from the German. Garden City, N.Y.: Doubleday, 1962. 304p.

3919.   White, Brian T. *Tanks and Other Tracked Vehicles in Service*. New York: Sterling, 1978. 155p.

3920.   Zaloga, Steve. *Modern Soviet Armor: Combat Vehicles of the U.S.S.R. and Warsaw Pact Today*. Englewood Cliffs, N.J.: Prentice-Hall, 1979. 88p.

ARTICLES

3921.   "Amphibious, Reconnaissance, and Patrol Personnel Carrier." *Soviet Military Translations*, no. 200 (September 1965), 20–23.

3922.   "Armor in the 1980's: An Overview." *Armor* 83 (July-August 1974), 46–51.

3923.   "Armored Personnel Carriers." In Bernard Fitzsimons, ed., *The Illustrated Encyclopedia of 20th Century Weapons and Warfare*. 24 vols. New York: Columbia House, 1978. II: 124–128.

3924.   "BMP." In Bernard Fitzsimons, ed., *The Illustrated Encyclopedia of 20th Century Weapons and Warfare.* 24 vols. New York: Columbia House, 1978. IV: 395–396.

3925.   "BTR." In Bernard Fitzsimons, ed., *The Illustrated Encyclopedia of 20th Century Weapons and Warfare.* 24 vols. New York: Columbia House, 1978. V: 476–478.

3926.   Babiasz, Frank, and Carl E. Daschke. "Threat: The Claw of the Bear." *U.S. Army Aviation Digest* 26 (March 1980), 14–16.

3927.   Bellany, Ian. "The Tank: A Theoretical Exploration of Its Limitations." *Journal of the Royal United Service Institute for Defence Studies* 119 (March 1974), 34–38.

3928.   Burney, John C. "Soviet Armor and Artillery." *Field Artilleryman* 20 (November 1961), 29–40.

3929.   Burtsev, Yuri. "Airborne Combat Vehicle [BMD-1] Described: Translated from *Znamenosets*, September 1980." *Translations on USSR Military Affairs,* no. 1550 (December 9, 1980), 28–32.

3930.   ———. "Infantry Combat Vehicle Characteristics Described: Translated from *Znamenosets*, July 1978." *Translations on USSR Military Affairs,* no. 1386 (October 16, 1978), 49–53.

3931.   Buyar, V. "APC's in Combat." *Soviet Military Review,* no. 10 (October 1980), 24–26.

3932.   Campbell, E. Gary. "Threat: So You Want to Buy a New Armored Infantry Combat Vehicle?" *U.S. Army Aviation Digest* 26 (April 1980), 28–30.

3933.   Cole, R. E. W. "Soviet [Armored] Equipment." *Military Review* 38 (July 1958), 76–82.

3934.   "Comparative Data: Current Armored Fighting Vehicles." *Armor* 79 (January-February 1970), 34–35.

3935.   "Confronting the Armor Gap: U.S. Lagging Behind Soviets in Tank Technology." *Time* 115 (January 21, 1980), 38.

3936.   Davenport, M. R. "Why Are Russian Tanks Better Than Ours?" *Saturday Evening Post* 223 (October 7, 1950), 30–31.

3937.   Davison, Michael S. "A Survey of Soviet Armor." *Armor* 60 (March-April 1951), 34–40.

3938.   "Details of Tanks in Service in NATO and the Warsaw Pact." *NATO's Fifteen Nations* 20 (February-March 1975), 47–56.

3939.   "Details of the Soviet T-72 Battle Tank." *International Defense Review* 10 (December 1977), 1031–1034.

3940.   Doubler, Michael. "Modern Tank Ammunition." *Strategy and Tactics*, no. 75 (July-August 1977), 38.

3941.   Dragunskiy, G. "Tank Capabilities: Translated from *Sovetskiy Patriot*, September 11, 1977." *Translations on USSR Military Affairs*, no. 1329 (February 10, 1978), 58–63.

3942.   Fein, Paul. "The BMD Airborne Infantry Combat Vehicle." *Review of the Soviet Ground Forces* 5 (March 1980), 27.

3943.   _____. "The T-64 and T-72 Tanks." *Review of the Soviet Ground Forces* 4 (November 1979), 37–44.

3944.   "Foreign Infantry Fighting Vehicles." *Army Research, Development, and Acquisition* 5 (March-April 1979), 20–21.

3945.   "Foreign Tank Destroyers." *Army Research, Development, and Acquisition* 5 (September-October 1979), 14–15.

3946.   "Foreign Trends in Fighting Machines." *Army Reservist* 25 (January 1979), 24–30.

3947.   Gratzl, J. "T-64: Some Thoughts on the New Soviet Battle Tank." *International Defense Review* 9 (February 1976), 24–26.

3948.   Gruzdev, B. "Why a Four-Stroke Diesel Engine?" *Soviet Military Review*, no. 5 (May 1972), 34–35.

3949.   Henderson, John D. "Soviet Tank Superiority." *Armor* 68 (November-December 1959), 16–18.

3950.   Holmes, David G. "The IFV on the Modern Battlefield." *Infantry* 70 (September-October 1980), 10–14.

3951.   "Infantry Combat Vehicle BMP-1 Described: Translated from *Soldat und Technik*, August 1979." *Translations on USSR Military Affairs*, no. 1483 (December 20, 1979), 23–26.

3952.   Krivoshein, G. "The T-55 Tank." *Soviet Military Review*, no. 5 (May 1974), 20–21.

3953.   McCaslin, James K. "The BMP in Combat." *Infantry* 67 (January-February 1977), 26–31.

3954.   McGuire, James D. "Soviet Amphibious Vehicles." *Automotive Industries* 123 (June 1960), 18–21.

3955. ———— . "Soviet Tanks." *Infantry* 52 (May-June 1962), 10–12.

3956. Miller, D. M. O. "The Development of the Russian Main Battle Tank, 1946–1977." *Journal of the Royal United Service Institute for Defence Studies* 123 (March 1978), 31–37.

3957. Miller, Martin J. "Russian Combat Vehicles." *Ordnance* 51 (July-August 1966), 49–54.

3958. ———— . "Soviet Personnel Carriers." *Ordnance* 53 (January-February 1969), 394–397.

3959. "The Modern Battle Tank: Current Types and Their Characteristics." *International Defense Review* 4 (December 1971), 581–590.

3960. Mostovenko, V. "The Soviet Heavy Tanks." *Soviet Military Review,* no. 2 (February 1968), 48–49.

3961. "The New Soviet Armor." *Armor* 77 (July-August 1968), 32–34.

3962. "The New Soviet T-72 Tank." *Army Reservist* 24 (March-April 1978), 26.

3963. "New Soviet T-72 Tanks Observed in Hungary: Translated from *Soldat und Technik,* July 1979." *Translations on USSR Military Affairs,* no. 1462 (September 7, 1979), 75–76.

3964. Odom, William E. "Armored Personnel Carriers in the Soviet Army." *Military Review* 45 (June 1965), 81–86.

3965. Ogorkiewicz, Richard M. "Armored Cars: Their Past and Their Future." *Armor* 60 (March-April 1951), 6–11.

3966. ———— . "Armored Infantry Carriers." *Army Quarterly* 81 (January 1961), 181–185.

3967. ———— . "The Evolving Battle Tank." *Military Review* 46 (February 1966), 94–99.

3968. ———— . "Future Infantry Armored Vehicles." *Armor* 87 (November-December 1979), 24–28.

3969. ———— . "The Future of the Battle Tank." *Journal of the Royal United Service Institute for Defence Studies* 116 (June 1971), 22–29.

3970. ———— . "The Infantry's Combat Vehicle." *Armor* 83 (September-October 1974), 16–20.

3971.   _____ . "Soviet Armor." *Armor* 70 (January-February 1961), 26–31.

3972.   _____ . "Soviet Tanks." In Basil H. Liddell-Hart, ed., *The Soviet Army*. London: Weidenfeld & Nicolson, 1956. pp. 295–306.

3973.   _____ . "Tanks in Tomorrow's Armies." *Military Review* 54 (February 1974), 20–26.

3974.   _____ . "Trends in Tank Technology." *Armor* 89 (July-August 1980), 8–14.

3975.   "PT-76." In Bernard Fitzsimons, ed., *The Illustrated Encyclopedia of 20th Century Weapons and Warfare*. 24 vols. New York: Columbia House, 1978. XX: 2150.

3976.   Pateyuk, Ye. "Amphibious Scout Car [BRDM-2] Characteristics Described: Translated from *Voyennyye Znaniya*, September 1978." *Translations on USSR Military Affairs*, no. 1403 (December 18, 1978), 1–5.

3977.   _____ . "Armored Personnel Carriers Described: Translated from *Voyennyye Znaniya*, March 1979." *Translations on USSR Military Affairs*, no. 1440 (May 24, 1979), 1–7.

3978.   _____ . "Infantry Combat Vehicle [BMP] Described: Translated from *Voyennyye Znaniya*, January 1979." *Translations on USSR Military Affairs*, no. 1420 (March 16, 1979), 1–6.

3979.   _____ . "Soviet-Made All-Terrain Vehicles." *Soviet Military Review*, no. 3 (March 1971), 35–37.

3980.   Pavlov, I. "Tank Fueling." *Soviet Military Review*, no. 9 (September 1972), 48–49.

3981.   Prow, John W. "What of Soviet Armor?" *Ordnance* 51 (March-April 1967), 485–489.

3982.   "Russian Medium- and Heavy-Tanks." *Illustrated London News* 217 (July 22, 1950), 140–141.

3983.   Ryan, Michael W. "T-62 Briefing." *Armor* 84 (November-December 1975), 44–45.

3984.   Ryazantsev, D. "Armored Personnel Carriers." *Soviet Military Review*, no. 5 (May 1980), 43–44.

3985.   _____ . "Infantry Fighting Vehicles." *Soviet Military Review*, no. 11 (November 1979), 24–26.

3986. ———— . "The T-62 Tank." *Soviet Military Review,* no. 3 (March 1980), 26–28.

3987. Schrier, F. "The Modern Battle Tank." *International Defense Review* 4 (December 1971), 581–586; 5 (February-June 1972), 59–66, 161–168, 284–291.

3988. "The Soviet Airborne's Fighting Vehicles." *Review of the Soviet Ground Forces* 1 (October 1977), 62–68.

3989. "Soviet Armor: A Survey of Developments since World War II." *Armor* 70 (January-February 1961), 26–31.

3990. "The Soviet BMP (Boievaia Machina Piekhotiy) Vehicle Family." *International Defense Review* 8 (December 1975), 896–898.

3991. "The Soviet Potential in Armor." *Armor* 67 (January-February 1958), 46–49.

3992. "The Soviet T-62 Tank Described: Translated from *Soldat und Technik,* September 1979." *Translations on USSR Military Affairs,* no. 1472 (October 31, 1979), 101–103.

3993. "Soviet Tanks Lack Finish, But Are Termed Efficient." *Science News Letter* 54 (November 27, 1948), 343.

3994. Sullivan, Roy F. "Comparing APC's: U.S.A.'s M113A1 vs. U.S.S.R.'s BTR-60." *Armor* 80 (November-December 1971), 48–51.

3995. ———— . "Soviet APC's Reveal a Shift in Tactics." *Infantry* 61 (November-December 1971), 30–31.

3996. "T-44 Through T-72." In Bernard Fitzsimons, ed., *The Illustrated Encyclopedia of 20th Century Weapons and Warfare.* 24 vols. New York: Columbia House, 1978. XXIII: 2465–2467.

3997. "The T-72: Soviet Medium Tank." *Armor* 87 (January-February 1978), 34–36.

3998. "Tank Battle: Which Is Best?" *U.S. News and World Report* 55 (August 26, 1963), 16.

3999. "The Tank on Tomorrow's Battlefield." *Armor* 81 (July-August 1972), 39–41.

4000. Teater, Donald L. "The T-72." *Armor* 87 (July-August 1978), 61–64.

4001. "Threat: The T-62." *Armed Forces Journal* 107 (May 16, 1970), 20.

4002.   Underhill, Garrett. "The New Soviet [Armored] Weapons." *Ordnance* 42 (July-August 1957), 57–61.

4003.   _____ . "Red Armor: Turretless Tanks." *Marine Corps Gazette* 39 (January 1955), 18–23.

4004.   United States. Department of the Army. "Armor." *Aviator's Recognition Manual.* FM 1-88. Washington, D.C., 1980. pp. 172–192.

4005.   _____ . "Armored Fighting Vehicles." *Opposing Forces: Europe.* FM 30-102. Washington, D.C., 1977. pp. 1/14–1/17.

4006.   _____ . "Identify Opposing Force (OPFOR) Armored Vehicles." *Soldier's Manual: Infantryman.* FM 7-11B 1/2. Washington, D.C., 1978. pp. 2-II-C-6/1–2-II-C-6/10.

4007.   _____ . "Identifying Opposing Force (OPFOR) Armored Vehicles." *Special Forces Soldier's Manual.* FM 31-11C-2. Washington, D.C., 1980. pp. 2/229–2/240.

4008.   _____ . "Light Armored Vehicles." *Aviator's Recognition Manual.* FM 1-88. Washington, D.C., 1980. pp. 284–304.

4009.   _____ . "Soviet Armored Vehicles." *Soviet Equipment Recognition Guide.* TC 30-3. Washington, D.C., 1975. pp. 25–44.

4010.   Vishnyakov, V. "Characteristics of T-62 Tank Described: Translated from *Znamenosets,* September 1978." *Translations on USSR Military Affairs,* no. 1405 (December 29, 1978), 1–5.

4011.   Von Senger und Etterlin, Fridolin M. "The Evolution of the Soviet Battle Tank. *Armor* 77 (January-April 1968), 22–27, 46–59.

4012.   Wade, Nicholas. "NATO Builds a Better Battle Tank, But May Still Lose the Battle." *Science* 201 (July 14, 1978), 136–140.

4013.   "Why the U.S. Is Rushing a New Supertank." *U.S. News and World Report* 86 (May 21, 1979), 8.

4014.   Zodorov, Rashko. "New Snow and Swamp Going Vehicles Described: Translated from *Serzhant,* November 1977." *Translations on USSR Military Affairs,* no. 1321 (January 9, 1978), 63–68.

4015.   Zyrzanov, A. "APC's in the Offensive." *Soviet Military Review,* no. 4 (April 1973), 18–20.

DOCUMENTS, PAPERS, AND REPORTS

4016.   McCaslin, James K. *Combat Infantry Vehicles (BMP) in Combat.* Research Report. New York: U.S. Army Institute for Advanced Russian and East European Studies, 1976. 24p.

4017.   United States. Department of Defense. Defense Intelligence Agency. *The Soviet Armed Forces: Medium Tank [T-62].* DIA-AP-220-3-70. Washington, D.C., 1970.

4018.   United States. Department of the Army. *The Soviet Main Battle Tank: Capabilities and Limitations.* TRADOC Bulletin, no. 10. Washington, D.C., 1979.

4019.   _____ . *Weapons, Tactics, Training: The BMP, Capabilities and Limitations.* TRADOC Bulletin, no. 7. Washington, D.C., 1977.

Further References

See also sections 2:D:4, 3:B:2, 4:C:1, 4:D:3, and 4:E:2:d:(3); for details of postwar tanks in action around the globe, check the various subsections in section 5.

5. Transport Vehicles

BOOKS

4020.   Foss, Christopher F. *Military Vehicles of the World.* New York: Scribners, 1976. 192p.

4021.   _____ , ed. *Jane's Military Vehicles and Ground Support Equipment.* New York: Franklin Watts, 1980–. v. 1–.

4022.   Vanderveen, Bart H., ed. *The Observer's Military Vehicles Directory.* London: Warne, 1972. 425p.

ARTICLES

4023.   Gusev, Vladimir. "Motor Transport Vehicles of Warsaw Pact Countries Described: Translated from *Za Rulem,* July 1979." *Translations on USSR Military Affairs,* no. 1456 (August 16, 1979), 51–54.

4024.   Ivanovskiy, V. "Military Tracked Transport Vehicles Described: Translated from *Za Rulem,* February 1978." *Translations on USSR Military Affairs,* no. 1435 (May 15, 1979), 43–47.

4025.   McGuire, James D. "Soviet Army Transport Vehicles." *Army Information Digest* 17 (June 1962), 19–23.

4026.   "Military Motor Vehicles: U.S.S.R." *Military Review* 45 (August 1965), 102–103.

4027.   Whetten, Lawrence L., and James L. Waddell. "Motor Vehicle Standardization in the Warsaw Pact: Problems and Limitations." *Journal of the Royal United Service Institute for Defence Studies* 124 (March 1979), 55–60.

DOCUMENTS, PAPERS, AND REPORTS

4028.   United States. Department of the Army. *Foreign Military Weapons and Equipment, Transport Vehicles, Pt. 1: U.S.S.R.* DA Pam 30-6-1. Washington, D.C., 1955. 109p.

Further References

See also section 4:D:1.

6. Uniforms, Medals, and Insignia

Soviet Army uniforms have not changed significantly since the Great Patriotic War, although, as in U.S. uniforms, there have been improvements in cloth, boots, and helmets.

A number of new orders and decorations plus insignia have been promulgated by the Russians since 1945. As with uniforms, the wearing of medals and display of crests is governed by regulations which change from time to time.

BOOKS

4029.   Cassin-Scott, Jack, and John Fabb. *Ceremonial Uniforms of the World.* New York: Hippocrene Books, 1974. 80p.

4030.   D'Ami, Rinaldo D. *World Uniforms in Color.* Translated from the Italian. 2 vols. London: Stephens, 1968–1969.

4031.   *Soviet Army Uniforms and Insignia, 1945–1975.* New York: Hippocrene Books, 1977. 91p.

ARTICLES

4032.   "The Commemoration Medal." *Soviet Military Review,* no. 7 (July 1975), 57.

4033.   "Decorations and Awards: Text of Revised Statute." *Translations on USSR Military Affairs,* no. 1527 (August 8, 1980), 29–43.

4034.   Hieronymussen, Paul. "Soviet Orders and Decorations." *Orders and Decorations of Europe in Color.* Translated from the Danish. New York: Macmillan, 1967. pp. 191–197.

4035.   "The Highest Award of the Motherland." *Soviet Military Review,* no. 3 (March 1980), 43–45.   The Order of Lenin.

4036.   Lebedev, V. "Decorations—Order of Lenin and Order of the Red Star: Translated from *Voyenno Istoricheskiy Zhurnal,* April 1980." *Translations on USSR Military Affairs,* no. 1525 (July 24, 1980), 106–112.

4037.   "Medals, Decorations—Wear Regulations Revised: Translated from *Krasnaya Zvezda*, March 30, 1980." *Translations on USSR Military Affairs*, no. 1521 (July 1, 1980), 81–87.

4038.   "New Awards for Valiant Service." *Soviet Military Review*, no. 1 (January 1975), 44–45.

4039.   "Order of the Red Star." *Soviet Military Review*, no. 4 (April 1980), 62.

4040.   "Orders and Medals of Ushakov and Nakhimov." *Soviet Military Review*, no. 2 (February 1979), 13.

4041.   "Orders of Military Valor." *Soviet Military Review*, no. 11 (November 1973), 16–17.   Orders of Victory and Glory.

4042.   Petrov, S. "Improvements in Military Clothing Noted: Translated from *Znamenosets*, October 1977." *Translations on USSR Military Affairs*, no. 1323 (January 11, 1978), 43–46.

4043.   _____ . "Military Uniforms—Dress Regulations: Translated from *Krasnaya Zvezda*, May 20, 1980." *Translations on USSR Military Affairs*, no. 1533 (September 12, 1980), 175–180.

4044.   "Rules for Wearing Orders and Medals: Translated from *Agitator Armii I Flota*, September 1977." *Translations on USSR Military Affairs*, no. 1324 (January 13, 1978), 37–39.

4045.   "Symbols of Military Valor and Courage." *Soviet Military Review*, no. 10 (October 1978), 14.

4046.   "Uniforms and Weapons of the Soviet Rifleman." *Army* 12 (May 1962), 67.

4047.   United States. Department of Defense. Defense Intelligence Agency. "Uniforms and Insignia." *Handbook on the Soviet Armed Forces*. DDB-2680-40-78. Washington, D.C., 1978. pp. 15/1–15/38.

4048.   "Warsaw Pact Military Clothing." *Army Research, Development, and Acquisition* 21 (September-October 1980), 22–23.

4049.   Werlich, Robert. "The Soviet Union." *Russian Orders, Decorations and Medals: Imperial Russia, the Provisional Government, and the Soviet Union*. Washington, D.C.: Quaker Press, 1968. pp. 102–139.

Further References

See also section 2:D:5.

5 / The Soviet Army and Military Assistance around the Globe, 1945 to the Present

Introduction

AT THE CONCLUSION of the Great Patriotic War, Soviet ground forces units occupied large sections of Eastern Europe, north China, and Korea. In China and Korea, they were largely withdrawn; however, as the result of coups and other arrangements, the Russian army found itself permanently located in many of the countries facing the U.S.S.R.'s western border. In the years immediately after the war, Stalin used these forces as a counterthreat to the nuclear umbrella maintained by the U.S. over Western Europe.

In addition to his Western Europe hostage strategy, Stalin courted a limited number of friends abroad, providing military aid to the Chinese and North Koreans, some of which was employed against U.N. troops in the Korean War.

This limited outward thrust changed rapidly when Nikita Khrushchev came to power. In addition to Soviet forces stationed in Eastern Europe, which even today include the Group of Soviet Forces in [East] Germany, the Northern Group of Forces (Poland), the Central Group of Forces (Czechoslovakia), and the Southern Group of Forces (Hungary), the Russians established the Warsaw Pact Treaty Organization in 1955 as a counter to the U.S.-sponsored NATO. The military establishments of the member-states of the Warsaw Pact are regarded by the Soviets as important strategic elements, and the current trend is toward an "integration" of forces, using common equipment and logistic support and forming a unified order of battle. The Warsaw Pact headquarters, under a first deputy U.S.S.R. minister of defense, is located in Moscow and issues plans and policies to the East European defense ministers down to various districts and field commands. Additionally, in each East European defense ministry there is a Soviet advisor of general officer rank who holds the position of representative of the Warsaw Pact Command.

341

The Russian government under Khrushchev also took more interest in supplying arms and advisors overseas. Help was sent not only to China, where it was withdrawn in the great 1960 schism, but to Indonesia, the Congo, Cuba, and Egypt, as examples. With the exception of the Soviet Army role in crushing the Hungarian revolt in 1956, Russian soldiers continued to train at home and maintained relatively low profiles when assigned as helpers elsewhere.

When Leonid Brezhnev and his followers took over from Khrushchev in 1964, they began a fifteen-year military buildup, to back a more activist foreign policy. Through this period, the balance of both conventional and nuclear power on the ground in Europe began to shift in the Russians' favor. Elsewhere, use of Soviet arms and advisors as tools of foreign policy increased manyfold. Assistance went, as it still does, to Cuba, North Vietnam, India, Syria, and assorted terrorist groups like the PLO and IRA. Soviet ground force combat experience was nil, except for the move into Czechoslovakia in 1968.

However, certain Soviet military personnel saw action. Advisors were on the ground and took losses in the 1967 and 1973 Middle East wars, the Indochina fighting, the Indo-Pakistani conflicts, and others. The Russian APC and AT-missile have been used in combat, and new items, such as the helicopter gunship, have been developed as the results of lessons learned.

As the Russian military continues its buildup, its involvement overseas seems less covert. Beginning in the mid-1970s, a new approach was employed when Soviet-trained and -equipped Cuban troops began to fight as proxies of Moscow in various African liberation conflicts. In many instances, Cuban troops were directed or otherwise assisted by regular Russian army personnel. By 1979–1980, Soviet ground forces were directly involved in combat on a large scale for the first time since the Great Patriotic War when large numbers were moved across the border into Afghanistan.

The references in this section, the largest in the volume, detail the role of the Soviet Army and military assistance in the foreign affairs of the Soviet Union. Following a general treatment on foreign policy, the balance of power, and military assistance, subsections are provided containing references pertaining to involvement around the globe. Here are data on the use of AT-missiles in the Middle East, Soviet-made tanks in Vietnam, and Cuban troops in Africa. Due to the large numbers of countries and the similarity in military assistance techniques, as also cited in 5:A, no individual subsection introductions are provided.

A. The Soviet Army as a Tool of Foreign Policy

1. General Works

BOOKS

4050.   Aspaturian, Vernon V. *Process and Power in Soviet Foreign Policy.* Boston, Mass.: Little, Brown, 1971. 939p.

4051.   Ayoob, Mohammed, ed. *Conflict and Intervention in the Third World.* New York: St. Martin's Press, 1980. 261p.

4052.   Booth, Ken. *The Military Instrument in Soviet Foreign Policy, 1917–1972.* London: Royal United Service Institute for Defence Studies, 1973.

4053.   Brown, Neville. *The Future Global Challenge: A Predictive Study of World Security, 1977–1990.* New York: Crane, Russak, 1977. 402p.

4054.   Buchan, Alastair F. *Power and Equilibrium in the 1970's.* Russell C. Leffingwell Lectures, 1972. New York: Praeger, 1972. 120p.

4055.   Clemens, Walter C., Jr. *The U.S.S.R. and Global Interdependence: Alternative Futures.* Washington, D.C.: American Enterprise Institute for Public Policy Research, 1978. 113p.

4056.   DeHuszar, George B., et al. *Soviet Power and Policy.* New York: T. Y. Crowell, 1955. 598p.

4057.   Donaldson, Robert H. *The Soviet Union in the Third World: Successes and Failures.* Boulder, Colo.: Westview Press, 1980. 350p.

4058.   Edmonds, Robin. *Soviet Foreign Policy, 1962–1973: The Paradox of Super Power.* London and New York: Oxford University Press, 1975. 197p.

4059.   Eide, Asbjorn, and Marek Thee, eds. *Problems of Contemporary Militarism.* New York: St. Martin's Press, 1980. 336p.

4060.   Griffith, William E., ed. *The Soviet Empire: Expansion and Detente.* Boston, Mass.: D. C. Heath, 1976. 417p.

4061.   Holbrand, Carstein. *Super Powers and International Conflict.* New York: St. Martin's Press, 1979. 178p.

4062.   Horelick, Arnold L. *Strategic Power and Soviet Foreign Policy.* Chicago, Ill.: University of Chicago Press, 1966. 225p.

4063. Howard, Michael, ed. *Restraints on War: Studies in the Limitation of Armed Conflict.* Oxford, Eng.: At the Clarendon Press, 1978. 192p.

4064. Jacobsen, Carl G. *Soviet Strategic Initiatives: Challenges and Response.* New York: Praeger, 1979. 168p.

4065. _____ . *Soviet Strategy—Soviet Foreign Policy: Military Considerations Affecting Soviet Policy-Making.* Glasgow, Scotland: The University Press, 1972. 232p.

4066. Kaplan, Stephen S., et al. *Diplomacy of Power: The Soviet Armed Forces as a Political Instrument.* Washington, D.C.: Brookings Institution, 1981. 733p.

4067. Lider, Julian. *On the Nature of War.* Brookfield, Vt.: Renouf/ U.S.A., 1979. 420p.

4068. McGowan, Pat, and Charles W. Kegley, Jr., eds. *Threats, Weapons and Foreign Policy.* Sage International Yearbook of Foreign Policy Studies, v. 5. Beverly Hills, Calif.: Sage, 1980. 324p.

4069. Mackintosh, John M. *The Strategy and Tactics of Soviet Foreign Policy.* Rev. ed. London and New York: Oxford University Press, 1963. 353p.

4070. Martin, Laurence W. *Arms and Strategy: The World Power Structure Today.* New York: David McKay, 1973. 320p.

4071. Modrzhinskaya, Ye. D., et al. *Problems of War and Peace.* Translated from the Russian. Moscow: Progress Publishers, 1972.

4072. Schurmann, Franz. *The Logic of World Power: An Inquiry into the Origins, Currents, and Contradictions of World Politics.* New York: Pantheon, 1974. 593p.

4073. Shanor, Donald R. *The Soviet Triangle: Russia's Relations with China and the West in the 1980's.* New York: St. Martin's Press, 1980. 288p.

4074. Stern, Ellen, ed. *The Limits of Military Intervention.* Sage Series on Armed Forces and Society, no. 12. Beverly Hills, Calif.: Sage, 1977. 400p.

4075. Stoessinger, John G. *Why Nations Go to War.* 2d ed. New York: St. Martin's Press, 1978. 246p.

4076. Taborsky, Edward. *Communist Penetration of the Third World.* New York: Robert Speller & Sons, 1973. 500p.

4077. Wesson, Robert G. *Soviet Foreign Policy in Perspective.* Homewood, Ill.: Dorsey Press, 1969. 472p.

4078.   Whetten, Lawrence L., ed. *The Political Implications of Soviet Military Power.* New York: Crane, Russak, 1976. 183p.

ARTICLES

4079.   Albrecht, Ulrich. "Red Militarism." *Journal of Peace Research* 17 (Spring 1980), 135–149.

4080.   Aspaturian, Vernon V. "International Politics and Foreign Policy in the Soviet System." In R. Barry Ferrell, ed., *Approaches to Comparative and International Politics.* Evanston, Ill.: Northwestern University Press, 1966. pp. 212–301.

4081.   _____ . "Soviet Global Power and the 'Correlation of Forces.'" *Problems of Communism* 29 (May-June 1980), 1–18.

4082.   Bochkarev, K. S. "On the Character and Types of War in the Modern Era." In William R. Kintner and Harriet F. Scott, eds., *The Nuclear Revolution in Soviet Military Affairs.* Norman: University of Oklahoma Press, 1968. pp. 65–82.

4083.   Booth, Ken. "Military Power, Military Force, and Soviet Foreign Policy." In Michael MccGwire, ed., *Soviet Naval Developments, Capability and Context.* New York: Praeger, 1973. pp. 31–56.

4084.   "Burdens of Empire: Too Much for the Kremlin?" *U.S. News and World Report* 90 (September 22, 1980), 28–30.

4085.   Chaplin, Dennis. "The Soviet Union's Indirect Strategy in the Third World." *Military Review* 57 (June 1977), 9–13.

4086.   Clemens, Walter C., Jr. "Soviet Policy in the Third World in the 1970's: Five Alternative Models." *Orbis* 13 (Summer 1969), 476–501.

4087.   Dinerstein, Herbert S. "The Soviet Employment of Military Strength for Political Purposes." *Annals of the American Academy of Political and Social Science* 318 (July 1958), 104–112.

4088.   _____ . "Soviet Goals and Military Force." *Orbis* 5 (Winter 1962), 425–436.

4089.   Dunn, Keith A. "Power Projection or Influence: Soviet Capabilities for the 1980's." *Naval War College Review* 32 (September-October 1980), 31–47.

4090.   Eliot, George F. "The Red Army and Soviet Policy." *American Mercury* 80 (October 1955), 93–99.

4091.   Erickson, John. "Detente, Deterrence, and 'Military Superiority': A Soviet Dilemma." *World Today* 21 (August 1965), 337–345.

4092. _____ . "Detente: Soviet Policy and Purpose." *Strategic Review* 4 (Spring 1976), 37–43.

4093. _____ . "The 'Military Factor' in Soviet Policy." *International Affairs* (London) 39 (April 1963), 214–226.

4094. Garthoff, Raymond L. "Military Influences and Instruments." In Ivo J. Lederer, ed., *Russian Foreign Policy: Essays in Historical Perspective.* New Haven, Conn.: Yale University Press, 1962. pp. 252–257.

4095. _____ . "Soviet Views on the Interrelation of Diplomacy and Military Strategy." *Political Science Quarterly* 94 (Fall 1979), 391–406.

4096. Gascogne, Alvary. "Russian Policy since 1945." *Journal of the Royal United Service Institution* 100 (February 1955), 24–35.

4097. Ginsburgs, George. "The Soviet Quest for Influence and Military Facilities in the Third World." In Michael MccGwire and John McDonnell, eds., *Soviet Naval Influence: Domestic and Foreign Dimensions.* New York: Praeger, 1977. pp. 455–458.

4098. Gray, Colin S. "Soviet Strategic Vulnerabilities." *Air Force Magazine* 62 (March 1979), 60–64.

4099. Hannah, Norman B. "Moscow's Outward Thrust." *National Review* 32 (September 5, 1980), 1073–1075.

4100. Haselkorn, Avigdor. "The Expanding Soviet Collective Security Network." *Strategic Review* 6 (Summer 1978), 62–73.

4101. _____ . "The 'External Function' of the Soviet Armed Forces." *Naval War College Review* 33 (January-February 1980), 35–45.

4102. _____ . "The Soviet Collective Security System." *Orbis* 19 (Spring 1975), 231–254.

4103. _____ . "Soviet Military Casualties in Third World Conflicts." *Conflict* 2 (1980), 73–87.

4104. Holloway, David. "Foreign and Defense Policy." In Archibald H. Brown and Michael Kaser, eds., *The Soviet Union since the Fall of Khrushchev.* New York: Free Press, 1975. pp. 49–76.

4105. _____ . "Military Power and Political Purpose in Soviet Policy." *Daedalus* 109 (Fall 1980), 13–30.

4106. _____ . "Strategic Concepts and Soviet Policy." *Survival* 13 (November 1971), 364–369.

4107. Hudson, George F. "Collective Security and Military Alliances." In Herbert Butterfield and Martin Wight, eds., *Diplomatic Investigations: Essays on the Theory of International Politics*. Cambridge, Mass.: Harvard University Press, 1966. Chpt. 8.

4108. Jacobsen, Carl G. "Soviet Strategic Objectives for the 1980's." *World Today* 35 (April 1979), 130–137.

4109. Jones, Christopher D. "Just Wars and Limited Wars: Restraints on the Use of the Soviet Armed Forces." *World Politics* 28 (October 1975), 44–68.

4110. Kaplan, Stephen S. "Military Blackmail, Kremlin Style: An Interview." *U.S. News and World Report* 90 (May 11, 1981), 32–33.

4111. Keep, John. "The Soviet Union and the Third World." *Survey*, no. 72 (Summer 1969), 19–38.

4112. Khibrikov, N. "Indoctrination Guide on the Soviet Role in National Liberation Movements: Translated from *Kommunist Vooruzhennykh Sil*, March 1978." *Translations on USSR Military Affairs*, no. 1354 (May 23, 1978), 92–102.

4113. Kime, Steve F. "Power Projection, Soviet Style." *Air Force Magazine* 63 (December 1980), 50–54.

4114. LaRocque, G. R. "Measuring Soviet Power: A Real World Appraisal." *Christianity and Crisis* 40 (May 26, 1980), 158–162.

4115. Lathrop, Gregory L. "Politics, Power Perception, and the Soviet Military." *Armed Forces and Society* 6 (Summer 1980), 695–700.

4116. Legvold, Robert. "The Super Rivals: Conflict in the Third World." *Foreign Affairs* 57 (Spring 1979), 755–778.

4117. McConnell, James M., and Bradford Dismukes. "The Soviet Diplomacy of Force in the Third World." *Problems of Communism* 28 (January-February 1979), 14–27.

4118. MccGwire, Michael. "The Overseas Role of a 'Soviet Military Presence.'" In Michael MccGwire and John McDonnell, eds., *Soviet Naval Influence, Domestic and Foreign Dimensions*. New York: Praeger, 1977. pp. 31–60.

4119. Mackintosh, Malcolm. "The Soviet Military's Influence on Foreign Policy." *Problems of Communism* 22 (September 1973), 1–26.

4120. Mozolev, M. "Role of the Army in Developing Countries Discussed: Translated from *Voyenno Istoricheskiy Zhurnal*, April 1980." *Translations on USSR Military Affairs*, no. 1525 (July 24, 1980), 68–78.

4121.   Nikitin, N. "Operational and Tactical Peculiarities of Local Wars." *Soviet Military Review,* no. 7 (July 1979), 46–47.

4122.   Papp, Daniel S. "Toward an Estimate of the Soviet Worldview." *Naval War College Review* 32 (November-December 1979), 60–78.

4123.   Peck, Edward. "Soviet Military Power and Political Influence." *NATO Review* 27 (April 1979), 14–18.

4124.   Pelliccia, Antonio. "Clausewitz and Soviet Politico-Military Strategy." *NATO's Fifteen Nations* 20 (December 1975–January 1976), 18–21.

4125.   Ra'anan, Uri. "Tactics and the Third World: Contradictions and Dangers." *Survey,* no. 57 (October 1965), 10.

4126.   Rubinstein, Alvin Z. "Soviet Policy in the Third World in Perspective." *Military Review* 58 (July 1978), 2–9.

4127.   Rybkin, Ye. "Rybkin on the Need for Contemporary Wars of National Liberation: Translated from *Voyenno Istoricheskiy Zhurnal,* November 1978." *Translations on USSR Military Affairs,* no. 1406 (January 2, 1979), 37–44.

4128.   Scribner, Jeffrey L. "The Soviet Military Buildup: A New Dimension in Foreign Policy." *Military Review* 51 (August 1971), 53–62.

4129.   Sella, Amnon. "Patterns of Soviet Involvement in Local Wars." *Journal of the Royal United Service Institute for Defence Studies* 124 (June 1979), 53–56.

4130.   Shackleton, N. A. "Soviet Strategy in the Cold War: A Reappraisal." *Canadian Army Journal* 18 (Fall 1964), 2–15.

4131.   Shulman, Marshall D. "Trends in Soviet Foreign Policy." In Michael MccGwire, Ken Booth, and John McDonnell, eds., *Soviet Naval Policy, Objectives and Constraints.* New York: Praeger, 1975. pp. 3–22.

4132.   Shumikhin, N. "Instructor Guide for Indoctrination on Contemporary Wars: Translated from *Kommunist Vooruzhennykh Sil,* October 1977." *Translations on USSR Military Affairs,* no. 1322 (January 9, 1978), 34–48.

4133.   Singleton, Seth. "Soviet Policy and Socialist Expansion in Asia and Africa." *Armed Forces and Society* 6 (Spring 1980), 339–369.

4134.   Smith, Hedrick. "Russia's Power Strategy." *New York Times Magazine* (January 27, 1980), 27–30, 42–47.

4135. "Soviet Geopolitical Momentum—Myth or Menace: Trends in Soviet Influence around the World, 1945–1980." *Defense Monitor* 9 (January 1980), 1–24.

4136. "Soviet Global Military Capability Gains." *Aviation Week and Space Technology* 108 (May 29, 1978), 60–61.

4137. "Soviet Military Might: A Soviet View." *Fortune* 99 (February 26, 1979), 46–53.

4138. Thomas, John R. "Soviet Foreign Policy and the Military." *Survey,* no. 17 (Summer 1971), 129–156.

4139. Twining, David T. "Soviet Activities in the Third World: A New Pattern." *Military Review* 60 (June 1980), 2–10.

4140. Valentia, Jiri. "From Prague to Kabul: The Soviet Style of Invasion." *International Security Review* 5 (Fall 1980), 114–141.

4141. "Where Soviets Flexed Their Military Muscle: 23 Examples of Russian Coercion." *U.S. News and World Report* 90 (May 11, 1981), 30–31.

4142. Whitney, Craig R. "The View from the Kremlin." *New York Times Magazine* (April 20, 1980), 30–33.

4143. Yost, Charles W. "Observing [Soviet] Close Encounters in the Third World." *International Security Review* 3 (Summer 1978), 187–192.

4144. Zagoria, Donald. "Into the Breach: New Soviet Alliances in the Third World." *Foreign Affairs* 57 (Spring 1979), 733–754.

DOCUMENTS, PAPERS, AND REPORTS

4145. Finley, David D. *Some Aspects of Conventional Military Capability in Soviet Foreign Relations.* ACIS Working Papers, no. 20. Los Angeles, Calif.: Center for International and Strategic Studies, University of California, 1980. 61p.

4146. Goldhamer, Herbert. *The Soviet Union in a Period of Strategic Parity.* RAND Report R-889-PR. Santa Monica, Calif.: RAND Corporation, 1971. 71p.

4147. Holst, Johan J. *Comparative U.S. and Soviet Deployments and Arms Limitations.* Chicago, Ill.: Center for Policy Study, University of Chicago, 1971. 60p.

4148. Jones, W. M. *Soviet Leadership Politics and Leadership Views on the Use of Military Force.* RAND Note N-1210-AF. Santa Monica, Calif.: RAND Corporation, 1979. 24p.

4149.   McConnell, Robert B. "Conventional Military Force and Soviet Foreign Policy." MA thesis, U.S. Naval Postgraduate School, 1978.

4150.   Novik, Nimrod. *On the Shores of Bab Al-Mandab: Soviet Diplomacy and Regional Dynamics.* Monograph, no. 26. Philadelphia, Pa.: Foreign Policy Research Institute, 1979. 83p.

4151.   Petersen, Charles W. *Third World Military Elites in Soviet Perspective.* Professional Paper. Alexandria, Va.: Institute of Naval Studies, Center for Naval Analysis, 1979. 57p.

4152.   *Prospects of Soviet Power in the 1980's: Papers from the International Institute for Strategic Studies 20th Annual Conference.* Adelphi papers, nos. 151–152. 2 vols. London, 1979.

4153.   Thompson, W. Scott. *Power Projection: A Net Assessment of U.S. and Soviet Capabilities.* New York: National Strategy Information Center, 1978. 39p.

4154.   ———. *The Projection of Soviet Power.* RAND Paper P-5988. Santa Monica, Calif.: RAND Corporation, 1977. 37p.

4155.   United States. Congress. House. Committee on International Relations. Subcommittee on Europe and the Middle East. *The Soviet Union—International Dynamics of Foreign Policy, Present and Future: Hearings.* 95th Cong., 2d sess. Washington, D.C.: U.S. Government Printing Office, 1978. 333p.

4156.   Whelan, Joseph G., and William B. Inglee. *The Soviet Union and the Third World: A Watershed in Great Power Policy.* Washington, D.C.: Congressional Research Service, Library of Congress, 1977. 186p.

4157.   Wolfe, Thomas W. *Worldwide Soviet Military Strategy and Policy.* RAND Paper P-5008. Santa Monica, Calif.: RAND Corporation, 1973. 38p.

Further References

See also section 1:A and various parts of this section.

2. The Military Balance

BOOKS

4158.   Baldwin, Hanson W. *The Great Arms Race: A Comparison of U.S. and Soviet Power Today.* New York: Praeger, 1958. 116p.

4159. Bertram, Christopher, ed. *Prospects of Soviet Power in the 1980's.* Hamden, Conn.: Shoestring Press, 1980. 128p.

4160. Bottome, Edgar M. *The Balance of Terror: A Guide to the Arms Race.* Boston, Mass.: Beacon Press, 1971. 215p.

4161. Carlton, David, and Carlo Schaerf, eds. *The Dynamics of the Arms Race.* London: Halsted Press, 1975. 244p.

4162. Chodes, John J. *The Myth of America's Military Power.* New York: Brandon House, 1973. 224p.

4163. Cline, Ray S. *World Power Assessment: A Calculus of Strategic Drift.* Boulder, Colo.: Westview Press, 1977. 206p.

4164. Collins, John M. *American and Soviet Military Trends since the Cuban Missile Crisis.* Washington, D.C.: Center for Strategic and International Studies, Georgetown University, 1978. 496p.

4165. _____ , and Anthony H. Cordesman. *Imbalance of Power: Shifting U.S.-Soviet Military Strength.* San Rafael, Calif.: Presidio Press, 1978. 316p.

4166. Daniel, Donald C., ed. *International Perceptions of the Superpower Military Balance.* New York: Praeger, 1978. 198p.

4167. Graham, Daniel O. *Shall America Be Defended?: SALT II and Beyond.* New Rochelle, N.Y.: Arlington House, 1979. 267p.

4168. Kirk, Grayson, and Nils Wessell, eds. *The Soviet Threat: Myths and Realities.* New York: Praeger, 1978. 192p.

4169. Liska, George. *The Quest for Equilibrium: America and the Balance of Power on Land and Sea.* Baltimore, Md.: Johns Hopkins University Press, 1977. 256p.

4170. Middleton, Drew. *Can America Win the Next War?* New York: Scribners, 1975. 271p.

4171. Myrdal, Alva. *The Game of Disarmament: How the United States and Russia Run the Arms Race.* New York: Pantheon, 1976. 397p.

4172. Peckman, Joseph A., ed. *Setting National Priorities: The 1980 Budget.* Washington, D.C.: Brookings Institution, 1979. 229p.

4173. Rummel, Rudolph J. *Peace Endangered: The Reality of Detente.* Beverly Hills, Calif.: Sage, 1976. 189p.

ARTICLES

4174.   American Enterprise Institute for Public Policy Research. "Who's First in Defense: The U.S. or the U.S.S.R.?" *AEI Round Table* (June 3, 1976), 1–39.

4175.   "An Appraisal of the Tactical Balance." *Aeronautics* 35 (February 1957), 54–57.

4176.   Aspin, Les. "Comparing Soviet and American Efforts." *NATO's Fifteen Nations* 21 (June-July 1976), 34–36.

4177.   _____ . "How to Look at the Soviet American Balance." *Foreign Policy,* no. 22 (Spring 1976), 96–106; no. 23 (Summer 1976), 32–52.

4178.   "Assessing the Balance of U.S., U.S.S.R., and P.R.C. General Forces." *Commander's Digest* 20 (February 17, 1977), 2–24.

4179.   Baldwin, Hanson W. "Comparative Armed Strengths: Reprinted from the *New York Times,* August 4 and 7, 1979." In Walter M. Daniels, ed., *Defense of Western Europe.* Reference Shelf, v. 22, no. 5. New York: H. W. Wilson, 1950. pp. 96–99.

4180.   Barrett, Raymond J. "A Balance of Powers." *U.S. Naval Institute Proceedings* 98 (April 1972), 18–24.

4181.   Bellany, Ian. "The Central Balance: Arms Race and Arms Control." In Carsten Holbrand, ed., *Super Powers and World Order.* Canberra, Aust.: Australian National University Press, 1971. pp. 41–63.

4182.   Bennett, Ralph K. "The U.S.-Soviet Military Balance: Who's Ahead?" *Reader's Digest* 113 (September 1976), 79–83.

4183.   Blechman, Barry M. "Handicapping the Arms Race: Are the Soviets Ahead?" *New Republic* 174 (January 3, 1976), 19–21.

4184.   Brock, William E. "The Shifting Balance." *Ordnance* 56 (March-April 1972), 366–368.

4185.   Brown, Harold. "The Balance between the United States and the Soviet Union: An Address, June 23, 1978." *Vital Speeches* 44 (July 15, 1978), 581–589.

4186.   _____ . "The Growing Soviet Threat, Even with an Arms Pact." *U.S. News and World Report* 86 (February 5, 1979), 33–34.

4187.   Burt, Richard. "Soviets' Military Buildup a Major Issue for Reagan: Reprinted from the *New York Times*, December 7, 1980." In U.S. Congress, Senate, Committee on Foreign Relations, *Nomination of Alexander M. Haig, Jr., to be Secretary of State: Hearings*. 97th Cong., 1st sess. Washington, D.C.: U.S. Government Printing Office, 1981. I: 296–300.

4188.   Cady, Steven E. "World Peace and the Soviet Military Threat." *Air University Review* 30 (January-February 1979), 94–98.

4189.   Citizens' Panel on Defense. "U.S. Superiority Has Ended: Summary of Statement." *U.S. News and World Report* 70 (April 5, 1971), 49–50.

4190.   Cobb, Tyrus W. "The Military Imbalance: Soviet Military Expansion during the Era of Detente." *Military Review* 57 (March 1977), 79–85.

4191.   ———. "Who's Out in Front?" *Army* 25 (January 1975), 12–18.

4192.   Collins, John M. "American and Soviet Armed Services: Strengths Compared, 1970–1976." *Congressional Record* 122 (August 5, 1976), S14064–S14104.

4193.   Dupuy, Trevor N. "The Credibility of Deterrence: A Comparison of the Combat Potentialities of the United States and the Soviet Union." *Strategy and Tactics*, no. 74 (May-June 1979), 23–30.

4194.   Foster, John S., Jr. "The Balance of Security." *Ordnance* 57 (July-August 1972), 44–47.

4195.   "Fresh Worry over Soviet Arms Buildup." *U.S. News and World Report* 72 (February 28, 1972), 24–26.

4196.   Fromm, Joseph. "New Alarm over Russian Threat: A Special Report." *U.S. News and World Report* 85 (October 30, 1978), 47–53.

4197.   Galen, Justin. "The Tactical Nuclear Balance." *Armed Forces Journal International* 115 (December 1977), 29–32; (January 1978), 20–24.

4198.   Garn, Jake. "Soviet Superiority: A Question for National Debate." *International Security Review* 4 (Spring 1979), 1–24.

4199.   Garrett, S. A. "Detente and the Military Balance." *Bulletin of the Atomic Scientists* 33 (April 1977), 10–20.

4200.   Garthoff, Raymond L. "The Concept of Balance of Power in Soviet Policy Making." *World Politics* 4 (October 1951), 256–268.

4201.   Gray, Colin S. "The Urge to Compete: Rationales for Arms Racing." *World Politics* 26 (January 1974), 595–611.

4202.   Haig, Alexander M., Jr. "Russia's Relentless Arms Buildup: An Interview." *U.S. News and World Report* 82 (January 17, 1977), 35–37.

4203.   Hessman, James D. "Arms, Men, and Military Budgets: Some Grim Facts and Sobering Conclusions about the Present Military 'Balance.'" *Sea Power* 19 (May 1976), 14–16.

4204.   _____ . "The Soviet Union Moves Ahead: On Land, on the Sea, and in the Air." *Armed Forces Journal* 107 (August 17, 1970), 28–37.

4205.   Hinterhoff, Eugene. "The Delicate Balance." *Military Review* 48 (December 1968), 78–85.

4206.   _____ . "The Soviet Threat since Czechoslovakia." *Military Review* 50 (June 1970), 68–73.

4207.   Hoffmann, Stanley. "Weighing the Balance of Power." *Foreign Affairs* 50 (July 1972), 618–643.

4208.   "If New Fighting Starts, Our Power and Russia's." *U.S. News and World Report* 21 (August 30, 1946), 14–15.

4209.   Ilke, Fred C. "What It Means to Be Number Two." *Fortune* 98 (November 20, 1978), 72–74.

4210.   International Institute for Strategic Studies. "The Military Balance." *Air Force Magazine* 55 (December 1972), 43–105; 56 (December 1973), 57–121; 59 (December 1976), 41–107.

4211.   _____ . "Tables of Comparative Strengths." *Air Force Magazine* 61 (December 1978), 122–127.

4212.   _____ . "The United States and the Soviet Union." *Air Force Magazine* 55 (December 1972), 46–52; 56 (December 1973), 60–67; 57 (December 1974), 44–49; 58 (December 1975), 46–51; 59 (December 1976), 44–50; 60 (December 1977), 62–65; 61 (December 1978), 64–70; 62 (December 1979), 64–70; 63 (December 1980), 64–70.

4213.   "Is the U.S. Forfeiting the Arms Race to Russia?" *U.S. News and World Report* 69 (October 19, 1971), 21–24.

4214.   Keegan, George J., Jr. "New Assessment Put on Soviet Threat: An Address." *Aviation Week and Space Technology* 106 (March 28, 1977), 38–43.

4215.   Kemp, Jack F. "The Soviet Threat." *AEI Defense Review* 2 (March 1978), 15–36.

4216. _____ . "The Soviet Military Threat to Our National Security: The Real Facts and Figures." *Congressional Record* 122 (June 16, 1976), H6008–H6013.

4217. Klare, M. T. "Soviet-U.S. Intervention Capabilities: The Power Projection Gap." *Nation* 228 (June 9, 1979), 671–676.

4218. Kolkowicz, Roman. "Strategic Parity and Beyond: Soviet Perspectives." *World Politics* 23 (April 1971), 431–451.

4219. Laird, Melvin R. "Why Soviet Arms Worry the U.S.: An Interview." *U.S. News and World Report* 72 (March 27, 1972), 41–46.

4220. Lemnitzer, Lyman. "Russia's Growing Power: An Interview." *U.S. News and World Report* 66 (May 12, 1969), 44–46.

4221. Levine, Isaac D. "Detente and Reality." *Strategic Review* 2 (Summer 1974), 44–50.

4222. "Living with the Soviet Superpower: A Symposium." *Foreign Policy,* no. 32 (Fall 1978), 22–106.

4223. Lowther, W. "Gathering Storm: Russia's Shift in the Balance of Terror." *Macleans* 91 (May 29, 1978), 22–24.

4224. Lucier, C. E. "Changes in Values of Arms Race Parameters." *Journal of Conflict Resolution* 23 (March 1979), 17–39.

4225. Mackintosh, Malcolm. "Moscow's View of the Balance of Power." *World Today* 29 (March 1973), 108–118.

4226. Martin, Laurence W. "The Changing Military Balance." *Proceedings of the American Academy of Political and Social Science* 29 (May 1969), 61–74.

4227. Moorer, Thomas H. "The Narrowing Gap." *Ordnance* 58 (July-August 1973), 30–32.

4228. Murphy, Charles J. V. "The Menace of Russia's Military Machine." *Reader's Digest* 103 (December 1973), 99–103.

4229. Nanes, Allan S. "American-Russian Arms Competition." *Current History* 37 (October 1959), 214–221.

4230. Nitze, Paul H. "The Global Military Balance." In Grayson Kirk and Nils H. Wessell, eds., *The Soviet Threat: Myths and Realities.* New York: Praeger, 1978. pp. 4–14.

4231. "Pentagon Size-Up: Where Russia Is Outstripping the U.S. in Military Might." *U.S. News and World Report* 80 (February 9, 1976), 20–21.

4232.   Rockingham-Gill, R. T. "The New East-West Military Balance." *East Europe* 4 (April 1964), 3–8.

4233.   Schemmer, Benjamin F. "U.S./U.S.S.R. Military Balance." *Armed Forces Journal International* 113 (March 1976), 18; (April 1976), 23–25; (May 1976), 24–28.

4234.   Schlesinger, James R. "Testing Time for America: The Russian Threat." *Fortune* 93 (February 1976), 74–77.

4235.   Seamans, Robert C. "The Growing Soviet Threat and What to Do about It." *Air Force and Space Digest* 53 (May 1970), 38–41.

4236.   "That Alarming Soviet Buildup." *Time* 107 (March 8, 1976), 35–36.

4237.   Ulsamer, Edgar. "The Accelerating Momentum of Soviet Military Might." *Air Force Magazine* 61 (March 1978), 34–41.

4238.   ———. "The Soviet Juggernaut: Racing Faster Than Ever." *Air Force Magazine* 59 (March 1976), 56–58.

4239.   ———. "The U.S.S.R.'s Military Shadow Is Lengthening." *Air Force Magazine* 60 (March 1977), 36–46.

4240.   ———. "World Hegemony through Military Superiority." *Air Force Magazine* 62 (March 1979), 40–47.

4241.   Vakhramyev, A. "Detente and the World Balance of Forces." *International Affairs* (Moscow), no. 1 (January 1979), 78–86.

4242.   Weeks, Albert L. "The Growth of Soviet Military Power." *American Legion Magazine* 91 (November 1971), 6–11.

4243.   Wheeler, Earle G. "Why Defense Planners Worry: An Interview." *U.S. News and World Report* 68 (April 20, 1970), 34–39.

4244.   Windsor, Philip. "The East-West Military Balance." *East Europe*, no. 7 (July 1964), 22–23.

4245.   Winston, D. C. "DOD Warns Congress of Soviet Gains." *Aviation Week and Space Technology* 96 (February 28, 1972), 18–19.

Documents, Papers, and Reports

4246.   Barnett, Frank R., et al. *The Military Unbalance: Is the U.S. Becoming a Second-Class Power?* New York: National Strategy Information Center, 1971. 65p.

4247.   Blechman, Barry M., et al. *Soviet Military Buildup and U.S. Defense Spending.* Washington, D.C.: Brookings Institution, 1977. 61p.

4248.   Committee on the Present Danger. *Is America Becoming Number 2?* Washington, D.C., 1978. 46p.

4249.   Daly, John C., et al. *Who's First in Defense: The U.S. or the U.S.S.R.?* Washington, D.C.: American Enterprise Institute for Public Policy Research, 1976. 39p.

4250.   Daniel, Donald C. *Perceptions of the Superpower Military Balance: Considerations and Evidence.* NPS 56-78-001. Monterey, Calif.: U.S. Naval Postgraduate School, 1978. 308p.

4251.   Dinerstein, Herbert S. *The United States and the Soviet Union: Standoff or Confrontation?* RAND Paper P-3046. Santa Monica, Calif.: RAND Corporation, 1965. 25p.

4252.   Jennings, Richard M. "U.S./Soviet Arms Competition, 1945–1972: Aspects of Its Nature, Control, and Results." PhD dissertation, Georgetown University, 1975.

4253.   Kintner, William R., and Robert L. Pfaltzgraff. *Soviet Military Trends: Implications for U.S. Security.* Analysis, no. 6. Washington, D.C.: American Enterprise Institute for Public Policy Research, 1971. 50p.

4254.   Korb, Laurence J. *The FY 1980–1984 Defense Program: Issues and Trends.* Washington, D.C.: American Enterprise Institute for Public Policy Research, 1979. 53p.

4255.   United States. Blue Ribbon Defense Panel. *Report.* Washington, D.C.: U.S. Government Printing Office, 1970. 237p.

4256.   ———. *Supplemental Statement to Report on the Shifting Balance of Military Power.* Washington, D.C.: U.S. Government Printing Office, 1970. 35p.

4257.   United States. Congress. House. Committee on Armed Services. *The Soviet Threat: Report.* 91st Cong., 2d sess. Washington, D.C.: U.S. Government Printing Office, 1970. 33p.

4258.   United States. Congress. Senate. Committee on Armed Services. *United States/Soviet Military Balance: A Frame of Reference for Congress.* Cmte. Print. 94th Cong., 1st sess. Washington, D.C.: U.S. Government Printing Office, 1976. 86p.   Written by John M. Collins and John S. Chwat.

4259.   United States. National Defense University. *Continuity and Change in the Eighties and Beyond: The Sixth National Security Conference.* Washington, D.C.: U.S. Government Printing Office, 1979. 222p.

Further References

See also section 1:A and other parts of this section.

3. Arms Transfers

BOOKS

4260.   Cahn, Anne H., et al. *Controlling Future Arms Trade.* New York: McGraw-Hill, 1977. 210p.

4261.   Cannizzo, Cindy, ed. *The Gun Merchants: Politics and Policies of the Major Arms Suppliers.* New York: Pergamon Press, 1980. 211p.

4262.   Frank, Lewis A. *The Arms Trade in International Relations.* New York: Praeger, 1969.

4263.   Goldman, Marshall I. *Soviet Foreign Aid.* New York: Praeger, 1967. 265p.

4264.   Harkavy, Robert E. *The Arms Trade and International Systems.* Boston, Mass.: Ballinger, 1975. 291p.

4265.   Joshua, Wynford, and Stephen P. Gilbert. *Arms for the Third World: Soviet Military Aid Diplomacy.* Baltimore, Md.: Johns Hopkins Press, 1969. 169p.

4266.   Kaldor, Mary, and Asbjorn Eide, eds. *The World Military Order: The Impact of Military Technology on the Third World.* New York: Praeger, 1979. 350p.

4267.   Neuman, Stephanie G., and Robert E. Harkavy, eds. *Arms Transfers in the Modern World.* New York: Praeger, 1979. 400p.

4268.   Ra'anan, Uri. *The U.S.S.R. Arms the Third World: Case Studies in Soviet Foreign Policy.* Cambridge, Mass.: M.I.T. Press, 1969. 256p.

4269.   Rubinstein, Alvin Z., ed. *Soviet and Chinese Influence in the Third World.* New York: Praeger, 1975. 246p.

4270.   Stockholm International Peace Research Institute. *The Arms Trade with the Third World.* Rev. and abr. ed. New York: Holmes & Meier, 1975. 362p.

ARTICLES

4271.   Bader, William B. "The Proliferation of Conventional Weapons." In Cyril E. Black and Richard A. Falk, eds., *The Future of the International Legal Order.* 3 vols. Princeton, N. J.: Princeton University Press, 1971. III: 210–223.

4272. Barrett, Raymond J. "The Arms Dilemma for the Developing World." *Military Review* 50 (April 1970), 28–55.

4273. _____ . "The Changing Role of the Military Advisor." *Military Review* 54 (September 1974), 25–30.

4274. Chaudhuri, J. N. "The International Arms Trade: The Recipient's Problem." *Political Quarterly* 43 (July-September 1972), 261–269.

4275. Cooper, Orah, and Carol Fogarty. "Soviet Economic and Military Aid to the Less-Developed Countries, 1954–1978." In U.S. Congress, Joint Economic Committee, *The Soviet Economy in a Time of Change: A Compendium of Papers.* 96th Cong., 1st sess. 2 vols. Washington, D.C.: U.S. Government Printing Office, 1979. II: 648–662.

4276. _____ . "Soviet Military and Economic Aid to the Less-Developed-Countries, 1954–1978." In Morris Bornstein, ed., *The Soviet Economy: Continuity and Change.* Boulder, Colo.: Westview Press, 1981. Chpt. 12.

4277. Finley, David D. "Conventional Arms in Soviet Policy." *World Politics* 33 (October 1980), 1–25.

4278. Gales, Robert R. "Soviet Foreign Assistance: A Glimpse of Its Structure and Species." *U.S. Air Force JAG Law Review* 15 (September 1973), 82–90.

4279. Gilbert, Stephen P. "Soviet-American Military Aid Competition in the Third World." *Orbis* 13 (Winter 1970), 1117–1137.

4280. _____ . "Wars of Liberation and Soviet Military Aid Policy." *Orbis* 10 (Fall 1966), 839–858.

4281. Heiman, Leo. "Moscow's Export Arsenal." *East Europe* 13 (May 1964), 2–11.

4282. Hinterhoff, Eugene. "The Soviet Military Aid and Its Implications." *NATO's Fifteen Nations* 6 (February-March 1962), 79.

4283. Husbands, J. L. "The Soviet Union in the Arms Trade." *Focus* 30 (March-April 1980), 7–9.

4284. Hutchings, Raymond. "Soviet Arms Exports to the Third World: A Pattern and Its Implications." *World Today* 84 (October 1978), 378–389.

4285. Kemp, Geoffrey. "Arms Traffic and Third World Conflicts." *International Conciliation,* no. 577 (March 1970), 1–80.

4286.   Ra'anan, Uri. "Soviet Arms Transfers and the Problem of Political Leverage." In Uri Ra'anan, Robert L. Pfaltzgraff, Jr., and Geoffrey Kemp, eds., *Arms Transfers to the Third World: The Military Buildup in Less-Industrial Countries.* Boulder, Colo.: Westview Press, 1979. Chpt. 7.

4287.   Ramazani, R. K. "Soviet Military Assistance to the Uncommitted Countries." *Midwest Journal of Political Science* 2 (November 1959), 356–373.

4288.   "Russia Puts on Old-Style Muscle: Military Aid Picking Up Speed." *Business Week* (March 2, 1968), 96–98.

4289.   Scharndorf, Werner. "East European Countries in the Forefront of Soviet Aid to the Third World." *Institute for the Study of the USSR Bulletin* 18 (February 1971), 28–31.

4290.   "Soviet Military Aid: Source of International Conflicts." *Military Review* 42 (February 1962), 33–51.

4291.   "Soviet Weapons Exports: Russian Roulette in the Third World." *Defense Monitor* 8 (January 1979), 1–57.

4292.   Starr, Richard F. "Soviet Weapons for the Third World." *Marine Corps Gazette* 57 (December 1973), 14–22.

4293.   Sumbatyan, Y. "The Army in the Developing Countries." *Soviet Military Review,* no. 8 (August 1975), 42–43.

4294.   Szulc, Tad. "From Russia with Love." *New York* 12 (September 24, 1979), 65.

4295.   Thayer, George. "The Communists as Arms Traders." *The War Business: The International Trade in Armaments.* New York: Simon & Schuster, 1970. pp. 324–358.

4296.   Wolynski, Alexander. "Soviet Aid to the Third World." *Conflict Studies,* no. 90 (December 1977), 1–20.

4297.   Yellon, R. A. "Shifts in Soviet Policies toward Developing Areas, 1964–1968." In W. Raymond Duncan, ed., *Soviet Policy in Developing Countries.* Waltham, Mass.: Ginn-Blaisdell, 1970. pp. 225–286.

4298.   Zorza, Victor. "Arms and the Soviet Union." *New Republic* 156 (January 14, 1967), 13–15.

DOCUMENTS, PAPERS, AND REPORTS

4299.   Finley, David D. *Conventional Arms in Soviet Foreign Policy.* ACIS Working Papers, no. 20. Los Angeles, Calif.: Center for International and Strategic Affairs, University of California, 1979. 51p.

4300.   Pajak, Roger F. "Soviet Military Aid: An Instrument of Soviet Foreign Policy toward the Developing Countries." PhD dissertation, American University, 1966.

4301.   Sutton, John L., and Geoffrey Kemp. *Arms to Developing Countries, 1945–1965.* Adelphi papers, no. 28. London: Institute for Strategic Studies, 1966. 45p.

4302.   United States. Central Intelligence Agency. National Foreign Assessment Center. *Arms Flows to LDCs: U.S.-Soviet Comparisons, 1974–77.* ER78-10494U. Washington, D.C.: Document Expediting Service, Exchange and Gift Division, Library of Congress, 1978. 13p.

4303.   _____ . *Communist Aid to the Less-Developed Countries of the Free World.* Research aid. Washington, D.C.: Document Expediting Project, Exchange and Gift Division, Library of Congress, 1976–. v. 1–.

Further References

See also 5:A:1 and other parts of this section.

B. Europe: The Warsaw Pact vs. the West

1. General Works

BOOKS

4304.   Bidwell, Shelford, ed. *World War 3: A Military Projection Founded on Today's Facts.* Englewood Cliffs, N. J.: Prentice-Hall, 1978. 207p.

4305.   Cave Brown, Anthony. *Dropshot: The American Plan for World War Three Against Russia in 1957.* New York: Dial Press, 1978. 330p.

4306.   Coffey, Joseph I. *Arms Control and European Security: A Guide to East-West Negotiations.* New York: Praeger, 1977. 271p.

4307.   DePorte, Anton W. *Europe between the Superpowers: The Enduring Balance.* New Haven, Conn.: Yale University Press, 1979. 256p.

4308.   Douglass, Joseph D., Jr. *Soviet Military Strategy in Europe.* Elmsford, N.Y.: Pergamon Press, 1978. 350p.

4309.   _____ . *The Soviet Theater Nuclear Offensive.* Studies in Communist Affairs, v. 1. Washington, D.C.: U.S. Government Printing Office, 1976. 127p.

4310.   Feis, Herbert. *From Trust to Terror: The Onset of the Cold War, 1945–1950.* New York: W. W. Norton, 1970. 428p.

4311.   Garnett, John C., ed. *The Defense of Western Europe: Papers Presented at the [British] National Defence College, Latimer, in September 1972.* New York: St. Martin's Press, 1974. 134p.

4312.   Gooch, John. *Armies in Europe.* London: Routledge & Kegan Paul, 1980. 296p.

4313.   Hackett, John W. *The Third World War: A Future History.* London: Hutchinson, 1978. 368p.   A fictional projection.

4314.   Leebaert, Derek, ed. *European Security: Prospects for the 1980's.* Boston, Mass.: Lexington Books, 1979. 320p.

4315.   Middleton, Drew. *The Defense of Western Europe.* New York: Appleton-Century-Crofts, 1952. 313p.

4316.   Myers, Kenneth A., ed. *N.A.T.O.—The Next 30 Years: The Changing Political, Economic, and Military Setting.* Boulder, Colo.: Westview Press, 1980. 440p.

4317.   Nalin, Y., and A. Nikolayev. *The Soviet Union and European Security.* Translated from the Russian. New York: Beekman House, 1973. 141p.

4318.   Pipes, Richard, ed. *Soviet Strategy in Europe.* New York: Published for the Strategic Studies Center of Stanford Research Institute by Crane, Russak, 1976. 316p.

4319.   Richardson, James L. *Germany and the Atlantic Alliance: The Interaction of Strategy and Politics.* Cambridge, Mass.: Harvard University Press, 1966. 403p.

4320.   Stockholm International Peace Research Institute. *Force Reductions in Europe.* New York: Humanities Press, 1974. 105p.

4321.   Wolfe, Thomas W. *Soviet Power and Europe, 1945–1970.* Baltimore, Md.: Johns Hopkins Press, 1970. 534p.

ARTICLES

4322.   Allen, Frank C. "Yugoslavia after Tito: The Soviet Threat." *Military Review* 58 (May 1978), 62–68.

4323.   Betit, Eugene D. "Soviet Tactical Doctrine and Capabilities and N.A.T.O.'s Strategic Defense." *Strategic Review* 4 (Fall 1976), 95–107.

4324.   Booth, Ken. "N.A.T.O. Ground Forces and the Soviet Threat." *Army Quarterly* 101 (July 1971), 426–436.

4325.   Borawski, John. "Mutual Force Reductions in Europe from a Soviet Perspective." *Orbis* 22 (Winter 1979), 845–873.

4326.   Brown,Dallas C., Jr. "Conventional Warfare in Europe: The Soviet View." *Military Review* 55 (February 1975), 58–71.

4327.   Buteux, Pierre. "Theater Nuclear Weapons and European Security." *Canadian Journal of Political Science* 10 (December 1977), 781–808.

4328.   Bykov, V. L. "The U.S.S.R. and Security in Europe: A Soviet View." *Annals of the American Academy of Political and Social Science* 414 (July 1974), 96–104.

4329.   Canby, Steven L. "Regaining a Conventional Military Balance in Europe: Precision-Guided Munitions and Immobilizing the Tank." *Military Review* 55 (June 1975), 26–38.

4330.   Clarke, Bruce C. "The Balance of Military Power in Europe." *NATO's Fifteen Nations* 7 (June-July 1962), 58–62.

4331.   _____ . "The Balance of Military Power in Europe." *Army* 13 (December 1962), 46–52.

4332.   Coffey, Joseph I. "Arms Control and the Military Balance in Europe." *Orbis* 17 (Spring 1973), 132–154.

4333.   Cohen, Samuel T. "Tactical Nuclear Weapons and U.S. Military Strategy." *Orbis* 15 (Spring 1971), 178–183.

4334.   Cross, Roy, and William Green. "If Russia Strikes in Europe." *Aero Digest* 61 (December 1950), 17–19.

4335.   DeBorchgrave, André. "The Nightmare for N.A.T.O." *Newsweek* 89 (February 7, 1977), 36–38.

4336.   Douglass, JosephD., Jr. "Soviet Nuclear Strategy in Europe: A Selective Targeting Doctrine?" *Strategic Review* 5 (Fall 1977), 19–32.

4337.   Dupuy, Trevor N. "Tactical Nuclear Combat." *Ordnance* 53 (November-December 1968), 292–296.

4338.   Dyer, Philip W. "Tactical Nuclear Weapons and Deterrence in Europe." *Political Science Quarterly* 92 (Summer 1977), 245–257.

4339.   Elliott, A. L. "The Calculus of Surprise Attack." *Air University Review* 30 (March-April 1979), 56–67.

4340.   Enthoven, Alain C. "Arms and Men: The Military Balance in Europe." *Interplay* 2 (October 1969), 11–14.

4341.   Erickson, John. "The European Military Balance." In Grayson Kirk and Nils H. Wessell, eds., *The Soviet Threat: Myths and Realities.* New York: Praeger, 1978. pp. 110–121.

4342.   _____ . "European Security: Soviet Preferences and Priorities." *Strategic Review* 4 (Winter 1976), 37–43.

4343.   _____ . "N.A.T.O.'s Balancing Act." *Current History* 77 (November 1979), 145–147.

4344.   _____ . "Soviet Military Capabilities in Europe." *Journal of the Royal United Service Institute for Defence Studies* 120 (March 1975), 65–69.

4345.   _____ . "Soviet Military Capabilities in Europe." *Military Review* 56 (January 1976), 58–65.

4346.   Fowler, Delbert M. "How Many Divisions?: A N.A.T.O.-Warsaw Pact Assessment." *Military Review* 52 (November 1972), 76–88.

4347.   Fromm, Joseph. "New Alarm over the Russian Threat." *U.S. News and World Report* 85 (October 30, 1978), 47–53.

4348.   Gallois, Pierre M. "Soviet Military Doctrine and European Defense." *Conflict Studies,* no. 96 (June 1978), 1–20.

4349.   Gill, R. Rockingham. "Europe's Military Balance since Czechoslovakia." *East Europe* 17 (October 1968), 17–21.

4350.   Goodpaster, Andrew J. "N.A.T.O. Today: The Russian Threat—An Address, September 2, 1971." *Vital Speeches* 37 (October 1, 1971), 43–49.

4351.   Gray, Colin S. "Theater Nuclear Weapons: Doctrines and Postures." *World Politics* 28 (January 1976), 300–314.

4352.   Gruenther, A. M. "Can Europe Be Defended?" *U.S. News and World Report* 35 (September 11, 1953), 44–51.

4353.   Hadley, Arthur T. "Our Underequipped, Unprepared N.A.T.O. Forces—The Surprising Soviet Lead in Technology and Tactics: Reprinted from the *Washington Post,* June 4–5, 1978." In U.S. Congress, Joint Economic Committee, Subcommittee on Priorities and Economy in Government, *Allocation of Resources in the Soviet Union and China, 1978: Soviet Union—Hearings.* 95th Cong., 2d sess. Washington, D.C.: U.S. Government Printing Office, 1978. IV: 103–111.

4354.   Haig, Alexander M., Jr. "Europe's New Balance of Power: An Interview." *U.S. News and World Report* 84 (June 5, 1978), 20–22.

4355. Hinterhoff, Eugene. "The Problem of the Defence of Europe." *NATO's Fifteen Nations* 12 (October-November 1967), 39, 42–44.

4356. _____ . "The Russian Threat since Czechoslovakia." *Military Review* 50 (June 1970), 68–73.

4357. Hunt, Kenneth. "The Soviet Theater Threat—Today and Tomorrow." *Conflict* 2 (1980), 149–158.

4358. International Institute for Strategic Studies. "The Military Balance between N.A.T.O. and the Warsaw Pact." *Air Force Magazine* 54 (December 1971), 104–110; 55 (December 1972), 68–71; 56 (December 1973), 80–85; 57 (December 1974), 96–103; 58 (December 1975), 96–104; 59 (December 1976), 98–106; 60 (December 1977), 118–126; 61 (December 1978), 111–116; 62 (December 1979), 120–125; 63 (December 1980), 121–124.

4359. Jones, David C. "Reappraising the Prospects for N.A.T.O." *Strategic Review* 2 (Fall 1974), 9–12.

4360. Kahler, Miles. "Rumors of War: The 1914 Analogy." *Foreign Affairs* 58 (Winter 1979–1980), 374–396.

4361. Keller, Jack B., Jr. "Opposing Forces Europe: A New Perspective." *Military Intelligence* 6 (October-December 1980), 51–52.

4362. Keller, John W. "The Czech Crisis and the European Balance of Power." *Midwest Quarterly* 11 (April 1970), 243–261.

4363. Khvostov, V. "The U.S.S.R. and European Security." *International Affairs* (Moscow), no. 2 (February 1968), 3–7.

4364. Kleiman, Robert. "How Strong Is Russia in Europe?" *U.S. News and World Report* 30 (May 4, 1951), 32–36.

4365. Kock, F. H. C. "Problems of Comparing Force Levels." *NATO Letter* 19 (March-April 1971), 19–22.

4366. Luttwak, Edward N. "Defense Reconsidered." *Commentary* 63 (March 1977), 51–58.

4367. Mackintosh, Malcolm. "Soviet Aims and Capabilities in Europe." *Journal of the Royal United Service Institution* 116 (March 1971), 22–30.

4368. Menaul, Stewart. "The Use of Nuclear Weapons in the European Theater." *NATO's Fifteen Nations* 20 (April-May 1975), 30–38.

4369.　　"Military Strength of the U.S.S.R. and the N.A.T.O. Powers." *Political Quarterly* 31 (January 1960), 71–88.

4370.　　Miller, Martin J. "N.A.T.O. and Communist Tanks." *Armor* 74 (May-June 1965), 15–18; (September-October 1965), 2–3.

4371.　　Montgomery, Bernard. "Russia's Rising Military Might." *U.S. News and World Report* 36 (June 4, 1954), 45.

4372.　　Moorer, Thomas H. "An Assessment of N.A.T.O. and Warsaw Pact Force Capabilities." *Defense Management Journal* 9 (October 1973), 7–11.

4373.　　"N.A.T.O., European Security, and the New Weapons Technology." *Orbis* 19 (Summer 1975), 461–532.

4374.　　Nitze, Paul. "The Relationship of Strategic and Theater Nuclear Forces." *International Security Review* 2 (Fall 1977), 122–132.

4375.　　Nunn, Sam. "Gearing Up to Deter Combat in Europe: An Address, September 11, 1976." *Vital Speeches* 43 (November 1, 1976), 49–52.

4376.　　———. "The New Soviet Threat to N.A.T.O." *Reader's Digest* 111 (July 1977), 73–77.

4377.　　———, and Dewey F. Bartlett. "N.A.T.O. and the New Soviet Threat: Excerpts from the Report, January 24, 1977." *Atlantic Community Quarterly* 15 (Spring 1977), 18–32.

4378.　　Owen, John. "N.A.T.O. and the Warsaw Pact." *Contemporary Review* 114 (March 1980), 123–128.

4379.　　Ranger, Robin. "M.B.F.R.: Political or Technical Arms Control?" *World Today* 30 (October 1974), 411–418.

4380.　　Rattinger, Hans. "Armament, Detente, and Bureaucracy: The Case of the Arms Race in Europe." *Journal of Conflict Resolution* 19 (December 1975), 571–595.

4381.　　"Russia's Edge in Men and Arms if War Comes: Line-up of Opposing Ground Forces." *U.S. News and World Report* 24 (April 2, 1948), 23–25.

4382.　　Saunders, Richard M. "The Soviet Buildup: Why Does the Threat Grow?" *Military Review* 60 (April 1980), 61–71.

4383.　　Schneider, William, Jr. "Changes in the Soviet Defense Posture in Europe." *Journal of Social and Political Studies* 2 (Summer 1977), 67–71.

4384.   Sixsmith, E. K. "The Military Situation in Europe." *Army Quarterly* 95 (January 1968), 134–138.

4385.   "Soviet Forces in Europe." *An Cosantoir* 12 (December 1952), 573–576.

4386.   Stevens, Philip. "N.A.T.O. and the Warsaw Pact: An Assessment." *Military Review* 58 (September 1978), 34–42.

4387.   Strafer, Kenneth J. "The Soviet Threat to Corps General Support Centers." *Army Logistician* 9 (July-August 1977), 6–9.

4388.   Turbiville, Graham H., Jr. "Intervention in Yugoslavia: An Assessment of the Soviet Military Option." *Strategic Review* 5 (Winter 1977), 62–73.

4389.   "The U.S.S.R. and the N.A.T.O. Powers: The Military Balance." *Air Force* 43 (March 1960), 38–45.

4390.   United States. Congressional Budget Office. "The Unfavorable Warsaw Pact/N.A.T.O. Force Ratio and NORTHAG Vulnerabilities." *Strengthening N.A.T.O.—POMCUS and Other Approaches: A Background Study.* Washington, D.C.: U.S. Government Printing Office, 1979. pp. 9–26.

4391.   Vigor, Peter H., and Christopher N. Donnelly. "The Soviet Threat to Europe." *Journal of the Royal United Service Institute for Defence Studies* 120 (March 1975), 69–75.

4392.   "Wave of Worries Piles Up for N.A.T.O." *U.S. News and World Report* 82 (January 17, 1977), 33–34.

4393.   Wolfe, Thomas W. "Trends in Soviet Thinking on Theater Warfare and Limited War." In John Erickson, ed., *The Military-Technical Revolution.* New York: Praeger, 1966. pp. 52–80.

4394.   Young, Frederick W. "The Military Balance in Europe." *Military Review* 58 (March 1978), 38–45.

DOCUMENTS, PAPERS, AND REPORTS

4395.   Bertram, Christopher, ed. *New Conventional Weapons and East-West Security.* New York: Praeger, 1979. 97p.

4396.   Brown, Neville. *European Security, 1972–1980.* London: Royal United Service Institute for Defence Studies, 1972. 168p.

4397.   Buchan, Alastair, et al. *The Soviet Threat to Europe: An Analysis of Soviet Potentials and Intentions.* London: Foreign Affairs Publishing, 1969. 78p.

4398.   Burrell, Raymond E. *Strategic Nuclear Parity and N.A.T.O. Defense Doctrine.* NSA Monograph 78-4. Washington, D.C.: Defense Directorate, National Defense University, 1978. 34p.

4399.   Cliffe, Trevor. *Military Technology and the European Balance.* Adelphi papers, no. 89. London: International Institute for Strategic Studies, 1972. 58p.

4400.   Davis, Jacquelyn K., and Robert L. Pfaltzgraff. *Soviet Theater Strategy: Implications for N.A.T.O.* Washington, D.C.: United States Strategic Institute, 1978. 54p.

4401.   Douglass, Joseph D., Jr. *The Soviet Theater Nuclear Offensive.* Research Note, no. 201. Arlington, Va.: System Planning Corporation, 1975. 88p.

4402.   Erickson, John. *Soviet Theater Warfare Capability.* Waverly Occasional Papers. Edinburgh, Scotland: Department of Politics, Edinburgh University, 1975.

4403.   Foster, R. B. *Soviet Reactions to U.S./N.A.T.O. Force Modernization.* DNA-4265F-1. 2 vols. Arlington, Va.: Strategic Studies Center, Sri International, 1977.

4404.   Gray, Colin S. *Defending N.A.T.O.-Europe: Forward Defense and Nuclear Strategy.* Croton-on-Hudson, N.Y.: Hudson Institute, 1977. 59p.

4405.   _____. *The Geopolitics of the Nuclear Era: Heartland, Rimlands, and the Technological Revolution.* New York: National Strategy Information Center, 1977. 70p.

4406.   McPeak, William S., Jr. *Surprise and the New Soviet Threat in Europe.* New York: U.S. Army Institute for Advanced Russian and East European Studies, 1977. 40p.

4407.   Prendergast, William B. *Mutual and Balanced Force Reduction: Issues and Prospects.* Washington, D.C.: American Enterprise Institute for Public Policy Research, 1978. 75p.

4408.   Royal United Service Institute for Defence Studies. *Report of a Seminar: The Future of the Battle Tank in a European Conflict.* London, 1975.

4409.   Snyder, Jack L. *The Soviet Strategic Culture: Implications for Limited Nuclear Operations.* RAND Report R-2154-AF. Santa Monica, Calif.: RAND Corporation, 1977. 40p.

4410.   Tillson, John C. F. *The Forward Defense of Europe.* ACIS Research Notes, no. 5. Los Angeles, Calif.: Center for International and Strategic Studies, University of California, 1979. 18p.

4411.   United States. Congress. House. Committee on Foreign Affairs. *N.A.T.O. and Western Security in the 1980's—The European Perspective: Report.* 96th Cong., 2d sess. Washington, D.C.: U.S. Government Printing Office, 1980. 78p.

4412.   United States. Congress. Senate. Committee on Armed Services. *N.A.T.O. and the New Soviet Threat: Report of Senator Sam Nunn and Senator Dewey F. Bartlett.* 95th Cong., 1st sess. Washington, D.C.: U.S. Government Printing Office, 1977. 78p.

4413.   United States. Congressional Budget Office. *Assessing the N.A.T.O./Warsaw Pact Military Balance.* Washington, D.C.: U.S. Government Printing Office, 1977. 60p.

4414.   Vernon, Graham D. *Soviet Options for War in Europe: Nuclear or Conventional?* NSA Monograph 79-1. Washington, D.C.: Research Directorate, National Defense University, 1979. 27p.

4415.   Vincent, R. J. *Military Power and Political Influence: The Soviet Union and Western Europe.* Adelphi papers, no. 119. London: International Institute for Strategic Studies, 1975.

4416.   Wolfe, Thomas W. *Soviet Attitudes toward M.B.F.R. and the U.S.S.R.'s Military Presence in Europe.* RAND Paper P-4819. Santa Monica, Calif.: RAND Corporation, 1972. 17p.

4417.   _____ . *Soviet Military Capabilities and Intentions in Europe.* RAND Paper P-5188. Santa Monica, Calif.: RAND Corporation, 1974. 42p.

Further References

See also section 5:A:1 and 2 and other parts of subsection 5:B.

2. The Warsaw Pact and Eastern Europe

a. GENERAL WORKS

BOOKS

4418.   Brown, James F. *The New Eastern Europe: The Khrushchev Era and After.* New York: Praeger, 1966. 306p.

4419.   Brzezinski, Zbigniew K. *The Soviet Bloc: Unity and Conflict.* Rev. and enl. ed. Cambridge, Mass.: Harvard University Press, 1967. 599p.

4420.   Byrnes, Robert F. *East Central Europe under the Communists.* 7 vols. New York: Praeger, 1956–1957.

4421.   Dornberg, John. *Eastern Europe: A Communist Kaleidoscope.* New York: Dial Press, 1980. 320p.

4422.   Fischer-Galati, Stephen A., ed. *Eastern Europe in the Sixties.* New York: Praeger, 1963. 239p.

4423.   Gluckstein, Ygael. *Stalin's Satellites in Europe.* Boston, Mass.: Beacon Press, 1952. 333p.

4424.   Kane, Robert S. *Eastern Europe, A to Z.* Garden City, N.Y.: Doubleday, 1968. 348p.

4425.   Mechan, John F. *The Warsaw Treaty Organization.* Boulder, Colo.: University of Colorado Press, 1970.

4426.   Owen, John. *Brassey's Warsaw Pact Infantry and Its Weapons.* Boulder, Colo.: Westview Press, 1976. 116p.

4427.   Remington, Robin A. *The Changing Soviet Perception of the Warsaw Pact.* Cambridge, Mass.: Center for International Studies, Massachusetts Institute of Technology, 1967.

4428.   _____ . *The Warsaw Pact: Case Studies in Communist Conflict Resolution.* Cambridge, Mass.: M.I.T. Press, 1971. 268p.

4429.   Schoepflin, George, ed. *The Soviet Union and Eastern Europe.* New York: Praeger, 1970. 614p.

4430.   Skilling, H. Gordon. *The Governments of Communist Eastern Europe.* New York: T. Y. Crowell, 1966. 256p.

4431.   Starr, Richard F. *Communist Regimes in Eastern Europe.* 3d ed., rev. Stanford, Calif.: Hoover Institution Press, 1978. 302p.

4432.   Steele, Jonathan, comp. *Eastern Europe Since Stalin.* London: David & Charles, 1974. 215p.

4433.   Wiener, Friedrich, and William J. Lewis. *The Warsaw Pact Armies: Organization, Concept of War, Weapons and Equipment.* Vienna, Austria: Carl Ueberreuter Publishers, 1977. 388p.   In English.

4434.   Antosyak, A. V. "The Warsaw Pact: A Defensive Alliance of Socialist States." *International Review of Military History,* no. 44 (1979), 220–232.

ARTICLES

4435.   "Armed Forces of the Warsaw Treaty Member Countries."
Soviet Military Review, no. 9 (September 1968), 22–23.

4436.   Baird, Gregory C. *"Glavnoe Komandovanie:* The Soviet Theater Command." *Naval War College Review* 32 (May-June 1980), 40–48.

4437.   Baranski, Wojcech. "Our Common Concern and Common Responsibility: Translated from *Kraznaya Zvezda,* August 14, 1968." *Current Digest of the Soviet Press* 20 (September 4, 1968), 5–6.

4438.   Baritz, Joseph J. "The Warsaw Pact and the Kremlin's European Strategy." *Institute for the Study of the USSR Bulletin* 17 (May 1970), 15–28.

4439.   Bender, Peter. "Inside the Warsaw Pact." *Survival* 12 (1970), 74–75, 253–269.

4440.   Boll, Michael M. "The Dilemma of the Warsaw Pact." *Military Review* 49 (July 1969), 89–95.

4441.   Braun, Aurel. "The Evolution of the Warsaw Pact." *Canadian Defence Quarterly* 3 (Winter 1973–1974), 27–36.

4442.   Garthoff, Raymond L. "The Military Establishment." *East Europe* 14 (September 1965), 2–12.

4443.   Gierek, Edward. "Important Factor of Peace and Internal Security." *World Marxist Review* 23 (May 1980), 3–5.

4444.   Gosztony, Peter I. "Shield and Sword: Thoughts on the 20th Anniversary of the Founding of the Warsaw Pact." *Military Review* 55 (December 1975), 81–92.

4445.   Griswold, Laurence. "The Warsaw Pact: Brood of the Bear." *Sea Power* 18 (April 1975), 27–32.

4446.   Gromyko, Andrei A. "The Warsaw Pact Is Twenty Years Old: Translated from *Pravda,* May 15, 1975." *Current Digest of the Soviet Press* 27 (June 11, 1975), 6–8.

4447.   Haigh, Patricia. "Reflections on the Warsaw Pact." *World Today* 24 (April 1968), 166–172.

4448.   Handler, M. S. "Satellite Armies Set at One Million: Reprinted from the *New York Times,* August 22, 1950." In Walter M. Daniels, ed., *Defense of Western Europe.* Reference Shelf, v. 22, no. 5. New York: H. W. Wilson, 1950. pp. 99–101.

4449.   Henning, Elaine M. "The Warsaw Pact: A Soviet Response." *Military Review* 55 (September 1975), 46–49.

4450.   Herspring, Dale R. "Technology and the Political Officer in the Polish and East German Armed Forces." *Studies in Comparative Communism* (Winter 1977), 393.

4451.   _____ . "The Warsaw Pact at 25." *Problems of Communism* 29 (September-October 1980), 1–15.

4452.   _____ , and Ivan Volgyes. "Political Reliability in the Eastern European Warsaw Pact Armies." *Armed Forces and Society* 6 (Winter 1980), 270–296.

4453.   Hinterhoff, Eugene. "The Military Potential of the Warsaw Pact." *East and West* 2 (July 1956), 22.

4454.   Holloway, David. "The Warsaw Pact in the Era of Negotiation." *Military Review* 53 (July 1973), 49–55.

4455.   Iakubovskiy, Ivan. "On Guard over the Gains of Socialism: Translated from *Pravda,* May 14, 1971." *Current Digest of the Soviet Press* 12 (June 25, 1971), 57–62.

4456.   Johnson, A. Ross. "Soviet-East European Military Relations: An Overview." In Dale R. Herspring and Ivan Volgyes, eds., *Civil-Military Relations in the Communist System.* Boulder, Colo.: Westview Press, 1978. Chpt. 12.

4457.   Jones, Christopher D. "Soviet Hegemony in Eastern Europe: The Dynamics of Political Autonomy and Military Intervention." *World Politics* 29 (January 1977), 216–241.

4458.   _____ . "The Warsaw Pact: Military Exercises and Military Interventions." *Armed Forces and Society* 7 (Fall 1980), 5–30.

4459.   Kamstra, Jerry. "Origins and Evolution of the Warsaw Pact." *Countermeasures* 2 (October 1976), 40–41.

4460.   Kime, Steve F. "The Kremlin and the Pact." *Defense '81,* no. 2 (February 1981), 10–13.

4461.   Kiraly, Bela K. "Why the Soviets Need the Warsaw Pact." *East Europe* 18 (April 1969), 8–17.

4462.   Korbonski, Andrzej. "The Warsaw Pact." *International Conciliation,* no. 573 (May 1969), 5–73.

4463.   Krisch, Henry. "Soviet Policy toward the Warsaw Pact." *Studies for a New Central Europe* 2 (Winter 1968–1969), 101–111.

4464. Krystev, T. "Warsaw Pact Deputy Chief of Staff on Mission and Tasks: Translated from *Sovetskiy Patriot,* May 14, 1978." *Translations on USSR Military Affairs,* no. 1369 (August 9, 1978), 59–63.

4465. Kulikov, Viktor G. "Kulikov on Warsaw Pact Tasks, Accomplishments: Translated from *Voyenno Istoricheskiy Zhurnal,* November 1977." *Translations on USSR Military Affairs,* no. 1326 (January 25, 1978), 42–52.

4466. _____ . "Marshal Kulikov on Warsaw Pact Tasks and Organization: Translated from *Agitator,* April 1980." *Translations on USSR Military Affairs,* no. 1529 (August 25, 1980), 105–111.

4467. _____ . "Marshal Kulikov on Warsaw Pact 25th Anniversary: Translated from *Voyenno Istoricheskiy Zhurnal,* May 1980." *Translations on USSR Military Affairs,* no. 1532 (September 10, 1980), 22–32.

4468. Kulski, W. W. "The Soviet System of Collective Security Compared With the Western System." *American Journal of International Law* 43 (July 1950), 453–476.

4469. Lider, Julian. "The Socialist Armed Forces." *On the Nature of Military Force.* Brookfield, Vt.: Renouf/U.S.A., 1980. Chpt. 5.

4470. Mackintosh, Malcolm. "The Evolution of the Warsaw Pact." In James L. Moulton, ed., *Brassey's Annual: The Armed Forces Yearbook.* New York: Praeger, 1969. pp. 127–141.

4471. _____ . "The Satellite Armies." In Basil H. Liddell-Hart, ed., *The Soviet Army.* London: Weidenfeld & Nicolson, 1956. pp. 6–13.

4472. _____ . "The Warsaw Pact Today." *Survival* 16 (May-June 1974), 122–126.

4473. Malakhov, G. "Warsaw Pact Organization and Tasks Discussed: Translated from *Kommunist Vooruzhennykh Sil,* July 1978." *Translations on USSR Military Affairs,* no. 1385 (October 11, 1978), 33–42.

4474. Mazza, Ugo. "The Eastern Alliance." *Armies and Weapons* 3 (July 15–September 15, 1974), 48–52.

4475. Merezhko, A. "Warsaw Pact—Tasks and Accomplishments Reviewed: Translated from *Kommunist Vooruzhennykh Sil,* May 1980." *Translations on USSR Military Affairs,* no. 1526 (July 31, 1980), 114–123.

4476. Orlov, A. "The Birth of Brotherhood." *Soviet Military Review,* no. 5 (May 1980), 9–11.

4477. Papp, Daniel S. "Dependence and Interdependence in the Warsaw Pact." *Parameters* 8 (June 1978), 57–70.

4478.   Papworth, Peter M. "The Integrity of the Warsaw Pact." *Air University Review* 28 (March-June 1977), 16–23, 47–59.

4479.   Patrick, Stephen B. "Red Star, White Star: Warsaw Pact and N.A.T.O. Forces in the 1970's." *Strategy and Tactics,* no. 36 (January-February 1973), 18–34.

4480.   Petersen, Philip A. "Military Intervention as a Solution to Soviet Problems in the Balkans." In Philip A. Petersen, ed., *Soviet Policy in the Post-Tito Balkans.* Studies in Communist Affairs, no. 4. Washington, D.C.: U.S. Government Printing Office, 1979. pp. 93–118.

4481.   Podkopayev, Leonid. "Unity among Warsaw Pact Countries Stressed: Translated from *Armeyski Kommunist,* no. 4, 1980." *Translations on USSR Military Affairs,* no. 1523 (July 9, 1980), 35–42.

4482.   Remington, Robin A. "The Warsaw Pact: Communist Coalition Politics in Action." In *The Yearbook of World Affairs, 1973.* New York: Praeger, 1974. pp. 153–172.

4483.   Rubin, F. "The Collective Treatment of Defence in the Warsaw Pact States." *Journal of the Royal United Service Institute for Defence Studies* 123 (December 1978), 43–49.

4484.   Shirk, Paul R. "The Warsaw Treaty Organization." *Military Review* 49 (May 1969), 28–37.

4485.   Smogorzewski, Kazimierz M. "The Soviet Satellite Armies in Europe." *Fortnightly* 176 (September 1951), 597–604; (October 1951), 657–666.

4486.   "Soviet Bloc Military Integration." *Intelligence Digest,* no. 320 (July 1965), 7–8.

4487.   Starr, Richard F. "The East European Alliance System." *U.S. Naval Institute Proceedings* 90 (September 1964), 26–39.

4488.   _____ . "How Strong Is the Soviet Bloc?" *Current History* 45 (October 1963), 209–215.

4489.   _____ . "Soviet Policies in Eastern Europe." *Current History* 77 (October 1979), 119–123; 79 (October 1980), 75–79.

4490.   _____ . "Soviet Relations with East Europe." *Current History* 74 (April 1978), 145–149.

4491.   Steger, George F. "A Warsaw Pact Front Commander's Concept." *Military Review* 58 (April 1978), 2–4.

4492.   Stevens, Leslie C. "The Present and Potential Military Capabilities of the Soviet Bloc." In Charles G. Haines, ed., *The Threat of Soviet Imperialism*. Baltimore, Md.: Johns Hopkins Press, 1954. pp. 188–199.

4493.   "Strengthening the Combat Readiness Is Our Chief Task: Translated from *Krasnaya Zvezda*, August 13, 1968." *Current Digest of the Soviet Press* 20 (September 4, 1968), 5.

4494.   Summerscale, Peter. "Eastern Europe in the Wake of Afghanistan." *World Today* 36 (May 1980), 172–179.

4495.   Thayer, C. W. "Can Russia Trust Her Slave Armies?" *Saturday Evening Post* 227 (August 7, 1954), 30.

4496.   Tiedtke, Jutta, and Stephen. "The Soviet Union's Internal Problems and the Development of the Warsaw Treaty Organization." In Egbert Jahn, ed., *Soviet Foreign Policy: Its Social and Economic Conditions*. New York: St. Martin's Press, 1978. pp. 114–157.

4497.   Titov, L. "Warsaw Pact—Purpose and Development Reviewed: Translated from *Agitator Armii I Flota*, February 1980." *Translations on USSR Military Affairs,* no. 1512 (May 2, 1980), 8–12.

4498.   "Trends in Warsaw Pact Military Developments." *NATO Review* 21 (July-August 1973), 8–11.

4499.   United States. Department of Defense. Defense Intelligence Agency. "The Warsaw Pact." *Handbook on the Soviet Armed Forces.* DDB-2680-40-78. Washington, D.C., 1978. pp. 3/1–3/5.

4500.   Van den Berk, L. J. M. "After the Biggest Manoeuvres in German History: Military Developments in Poland, Czechoslovakia, and East Germany." *NATO's Fifteen Nations* 11 (June-July 1966), 102–104.

4501.   Volz, Arthur G. "Standardization in the Warsaw Pact." *Armor* 88 (March-April 1979), 22–26.

4502.   Wandycz, P. S. "The Soviet System of Alliances in East-Central Europe." *Journal of Central European Affairs* 16 (July 1956), 177–184.

4503.   "The Warsaw Pact." *Military Review* 47 (October 1967), 18–21.

4504.   "Warsaw Pact Military Power." *NATO Review* 20 (July-August 1972), 13–16.

4505.   Whetten, Lawrence L. "The Warsaw Pact Threat in the 1970's." *NATO's Fifteen Nations* 15 (October-November 1970), 20–28.

4506.   Williams, Forrest D. "The Warsaw Pact: 6'6" and Growing." *U.S. Army Aviation Digest* 27 (February 1981), 33–35.

4507.   Wolfe, Thomas W. "The Warsaw Pact in Evolution." *World Today* 22 (May 1966), 191–198.

4508.   ———. "The Warsaw Pact in Evolution." In Kurt London, ed., *Eastern Europe in Transition*. Baltimore, Md.: Johns Hopkins Press, 1966. pp. 207–235.

4509.   Zhukov, Georgiy K. "A Reliable Instrument of Peace—The Warsaw Treaty Organization: Twenty Years." *International Affairs* (Moscow), no. 6 (June 1975), 48–56.

DOCUMENTS, PAPERS, AND REPORTS

4510.   Burt, Donald L. *The Warsaw Treaty Organization: An Appraisal.* Professional Study, no. 4087. Maxwell AFB, Ala.: Air War College, Air University, 1971. 30p.

4511.   Canby, Steven L. *N.A.T.O. Military Policy—Obtaining Conventional Comparability with the Warsaw Pact: A Report.* RAND Report R-1088-ARPA. Santa Monica, Calif.: RAND Corporation, 1973. 94p.

4512.   Erickson, John. *Soviet-Warsaw Pact Force Levels.* Report, no. 76-2. Washington, D.C.: United States Strategic Institute, 1976. 40p.

4513.   Johnson, A. Ross. *East European Military Establishments: The Warsaw Pact Northern Tier [of Czechoslovakia, East Germany, and Poland].* RAND Report R-2417/1-AF/FF. Santa Monica, Calif.: RAND Corporation, 1980. 218p.

4514.   ———. *Has East Central Europe Become a Liability to the U.S.S.R.: The Military Aspect.* RAND Paper P-5383. Santa Monica, Calif.: RAND Corporation, 1975. 29p.

4515.   ———. *Soviet-East European Military Relations: An Overview.* RAND Paper P-5383-1. Santa Monica, Calif.: RAND Corporation, 1977. 29p.

4516.   ———. *The Warsaw Pact's Campaign for "European Security."* RAND Report R-565-PR. Santa Monica, Calif.: RAND Corporation, 1970. 91p.

4517.   Kanet, Roger E. *East Europe and the Warsaw Treaty Organization: The Question of Reliability.* Research Memorandum. Carlisle Barracks, Pa.: Strategic Studies Institute, U.S. Army War College, 1978. 21p.

4518.   Kolkowicz, Roman, ed. *The Warsaw Pact: Report on a Conference on the Warsaw Treaty Organization, Held at the Institute for Defense Analysis, May 17–19, 1967.* Research Paper, no. P-496. Arlington, Va.: International and Social Studies Division, Institute for Defense Analysis, 1969.

4519.   Korbonski, Andrzej. *The Warsaw Pact.* New York: Carnegie Endowment for International Peace, 1969. 73p.

4520.   Mackintosh, Malcolm. *The Evolution of the Warsaw Pact.* Adelphi papers, no. 58. London: Institute for Strategic Studies, 1969. 25p.

4521.   North Atlantic Treaty Organization. Information Service. *The Atlantic Alliance and the Warsaw Pact: A Comparative Study.* Brussels, Belgium, [1972?]. 30p.

4522.   Stakutis, V. J. *The Effect of Weather on N.A.T.O./Warsaw Pact Air/Ground Operations.* MTR-3300-ESD-TR-76-292. Bedford, Mass.: Mitre Corporation, 1977. 90p.

4523.   United States. Congress. House. Committee on Armed Services. Special Subcommittee on National Defense Posture. *Review of a Systems Analysis Evaluation of N.A.T.O. vs. Warsaw Pact Conventional Forces: A Report.* 90th Cong., 2d sess. Washington, D.C.: U.S. Government Printing Office, 1968. 15p.

4524.   United States. Congress. Senate. Committee on Government Operations. Subcommittee on National Security and International Operations. *The Warsaw Pact—Its Role in Soviet Bloc Affairs: A Study.* 89th Cong., 2d sess. Washington, D.C.: U.S. Government Printing Office, 1966. 49p.

4525.   United States. Department of Defense. Defense Intelligence Agency. *Soviet/Warsaw Pact Ground Force Camouflage and Concealment Techniques.* DDI-1100-161-78. Washington, D.C., 1978. 34p.

4526.   United States. Department of the Army. *Opposing Forces: Europe.* FM 30-102. Washington, D.C., 1977.   Various paging.

4527.   Wise, R. A., et al. *A Model of Vehicle Activity in the Warsaw Pact Tactical Rear during a Conventional Attack Against N.A.T.O.* RAND Report R/N-1495-AF. Santa Monica, Calif.: RAND Corporation, 1980. 120p.

4528.   Wolfe, Thomas W. *The Evolving Nature of the Warsaw Pact.* RAND Memorandum RM-4835-PR. Santa Monica, Calif.: RAND Corporation, 1965.

4529.   _____ . *The Role of the Warsaw Pact in Soviet Policy.* RAND Paper P-4973. Santa Monica, Calif.: RAND Corporation, 1973. 19p.

Further References

See also sections 5:A:2 and 5:B:1, and other parts of this section.

b. CZECHOSLOVAKIA (INCLUDING THE 1968 INVASION)

BOOKS

4530.   Chapman, Colin. *August 21st: The Rape of Czechoslovakia.* Philadelphia, Pa.: Lippincott, 1968. 123p.

4531.   Czechoslovak Academy of Sciences. Institute of History. *The Czech Black Book.* Edited by Robert Littell. New York: Praeger, 1969. 303p.

4532.   Czerwinski, Edward J., and Janusz Piekalkiewicz, eds. *The Soviet Invasion of Czechoslovakia: Its Effects on Eastern Europe.* New York: Praeger, 1972. 210p.

4533.   Hejzlar, Zdenek, and Vladimir V. Kusin. *Czechoslovakia, 1968–1969.* New York: Garland, 1975. 316p.

4534.   Kalvoda, Josef. *Czechoslovakia's Role in Soviet Strategy.* Washington, D.C.: University Press of America, 1978. 396p.

4535.   Levine, Isaac D. *Intervention.* New York: David McKay, 1969. 152p.

4536.   Levy, Alan. *Rowboat to Prague.* New York: Grossman, 1972. 531p.

4537.   Mastny, Vojtech, ed. *Czechoslovakia: Crisis in World Communism.* New York: Facts on File, 1972. 392p.

4538.   Mejerik, Avraham G., ed. *Invasion and Occupation of Czechoslovakia and the U.N.* New York: International Review Service, 1968. 123p.

4539.   Mňackŏ, Ladislav. *The Seventh Night.* New York: E. P. Dutton, 1969. 220p.

4540.   Schwartz, Harry. *Prague's 200 Days: The Struggle for Democracy in Czechoslovakia.* New York: Praeger, 1969. 274p.

4541.   Skilling, H. Gordon. *Czechoslovakia's Interrupted Revolution.* Princeton, N.J.: Princeton University Press, 1976. 924p.

4542.   Szulc, Tad. *The Invasion of Czechoslovakia, August 1968.* New York: Franklin Watts, 1974. 66p.

4543. _____ . *Czechoslovakia since World War II.* New York: Viking Press, 1971. 503p.

4544. Valentia, Jiri. *Soviet Intervention in Czechoslovakia, 1968: Anatomy of a Decision.* Baltimore, Md.: Johns Hopkins University Press, 1979. 209p.

4545. Weisskoff, Kurt. *The Agony of Czechoslovakia.* London: Elik Books, 1968. 234p.

4546. Windsor, Philip, and Adam Roberts. *Czechoslovakia, 1968: Reform, Repression, and Resistance.* New York: Published for the Institute for Strategic Studies by Columbia University Press, 1969. 199p.

4547. Zartman, I. William. *Czechoslovakia: Intervention and Impact.* New York: New York University Press, 1970. 127p.

4548. Zeman, Zybněk A. B. *Prague Spring.* New York: Hill & Wang, 1969. 167p.

ARTICLES

4549. "Autumn for Czechoslovakia." *Agenor* 12 (October 1969), 38–41.

4550. Beer, Fritz. "Ten Weeks That Shook Czechoslovakia." *Survival* 10 (1968), 56–66.

4551. "Brutal and Stupid." *Nation* 207 (September 2, 1968), 162–164.

4552. Bryant, Christopher. "Czechoslovakia under the Occupation." *East Europe* 17 (November 1968), 12–17.

4553. _____ . "Prague Summer, 1968." *East Europe* 17 (September 1968), 7–10.

4554. "Chronology of the Czechoslovak-Soviet Confrontation, July–August 1968." *World Today* 24 (September 1968), 359.

4555. "A Chronology of Occupation." *East Europe* 17 (October 1968), 38–46.

4556. "Confrontation in Czechoslovakia." *Newsweek* 72 (August 5, 1968), 34.

4557. "The Czechoslovak Crisis." *Institute for the Study of the USSR Bulletin* 15 (September 1968), 5–9.

4558. "Czechs vs. Soviets: Defiance Rises." *U.S. News and World Report* 65 (November 18, 1968), 8.

4559.   Dawisha, Karen. "Soviet Security and the Role of the Armed Forces: The 1968 Czechoslovak Crisis." *British Journal of Political Science* 10 (July 1980), 341–363.

4560.   Djilas, Milovan. "Russia's Dangerous New Doctrine of Conquest." *Reader's Digest* 94 (January 1968), 43–47.

4561.   "Documents on Czechoslovakia." *International Legal Materials* 7 (November 1968), 1265–1339.

4562.   Floyd, David. "The Czech Crisis of 1968." In James L. Moulton, ed., *Brassey's Annual: The Armed Forces Yearbook.* New York: Praeger, 1969. pp. 33–46.

4563.   "Forces of Warsaw Alliance Occupy Czechoslovakia." *Current Digest of the Soviet Press* 20 (September 11, 1968), 1–17.

4564.   Gill, R. Rockingham. "Czechoslovakia: Will the Soviet Army Intervene?" *East Europe* 17 (July 1968), 2–6.

4565.   Goglev, M. "Central Group of Forces—Cooperative Efforts Noted: Translated from *Kommunist Vooruzhennykh Sil,* May 1980." *Translations on USSR Military Affairs,* no. 1526 (July 31, 1980), 124–132.

4566.   Heiman, Leo. "Soviet Invasion Weaknesses." *Military Review* 49 (August 1969), 38–45.

4567.   Hester, Hugh. "The Soviet Invasion of Czechoslovakia." *New Man* 20 (October-December 1968), 4–7.

4568.   Hinterhoff, Eugene. "Military Implications of the Soviet Invasion of Czechoslovakia." *Contemporary Review* 213 (November 1968), 235–240.

4569.   "Invasion: Prague's Own Story." *Newsweek* 72 (December 16, 1968), 54–55.

4570.   Kadish, Alan. "The Rape of Czechoslovakia." In Philip de St. Croix, ed., *Airborne Operations: An Illustrated Encyclopedia of the Great Battles of Airborne Forces.* New York: Crown, 1978. pp. 204–209.

4571.   Kalb, Marvin. "Enough Comrades." *New Republic* 159 (September 14, 1968), 10–15.

4572.   Karber, Philip A. "Czechoslovakia: A Scenario of the Future." *Military Review* 49 (February 1969), 11–21.

4573.   Kholodul'kin, V. "Combat Training—Soviet-Czech Exercise Described: Translated from *Krasnaya Zvezda,* June 14, 1980." *Translations on USSR Military Affairs,* no. 1539 (October 15, 1980), 44–46.

4574.   Kiraly, Bela K. "Budapest, 1956—Prague, 1968: Parallels and Contrasts." *Problems of Communism* 18 (July-August 1969), 52–66.

4575.   Kopkind, Andrew. "From Protest to Resistance: Prague under Red Guns." *Ramparts* 7 (September 28, 1968), 4–6.

4576.   Kotsch, William. "The Tanks of August 1968." *U.S. Naval Institute Proceedings* 95 (May 1969), 86–93.

4577.   Lichtheim, George. "Czechoslovakia, 1968." *Commentary* 46 (November 1968), 63–72.

4578.   "Living with the Russians." *Time* 92 (September 13, 1968), 26–27.

4579.   "Moscow's Reporting of the Invasion and Its Causes." *Current Digest of the Soviet Press* 20 (September 11, 1968), 18–23.

4580.   "The New Red Revolution—A Test of Nerves: Czech Courage vs. Soviet Steele." *U.S. News and World Report* 65 (August 5, 1968), 58–60.

4581.   North Atlantic Treaty Organization. "N.A.T.O. Communiqué on Czechoslovakia, November 16, 1968." *Current History* 56 (April 1969), 239–241.

4582.   Paul, David W. "Soviet Foreign Policy and the Invasion of Czechoslovakia." *International Studies Quarterly* 15 (June 1971), 159–202.

4583.   Polk, James H. "Reflections on the Czechoslovakia Invasion, 1968." *Strategic Review* 5 (Winter 1977), 30–37.

4584.   "The Rape of Czechoslovakia." *Reader's Digest* 93 (November 1968), 89–94.

4585.   Remington, Robin A. "Czechoslovakia and the Warsaw Pact." *East European Quarterly* 3 (1970), 315–336.

4586.   Roling, B. V. A. "The Russian Invasion of Czechoslovakia: Precautionary Measure, Not a Crusade." *Insight and Opinion* 3 (Fall 1968), 77.

4587.   Rothschild, Joseph. "The Soviet Union and Czechoslovakia." In Steven L. Spiegel and Kenneth N. Waltz, eds., *Conflict in World Politics.* Cambridge, Mass.: Winthrop, 1971. pp. 115–138.

4588.   "Russians Go Home." *Time* 92 (August 30, 1968), 22–28.

4589.   Shub, Anatole. "The Lessons of Czechoslovakia." *Foreign Affairs* 47 (January 1969), 266–280.

4590.   Sparn, Edwin. "The Czech Crisis: On-the-Spot Reports." *Senior Scholastic* 93 (September 20, 1968), 32–33.

4591.   Stolley, R. B. "The Tense Czech Watch on the Red Army." *Life* 65 (August 2, 1968), 24–27.

4592.   Taylor, Richard K. "Czech Revolution—Resisting the Invaders." *Liberation* 13 (October 1968), 21–28.

4593.   Tessadori, Henry J. "Soviet Foreign Policy as Reflected in the Hungarian and Czech Crises." *Naval War College Review* 22 (February 1969), 59–90.

4594.   "The Ugly Arrogance of Force." *Newsweek* 72 (September 9, 1968), 59–60.

4595.   Valentia, Jiri. "Bureaucratic Politics Paradigm and the Soviet Invasion of Czechoslovakia." *Political Science Quarterly* 94 (Spring 1979), 55–76.

4596.   Von Kuehnelt-Leddihn, E. M. "Invasion by Prisoners." *National Review* 20 (October 8, 1968), 1013.

4597.   Wayper, C. L. "International Affairs: Czechoslovakia—The Acid Test." *Royal Air Forces Quarterly* 8 (Winter 1968), 251–253.

4598.   Whetten, Lawrence L. "Civilian Resistance in Czechoslovakia." *World Today* 25 (February 1969), 52–68.

4599.   _____ . "Military Aspects of the Soviet Occupation of Czechoslovakia." *World Today* 25 (February 1969), 50–68.

4600.   "Woe to the Victors." *Newsweek* 72 (September 16, 1968), 45–46.

DOCUMENTS, PAPERS, AND REPORTS

4601.   Eidlin, Fred H. "The Logic of 'Normalization': The Soviet Intervention in Czechoslovakia of 21 August 1968." PhD dissertation, University of Toronto, 1980.

4602.   Herrick, R. Waring. *The Soviet Intervention in Czechoslovakia.* New York: Radio Liberty Committee, 1968. 11p.

4603.   Menges, Constantine. *Prague Resistance, 1968: The Ingenuity of Conviction.* RAND Paper P-3980. Santa Monica, Calif.: RAND Corporation, 1968. 15p.

4604.   Schuler, Wendell L. *An Analysis of the 1968 Invasion of Czecho-slovakia.* Research Study, no. 1725-71. Maxwell AFB, Ala.: Air Command and Staff College, Air University, 1971. 61p.

4605.   United States. Congress. Senate. Committee on Foreign Relations. *Czechoslovakia, 1968: Report.* 90th Cong., 2d sess. Washington, D.C.: U.S. Government Printing Office, 1968. 8p.

4606.   _____ . Committee on Government Operations. Subcommittee on National Security and International Operations. *Czechoslovakia and the Brezhnev Doctrine: Report.* 91st Cong., 1st sess. Washington, D.C.: U.S. Government Printing Office, 1969. 61p.

Further References

See also sections 5:A:1, 5:B:1, and 5:B:2:a.

c. East Germany (including the Berlin Crises)

BOOKS

4607.   Baring, Arnulf. *Uprising in East Germany, June 17, 1953.* Translated from the German. Ithaca, N.Y.: Cornell University Press, 1972. 194p.

4608.   Cate, Curtis. *The Ides of August: The Berlin Wall Crisis, 1961.* New York: Evans, 1978. 544p.

4609.   Charles, Max. *The Berlin Blockade.* London: Wingate, 1959. 175p.

4610.   Childs, David. *East Germany.* New York: Praeger, 1969. 275p.

4611.   Clay, Lucius D. *Decision in Germany.* Garden City, N.Y.: Doubleday, 1950. 522p.

4612.   _____ . *The Papers of General Lucius D. Clay.* 2 vols. Bloomington: Indiana University Press, 1974.

4613.   Collier, Richard. *Bridge across the Sky: The Berlin Blockade and Airlift, 1948–1949.* New York: McGraw-Hill, 1978. 239p.

4614.   Davison, W. Phillips. *The Berlin Blockade.* Princeton, N.J.: Princeton University Press, 1958. 423p.

4615.   Forster, Thomas M. *The East German Army: A Pattern of a Communist Military Establishment.* South Brunswick, N.J.: A. S. Barnes, 1968. 255p.

4616. Friedmann, Wolfgang. *The Allied Military Government of Germany.* London: Stevens, 1947. 362p.

4617. Hildebrandt, Rainer. *The Explosion: The Uprising behind the Iron Curtain.* Translated from the German. New York: Duell, Sloan & Pearce, 1955. 198p. The June 1953 workers insurrection in East Germany.

4618. Howley, Frank. *Berlin Command.* New York: G. P. Putnam, 1950. 276p.

4619. Klimov, Gregory. *The Terror Machine: The Inside Story of the Soviet Administration of Germany.* New York: Praeger, 1953. 400p.

4620. Man, John. *Berlin Blockade.* Ballantine's Illustrated History of the Violent Century, Politics in Action Book, no. 10. New York: Ballantine Books, 1973. 156p.

4621. Mander, John. *Berlin: The Eagle and the Bear.* London: Barrie and Rockcliff, 1959. 193p.

4622. Moreton, N. Edwina. *East Germany and the Warsaw Alliance: The Politics of Detente.* Boulder, Colo.: Westview Press, 1978. 267p.

4623. Morris, Eric. *Blockade: Berlin and the Cold War.* New York: Stein & Day, 1973. 278p.

4624. Nettl, J.P. *The Eastern Zone and Soviet Policy in Germany, 1945–1950.* London: Oxford University Press, 1951. 324p.

4625. Schick, Jack M. *The Berlin Crisis, 1958–1962.* Philadelphia: University of Pennsylvania Press, 1971. 266p.

4626. Schneider, Eberhard. *The G.D.R.: The History, Politics, Economy, and Society of East Germany.* New York: St. Martin's Press, 1978. 121p.

4627. Scriabine, Helene. *Allies on the Rhine, 1945–1950.* Translated from the French. Carbondale: Southern Illinois University Press, 1980. 158p.

4628. Slusser, Robert M. *The Berlin Crisis of 1961: Soviet-American Relations and the Struggle for Power in the Kremlin, June-November 1961.* Baltimore, Md.: Johns Hopkins University Press, 1973. 509p.

4629. Smith, Jean E. *The Defense of Berlin.* Baltimore, Md.: Johns Hopkins Press, 1963. 431p.

4630. _____ . *Germany beyond the Wall.* Boston, Mass.: Little, Brown, 1969. 338p.

4631. *The Soviet Stand on Germany.* Documents on Current History, no. 17. New York: Crosscurrents Press, 1961. 157p.

4632. Windsor, Philip. *City on Leave: A History of Berlin, 1945 –1962.* New York: Praeger, 1963. 275p.

ARTICLES

4633. Bell, J. Bowyer. "Berlin." *Besieged: Seven Cities under Siege.* Philadelphia, Pa.: Chilton Books, 1966. Chpt. 7.

4634. "Berlin: The Military Outlook." *Time* 73 (March 9, 1959), 12–13.

4635. Chervov, Nikolai. "Troop Withdrawal from East Germany Discussed—An Interview: Translated from *Novosti Daily Review,* August 1, 1980." *Translations on USSR Military Affairs,* no. 1530 (August 27, 1980), 68–72.

4636. Chopra, Maharaj K. "East German Security." *Military Review* 51 (October 1971), 12–20.

4637. Clay, Lucius D. "Berlin." *Foreign Affairs* 41 (October 1962), 47–58.

4638. Danilov, A. "Training Activities in Group of Soviet Forces in Germany: Translated from *Sovetskiy Voin,* January 1978." *Translations on USSR Military Affairs,* no. 1342 (March 29, 1978), 71–78.

4639. Flavin, Martin. "Red Blunders in Berlin." *Harper's* 203 (November 1951), 37–44.

4640. Geisenheyner, Stefan. "Soviet Forces in East Germany." *Air Force and Space Digest* 53 (February 1970), 21.

4641. Grigorkin, M. "An Army to Protect Socialism." *Soviet Military Review,* no. 2 (February 1971), 40–43.

4642. Grinkevich, D. "Staff Work Effectiveness in Group of Soviet Forces in Germany Discussed: Translated from *Krasnaya Zvezda,* July 2, 1978." *Translations on USSR Military Affairs,* no. 1387 (October 18, 1978), 4–9.

4643. Herspring, Dale R. "The Effect of Detente on Professionalism and Political Control in the East German Army." *Naval War College Review* 28 (Winter 1976), 10–20.

4644. Herz, John H. "Berlin and the Soviet Zone." In Gwendolen M. Carter and John H. Herz, eds., *Major Foreign Powers.* 4th ed. New York: Harcourt, Brace & World, 1962. pp. 459–473.

4645.   Howley, Frank L. "I've Talked 1,000 Hours with the Russians." *Reader's Digest* 54 (May 1949), 73–78.

4646.   _____ . "My Four-Year War with the Russians." *Collier's* 124 (November 5, 1949), 13–14; (November 12, 1949), 18–19; (November 19, 1949), 30; (November 26, 1949), 22; (December 3, 1949), 30–31.

4647.   Hudson, George F. "Berlin: The Menaced City." *Commentary* 27 (April 1959), 310–316.

4648.   Ivanovskiy, Yevgeniy. "Soviet General in the G.D.R. Writes on Red Army Anniversary: Translated from *Neues Deutschland,* February 20, 1978." *Translations on USSR Military Affairs,* no. 1339 (March 20, 1978), 74–78.

4649.   Jokel, G., et al. "Soviet-East German Armed Forces Cooperation Recounted: Translated from *Voyenno Istoricheskiy Zhurnal,* July 1978." *Translations on USSR Military Affairs,* no. 1387 (October 18, 1978), 44–54.

4650.   Mednikov, I. "Group of Soviet Forces in Germany—Tasks and Accomplishments: Translated from *Agitator Armii I Flota,* January 1978." *Translations on USSR Military Affairs,* no. 1336 (March 10, 1978), 77–81.

4651.   "The Modernization of Soviet Forces in Germany." *Marine Corps Gazette* 46 (August 1962), 12.

4652.   Nagornyy, V. "[General Aleksey A.] Yepishev Visits Group of Soviet Forces in Germany, 10–14 February: Translated from *Krasnaya Zvezda,* February 16, 1978." *Translations on USSR Military Affairs,* no. 1335 (March 7, 1978), 89–91.

4653.   _____ . "River Crossing Exercise in the Group of Soviet Forces in Germany Described: Translated from *Krasnaya Zvezda,* July 16, 1978." *Translations on USSR Military Affairs,* no. 1385 (October 11, 1978), 13–16.

4654.   "Order of Battle in East Germany." *Time* 56 (August 7, 1950), 26.

4655.   Palmer, Dave R. "Armor behind the Iron Curtain: Berlin." *Armor* 70 (January-February 1961), 46–48.

4656.   Pendergast, Kerry, and David Ritchie. "Berlin '85: The Enemy at the Gates." *Strategy and Tactics,* no. 79 (March-April 1979), 4–14.

4657.   "The Soviet Army in Germany." *Military Review* 41 (November 1961), 92–96.

4658.   Union of Soviet Socialist Republics. Ministry of Defense. "Agreement Concerning Questions Connected with the Presence of Soviet Forces on East German Territory, 1957." *American Journal of International Law* 52 (January 1958), 210–215.

4659.   Wolfe, Thomas W. "The Soviet Union's Strategic Stake in the G.D.R." *World Today* 27 (August 1971), 340–350.

DOCUMENTS, PAPERS, AND REPORTS

4660.   Baras, Victor. "East Germany in Soviet Foreign Policy: The Objectives of the New Course and the Impact of the Uprising of June 17, 1953." PhD dissertation, Cornell University, 1973.

4661.   Croan, Melvin. *East Germany: The Soviet Connection.* Washington Papers, v. 4, no. 36. Beverly Hills, Calif.: Sage, 1976. 71p.

4662.   Finke, Blythe F. *Berlin: Divided City.* Topics of Our Time, no. 1. Charlottesville, N.Y.: SamHar Press, 1973. 29p.

4663.   Harrell, Edward J. "Berlin: Rebirth, Reconstruction, and Division, 1945–1948—A Study of Allied Cooperation and Conflict." PhD dissertation, Florida State University, 1965.

4664.   McCauley, Martin. *East Germany: The Dilemmas of Division.* Conflict Studies, no. 119. London: Institute for the Study of Conflict, 1980. 19p.

4665.   Skowronets, Paul G. "U.S.-Soviet Military Liaison in Germany since 1947." PhD dissertation, University of Colorado, 1976.

4666.   United States. Department of Defense. Defense Intelligence Agency. *The East German Workers' Militia (Kampfgruppen).* DDI-1100-162-77. Washington, D.C., 1977.

Further References

See also sections 2:C:3:i, 5:A, and 5:B:2:a.

d. HUNGARY (INCLUDING THE 1956 INVASION)

BOOKS

4667.   Barber, Noel. *Handful of Ashes: A Personal Testament of the Battle of Budapest.* London: Wingate, 1957. 130p.

4668.   _____ . *Seven Days of Freedom: The Hungarian Uprising, 1956.* New York: Stein & Day, 1974. 266p.

4669.   Beke, Laszlo, pseud. *Student's Diary: Budapest, October 16–November 1, 1956.* Translated from the Hungarian. New York: Viking Press, 1957. 125p.

4670.   Heller, Andor. *No More Comrades.* Chicago, Ill.: Regnery, 1957. 175p.

4671.   Ignotus, Pavl. *Hungary.* New York: Praeger, 1972. 333p.

4672.   Letlis, Richard, and W. E. Morris, eds. *The Hungarian Revolt.* New York: Scribners, 1961. 219p.

4673.   Lomax, Bill. *Hungary, 1956.* New York: St. Martin's Press, 1977. 222p.

4674.   Marton, Endre. *The Forbidden Sky.* Boston, Mass.: Little, Brown, 1971. 306p.

4675.   Meray, Tibor. *That Day in Budapest, October 23, 1956.* Translated from the Hungarian. New York: Funk & Wagnalls, 1969. 503p.

4676.   _____ . *Thirteen Days That Shook the Kremlin.* Translated from the Hungarian. New York: Praeger, 1959. 290p.

4677.   Mikes, George. *The Hungarian Revolution.* London: Deutsch, 1957. 192p.

4678.   Pryce-Jones, David. *The Hungarian Revolution.* London: Benn, 1969. 128p.

4679.   Radvanyi, Janos. *Hungary and the Superpowers: The 1956 Revolution and Realpolitik.* P-111. Stanford, Calif.: Hoover Institution Press, 1972. 197p.

4680.   Szabo, Tamas, pseud. *Day on the Rooftop.* Translated from the French. Boston, Mass.: Little, Brown, 1958. 180p.

4681.   Urban, George. *Nineteen Days: A Broadcaster's Account of the Hungarian Revolution.* London: Heinemann, 1957. 361p.

4682.   Zinner, Paul E. *Revolution in Hungary.* New York: Columbia University Press, 1962. 380p.

ARTICLES

4683.   Agee, Joel. "Waking Up." *Harper's* 262 (May 1981), 57–60.

4684.   Auer, Paul. "Hungary Ten Years Ago." *Central Europe Journal* 14 (October 1966), 301–304.

4685.   Babynin, Ye. "Motorized Infantry Regiment Training in Southern Group of Forces: Translated from *Krasnaya Zvezda,* December 1, 1977." *Translations on USSR Military Affairs,* no. 1338 (March 16, 1978), 18–22.

4686.   Bailey, George. "The Road to Dishonor That Ended in Budapest." *Reporter* 16 (April 18, 1957), 10–13.

4687.   "The Battle of Budapest." *Illustrated London News* 224 (November 24, 1956), 879–881.

4688.   Bertalen-Istvan, Bela. "Journalist Describes Visit to Army Unit Stationed in Hungary: Translated from *Magyar Nemzet,* February 7, 1978." *Translations on USSR Military Affairs,* no. 1343 (April 7, 1978), 121–124.

4689.   Burks, E. C. "I Saw Budapest Crushed." *U.S. News and World Report* 41 (November 23, 1956), 58–60.

4690.   Deutscher, Isaac. "October Revolution—New Style." *Reporter* 15 (November 15, 1956), 14–17.

4691.   "Five Days of Freedom." *Time* 68 (November 12, 1956), 40.

4692.   "Freedom's Choice: The Hungarian Freedom Fighters." *Time* 69 (January 7, 1957), 18–22.

4693.   "How the Youth of Hungary Fought Off Russia's Army." *U.S. News and World Report* 41 (November 9, 1956), 46–50.

4694.   "The Hungarian Revolution." *World Today* 13 (January 1957), 3–16.

4695.   Krivda, F. "Southern Group of Forces Commander on Training Results: Translated from *Krasnaya Zvezda,* January 21, 1978." *Translations on USSR Military Affairs,* no. 1349 (May 2, 1978), 45–51.

4696.   Listowel, Judith. "Hungary's Terrible Ordeal." *Saturday Evening Post* 229 (January 5, 1957), 32–33; (January 12, 1957), 26–27.

4697.   Mydans, Carl M., and Shelly. "Revolt in Hungary." *The Violent Peace.* New York: Atheneum, 1968. Chpt. 12.

4698.   "Revolt Rocks Hungary." *Senior Scholastic* 69 (November 8, 1956), 18–20.

4699.   "Revolution." *Time* 68 (November 5, 1956), 30–32.

4700.   "The Soviet Intervention, November 4–5." In Paul E. Zinner, ed., *National Communism and Popular Revolt in Eastern Europe: A Selection of Documents on Events in Poland and Hungary, February–November 1956.* New York: Columbia University Press, 1956. pp. 472–485.

4701.   "Tanks and Yet More Tanks Raze Hungary." *Life* 41 (November 26, 1956), 28–32.

4702.   Union of Soviet Socialist Republics. Ministry of Defense. "Agreement on the Legal Status of the Soviet Forces Temporarily Present on the Territory of the Hungarian People's Republic, 1957." *American Journal of International Law* 52 (January 1958), 215–221.

4703.   Vizinczey, Stephen. "Budapest, 1956: Memoirs of a Freedom Fighter." *Horizon* 18 (Autumn 1976), 56–63.

4704.   "The War Waged by the Soviet Army." *U.S. News and World Report* 42 (June 28, 1957), 92–94.

4705.   Wright, Quincy. "Intervention, 1956." *American Journal of International Law* 51 (April 1957), 257–276.

DOCUMENTS, PAPERS, AND REPORTS

4706.   Nagly, Ernest A. *Crisis Decision Setting and Response: The Hungarian Revolution.* NSA 78-1. Washington, D.C.: Research Directorate, National Defense University, 1978. 39p.

Further References

See also the bibliographies cited in section 1:A and more general references in 2:C:3:h:(4), 5:B:1, and 5:B:2:a.

e. RUMANIA AND BULGARIA

BOOKS

4707.   Kosev, Dimitur. *A Short History of Bulgaria.* Sofia: Foreign Languages Press, 1963. 461p.

ARTICLES

4708.   Carp, Mircea, and Basil Ratziu. "The Armed Forces." In Alexandre Cretzianu, ed., *Captive Rumania: A Decade of Soviet Rule.* New York: Praeger, 1956. pp. 355–374.

4709.   Seton-Watson, Hugh. "Soviet Occupation in Rumania, Bulgaria, and Hungary." In John D. Montgomery and Albert O. Hirschman, eds., *Public Policy, 1968.* Cambridge, Mass.: Harvard University Press, 1968. pp. 145–163.

4710. Vucinich, W. S. "Soviet Rumania, 1944–1951." *Current History* 22 (February 1952), 85–91.

DOCUMENTS, PAPERS, AND REPORTS

4711. Foster, William F. "A Comparison of Soviet Reaction to Change in Rumania and Czechoslovakia in the 1960's." PhD dissertation, American University, 1974.

Further References

See also sections 2:C:3:h:(4) and 5:B:2:a.

f. POLAND

BOOKS

4712. Benes, Vaclav L., and Norman J. G. Ponds. *Poland.* New York: Praeger, 1970. 416p.

ARTICLES

4713. Brecher, John. "How Moscow Would Invade." *Newsweek* 96 (December 15, 1980), 40–41.

4714. Herspring, Dale R. "The Polish Military and the Policy Process." In Maurice D. Simon and Roger E. Kanet, eds., *Background to Crisis: Policies and Politics in Poland.* Boulder, Colo.: Westview Press, 1980.

4715. Kulishev, O. "Commander of Northern Group of Forces on Training Objectives: Translated from *Krasnaya Zvezda*, December 2, 1977." *Translations on USSR Military Affairs*, no. 1339 (March 20, 1978), 3–7.

4716. Migunov, A. "Northern Group of Forces—Soviet-Polish Ties Described: Translated from *Kommunist Vooruzhennykh Sil,* July 1980." *Translations on USSR Military Affairs,* no. 1541 (October 28, 1980), 36–41.

4717. Pastukhovskiy, G. "Living Conditions in Northern Group of Forces: Translated from *Krasnaya Zvezda*, December 8, 1977." *Translations on USSR Military Affairs,* no. 1344 (April 7, 1978), 13–16.

4718. Pimenov, A. "Correspondent Describes Soviet-Polish Joint Exercise: Translated from *Krasnaya Zvezda*, June 25, 1978." *Translations on USSR Military Affairs,* no. 1362 (July 12, 1978), 47–48.

4719. ————. "A Tank Regiment in Northern Group of Forces: Translated from *Krasnaya Zvezda*, October 20, 1977." *Translations on USSR Military Affairs,* no. 1327 (January 27, 1978), 39–42.

4720.   "Poised to Strike in Poland." *U.S. News and World Report* 89 (December 26, 1980), 26.

4721.   Rizatdinov, R. "Training Methods and Tasks in Northern Group of Forces Discussed: Translated from *Kommunist Vooruzhennykh Sil,* December 1978." *Translations on USSR Military Affairs,* no. 1421 (March 20, 1979), 9–17.

4722.   Sancton, T. A. "New Invasion Jitters," *Time* 117 (April 13, 1981), 60–62.

4723.   "Sheltered Strangers." *Time* 117 (February 9, 1981), 32–33.   The Soviet Army Northern Group of Forces in Poland.

4724.   Smith, Stephen. "Poland: Red Alert from Moscow." *Time* 116 (December 15, 1980), 42–43.

4725.   Strasser, Steven. "Brezhnev Takes Aim at Poland." *Newsweek* 96 (December 15, 1980), 38–47.

4726.   Union of Soviet Socialist Republics. Ministry of Defense. "Agreement on the Legal Status of Soviet Troops Temporarily Stationed in Poland, 1956." *American Journal of International Law* 52 (January 1958), 221–227.   Reprinted in *Current History* 32 (March 1958), 179–182.

4727.   Wojniak, Marian, pseud. "The Soviet Presence in Legnica." *East Europe* 18 (March 1969), 18–22.   Then headquarters of Northern Group of Forces.

DOCUMENTS, PAPERS, AND REPORTS

4728.   DeWeydenthal, Jan B. *Poland: Communism Adrift.* Washington Papers, no. 72. Beverly Hills, Calif.: Sage, 1979. 88p.

Further References

See also sections 2:C:3:h:(1) and 5:B:2:a.

3. Northern Europe

ARTICLES

4729.   Araldsen, O. P. "Norwegian Defense Problems." *U.S. Naval Institute Proceedings* 84 (October 1958), 38–47.

4730.   _____ . "The Soviet Union and the Arctic." *U.S. Naval Institute Proceedings* 93 (June 1967), 48–57.

4731.   Breyer, Siegfried. "Soviet Power in the Baltic." *Military Review* 42 (January 1962), 41–47.

4732.   Brundtland, Arne O. "The Nordic Balance." *Cooperation and Conflict* 2 (1966), 30–63.

4733.   Chabanier, A. "Soviet Strength in the Baltic Area." *Military Review* 37 (February 1957), 45–101.

4734.   Dewey, Arthur E. "The Nordic Balance." *Strategic Review* 4 (Fall 1976), 49–60.

4735.   Dobbs, Theodore. "Baltic Defense." *Marine Corps Gazette* 47 (July 1963), 20–24.

4736.   Erickson, John. "The Northern Theater: Soviet Capabilities and Concepts." *Strategic Review* 4 (Summer 1976), 67–82.

4737.   Furlong, R. D. M. "The Strategic Situation in Northern Europe." *International Defense Review* 12 (June 1979), 899–910.

4738.   Geisenheyner, Stefan. "N.A.T.O.'s Northern Flank: Vital, But Increasingly Vulnerable." *Air Force Magazine* 54 (July 1971), 56–61.

4739.   Gilberg, Trond, et al. "The Soviet Union and Northern Europe." *Problems of Communism* 30 (March-April 1981), 1–24.

4740.   Griswold, Laurence. "The Cold Front: U.S.S.R. Has the Strategic Advantage above the Arctic Circle." *Sea Power* 15 (December 1972), 18–23.

4741.   Haworth, David. "Denmark Feels the Heat of Warsaw Pact Baltic Exercises: Reprinted from the *Washington Post,* December 28, 1976." *U.S. Naval Institute Proceedings* 103 (March 1977), 108–109.

4742.   Holst, Johan J. "The Soviet Union and Nordic Security." *Cooperation and Conflict* 7 (1971), 137–145.

4743.   Lindberg, Folke. "Power Politics and the Baltic." *American-Scandinavian Review* 54 (June 1966), 158–168.

4744.   Maconochie, Alexander K. "Across or Along?: Soviet Amphibious Options in Northwestern Europe." *U.S. Naval Institute Proceedings* 106 (April 1980), 46–50.

4745.   Morgan, Henry G., Jr. "Soviet Policy in the Baltic." *U.S. Naval Institute Proceedings* 86 (April 1960), 82–89.

4746.   Moulton, James L. "The Defense of Northwestern Europe and the North Sea." In Frank Uhlig, Jr., ed., *The Naval Review, 1971.* Annapolis, Md.: U.S. Naval Institute, 1971. pp. 80–98.

4747. "N.A.T.O.'s Northern Flank." *Royal Air Forces Quarterly* 10 (Summer 1970), 133–143.

4748. Orvik, Nils. "Scandinavia, N.A.T.O. and Northern Security." *International Journal* 20 (Summer 1966), 380–396.

4749. _____. "Soviet Approaches to N.A.T.O.'s Northern Flank." *International Journal* 20 (Winter 1964–1965), 54–67.

4750. Romaneski, Albert L. "The Nordic Balance in the 1970's." *U.S. Naval Institute Proceedings* 99 (August 1973), 32–41.

4751. Sjaastad, Anders C. "Security Problems on the Northern Flank." *World Today* 35 (April 1979), 137–149.

4752. Sterne, Joseph R. L. "Soviet Forces Strengthened in Northern Peninsula Area: Reprinted from the *Baltimore Sun,* April 30, 1972." *U.S. Naval Institute Proceedings* 98 (September 1972), 115–116.

4753. Sullivan, William K. "Soviet Strategy and N.A.T.O.'s Northern Flank." *Naval War College Review* 32 (June-July 1979), 26–38.

4754. Walker, Walter. "The Challenge in the North." *NATO's Fifteen Nations* 16 (April-May 1971), 44–50.

4755. _____. "The Defence of the Northern Flank." *Journal of the Royal United Service Institution* 118 (September 1973), 21–30.

4756. _____. "Problems in the Defence of N.A.T.O.'s Northern Flank." *Journal of the Royal United Service Institution* 115 (September 1970), 13–23.

4757. Wettern, Desmond. "Amphibious Warfare: The Northern Flank." *NATO's Fifteen Nations* 23 (April-May 1978), 28–33.

4758. _____. "N.A.T.O.'s Northern Flank." *U.S. Naval Institute Proceedings* 95 (July 1969), 52–59.

DOCUMENTS, PAPERS, AND REPORTS

4759. Himma, Einar. *An Evaluation of the Anti-Soviet Guerrilla Warfare Potential in Soviet Estonia.* Student Essay. Carlisle Barracks, Pa.: Strategic Studies Institute, U.S. Army War College, 1974. 37p.

4760. Hunt, Herman L. "Policy and Posture of N.A.T.O. on the Northern Flank: An Appraisal." MA thesis, U.S. Naval War College, 1972.

4761. Leighton, Margaret. *The Soviet Threat to N.A.T.O.'s Northern Flank.* New York: National Strategy Information Center, 1979. 95p.

4762.   Ulstein, Egil. *Nordic Security.* Adelphi papers, no. 81. London: International Institute for Strategic Studies, 1971. 34p.

Further References

See also section 5:B:1.

4. Central Europe

BOOKS

4763.   Close, Robert. *Europe without Defense: 48 Hours That Could Change the Face of the World.* Translated from the French. London and New York: Pergamon Press, 1979. 278p.

4764.   Cordier, Sherwood S. *Calculus of Power: The Current Soviet-American Conventional Military Balance in Central Europe.* 3d ed. Washington, D.C.: University Press of America, 1980. 150p.

4765.   Pratt, Clayton A. *The Military Use by Warsaw Treaty Organization Forces of 20th Century Operational Routes in the Benelux and Northern Germany.* Laramie: University of Wyoming Press, 1977. 116p.   A hypothetical study.

ARTICLES

4766.   Bennecke, Juergen. "The Challenge in the Center." *NATO's Fifteen Nations* 16 (April-May 1971), 52–56.

4767.   Brown, Neville. "The Armies in Central Europe." *Journal of the Royal United Service Institution* 108 (November 1963), 341–348.

4768.   Coffey, Kenneth J. "Defending Europe Against a Conventional Attack." *Air University Review* 31 (January-February 1980), 47–59.

4769.   Cranford, Jack. "Terrain vs. Armor: Rhine to Russia." *Armor* 70 (January-February 1961), 49–51.

4770.   Davison, Michael S. "The Military Balance in Central Army Group." *Strategic Review* 2 (Fall 1974), 13–18.

4771.   DeMaiziere, Ulrich. "A German View of the Strategic Situation in Central Europe." In Royal United Service Institute for Defence Studies, eds., *R.U.S.I. and Brassey's Annual, 1977–1978.* Boulder, Colo.: Westview Press, 1977. 113–123.

4772.   Genesti, Marc. "The Nuclear Land Battle." *Strategic Review* 4 (Winter 1976), 79–85.

4773.   Hofmann, Kurt. "The Battlefield of the 1980's." *International Defense Review* 10 (June 1977), 431–435.

4774.   Ledbetter, Homer M. "Armored Assault across Europe: Can It Be Stopped?" *Armor* 83 (September-October 1974), 12–15.

4775.   McCaffrey, Barry R. "Infantry on the High-Intensity Battlefield of Central Europe." *Military Review* 58 (January 1978), 3–6.

4776.   McMichael, Scott R. "The Soviet Theater Nuclear Offensive and the European Battlefield." *Field Artillery Journal* 47 (September-October 1979), 24–27.

4777.   Marriott, John. "The Antitank Problem." *NATO's Fifteen Nations* 17 (April-May 1972), 72–82.

4778.   Michie, Allan A. "Russia Could Take Europe in Three Weeks." *Collier's* 126 (December 30, 1950), 9–11.

4779.   Miller, D. M. O. "Strategic Factors Affecting a Soviet Conventional Attack in Western Europe." *International Defense Review* 11 (June 1978), 553–559.

4780.   Myer, Allan A. "The Balance in Central Europe: Reflections through the Soviet Prism." *Naval War College Review* 33 (November-December 1980), 15–43.

4781.   Polk, James H. "The North German Plain Attack Scenario: Threat or Illusion?" *Strategic Review* 8 (Summer 1980), 60–66.

4782.   _____ . "The Realities of Tactical Nuclear Weapons." *Orbis* 17 (Summer 1973), 439–447.

4783.   Pratt, Clayton A. "The Benelux and Northern German Plains Avenue of Approach." *Military Review* 58 (June 1978), 2–8.

4784.   Rasmussen, Robert D. "The Central European Battlefield: Doctrinal Implications for Counterair-Interdiction." *Air University Review* 29 (July-August 1978), 2–20.

4785.   Richardson, James L. "The Soviet Threat." *Germany and the Atlantic Alliance: The Interaction of Strategy and Politics.* Cambridge, Mass.: Harvard University Press, 1966. Chpt. 2.

4786.   Syrett, David. "An Inconsequent Debate: Blitzkrieg, PGM's [Precision-Guided Munitions] and Central Europe." *Military Review* 57 (July 1977), 12–15.

4787.   Turbiville, Graham H., Jr. "Invasion in Europe: A Scenario." *Army* 26 (November 1976), 16–21.

4788.   United States. Congressional Budget Office. "The Fire Power Balance in Central Europe." *United States Air and Ground Conventional Forces for N.A.T.O.: Firepower Issues.* Washington, D.C.: U.S. Government Printing Office, 1978. pp. 3–8.

4789.   Von Wyszecki, Fritz. "Armored Warfare: Trends in Central Europe." *Military Review* 48 (November 1968), 76–79.

4790.   Woller, Rudolf. "The Red Army in the Rhineland: How It Could Happen." *Atlas* 17 (January 1969), 30–32.

DOCUMENTS, PAPERS, AND REPORTS

4791.   Becker, Abraham S. *Strategic Breakout as a Soviet Policy Option.* RAND Report R-2097-ACDA. Santa Monica, Calif.: RAND Corporation, 1977. 56p.

4792.   Braddock, J. V., and N. F. Wikner. *An Assessment of Soviet Forces Facing N.A.T.O.—The Central Region—And Suggested N.A.T.O. Initiatives.* DNA-4343F. Alexandria, Va.: Santa Fe Corporation, 1977. 87p.

4793.   Brown, Rex V., et al. *The Timeliness of a N.A.T.O. Response to an Impending Warsaw Pact Attack.* N-00014-76-C-0074. Maclean, Va.: Decisions and Designs, 1975. 68p.

4794.   DeMaizier, Ulrich. *The Rational Deployment of Forces on the Central Front.* Translated from the French. Document Series, no. 663. Paris, France: Western European Union Assembly, 1975.

4795.   Fischer, Robert L. *Defending the Central Front: The Balance of Forces.* Adelphi papers, no. 127. London: International Institute for Strategic Studies, 1976. 43p.

4796.   Rainville, R. C. *The Changing Military Equation in Central Europe.* Military Issues Research Memorandum. Carlisle Barracks, Pa.: Strategic Studies Institute, U.S. Army War College, 1978. 30p.

Further References

See also sections 4:B, 5:A and B.

5. Southern Europe

ARTICLES

4797.   Geisenheyner, Stefan. "The Growing Threat to N.A.T.O.'s Southern Flank." *Air Force and Space Digest* 52 (January 1969), 40–44.

4798. Hinterhoff, Eugene. "The Complex Problems of the Southern N.A.T.O. Flank." *NATO's Fifteen Nations* 17 (April-May 1972), 32–39.

4799. Johnson, Means, Jr. "N.A.T.O.'s Southern Front: Where the Soviets Show Big Gains." *U.S. News and World Report* 78 (June 2, 1975), 22–23.

4800. _____. "N.A.T.O.'s Southern Region: Problems and Prospects." *U.S. Naval Institute Proceedings* 101 (January 1975), 47–51.

4801. Locksley, Norman. "N.A.T.O.'s Southern Exposure." *U.S. Naval Institute Proceedings* 88 (November 1962), 41–54.

DOCUMENTS, PAPERS, AND REPORTS

4802. Gasteyger, Curt W. *Conflict and Tension in the Mediterranean.* Adelphi papers, no. 51. London: Institute for Strategic Studies, 1968. 18p.

Further References

See also section 5:A.

C. Cuba

1. General Works

BOOKS

4803. Blasier, Cole. *Cuba in the World.* Pittsburgh, Pa.: University of Pittsburgh Press, 1979. 343p.

4804. Levesque, Jacques. *The U.S.S.R. and the Cuban Revolution: Soviet Ideology and Strategic Perspectives.* New York: Praeger, 1978. 220p.

4805. Rivero, Nicholas. *Castro's Cuba: An American Dilemma.* Washington, D.C.: R. B. Luce, 1962. 239p.

4806. Sobel, Lester A., ed. *Cuba, the U.S., and Russia, 1963–1969.* New York: Facts on File, 1964. 138p.

4807. Tetlow, Edwin. *Eye on Cuba.* New York: Harcourt, Brace, 1966. 291p.

ARTICLES

4808. "Again, a Challenge in Cuba." *U.S. News and World Report* 87 (September 10, 1979), 17–18. Disposition of a Soviet combat brigade.

4809.   "Background on the Question of Soviet Troops in Cuba."
Department of State Bulletin 79 (November 1979), 9–11.

4810.   Bhattacharya, Sauripada. "Cuban-Soviet Relations under
Castro, 1959–1964." *Studies on the Soviet Union* 4 (March 1965), 27–36.

4811.   Blasier, Cole. "The Cuban-Soviet Link." *Problems of Communism* 27 (November-December 1978), 59–62.

4812.   "Building Up Again?: Russia's Military Presence in Cuba."
Time 81 (February 8, 1963), 32.

4813.   Butler, David. "Russia's Cuban Brigade." *Newsweek* 94 (September 10, 1979), 18–19.

4814.   Connell-Smith, Gordon. "Castro's Cuba in World Affairs,
1959–1979." *World Today* 35 (January 1979), 15–23.

4815.   Crozier, Brian. "Soviet Pressures in the Caribbean: The Satel-
lisation of Cuba." *Conflict Studies,* no. 14 (May 1973), 1–20.

4816.   "Cuba under the Lens: No Missiles, But. . . ." *Newsweek* 69
(February 18, 1963), 19–22.

4817.   Deming, Angus. "Carter's Cuban Dilemma: Soviet Troops."
Newsweek 94 (October 8, 1979), 24–25.

4818.   Dominguez, J. I. "Cuban Foreign Policy." *Foreign Affairs* 57
(Fall 1978), 83–108.

4819.   Fenton, Leslie K. "The Umpteenth Cuban Confrontation."
U.S. Naval Institute Proceedings 106 (July 1980), 40–45.

4820.   Fontaine, Roger. "The Standoff in Cuba." *New Leader* 62
(September 24, 1979), 4–6.

4821.   Garcia Marquez, Gabriel. "Operation Carlota." *New Left Review* (February-April 1977), 123–137.

4822.   Gleichauf, Justin F. "The Red Presence in Cuba: The Genesis
of a Crisis." *Army* 29 (November 1979), 34–38.

4823.   "The Hardening Soviet Base in Cuba." *Time* 81 (February 15,
1963), 23.

4824.   Heinl, Robert D., Jr. "Cuba: Russia's Foreign Legion." *Sea
Power* 19 (March 1976), 44–45.

4825.   Keating, Kenneth B. "The Latest Facts on Russia's Cuban
Base." *U.S. News and World Report* 54 (February 11, 1963), 43–45.

4826.   Mesa-Lago, Carmelo. "The Sovietization of the Cuban Revolution." *World Affairs* 136 (Summer 1973), 3–35.

4827.   Rees, John. "Cuba Becomes a Soviet Base under Fidel Castro." *American Opinion* 22 (December 1979), 5–10.

4828.   Reisman, Michael. "Fidel's Little Helpers." *New Republic* 181 (November 24, 1979), 17–18.

4829.   Robinson, Clarence A., Jr. "U.S.S.R. Cuba Force Clouds Debate on SALT." *Aviation Week and Space Technology* 111 (September 10, 1979), 16–19.

4830.   "Russia Tightens Her Grip on Castro." *U.S. News and World Report* 71 (August 23, 1971), 34–35.

4831.   "Russians in Our Back Yard to Stay?" *U.S. News and World Report* 87 (October 15, 1979), 23–26.

4832.   Sauvage, Leo. "Castro's Foreign Legion." *Reporter* 27 (September 27, 1963), 21–24.

4833.   "The Storm Over Cuba." *Time* 114 (September 17, 1979), 12–15.

4834.   Szulc, Tad. "Outfoxed by Fidel: Soviet Combat Troops in Cuba." *New Republic* 181 (September 22, 1979), 14–15.

4835.   "Those Troops in Cuba." *Progressive* 43 (November 1979), 11–12.

4836.   Tretiak, Daniel. "Cuba and the Soviet Union: The Growing Accommodation, 1964–1965." *Orbis* 11 (Summer 1967), 439–458.

4837.   United States. Department of State. "Sino-Soviet Bloc Military Aid to Cuba Summarized." *Department of State Bulletin* 46 (April 16, 1962), 644–646.

4838.   "What Kind of a Soviet Base Is Cuba Now?" *U.S. News and World Report* 53 (November 19, 1962), 83–85.

4839.   "Why the Soviets Are Rushing a Military Buildup in Cuba." *U.S. News and World Report* 54 (February 11, 1963), 42–43.

4840.   Wilson, Desmond P., Jr. "Strategic Projections and Policy Options in the Soviet-Cuban Relationship." *Orbis* 12 (Summer 1968), 504–517.

DOCUMENTS, PAPERS, AND REPORTS

4841.   Gonzales, Edward, and David Ronfeldt. *Post-Revolutionary Cuba in a Changing World.* RAND Report R-1844-ISA. Santa Monica, Calif.: RAND Corporation, 1975. 78p.

4842.   Harvey, Mose L. *Soviet Combat Troops in Cuba: Implications of the Carter Solution for the U.S.S.R.* Washington, D.C.: Advanced International Studies Institute, 1979. 54p.

4843.   Tretiak, Daniel. *Cuba and the Soviet Union: The Growing Accommodation.* RAND Memorandum, RM-4935-PR. Santa Monica, Calif.: RAND Corporation, 1966. 61p.

4844.   United States. Central Intelligence Agency. National Foreign Assessment Center. *Cuban Chronology.* Reference aid. Washington, D.C.: Document Expediting Project, Exchange and Gift Division, Library of Congress, 1978. 94p.

4845.   _____ . *The Cuban Economy: A Statistical View, 1968–1976.* Research aid. Washington, D.C.: Document Expediting Project, Exchange and Gift Division, Library of Congress, 1976. 17p.

4846.   United States. Congress. House. Committee on Foreign Affairs. Subcommittee on Inter-American Affairs. *Impact of Cuban-Soviet Ties in the Western Hemisphere, Spring 1979: Hearings.* 96th Cong., 1st sess. Washington, D.C.: U.S. Government Printing Office, 1979. 50p.

4847.   _____ . *Soviet Activities in Cuba: Hearings.* 93d Cong., 1st sess. Washington, D.C.: U.S. Government Printing Office, 1974. 23p.

Further References

See also sections 5:A:1 and 3, and 5:F.

2. The Missile Crisis, 1962

BOOKS

4848.   Abel, Elie. *The Missile Crisis.* New York: McClelland, 1966. 220p.

4849.   Daniel, James, and John G. Hubble. *Strike in the West: The Complete Story of the Cuban Missile Crisis.* New York: Holt, 1963. 180p.

4850.   Detzer, David. *The Brink: The Cuban Missile Crisis, 1962.* New York: T. Y. Crowell, 1979. 304p.

4851.   Larson, David L., ed. *The Cuban Crisis of 1962: Selected Documents and Chronology.* Boston, Mass.: Houghton Mifflin, 1963. 333p.

ARTICLES

4852.   Crosby, Ralph D., Jr. "The Cuban Missile Crisis: A Soviet View." *Military Review* 56 (September 1976), 58–70.

4853.   Pederson, John C. "Soviet Reporting of the Cuban Crisis." *U.S. Naval Institute Proceedings* 91 (October 1965), 54–63.

DOCUMENTS, PAPERS, AND REPORTS

4854.   Horelick, Arnold L. *The Cuban Missile Crisis: An Analysis of Soviet Calculations and Behavior.* RAND Memorandum RM-3779-PR. Santa Monica, Calif.: RAND Corporation, 1963. 60p.

4855.   United States. Congress. Senate. Committee on Armed Services. Subcommittee on the Cuban Military Buildup. *Interim Report.* 88th Cong., 1st sess. Washington, D.C.: U.S. Government Printing Office, 1963. 18p.

Further References

See supplementary citations in sections 5:C:1 and 7:B:2:b, and the author's *Soviet Air and Strategic Missile Forces* (Santa Barbara, Calif.: ABC-Clio, 1981).

D. The Middle East

1. Helping the Arabs

a. GENERAL WORKS

BOOKS

4856.   Bar-Simon-Tov, Yaacov. *The Israeli-Egyptian War of Attrition, 1969–1970: A Case Study of Limited Local War.* New York: Columbia University Press, 1980. 256p.

4857.   Bell, J. Bowyer. *The Long War: Israel and the Arabs since 1946.* Englewood Cliffs, N.J.: Prentice-Hall, 1969. 467p.

4858.   Brecker, Michael. *Decisions in Crisis: Israel, 1967 and 1973.* Berkeley, Calif.: University of California Press, 1977. 500p.

4859.   Confino, Michael, and Shimon Shamir, eds. *The U.S.S.R. and the Middle East.* Israel Program for Scientific Translations. New York: Wiley, 1973. 441p.

4860. Congressional Quarterly, Editors of. *The Middle East: U.S. Policy, Israel, Oil, and the Arabs.* 4th ed. Washington, D.C., 1979. 252p.

4861. Donovan, John, ed. *U.S. and Soviet Policy in the Middle East, 1957–1966.* New York: Facts on File, 1974. 218p.

4862. Dupuy, Trevor N. *Elusive Victory: The Arab-Israeli Wars, 1947–1974.* New York: Harper & Row, 1978. 669p.

4863. Freedman, Robert O. *Soviet Policy toward the Middle East since 1970.* Rev. ed. New York: Praeger, 1978. 400p.

4864. _____ . *World Politics and the Arab-Israeli Conflict.* New York and London: Pergamon Press, 1979. 358p.

4865. Geyer, Georgie A. *The New One Hundred Years War.* Garden City, N.Y.: Doubleday, 1972. 318p.

4866. Glassman, Jon D. *Arms for the Arabs: The Soviet Union and War in the Middle East.* Baltimore, Md.: Johns Hopkins University Press, 1976. 243p.

4867. Golan, Galia. *Yom Kippur and After: The Soviet Union and the Middle East Crisis.* Cambridge, Eng.: At the University Press, 1977. 350p.

4868. Haykal, Muhammad H. *The Sphinx and the Commissar: The Rise and Fall of Soviet Influence in the Middle East.* New York: Harper & Row, 1979. 304p.

4869. Hurewitz, J. C. *Middle East Politics: The Military Dimension.* New York: Octagon Books, 1974. 551p.

4870. Jabber, Paul. *Not by War Alone: The Politics of Arms Control in the Middle East.* Berkeley, Calif.: University of California Press, 1980.

4871. Kass, Ilana. *Soviet Involvement in the Middle East: Policy Formulation, 1966–1973.* Boulder, Colo.: Westview Press, 1978. 273p.

4872. Klieman, Aaron S. *Soviet Russia and the Middle East.* Baltimore, Md.: Johns Hopkins Press, 1970. 101p.

4873. Laqueur, Walter. *The Struggle for the Middle East: The Soviet Union in the Mediterranean, 1948–1968.* New York: Macmillan, 1969. 360p.

4874. _____ . *The Struggle for the Middle East: The Soviet Union in the Mediterranean, 1958–1973.* Rev. ed. Harmondsworth, Eng.: Penguin Books, 1972. 267p.

4875.		Lenczowski, George. *Soviet Advances in the Middle East.* Foreign Affairs Studies, no. 2. Washington, D.C.: American Enterprise Institute for Public Policy Research, 1972. 176p.

4876.		McLane, Charles B. *Soviet-Middle East Relations.* London: Asian Research Centre, 1973. 126p.

4877.		McLaurin, Ronald D. *The Middle East in Soviet Policy.* Boston, Mass.: D. C. Heath, 1975. 206p.

4878.		Mangold, Peter. *Superpower Intervention in the Middle East.* New York: St. Martin's Press, 1978. 209p.

4879.		Moore, John N., ed. *The Arab-Israeli Conflict: Readings and Documents.* Rev. ed. Princeton, N.J.: Princeton University Press, 1977. 1,285p.

4880.		Quarrie, Bruce. *Tank Battles in Miniature, No. 5: A Wargamer's Guide to the Arab-Israeli Wars, 1948–1978.* New York: Arbor House, 1978. 144p.

4881.		Ro'i, Yaacov. *From Encroachment to Involvement: A Documentary Study of Soviet Politics in the Middle East, 1945–1973.* London: Halsted Press, 1974. 616p.

4882.		———— , ed. *Limits to Power: Soviet Policy in the Middle East.* New York: St. Martin's Press, 1979. 376p.

4883.		Sella, Amnon. *Soviet Political and Military Conduct in the Middle East.* New York: St. Martin's Press, 1980. 300p.

4884.		Smolansky, Oles M. *The Soviet Union and the Arab East under Khrushchev.* Cranbury, N.J.: Bucknell University Press, 1974. 326p.

4885.		Snider, Lewis W. *Arabesque: Untangling the Patterns of Supply of Conventional Arms to Israel and the Arab States and the Implications for United States Policy of Supply of "Lethal" Weapons to Israel.* Monograph Series in World Affairs, v. 15, no. 1. Denver, Colo.: Colorado Seminary, University of Denver, 1977. 151p.

4886.		Von Pivka, Otto. *Armies of the Middle East.* New York: Mayflower Books, 1979. 168p.

4887.		Wagner, Abraham K. *Crisis Decisionmaking: Israel's Experience in 1967 and 1973.* New York: Praeger, 1974. 186p.

4888.		Whetten, Lawrence L. *The Canal War: Four-Power Conflict in the Middle East, 1967–1973.* Cambridge, Mass.: M.I.T. Press, 1974. 520p.

4889.   Williams, Louis, ed. *Military Aspects of the Arab-Israeli Conflict.* Tel Aviv, Israel: University Publishing Projects, 1975. 265p.

ARTICLES

4890.   Adomeit, Hannes. "Soviet Policy in the Middle East: Problems of Analysis." *Soviet Studies* 27 (April 1975), 288–305.

4891.   Allon, Yigel. "The Soviet Involvement in the Arab-Israeli Conflict." In Michael Confino and Shimon Shamir, eds., *The U.S.S.R. and the Middle East.* Israel Program for Scientific Translations. New York: Wiley, 1973. p. 152.

4892.   Alsop, Joseph. "Reading Soviet Intentions." *New Republic* 163 (October 3, 1970), 17–19.

4893.   Anthem, Thomas. "Russia in the Med." *Contemporary Review* 212 (March 1968), 132–137.

4894.   "Arms in the Middle East: A Special Report." *Moment* 2 (December 1976), 15–20.

4895.   Azar, Edward E. "Soviet and Chinese Roles in the Middle East." *Problems of Communism* 28 (May-June 1979), 18–30.

4896.   Blixt, Melvin D. "Soviet Objectives in the Eastern Mediterranean." *Naval War College Review* 21 (March 1969), 4–24.

4897.   Brown, Neville. "American and Soviet Weapons in Israeli and Arab Hands." *New Middle East* 20 (1970), 11–15.

4898.   _____ . "The Real Capabilities of Soviet and U.S. Weapons in the Middle East and How the Two Sides Use Them: A New Approach to Assessing the Aerial Power Balance." *New Middle East* 20 (1970), 11–14.

4899.   Chung-kiang, Ting. "Russia and the Mediterranean: A Report to the Council of N.A.T.O. Foreign Ministers." *Asian Outlook* 5 (August 1970), 14–17.

4900.   Coleman, H. J. "Mideast Power Structure Shifting." *Aviation Week and Space Technology* 98 (March 26, 1973), 12–13.

4901.   Cordesman, Anthony H. "The Arab-Israeli Balance: How Much Is Too Much?" *Armed Forces Journal* 115 (October 1977), 32–41.

4902.   Cottrell, Alvin J. "The Soviet Union in the Middle East." *Orbis* 14 (Fall 1970), 588–589.

4903.   Dawisha, Karen. "Soviet Policy in the Middle East: Present Dilemmas and Future Trends." *Journal of International Studies* 6 (Autumn 1977), 182–189.

4904.   "The Defence Forces of the Muslim World." *Islamic Defence and Aviation Review* 1 (1979), 6–12.

4905.   DeVore, Ronald M. "Arab-Israeli Arms Race and the Superpowers." *Current History* 66 (February 1974), 70–73.

4906.   Dimant-Kass, Ilana. "The Soviet Military and Soviet Policy in the Middle East." *Soviet Studies* 26 (October 1974), 502–521.

4907.   "Firepower Grows in the Tinderbox." *Business Week* (July 18, 1970), 72–73.

4908.   Forsythe, David P. "The Soviets and the Arab-Israeli Conflict." *World Affairs* 14 (Fall 1971), 132–142.

4909.   Freedman, Robert O. "Soviet Policy Toward the Middle East from the Exodus of 1972 to the Yom Kippur War." *Naval War College Review* 27 (January-February 1975), 32–53.

4910.   _____ . "Soviet Policy toward the Middle East since the October 1973 Arab-Israeli War." *Naval War College Review* 29 (Fall 1976), 61–103.

4911.   _____ . "The Soviet Union and the Middle East: The High Cost of Influence." *Naval War College Review* 24 (January 1972), 15–34.

4912.   Gabelic, Andro. "The U.S.S.R.: New Ascent in Strategy." *Review of International Affairs* 18 (November 20, 1967), 16–18.

4913.   Golan, Galia. "Soviet Policy in the Middle East: Growing Difficulties and Changing Interests." *World Today* 33 (September 1977), 335–342.

4914.   Griswold, Laurence. "The Bear in the Burnoose: A First Hand Report on Russia's Arab Bases." *Sea Power* 14 (September 1971), 16–23.

4915.   Heiman, Leo. "Armored Forces in the Middle East." *Military Review* 48 (November 1968), 11–19.

4916.   Hinterhoff, Eugene. "The Soviet Presence in the Mediterranean." *Orbis* 13 (Spring 1969), 261–269.

4917.   Jabber, Paul. "Not by War Alone: Curbing the Arab-Israeli Arms Race." *Middle East Journal* 28 (Summer 1974), 233–247.

4918. Joshua, Wynford. "Arms for the Love of Allah." *U.S. Naval Institute Proceedings* 96 (March 1970), 30–39.

4919. _____ . "The Middle East in Soviet Strategy." *Strategic Review* 2 (Spring 1974), 51–67.

4920. Kemp, Geoffrey. "Middle East Strategy and Arms Levels, 1945–1967." In J. C. Hurewitz, ed., *Soviet-American Rivalry in the Middle East*. New York: Praeger, 1969. pp. 21–36.

4921. Kilmarx, Robert A., and Alvin J. Cottrell. "The U.S.S.R. and the Middle East." *Air Force Magazine* 53 (August 1970), 40–46.

4922. Kimche, Jan. "The Superpowers in the Middle East—Backstage." *Midstream* 21 (June-July 1975), 7–13.

4923. Laqueur, Walter. "Russia Enters the Middle East." *Foreign Affairs* 47 (January 1969), 296–308.

4924. Lenczowski, George. "The Middle East in Soviet Strategy." *Problems of Communism* 27 (November-December 1978), 49–53.

4925. Limoli, Salvatore. "Twenty Years of History in the Mediterranean, 1948–1968." *NATO's Fifteen Nations* 13 (December 1968–January 1969), 54–64.

4926. "The Middle East: Background to the Russian Intervention." *World Today* 11 (November 1955), 463–477.

4927. "The Middle East: The Military Dimension." *Journal of Palestine Studies* 4 (Summer 1975), 3–25.

4928. Nes, David G. "The Soviets in the Middle East." *Military Review* 52 (June 1972), 80–85.

4929. "New Threat: Red Bases in Morocco." *U.S. News and World Report* 53 (September 17, 1962), 43.

4930. O'Ballance, Edgar. "The Middle East Arms Race." *Army Quarterly* 78 (July 1964), 210–214.

4931. Pajak, Roger F. "Soviet Arms Aid in the Middle East since the October War." In U.S. Congress, Joint Economic Committee, *The Political Economy of the Middle East, 1973–1978: A Compendium of Papers*. 96th Cong., 2d sess. Washington, D.C.: U.S. Government Printing Office, 1980. pp. 445–485.

4932. Pierre, Andrew J. "Beyond the 'Plane Package': Arms and Politics in the Middle East." *International Security Review* 3 (Summer 1978), 148–161.

4933.   Ra'anan, Uri. "Soviet Decision-Making in the Middle East, 1969–1973." In Michael MccGwire, Ken Booth, and John McDonnell, eds., *Soviet Naval Policy, Objectives and Constraints*. New York: Praeger, 1975. pp. 182–210.

4934.   _____ . "The U.S.S.R. and the Middle East: Some Reflections on the Soviet Decision-Making Process." *Orbis* 17 (Fall 1973), 946–977.

4935.   _____ . "Soviet Global Policy and the Middle East." *Naval War College Review* 24 (September 1971), 19–29.

4936.   Rey, Gabriel. "The Arms Balance in the Middle East." *Israel Horizons* 17 (March 1969), 8–15.

4937.   Rosen, Steven J. "What the Next Arab-Israeli War Might Look Like." *International Security* 2 (Spring 1978), 149–171.

4938.   Rubinstein, Alvin Z. "The Evolution of Soviet Strategy in the Middle East." *Orbis* 24 (Summer 1980), 323–337.

4939.   _____ . "The Soviet Union and the Eastern Mediterranean, 1968–1978." *Orbis* 23 (Summer 1979), 299–315.

4940.   "Russia Moves Deeper into the Mideast Conflict." *U.S. News and World Report* 68 (April 6, 1970), 54–55.

4941.   Sella, Amnon. "Patterns of Soviet Involvement in Local War." *Journal of the Royal United Service Institute for Defence Studies* 224 (June 1979), 53–56.

4942.   Smolansky, Oles M. "Moscow and the Arab-Israeli Sector." *Current History* 71 (October 1976), 105–108.

4943.   _____ . "Soviet Policy in the Middle East and Africa." *Current History* 75 (October 1978), 113–116.

4944.   _____ . "The United States and the Soviet Union in the Middle East." In Grayson Kirk and Nils H. Wessell, eds., *The Soviet Threat: Myths and Realities*. New York: Praeger, 1978. pp. 99–109.

4945.   "Soviet Power in the Middle East." *Newsweek* 73 (February 17, 1969), 46.

4946.   Stolley, R. B. "Russia in the Middle East." *Life* 65 (November 29, 1968), 22–31.

4947.   Tekiner, Sueleyman. "Soviet Policy toward the Arab East." *Institute for the Study of the U.S.S.R. Bulletin* 15 (February 1968), 29–37.

4948.   Ulin, Robert R. "The Weapons Connection." *Military Review* 59 (November 1979), 55–65.

4949.   "War and the Weapons Makers: Who Supplies Arms for the Mideast War?" *Business Week* (October 20, 1973), 32–33.

4950.   Weller, Jac. "New Military Equipment." *Infantry* 64 (May-June 1974), 18–21.

4951.   Whetten, Lawrence L. "The Mediterranean Threat: Has Strategic Parity Been Achieved?" *Survey*, no. 74/75 (Winter-Spring 1970), 270–281.

4952.   _____ . "The Military Consequences of Mediterranean Superpower Parity." *New Middle East*, no. 38 (November 1971), 14–25.

4953.   _____ . "Soviet Strategy." *Survival* 12 (August 1970), 252–260.

4954.   _____ . "Strategic Parity in the Middle East." *Military Review* 50 (September 1970), 24–31.

4955.   "Who Has Been Arming the Middle East?" *Business Week* (July 18, 1970), 72–73.

4956.   Winston, D. C. "Soviet Mideast Buildup Shows Tactical Shift." *Aviation Week and Space Technology* 87 (November 6, 1967), 19–20.

4957.   _____ . "Soviet-Yugoslav Buildup for Mideast Worries the West." *Aviation Week and Space Technology* 99 (November 19, 1973), 18–19.

4958.   Yodfat, Aryeh Y. "Soviet Policy in the Middle East: Before October 1973 and After." *New Outlook* 17 (November-December 1974), 31–56.

DOCUMENTS, PAPERS, AND REPORTS

4959.   Becker, Abraham S. *Arms Transfers, Great Power Intervention, and Settlement of the Arab-Israeli Conflict*. RAND Paper P-5901. Santa Monica, Calif.: RAND Corporation, 1978. 25p.

4960.   _____ . *The Superpowers in the Arab-Israeli Conflict, 1970–1973*. RAND Paper P-5167. Santa Monica, Calif.: RAND Corporation, 1973. 67p.

4961.   _____ , and Arnold L. Horelick. *Soviet Policy in the Middle East*. RAND Report R-504-FF. Santa Monica, Calif.: RAND Corporation, 1970. 115p.

4962.   Chase, Alan C. *Soviet Military Goals in the Middle East.* Research Study. Maxwell AFB, Ala.: Air Command and Staff College, Air University, 1972. 79p.

4963.   Churba, Joseph. *Soviet Penetration into the Middle East.* Documentary Research Study AU-203-68-ASI. Maxwell AFB, Ala.: Documentary Research Division, Aerospace Studies Institute, Air University, 1968. 113p.

4964.   Glassman, Jon D. "Arms for the Arabs: The Soviet Union and War in the Middle East." PhD dissertation, Columbia University, 1976.

4965.   Hatzilambrou, Lambros. "Soviet Foreign Policy in the Eastern Mediterranean: A Systemic Approach." PhD dissertation, Howard University, 1976.

4966.   Hunter, Robert E. *The Soviet Dilemma in the Middle East.* Adelphi papers, nos. 59–60. 2 vols. London: Institute for Strategic Studies, 1969.

4967.   Kemp, Geoffrey. *Arms and Security: The Egypt-Israel Case.* Adelphi papers, no. 52. London: Institute for Strategic Studies, 1968. 27p.

4968.   Meltzer, Ronald M. "The Middle East Arms Race: Suppliers and Recipients." MA thesis, San Diego State University, 1970.

4969.   *The Middle East and the International System.* Adelphi papers, nos. 114–115. 2 vols. London: International Institute for Strategic Studies, 1975.

4970.   Milstein, Jeffrey S. *Soviet and American Influences on the Arab-Israeli Arms Race: A Quantitative Analysis.* New Haven, Conn.: Department of Political Science, Yale University, 1970. 27p.

4971.   Near East Report, Editors of. *The Arms Race in the Near East: A Special Survey.* Washington, D.C., 1967. 28p.

4972.   Pajak, Roger F. *Soviet Arms Aid in the Middle East.* Washington, D.C.: Center for Strategic and International Studies, Georgetown University, 1976. 45p.

4973.   Pierce, Max R. *Soviet Involvement in Egypt, Syria, and Iraq.* Research Study. Maxwell AFB, Ala.: Air Command and Staff College, Air University, 1973. 53p.

4974.   Tahtinen, Dale R. *The Arab-Israeli Military Balance since October 1973.* Foreign Affairs Studies, no. 1. Washington, D.C.: American Enterprise Institute for Public Policy Research, 1974. 43p.

4975. _____ . *Arab-Israel Military Status in 1976*. Foreign Affairs Studies, no. 30. Washington, D.C.: American Enterprise Institute for Public Policy Research, 1976. 31p.

4976.   United States. Central Intelligence Agency. Office of Political Research. *Issues in the Middle East: Atlas*. Washington, D.C., 1973. 40p.

4977.   United States. Congress. House. Committee on Foreign Relations. Subcommittees on Europe and the Near East. *Soviet Involvement in the Middle East and the Western Response: Joint Hearings*. 92d Cong., 1st sess. Washington, D.C.: U.S. Government Printing Office. 1971. 219p.

4978. _____ . Subcommittee on the Near East. *The Continuing Near East Crisis: Background Information*. Washington, D.C.: U.S. Government Printing Office, 1969. 40p.

4979. _____ . *The Middle East in Crisis —Problems and Prospects: Report*. 92d Cong., 1st sess. Washington, D.C.: U.S. Government Printing Office, 1971. 28p.

4980.   Whetten, Lawrence L. *The Soviet Presence in the Eastern Mediterranean*. New York: National Strategy Information Center, 1971. 50p.

4981.   Wolfe, Thomas W. *Soviet Goals and Policies in the Middle East*. RAND Paper P-4472. Santa Monica, Calif.: RAND Corporation, 1970. 27p.

Further References

See also section 5:A and other parts of this section.

b. SPECIFIC NATIONS

(1). Egypt

BOOKS

4982.   Baker, Raymond W. *Egypt's Uncertain Revolution under Nasser and Sadat*. Cambridge, Mass.: Harvard University Press, 1978. 290p.

4983.   Bar-Simon-Tov, Yaacov. *The Israeli-Egyptian War of Attrition, 1969–1970: A Case Study of Limited Local War*. New York: Columbia University Press, 1980. 248p.

4984.   Dawisha, Karen. *Soviet Foreign Policy towards Egypt*. New York: St. Martin's Press, 1979. 276p.

4985.	Heikal, Mohamed. *The Road to Ramadan.* New York: Quadrangle Books, 1975. 285p.

4986.	Nutting, Anthony. *Nasser.* New York: E. P. Dutton, 1972. 493p.

4987.	Rubinstein, Alvin Z. *Red Star on the Nile: The Soviet-Egyptian Influence Relationship since the June War.* Princeton, N.J.: Princeton University Press, 1977. 383p.

4988.	Sadat, Anwar. *In Search of Identity: An Autobiography.* New York: Harper & Row, 1978. 360p.

ARTICLES

4989.	Alsop, Joseph. "Russia's Menacing New Challenge in the Middle East." *Reader's Digest* 97 (August 1970), 47–51.

4990.	Ballis, William B. "Soviet Foreign Policy toward Developing States: The Case of Egypt." *Institute for the Study of the USSR Bulletin* 15 (March 1968), 84–113.

4991.	Beecher, William. "The Watch on the Suez: Egypt's Noisy Silent Partner." *Army* 21 (November 1971), 10–13.

4992.	Cottrell, Alvin J. "Soviet-Egyptian Relations." *Military Review* 49 (December 1969), 69–76.

4993.	Cox, Frederick J. "The Russian Presence in Egypt." *Naval War College Review* 22 (February 1970), 45–53.

4994.	DeBorchgrave, André. "The Kremlin's Mideast Gamble." *Newsweek* 75 (June 1, 1970), 37–42.

4995.	"Egypt Displays Soviet-Supplied Weapons." *Aviation Week and Space Technology* 101 (August 26, 1974), 14–18.

4996.	"Electronic Summer." *Time* 95 (April 6, 1970), 38.

4997.	Evron, Yair. "The Soviet Union in Egypt." *Survival* 12 (August 1970), 259–262.

4998.	Freedman, Robert O. "Soviet Policy toward Sadat's Egypt from the Death of Nasser to the Fall of General Sadek." *Naval War College Review* 26 (November-December 1973), 63–79.

4999.	"The Growing Soviet Commitment: Training Programs and Missile Sites in Egypt." *Time* 95 (April 13, 1970), 33.

5000.	Hottinger, Arnold. "Cairo's Ties to Moscow." *Swiss Review of World Affairs* 19 (November 1969), 7–8.

5001.   Kapeliuk, Amnon. "The Egyptian-Russian Conflict: Origins and Development." *New Outlook* 15 (September 1972), 8–18.

5002.   Kolcum, E. H. "Soviets Accelerating Mideast Drive." *Aviation Week and Space Technology* 92 (May 18, 1970), 9, 14–18.

5003.   _____ . "Soviets Shifting Mideast Balance." *Aviation Week and Space Technology* 92 (May 11, 1970), 18–21.

5004.   _____ . "Soviets Spur Arms Flow to Egypt." *Aviation Week and Space Technology* 94 (April 19, 1971), 9, 14–16.

5005.   "Living on the Brink of War." *U.S. News and World Report* 70 (March 15, 1971), 78–82.

5006.   "Middle East: That Electronic Summer." *Time* 96 (July 20, 1970), 18–19.

5007.   "Moscow-on-the-Nile." *Time* 95 (June 22, 1970), 31.

5008.   "Of Mosques and MIG's: Moscow's Growing Military Role in Egypt." *Time* 95 (June 1, 1970), 19–20.

5009.   Oliver, Luis G. "Tactical Electronic Warfare: E.C.M. are Good When You Know How to Use Them." *TacAir Warfare Center Quarterly Report* 2 (Spring 1971), 4–9.

5010.   Pajak, Roger F. "Soviet Arms and Egypt." *Survival* 17 (July-August 1975), 166.

5011.   Ra'anan, Uri. "Genesis of an Arms Deal: Egypt, 1955." *The U.S.S.R. Arms the Third World: Case Studies in Soviet Foreign Policy.* Cambridge, Mass.: M.I.T. Press, 1969.

5012.   _____ . "The Soviet-Egyptian Rift." *Commentary* 61 (June 1976), 29–35.

5013.   "Relief for Egypt—Anxiety for Israel." *Time* 95 (May 11, 1970), 43–44.

5014.   Rubenstein, Alvin Z. "Moscow and Cairo: Currents of Influence." *Problems of Communism* 23 (July-August 1974), 17–28.

5015.   "SAM's, MIG's, Russians: Soviet Troops in Egypt." *Newsweek* 75 (May 11, 1970), 59–60.

5016.   Singh, K. R. "Soviet-U.A.R. Relations." *India Quarterly* 25 (April-June 1969), 139–152.

5017.   "Sparring along the Canal." *Newsweek* 78 (September 27, 1971), 46.

5018.   "The Suez Canal: Key to Russia's Strategy in the Mideast?" *U.S. News and World Report* 68 (June 22, 1970), 22–24.

5019.   Werth, Alexander. "Russia on the Nile." *Nation* 206 (February 12, 1968), 198–201.

5020.   Whetten, Lawrence L. "June 1967 to June 1971: Four Years of Canal War Reconsidered." *New Middle East,* no. 33 (June 1971), 15–25.

5021.   _____ . "Sadat's Strategic Options in the Canal War." *World Today* 29 (February 1973), 58–67.

5022.   Yodfat, Aryeh Y. "Arms and Influence in Egypt: The Record of Soviet Military Assistance since June 1967." *New Middle East,* no. 10 (July 1969), 27–33.

DOCUMENTS, PAPERS, AND REPORTS

5023.   Burnett, John H., Jr. "Soviet-Egyptian Relations during the Khrushchev Era: A Study in Soviet Foreign Policy." PhD dissertation, Emory University, 1966.

5024.   Horelick, Arnold L. *Moscow's Rift with Sadat: Implications for Soviet Middle East Policy.* RAND Paper P-5666. Santa Monica, Calif.: RAND Corporation, 1976. 29p.

5025.   Ramet, Pedro. *Sadat and the Kremlin.* Santa Monica, Calif.: California Seminar on Arms Control and Foreign Policy, 1980. 66p.

Further References

See also section 5:D:1:a.

(2). Syria/Jordan/Libya

BOOKS

5026.   First, Ruth. *Libya: The Elusive Revolution.* New York: Holmes & Meier, 1975. 294p.

5027.   Rabinovich, Itamar. *The Soviet Union and Syria in the 1970's: A Study of Influence.* New York: Praeger, 1980. 200p.

ARTICLES

5028.   Bodansky, Yossef. "The Soviet Military Presence in Libya." *Armed Forces Journal International* 118 (November 1980), 89–90.

5029.   Golan, Galia. "Syria and the Soviet Union since the Yom Kippur War." *Orbis* 21 (Winter 1978), 777–801.

5030.   "The Making of a Russian Base: How the Reds Are Winning Syria." *U.S. News and World Report* 43 (October 18, 1957), 96–100.

5031.   Mangold, Peter. "The Soviet-Syrian Military Relationship, 1955–1977." *Journal of the Royal United Service Institute for Defence Studies* 122 (September 1977), 27–33.

5032.   Pajak, Roger F. "Soviet Arms Aid to Libya." *Military Review* 56 (July 1976), 82–87.

5033.   _____ . "Soviet Military Aid to Iraq and Syria." *Strategic Review* 4 (Winter 1976), 51–59.

5034.   Rudolph, James D. "National Security." In Richard F. Nyrop, ed., *Syria: A Country Study*. Washington, D.C.: U.S. Government Printing Office, 1978. pp. 191–255.

Further References

See also section 5:D:1:a.

2. The Arab-Israeli Wars, 1967 and 1973

a. THE SIX-DAY WAR, 1967

BOOKS

5035.   *The Arab-Israeli Conflict: The 1967 Campaign*. New York: Scribners, 1968. 55p.

5036.   Barker, Arthur J. *Six-Day War*. Ballantine's Illustrated History of the Violent Century. New York: Ballantine Books, 1974. 159p.

5037.   Dayan, David. *Strike First!: A Battle History of Israel's Six-Day War*. New York: G. P. Putnam, 1968. 292p.

5038.   Dayan, Moshe. *Diary of the Sinai Campaign*. New York: Harper & Row, 1966. 236p.

5039.   Kosut, Hal, ed. *Israel and the Arabs: The June 1967 War*. New York: Facts on File, 1974. 185p.

5040.   O'Ballance, Edgar. *The Third Arab-Israeli War*. Hamden, Conn.: Shoe String Press, 1972. 288p.

5041.   Young, Peter. *The Israeli Campaign, 1967*. London: Kimber, 1967. 192p.

ARTICLES

5042.   Badeau, J. S. "The Arabs, 1967." *Atlantic* 220 (December 1967), 102–110.

5043.   Doran, C. F. "Leading Indicators of the June War." *International Journal of Middle East Studies* 11 (February 1980), 23–58.

5044.   "The Israeli Thrust." *Life* 62 (June 16, 1967), 26–38D.

5045.   Kotch, W. J. "The Six-Day War of 1967." *U.S. Naval Institute Proceedings* 94 (June 1968), 72–81.

5046.   Liddell-Hart, Basil H. "Strategy of a War." *Encounter* 20 (February 1968), 16–20.

5047.   "Lightning in the Desert: The Story of the Israeli Victory." *U.S. News and World Report* 62 (June 19, 1967), 62–63.

5048.   "The Quickest War." *Time* 89 (June 16, 1967), 22–28.

5049.   Shoemaker, R. "The Arab-Israeli War." *Military Review* 48 (August 1968), 56–69.

5050.   "Terrible Swift Sword: How the War Was Won." *Newsweek* 69 (June 19, 1967), 24–29.

5051.   "The Three-Day Blitz from Gaza to Suez." *U.S. News and World Report* 62 (June 19, 1967), 33–37.

5052.   Tuchman, Barbara W. "Israel's Swift Sword." *Atlantic* 220 (September 1967), 56–62.

5053.   Yost, Charles W. "The Arab-Israeli War." *Foreign Affairs* 46 (January 1968), 304–346.

Further References

See also section 5:D:1:a.

b. THE YOM KIPPUR WAR, 1973

BOOKS

5054.   Adan, Avraham. *On the Banks of the Suez: An Israeli General's Personal Account of the Yom Kippur War.* San Rafael, Calif.: Presidio Press, 1980. 512p.

5055. Amos, John W., 2d. *Arab-Israeli Military-Political Relations: Arab Perceptions and the Politics of Escalation.* New York and London: Pergamon Press, 1979. 382p.

5056. Barker, Arthur J. *Yom Kippur War.* Ballantine's Illustrated History of the Violent Century, Campaign Book, no. 29. New York: Ballantine Books, 1974. 159p.

5057. Bullock, John. *The Making of a War.* London: Longmans, Green, 1974. 220p.

5058. Dayan, Yael. *Three Weeks in October.* New York: Delacorte, 1979.

5059. El-Badri, Hassan. *Ramadan War, 1973.* Translated from the Arabic. New York: Hippocrene Books, 1978. 239p.

5060. El-Shazly, Saad. *The Crossing of the Suez.* San Francisco, Calif.: American Mideast Research, 1980. 300p.

5061. Herzog, Chaim. *The War of Atonement, October 1973.* Boston, Mass.: Little, Brown, 1975. 300p.

5062. Kohler, Foy D.; Leon Gouré; and Mose L. Harvey. *The Soviet Union and the October 1973 Middle East War: The Implications for Detente.* Miami, Fla.: Center for Advanced International Studies, University of Miami, 1974. 127p.

5063. London Sunday Times, Insight Team of the. *The Yom Kippur War.* Garden City, N.Y.: Doubleday, 1974. 514p.

5064. O'Ballance, Edgar. *No Victor, No Vanquished: The Yom Kippur War.* San Rafael, Calif.: Presidio Press, 1979. 383p.

5065. Palit, D. K. *Return to Sinai: The Arab Offensive, October 1973.* New Delhi, India: Palit & Palit, 1974. 172p.

5066. Schiff, Zeev. *October Earthquake: Yom Kippur, 1973.* Tel Aviv, Israel: University Publishing Projects, 1974.

5067. Schmidt, Dana A. *Armageddon in the Middle East.* New York: John Day, 1974. 269p.

5068. Sobel, Lester A., ed. *Israel and the Arabs: The October 1973 War.* New York: Facts on File, 1974. 185p.

5069. Williams, Louis, ed. *Military Aspects of the Israeli-Arab Conflict.* Tel Aviv, Israel: University Publishing Projects, 1975. 265p.

ARTICLES

5070.   "Arabs vs. Israelis in a Suez Showdown." *Time* 102 (October 29, 1973), 22–30.

5071.   Barclay, C. N. "Lessons from the October War: Learning the Hard Way." *Army* 24 (March 1974), 25–29.

5072.   Barker, Arthur J. "Aspects of the October 1973 War." *Royal Air Forces Quarterly* 14 (Winter 1974), 301–307.

5073.   "Black October: Old Enemies at War Again." *Time* 102 (October 15, 1973), 30–32.

5074.   Brower, Kenneth S. "Armor in the October War." *Armor* 83 (May-June 1974), 10–15.

5075.   ———. "The Yom Kippur War." *Military Review* 54 (March 1974), 25–33.

5076.   Burke, John T. "Precision Weaponry: The Changing Nature of Modern Warfare." *Army* 24 (March 1974), 12–16.   Examines Arab use of Soviet-made antitank missiles.

5077.   Cox, Richard. "The October War's Military Lessons." *International Perspectives* 2 (March-April 1974), 32–35.

5078.   Crump, Roger L. "The October War: A Postwar Assessment." *Military Review* 54 (August 1974), 12–26.

5079.   "Deadly New Weapons: Their Use in the Israel-Arab War." *Time* 102 (October 22, 1973), 37–38.

5080.   Deane, John R., Jr. "Armor Today and the October War." *Armor* 83 (July-August 1974), 35–39.

5081.   Deborchgrave, André. "Dispatches from the Front." *Newsweek* 82 (November 5, 1973), 48–50.

5082.   "The Desert as a Proving Ground: The Use of Newest Weaponry." *Time* 102 (October 29, 1973), 43–44.

5083.   "A Diary of the Fourth Arab-Israeli War." *Army Quarterly* 104 (January 1974), 168–189.

5084.   "The Duel on Mount Herman." *Newsweek* 83 (April 29, 1978), 39–40.

5085.   Dupuy, Trevor N. "The War of Ramadan: An Arab Perspective of the October War." *Army* 25 (March 1975), 13–22.

5086.   Eaker, Ira C. "The Fourth Arab-Israeli War." *Strategic Review* 2 (Winter 1974), 18–25.

5087.   Forsyth, Robert W., and John P. "The Cheap Shot." *Armor* 83 (March-April 1974), 35–37.   Arab antitank missiles.

5088.   Ghazala, Mohamed A. H. A. "The Suez Crossing: An Interview." *Military Review* 59 (November 1979), 2–7.

5089.   "The Great Armoured Battles: October 14, 1973." *Born in Battle Magazine* (November 1979), *passim.*

5090.   Handel, Michael I. "Yom Kippur and the Inevitability of Surprise." *International Studies Quarterly* 21 (September 1977), 461–502.

5091.   Hein, K. P. "Old Lessons Learned." *Armor* 84 (September-October 1975), 30–36.

5092.   Herzog, Chaim. "The Middle East War, 1973." *Journal of the Royal United Service Institute for Defence Studies* 120 (March 1975), 3–13.

5093.   Latter, B. "Lessons for N.A.T.O. in the Yom Kippur War." *Royal Air Forces Quarterly* 16 (Winter 1976), 380–385.

5094.   "Looking Back in Anger: The Report of the Agranat Commission of Inquiry." *Time* 103 (April 15, 1974), 42.

5095.   McKenzie-Smith, Robert H. "Crisis Decisionmaking in Israel: The Case of the October 1973 Middle East War." *Naval War College Review* 29 (Summer 1976), 39–52.

5096.   Marshall, Samuel L. A. "Egypt's Two-Week Military Myth." *New Leader* 57 (November 12, 1973), 7–12.

5097.   _____ . "Reading the Mideast War: Reality in a Game of Confusion." *New Leader* 56 (October 29, 1973), 4–7.

5098.   Meir, Golda. "The Yom Kippur War." *My Life.* New York: Dell, 1975. pp. 405–437.

5099.   Middleton, Drew. "Who Lost the Yom Kippur War?" *Atlantic* 133 (March 1974), 45–47.

5100.   "Missing the Arabs' War Signals." *Time* 102 (October 22, 1973), 48–49.

5101.   Morony, T. L. "Artillery Support in the Yom Kippur War." *Field Artillery Journal* 43 (September-October 1975), 40–43.

5102.   "The October War and Its Aftermath." *Journal of Palestine Studies* 3 (Winter 1974), 3–129.

5103.   O'Neill, Bard E. "The October War: A Political-Military Assessment." *Air University Review* 25 (July-August 1974), 27–35.

5104.   Pa'il, Meir. "Political and Military Reflections in the Wake of the War of October 1973." *New Outlook* 16 (December 1973), 4–17.

5105.   Perimutter, Amos. "Israel's Fourth War, October 1973: Political and Military Misperceptions." *Orbis* 19 (Summer 1975), 434–460.

5106.   Quandt, William B. "Soviet Policy in the October Middle East War." *International Affairs* (London) 53 (July 1977) 377–389; (October 1977), 587–603.

5107.   Record, Jeffrey. "The October War: Burying the Blitzkrieg." *Military Review* 56 (April 1976), 19–21.

5108.   "Restocking the Arsenals." *Newsweek* 82 (October 29, 1973), 50.

5109.   Rodwell, Robert R. "The Mideast War: A Damned Close-Run Thing." *Air Force Magazine* 57 (February 1974), 36–41.

5110.   Ropelewski, R. R. "Egypt Assesses Lessons of October War." *Aviation Week and Space Technology* 99 (December 17, 1973), 14–17.

5111.   Safran, Nadev. "Trial by Ordeal: The Yom Kippur War, October 1973." *International Security Review* 3 (Fall 1977), 133–170.

5112.   Sagan, S. D. "Lessons of the Yom Kippur Alert." *Foreign Policy*, no. 36 (Fall 1979), 160–177.

5113.   Shlaim, Avi. "Failures in National Intelligence Estimates: The Case of the Yom Kippur War." *World Politics* 28 (April 1976), 348–380.

5114.   Singh, K. R. "Ground Attack vs. Anti-Aircraft Defense." *India Quarterly* 30 (April-June 1975), *passim*.

5115.   Slominski, Martin J. "The Soviet Military Press and the October War." *Military Review* 54 (May 1974), 39–47.

5116.   "Soviet Aid Sparks Arab Gains." *Aviation Week and Space Technology* 99 (October 15, 1973), 12–14.

5117.   "Special Report: Mideast War." *Aviation Week and Space Technology* 99 (October 15, 1973), 7, 12–18.

5118.   Thompson, Anthony. "What the Mideast War Showed." *International Socialist Review* 34 (December 1973), 18–24.

5119.   Timmons, Richard F. "AT Missiles in the Yom Kippur War." *Infantry* 64 (January-February 1974), 18–21.

5120.   Toepfer, Horst. "The 1973 Mideast War." *Field Artillery Journal* 42 (November-December 1974), 36–43; 43 (January-February 1975), 6–13; (March-April 1975), 12–19.

5121.   Toyne-Sewell, T. P. "The War of Atonement and Its Lessons." *Army Quarterly* 106 (January 1976), 67–71.

5122.   Turley, G. H. "Time of Change in Modern War." *Marine Corps Gazette* 58 (December 1974), 16–20.

5123.   Viksne, J. "The Yom Kippur War in Retrospect: Electronic Warfare." *Army Journal,* no. 324 (May 1976), 25–28.

5124.   Wakebridge, Charles. "The Syrian Side of the Hill." *Military Review* 56 (April 1976), 19–21.

5125.   _____ . "A Tank Myth or a Missile Mirage." *Military Review* 56 (August 1976), 3–11.

5126.   Walszyk, Thomas. "The October War: Doctrine and Tactics in the Yom Kippur Conflict, 6 to 24 October 1974." *Strategy and Tactics,* no. 61 (March-April 1977), 4–18, 39.

5127.   Weller, Jac. "The Arab Improvement—Good, but Not Good Enough." *National Guardsman* 28 (May 1974), 2–8.

5128.   _____ . "Infantry in the October War: Foot Soldiers in the Desert." *Infantry* 24 (August 1974), 21–26.

5129.   _____ . "Middle East Tank Killers." *Journal of the Royal United Service Institute for Defence Studies* 119 (December 1974), 28–33.

5130.   _____ . "Tanks in the Middle East War." *Military Review* 56 (May 1976), 11–23.

5131.   Whetten, Lawrence L., and Michael Johnson. "Military Lessons of the Yom Kippur War." *World Today* 30 (March 1974), 101–110.

5132.   Williams, Philip. "Detente and the Yom Kippur War: From Crisis Management to Crisis Prevention." *Royal Air Forces Quarterly* 16 (Autumn 1976), 227–233.

5133.   "The World Will No Longer Laugh: The Strength of the Arab Military Force." *Time* 102 (October 22, 1973), 49–50.

5134.   "The Yom Kippur War." *Infantry* 64 (May-June 1974), 12–17.

5135.   "The Yom Kippur War." *Midstream* 19 (December 1973), 3–70.

DOCUMENTS, PAPERS, AND REPORTS

5136.   Golan, Galia. *The Soviet Union and the Arab-Israeli War of October 1973*. Jerusalem Papers on Peace Problems, no. 7. Jerusalem: Hebrew University of Jerusalem, 1974. 31p.

5137.   Handel, Michael I. *Perception, Deception, and Surprise: The Case of the Yom Kippur War*. Jerusalem Papers on Peace Problems, no. 19. Jerusalem: Hebrew University of Jerusalem, 1976. 33p.

5138.   Israel. Agranat Commission of Inquiry. *Interim Report*. Jerusalem, April 1, 1974.

5139.   Jarjura, Sana. "The Yom Kippur War: Conflict Resolution through Combat." MA thesis, California Institute of Asian Studies, 1979.

5140.   Mergien, A. *Military Lessons of the October War*. Adelphi papers, no. 114. London: International Institute for Strategic Studies, 1975. 28p.

5141.   Monroe, Elizabeth, and Anthony H. Farrar-Hockley. *The Arab-Israel War, October 1973: Background and Events*. Adelphi papers, no. 111. London: International Institute for Strategic Studies, 1975.

5142.   Quandt, William B. *Soviet Policy in the October 1973 War*. RAND Research Study RS-1864-ISA. Santa Monica, Calif.: RAND Corporation, 1976. 39p.

5143.   United States. Congress. House. Committee on Foreign Relations. Subcommittee on the Near East and South Asia. *The Impact of the October Middle East War: Hearings*. 93d Cong., 1st sess. Washington, D.C., 1973. 159p.

5144.   United States. Department of Defense. Defense Intelligence Agency. *A Summary of Lessons Learned in the Arab-Israeli War of 1973*. DI-646-71-74. Washington, D.C., 1974. 47p.

5145.   Van Creveid, Martin L. *Military Lessons of the Yom Kippur War: Historical Perspectives*. Washington papers, v. 3, no. 4. Los Angeles, Calif.: Sage, 1975. 60p.

Further References

See also sections 4:E:2:e, 4:F:2, and 5:D:1:a and b.

E. The Persian Gulf and the Horn of Africa

1. General Works

BOOKS

5146.   Cottrell, Alvin J., ed. *The Persian Gulf States: A General Survey.* Baltimore, Md.: Johns Hopkins University Press, 1980. 736p.

5147.   Farer, Tom J. *War Clouds on the Horn of Africa.* Washington, D.C.: Carnegie Endowment for International Peace, 1976. 176p.

5148.   Legum, Colin. *The Horn of Africa in Continuing Crisis.* New York: Holmes & Meier, 1979. 186p.

5149.   Long, David E. *The Persian Gulf.* Boulder, Colo.: Westview Press, 1976. 182p.

5150.   Mughisuddin, Mohammed, ed. *Conflict and Cooperation in the Persian Gulf.* New York: Praeger, 1976. 192p.

5151.   Noyes, James H. *Clouded Lens: Persian Gulf Security and U. S. Policy.* Stanford, Calif.: Hoover Institution Press, 1979. 165p.

5152.   Page, Stephen. *The U.S.S.R. and Arabia: The Development of Soviet Policies and Attitudes towards the Countries of the Arabian Peninsula, 1955–1970.* London: Central Asian Research Center, in Association with the Canadian Institute of International Affairs, 1971. 149p.

5153.   Yodfat, Aryeh, and Mordechai Abir. *In the Direction of the Persian Gulf: The Soviet Union and the Persian Gulf.* London: Cass, 1977. 167p.

ARTICLES

5154.   Becker, Abraham S. "Oil and the Persian Gulf in Soviet Policy in the 1970's." In Michael Confino and Shimon Shamir, eds., *The U.S.S.R. and the Middle East.* New York: Wiley, 1973. pp. 173–214.

5155.   Brown, Harold. "The Persian Gulf and Southwest Asia: Interests and Strategies." *Defense '80,* no. 6 (June 1980), 1–7.

5156.   Creekman, Charles T. "Sino-Soviet Competition in the Yemans." *Naval War College Review* 32 (June-July 1979), 73–82.

5157.   Croizat, Victor J. "Stability in the Persian Gulf." *U.S. Naval Institute Proceedings* 99 (July 1973), 48–59.

5158.   David, Steven. "Realignment in the Horn: The Soviet Advantage." *International Security Review* 4 (Fall 1979), 69–90.

5159.   Griswold, Laurence. "The Bear on the Roof: Soviet Power Encircles the Persian Gulf." *Sea Power* 15 (June 1972), 20–25.

5160.   Harrigan, Anthony. "Security Interests in the Persian Gulf and Western Indian Ocean." *Strategic Review* 1 (Fall 1973), 13–22.

5161.   Hurewitz, J. C. "The Persian Gulf: British Withdrawal and Western Security." *Annals of the American Academy of Political and Social Science* 401 (May 1972), 106–115.

5162.   Legum, Colin. "International Dimensions of the Power Struggle in the Horn of Africa." *Atlantic Community Quarterly* 17 (Fall 1979), 257–264.

5163.   Luttwak, Edward N. "Cubans in Arabia [Yeman]?" *Commentary* 68 (December 1979), 62–66.

5164.   Mullin, David. "The U.S.-Soviet Struggle to Control the Horn of Africa." *U.S. News and World Report* 83 (August 29, 1977), 43–45.

5165.   Price, David L. "Moscow and the Persian Gulf." *Problems of Communism* 28 (March-April 1979), 1–13.

5166.   Remnek, Richard B. "Soviet Policy in the Horn of Africa: The Decision to Intervene." In Robert H. Donaldson, ed., *The Soviet Union in the Third World.* Boulder, Colo.: Westview Press, 1981. Chpt. 6.

5167.   Sheldon, L. G., Jr. "The Sino-Soviet Split: The Horn of Africa, November 1977–February 1979." *Naval War College Review* 32 (May-June 1979), 78–87.

5168.   "Shifting Sands on the Horn." *Time* 110 (August 22, 1977), 34.

5169.   Smolansky, Oles M. "Moscow and the Persian Gulf: An Analysis of Soviet Ambitions and Potential." *Orbis* 14 (Spring 1970), 92–108.

5170.   Standish, J. F. "The Pursuit of Peace in the Persian Gulf." *World Politics* 32 (December 1969), 235–244.

5171.   Tasker, R. "Facing Moscow's Pincer Movement." *Far Eastern Economic Review* 108 (May 9, 1980), 21–25.

5172.   Vanneman, Peter, and Martin James. "The Soviet Thrust into the Horn of Africa: The Next Targets." *Strategic Review* 6 (Spring 1978), 33–40.

5173.   Watt, Donald C. "The Persian Gulf: Cradle of Conflict?" *Problems of Communism* 21 (May-June 1972), 32–40.

5174.   Whetten, Lawrence L. "The Soviet-Cuban Presence in the Horn of Africa." *Journal of the Royal United Service Institute for Defence Studies* 123 (September 1978), 39–45.

5175.   Wohlstetter, Albert. "Half Wars and Half Policies in the Persian Gulf." In W. Scott Thompson, *National Security for the 1980's: From Weakness to Strength.* San Francisco, Calif.: Institute for Contemporary Studies, 1980. Chpt. 7.

5176.   Woodward, Peter. "Conflict in the Horn of Africa." *Contemporary Review* 231 (December 1977), 281–285.

5177.   Wright, Denis. "The Changing Balance of Power in the Persian Gulf." *Asian Affairs* 60 (October 1973), 255–262.

5178.   Yodfat, Aryeh. "The U.S.S.R. and the Persian Gulf Area." *Australian Outlook* 33 (April 1979), 60–72.

DOCUMENTS, PAPERS, AND REPORTS

5179.   Becker, Abraham S. *Oil and the Persian Gulf in Soviet Policy in the 1970's.* RAND Paper P-4743. Santa Monica, Calif.: RAND Corporation, 1971. 45p.

5180.   Bell, J. Bowyer. *The Horn of Africa: Strategic Magnet in the Seventies.* Strategy papers, no. 21. New York: Published for the National Strategy Information Center by Crane, Russak, 1973. 55p.

5181.   Hensel, Howard M. "Soviet Policy in the Persian Gulf, 1968–1975." PhD dissertation, University of Virginia, 1976.

5182.   O'Neill, Bard E. *Petroleum and Security: The Limitations of Military Power in the Persian Gulf.* NSA Monograph 77-4. Washington, D.C.: Research Directorate, National Defense University, 1977. 22p.

Further References

See also section 5:A.

2. The Persian Gulf War, 1980–1981

5183.   Davidson, Spencer. "War in the Persian Gulf." *Time* 116 (October 6, 1980), 34–47.

5184.   Dawisha, Karen. "Moscow and the Gulf War." *World Today* 37 (January 1981), 8–14.

5185.   Johnson, Marguerite. "The Blitz Bogs Down." *Time* 116 (October 13, 1980), 46–49.

5186.   Levin, Bob. "Iraq's Ambitious War Aims." *Newsweek* 96 (October 6, 1980), 37–38.

5187.   "The Mideast Cauldron." *U.S. News and World Report* 90 (October 13, 1980), 22–25.

5188.   Petrossian, Vahe. "The Gulf War." *World Today* 36 (November 1980), 415–417.

5189.   Strasser, Steven. "Fighting to a Standstill." *Newsweek* 96 (October 13, 1980), 50–54.

5190.   _____ . "The Gulf War: Rising Risks." *Newsweek* 96 (October 20, 1980), 40–44.

5191.   _____ . "The War in the Oil Fields." *Newsweek* 96 (October 6, 1980), 28–35.

5192.   Talbott, Strobe. "Will the Gulf Explode?" *Time* 116 (October 27, 1980), 38–39.

5193.   Wright, Claudia. "Implications of the Iran-Iraq War." *Foreign Affairs* 59 (Winter 1980-1981), 275–303.

Further References

See also section 5:E:3:c.

3. *Specific Nations*

a. SOMALIA

ARTICLES

5194.   Bell, J. Bowyer. "Strategic Implications of the Soviet Presence in Somalia." *Orbis* 19 (Summer 1975), 402–411.

5195.   Chaplin, Dennis. "Somalia and the Development of Soviet Activity in the Indian Ocean." *Military Review* 55 (July 1975), 3–9.

5196.   Crozier, Brian. "The Soviet Presence in Somalia." *Conflict Studies*, no. 54 (February 1975), 3–19.

5197.   Hughes, A. J. "Somalia's Socialist Road." *Africa Report* 22 (March 1977), 41–49.

5198.   Legum, Colin. "Horning In." *New Republic* 177 (October 1, 1977), 18–21.

5199.   Mullin, Dennis. "That Russian Base in Somalia: What Our Man Found on the Scene." *U.S. News and World Report* 79 (July 21, 1975), 58–60.

5200.   Payton, Gary D. "The Soviet Military Presence Abroad: The Lessons of Somalia." *Military Review* 59 (January 1979), 67–77.

5201.   "The Russians on Africa's Horn." *Time* 106 (July 21, 1975), 29–30.

DOCUMENTS, PAPERS, AND REPORTS

5202.   United States. Congress. Senate. Committee on Armed Services. *The Soviet Military Capability in Berbera, Somalia: Report.* Washington, D.C.: U.S. Government Printing Office, 1975. 29p.

Further References

See section 5:E:1.

b. ETHIOPIA

BOOKS

5203.   Sherman, Richard. *Eritrea: The Unfinished Revolution.* New York: Praeger, 1980. 197p.

5204.   Spencer, John H. *Ethiopia, the Horn of Africa, and U.S. Policy.* Cambridge, Mass.: Institute for Foreign Policy Analysis, 1977. 70p.

ARTICLES

5205.   Carroll, Robert. "War in the Horn." *Newsweek* 91 (February 13, 1978), 45.

5206.   Connell, Dan. "The Eritrean Battle Front: The Cubans Move In." *Nation* 226 (May 6, 1978), 530–533.

5207.   DeBorchgrave, André. "Counterattack in the Horn." *Newsweek* 91 (February 20, 1978), 39–40.

5208.   Legum, Colin. "Cubans in Ethiopia." *New Republic* 176 (June 11, 1977), 15–16.

5209.   _____ . "Next: Eritrea." *New Republic* 178 (April 8, 1978), 13–15.

5210.   Mullin, Dennis. "Another Place the Kremlin Is Bogged Down." *U.S. News and World Report* 88 (March 3, 1980), 23.

5211.   Papp, Daniel S. "The Soviet Union and Cuba in Ethiopia." *Current History* 76 (March 1979), 110–114.

5212.   Payton, Gary D. "The Soviet-Ethiopian Liaison." *Air University Review* 31 (November-December 1979), 66–73.

Further References

See also section 5:E:1.

c. IRAQ

BOOKS

5213.   O'Ballance, Edgar. *The Kurdish Revolt, 1961–1970.* London: Faber & Faber, 1973. 196p.

5214.   Penrose, Edith, and E. F. *Iraq: International Relations and National Development.* Boulder, Colo.: Westview Press, 1978. 569p.

5215.   Smolansky, Oles M. *The Soviet Union and Iraq, 1968–1979.* New York: Praeger, 1980. 200p.

ARTICLES

5216.   Cooley, John K. "Conflict within the Iraqi Left." *Problems of Communism* 29 (January-February 1980), 87–93.

5217.   Freedman, Robert O. "Soviet Policy toward Ba'athist Iraq, 1968–1978." In Robert H. Donaldson, ed., *The Soviet Union in the Third World.* Boulder, Colo.: Westview Press, 1981. Chpt. 8.

5218.   Kuchin, V. "Fruitful Cooperation." *Soviet Military Review,* no. 3 (March 1977), 48–50.

5219.   O'Ballance, Edgar. "The Kurdish Factor in the Gulf." *Army Quarterly* 104 (October 1974), 561–570.

5220.   "Soviet and American Military Bases in Iraq and Saudi Arabia." *International Currency Review* 12 (January 1980), 40–44.

5221.   Wright, Claudia. "Iraq: New Power in the Middle East." *Foreign Affairs* 58 (Winter 1979), 257–277; (Spring 1980), 966–969.

5222.   Yodfat, Aryeh Y. "Iraq—Russia's Other Middle East Pasture." *New Middle East,* no. 38 (November 1971), 26–30.

5223.   ———. "Unpredictable Iraq Poses a Russian Problem." *New Middle East,* no. 13 (October 1969), 17–20.

DOCUMENTS, PAPERS, AND REPORTS

5224.   Fukuyama, Y. F. *The Soviet Union and Iraq since 1968*. RAND
Note N-1524-AF. Santa Monica, Calif.: RAND Corporation, 1980. 81p.

5225.   Helmlinger, R. B. *Iranian-Iraqi Antagonism: Source for U.S.-
U.S.S.R. Confrontation*. Carlisle Barracks, Pa.: Strategic Studies Institute, U.S. Army War College, 1974. 39p.

Further References

See also sections 5:E:1 and 5:E:2.

F. Africa

1. General Works

BOOKS

5226.   Adelman, Kenneth L. *African Realities*. New York: Crane,
Russak, 1980. 192p.

5227.   Albright, David E., ed. *Communism in Africa*. Bloomington:
Indiana University Press, 1980. 277p.

5228.   Cohn, Helen D. *Soviet Policy toward Black Africa: The Focus on
National Integration*. New York: Praeger, 1972. 316p.

5229.   Legum, Colin, et al. *Africa in the 1980's: A Continent in Crisis*.
New York: McGraw-Hill, 1979. 232p.

5230.   Stevens, Christopher. *The Soviet Union and Black Africa*. New
York: Holmes & Meier, 1976. 236p.

5231.   Stockholm International Peace Research Institute. *Southern
Africa, the Escalation of a Conflict: A Politico-Military Study*. New York:
Praeger, 1976. 235p.

5232.   Weinstein, Warren, ed. *Chinese and Soviet Aid to Africa*. New
York: Praeger, 1975. 316p.

5233.   _____ , and Thomas H. Henriksen, eds. *Soviet and Chinese
Aid to African Nations*. New York: Praeger, 1979. 215p.

ARTICLES

5234.   "Africa: A Vietnam for Russia and Cuba?" *U.S. News and
World Report* 84 (February 6, 1978), 27–28.

5235.   Albright, David E. "Soviet Policy." *Problems of Communism* 27 (January 1978), 20–39.

5236.   Amery, Julian. "Soviet Imperialism in Africa." *NATO's Fifteen Nations* 23 (June-July 1978), 28–30.

5237.   "Another Challenge: How to Deal with the Russians in Africa." *U.S. News and World Report* 84 (February 27, 1978), 22–24.

5238.   Baker, Ross K. "Soviet Military Assistance to Tropical Africa." *Military Review* 48 (July 1968), 76–81.

5239.   Bienen, Henry. "Perspectives on Soviet Intervention in Africa." *Political Science Quarterly* 95 (Spring 1980), 29–42.

5240.   Bissell, Richard. "Soviet Policies in Africa." *Current History* 77 (October 1979), 110–114.

5241.   Brayton, Abbot A. "Soviet Involvement in Africa." *Journal of Modern African Studies* 17 (June 1979), 253–269.

5242.   Burns, Robert T. "Soviet-Cuban Enterprises in Africa." *U.S. Naval Institute Proceedings* 105 (July 1979), 28–33.

5243.   Campbell, J. C. "Soviet Policy in Africa and the Middle East." *Current History* 73 (October 1977), 100–104.

5244.   Carney, Joseph P. "The U.S.S.R. and Africa's Wars of Liberation." *Thought* 46 (Winter 1971), 592–610.

5245.   "Cubans, Cubans Everywhere." *Time* 109 (March 28, 1977), 33–34.

5246.   Deming, Angus. "Cubans in Africa." *Newsweek* 91 (March 13, 1978), 36–37.

5247.   Durch, William J. "The Cuban Military in Africa and the Middle East: From Algeria to Angola." *Studies in Comparative Communism* 11 (Spring-Summer 1978), 34–74.

5248.   Farer, Tom J. "Soviet Strategy and Western Fears." *Africa Report* 23 (November 1978), 4–8.

5249.   Fontaine, Roger W. "Cuban Strategy in Africa: The Long Road to Ambition." *Strategic Review* 6 (Summer 1978), 18–27.

5250.   Gann, Lewis H. "The Military Outlook: Southern Africa." *Military Review* 52 (July 1972), 59–72.

5251.   Geyer, Georgie A. "Cubans in Africa: What Are They Up To?" *New Republic* 176 (April 2, 1977), 11–13.

5252.   Gonzales, Edward. "The Complexities of Cuban Foreign Policy." *Problems of Communism* 26 (November-December 1977), 1–15.

5253.   Grabendorff, Wolf. "Cuba's Involvement in Africa: An Interpretation of Objectives, Reactions, and Limitations." *Journal of Inter-American Studies* 22 (February 1980), 3–29.

5254.   Gutteridge, William F. "The Political Role of African Armed Forces: The Impact of Foreign Military Assistance." *African Affairs* 66 (April 1967), 43–101.

5255.   Howe, R. W. "Cuba: Private Gutierrez Goes to War." *Atlantic* 242 (November 1978), 16–17.

5256.   Kapcia, A. M. "Cuba's African Involvement: A New Perspective." *Survey* 24 (Spring 1979), 142–159.

5257.   Klimov, Andrei. "Africa Rejects 'Absolute Neutrality.'" *Soviet Military Review*, no. 1 (January 1972), 57–58.

5258.   Kossow, Arabel G. "Soviet and Radical Arab Designs on the Saharan Belt." *Armed Forces Journal International* 117 (June 1980), 22.

5259.   Legum, Colin. "The African Crisis." *Foreign Affairs* 57 (February 1979), 633–651.

5260.   _____ . "The African Environment." *Problems of Communism* 27 (January-February 1978), 1–19.

5261.   _____ . "The Soviet Union, China, and the West in Southern Africa." *Foreign Affairs* 54 (July 1976), 745–762.

5262.   Marchand, Jean. "The Soviet Union and the Dark Continent." *Military Review* 43 (October 1963), 53–61.

5263.   Natufe, O. Igho. "Nigeria and Soviet Attitudes to African Military Regimes, 1965–1970." *Survey* 21 (Winter 1976), 93–111.

5264.   Newsom, David D. "Communism in Africa." *Department of State Bulletin* 79 (December 1979), 29–32.

5265.   O'Ballance, Edgar. "The Cuban Factor." *Journal of the Royal United Service Institute for Defence Studies* 123 (September 1978), 46–51.

5266.   Paris, Henri. "Soviet Activities in Africa Discussed: Translated from *Defense Nationale*, November 1980." *Translations on USSR Military Affairs*, no. 1557 (January 16, 1981), 1–8.

5267.   Portell-Vila, Herminio. "Cuba's Adventure in Africa." *International Security Review* 4 (Spring 1979), 26–59.

5268.   Rees, David. "Russia's Ruthless Reach into Africa." *Reader's Digest* 111 (November 1977), 169–174.

5269.   _____ . "Soviet Strategic Penetration of Africa." *Conflict Studies,* no. 77 (November 1976), 1–20.

5270.   "Russia's Dangerous Game: A Bold Gamble for Africa." *U.S. News and World Report* 79 (December 15, 1975), 43–45.

5271.   Rustin, Bayard, and Carl Gershman. "Africa, Soviet Imperialism, and the Retreat of American Power." *Commentary* 64 (October 1977), 33–43.

5272.   Samuels, Michael A., et al. "Implications of Soviet and Cuban Activities in Africa for U.S. Policy." *Africa Report* 25 (January-February 1980), 51–53.

5273.   "The Soviets in Africa." *Newsweek* 89 (April 4, 1977), 43.

5274.   Stainforth, Charles. "The Cuban Catspaw." *Army Quarterly* 109 (January 1979), 6–10.

5275.   Szulc, Tad. "Russia's African Ambitions." *New Republic* 178 (May 6, 1978), 14–15.

5276.   _____ . "The Soviet Master Plan in East Africa." *New York* 11 (February 27, 1978), 6.

5277.   Thom, William G. "Trends in Soviet Support for African Liberation." *Air University Review* 25 (July-August 1974), 36–43.

5278.   Thomas, Hugh. "Cuba in Africa." *Survey* 23 (Autumn 1978), 181–188.

5279.   _____ . "Cuba's Civilizing Mission." *Encounter* 50 (February 1978), 51–55.

5280.   Thompson, W. Scott. "The Soviet-Cuban Experience in Africa, 1974–1978: Implications for South Africa." In Richard E. Bissell and Chester A. Crocker, eds., *South Africa into the 1980's.* Boulder, Colo.: Westview Press, 1979. Chpt. 7.

5281.   Tomlinson, K. Y. "Can We Stop the Soviet Arms Machine in Africa?" *Reader's Digest* 113 (September 1978), 153–158.

5282.   "What Can Be Done?: Responding to Soviet-Cuban Involvement in Africa." *National Review* 30 (June 23, 1978), 761–762.

5283.   Whitaker, Paul M. "Arms and Nationalists: Who Helps?" *Africa Report* 15 (1970), 12–14.

5284.   Yodfat, Aryeh Y. "The U.S.S.R. and the North African Countries." *International Spectator* 25 (1971), 2126–2143.

DOCUMENTS, PAPERS, AND REPORTS

5285.   Copson, Raymond W. *Africa: Soviet-Cuban Role.* CRS Issue Brief 78077. Washington, D.C.: Foreign Affairs and National Defense Division, Congressional Research Service, Library of Congress, 1978.

5286.   Durch, William J. *The Cuban Military in Africa and the Middle East, from Algeria to Angola.* Professional paper, no. 201. Arlington, Va.: Center for Naval Analysis, Department of the Navy, 1977. 67p.

5287.   Legum, Colin, and Tony Hodges. *After Angola: The War over Southern Africa.* New York: Holmes & Meier, 1976. 85p.

5288.   Leogrande, William M. *Cuba's Policy in Africa, 1959–1980.* Policy Papers in International Affairs, no. 13. Berkeley: Institute of International Studies, University of California, 1980. 80p.

5289.   Ra'anan, G. *The Evolution of the Soviet Use of Surrogates in Military Relations with the Third World, with Particular Emphasis on Cuban Participation in Africa.* RAND Paper P-6420. Santa Monica, Calif.: RAND Corporation, 1979. 97p.

5290.   Samuels, Michael A., et al. *Implications of Soviet and Cuban Activities in Africa for United States Policy.* Significant Issues Series, v. 1, no. 5. Washington, D.C.: Center for Strategic and International Studies, Georgetown University, 1980. 73p.

Further References

See also sections 5:A, D, and E.

2. Specific Nations

a. ANGOLA

BOOKS

5291.   Harsch, Ernest, and Tony Thomas. *Angola: The Hidden History of Washington's War.* New York: Pathfinder Press, 1976. 157p.

5292.   Heimer, F. W. *The Decolonization Conflict in Angola, 1974–1976: An Essay in Political Sociology.* International Studies in Contemporary Africa, no. 2. Geneva, Switz.: Institut Universitaire de Hautes Etudes Internationales, 1979. 117p.

5293. Henderson, Lawrence. *Angola: Five Centuries of Conflict.* Ithaca, N.Y.: Cornell University Press, 1979. 256p.

5294. Klinghoffer, Arthur J. *The Angolan War: A Study of Soviet Policy in the Third World.* Boulder, Colo.: Westview Press, 1980. 231p.

5295. Martin, Phyllis M. *Historical Dictionary of Angola.* Metuchen, N.J.: Scarecrow Press, 1980. 196p.

ARTICLES

5296. "Angola." *Africa Report* 21 (January-February 1976), 2–17.

5297. "Angola—Reiterating the Soviet Position: Translated from *Pravda,* January 3, 1976." *Current Digest of the Soviet Press* 28 (February 4, 1976), 4–5.

5298. Baynham, S. J. "International Politics and the Angolan Civil War." *Army Quarterly* 107 (January 1977), 25–32.

5299. Bender, Gerald J. "Angola, the Cubans, and American Anxieties." *Foreign Policy,* no. 31 (Summer 1977), 3–30.

5300. Bissell, Richard E. "Southern Africa: Testing Detente." In Grayson Kirk and Nils H. Wellman, eds., *The Soviet Threat: Myths and Realities.* New York: Praeger, 1978. pp. 88–98.

5301. Chapman, Michael. "The Civil War in Angola." In Royal United Service Institution, eds., *R.U.S.I. and Brassey's Annual, 1976/77.* Boulder, Colo.: Westview Press, 1976. pp. 36–47.

5302. Dobert, Margarita. "Government and Politics." In Irving Kaplan, ed., *Angola: A Country Study.* Washington, D.C.: U.S. Government Printing Office, 1978. pp. 117–164.

5303. Ebinger, Charles K. "External Intervention in Internal War: The Politics and Diplomacy of the Angolan Civil War." *Orbis* 20 (Fall 1976), 669–699.

5304. Henriksen, Thomas H. "Angola and Mozambique: Intervention and Revolution." *Current History* 71 (November 1976), 153–157.

5305. Hodges, Tony. "The Struggle for Angola: How the World Powers Entered." *Round Table,* no. 262 (1976), 173–184.

5306. Howe, John. "Angola: A Long and Bitter Civil War." *African Development* 9 (November 1975), 15.

5307. Ignatyev, Oleg. "Angola Retrospect." *New Times* (Moscow), no. 34 (August 1976), 27–30.

5308.   Klinghoffer, Arthur J. "The Soviet Union and Angola." In Robert H. Donaldson, ed., *The Soviet Union in the Third World.* Boulder, Colo.: Westview Press, 1981. Chpt. 5.

5309.   Larrabee, Steven. "Moscow, Angola, and the Dialectics of Detente." *World Today* 32 (May 1976), 173–182.

5310.   Lowenthal, Mark M. "Foreign Assistance in the Angolan Civil War: Chronology of Reported Events, 1957–1976." In U.S. Congress, House, Special Subcommittee on Investigations, *Mercenaries in Africa: Hearings.* 94th Cong., 2d sess. Washington, D.C.: U.S. Government Printing Office, 1976. pp. 35–69.

5311.   Marcum, John A. "Angola: Division or Unity?" In G. M. Carter and P. O'Meara, eds., *Southern Africa in Crisis.* Bloomington: Indiana University Press, 1977. pp. 136–162.

5312.   _____ . "The Lessons of Angola." *Foreign Affairs* 54 (April 1976), 407–425.

5313.   Papp, Daniel S. "Angola, National Liberation, and the Soviet Union." *Parameters* 8 (March 1978), 26–39.

5314.   Petersen, Charles W. "The Military Balance in Southern Africa." In C. P. Potholm and Richard Dale, eds., *Southern Africa in Perspective.* New York: Free Press, 1972. pp. 298–317.

5315.   Reed, David. "Angola's Made-in-Moscow War." *Reader's Digest* 108 (June 1976), 83–88.

5316.   Stevens, Christopher. "The Soviet Union and Angola." *African Affairs* 75 (April 1976), 137–151.

5317.   "U.S.S.R.-Angola." *Soviet Military Review,* no. 9 (September 1977), 59.

5318.   Uralov, K. "New Advances in Angola." *International Relations* (Moscow), no. 8 (August 1976), 76–80.

5319.   Valentia, Jiri. "The Soviet-Cuban Intervention in Angola." *U.S. Naval Institute Proceedings* 106 (April 1980), 51–57.

5320.   _____ . "The Soviet-Cuban Intervention in Angola, 1975." *Studies in Comparative Communism* 11 (Spring-Summer 1978), 3–33.

5321.   Vanneman, Peter, and Martin James. "The Soviet Intervention in Angola: Intentions and Implications." *Strategic Review* 4 (Summer 1976), 92–103.

5322.   Volkov, Valery. "The Enemy in Retreat: A Report from the Southern Front in Angola." *New Times* (Moscow), no. 8 (February 1976), 6–7.

5323.   _____ . "Two Weeks on Angola's Fighting Fronts." *New Times* (Moscow), no. 11 (March 1976), 23–26.

DOCUMENTS, PAPERS, AND REPORTS

5324.   Crocker, Chester A. *Report on Angola.* CSIS Report. Washington, D.C.: Center for Strategic and International Studies, Georgetown University, 1976.

5325.   United States. Congress. Senate. Committee on Foreign Relations. Subcommittee on African Affairs. *Angola: Hearings.* 94th Cong., 2d sess. Washington, D.C.: U.S. Government Printing Office, 1976. 212p.

Further References

See also section 5:F:1.

b. THE CONGO

BOOKS

5326.   Abi-Saab, Genges. *The United Nations Operation in the Congo, 1960–1964.* London and New York: Oxford University Press, 1978. 200p.

5327.   Dayal, Rajeshwar. *Mission for Hammerskjold: The Congo Crisis.* Princeton, N.J.: Princeton University Press, 1976. 335p.

5328.   Facts on File, Editors of. *Revolt in the Congo.* New York: Facts on File, 1977. 187p.

5329.   Gordon, King. *The United Nations in the Congo: A Quest for Peace.* Washington, D.C.: Carnegie Endowment for International Peace, 1962. 184p.

5330.   House, Arthur H. *The U.N. in the Congo: The Political and Civilian Efforts.* Washington, D.C.: University Press of America, 1978. 435p.

5331.   Lefever, Ernest W., and Wynford Joshua. *United Nations Peace-Keeping in the Congo, 1960–1964: An Analysis of Political, Executive, and Military Control.* 4 vols. Washington, D.C.: Brookings Institution, 1966.

DOCUMENTS, PAPERS, AND REPORTS

5332.   United States. Congress. House. Committee on Foreign Affairs. *Immediate and Future Problems in the Congo: Hearings.* 88th Cong., 1st sess. Washington, D.C.: U.S. Government Printing Office, 1963. 22p.

5333.   United States. Department of State. Bureau of Intelligence and Research. *Chronology of Significant Events in the Congo, January 1959–December 21, 1961.* Research Memorandum, no. RAF-16. Washington, D.C., 1961. 32p.

Further References

See also section 5:F:1.

G. Asia

1. General Works

BOOKS

5334.   Sen Gupta, Bhabani. *Soviet-Asian Relations in the 1970's and Beyond.* New York: Praeger, 1976. 200p.

5335.   _____ . *The U.S.S.R. in Asia: An Interperceptional Study of Soviet-Asian Relations, with a Critique of the Soviet Role in Afghanistan.* Rev. ed. New Delhi, India: Young Asia Publications, 1980. 502p.

ARTICLES

5336.   Carpenter, Cliffton C. "The Inner Asian Frontier: A Cradle of Conflict." *Strategic Review* 5 (Winter 1977), 90–99.

5337.   Hannah, Norman B. "Russia's Outward Thrust." *National Review* 32 (September 5, 1980), 1073–1077.

5338.   Rahul, Ram. "The Struggle for Central Asia." *International Studies* (New Delhi) 18 (January-March 1979), 1–12.

5339.   Wallace, James. "Russia's Thrust on the Rim of Asia." *U.S. News and World Report* 89 (December 8, 1980), 34–35.

DOCUMENTS, PAPERS, AND REPORTS

5340.   Choudhury, Golam W. *Brezhnev's Collective Security Plan for Asia.* Washington, D.C.: Center for Strategic and International Studies, Georgetown University, 1976.

5341.   Gilbert, Stephen P., and Wynford Joshua. *Guns and Rubles: Soviet Aid Diplomacy in Neutral Asia.* Monograph series, no. 6. New York: American-Asian Educational Exchange, 1970. 60p.

5342.   United States. Department of Defense. Defense Intelligence Agency. *Soviet Forces in Asia.* DST-1710-D-979-79-7. Washington, D.C., 1979.

Further References

See also section 5:A.

2. *Specific Nations*

a. CHINA

BOOKS

5343.   An, Tai-sung. *The Sino-Soviet Territorial Dispute.* Philadelphia, Pa.: Westminster Press, 1973. 254p.

5344.   Carr, Gerard H. *The Chinese Red Army: Campaigns and Politics since 1949.* New York: Schocken Books, 1974. 175p.

5345.   Clemens, Walter C., Jr. *The Arms Race and Sino-Soviet Relations.* Stanford, Calif.: Hoover Institution Press, 1968. 335p.

5346.   Clubb, O. Edmund. *China and Russia: "The Great Game."* New York: Columbia University Press, 1971. 578p.

5347.   Ginsburgs, George, and Carl F. Pinkele. *The Sino-Soviet Territorial Dispute, 1949–1964.* New York: Praeger, 1978. 159p.

5348.   Jackson, William A. D. *The Russo-Chinese Borderlands: Zone of Peaceful Contact or Potential Conflict.* 2d ed. Princeton, N.J.: Van Nostrand, 1968. 156p.

5349.   Louis, Victor. *The Coming Decline of the Chinese Empire.* New York: Times Books, 1979. 198p.

5350.   Middleton, Drew. *The Duel of the Giants: China and Russia in Asia.* New York: Scribners, 1978. 231p.

5351.   Myrdal, Jan. *The Silk Road.* New York: Pantheon Books, 1980. 292p.

5352.   Petrov, Vladimir, ed. *Sino-Soviet Relations, 1945–1970.* Translated from the Russian. Bloomington: Indiana University Press, 1975. 364p.

5353.   Rothenberg, Morris. *Whither China: The View from the Kremlin.* Miami, Fla.: Center for Advanced International Studies, University of Miami, 1977. 286p.

5354.   Salisbury, Harrison E. *War between Russia and China.* New York: W. W. Norton, 1969. 224p.

5355.   Sulzberger, Cyrus L. *The Coldest War: Russia's Game in China.* New York: Harcourt Brace Jovanovich, 1974. 113p.

5356.   Yin, John. *The Sino-Soviet Dialogue on the Problem of War.* The Hague, Neth.: Nijhoff, 1971. 247p.

ARTICLES

5357.   Aarestad, James H. "The Sino-Soviet Border Dispute." *Forum,* no. 13 (Fall 1971), 92–100.

5358.   Alsop, Joseph. "Go vs. No Go." *New York Times Magazine* (March 11, 1973), 30–31.

5359.   "The Battle for the Backyards." *Time* 93 (April 3, 1969), 38.

5360.   "The Battle on the Sino-Soviet Border." *Time* 94 (August 22, 1969), 33.

5361.   Berton, Peter. "The Border Issue, China and the Soviet Union." *Studies in Comparative Communism* 2 (March-April 1969), 131–149.

5362.   "The Border Issue, China and the Soviet Union, March-October 1969: Documents." *Studies in Comparative Communism* 2 (March-April 1969), 150–382.

5363.   Brown, Neville. "The Myth of an Asian Diversion." *Journal of the Royal United Service Institute for Defence Studies* 118 (September 1973), 48–51.

5364.   Chaplin, Dennis. "The Sino-Soviet Conflict: How Soon?" *Military Review* 54 (January 1974), 34–38.

5365.   "China vs. K[hrushchev]: Point of No Return?" *Newsweek* 61 (March 25, 1963), 41–42.

5366.   "China vs. Russia: The New Game." *U.S. News and World Report* 55 (July 29, 1963), 27–30.

5367.   "Chinese Protests to U.S.S.R. over the Border Incidents of June 10." *Peking Review* 13 (June 1969), 4–5.

5368.   Clubb, O. Edmund. "The Sino-Soviet Frontier." *Military Review* 44 (July 1964), 3–13.

5369. Connors, Michael. "China and Russia: Prospects for War." *America* 138 (June 24, 1978), 501–503.

5370. Currie, J. H. C. "The Current Sino-Soviet Situation from the Point-of-View of the Russians." *Army Quarterly* 107 (January 1977), 67–70.

5371. Dinerstein, Herbert S. "The Soviet Union and China." In Steven L. Speigel and Kenneth N. Waltz, eds., *Conflict in World Politics.* Cambridge, Mass.: Winthrop, 1971. pp. 78–98.

5372. Erickson, John. "The Dislocation of an Alliance: Sino-Soviet Relations, 1960–1961." *Survey of International Affairs, 1961.* London and New York: Oxford University Press, 1965. pp. 149–210.

5373. "Even Money: The Sino-Soviet Battlefield." *Newsweek* 73 (March 17, 1969), 58–59.

5374. Fitzgerald, C. P. "The Sino-Soviet Border Conflict." *Pacific Community* 1 (1970), 271–283.

5375. _____ . "Tension on the Sino-Soviet Border." *Foreign Affairs* 45 (July 1967), 683–693.

5376. Ford, Harold P. "The Eruption of Sino-Soviet Politico-Military Problems." In Raymond L. Garthoff, ed., *Sino-Soviet Military Relations.* New York: Praeger, 1966. pp. 100–114.

5377. _____ . "Modern Weapons and the Sino-Soviet Estrangement." *China Quarterly,* no. 18 (April-June 1964), 160–173.

5378. Fromm, Joseph. "Russia vs. China in a Big War?: It's a Real Worry to Many." *U.S. News and World Report* 75 (August 27, 1973), 32–33.

5379. Galay, Nikolay. "The Moscow-Peking Cold War Flares Up." *Institute for the Study of the USSR Bulletin* 11 (May 1964), 21–25.

5380. Garthoff, Raymond L. "Politico-Military Issues in the Sino-Soviet Debate, 1963–1965." In Raymond L. Garthoff, ed., *Sino-Soviet Military Relations.* New York: Praeger, 1966. pp. 171–183.

5381. _____ . "Sino-Soviet Military Relations." *Annals of the American Academy of Political and Social Science* 349 (September 1963), 81–94.

5382. _____ . "Sino-Soviet Military Relations." *Military Review* 44 (January 1964), 80–93.

5383. Gelman, Harry. "The Conflict: A Survey." *Problems of Communism* 13 (March-April 1964), 3–15.

5384. _____ . "Outlook for Sino-Soviet Relations." *Problems of Communism* 28 (September-December 1979), 50–66.

5385. Gibson, Sherri. "Sino-Soviet Military Relations, 1946–1966." *Journal of International and Comparative Studies* 2 (Spring 1969), 24–30.

5386. Ginsburgs, George. "The Dynamics of the Sino-Soviet Territorial Dispute: The Case of the River Islands." In Jerome A. Cohen, ed., *The Dynamics of China's Foreign Policy.* Cambridge, Mass.: East Asian Research Center, Harvard University, 1970. pp. 1–20.

5387. Gittings, John. "The Giants Clash." *Far Eastern Economic Review* 63 (March 13, 1969), 446–449. On the Ussuri River.

5388. Gorbachev, B. "Comments on the Role of the Army in China: Translated from *Znamenosets,* August 1978." *Translations on USSR Military Affairs,* no. 1391 (October 30, 1978), 74–79.

5389. Green, William C., and David S. Yost. "Soviet Military Options Regarding China." In Douglas T. Stuart and William T. Tow, eds., *China, the Soviet Union, and the West: Strategic and Political Dimensions for the 1980's.* Boulder, Colo.: Westview Press, 1981. Chpt. 9.

5390. Gurtov, Melvin, and Byong-moo Hwang. "The 1969 Sino-Soviet Border Clashes." *China under Threat: The Politics of Strategy and Diplomacy.* Baltimore, Md.: Johns Hopkins University Press, 1980. Chpt. 5.

5391. Hinton, Harold C. "Conflict on the Ussuri: A Clash of Nationalisms." *Problems of Communism* 20 (January-April 1971), 45–59.

5392. _____ . "Perspectives on the Sino-Soviet Conflict." *Problems of Communism* 29 (May 1980), 72–75.

5393. Horowitz, David. "Analysis: Behind the Sino-Soviet Dispute." *Ramparts* 7 (June 1969), 39–43.

5394. Hunt, Kenneth. "The Chinese Armed Forces and the Soviet Union." *NATO's Fifteen Nations* 23 (June-July 1978), 72–75.

5395. _____ . "Sino-Soviet Theater Force Comparisons." In Douglas T. Stuart and William T. Tow, eds., *China, the Soviet Union, and the West: Strategic and Political Dimensions for the 1980's.* Boulder, Colo.: Westview Press, 1981. Chpt. 6.

5396. Hyland, William G. "The Sino-Soviet Conflict: A Search for New Security Strategies." *Strategic Review* 7 (Fall 1979), 51–62.

5397. "If China and Russia Fight." *Newsweek* 74 (August 18, 1969), 35.

5398.   "Itchy Trigger Fingers along the Sinkiang Border." *Business Week* (March 19, 1979), 53.

5399.   Jones, P. H. M. "Drums along the Amur." *Far Eastern Economic Review* 46 (October 15, 1964), 137–140.

5400.   Kanet, Roger E. "The Soviet Union and China: Is War Inevitable?" *Current History* 65 (October 1973), 145–149.

5401.   Karnow, Stanley. "Sinkiang: Soviet Rustlers in China's Wild West." *Reporter* 30 (June 18, 1964), 36–39.

5402.   Kefner, John. "The Dragon and the Bear: Asian Perceptions of a Sino-Soviet War." *America* 137 (September 24, 1977), 162–164.

5403.   _____ . "Will the Soviets Attack China?" *America* 134 (May 15, 1976), 421–423.

5404.   Kennedy, William V. "The Defense of China's Homeland." In Ray Bonds, ed., *The Chinese War Machine*. London: Salamander Books, 1979. pp. 92–113.

5405.   Kirby, E. Stuart. "The Sino-Soviet Frontier: Some Russian Viewpoints." *Journal of the Royal United Service Institute for Defence Studies* 119 (March 1974), 61–62.

5406.   Kux, Ernst. "Tension on the Ussuri." *Military Review* 49 (June 1969), 25–28.

5407.   Landes, Burrell H. "Sino-Soviet Relations since the Death of Mao Zedong." *Naval War College Review* 32 (September-October 1979), 29–47.

5408.   Leedeen, Michael. "How the Russian-Chinese War Would be Fought." *New York* 11 (June 19, 1978), 51–57.

5409.   Litvinoff, Boris. "Will There Be a Russo-Chinese War?" *NATO's Fifteen Nations* 15 (June-July 1970), 16–18.

5410.   Lu, Ta. "The Moscow-Peking Military Relationship." *Issues and Studies* 1 (October 1964), 17–21.

5411.   Lushev, P. "Central Asia Commander Hits Maoists, Notes Eastern Vigil: Translated from *Kazakhstanskaya Pravda*, February 22, 1978." *Translations on USSR Military Affairs*, no. 1341 (March 28, 1978), 43–45.

5412.   Luttwak, Edward N. "Against the China Card." *Commentary* 66 (October 1978), 37–40; 67 (January 1979), 4–8.

5413.   MacCaskill, Douglas C. "The Soviet Union's Second Front: Manchuria." *Marine Corps Gazette* 59 (January 1975), 18–26.

5414.   Mackintosh, Malcolm. "The Military Aspects of the Sino-Soviet Dispute." *Bulletin of the Atomic Scientists* 21 (October 1965), 14–18.

5415.   _____ . "The Soviet Generals' View of China in the 1960's." In Raymond L. Garthoff, ed., *Sino-Soviet Military Relations*. New York: Praeger, 1966. pp. 183–193.

5416.   Markish, David. "Where China Begins." *Encounter* 42 (February 1974), 71–75.

5417.   Marks, Donald M. "The Ussuri River Incident as a Factor in Chinese Foreign Policy." *Air University Review* 22 (July-August 1971), 53–63.

5418.   Martin, Robert P. "Where Danger Grows on a 4,500-Mile Border, Between Communist Russia and Red China." *U.S. News and World Report* 59 (December 6, 1965), 44–47.

5419.   Maxwell, Neville. "The Chinese Account of the 1969 Fighting at Chenpao." *China Quarterly,* no. 56 (October-December 1973), 730–739.

5420.   Mayer, Peter. "A Note on the Amur/Ussuri Sector of the Sino-Soviet Boundaries." *Modern China* 1 (January 1975), 116–126.

5421.   _____ . "Why the Ussuri?" *Military Review* 50 (January 1970), 22–32.

5422.   "The Mounting Military Conflict between the Chinese Communists and Soviet Russia." *Asian Outlook* 4 (March 1969), 16–20.

5423.   Nan, Kung-po. "War Posture between the Chinese Communists and Soviet Russia." *Asian Outlook* 5 (January 1970), 9–12.

5424.   Nihart, Brooke. "The Sino-Soviet Conflict." *Armed Forces Journal* (January 24, 1970), 352–354.

5425.   Ou-Yang, Wu-Wei. "Sino-Soviet Border Problems." *Issues and Studies* 1 (October 1964), 26–30.

5426.   Patrick, Stephen B. "The China War: Sino-Soviet Conflict in the 1980's." *Strategy and Tactics,* no. 76 (September-October 1979), 4–22.

5427.   _____ . "The East Is Red: Potential for Sino-Soviet Conflict." *Strategy and Tactics,* no. 42 (January-February 1974), 4–19.

5428.   Petersen, Philip A. "Possible Courses of a Military Conflict between the U.S.S.R. and P.R.C." *Military Review* 57 (March 1977), 28–37.

5429.   Petrov, Yu. "Political Indoctrination—China as a Military Threat: Translated from *Kommunist Vooruzhennykh Sil,* April 1980." *Translations on USSR Military Affairs,* no. 1528 (August 14, 1980), 32–46.

5430.   Pollack, Jonathan D. "Sino-Soviet Relations." In Grayson Kirk and Nils H. Wessell, eds., *The Soviet Threat: Myths and Realities.* New York: Praeger, 1978. pp. 30–46.

5431.   Portisch, Hugo. "The Chinese-Soviet Gap Widens." *Saturday Review* 49 (July 2, 1966), 8–12.

5432.   Possnoy, Stefan T. "Peking and Moscow: The Permanence of Conflict." *Modern Age* 16 (Spring 1972), 130–145.

5433.   Rahul, Ram. "No Sino-Soviet War." *China Report* 5 (September-October 1971), 18–20.

5434.   Rhee, Tong-chin. "The Sino-Soviet Conflict and the Balance of Power." *Military Review* 50 (November 1970), 23–31.

5435.   _____ . "The Sino-Soviet Military Conflict and the Global Balance of Power." *World Today* 26 (January 1970), 29–37.

5436.   Roucek, Joseph S. "Territorial Claims and the Sino-Soviet Conflict." *Ukrainian Quarterly* 21 (Winter 1965), 357–370.

5437.   "Russia's Second Front: The Border with Red China." *Newsweek* 53 (May 25, 1959), 54–57.

5438.   Salisbury, Harrison E. "Russia vs. China: Global Conflict?" *Antioch Review* 27 (Winter 1967-1968), 425–439.

5439.   Scalapino, Robert A. "The Sino-Soviet Relationship: Reflections upon Its Past and Future." *Strategic Review* 5 (Fall 1977), 45–63.

5440.   Schapiro, Leonard. "The Border Issue, China and the Soviet Union: Communists in Collision." *Studies in Comparative Communism* 2 (March-April 1969), 121–130.

5441.   "The Search for Lebensraum?: The Struggle between Russia and Red China." *Time* 84 (September 18, 1969), 40–41.

5442.   "The Sino-Soviet Border Dispute." *Military Review* 50 (January 1970), 77–83.

5443.   "The Soviet-Chinese Border Clash on Damansky Island: Translated from Various Sources." *Current Digest of the Soviet Press* 21 (March 26, 1969), 3–10; (April 2, 1969), 3–10; April 9, 1969), 3–9; (April 16, 1969), 3–5.

5444.   "Soviet Note on Border Conflict with China." *Current Digest of the Soviet Press* 21 (July 1969), 9–13.

5445.   Spurr, R. "Building Up More Border Muscle." *Far Eastern Economic Review* 101 (September 15, 1978), 38.

5446.   "Statements on the Sino-Soviet Border Clashes: Excerpts from the Official Government Statements." *Current History* 57 (October 1969), 241–244.

5447.   Stockwell, Charles W. "Menacing Bears and Paper Dragons." *Military Review* 48 (July 1968), 47–53.

5448.   Summers, Harry G., Jr. "Power: The Crucible of Conflict in the Sino-Soviet Dispute." *Military Review* 51 (March 1971), 56–66.

5449.   Thach, Joseph E., Jr. "Modernization and Conflict: Soviet Military Assistance to the P.R.C., 1950–1960." *Military Review* 58 (January 1978), 72–92.

5450.   Tretiak, Daniel. "China's New Frontier Trouble: The Border Area of Sinkiang." *Far Eastern Economic Review* 42 (October 10, 1963), 60–62.

5451.   Vertelko, I. P. "Frontier Sentinals: An Interview." *Soviet Military Review*, no. 5 (May 1978), 12–14.

5452.   "Violence on the Sino-Soviet Border." *Time* 93 (March 14, 1969), 32–33.

5453.   Volkogonov, D. "Sino-Soviet Relations—Maoist Policies Criticized: Translated from *Kommunist Vooruzhennykh Sil,* May 1980." *Translations on USSR Military Affairs,* no. 1526 (July 31, 1980), 136–148.

5454.   "Where Troops of Red China and Soviet Russia Stand Toe-to-Toe." *U.S. News and World Report* 56 (January 6, 1964), 53–54.

5455.   "Why Russia and China Prepare for War." *U.S. News and World Report* 67 (September 15, 1969), 32–34.

5456.   Wolf, John B. "The Bear and the Dragon." *U.S. Naval Institute Proceedings* 95 (November 1969), 84–91.

5457.   Zagoria, Donald A. "The Soviet Quandry in Asia: Sino-Soviet Relations." *Foreign Affairs* 56 (January 1978), 306–323.

446   *Asia*

DOCUMENTS, PAPERS, AND REPORTS

5458.   Dervaes, Arthur S. *U.S. Response to a Sino-Soviet Armed Conflict.* Research Study. Maxwell AFB, Ala.: Air Command and Staff College, Air University, 1974. 77p.

5459.   Doolin, Dennis J. *Territorial Claims in the Sino-Soviet Conflict: Documents and Analysis.* Studies, no. 7. Stanford, Calif.: Hoover Institution Press, 1965. 77p.

5460.   Dzirkals, Lilita. *Soviet Policy Statements and Military Deployments in Northeast Asia.* RAND Paper P-6229. Santa Monica, Calif.: RAND Corporation, 1978. 31p.

5461.   Ginsburgs, George. *The Damansky-Chenpao Island Incidents: A Case Study of Syntactic Patterns in Crisis Diplomacy.* Asian Studies Occasional Papers, no. 6. Edwardsville: Southern Illinois University at Edwardsville, 1973. 41p.

5462.   Hinton, Harold C. *The Sino-Soviet Confrontation: Implications for the Future.* Strategy papers, no. 29. New York: Published for the National Strategy Information Center by Crane, Russak, 1976. 29p.

5463.   Robinson, Thomas W. *The Sino-Soviet Border Dispute: Background, Development, and the March 1969 Clashes.* RAND Memorandum RM-6171-PR. Santa Monica, Calif.: RAND Corporation, 1970. 74p.

5464.   United States. Congress. House. Committee on Foreign Affairs. Subcommittee on the Far East and the Pacific. *The Sino-Soviet Conflict: Report.* 89th Cong., 1st sess. Washington, D.C.: U.S. Government Printing Office, 1965. 412p.

5465.   _____ . Committee on International Relations. Subcommittee on Future Foreign Policy Research and Development. *United States-Soviet Union-China, the Great Power Triangle: Hearings.* 94th Cong., 2d sess. 2 vols. Washington, D.C.: U.S. Government Printing Office, 1976.

5466.   United States. Department of State. Bureau of Intelligence and Research. Office of the Geographer. *China-U.S.S.R. Boundary.* International Boundary Study, no. 64. Rev. ed. Washington, D.C., 1978. 23p.

5467.   Wirdnam, Kenneth A. C. *The Sino-Soviet Dispute: Jaw-Jaw or War-War in the 1970's?* Professional Study, no. 4270. Maxwell AFB, Ala.: Air War College, Air University, 1971. 21p.

5468.   Wolfe, Thomas W. *The Soviet Union and the Sino-Soviet Dispute.* RAND Paper P-3203. Santa Monica, Calif.: RAND Corporation, 1965. 63p.

5469.   Zhanuzakov, Tel'man. *Combat on the Border: A Kazakh-Language Newspaper's [Qazaq Edibizeti] Account of Fighting on the Sino-Soviet Border, August 13, 1969.* New York: Radio Liberty Committee, 1969. 6p.

Further References

See also section 5:A.

b. NORTH KOREA AND THE KOREAN WAR

BOOKS

5470.   Gardner, Lloyd C., comp. *The Korean War.* New York: Quadrangle Books, 1972. 242p.

5471.   George, Alexander L. *The Chinese Communist Army in Action: The Korean War and Its Aftermath.* New York: Columbia University Press, 1967. 255p.

5472.   Higgins, Trumbull. *Korea and the Fall of MacArthur: A Precis in Limited War.* New York and London: Oxford University Press, 1960. 229p.

5473.   MacArthur, Douglas. *Reminiscences.* New York: McGraw-Hill, 1964. 438p.

5474.   _____ . *A Soldier Speaks: Public Papers.* New York: Praeger, 1965. 367p.

5475.   McGovern, James. *To the Yalu: From the Chinese Invasion of Korea to MacArthur's Dismissal.* New York: W. W. Morrow, 1972. 225p.

5476.   Marshall, Samuel L. A. *The River and the Gauntlet: Defeat of the Eighth Army by the Chinese Communist Forces, November 1950, in the Battle of the Congchon River, Korea.* New York: William Morrow, 1953. 385p.

5477.   Paige, Glenn D. *The Korean Decision, June 24–30, 1950.* New York: Free Press, 1968. 394p.

5478.   Rees, David. *Korea: The Limited War.* New York: St. Martin's Press, 1964. 511p.

5479.   Ridgeway, Matthew B. *The Korean War.* Garden City, N.Y.: Doubleday, 1967. 291p.

5480.   Spanier, John W. *The Truman-MacArthur Controversy and the Korean War.* Cambridge, Mass.: Harvard University Press, 1959. 311p.

5481.   Whiting, Allen S. *China Crosses the Yalu: The Decision to Enter the Korean War.* 2d ed. Stanford, Calif.: Stanford University Press, 1968. 219p.

ARTICLES

5482.   Campbell, J. W. "What the Russians Have Learned in Korea." *Yale Review* 42 (December 1952), 226–235.

5483.   "Exhibit A: Soviet War Materiel." *Time* 56 (October 2, 1950), 20.

5484.   Manchester, William. "Sunset Gun, 1950–1951." *American Caesar: Douglas MacArthur, 1880–1964.* Boston, Mass.: Little, Brown, 1978. pp. 545–629.

5485.   O'Neill, Robert. "The Chongchon River." In Noble Frankland and Christopher Dowling, eds., *Decisive Battles of the 20th Century.* New York: David McKay, 1976. pp. 289–304.

5486.   Raymond, Ellsworth L. "Korea: Stalin's Costly Miscalculation." *U.N. World* 6 (March 1952), 28–31.

5487.   Ruetten, R. T. "General Douglas MacArthur's 'Reconnaissance in Force': The Rationalization of a Defeat in Korea." *Pacific Historical Review* 36 (1967), 79–93.

5488.   Seung-Kwon, Synn. "Reflections on the Korean War: Soviet-North Korean Relations." *East Asian Review* 1 (Autumn 1974), 267–285.

5489.   Soltys, Andrew T. "Enemy Antiaircraft Defenses in North Korea." *Air University Quarterly Review* 7 (Spring 1954), 75–82.

5490.   Spahr, William J. "The Military-Security Aspects of Soviet Relations with North Korea." *Journal of Korean Affairs* (April 1974), 1–8.

DOCUMENTS, PAPERS, AND REPORTS

5491.   Stelmach, Daniel S. "The Influence of Soviet Armored Tactics on the North Korean Invasion of 1950." PhD dissertation, St. Louis University, 1973.

5492.   United States. Congress. Senate. Committee on Armed Services. *The Military Situation in the Far East and the Relief of General Douglas MacArthur.* 5 vols. 92d Cong., 1st sess. Washington, D.C.: U.S. Government Printing Office, 1951.   Reprinted on 8 rolls of 35mm microfilm in 1977 by University Publications of America (Washington, D.C.).

Further References

See also sections 5:A, 5:G:1, and 5:G:2:a.

c. INDOCHINA

BOOKS

5493.   Brown, Weldon A. *The Last Chopper: The Denouement of the American Role in Vietnam, 1964–1975*. Port Washington, N.Y.: Kennikat Press, 1976. 359p.

5494.   _____ . *Prelude to Disaster: The American Role in Vietnam, 1940–1963*. Port Washington, N.Y.: Kennikat Press, 1975. 278p.

5495.   Cooper, Chester L. *The Last Crusade: America in Vietnam*. New York: Dodd, Mead, 1970. 559p.

5496.   Emerson, Gloria. *Winners and Losers: Battles, Retreats, Gains, Losses, and Ruins from a Long War*. New York: Harcourt, Brace, 1978. 448p.

5497.   Facts on File, Editors of. *South Vietnam: U.S.-Communist Confrontation in Southeast Asia, 1961–1973*. 7 vols. New York: Facts on File, 1977.

5498.   Fall, Bernard B. *Hell in a Very Small Place: The Siege of Dien Bien Phu*. Philadelphia, Pa.: Lippincott, 1967. 515p.

5499.   Fitzgerald, Frances. *Fire in the Lake*. Boston, Mass.: Little, Brown, 1972. 491p.

5500.   Giap, Vo Nguyen. *People's War, People's Army*. Translated from the Vietnamese. New York: Praeger, 1962. 217p.

5501.   Halberstam, David. *The Best and the Brightest*. New York: Random House, 1972. 688p.

5502.   Hoopes, Townsend. *The Limits of Intervention*. Rev. ed. New York: David McKay, 1973. 264p.

5503.   Kirk, Donald. *The Wider War: The Struggle for Cambodia, Thailand, and Laos*. New York: Praeger, 1971. 305p.

5504.   Kun, Joseph C. *Communist Indochina: Problems, Policies, and Superpower Involvement*. Washington, D.C.: Center for Strategic and International Studies, Georgetown University, 1976.

5505.   Lewy, Guenther. *America in Vietnam*. New York and London: Oxford University Press, 1979. 540p.

5506.   McLean, Donald B. *Guide to Viet Cong Ammunition.* Forest Grove, Oreg.: Normount Technical Publications, 1971. 143p.

5507.   Milheev, Iuri. *On the Side of a Just Cause: Soviet Assistance to the Heroic Vietnamese People.* Translated from the Russian. Moscow: Progress Publishers [197?]. 127p.

5508.   O'Ballance, Edgar. *The Indochina War, 1945–1954.* London: Faber & Faber, 1965. 285p.

5509.   _____ . *The Wars in Vietnam, 1954–1973.* New York: Hippocrene Books, 1975. 204p.

5510.   Sharp, U.S. Grant. *U.S. Strategy for Defeat: Vietnam in Retrospect.* San Rafael, Calif.: Presidio Press, 1978. 324p.

5511.   Van Dyke, Jon M. *North Vietnam's Strategy for Survival.* Mt. View, Calif.: Pacific Press, 1972. 336p.

5512.   Van Tien, Dung. *Our Great Spring Victory: An Account of the Fall and Liberation of South Vietnam.* Translated from the Vietnamese. New York: Monthly Review Press, 1977. 275p.

5513.   Warner, Denis. *Certain Victory: How Hanoi Won the War.* Kansas City, Mo.: Sheed Andrews & McMeel, 1978. 295p.

5514.   Westmoreland, William C. *A Soldier Reports.* Garden City, N.Y.: Doubleday, 1976. 446p.

5515.   Zagoria, Donald S. *The Vietnam Triangle: Moscow-Peking-Hanoi.* New York: Pegasus Books, 1961.

ARTICLES

5516.   Allen, William A. "Spring 1972 Northern Invasion Repulsed." In Ray Bonds, ed., *The Vietnam War: An Illustrated History of the Conflict in Southeast Asia.* New York: Crown, 1979. pp. 218–227.

5517.   "Army Cobras Blast Tanks at An Loc." *Aviation Week and Space Technology* 96 (May 22, 1972), 14–15.

5518.   "The Army's Tank Aces." *Armed Forces Journal* 109 (July 1972), 15–16.

5519.   Ballis, William B. "Relations between the U.S.S.R. and Vietnam." *Studies on the Soviet Union* 6 (February 1966), 43–57.

5520.   "The Battle of Saigon." *Journal of Contemporary Asia* 5 (Fall 1975), 393–396.

5521.   Bellows, Thomas J. "Proxy War in Indo-China." *Asian Affairs* 7 (September-October 1979), 13–30.

5522.   _____. "Southeast Asia Today." *Air University Review* 31 (September-October 1980), 83–92.

5523.   Bouscaren, A. T. "All Quiet on the Eastern Front: What Happened?" *National Review* 27 (June 20, 1975), 660–666.

5524.   Bowers, Ray L. "Defeat and Retaliation: The Communist Triumph." In Ray Bonds, ed., *The Vietnam War: An Illustrated History of the Conflict in Southeast Asia.* New York: Crown, 1979. pp. 228–237.

5525.   Brown, F. C. "North Vietnamese Army Armor." *Military Journal* 2 (Spring-Summer, Winter 1978-1979), 14–15, 29, 31–33, 43, 31–34, 50.

5526.   Chanda, Nayan. "An Alliance Based on Mutual Need." *Far Eastern Economic Review* 105 (August 24, 1979), 22–24.   Alliance between Vietnam and the U.S.S.R.

5527.   _____. "The Ho Chi Minh Campaign: How the South Was Won." *Far Eastern Economic Review* 89 (September 12, 1975), 35–39.

5528.   Clarke, P. C. "The Battle That Saved Saigon: An Loc." *Reader's Digest* 102 (March 1973), 151–156.

5529.   Daley, Jerome R. "The AH-G1 [Hueycobra] Versus Enemy Tanks at An Loc: An Address to the U.S. Armor Association, May 19, 1972." *Armor* 81 (July-August 1972), 42–43.

5530.   Donnell, J. C. "South Vietnam in 1975: The Year of Communist Victory." *Asian Survey* 16 (January 1976), 1–13.

5531.   Duncanson, Dennis J. "Vietnam and Foreign Powers." *International Affairs* (London) 45 (1969), 413–423.

5532.   "The End in Vietnam." *U.S. News and World Report* 78 (May 12, 1975), 16–19.

5533.   "The Enemy's New Weapons." *Time* 91 (March 15, 1968), 21–22.

5534.   Halloran, Bernard F. "Soviet Armor Comes to Vietnam: A Surprise That Needn't Have Been [after Korea]." *Army* 22 (August 1972), 19–23.

5535.   Horn, Robert C. "Soviet-Vietnam Relations and the Future of Southeast Asia." *Pacific Affairs* 51 (Winter 1978-1979), 585–605.

5536.   Hosmer, Stephen T.; Konrad Kellen; and Brian M. Jackson. "The Fall of South Vietnam." *Conflict* 2 (1980), 1–8.

5537.   Howard, John D. "An Loc: A Study of U.S. Power." *Army* 25 (September 1975), 18–24.

5538.   _____ . "They Were 'Good Ol' Boys'!: An Infantryman Remembers An Loc and the Air Force." *Air University Review* 26 (January-February 1975), 26–39.

5539.   Ivanov, O. "Battery in a Rice Paddy." *Soviet Military Review*, no. 6 (June 1969), 51–52.

5540.   _____ . "The Lessons of Vietnam." *Soviet Military Review*, no. 4 (April 1976), 44–46.

5541.   McGovern, Raymond L. "Moscow and Hanoi." *Problems of Communism* 16 (May-June 1967), 64–71.

5542.   McLane, Charles B. "The Russians and Vietnam: Strategies of Indirection." *International Journal* (Toronto) 24 (Winter 1969), 47–64.

5543.   Mendenhall, Joseph A. "Communist Vietnam and the [Cambodian] Border War: Victim or Aggressor?" *Strategic Review* 6 (Summer 1978), 56–61.

5544.   Miller, David C. "Weapons of the Communist Forces." In Ray Bonds, ed., *The Vietnam War: An Illustrated History of the Conflict in Southeast Asia*. New York: Crown, 1979. pp. 24–25.

5545.   Noorani, A. G. "Soviet Ambitions in Southeast Asia." *International Security Review* 4 (Winter 1979-1980), 31–59.

5546.   O'Ballance, Edgar. "Sino-Soviet Influence on the War in Vietnam." *Contemporary Review*, no. 210 (1967), 176–187.

5547.   Parry, Albert. "Soviet Aid to Vietnam." *Reporter* 36 (January 1967), 28–32.

5548.   Pike, Douglas. "The U.S.S.R. and Vietnam: Into the Swamp." *Asian Survey* 19 (December 1979), 1159–1170.

5549.   Ranch, R. "A Record of Sheer Endurance: The Siege of An Loc." *Time* 99 (June 26, 1972), 25–26.

5550.   "The Reds' Big Drive in Vietnam." *U.S. News and World Report* 78 (January 27, 1975), 26–27.

5551.   "Russia: The Enemy in Vietnam." *U.S. News and World Report* 62 (January 30, 1967), 27–29.

5552.   "Russia's Options." *Newsweek* 98 (March 5, 1979), 28–29.   During the Sino-Vietnam border war.

5553.   Saar, John. "A Nervous Air Mission to An Loc and Back." *Life* 72 (May 12, 1972), 36–37.

5554.   _____ . "Report from the [An Loc] Inferno." *Life* 72 (April 28, 1972), 30–36.

5555.   _____ . "The Shock of War: The Battle for An Loc." *Life* 72 (May 12, 1972), 34B–40.

5556.   Sen Gupta, Bhabani. "The Soviet Union and Vietnam." *International Studies* (New Delhi) 12 (October-December 1973), 559–567.

5557.   "Tactical Air Action Blunts Armored Drive [on An Loc]." *Aviation Week and Space Technology* 96 (May 15, 1972), 17–18.

5558.   Thomas, John R. "Soviet Russia and Southeast Asia." *Current History* 55 (November 1968), 275–280.

5559.   Timmes, Charles J. "Vietnam Summary: Military Operations after the [1973] Cease-Fire Agreement." *Military Review* 56 (August 1976), 63–75; (September 1976), 21–29.

5560.   Turley, G. H. "The Easter Invasion, 1972." *Marine Corps Gazette* 57 (March 1973), 18–29.

5561.   Ulmer, Walter F., Jr. "Notes on Enemy Armor at An Loc." *Armor* 82 (January-February 1973), 14–20.

5562.   United States. Central Intelligence Agency. "Communist Military and Economic Aid to North Vietnam, 1970–1974." *Congressional Record* 121 (March 7, 1975), 5767–5768.

5563.   Ward, Ian, and Brian Crozier. "North Vietnam's Blitzkrieg: An Interim Assessment." *Conflict Studies*, (October 1972), 1–18.

5564.   Weller, Jac. 'Enemy Weapons in Vietnam." *Ordnance* 53 (September-October 1968), 172–175.

5565.   Willenson, Ken, et al. "La Guerre est Finie." *Newsweek* 85 (May 5, 1975), 22–23.

5566.   _____ . "The Siege of Saigon." *Newsweek* 85 (April 21, 1975), 31.

5567. _____ . "Vietnam's Last Battle." *Newsweek* 85 (April 18, 1975), 18–19.

5568. _____ . "Why the ARVN Broke." *Newsweek* 85 (April 7, 1975), 41.

DOCUMENTS, PAPERS, AND REPORTS

5569. Nathan, K. Soosay. "Detente and Soviet Policy in Southeast Asia." PhD dissertation, Claremont Graduate School, 1975.

5570. United States. Central Intelligence Agency. Office of Basic and Geographic Intelligence. *Indochina Atlas.* Washington, 1970. 17p.

5571. United States. Department of Defense. *United States-Vietnam Relations, 1945–1967.* 12 vols. Washington, D.C.: U.S. Government Printing Office, 1971.   Other editions, abridged, include *The Pentagon Papers: The Defense Department History of United States Decisionmaking on Vietnam,* The Senator [Mike] Gravel Edition, 5 vols. (Boston, Mass.: Beacon Press, 1971), and Neil Sheehan et al., *The Pentagon Papers, the Secret History of the Vietnam War: The Complete and Unabridged Series as Published by the New York Times* (New York: Quadrangle Books, 1971), 677p.

5572. United States. Department of the Army. *Weapons and Equipment Recognition Guide: Southeast Asia.* Washington, D.C., 1966. 318p.

Further References

See also sections 5:A and 5:G:1 and the bibliographies noted in section 1:A.

d. THE INDO-PAKISTANI CONFLICTS

BOOKS

5573. Arora, J. S. B. *War with Pakistan, 1971.* New Delhi, India: Army Publishers, 1972. 208p.

5574. Ayoob, Mohammed. *The Liberation War.* New Delhi, India: Chand, 1972. 292p.

5575. Banerjee, Jyotirmey. *India in Soviet Global Strategy: A Conceptual Study.* Columbia, Mo.: South Asia Books, 1977. 201p.

5576. Choudhary, Sukhbir. *The Indo-Pakistani War and the Big Powers.* New Delhi, India: Trimurte Publications, 1972. 195p.

5577. Choudhury, Golam W. *India, Pakistan, Bangladesh, and the Major Powers.* New York: Free Press, 1975. 276p.

5578.   Drieberg, Trevor. *Towards Closer Indo-Soviet Co-Operation.* New Delhi, India: Vikas, 1974. 182p.

5579.   Jackson, Robert. *South Asian Crisis: India, Pakistan, and Bangladesh—A Political and Historical Analysis of the 1971 War.* New York: Praeger, 1975. 240p.

5580.   Jain, Rajendra K. *Soviet-South Asian Relations, 1947–1978.* 2 vols. New York: Humanities Press, 1979.

5581.   Kapur, Harish. *The Soviet Union and the Emerging Nations: A Case Study of Soviet Policy toward India.* London: Joseph, 1972. 124p.

5582.   Kaushik, Devendra. *Soviet Relations with India and Pakistan.* New York: Harper & Row, 1971. 119p.

5583.   Mellor, John W., ed. *India: A Rising Middle Power.* Boulder, Colo.: Westview Press, 1979. 374p.

5584.   Palit, Dharitri. *The Lightning Campaign: The Indo-Pakistan War, 1971.* Compton, Chamberlayne, Eng.: Compton Press, 1972. 172p.

5585.   Ray, Hemen. *Indo-Soviet Relations, 1955–1971.* Bombay, India: Jaico Publishing House, 1973. 302p.

5586.   Siddiqui, Kalim. *Conflict, Crisis, and War in Pakistan.* New York: Praeger, 1972. 217p.

5587.   Singh, K. R. *Politics of the Indian Ocean.* New Delhi, India: Thomson Press, 1974. 252p.

5588.   Taktimen, Dale R., and John Lenczowski. *Arms in the Indian Ocean: Interests and Challenges.* Washington, D.C.: American Enterprise Institute for Public Policy Research, 1977. 84p.

5589.   Vali, Ferenc A. *Politics of the Indian Ocean Area: The Balance of Power.* New York: Macmillan, 1976. 272p.

5590.   Ziring, Lawrence, ed. *The Sub-Continent in World Politics: India, Its Neighbors, and the Great Powers.* New York: Praeger, 1978. 240p.

ARTICLES

5591.   Barclay, Cyril N. "The Indo-Pakistani War." *Army* 22 (May 1972), 20–26.

5592.   Barnds, William J. "The Soviet Union Chooses India." *India, Pakistan, and the Great Powers.* New York: Praeger, 1972. Chpt. 5.

5593.   _____. "The U.S.S.R., China, and South Asia." *Problems of Communism* 26 (November-December 1977), 44–59.

5594.   Bowles, Chester. "America and Russia in India." *Foreign Affairs* 49 (July 1971), 639–651.

5595.   Budhraj, Vijay Sen. "The Evolution of Russia's Pakistan Policy." *Australian Journal of Politics and History* 16 (December 1973), 343–360.

5596.   _____ . "From Tashkent to the Treaty of Peace, Friendship, and Co-Operation: A Study of Recent Trends in Moscow's South Asian Policy." *Indian Journal of Political Science* 32 (October-December 1971), 487–501.

5597.   _____ . "Moscow and the Birth of Bangladesh." *Asian Survey* 13 (May 1973), 482–495.

5598.   Chau, P. R. "Indo-Soviet Military Cooperation, 1947–1974: A Review." *Asian Survey* 19 (March 1979), 50–70.

5599.   Choudhury, Golam W. "The Dismemberment of Pakistan, 1971." *Orbis* 18 (Spring 1974), 179–200.

5600.   _____ . "Moscow's Influence in the Indian Subcontinent." *World Today* 28 (July 1972), 304–311.

5601.   Clubb, O. Edmund. "China, Russia, and East Asia." *Pacific Community* 3 (July 1972), *passim.*

5602.   Costa, Benedict. "The 14-Day War: Blow-by-Blow." *Illustrated Weekly of India* 93 (January 16, 1972), 6–17.

5603.   Dil, Shaheen. "The Extent and Nature of Soviet Involvement in the Bangladesh Crisis." *Asia Quarterly,* no. 3 (Fall 1973), 243–259.

5604.   Hanne, William G. "From Moscow: South by Southeast." *Military Review* 56 (January 1976), 47–55.

5605.   Hasan, Zubeida. "Soviet Arms Aid to Pakistan and India." *Pakistan Horizon* 21 (April 1969), 344–355.

5606.   "Help from Russia? India's Army." *Newsweek* 59 (June 25, 1962), 43.

5607.   Horn, Robert C. "Indian-Soviet Relations in 1969: A Watershed Year?" *Orbis* 19 (Winter 1976), 1539–1543.

5608.   "The India-Pakistan War: A Soviet View." *Current Digest of the Soviet Press* 23 (January 11, 1972), 8–10.

5609.   Jackson, Robert. "The Great Powers and the Indian Sub-Continent." *International Affairs* (London) 48 (January 1973), 35–50.

5610. _____ . "The Strategic Outlook for the Indian Sub-Continent." *Asian Affairs* 59 (October 1972), 259–269.

5611. Jukes, Geoffrey. "The Soviet Union and the Indian Ocean." *Survival* 13 (November 1971), 370–375.

5612. Kapur, Harish. "India and the Soviet Union." *Survey* 16 (Winter 1971), 189–215.

5613. Kaul, Ravi. "The Indo-Pakistani War and the Changing Balance of Power in the Indian Ocean." In Frank Uhlig, Jr., ed., *The Naval Review, 1973*. Annapolis, Md.: U.S. Naval Institute, 1973. pp. 172–195.

5614. Menon, M. Rajan. "The Military and Security Dimensions of Soviet-Indian Relations." In Robert H. Donaldson, ed., *The Soviet Union in the Third World*. Boulder, Colo.: Westview Press, 1981. Chpt. 12.

5615. Mustafa, Zubeida. "The U.S.S.R. and the Indo-Pakistan War, 1971." *Pakistan Horizon* 25 (Spring 1972), 45–52.

5616. Qureshi, Khalida. "Arms Aid to India and Pakistan." *Pakistan Horizon* 20 (February 1967), 137–150.

5617. Rajasekhariah, A. M. "Soviet Arms Supply to Pakistan: Motives and Implications." *Modern Review* 123 (October 1968), 706–710.

5618. Rikhye, Ravi. "Why India Won: The 14-Day War." *Armed Forces Journal* 109 (April 1972), 38–41.

5619. Sagar, Imrose. "Indo-Soviet Strategic Interests and Collaboration." *Naval War College Review* 34 (January-February 1981), 13–33.

5620. Sen Gupta, Bhabani. "Moscow and Bangladesh." *Problems of Communism* 24 (March-April 1975), 56–68.

5621. Sharma, B. L. "Soviet Arms for Pakistan." *United Service Institute of India Journal* 98 (July-September 1968), 223–238.

5622. Wheeler, Geoffrey. "The Indian Ocean Area: Soviet Aims and Interests." *Asian Affairs* 59 (October 1972), 270–274.

DOCUMENTS, PAPERS, AND REPORTS

5623. Belke, Reece G. *Military Power in the Indian Ocean: A Comparative Analysis Between United States and Soviet Realization*. Research Report, no. 3715. Maxwell AFB, Ala.: Air Command and Staff College, Air University, 1969. 71p.

5624. Bhargava, G. S. *India's Security in the 1980's*. Adelphi papers, no. 124. London: International Institute for Strategic Studies, 1976. 35p.

5625.   Donaldson, Robert H. *The Soviet-Indian Alignment: Quest for Influence.* Denver, Colo.: Graduate School of International Studies, University of Denver, 1979. 70p.

5626.   Millar, Thomas B. *Soviet Policies in the Indian Ocean Area.* Canberra Papers on Strategy and Defense, no. 7. Canberra: Australian National University Press, 1970. 22p.

5627.   United States. Congress. House. Committee on Foreign Affairs. Subcommittee on National Security and Scientific Developments. *The Indian Ocean, Political and Strategic Future: Hearings.* 92d Cong., 1st sess. Washington, D.C.: U.S. Government Printing Office, 1971. 242p.

5628.   Vogler, Charles C. *Soviet Expansion in South Asia.* Professional Study. Maxwell AFB, Ala.: Air War College, Air University, 1972. 68p.

5629.   Wannitikul, Udsaner. "Indo-Soviet Relations: The Implications of Soviet-United States Rivalry in the Indian Ocean, 1968–1976." MA thesis, North Texas State University, 1978.

Further References

See also section 5:A.

e. AFGHANISTAN

BOOKS

5630.   Griffiths, John C. *Afghanistan: Key to a Continent.* Boulder, Colo.: Westview Press, 1981. 200p.

5631.   Srivastava, Mahavir P. *Soviet Intervention in Afghanistan.* New Delhi, India: Ess Ess Publications, 1980. 128p.

ARTICLES

5632.   "Afghan Report: A War Russia Can't Win." *U.S. News and World Report* 88 (March 3, 1980), 21–22.

5633.   "The Afghanistan Takeover: Why Russians Acted." *U.S. News and World Report* 88 (January 14, 1980), 22–26.

5634.   "Afghanistan: The Soviets Dig in Deeper." *Time* 115 (January 21, 1980), 36–38.

5635.   "Afghanistan's Forgotten War: Advantages for Russia." *U.S. News and World Report* 90 (October 13, 1980), 25.

5636.   Ali, S. "Accepting the Limits of Aid." *Far Eastern Economic Review* 105 (August 31, 1979), 27–28.

5637.   Aspaturian, Vernon V. "Moscow's Afghan Gamble." *New Leader* 63 (January 28, 1980), 7–13.

5638.   "Back to Maps and Raw Power." *Time* 115 (January 21, 1980), 24.

5639.   Binyon, Michael. "Afghanistan: A Major Miscalculation." *World Press Review* 28 (Febraury 1981), 41–42.

5640.   "Bogged Down in Afghanistan." *U.S. News and World Report* 89 (December 22, 1980), 26.

5641.   Bonfante, J. "Moscow's Military Deadlock." *Time* 116 (August 25, 1980), 34.

5642.   Came, B. "On the Run with the Rebels." *Newsweek* 95 (March 24, 1980), 57.

5643.   Chaffetz, David. "Afghanistan in Turmoil." *International Affairs* (London) 56 (January 1980), 15–36.

5644.   Cheema, Pervaiz I. "The Afghan Crisis." *Islamic Defence and Aviation Review* 5 (February 1980), 11–19.

5645.   "The Chill of a New Cold War." *Newsweek* 95 (January 14, 1980), 24–27.

5646.   Collins, Joseph J. "The Soviet Invasion of Afghanistan: Methods, Motives, and Ramifications." *Naval War College Review* 33 (November-December 1980), 53–62.

5647.   Crozier, Brian. "Moscow's Imperial Burden." *National Review* 32 (October 17, 1980), 1248–1249.

5648.   Dallin, Alexander. "Russia's Afghanistan Move." *Center Magazine* 13 (May 1980), 2–6.

5649.   DeBorchgrave, André. "The 'New' Afghanistan." *Newsweek* 95 (January 21, 1980), 34–35.

5650.   _____ . "Russia's New Frontiers." *Newsweek* 95 (January 28, 1980), 40.

5651.   "The Carnage in Kabul." *Newsweek* 95 (March 10, 1980), 57.

5652.   "Deeper into the Quagmire." *Time* 115 (March 3, 1980), 34–35.

5653.   Deming, Angus. "Soviets Dig in Deeper." *Newsweek* 95 (March 3, 1980), 24–25.

5654.   Fink, D. E. "Afghan Operations Jeopardized." *Aviation Week and Space Technology* 113 (September 22, 1980), 24–25.

5655.   _____ . "Afghanistan Invasion Likened to 1968 [Czech] Action." *Aviation Week and Space Technology* 113 (July 14, 1980), 20–23.

5656.   Foot, Rosemary. "The Changing Pattern of Afghanistan: Relations with Its Neighbors." *Asian Affairs* 11 (February 1980), 55–62.

5657.   Freistetter, Franz. "The Battle in Afghanistan: A View from Europe." *Strategic Review* 9 (Winter 1981), 36–43.

5658.   Furlong, Robert D. M., and Theodor Winkler. "The Soviet Invasion of Afghanistan." *International Defense Review* 13 (February 1980), 168–170.

5659.   Garrity, Patrick J. "The Soviet Military Stake in Afghanistan, 1956–1979." *Journal of the Royal United Service Institution for Defence Studies* 125 (September 1980), 31–36.

5660.   Gelb, L. H. "Keeping Cool at the Khyber Pass." *Foreign Policy*, no. 38 (Spring 1980), 3–18.

5661.   Girardet, E. "With the Afghan Rebels in a Nasty, No-Win War." *U.S. News and World Report* 88 (June 9, 1980), 53–54.

5662.   _____ . "With Afghan Rebels: Ready, Willing—Able?" *U.S. News and World Report* 88 (February 18, 1980), 38–39.

5663.   Griffiths, D. R. "Afghan Problems Stall Soviets." *Aviation Week and Space Technology* 113 (April 21, 1980), 18–19.

5664.   Haggerty, Jerome J. "Afghanistan: The Great Game." *Military Review* 60 (August 1980), 37–44.

5665.   Halliday, Fred. "War and Revolution in Afghanistan." *New Left Review* (January-February 1980), 20–41.

5666.   Hansen, Jim. "U.S.S.R.-Afghanistan: Perspectives on the Conflict." *Military Intelligence* 6 (April-June 1980), 43–44.

5667.   Heuer, Richard J., Jr. "Analyzing the Soviet Invasion of Afghanistan: Hypotheses from the Causal Attribution Theory." *Studies in Comparative Communism* 13 (Winter 1980), 347–355.

5668.   "How the Soviet Army Crushed Afghanistan." *Time* 115 (January 14, 1980), 20–23.

5669.   Hussein, Mushahid. "Red Star over Kabul." *Arabia: The Islamic World Review* 1 (February 1981), 12–13.

5670.   Hyman, Anthony. "Afghan/Pakistan Border Disputes." *Asian Affairs* 11 (October 1980), 264–275.

5671.   Jabarov, Akbar. "Friends and Enemies of Afghanistan." *Soviet Military Review,* no. 4 (April 1980), 51–53.

5672.   Jacobs, G. "The Afghan Armed Forces—To the Soviet Invasion 1980." *Asian Defense Journal,* no. 6 (November-December 1980), 74–75.

5673.   Khalilzad, Zalmay. "Soviet-Occupied Afghanistan." *Problems of Communism* 29 (November-December 1980), 23–40.

5674.   _____ . "The Super Powers and the Northern Tier." *International Security Review* 4 (Winter 1979-1980), 6–30.

5675.   Khorobryy, A. "Helicopter Unit Activities in Afghanistan Described: Translated from *Kryl'ya Rodiny,* September 1980." *Translations on USSR Military Affairs,* no. 1556 (January 14, 1981), 17–21.

5676.   Kline, David. "Inside Afghanistan." *Macleans* 93 (April 21, 1980), 28–31.

5677.   Kwitny, Jonathan. "Afghanistan: Crossroads of Conflict." In Stephen L. Spiegel, ed., *At Issue: Politics in the World Arena.* 3d ed. New York: St. Martin's Press, 1980. Chpt. 4.

5678.   Luttwak, Edward N. "After Afghanistan, What?" *Commentary* 69 (April 1980), 40–49.

5679.   "The Making of a Quagmire." *Newsweek* 95 (May 26, 1980), 46–47.

5680.   Martin, Robert P. "In Kabul: Russia Digs in for a Long Stay." *U.S. News and World Report* 88 (January 21, 1980), 20–21.

5681.   _____ . "Russia's No-Win War in Afghanistan." *U.S. News and World Report* 87 (October 15, 1979), 89–90.

5682.   Mather, I. "A Quagmire of a Different Sort." *Macleans* 93 (February 4, 1980), 28–30.

5683.   "Moscow Counts Its Dead." *Newsweek* 95 (February 25, 1980), 54.

5684.   "Moscow's Defensive Offensive." *Time* 115 (February 11, 1980), 38.

5685.   "Moscow's Murky Morass." *Time* 115 (February 25, 1980), 32–33.

5686.   Muskie, Edmund S. "Afghanistan Briefing." *Department of State Bulletin* 80 (August 1980), 71–72.

5687.   Nations, Robert. "A Grassroots Challenge to Moscow." *Far Eastern Economic Review* 107 (March 7, 1980), 12–13.

5688.   Nielsen, John, et al. "Russia's Afghan Coup." *Newsweek* 95 (January 7, 1980), 18–22.

5689.   _____ . "Soviet Afghanistan." *Newsweek* 95 (January 14, 1980), 28–30.

5690.   Niesewand, Peter. "The Ugly Mood of Moscow's Troops." *Macleans* 93 (January 28, 1980), 26–29.

5691.   O'Ballance, Edgar. "Soviet Tactics in Afghanistan." *Military Review* 60 (August 1980), 45–52.

5692.   Overholt, William H. "The Geopolitics of the Afghan War." *Asian Affairs* 7 (March-April 1980), 205–217.

5693.   Paul, Anthony. "The Soviets' Afghan Quagmire." *World Press Review* 27 (July 1980), 25–27.

5694.   _____ . "Will We Hear Their Cry?" *Reader's Digest* 118 (April 1981), 123–128.

5695.   Peer, Elizabeth. "Moscow's Friend in Need." *Newsweek* 96 (October 27, 1980), 73–74.

5696.   Petrov, Vladimir. "The Soviet Intervention in Afghanistan." In Franklin D. Margiotta, ed., *Evolving Strategic Realities: Implications for U.S. Policy Makers.* Washington, D.C.: Research Directorate, National Defense University, 1980. pp. 34–39.

5697.   Ram, M. "Division over the Soviet Presence." *Far Eastern Economic Review* 108 (May 16, 1980), 22–23.

5698.   _____ . "The Soviet Union's Broken Record." *Far Eastern Economic Review* 108 (June 20, 1980), 32–33.

5699.   Ramati, Yohanan. "The Gambit in Afghanistan." *Midstream* 26 (April 1980), 3–7.

5700.   "The Red Spring Offensive." *Newsweek* 95 (March 17, 1980), 51–52.

5701.   Roucek, Joseph S. "Afghanistan in Geopolitics." *Ukrainian Quarterly* 36 (Summer 1980), 150–163.

5702.   Rubinstein, Alvin Z. "Soviet Imperialism in Afghanistan." *Current History* 79 (October 1980), 80–83.

5703.   "Russia's Afghan Coup." *Newsweek* 95 (January 7, 1980), 18–19.

5704.   "Russia's Nightmare in Afghanistan." *U.S. News and World Report* 88 (March 10, 1980), 32.

5705.   Saint Brides, John M. C. J. "Afghanistan: The Empire Plays to Win." *Orbis* 24 (Fall 1980), 533–540.

5706.   Sareen, R. "Shroud of Insecurity." *Time* 117 (April 27, 1981), 43.

5707.   Shaw, John. "All the Guns, But No Power." *Far Eastern Economic Review* 108 (April 18, 1980), 25.

5708.   _____ . "Frightened City [Kabul] under the Gun." *Time* 115 (April 7, 1980), 40–41.

5709.   "60 Minutes Brings Back the Afghan War." *Broadcasting* 98 (April 14, 1980), 84.

5710.   "Soviet Afghanistan." *Newsweek* 95 (January 14, 1980), 28.

5711.   "The Soviet Invasion of Afghanistan: Special Section." *Department of State Bulletin* 80 (January 1980), A–D.

5712.   "The Soviet Status in Afghanistan." *Defense and Foreign Affairs Digest* 8 (February 1980), 36–38.

5713.   "The Soviets Dig in Deeper." *Time* 115 (January 21, 1980), 36–38.

5714.   "Stamping Out the Flickers of Revolt." *Far Eastern Economic Review* 107 (February 1, 1980), 11–12.

5715.   Steif, William. "At the Front in Afghanistan." *Progressive* 44 (April 1980), 16–21.

5716.   Tahir-Kheli, Shirin. "The Southern Flank of the U.S.S.R." *Naval War College Review* 31 (Winter 1979), 30–40.

5717.   _____ . "The Soviet Union in Afghanistan: Benefits and Costs." In Robert H. Donaldson, ed., *The Soviet Union in the Third World.* Boulder, Colo.: Westview Press, 1981. Chpt. 11.

5718.   Taylor, James E. "Afghanistan: Eyewitness Story of the Soviet Invasion." *Department of State News Letter* 221 (March 1980), 4–5.

5719.   Teicher, Howard. "The Soviet Union in Afghanistan: The Political-Military Costs." *Leviathan* 3 (Fall 1980), 28–32.

5720.   Tulenko, Thomas. "Two Invasions of Afghanistan." *History Today* 30 (June 1980), 7–12.

5721.   Valentia, Jiri. "The Soviet Invasion of Afghanistan: The Difficulty of Knowing Where to Stop." *Orbis* 24 (Summer 1980), 201–218.

5722.   Van Hollen, Eliza. "Afghanistan: A Year of Occupation." *Department of State Bulletin* 81 (March 1981), 18–22.

DOCUMENTS, PAPERS, AND REPORTS

5723.   Deupree, Louis. *Red Flag over the Hindu Kush.* Report 1980/27. Washington, D.C.: American University Field Staff, 1980. 10p.

5724.   Heller, Mark. *The Soviet Invasion of Afghanistan: Motivations and Implications.* CCS Memo, no. 2. Tel Aviv, Israel: Center for Strategic Studies, Tel Aviv University, 1980. 40p.

5725.   United States. Congress. House. Committee on Foreign Affairs. Subcommittee on Europe and the Middle East. *East-West Relations in the Aftermath of the Soviet Invasion of Afghanistan: Hearings.* 96th Cong., 2d sess. Washington, D.C.: U.S. Government Printing Office, 1980. 125p.

5726.   United States. Library of Congress. Congressional Research Service. Foreign Affairs and National Defense Division. *Afghanistan: Soviet Invasion and U.S. Response.* Issue Brief, no. 80006. Washington, D.C., 1980.

5727.   Volkov, Ye., et al., eds. *The Truth about Afghanistan: Documents, Facts, and Eyewitness Reports.* Translated from the Russian. Moscow: Novosti Press Agency Publishing House, 1980. 157p.

H. The Pacific Area

1. Indonesia

BOOKS

5728.   Facts on File, Editors of. *Indonesia: The Sukarno Years.* New York: Facts on File, 1977. 140p.

5729.   Hughes, John. *Indonesian Upheaval.* New York: David McKay, 1967. 304p.

5730.   Mahajani, Usla. *Soviet and American Aid to Indonesia, 1949–1968.* Athens: Ohio University Press, 1972.

5731.   Stevenson, William. *Birds Nest in Their Beards.* Boston, Mass.: Houghton Mifflin, 1964. 280p.

5732.   Sukarno. *Sukarno: An Autobiography.* Indianapolis, Ind.: Bobbs-Merrill, 1965. 324p.

ARTICLES

5733.   "Eyes Left: Arms to Indonesia." *Newsweek* 51 (January 6, 1958), 26.

5734.   Martin, Robert P. "The War Russia Is Trying to Start: The Indonesian-Dutch Quarrel." *U.S. News and World Report* 52 (April 23, 1962), 55–56.

5735.   O'Ballance, Edgar. "Indonesia." *Quarterly Review,* no. 651 (January 1967), 13–22.

5736.   Pauker, Guy J. "The Soviet Challenge in Indonesia." *Foreign Affairs* 40 (July 1962), 612–626.

5737.   Ra'anan, Uri. "Relations between Recipients and Donors: Indonesia, 1956–1960." *The U.S.S.R. Arms the Third World: Case Studies in Soviet Foreign Policy.* Cambridge, Mass.: M.I.T. Press, 1969. pp. 175–247.

5738.   "Red Arms for Sukarno." *U.S. News and World Report* 44 (March 28, 1958), 69.

5739.   "The Tilt toward Moscow: Arms for Indonesia." *Newsweek* 57 (January 30, 1961), 36.

DOCUMENTS, PAPERS, AND REPORTS

5740.   Horn, Robert C. "Soviet-Indonesian Relations, 1956–1966: A Case Study of Soviet Foreign Policy." PhD dissertation, Fletcher School of Law and Diplomacy, 1969.

2. Japan and the Kuriles

BOOKS

5741.   Swearingen, Rodger. *The Soviet Union and Postwar Japan: Escalating Challenge and Response.* Publication, no. 197. Stanford, Calif.: Hoover Institution Press, 1978. 340p.

ARTICLES

5742.   "Echoes of Cuba: The Soviet Military Buildup on Shikotan and Two Other Isles in the Southern Kuriles." *Time* 114 (October 15, 1979), 64.

5743.   "The Soviets Accelerate Buildup in the Kuriles." *Aviation Week and Space Technology* 111 (October 22, 1979), 24.

5744.   Stephen, John J. "Sakhalin Island: Soviet Outpost in Northeast Asia." *Asian Survey* 10 (1970), 1090–1100.

5745.   Talbott, Stephen. "Soviets Stir Up the Pacific." *Time* 117 (March 23, 1981), 53–55.

Further References

See also section 5:G:1.

Appendix I: List of Journals Consulted

AEI Defense Review
AEI Round Table
AFV-G2
Aero Digest
Aeronautics
Aerospace Historian
Africa Report
African Affairs
African Development
Agenor
Air Defense Magazine
Air Force and Space Digest
Air Force Magazine
Air University Quarterly Review
Air University Review
Airman
America
American Historical Review
American Journal of International Law
American Legion Magazine
American Magazine
American Mercury
American Opinion
American Rifleman
American-Scandinavian Review
American Slavic Review
An Cosantoir
Annals of the American Academy of Political and Social Science
Antiaircraft Journal
Antioch Review
Arabia: The Islamic World Review
Armada International

Armed Forces and Society
Armed Forces Journal
Armed Forces Journal International
Armies and Weapons
Armor
Armored Cavalry Journal
Army
Army Information Bulletin
Army Information Digest
Army Logistician
Army Quarterly
Army Research, Development, and Acquisition
Army Reservist
Asia
Asia Quarterly
Asian Affairs
Asian Defense Journal
Asian Outlook
Asian Survey
Atlantic
Atlantic Community Quarterly
Atlas
Australian Journal of Politics and History
Australian Outlook
Automotive Industries
Aviation Week and Space Technology
Born in Battle Magazine
British Journal of International Studies
British Journal of Political Science
Broadcasting
Bulletin of the Atomic Scientists
Business Week
Canadian-American Slavic Studies
Canadian Army Journal
Canadian Defence Quarterly
Canadian Journal of Political Science
Cavalry Journal
Center Magazine
Central Europe Journal
Challenge
China Quarterly
China Report
Christianity and Crisis

Coast Artillery Journal
Collier's
Combat Forces Journal
Command and General Staff School Quarterly
Commander's Digest
Commentary
Comparative Politics
Comparative Strategy
Conflict
Conflict Studies
Congressional Digest
Congressional Record
Contemporary Review
Cooperation and Conflict
Countermeasures
Current Digest of the Soviet Press
Current History
Daedalus
Defense and Foreign Affairs Digest
Defense '80
Defense '81
Defense Management Journal
Defense Monitor
Department of State Bulletin
Department of State News Letter
Dissent
Dublin Review
East and West
East Asian Review
East Europe
Eastern Europe
Encounter
Engineer
Far Eastern Economic Review
Field Artillery Journal
Field Artilleryman
Fighting Forces
Focus
Foreign Affairs
Foreign Policy
Fortnightly
Fortune
Forum

Free World
Geographic Review
Harper's
Historian
History, Numbers and War
History Today
Hungarian Quarterly
Illustrated London News
Illustrated Weekly of India
India Quarterly
Indian Journal of Political Science
Infantry
Infantry Journal
Infantry School Quarterly
Insight and Opinion
Institute for the Study of the USSR Bulletin
Intelligence Digest
Interavia
International Affairs (London)
International Affairs (Moscow)
International Conciliation
International Currency Review
International Defense Review
International Journal (Toronto)
International Journal of Middle East Studies
International Legal Materials
International Perspectives
International Review of Military History
International Socialist Review
International Socialist Review
International Spectator
International Studies (New Delhi)
International Studies Quarterly
Interplay
Interplay of European-American Affairs
Islamic Defence and Aviation Review
Israel Horizons
Issues and Studies
Journal of Central European Affairs
Journal of Conflict Resolution
Journal of Contemporary Asia
Journal of Contemporary History
Journal of Economic History

Journal of Inter-American Studies
Journal of International Affairs
Journal of International Studies
Journal of Korean Affairs
Journal of Modern History
Journal of Palestine Studies
Journal of Peace Research
Journal of Politics
Journal of Social and Political Studies
Journal of the Royal Artillery
Journal of the Royal United Services Institute for Defence Studies
Judge Advocate General's Bulletin
Leviathan
Liberation
Life
Macleans
Marine Corps Gazette
Middle East Journal
Midstream
Midwest Journal of Political Science
Midwest Quarterly
Military Affairs
Military Engineer
Military Intelligence
Military Reports on the United Nations
Military Review
Missiles and Rockets
Modern Age
Modern China
Moment
Nation
National Defence
National Guardsman
National Review
NATO Letter
NATO Review
NATO's Fifteen Nations
Naval War College Review
Navy
New Leader
New Left Review
New Man
New Middle East

New Outlook
New Republic
New Times (Moscow)
New York
New York Times Magazine
Newsweek
19th Century
Orbis
Ordnance
Pacific Affairs
Pacific Community
Pacific Historical Review
Pakistan Horizon
Parameters
Pegasus
Peking Review
The Pointer
Polish Western Affairs
Political Quarterly
Political Science Quarterly
Popular Mechanics
Popular Science
Problems of Communism
Proceedings of the American Academy of Political and Social Science
Product Engineering
Progressive
Quarterly Review
Queen's Quarterly
RCAF Staff College Journal
Ramparts
Reader's Digest
Reporter
Reserve Officer
Review (Jugoslav Affairs)
Review of the Soviet Ground Forces (U.S. Defense Intelligence Agency)
Round Table
Royal Air Forces Quarterly
Royal Engineers' Journal
Russian Review
Saturday Evening Post
Saturday Review
Scholastic
School and Society

Science
Science Digest
Science News Letter
Sea Power
Senior Scholastic
Services and Territorial Magazine
Signal
Slavic Review
Social Justice Review
Soldiers
Soviet Literature
Soviet Military Review
Soviet Military Translations (U.S. Commerce Department, Joint
    Publications Research Service)
Soviet Studies
Strategic Review
Strategy and Tactics
Studies for a New Central Europe
Studies in Comparative Communism
Studies in Soviet Thought
Studies on the Soviet Union
Survey
Survey Graphic
Survival
Swiss Review of World Affairs
TacAir Warfare Center Quarterly Report
Tactical and Technical Trends
Tank
Technology and Armament
Thought
Time
Times Literary Supplement
Translations on USSR Military Affairs (U.S. Commerce Department, Joint
    Publications Research Service)
Travel
20th Century
U.N. World
U.S. Air Force JAG Law Review
U.S. Army Aviation Digest
U.S. Army Combat Forces Journal
U.S. Naval Institute Proceedings
U.S. News and World Report
Ukrainian Quarterly

United Service Institute of India Journal
Virginia Quarterly Review
Vital Speeches
World Marxist Review
World Politics
World Press Review
World Today
World War Enthusiast, 1939–1945
World War II Journal
World War II Magazine
Yad Vasem Bulletin
Yad Vasem Studies
Yale Review

Appendix II: Selected Soviet Military Lives: A Biographical Directory

Introduction

COMPILING A COMPENDIUM of Soviet military figures, to complement especially section 1:G, "Biography," turned out to be somewhat more difficult than expected.

Although much is available on certain Soviet marshals and other defense-related leaders or inventors, surprisingly little exists in English on current Russian military men below the rank of full general. What is available is often spotty at best and does not always cover those holding the most recent or highest positions. Nevertheless, data was obtained for 120 individuals of varying importance. Unfortunately, some listings are more complete than others.

Symbols

A: awards
Acad.: Academy
Admin.: Administration
B: Birth
Bd.: Board/Directorate
Bye.: Byelorussian
bttn.: battalion
CC: Central Committee
cand.: candidate
Cent.: Central
Chmn.: Chairman
CO: Commanding Officer
Col: Colonel
Col. Gen.: Colonel General
CP: Communist Party
CPSU: Communist Party of the Soviet Union
Comm.: Commission

Comr.: Commissar
convoc.: convocation/convention/meeting
CoS: Chief of Staff
DC: Deputy Commander
del.: delegate/delegation
Dep./dep.: deputy
div.: division
ED: education
Engr.: Engineers, Engineering
Est.: Estonian
FDC: First Deputy Commander
Geo.: Georgian
HQ: Headquarters
Inft.: infantry
Lat.: Latvian
Lt.: Lieutenant
MD: Military District
MS: Military Service
Mil.: Military
Mjr.: Major
NCO: Noncommissioned Officer
O.: Order of
PO/po: Party Office/political officer
Pop./Peo.: Popular/Peoples
R: Rank (final or most recent)
RSFSR: Russian Soviet Federal Socialist Republic
regt.: regiment
ret.: retired
so: staff officer
sqn.: squadron
Supr. Sov.: Supreme Soviet
Ukr.: Ukrainian

Nikolai N. Alekseyev

B: June 13, 1914
MS: Unknown until 1941; CO, various artillery units, 1941–1945; electronics R & D, 1945–1968; Soviet del., SALT, 1969; Dep. USSR Minister of Defense (for Armaments), 1970–.
R: Col. Gen. of Engr.-Technical Troops
A: O. Red Banner; other decorations and medals
PO: Member, CPSU, 192?; Dep., RSFSR Supr. Sov. convoc., 1975–

Aleksandr T. Altunin

B: August 14, 1921
ED: Graduate, Frunze Mil. Acad. and Acad. of the General Staff
MS: Joined Red Army, 1939; train engr., CO of a bttn. and DC of a regt., 1940–1945; field and so, 1945–1968; CO, North Caucasus MD, 1968–1970; Head of Personnel Admin., USSR Ministry of Defense, 1971–1972; Head, USSR Civil Defense and Dep. USSR Minister of Defense, 1972–
R: General
A: O. Red Banner; other decorations and medals
PO: Member, CPSU, 1943; memb., CC, CPSU, 1976–

Alexei I. Antonov

B: 1896
MS: Joined Red Army, 1920; field and so, 1921–1941; CoS, Southern, North Caucasus, Transcaucasus, Voronezh Fronts, 1941–1942; Dep. CoS and Chief, Operations Dept., Red Army, 1943–1945; Soviet military del. to Moscow, Yalta, and Potsdam conferences, 1943–1945; CO, Transcaucasian MD, 1946–1954; CoS, Warsaw Pact Forces, and FDC, General Staff, USSR Armed Forces, 1955–1962; died 1962.
R: General
A: O. Lenin; other decorations and medals
PO: Member, CPSU, 192?

Amazasp K. Babadzhanyan

B: Armenia, 1906
ED: Graduate, Frunze Mil. Acad., 1948, and Acad. of the General Staff
MS: Joined Red Army, 1924; CO of a company, bttn., and aide to a regt. CO, 1925–1941; CO of a regt., brig., div. and corps, 1941–1945; field CO, 1949–1959; CO, Odessa MD, 1959–1967; Head, Malinovskiy Acad. for Armored Divisions, 1968–.
R: Chief Marshal of Tank Troops
A: O. Lenin; O. Red Banner; other decorations and medals
PO: Member, CPSU, 1928; memb., CC, Ukr. CP, 1960–1968

Ivan Kh. Bagramyan

B. Kirovabad, Armenia, December 2, 1897
ED: Graduate, cadet school, 1917; cavalry officer's school, 1925; Frunze Mil. Acad., 1934; Acad. of the General Staff, 1938
MS: Tsarist army volunteer, 1915–1917; joined Red Army, 1920; field officer, Transcaucasus, 1920–1934; CoS, 5th Cav., II Corps, 1934–1936; memb., Operations Dept., Kiev MD, 1936–1940; dep. CoS then CoS, Southwestern Front, 1941–1943; CO, 11th Guards Army, 1943; CO, 1st Baltic Front, 1944–1945; CO, Baltic MD, 1945–1954; Chief Inspector, Main Inspectorate, USSR Ministry of Defense, 1954–1956; Head, Acad. of the General Staff, 1956–1958; Dep. USSR Minister of Defense, 1958–1968; Inspector-General, Main Inspectorate, USSR Ministry of Defense, 1968–
R: Marshal of the Soviet Union
A: O. Lenin (4); O. Red. Banner (3); O. Suvorov (2); O. Kutuzov; Hero of the Soviet Union; other decorations and medals
PO: Member, CPSU, 1941; memb., CC, Latvian CP, 1954–1955; cand. memb., CC, CPSU, 1952–1961; memb., CC, CPSU, 1961–1968; dep., USSR Supr. Sov. convoc., 1946–

Pavel I. Batov

B: Yaroslavl Guberniya, June 1, 1897
ED: Graduate, Frunze Mil. Acad., 1928
MS: Drafted into Tsarist Army and later wounded, 1915–1916; joined Red Guards, 1917; fought in Civil War, 1918–1920; Head of a regt. school, CO of a bttn. and regt., and CO, Moscow Proletarian Div., 1920–1927; CoS then CO of a regt., CoS then CO, 15th Sivash Inft. Div., 1928–1935; Dep. CO, 12th International Brig. in Spain, 1936–1937; CO of a div., including service in Russo-Finnish War, 1938–1940; CO of a corps, Dep. CO of an army, CO, 51st Independent Army while simultaneously Dep. CO, Red Army Forces in the Crimea, then Dep. CO, Bryansk Front, 1940–1942; CO, 65th Army on Don and 1st Bye. Fronts, 1942–1945; CO of an army, Soviet occupation forces, Germany, 1945–1948; CO, Group of Soviet Forces, Kaliningrad Oblast, then FDC, Group of Soviet Forces in Germany, 1949–1950; so, USSR Ministry of Defense, 1950–1955; CO, Transcarpathian MD, 1955–1958; CO, Baltic MD, 1959–1960; CO, Southern Group of Forces (Hungary), 1961–1962; CoS, Warsaw Pact Forces and 1st Dep. Chief, General Staff, USSR Armed Forces, 1962–1965; Inspector-General, Main Inspectorate, USSR Ministry of Defense, 1965–

R: General
A: Hero of the Soviet Union (2); O. Lenin (6); O. Red Banner (3); O. Suvurov (3); other decorations and medals
PO: Member, CPSU, 1929; memb., CC, Ukr. CP, 1956–1959; dep. USSR Supr. Sov. convoc., 1937–1966

Piotr A. Belik

B: October 6, 1909
ED: Graduate, Mil. Acad. of Tank Troops, 1945; Acad. of the General Staff, 1953
MS: Joined Red Army, 1927; field officer, 1927–1941; CO, various units, Western, Bryansk, Southwestern, and 3rd Ukr. Fronts, 1941–1945; CO, various units then FDC, Group of Soviet Forces in Germany, 1946–1966; CO, Transbaikal MD, 1966–
R: General
A: Hero of the Soviet Union; O. Lenin; other decorations and medals
PO: Member, CPSU, 1929; dep., USSR Supr. Sov. convoc., 1970–; memb., Cent. Auditing Comm., CPSU, 1971–

Afanasiy P. Beloborodov

ED: Graduate, Frunze Mil. Acad., 1928
MS: Unknown before 1939; CO, 78th Div., 1939–1941; CO, 9th Guards Div., 1941–1943; CO, 43rd Army, 1944–1945; CO of an army, Soviet occupation forces in Manchuria, 1945; CO, special Group of Soviet Forces, Port Arthur, 1946–1955; CO, Voronezh MD, 1956–1957; Head, Main Personnel Bd., USSR Ministry of Defense, 1957–1963; CO, Moscow MD, 1963–1971; Ret. 1972
R: General
A: Hero of the Soviet Union; O. Lenin (3); O. Red Banner; other decorations
PO: Member, CPSU, 1926; dep., USSR Supr. Sov. convoc., 1950–1954; dep., RSFSR Supr. Sov. convoc., 1959–1963; del., CPSU Congress, 1956–1961

Stepan E. Belonozhko

B: 1919
ED: Graduate, Frunze Mil. Acad. and Acad. of the General Staff
MS: Joined Red Army, 1937; field officer, 1938–1941; CoS, various

units, 1941–1945; field and so, 1945–1968; FDC, Turkestan MD, 1968–1969; CO, Turkestan MD, 1969–
R: Col. Gen.
A: Various medals
PO: Member, CPSU, 1943; memb., CC, Uzbek CP, 1971; dep., USSR Supr. Sov. convoc., 1970–

Nikolai Berzarin

B: 1904
MS: Unknown until 1938; CO, 32nd Inft. div., Lake Khassan incident, 1938; CO, various armies, 1939–1945; CO, Soviet occupation forces, Berlin, 1945; killed in motorcycle accident, 1945
R: Col. Gen.
A: Hero of Soviet Union; O. Lenin; other decorations

Leonid I. Brezhnev

B: Dneprodzerzhinsk, Ukraine, December 19, 1906
ED: Graduate, Dneprodzerzhinsk Metallurgical Institute, 1935
MS: Civilian politician and executive, 1927–1935; soldier, Red Army, 1935–1936; civilian politician, 1937–1941; Dep. Chief., Pol. Admin., Southern Front, 1941–1942; Head, Pol. Dept., 18th Army, later Head, Pol. Dept., 4th Ukr. Front, 1942–1945; Head, Pol. Admin., Carpathian MD, 1945–1946; civilian politician, 1946–1952; FDC, Main Pol. Admin., Soviet Army and Navy, 1953–1954; civilian politician, rising to status of CPSU Party Chairman, 1964–, and USSR President, 1977–
R: Marshal of the Soviet Union
A: Hero of the Soviet Union; Hero of Socialist Labor; O. Lenin (5); Gold Star Medal (2); O. Red Banner (2); numerous other decorations.
PO: Member, CPSU, 1931; local and national CP offices, del. and dep. to various local and national CP congresses and convoc.

Semen M. Budennyi

B: Kosiurin, Rostov Oblast, 1883
ED: Graduate, Frunze Mil. Acad., 1932
MS: Cavalryman, Russo-Japanese War, 1905–1908; NCO, Maritime Dragoons Regt., 1908–1917; joined Red Army, 1917; CO of a cav. brig. and div., 1918–1919; CO, 1st Cav. Army, 1919–1920; memb., mil. coun-

cil, North Caucasian MD and memb., Rev. Mil. Council of the USSR, 1921–1922; asst. to CO, Red Army Cav., 1922–1924; Inspector and Dir. of Maintenance, Red Army Cav., 1924–1937; CO, Moscow MD, 1937–1939; Dep., later First Dep., Pop. Comr. of Defense, 1939–1941; CO of various units, Southwest Flank and Western Reserve Front, 1941–1942; CO, North Caucasian Front, 1942; relieved, 1942; CO, Red Army Cav., 1943–1953; Ret., 1953; died October 26, 1973.

R: Marshal of the Soviet Union

A: Hero of the Soviet Union (2); O. Lenin (7); O. Red Banner (6); Gold Star Medal (2); other decorations and medals.

PO: Member, CPSU, 1919; memb., All-Russian CC Executive and CC, CPSU, 1920–1937; cand. memb., then memb., All-Union CP(B), 1934–1939, 1952–1973; memb., CC, CPSU, 1939–1952; del., CPSU Congresses, 1938–1973

Nikolai A. Bulganin

B: Gorky, June 11, 1895

MS: Civilian politician, 1918–1941; memb., mil. council, Western, 2d Baltic, and 1st Bye. Fronts, 1941–1944; Dep. Pop. Comr. of Defense and memb., State Cmte. for Defense, 1944–1946; First Dep. Minister, USSR Armed Forces, 1946–1947; Dep. Chmn., USSR Council of Ministers, 1947–1955; USSR Minister of Defense, 1947–1955; Chmn., USSR Council of Ministers, 1955–1958; dismissed, 1958; ret. 1960; died February 24, 1975.

R: Marshal of the Soviet Union

A: Hero of Socialist Labor; O. Lenin (2); O. Red Banner; O. Suvorov; O. Kutuzov (2); O. Red Star; other decorations and medals

PO: Member, CPSU, 1917; memb., CC, CPSU, 1939–1961; deleg., CPSU Congress, 1946–1958; dep., USSR Supr. Sov. convoc., 1946–1958

Ivan D. Chernyakhovsky

B: Uman, 1906

MS: Unknown until 1942; CO, 60th Army, 1943; CO, 3rd Bye. Front, 1944–1945; died February 18, 1945 as the result of wounds received in combat near Mehlsack, East Prussia.

R: General

A: Hero of the Soviet Union; O. Lenin; other decorations and medals

Mikhail N. Chistyakov

B: November 18, 1896
ED: Graduate, Red Army Artillery Acad., 1922
MS: Tsarist officer, 1915–1917; joined Red Guard, 1918; fought in Civil War, 1918–1921; CO of an artillery regt., div., corps, then Head, Higher Artillery Acad. and Chief, Bd. for Artillery Combat Training, 1923–1941; CO, Red Army Artillery, CO of artillery for various fronts, then Dep. CO, Red Army Artillery, 1941–1944; CO of artillery, Far Eastern Forces, 1945; Head, Artillery Combat Training and CO, Red Army artillery schools, 1946–1957; so, USSR Ministry of Defense, 1957–1966; Inspector-Advisor, Main Inspectorate, USSR Ministry of Defense, 1966–.
R: Marshal of Artillery
A: O. Lenin (2); other decorations and medals
PO: Member, CPSU, 1944

Vasiliy I. Chuikov

B: Moscow Oblast, February 12, 1900
ED: Graduate, Frunze Mil. Acad., 1927
MS: Joined Red Army, 1918; CO, 28th Rifle Regt., 1919; CO, various units, Soviet-Polish War, 1920; CO of a mechanized brig., various other units, 1928–1938; CO, rifle corps and army group, Special Bye. MD, 1938–1939; CO, 4th Army in occupation of western Bye. and Russo-Finnish War, 1939–1940; Soviet mil. attaché to China and chief mil. advisor to Chiang Kai-shek, 1941–1942; Dep. CO then CO, 64th and 62nd Armies in defense of Stalingrad, 1942–1943; CO, 8th Guards Army, 1943–1945; CO, Soviet occupation force, Thuringia, 1945–1946; Dep. CO, Soviet Ground Forces, 1946–1949; CO, Group of Forces in Germany and Chmn., Soviet Control Commission, East Germany, 1949–1953; CO, Kiev MD, 1953–1960; CO, Soviet Ground Forces, 1960–1964; Head, Soviet Civil Defense and Dep. USSR Minister of Defense, 1964–1972; Inspector General, Main Inspectorate, USSR Ministry of Defense, 1972–.
R: Marshal of the Soviet Union
A: Hero of the Soviet Union (2); O. Lenin (5); O. Red Banner (4); O. Suvorov (3); O. October Revolution; other decorations and medals
PO: Member, CPSU, 1919; memb., CC, Ukr. CP, 1954–1961; cand. memb., CC, CPSU, 1952–1961; memb., CC, CPSU, 1961–1972; dep., USSR Supr. Sov. convoc., 1946–

David A. Dragunskiy

B: Bryansk Oblast, February 15, 1910
ED: Graduate, Frunze Mil. Acad., 1941; Acad. of the General Staff, 1950
MS: Joined Red Army, 1933; NCO, various units, 1933–1938; fought in Lake Khasan incident, 1938; CO, tank bttn., Western Front, so, Northern Caucasus, Kalinin, and Voronezh Fronts, then CO, tank regt., 1st Ukr. Front, 1941–1945; CO, Yerevan and Tbilisi garrisons, 1945–1969; Head, "Vystrel" Higher Officers' courses, 1969–.
R: Col. Gen. of Tank Troops
A: Hero of the Soviet Union (2); O. Lenin; O. Red Banner (3); other decorations and medals.
PO: Member, CPSU, 1931; memb., CC, Armenian CP, 1961–1965; memb., Central Auditing Comm., CPSU, 1971–

Aleksei A. Epishev

B: Astrakhan, 1908
ED: Graduate, Mil. Acad. for Mechanization and Motorization of the Red Army, 1938
MS: Red Army po, 1930–1938, 1943–1946; civilian politician and diplomat, 1939–1942, 1946–1962; Head, Main Pol. Bd., Soviet Army and Navy, 1962–.
R: General
A: O. Lenin, O. Red Banner; other decorations and awards
PO: Member, CPSU, 1929; dep., USSR Supr. Sov. convoc., 1937–1946, 1950–1958, 1962–; Ukr. CP political posts, 1938–1964

Ivan I. Fedyuninsky

B: 1900
MS: Joined Red Army, 1919; field and so, 1919–1938; CO, div. and corps, 1939–1941; CO, 42nd and 54th Armies, Leningrad Front, then 11th Army, Western Front, 1941–1943; CO, 2d Assault Army, 1944–1945; CO of an army, Soviet occupation forces in Poland, then Dep. CO, Group of Soviet Forces in Germany, 1949–1951; Dep. CO, Transcaucasian MD, 1952–1956; CO, Turkestan MD., 1957–1969; ret., 1969
R: General
A: Hero of the Soviet Union; O. Lenin (3); O. Red Banner (2); other decorations and medals

PO: Member, CPSU, 1930; dep., USSR Supr. Sov. convoc., 1958–1969; del., CPSU Congress, 1956–1967; dep. Geo. Supr. Sov. convoc., 1955; memb., CC, Geo. CP, 1956–1957; memb., CC, Uzbek CP, 1960–1969

Ivan I. Fesin

B: Rostov Oblast, 1904
ED: Graduate, Mil. Infantry School, 1930; Frunze Mil. Acad., 1941; Acad. of the General Staff, 1949
MS: Joined Red Army, 1926; soldier and NCO, various units, 1926–1937; CO, regt., motorized inft. brig., and inft. div. on Northwestern, Voronezh, Southwest, 2d and 3d Ukr. Fronts, 1941–1945; CO, Moscow Inft. School, 1946–1950; instructor, Moscow Inft. School, 1950–ret.
R: Mjr. General.
A: Hero of the Soviet Union (2); O. Lenin (2); other decorations and awards
PO: Member, CPSU, 1929

Kuzma N. Galitskiy

B: 1897
ED: Graduate, Mil. Engr. Acad., 1935
MS: Unknown until 1944; CO, 2d Guards Army, 1945; CO, Soviet occupation forces, East Prussia, 1945–1946; CO, Ciscarpathian MD, 1946–1954; CO, Odessa MD, 1954–1955; Head, Kuybyshev Mil. Engr. Acad., 1955–1957; CO, Transcaucasian MD., 1957–1961; no information after 1961
R: General
A: O. Lenin; O. Suvorov; O. Kutuzov; other decorations and medals
PO: Member, CPSU, 1918; memb., CC, Ukr. CP, 1949–1954; dep., USSR Supr. Sov. convoc., 1950–1958; del., CPSU Congress, 1956–1959; memb., CC, Geo. CP, 1957–1961

Anton I. Gastilovich

B: 1902
ED: Graduate, Frunze Mil. Acad., 1931; Acad. of the General Staff, 1938
MS: Joined Red Army, 1919; fought in Civil War, 1919–1920; soldier and NCO, 1921–1927; Head, Operations Staff, 45th Div., 1931; so,

Operations Staffs, Ukr. and Kiev MDs, 1932–1934; CO, regt., 1935–1936; field and so, Ukr. MD, 1938–1941; CO, 17th Independent Guards Corps and later, 18th Army, 1941–1945; author-instructor then Dep. CO, Acad. of the General Staff, 1945–ret.
R: Col. Gen.
A: O. Lenin; O. Red Banner; other decorations and medals
PO: Member, CPSU, 1919

Ivan A. Gerasimov

B: 1921
ED: Graduate, Frunze Mil. Acad. and Acad. of the General Staff
MS: Unknown until 1969; CO, 1st Tank Army, Group of Soviet Forces in Germany, 1969–1971; CO, Transcarpathian MD, 1972–1973; CO, Northern Group of Forces (Poland), 1973–1975; CO, Kiev MD, 1976–
R: General
A: O. Red Star; other decorations and awards
PO: Member, CPSU, 194?; memb., CC, Ukr. CP, 1976–

Andrey L. Getman

B: Sumy Oblast, October 5, 1903
ED: Graduate, Red Warrant Officer's course, 1926; Mil. Acad. of Armored Troops, 1937
MS: Joined Red Army, 1924; field and so, 1926–1935; CoS then CO, an armored brig., Leningrad and Far East MD, 1937–1941; CO, an armored brig., later CO, 112th Armored Div. of 5th Army and of an armored corps, 1st Armored Army, 1941–1944; FDC of an armored army, 1945; CO, armored troops, various MD, 1945–1948; CoS, Red Army Tank Troops, 1948–1954; Dep. CO, Soviet Armored Troops, 1954–1956; CO, Soviet forces in Rumania, 1956–1958; CO, Carpathian MD, 1958–1964; Chmn., DOSAAF, 1964–1971; Inspector-Advisor, Main Inspectorate, USSR Ministry of Defense, 1972–.
R: Col. Gen. of Tank Troops
A: O. Lenin (3); O. Red Banner (4); other decorations and medals
PO: Member, CPSU, 1927; dep., USSR Supr. Sov. convoc., 1958–1962; cand. memb., CC, CPSU, 1961–1971; memb., CC, Ukr. CP, 1961–1971

Filipp I. Golikov

B: July 16, 1900
ED: Graduate, Frunze Mil. Acad., 1933
MS: Joined Red Army, 1918; fought in Civil War then field or so, 1919–1929; so, 1933–1939; Dep. CoS, Soviet General Staff, 1940–1941; Head, G. R. U. and Head, Soviet Mil. Mission (Lend-Lease) to U.S., then CO, 10th Army, 1941; CO, Bryansk and Voronezh Fronts, 1942–1943; Chief, Soviet Repatriation Mission, 1944–1946; Dep. Pop. Comr. of Defense (for Personnel) and Chief, Main Personnel Bd., Red Army, 1943–1950; CO of an army, 1950–1956; Chief, Armored Forces Mil. Acad., 1956–1958; Head, Main Pol. Bd., Soviet Army and Navy, 1958–1962; Inspector-General, Main Inspectorate, USSR Ministry of Defense, 1962–; died July 1980.
R: Marshal of the Soviet Union
A: Hero of the Soviet Union; O. Lenin (4); O. Red Banner (4); other decorations and medals.
PO: Member, CPSU, 1918; dep., USSR Supr. Sov. convoc., 1937, 1954–1962; memb., CC, CPSU, 1961–1962

Aleksandr V. Gorbatov

B: 189?
MS: Joined Red Army, 1918; fought in Civil War, 1919–1921; field and so, 1922–1938; CO of a brig., 1939–1940; CO of a div. and a corps, 1941–1942; CO, 3d Army, 1943–1945; CO, Kaliningrad Group, 1945–1950; CO, USSR Airborne Troops, 1950–1955; so, USSR Ministry of Defense, 1956–1961; no information after 1961.
R: Col. Gen.
A: Hero of the Soviet Union; O. Lenin (2); O. Suvurov; O. Kutuzov; other decorations and medals
PO: Member, CPSU, 1919; memb., CC, Lat. CP, 1958; dep., USSR Supr. Sov. convoc., 1950–1958; cand. memb., CC, CPSU, 1952–1961

Artem G. Gornyy

B: April 9, 1912
MS: Unknown before 1958; USSR Chief Mil. Procurator, 1958–
R: Col. Gen. of Justice
A: O. Red Star; other decorations and medals
PO: Member, CPSU, 19?

Anatoliy A. Gorpenko

B: 1916
ED: Graduate, Kharkov Inst. of Art
MS: Grekov Studio of War Artists, 1940–; painter of personally-observed battle scenes, 1941–1944; helped design Berlin memorial to Soviet war dead, 1945; battle artist, 1945–.
R: Civilian attached to Soviet Army
A: Stalin Prize, 1949–1950

Leonid A. Govorov

B: 1897
MS: Joined Red Army, 1919; fought in Civil War, 1919–1921; artillery field and so, 1920–1940; artillery officer, Western Front, 1941; CO, 5th Army, 1941; CO, Leningrad Front, 1942–1945; no information after 1945; died 1955
R: Marshal of Artillery
A: Hero of the Soviet Union; O. Lenin; other decorations and medals

Andrei A. Grechko

B: Kiubyshevo, Rostov-on-Don, October 17, 1903
ED: Graduate, Frunze Mil. Acad., 1936; Acad. of the General Staff, 1941
MS: Joined Red Army, 1919; soldier, platoon leader, sqn. CO, then so, 1919–1939; CO of an inft. regt., Russo-Finnish War, 1939–1940; corps so, 1940–1941; CO, 34th Cavalry Div., 1941; CO, 5th Cavalry Corps., then 12th, 47th, and 18th Armies, 1942; CO, 56th Army then Dep. CO, 1st Ukr. Front, 1943; CO, 1st Guards Army, 1943–1945; CO, Kïev MD, 1945–1953; CO, Group of Soviet Forces in Germany, 1953–1957; CO, Soviet Ground Forces, 1957–1960; CO, Warsaw Pact Forces, 1960–1967; USSR Minister of Defense, 1967–1976; died April 26, 1976.
R: Marshal of the Soviet Union
A: Hero of the Soviet Union; O. Lenin (5); O. Red Banner (3); O. Red Star; other decorations and medals
PO: Member, CPSU, 1928; memb., CC, Ukr. CP, 1949–1952; cand. memb., CC, CPSU, 1952–1961; memb., CC, CPSU, 1961–1976; memb., Politburo, CC, CPSU, 1973–1976

Anatoliy I. Gribkov

B: March 23, 1919
ED: Graduate, Frunze Mil. Acad., 1942; Acad. of the General Staff, 1951
MS: Unknown before 1942; so and CoS, various units, 1942–1973; CoS, Warsaw Pact Forces, 1973–1976; FDC, Warsaw Pact Forces and FDC, Soviet General Staff, 1976–.
R: General
A: O. Lenin; other decorations and medals
PO: Member, CPSU, 1941; memb., CC, CPSU, 1976–

Piotr G. Grigorenko

B: Borisovka, 1907
ED: Graduate, Acad. of the General Staff, 1939
MS: Unknown before 1939; field and so, Far East MD, 1940–1943; field and so, Western Front, 1943–1945; field and so, later Prof. Chmn. of Cybernetics, 1945–1961; ret. as a "troublemaker," 1961
R: General
A: Five orders and 6 medals
PO: Member, CPSU, 1927; del., CPSU Congress, 1956–1961; called for reform at 1961 CPSU Congress, which led to his dismissal from active service; founded "Fighting League for the Reestablishment of Leninism," 1962; arrested and committed to a psychiatric clinic, 1964; released, 1965; rearrested and recommitted, 1969; released, 1974

Josif I. Gusakovsky

B: December 25, 1904
ED: Graduate, Acad. of the General Staff, 193?
MS: Joined Red Army, 1928; field and so, 1928–1936; arrested, imprisoned, and released, 1937–1938; Dep. CoS of a tank sqn., CoS of a tank regt., then a tank brig., 1940–1942; CO, 44th Guards Tank Brig., 1st Tank Army, 1944–1945; CO of a div. then of an army, 1945–1957; CO, Riga Garrison and FDC, Baltic MD, 1958–1959; CO, Baltic MD, 1959–1963; Head, Main Personnel Admin., USSR Ministry of Defense, 1963–1970; Inspector-Advisor, Main Inspectorate, USSR Ministry of Defense, 1970–
R: Col. Gen. of Tank Troops

A: Hero of the Soviet Union (2); O. Lenin (2); O. Red Banner (4); other decorations and medals
PO: Member, CPSU, 1931; memb., CC, Lat. CP, 1960–1963; del., CPSU Congress, 1956–1961; dep., USSR Supr. Sov. convoc., 1962–1970

Ivan I. Iakubovskiy

B: Byelorussia, 1912
ED: Graduate, Inft. School, 1932; Acad. of the General Staff, 1948
MS: Joined Red Army, 1932; platoon and company CO, 1932–1941; field officer, 1941–1945; CO of armored troops in Transcarpathian MD, later FDC, Group of Soviet Forces in Germany, 1945–1959; CO, Group of Soviet Forces in Germany, 1960–1965; CO, Kiev MD, 1965–1967; CO, Warsaw Pact Forces and USSR 1st Dep. Minister of Defense, 1967–1976; died November 30, 1976.
R: Marshal of the Soviet Union
A: O. Lenin (3); O. Red Banner; other decorations and medals
PO: Member, CPSU, 1937; dep., RSFSR Supr. Sov. convoc., 1955–1963; dep., USSR Supr. Sov. convoc., 1962–1976; memb., CC, Ukr. CP, 1966–1971; memb., CC, CPSU, 1961–1976

Ilya I. Ivanov

B: St. Petersburg, 1899
ED: Graduate, Petrograd Artillery course, 1921; Drerzhinsky Artillery Acad., 1928
MS: Joined Red Army, 1918; artillery officer in Civil War later a battery CO, 1919–1936; instructor, Drerzhinsky Artillery Acad., 1932–1937; artillery designer, 1937–ret.
R: Lt. Gen. of Engineering-Technical Troops
A: O. Lenin (4); Stalin Prize (2); Hero of Socialist Labor; other decorations
PO: Member, CPSU, 1946

Yvgeniy F. Ivanovskiy

B. Byelorussia, March 7, 1918
ED: Graduate, Acad. Motorization and Mechanization of the Red Army, 1941; Acad. of the General Staff, 1958

MS: Joined Red Army, 1936; CoS then CO of a tank bttn., a tank reconnaissance corps, and a tank brig. on the Western, Stalingrad, Southwestern, 1st and 2d Bye. Fronts, 1941–1945; Dep. CO then CO, armored troops of a MD, CoS then CO of a div., Dep. CoS of a MD, then FDC, Moscow MD, 1946–1968; CO, Moscow MD, 1968–1972; CO, Group of Soviet Forces in Germany, 1973–
R: General
A: O. Red Star; other decorations and medals
PO: Member, CPSU, 1941; dep., USSR Supr. Sov. convoc., 1970–; memb., CC, CPSU, 1971–

Petr I. Ivashutin

B: 1903
MS: Joined Red Army, 1931; so, 1932–1941; so, Transcaucasian, Caucasian, Crimean, North Caucasian, Southwestern, and 3d Ukr. Fronts, 1941–1945; G.R.U.-K.G.B. officer, 1945–1955; Dep. Chmn., K.G.B., 1956–1958; 1st Dep. Chmn., K.G.B., 1959–1962; Chief, Main Intelligence Directorate (G.R.U.), USSR Ministry of Defense, 1963–
R: General
PO: Member, CPSU, 1930

Mikhail T. Kalashnikov

B: Altai Krai, November 10, 1919
MS: Designer of small arms, including the AK series
A: Hero of Socialist Labor; O. Lenin (2); Stalin Prize; other decorations
PO: Member, CPSU, 1953

Mikhail Y. Katukov

B: October 9, 1901
ED: Graduate, School of Red Army Commanders; Armored Troops Mil. Acad.; Acad. of the General Staff
MS: Joined Red Army, 1919; fought in Civil War, 1919–1921; inft. officer, 1921–1932; transferred to and served in armor, 1933–1940; CO, 4th Tank Brig., 1941; CO of a tank corps, 1942–1943; CO, 1st Guards Tank Army, 1943–1945; CO, 1st Guards Tank Army in Soviet occupation forces, Germany, 1949; recalled, 1949; so, USSR Ministry of

Defense, 1949–1964; CoS, Warsaw Pact Forces and 1st Dep. Chief, Soviet General Staff, 1965–1968; Inspector-Advisor, Main Inspectorate, USSR Ministry of Defense, 1968–.
R: Marshal of Tank Troops
A: Hero of the Soviet Union (2); O. Lenin (2); other decorations and medals
PO: Member, CPSU, 1932; dep., Bye. Supr. Sov. convoc., 1955

K. Petrovich Kazakov

B: November 18, 1902
ED: Graduate, Frunze Mil. Acad., 1936
MS: Joined Red Army, 1921; artilleryman, 1921–1932, 1936–1941; CO of an artillery regt., then Head, artillery operations depts., various fronts, 1941; chief artillery officer, Stalingrad, 1942–1943; artillery officer, Leningrad and Estonia, 1943–1944; artillery officer, East Prussia and Manchuria, 1945; CO of artillery, Maritime MD, 1945–1957; so, USSR Ministry of Defense, 1958–1962; CO, Soviet Missile and Artillery Troops, 1963–1968; Inspector-Advisor, Main Inspectorate, USSR Ministry of Defense, 1969–
R: Marshal of Artillery
A: O. Lenin; O. Red Banner; other decorations and medals
PO: Member, CPSU, 1920

Vasiliy I. Kazakov

B: 1898
ED: Graduate, Petrograd Artillery School, 1918; Frunze Mil. Acad., 1934
MS: Joined Red Army, 1919; CO, artillery battery in the Civil War, 1919–1921; artillery officer, 1922–1932; CO of an artillery regt., Proletarian Div., 1933–1939; CO, 7th Motorized Corps in the Moscow MD and later the Russo-Finnish War, 1939–1940; CO, 16th Army artillery, 1941–1942; CO of artillery on the Bryansk, Stalingrad, Don, Center, and 1st Bye. Fronts, 1942–1945; CO of artillery, Soviet occupation forces, Germany, 1945–1949; FDC, Soviet Artillery, 1950–1959; CO, Soviet Artillery, 1955–1962; ret. 1962
R: Marshal of Artillery
A: Hero of the Soviet Union; O. Lenin (4); O. Red Banner (4); other decorations
PO: Member, CPSU, 1932; dep., USSR Supr. Sov. convoc., 1946

Georgiy I. Khetagurov

B: 1903
ED: Civilian college graduate
MS: Joined Red Army, 1920; troop and battery CO, 1920–1930; CO of a regt., then CO of artillery in a regt., div., and corps, 1931–1940; CO of artillery in a mechanized corps, CoS of an army, CO of a div. and a corps, Dep. CO of an army, later CO of an army, 1941–1945; so and CO of artillery, various MD, 1945–1955; CO, Northern Group of Forces (Poland), 1956–1963; CO, Baltic MD, 1963–ret.; no information after 1969
R: Col. General of Artillery
A: Hero of the Soviet Union; O. Lenin; other decorations and medals
PO: Member, CPSU, 1929; USSR Supr. Sov. convoc., 1958–1962; del., CPSU Congress, 1956–1963; memb., CC, Lat. CP, 1963–ret.

Nikita S. Khrushchev

B: Kursk Oblast, 1894
ED: Graduate, Workers Facility, Donets Industrial Institute, Stalino, 1925
MS: Partisan CO in Civil War, 1918–1921; civilian politician, 1921–1941; po and memb., Mil. Council, Southwestern, Stalingrad, and 1st Ukr. Fronts, 1941–1945; civilian politician and government official, then 1st Secretary, CC, CPSU, 1945–1964; ret., 1964; died October 1971
R: Lt. Gen.
A: Hero of the Soviet Union; O. Lenin (6); O. Red Banner; other decorations
PO: Member, CPSU, 1934; del. and dep. to regional and national CPSU Congresses and convoc. and USSR Supr. Sov. convoc., 1934–1964

Ivan S. Konev

B: Kirov Oblast, November 27, 1897
ED: Graduate, Frunze Mil. Acad., 1926; Special facility, Frunze Mil. Acad., 1934–1935.
MS: Tsarist soldier, 1914–1918; joined Red Army, 1919, CO of a com-

pany in the Civil War, 1919–1921; CO of a corps then of armored trains, 1921–1925; CO of a regt. and a div., 1926–1934; CO, 2d Red Banner Far Eastern Army, 1935–1938; CO, Transbaikal, then Transcaucasian MD, 1938–1941; CO, 19th Army then Western Front, 1941; CO, Kalinin Front, 1941–1943; CO, 2d Ukr. Front, 1943–1944; CO, 1st Ukr. Front, 1944–1945; CO, Soviet occupation forces, Austria-Hungary, 1945–1946; CO, Soviet Ground Forces, 1946–1950; USSR Dep. Minister of Defense, 1946–1952; Chief Inspector for Coordinating Military Efforts of the Eastern European States, 1950–1952; CO, Carpathian MD, 1952–1954; USSR Dep. Minister of Defense (for Troop Training), 1954–1955; CO, Warsaw Pact Forces and USSR 1st Dep. Minister of Defense, 1955–1960; sick leave, 1960–1961; CO, Group of Soviet Forces in Germany, 1961–1962; General-Inspector, Main Inspectorate, USSR Ministry of Defense, 1962–1973; died May 21, 1973
R: Marshal of the Soviet Union
A: Hero of the Soviet Union (2); O. Lenin (6); O. Red Banner (3); O. Red Star (3); O. Suvurov (3); O. Kutuzov (2); other decorations and medals
PO: Member, CPSU, 1918; dep. to all USSR Supr. Sov. convoc., 1946–1973; del., CPSU Congress, 1959–1961, cand. memb., CC, Ukr. CP, 1954

Petr K. Koshevoi

B: Kirovograd Oblast, 1904
ED: Graduate, Frunze Mil. Acad., 1939; Acad. of the General Staff, 1948
MS: Joined Red Army, 1920; NCO in Civil War, 1920–1921; CO of a platoon and a regt. school, CoS of a regt., CoS of a div. then CO of a div., 1921–1941; CO, 24th Inft. Div., 1941–1943; CO, 63rd Inft. Corps, 1943–1945; so and CO, various units, 1945–1954; FDC, Group of Soviet Forces in Germany, 1955–1957; CO, Siberian MD, 1957–1960; CO, Kiev MD, 1960–1965; CO, Group of Soviet Forces in Germany, 1965–1973; ret. 1973
R: General
A: Hero of the Soviet Union (2); O. Lenin (4); other decorations and medals
PO: Member, CPSU, 1925; dep., RSFSR Supr. Sov. convoc., 1955–1959; memb., CC, Ukr. CP, 1963; del., CPSU Congress, 1959–1973; cand. memb., CC, CPSU, 1965–1973

Sydir A. Kovpak

B. Poltava Oblast, 1887
MS: Partisan CO, 1918–1919; NCO, Red Army, 1919; civilian politician, 1920–1941; CO, various partisan units, 1941–1945; ret. 1945; no information after 1961
R: Mjr. Gen.
A: Hero of the Soviet Union (2); O. Lenin (2); Gold Star Medal; other decorations
PO: Member, CPSU, 1919; dep., USSR Supr. Sov. convoc., 1946–1958; del., CPSU Congress, 1959; dep., Ukr. Supr. Sov. convoc., 1947–1960; memb., CC, Ukr. CP, 1956–1960

Mikhail M. Kozlov

B: 1917
MS: Unknown before 1973; Dep. CoS, Soviet Army and Navy, 1973–1974; 1st Dep. CoS, Soviet Army and Navy, 1974–
R: Col. General
PO: Member, CPSU, 19?; cand. memb., CC, CPSU, 1976–

Yakov G. Krezzer

B: 1905
ED: Graduate, Acad. of the General Staff, 1949
MS: Joined Red Army, 1921; field and so, 1925–1937; CO, 1st Moscow Proletarian Div., later 1st Moscow Motorized Inft. Div., 1938–1941; Dep. CO then CO, 2d Guards Army, 1942–1943; CO, 51st Army, 1943–1945; CO of an army, Kiev MD, 1945–1955; CO, Southern Urals MD, 1956–1958; CO, Transbaikal MD, 1958–1959; CO, Urals MD, 1959–1960; CO, Far East MD, 1961–ret.
R: General
A: Hero of the Soviet Union; O. Lenin; O. Red Banner (3); other decorations
PO: Member, CPSU, 1925; memb., CC, Ukr. CP, 1954; dep., Ukr. Supr. Sov. convoc., 1955; dep., RSFSR Supr. Sov. convoc., 1959; dep., USSR Supr. Sov. convoc., 1961; del., CPSU Congress, 1959–ret.; memb., Cent. Auditing Comm., CPSU, 1961–ret.

Fedor F. Krivda

MS: Unknown before 1976; CO, Group of Southern Forces (Hungary), 1976–
R: Col. Gen.

Nikolai I. Krylov

B: Galyaevka, Saratov Guberniya, 1903
ED: Secondary
MS: Joined Red Army, 1919; fought in Civil War, 1919–1921; field and so, Far East frontier, 1921–1937; CO of an inft. div., 1938–1941; CoS, Odessa Fortified Area and 1st Black Sea Army, 1941; CoS, 62nd Army, 1942–1943; CO, 21st Army, 1943; CO, 5th Army, 1944–1945; CO, Special Army Group, Sakhalin and Kurile Islands, and FDC, Far East MD, 1945–1955; CO, Urals MD, 1955–1957; CO, Leningrad MD, 1957–1960; CO, Moscow MD, 1960–1963; headed a mil. delegation to Sweden, 1958; CO, Strategic Rocket Forces and Dep., USSR Minister of Defense, 1963–1972; died January 1972
R: Marshal of the Soviet Union
A: Hero of the Soviet Union (2); O. Lenin (4); O. Red Banner (4); other decorations and medals
PO: Member, CPSU, 1927; dep., USSR Supr. Sov. convoc., 1950–1972; del., CPSU Congress, 1956–1961; memb., CC, CPSU, 1961–1972

Viktor G. Kulikov

B: July 5, 1921
ED: Graduate, Groznyy Mil. Acad., 1941; Frunze Mil. Acad., 1953; Acad. of the General Staff, 1959
MS: Joined Red Army, 1939; CO of an inft. sqn., 1941; CO, various tank units, Dep. CoS then CoS of a tank brig., 1941–1946; CO of a regt., CoS of a div., CO of a div., Dep. CO, FDC, then CO of an army, 1953–1967; CO, Kiev MD, 1967–1969; CO, Group of Soviet Forces in Germany, 1969–1971; Chief, Soviet General Staff and 1st Dep. USSR Minister of Defense, 1971–1977; CO, Warsaw Pact Forces, 1977–
R: Marshal of the Soviet Union
A: O. Lenin; O. Red Banner (3); other decorations and medals
PO: Member, CPSU, 1942; dep., USSR Supr. Sov. convoc., 1970–; memb., CC, CPSU, 1971–

Oleg F. Kulishev

B: 1929
MS: Unknown before 1976; CO, Northern Group of Forces (Poland),
1976–1977; CO, Transcaucasian MD, 1978–
R: Col. Gen.

Vladimir V. Kurasov

B: 1897
ED: Graduate, Frunze Mil. Acad., 1932; Acad. of the General Staff,
1938
MS: Unknown before 1941; CoS, various armies and fronts, incl. 1st
Baltic Front, 1941–1945; CoS, Soviet Central Group of Occupation
Forces (Hungary-Austria-Rumania), 1945–1946; CO, Soviet occupa-
tion forces and USSR Supr. CO, Austria, 1946–1949; Head, Acad. of
the General Staff, 1949–1956; Dep. CoS, Soviet General Staff, 1956–
ret.
R: General
A: O. Lenin; O. Red Banner; other decorations and medals
PO: Member, CPSU, 1928

Semen K. Kurkotkin

B: February 13, 1917
MS: Joined Red Army, 1937; tank officer, 1938–1941; CO, various
tank units, 1941–1954; CO of tank troops, Group of Soviet Forces in
Germany, 1955–1965; FDC, Group of Soviet Forces in Germany,
1966–1967; CO, Transcaucasian MD, 1968–1971; CO, Group of Soviet
Forces in Germany, 1971–1972; Chief of Rear Services and Dep. USSR
Minister of Defense, 1972–
R: General
A: O. Lenin; O. Red Banner; other decorations and medals
PO: Member, CPSU, 1940; memb., CC, CPSU, 1973–

Pavel A. Kurochkin

B: 1900
ED: Graduate, Frunze Mil. Acad.; Acad. of the General Staff, 1938
MS: Joined Red Army, 1918; fought in Civil War, 1919–1921; field and
so, 1921–1929; so, 1930–1938; instructor, Frunze Mil. Acad., 1938–

1939; CO, 20th Army, 1940–1941; CO, Northwestern Front, 1941–1943; CO, 11th Army then CO, Northwestern Front, 1943; CO, 2d Bye. Front, and later, 60th Army, 1944–1945; CO, Kuban MD, 1946–1947; instructor later Head, Frunze Mil. Acad., 1948–ret.
R: General
A: Hero of the Soviet Union; O. Lenin; other decorations and medals
PO: Member, CPSU, 1920; dep., USSR Supr. Sov. convoc., 1946; del., CPSU Congress, 1959–1961

Petr M. Kurochkin

B: 1897
ED: Graduate, Mil. Electr. Eng. Acad., 1932
MS: Joined Red Army, 1918; fought in Civil War, 1919–1921; signals officer, 1919–1951; signals instructor, Frunze Mil. Acad., 1952–ret.
R: Lt. Gen. of Signal Troops
A: O. Lenin; other decorations and medals

Vasiliy Kuznetsov

B: 1894
MS: Joined Red Army, 1918; fought in Civil War, 1919–1921; field and so, 1921–1941; field officer, Western Front, 1941; CO, 1st Guards Army, 1942–1943; Dep. CO, Southwestern Front, 1943–1945; no information after 1945; died 1964
R: General

Petr N. Lashchenko

B: Turia, Chernigov Oblast, December 19, 1910
ED: Graduate, Frunze Mil. Acad., 1940; Acad. of the General Staff, 1951
MS: Unknown before 1944; wounded in action, July 1944; field and so, 194?–1958; FDC, Kiev and Transcarpathian MD, 1959–1964; CO, Transcarpathian MD, 1964–1968; FDC, Soviet Ground Forces, 1968–1975; Inspector-Advisor, Main Inspectorate, USSR Ministry of Defense, 1976–
R: General
A: Hero of the Soviet Union; O. Lenin (4); O. Red Banner (3); other decorations and medals
PO: Member, CPSU, 1931

Dmitriy D. Lelyushenko

ED: Graduate, Frunze Mil. Acad., 1929
MS: Joined Red Army, 1918; fought in Civil War, 1919–1921; field officer, Far East frontier, 1922–1926, 1930–1941; CO of an army, Western Front, 1941–1942; CO, 4th Tank Army, 1943–1945; CO, 4th Tank Army, Saxony, 1945–1947; memb., mil. council, various MD, and so, USSR Ministry of Defense, 1947–1956; CO, Transbaikal MD, 1956–1958; CO, Urals MD, 1958–1960; Chmn., COSAAF, 1960–ret.
R: General
A: O. Lenin (2); O. Suvurov; other decorations and medals
PO: Member, CPSU, 1929; dep., RSFSR Supr. Sov. convoc., 1951–1955; dep., USSR Supr. Sov. convoc., 1958; del., CPSU Congress, 1956–1959

Dmitriy I. Litovtsev

MS: armored officer, various units, 1941–1967; Dep. CO, Central Group of Forces (Czechoslovakia), 1968–1970; CO, Northern Caucasus MD, 1970–1975; Soviet rep. for Czechoslovakia, Joint Warsaw Pact Forces Supreme Command, 1976–
R: Col. Gen. of Tank Troops

Oleg A. Losik

B: December 4, 1915
ED: Graduate, Saratov Tank School, 1938; Acad. of the General Staff, 1950
MS: Joined Red Army, 1935; field and so, 1939–1964; FDC, Far East MD, 1965–1967; CO, Far East MD, 1967–1969; Head, Malinovskiy Armored Troops Acad., 1969–
R: Marshal of Tank Troops
A: Hero of the Soviet Union; O. Lenin; other decorations and medals
PO: Member, CPSU, 193?

Rodion Y. Malinovskiy

B: Odessa, November 22, 1898
ED: Graduate, special officers course, 1922; Frunze Mil. Acad., 1930
MS: Tsarist soldier, 1914–1917; NCO with Russian Expeditionary

Corps, France, 1917–1918; joined Red Army, 1918; CO of a company, a bttn., and a regt. in Civil War, 1918–1921; field officer, 1922–1929; CoS of a cavalry regt., so in a MD, and CoS of a cavalry corps, 1930–1936; advisor-volunteer, Spanish Civil War, 1937–1938; instructor, Frunze Mil. Acad., 1939–1941; CO, 6th and 12th Armies, 1941; CO, Southern Front, Don Group, and 66th Army, 1942; CO, 66th and 2d Guards Armies and Southwestern Front, 1943; CO, 2d Ukr., Front, 1944–1945; CO, Transbaikal Front then Far East MD, 1945–1956; CO, Soviet Ground Forces and 1st Dep. USSR Minister of Defense, 1956–1957; USSR Minister of Defense, 1957–1967; died March 31, 1967.
R: Marshal of the Soviet Union
A: Hero of the Soviet Union (2); O. Lenin (7); O. Red Star (3); other decorations and medals
PO: Member, CPSU, 1926; dep., USSR Supr. Sov. convoc., 1946–1967; del., CPSU Congress, 1952–1967; memb., CC, CPSU, 1956–1967

Aleksandr M. Mayorov

B: 1920
ED: Graduate, Frunze Mil. Acad., 1951; Acad. of the General Staff, 1963
MS: Joined Red Army, 1940; CO and Engineer CO, Voronezh, Western, 1st and 2d Ukr. Fronts, 1941–1945; CO, engr. bttn., so, and FDC, Central Group of Forces (Czechoslovakia), 1945–1968; CO, Central Group of Forces (Czechoslovakia), 1968–1972; CO, Baltic MD, 1972–
R: General
A: O. Lenin; other decorations and medals
PO: Member, CPSU, 1943; dep., USSR Supr. Sov. convoc., 1970–; cand. memb., CC, CPSU, 1971; memb., CC, Lat. CP, 1972–

Kirill A. Meretskov

B: Moscow, 1897
ED: Graduate, Red Army Mil. Acad., 1921
MS: Joined Red Army, 1918; fought in Civil War, 1919–1921; field and so, 1921–1935; CoS, Bye. MD, 1936–1938; CO, Volga and Leningrad MD, 1938–1939; CO, of an army, Russo-Finnish War, 1939–1940; CoS, Soviet General Staff, and Dep. USSR Pop. Comr. of Defense, 1940–1941; CO, Volkhov, Karelian, and 1st Far Eastern Fronts, 1941–1945; CO, Maritime and Moscow MD, 1946–1947; CO, Northern MD, 1947–1955; assistant to USSR Minister of Defense (for higher mil.

schools), 1955–1958; Chmn., Soviet War Veterans Comte., 1958–1961; no information after 1961
R: Marshal of the Soviet Union
A: Hero of the Soviet Union; O. Lenin (5); other decorations and medals
PO: Member, CPSU, 1917; memb., CC, CPSU, 1939, 1952; dep., USSR Supr. Sov. convoc., 1937, 1946–1961; memb., Cent. Auditing Comm., CPSU, 1956–1961

Aleksandr A. Morozov

B: Kharkov, October 29, 1904
ED: Graduate, Moscow Higher Technical School, 1936
MS: Head, design bureau, then Chief Designer, Kharkov Tank Plant no. 183, 1936–ret.; designed T-60, T-34, Su-85, Su-100, and T-54 armored vehicles
R: Mjr. Gen. of Tank Troops
A: Hero of Socialist Labor; Stalin Prize (3); Lenin Prize; O. Lenin (2); other decorations and medals
PO: Member, CPSU, 1943; dep., USSR Supr. Sov. convoc., 1958

Kirill S. Moskalenko

B: Donets Oblast, May 5, 1902
ED: Graduate, Dzerzhinski Artillery Acad., 1939
MS: Joined Red Army, 1920; cadet, CO of a platoon and battery, 1st Cavalry Army, 1920–1927; CO of a battery, CoS then CO of an artillery regt. then an artillery Brig., 1927–1938; CO, motorized brig., a rifle then a cavalry corps, later an army, 1938–1941; CO of artillery on the Southwestern, Stalingrad, Voronezh, 1st and 4th Ukr. Fronts, 1941–1945; CO, anti-aircraft artillery, Moscow MD, 1945–1953; CO, Moscow MD, 1953–1960; CO, Strategic Rocket Forces and Dep. USSR Minister of Defense, 1960–1962; Chief Inspector, Main Inspectorate, USSR Ministry of Defense, 1962– and Dep. USSR Minister of Defense, 1966–
R: Marshal of the Soviet Union
A: Hero of the Soviet Union; O. Lenin (5); O. Red Banner (5); O. Suvurov (2); O. Kutuzov (2); other decorations and medals
PO: Member, CPSU, 1926; dep., USSR Supr. Sov. convoc., 1946–1962; memb., CC, CPSU, 1960–

Vasiliy P. Mzhavanadze

B: Kutaisi, 1902
ED: Graduate, Geo. Mil. School, 1927; Lenin Mil.-Pol. Acad., 1937
MS: Joined Red Army, 1924; field and po, 1927–1936; CO of a regt.,
Leningrad MD, 1937–1939; po then CO, Baltic MD, 1939–1941; CO of
an inft. corps and div., Maritime Operational Group, later CO of 42d,
2d Assault, and 21st Armies, 1942–1945; Dep. CO, Kharkov, Kiev, and
Carpathian MD, 1946–1953; civilian politician, 1954–ret.
R: Lt. Gen.
A: Hero of Socialist Labor; O. Lenin; O. Kutuzov; O. Suvorov; other
decorations and medals
PO: Member, CPSU, 1927; memb., CC, Ukr. CP, 1952; 1st Sec., CC,
Geo. CP, 1953; memb., CC, CPSU, 1956–ret.; dep., Ukr. Supr. Sov.
convoc., 1947–1951; dep., Geo. Supr. Sov. convoc., 1955–ret.; dep.,
USSR Supr. Sov. convoc., 1952–ret.; del., CPSU Congress, 1953–ret.

Nikolay A. Nachinkin

B: November 1907
MS: Unknown before 1956; Head, political Bd. and memb., mil. council, Bye. MD, 1957–1961; Dep. Head, Main Political Bd., Soviet Army
and Navy, 1961–1974; Consultant, Main Inspectorate, USSR Ministry
of Defense, 1974–
R: Col. Gen.
PO: Member, CPSU, 1926; del., CPSU Congress, 1959–1974; dep.,
Bye. Supr. Sov. convoc., 1959; dep., RSFSR Supr. Sov. convoc., 1963;
dep., USSR Supr. Sov. convoc., 1961–1974

Viktor T. Obukhov

B: Orenburg Oblast, 1898
ED: Graduate, Frunze Mil. Acad., 1934
MS: Joined Red Army, 1918; fought in Civil War, 1919–1921; helped
quash Basmachi movement, Turkestan, 1920; field officer, 1920–1938;
fought at Khalkin-Goll, 1939; field officer, various units, 1939–1941;
CO, 26th Tank Div., 1941; wounded, 1941–1942; DC of a tank army
then CO, 3d Guards Mechanized Corps, 1943–1945; CO, various tank
units later FDC, Soviet Armored Forces, 1945–1964; no information
after 1965

R: Col. Gen. of Tank Troops
A: Hero of the Soviet Union; O. Lenin; O. Red Banner; other decorations
PO: Member, CPSU, 1918; del., CPSU Congress, 1956

Nikolay V. Ogarkov

B: Moloko, Kalinin Oblast, October 30, 1917
ED: Graduate, Mil. Engr. Acad., 1941; Acad. of the General Staff, 1959
MS: Joined Red Army, 1938; regt., brig., div. engineer, 1941–1945; engineer officer, 1945–1948; so, Far East MD, 1949–1953; dep. then CoS of a MD, 1953–1957; CO of a div., 1959–1961; CoS then FDC, Bye. MD, 1961–1965; CO, Volga MD, 1965–1968; 1st Dep. CoS, Soviet General Staff, 1968–1977; Dep. USSR Minister of Defense (portfolio unknown), 1974–1976; Chief, Soviet General Staff and 1st Dep., USSR Minister of Defense, 1977–
R: Marshal of the Soviet Union
A: Hero of the Soviet Union; O. Lenin; O. Red Banner; O. Red Star; other decorations and medals
PO: Member, CPSU, 1945; dep., Bye. Supr. Sov. convoc., 1963–1967; dep., USSR Supr. Sov. convoc., 1966–; cand. memb., CC, CPSU, 1966–1971; memb., CC, CPSU, 1971–

Vasiliy V. Okunev

B: April 20, 1920
ED: Graduate, Dzerzhinski Artillery School, 1950; Acad. of the General Staff, 1961
MS: Joined Red Army, 1936; NCO and officer, CO of an antiaircraft tank sqn., later CO of an antiaircraft div., 1936–1944; CO of an artillery regt., CoS, FDC, and CO of various antiaircraft units, a div., and AA in a MD, 1944–1966; CO, Moscow Antiaircraft Defense District (PVO), 1966–1970; CO, Soviet SAM Expeditionary Corps, Egypt, 1970–1972; so, USSR Ministry of Defense, 1972–1974; FDC, USSR Antiaircraft Defense Troops (PVO), 1974–1976; Inspector-Advisor, Main Inspectorate, USSR Ministry of Defense, 1976–
R: Col. Gen. of Artillery
A: O. Red Banner; other decorations and medals
PO: Member, CPSU, 1941; cand. memb., CC, CPSU, 1971–1976; dep., USSR Supr. Sov. convoc., 1970–1976; del., CPSU Congress, 1966–1971; memb., Cent. Auditing Comm., CPSU, 1966–1971

Ivan G. Pavlovskiy

B: Teremkovtsky, Khmelnitskiy Oblast, February 24, 1909
ED: Graduate, Frunze Mil. Acad., 1941; Acad. of the General Staff, 1948
MS: Joined Red Army, 1931; soldier and NCO, 1932–1939; CoS and CO of a regt., then CO of a regt., later a div., 1941–1945; CO of a div., a corps, and an army, 1945–1958; FDC, Transcaucasian MD, 1958–1961; CO, Volga MD, 1961–1963; CO, Far East MD, 1963–1967; CO, Soviet Ground Forces and Dep. USSR Minister of Defense, 1967–.
R: General
A: Hero of the Soviet Union; O. Lenin (2); O. Red Banner (6); O. Suvorov; O. Red Star; other decorations and medals.
PO: Member, CPSU, 1939; dep., Armenian Supr. Sov. convoc., 1955–1959; dep., USSR Supr. Sov. convoc., 1962–; memb., Cent. Auditing Comm., CPSU, 1966–1971; memb., CC, CPSU, 1971–.

Dmitri Pavlov

MS: Joined Red Army, 1919; fought in Civil War, 1919–1920; field and so, 1922–1936; volunteer-advisor, Spanish Civil War, 1937–1938; field officer, Russo-Finnish War, 1939–1940; CO, Western Front, 1941; relieved of his command and, together with his CoS and the CO of 4th Army, executed for incompetence, July 1941
R: General

Ivan T. Peresypkin

B: Protasovo, Orel Oblast, June 18, 1904
ED: Graduate, Red Army Mil.-Pol. School, 1924; Mil. Electrotech.-Communications Acad., 1937
MS: Joined Red Army, 1919; fought in Civil War, 1919–1920; po, 1924–1932; CO, Communications Research Institute then CO, Red Army Communications Bd., 1937–1939; USSR Pop. Comr. of Communications, 1939–1941; Dep. USSR Pop. Comr. of Defense and Chief, Red Army Communications Bd., 1941–1945; CO, Soviet Army Signal Troops, 1946–1957; signals advisor, North Korean Peoples Army, 1950–1953; scientific-advisor, USSR Ministry of Defense, 1957–1958; Inspector-Advisor, Main Inspectorate, USSR Ministry of Defense, 1958–
R: Marshal of Signal Troops

A: O. Lenin (4); O. Red Banner (2); O. Red Star; other decorations and medals
PO: Member, CPSU, 1925; dep., USSR Supr. Sov. convoc., 1946; memb., Cent. Auditing Comm., CPSU, 1941–1952

Fedor F. Petrov

B: St. Petersburg, 1902
ED: Graduate, Leningrad Polytechnical Institute, 1931
MS: Joined Red Guards, 1918; employed at Kronstadt artillery repair shop, 1919–1921; employed at Tula munitions plant, 1922–1929; designer of Red Army artillery, 1932–ret.
R: Mjr. Gen. of Engineer-Technical Troops
A: Stalin Prize (3); O. Lenin (2); Hero of Socialist Labor; other decorations and medals.
PO: Member, CPSU, 1942; dep., USSR Supr. Sov. convoc., 1946 and 1954.

Ivan V. Petrov

B: Voronezh Oblast, 1906
ED: Graduate, Mil. Conducting Facility, Moscow University, 1936
MS: Joined Red Army, 192?; trainee, musician, master sergeant on band duty, 192?–1933; mil. band conductor, 1936–1943; Head, Higher School of Mil. Conductors, 1944–1950; Soviet Army inspector of bands, 1950–1953; Chief Conductor, Soviet Army and Head, Mil. Band Service, USSR Ministry of Defense, 1954–1976; ret. 1977
R: Mjr. Gen.
A: Various decorations and medals

Vasiliy I. Petrov

B: Chernolesskoe, Stavropol Krai, January 15, 1917
ED: Graduate, Frunze Mil. Acad., 1941; Acad. of the General Staff, 1969
MS: Joined Red Army, 1939; field officer, Southern, Crimean, North Caucasian, Transcaucasian, Steppe, Voronezh, 1st and 2d Ukr. Fronts, 1941–1945; field and so, 1946–1965; CoS and FDC, Far East MD,

1966–1972; CO, Far East MD, 1972–1976; FDC, Soviet Ground Forces, 1976–
R: General
A: O. Lenin; O. Red Banner; O. Red Star (2); other decorations and medals
PO: Member, CPSU, 1944; memb., CC, CPSU, 1976–

Pavel P. Poluboyarov

B: Tula, June 16, 1901
ED: Graduate, Armored Vehicle School, 1926; Mil. Acad. of Motorization and Mechanization, 1938; Acad. of the General Staff, 1941
MS: Joined Red Army, 1919; fought in Civil War, 1919–1921; tank officer, 1927–1941; CO of various armored units, later the 17th Tank Corps, 1941–1945; Dep. CO, then FDC, Red Army Tank and Mechanized Troops, 1949–1954; CO, Tank Troops, 1954–1968; Inspector-Advisor, Main Inspectorate, USSR Ministry of Defense, 1969–
R: Marshal of Tank Troops
A: Hero of the Soviet Union; O. Lenin (3); O. Red Banner (5); O. Red Star (2); O. Suvorov (2); O. Kutuzov; other decorations and medals.
PO: Member, CPSU, 1920; dep., Bye. Supr. Sov. convoc., 1947; dep., RSFSR Supr. Sov. convoc., 1955–; del., CPSU Congress, 1961.

Stanislav G. Poplavskiy

B: Podolshchina, Ukraine, 1902
ED: Graduate, Frunze Mil. Acad., 1937
MS: Joined Red Army, 1919; fought in Civil War, 1919–1921; warrant officer, 99th Div., instructor of tactics and Polish language, Frunze Mil. Acad., and so, 1921–1941; CO of a regt., CoS of a div., CO of a div., 1941–1943; attached to Polish forces in the Red Army then CO, 2d Polish Army, 1943–1944; CO, 1st Polish Army, 1944–1945; CO, Wroclaw MD, 1945–1947; CO, Polish Ground Forces, 1947–1956; relieved of command, 1956; so, USSR Ministry of Defense, 1956–ret.
R: General
A: Hero of the Soviet Union; O. Lenin (3); O. Red Banner (3); O. Suvorov; other decorations and medals.
PO: Member, CPSU, 192?

Markian M. Popov

B: 1902
ED: Graduate, Frunze Mil. Acad., 1936
MS: Joined Red Army, 1920; soldier and NCO, 1921–1932; CoS of various units in a MD, 1936–1939; CO, Leningrad MD, 1940–1941; CO, Northern and Leningrad Fronts, 1941–1942; Dep. CO, Stalingrad Front, CO, 5th Assault Army, Dep. CO, Southwestern Front, and CO, Bryansk Front, 1942–1943; CO, 2d Baltic Front, then demoted to CoS, Leningrad Front, 1943–1945; CO, Tauria MD, 1946–1955; so, USSR Ministry of Defense, 1955–ret.
R: General
A: O. Lenin (4); O. Red Banner (3); other decorations and medals
PO: Member, CPSU, 192?; dep., USSR Supr. Sov. convoc., 1946–1958

Aleksey I. Proshlyakov

B: 1901
MS: Unknown before 1936; CO, engineer troops of an army, 1936–1941; Head, Engineer Bd., Southern Front, later Chief of Engineer Troops, Southern, Stalingrad, Don, Center, and 1st Bye. Fronts, 1941–1945; Chief of Engineer Troops, Group of Soviet Forces in Germany, then Chief, Bd. of Combat Training, Soviet Army Engineer Troops, 1945–1961; CO, Soviet Army Engineer Troops, 1961–
R: Marshal of Engineer Troops
A: Hero of the Soviet Union; O. Lenin; O. Red Banner; other decorations
PO: Member, CPSU, 1921; del., CPSU Congress, 1961

Aleksei I. Radziyevsky

B: Uman, August 13, 1911
ED: Graduate, Red Army Cavalry School, 1931; Frunze Mil. Acad., 1938; Acad. of the General Staff, 1941
MS: Details unknown before 1941; field officer, 1941–1949; CO, Northern Group of Forces (Poland), 1950–1952; CO, Turkman MD, 1952–1953; CO, Soviet Tank Troops, 1953–1954; CO, Odessa MD, 1954–1959; FDC, Acad. of the General Staff, 1959–1968; Head, Main Administration for Mil. Educational Institutions, USSR Ministry of Defense, 1968–1969; Head, Frunze Mil. Acad., 1969–
R: General

A: O. Lenin; O. Red Banner (6); O. Suvorov (2); O. Kutuzov; O. Red Star; other decorations and medals
PO: Member, CPSU, 1931

Aleksandr I. Rodimtsev

B: Kalinin Oblast, 190?
ED: Graduate, Frunze Mil. Acad., 1938; Acad. of the General Staff, 1949
MS: Joined Red Army, 1919; fought in Civil War, 1919–1921; field and so, 1922–1935; volunteer-advisor, Spanish Civil War, 1936–1938; field officer, 1939–1941; CO, 1st Guards Div., 1941–1944; CO, 33d Rifle Corps, 1944–1945; ret., 1945–1955; Dep. CO, Northern MD, 1956–1957; Mil. Attaché and Head, Soviet Mil. del., Albania, 1957–1958; ret. 1958
R: Lt. Gen.
A: Hero of the Soviet Union (2); O. Lenin (2); O. Red Banner; other decorations
PO: Member, CPSU, 1919; dep., USSR Supr. Sov. convoc., 1950

Konstantin K. Rokossovskiy

B: Velikie Luki, December 21, 1896
ED: Graduate, Frunze Mil. Acad., 1929
MS: Tsarist cavalry NCO, 1914–1918; joined Red Guard, 1918; CO of a cavalry regt. in the Civil War, 1918–1920; so and CO, troops fighting along the Chinese-Eastern RR, 1920–1929; CO, various units, Far East, CO of a corps, Leningrad MD, CO of an army, Far East, 1930–1937; imprisoned later released, 1937–1938; CO of a motorized corps in the Soviet occupation of eastern Poland, 1939; field CO, 1940–1941; CO, 6th Mechanized Corps, an army on the Western Front, and the 16th Army at Moscow, 1941–1942; CO, Bryansk, Don, Center, 1st and 2d Ukr. Fronts, 1942–1945; CO, Soviet occupation forces in Poland, 1945–1949; Dep. Chmn. Pol. Council of Ministers and Polish Minister of Defense, 1949–1956; expelled from Poland, 1956; Dep. USSR Minister of Defense, 1956–1958; CO, Transcaucasian MD, 1957–1958; Inspector General, Main Inspectorate, USSR Ministry of Defense, 1958–1968; died August 3, 1978
R: Marshal of the Soviet Union

A: Hero of the Soviet Union (2); O. Lenin (6); O. Red Banner (6); other decorations and medals
PO: Member, CPSU, 1919; dep., USSR Supr. Sov. convoc., 1937, 1946–1968; cand. memb., CC, CPSU, 1961–1968

Pavel A. Rotmistrov

B: Kalinin Oblast, July 6, 1901
ED: Graduate, Frunze Mil. Acad., 1930
MS: Joined Red Army, 1918; fought in Civil War, 1919–1921; field officer, various armored units, 1922–1938; CO of an armored brig. and div., Russo-Finnish War, 1939–1940; CoS, 3d Mechanized Corps then CO, 8th Guards Tank Brig., 1940–1941; CO, 3d and 7th Tank Guards Brigs., 1942; CO, 3d Tank Guards Corps, 5th Guards Tank Army, 1943–1944; CO, Red Army Tank Troops, 1944–1945; CO of tank troops, Group of Soviet Forces in Germany and then Far East MD, 1945–1948; Chief of officer training, Main Administration, Soviet Army Tank Troops, 1948–1952; Head, Stalin Armored Forces Acad., 1952–1955; CO, Soviet tank troops and Head, Main Administration, Soviet Army Tank Troops, 1955–1958; Head, Mil. Acad. for Tank Troops, 1958–1964; aide to USSR Minister of Defense (for higher mil. educational facilities), 1964–1968; Inspector General, Main Inspectorate, USSR Ministry of Defense, 1968–
R: Chief Marshal of Tank Troops
A: Hero of the Soviet Union; O. Lenin (5); O. Red Banner (4); other decorations
PO: Member, CPSU, 1919

Pavel Rybalko

B: 1894
MS: Joined Red Army, 1918; fought in Civil War, 1919–1921; field and so, 1922–1940; instructor, Frunze Mil. Acad., 1941–1942; CO, 5th and 3d Guards Tank Armies, 1942–1945; no information after 1945; died 1948
R: General

Aleksandr N. Saburov

B: 1908
MS: Joined Red Army, 1931; field officer, 1932–1941; CO, partisan units, Ukr. and Bryansk Oblast, 1941–1945; civilian official, Ukr., 1945–ret.
R: Mjr. Gen.
A: Hero of the Soviet Union; O. Lenin; other decorations and medals
PO: Member, CPSU, 1932; dep., USSR Supr. Sov. convoc., 1946–1954.

Grigoriy I. Salmanov

B: 1922
ED: Graduate, Frunze Mil. Acad., 1949; Acad. of the General Staff, 1964
MS: Joined Red Army, 1940; CO of a platoon and company, CoS and DC of a bttn., and Dep. Head of a corps department, Western, Central, 1st and 2d Bye. Fronts, 1941–1945; CO of a bttn., CoS of a regt., CO of various regts., CoS of a mechanized div., CO of a rifle div., FDC of a MD, 1945–1969; CO, Kiev MD, 1969–1975; Dep. CO of Soviet Ground Forces (for combat training), 1975–
R: Col. Gen.
A: O. Red Star; other decorations and medals
PO: Member, CPSU, 194?; memb., CC, Ukr. CP, 1971–1976; dep., USSR Supr. Sov. convoc., 1970–; cand. memb., CC, CPSU, 1971–

Boris M. Shaposhnikov

B: 1882
MS: Joined Red Army, 1918; fought in Civil War, 1919–1921; field and so, 1922–1932; Dep. Peo. Comr. Defense, 1932–1940; CoS, Soviet General Staff, 1940–1941; Dep. Peo. Comr. Defense, 1942; Head, Voroshilov Mil. Acad., 1943–1945; died 1945
R: Marshal of the Soviet Union
A: O. Lenin; other decorations and medals
PO: Member, CPSU, 1918

Ivan E. Shavrov

B: March 27, 1916
ED: Graduate, Mil. Acad. for Tank Troops, 1941; Acad. of the General Staff, 1948
MS: Joined Red Army, 1935; CoS of a tank corps and tank army, Southwestern, Southern, Stalingrad, Don, 4th Ukr., 1st and 2d Baltic Fronts, 1941–1945; so, CO of a div., and FDC, Group of Soviet Forces in Germany, 1945–1967; CO, various units and FDC of a MD, 1968–1973; Head, Acad. of the General Staff, 1973–
R: General
A: O. Red Star; other decorations and medals
PO: Member, CPSU, 1940; memb., CC, Est. CP, 1966–1976; dep., USSR Supr. Sov. convoc., 1970; memb., CC, CPSU, 1971–

Sergei M. Shtemenko

B: Volgograd Oblast, 1907
ED: Graduate, Moscow Artillery School, 1926; Mil. Acad. of Tank Troops, 1937; Acad. of the General Staff, 1938
MS: Joined Red Army, 1926; CO of a platoon, CoS of a div., Dep. CoS of a regt., 1926–1937; CO, tank bttn., 1937–1938; memb., then Head, Operations Department, Soviet General Staff, 1938–1945; memb., Soviet General Staff, CoS later FDC of a MD, 1945–1948; CoS, Group of Soviet Forces in Germany, 1952–1953; after Stalin's death, demoted and removed from public view, 1953–1956; Head, Main Intelligence Directorate (G.R.U.), USSR Ministry of Defense, 1957; CO, Southern Group of Forces (Hungary), 1958–1960; Dep. CO, Volga MD, 1960–1961; FDC, Transcaucasian MD, 1961–1962; CO, Tbilisi Garrison, 1963–1965; Dep. CoS, Soviet Ground Forces, 1965–1968; 1st Dep. CoS, Soviet Ground Forces then CoS, Warsaw Pact Forces and 1st Dep. Chief, Soviet General Staff, 1968–1976; died April 23, 1976
R: General
A: O. Lenin; O. Red Banner (2); O. Suvurov (2); O. Kutuzov; other decorations
PO: Member, CPSU, 1930; cand. memb., CC, CPSU, 1952; cand. memb., CC, Geo. CP, 1961–1963.

Nikolay K. Silchenko

B: 1919
MS: Unknown before 1966; FDC, Urals MD, 1966–1970; CO, Urals

MD, 1970–
R: Col. Gen.
A: O. Red Star; other decorations and medals

Sergei L. Sokolov

B: July 1, 1911
ED: Graduate, Mil. Acad. of Armored and Mechanized Troops, 1947; Acad. of the General Staff, 1951
MS: Joined Red Army, 1932; NCO and field officer, CoS of a regt. and a bd., CO, tank troops, Karelian Front, 1933–1945; CO of a regt., CoS of a div., CO of a div., CoS then CO of an army, and FDC of a MD, 1945–1965; CO, Leningrad MD, 1965–1967; 1st Dep. USSR Minister of Defense, 1967–
R: Marshal of the Soviet Union
A: O. Red Banner, O. Lenin; O. Red Star (2); other decorations and medals
PO: Member, CPSU, 1937; cand. memb., CC, CPSU, 1966–1968; memb., CC, CPSU, 1968–

Vasiliy D. Sokolovskiy

B: Kozliki, Grodno Guberniya, July 20, 1897
ED: Graduate, Acad. of the General Staff, 1921
MS: Joined Red Army, 1918; CO of a company, bttn., and brig. in the Civil War, 1919–1921; CoS then CO of a div., CO, Fergana and Samarkand Oblast MD, 1922–1929; so, 1930–1933; so then CoS of a MD, 1934–1941; CoS, Western Front, 1941–1943; CO, Western Front, 1943–1944; CoS, 1st Ukr. Front then Dep. CO, 1st Bye. Front, 1944–1945; FDC then CO, Soviet occupation forces and Head, Soviet Mil. Administration, Germany, 1945–1949; Chief, Soviet General Staff and 1st USSR Dep. Minister of Defense, 1950–1960; Inspector General, Main Inspectorate, USSR Ministry of Defense, 1960–1968; died May 10, 1968
R: Marshal of the Soviet Union
A: Hero of the Soviet Union; O. Lenin (7); other decorations and medals
PO: Member, CPSU, 1931; dep., USSR Supr. Sov. convoc., 1946–1968; del., CPSU Congress, 1952–1961; cand. memb., CC, CPSU, 1952–1961

Gennadiy V. Sredin

B: 1917
ED: Graduate, Mil.-Pol. Acad., 1962
MS: Unknown before 1964; memb., Mil. Council and Head, Pol. Admin., Group of Southern Forces (Hungary), 1964–1967; memb., Mil. Council and Head, Pol. Admin., Carpathian MD, 1968–1971; Dep. Head, Main Pol. Admin., Soviet Army and Navy, 1972–1974; FDC, Main Pol. Admin., Soviet Army and Navy, 1974–
R: Col. Gen.
PO: Member, CPSU, 1940

Pavel G. Stolypin

B: 1899
ED: Graduate, Leningrad Mil. Medical Acad., 1927
MS: Joined Red Army, 1919; po, 1919–1922; medical officer, various units, 1927–1941; Head, Medical Services, Northwestern, Steppe, 2d Ukr., and Transbaikal Fronts, 1941–1945; Head, Far East Mil. Medical Inspectorate, Head, Leningrad Mil. Medical Acad., and Head, Main Mil. Medical Bd., 1945–1963; ret. 1963
R: Lt. Gen., Medical Corps
PO: Member, CPSU, 1919

Andrey T. Stuchenko

B: 1904
ED: Graduate, Frunze Mil. Acad., 1938; Acad. of the General Staff, 1953
MS: Joined Red Army, 1921; officer, Chapaev Div., 1921–1922; field and so, 1923–1934; 1938–1941; CO of a regt., a div., and a corps, 1941–1945; CO of a corps, 1947–1951; CO of an army, 1953–1954; FDC of a MD, 1955–1956; CO, Northern Group of Forces (Poland), 1956–1959; CO, Volga MD, 1960–1961; CO, Transcaucasian MD, 1961–ret.; no information after 1965
R: General
A: O. Lenin; O. Red Banner (3); other decorations and medals
PO: Member, CPSU, 1929; dep., USSR Supr. Sov., convoc., 1962; del., CPSU Congress, 1956–1962; cand. memb., CC, CPSU, 1961–ret.; memb., CC, Geo. CP, 1961–ret.

Semen K. Timoshenko

B: Odessa, February 18, 1895
ED: Graduate, Higher Mil. Acad., 1922; Advanced Training Course for Officers, 1927; Comr.-Cmdrs. Course, Mil.-Pol. Acad., 1930
MS: Cavalryman, Tsarist Army, 1915–1918; joined Red Army, 1918; CO of a platoon and sqn., CO of the 1st Crimean Revolutionary Guards Cavalry Regt., CO of a brig., 1st Cavalry Army, and CO of a cavalry corps, 1918–1921; CO of a div. and a corps, 1922–1932; Dep. CO, Bye. MD, 1933–1935; Dep. CO, Kiev MD, 1935–1937; CO, North Caucasian then Kharkov MD, 1937–1938; CO, Kiev Special MD, 1938–1939; CO, Ukr. Front, Soviet-Polish War, 1939; CO, Northwestern Front, Russo-Finnish War, 1939–1940; USSR Pop. Comr. of Defense, 1940–1941; USSR Pop. Comr. of Defense, CO, Western Front then Western Strategic Flank, 1941; CO, Stalingrad Front, 1942; CO, Northwestern Front, 1943; Stavka repr., 2d, 3d, and 4th Ukr. Fronts, 1943–1945; CO, Baranovichi and South Urals MD, 1945–1948; CO, Bye. MD, 1949–1960; Inspector-General, USSR Ministry of Defense, 1961–1970; died March 31, 1970
R: Marshal of the Soviet Union
A: Hero of the Soviet Union; O. Lenin (4); O. Red Banner (6); O. Suvorov (2); other decorations and medals
PO: Member, CPSU, 1919; cand. memb., CC, CPSU, 1952–1961; memb., CC, Bye. CP, 1939–1960; del., CPSU Congress, 1956–1961

Fydor I. Tolbukhin

B: 1894
ED: Graduate, Frunze Mil. Acad., 1934
MS: Joined Tsarist Army, 1914; wounded, later returning to combat, 1914–1917; joined Red Army, 1918; fought in Civil War, 1919–1921; no information until 1942; CO, 57th Army, 1942–1943; CO, Southern Front, 1943–1945; CO, Soviet occupation forces, Bulgaria and Rumania, 1946–1949; died October 17, 1949
R: Marshal of the Soviet Union
A: Hero of the Soviet Union; O. Lenin; other decorations and medals

Vladimir F. Tolubko

B: Krasnograd, November 25, 1914
ED: Graduate, Acad. of Tank and Armored Troops, 1941; Acad. of the General Staff, 1951; Higher Course, Acad. of the General Staff, 1968

MS: Joined Soviet Army, 1932; soldier, officer cadet, tank, platoon, company CO, 1932–1938; tank sqn. CO, CoS of a tank div., CO of a tank brig., and CoS of a tank corps on the Leningrad, Kalinin, and 3d Ukrainian Fronts, 1941–1945; CoS of a div., CoS and FDC of a corps, aide to the Supr. CO, Soviet Forces in Germany, then CO of an army, 1946–1960; FDC, SRF, 1960–1968; CO, Siberian MD, 1968; CO, Far Eastern MD, 1969–1972; CO, SRF and Dep. USSR Minister of Defense, 1972–
R: General of the Army
A: O. Lenin (2); O. Red Banner (4); O. Red Star (2); other decorations, orders, and medals
PO: Member, CPSU, 1939; dep., USSR Supr. Sov. 1970 convoc.; cand., memb., CC, CPSU, 1971–1976; memb., CC, CPSU, 1976–

Ivan M. Tretiak

B: Malaia Popovka, Poltava Oblast, February 2, 1923
ED: Graduate, Frunze Mil. Acad., 1949; Acad. of the General Staff, 1959
MS: Joined Red Army, 1939; CO of a company, Dep. CO of a bttn. and a regt., CO of a regt., 1941–1945; CO of a regt., CoS, DC, and CO, various units, 1945–1967; CO, Bye. MD, 1967–1976; CO, Far East MD, 1976–
R: General
A: Hero of the Soviet Union; O. Lenin (2); O. Red Banner (3); O. Red Star (2); other decorations and medals
PO: Member, CPSU, 1943; dep., USSR Supr. Sov. convoc., 1966–; cand. memb., CC, CPSU, 1971–1976; memb., CC, CPSU, 1976–; memb., CC, Bye. CP, 1967–1976

Ivan V. Tyulenov

B: Ulyanovsk Oblast, 1892
ED: Graduate, Red Army Mil. Acad., 1922
MS: Participated in October Revolution and joined Red Guard, 1917; CO of a cavalry brig. and helped in suppression of Kronstadt and Antonov revolts, 1918–1921; CO of a cavalry brig., div., and corps, 1922–1937; Dep. Inspector of Red Army Cavalry, 1938–1941; CO, Southern and Transcaucasian Fronts and Transcaucasian MD, 1941–1945; memb., Mil. Council, various MDs, 1946–1955; so, USSR Ministry of Defense, 1956–1958; ret. 1958

R: General
A: O. Lenin (2); O. Red Star; other decorations and medals
PO: Member, CPSU, 1918; dep., USSR Supr. Sov. convoc., 1946

Dmitriy F. Ustinov

B: October 30, 1908
ED: Graduate, Leningrad Mil.-Technical Institute, 1934
MS: Civilian defense worker/manager, 1935–1940; Dep. Pop. Comr. of Defense (for Armaments), 1941–1952; Head, Ministry of Defense Industries, 1953–1963; 1st Dep. Chmn., USSR Council of Ministers and Chmn., USSR Supr. National Economic Council, 1963–1965; government official, various posts, 1965–1976; USSR Minister of Defense, 1976–
R: Marshal of the Soviet Union
A: Hero of the Soviet Union; O. Lenin (8); O. Red Banner; Hero of Socialist Labor; other decorations and medals
PO: Member, CPSU, 1927; memb., CC, CPSU, 1952–; sec. and cand. memb., CC Politburo, CPSU, 1965–1976; memb., CC Politburo, CPSU, 1976–

Valentin I. Varennikov

B: Krasnodar, December 15, 1923
ED: Graduate, Frunze Mil. Acad., Acad. of the General Staff
MS: Joined Red Army, 1941; artillery officer, Stalingrad, Southwestern, 3d and 1st Bye. Fronts, 1941–1945; field and so, 1945–1970; FDC, Group of Soviet Forces in Germany, 1971–1973; CO, Carpathian MD, 1973–
R: General
A: O. Red Banner (4); other decorations and medals
PO: Member, CPSU, 1944; dep., USSR Supr. Sov. convoc., 1978–

Sergey S. Varentsov

B: 1901
ED: Graduate, Higher Artillery School, 1930; Acad. of the General Staff, 1951
MS: Joined Red Army, 1919; fought in Civil War, 1919–1921; artilleryman, 1921–1926; CO of artillery in a div., an army, and a corps,

1931–1941; CO of artillery, Voronezh and 1st Ukr. Fronts, 1942–1945; CO of artillery, Central Army Group (Austria and Hungary) then CO of artillery in a MD, 1945–1951; Chief, Main Artillery Bd., 1952–1955, Dep. CO of artillery, Soviet Ground Forces, 1955–1961; CO of artillery, Soviet Ground Forces, 1961–
R: Chief Marshal of Artillery
A: Hero of the Soviet Union; O. Lenin (3); other decorations and medals
PO: Member, CPSU, 1941; dep., RSFSR Supr. Sov. convoc., 1955–1959; cand. memb., CC, CPSU, 1961–

Semen P. Vasigin

B: February 15, 1910
MS: Joined Red Army, 1932; po, 1933–1941; Head, pol. dept. of a div. and a corps, 1941–1945; Head, Pol. Admin. and memb., Mil. Council, various MD, 1948–1958; Head, Pol. Admin., Soviet Ground Forces and Dep. CO, Main Pol. Directorate, USSR Ministry of Defense, 1967–
R: General
A: O. Lenin; O. Red Banner (2); other decorations and medals
PO: Member, CPSU, 1932; dep., USSR Supr. Sov. convoc., 1954–; memb., Cent. Auditing Comm., CPSU, 1966–

Aleksandr M. Vasilevskiy

B: Ivanovo Oblast, September 30, 1895
ED: Graduate, Leningrad Mil. School, 1914; Acad. of the General Staff, 1937
MS: Tsarist officer, 1914–1918; joined Red Army, 1918; CO of a company, bttn. and a regt., 1918–1931; so, Pop. Comr. of Defense (for combat training) and in Volga MD, 1931–1936; so, Soviet General Staff, 1936–1941; Dep. Chief, Soviet General Staff, 1941–1942; Chief, Soviet General Staff and 1st Dep. Pop. Comr. Defense, then CO, 3d Bye. Front, later Far Eastern Forces, 1942–1945; Chief, Soviet General Staff and 1st Dep. Minister of the Armed Forces, 1946–1949; USSR Minister of Armed Forces, 1949–1950; USSR Minister of Defense, 1950–1953; 1st Dep. USSR Minister of Defense, 1953–1957; ret. 1957–1958; Inspector General, Main Inspectorate, USSR Ministry of Defense, 1959–1977; died December 5, 1977
R: Marshal of the Soviet Union
A: Hero of the Soviet Union (2); O. Lenin (4); O. Red Banner (2); O.

Suvurov (2); O. Red Star; other decorations and medals
PO: Member, CPSU, 1938; dep., USSR Supr. Sov. convoc., 1946–1954;
memb., CC, CPSU, 1953–1957

Nikolai F. Vatutin

B: 1901
ED: Graduate, Frunze Mil. Acad., 1929
MS: Served in Tsarist Army, 1914–1917; joined Red Army, 1918;
fought in Civil War, 1919–1921; NCO, 1922–1925; service unknown,
1929–1941; Head, Operations Dept., Soviet General Staff, 1941; CO,
Voronezh and Southwestern Fronts, 1942–1944; killed in action near
Rovno, April 14, 1944
R: General
A: Hero of the Soviet Union; O. Lenin; other decorations and medals

Andrey Y. Vedenin

B: 1901
ED: Graduate, Advanced Inft. Course, 1941
MS: Joined Red Army, 1919; fought in Civil War, 1919–1921; service
unknown, 1922–1940; CO, 999th Inft. Regt., 1941–1943; CO, 3d
Mountain Inft. Corps, 1944–1945; field and so, 1945–1952; CO, Mos-
cow Kremlin, 1953–ret.
R: Lt. Gen.
A: O. Lenin (2); other decorations and medals
PO: Member, CPSU, 1919; dep., Moscow City Soviet, 1955

Vasiliy I. Vinogradov

B: 1895
ED: Graduate, Moscow Mil. Acad., 1923
MS: Joined Red Army, 1918; fought in Civil War, 1919–1921; field and
supply officer, 1923–1938; fought in Russo-Finnish War, 1939–1940;
Head, various departments then Dep. Head, Red Army Service and
Supply Bd., 1941–1945; Head, Operations Dept., Far East Service and
Supply Bd., 1945–1953; Head, Main Soviet Army Service and Supply
Bd., 1953–ret.
R: Col. Gen.
A: O. Lenin; O. Red Star; other decorations and medals
PO: Member, CPSU, 1920; dep., RSFSR Supr. Sov. convoc., 1955

Andrei A. Vlasov

B: 1900
MS: Unknown until 1938; mil. advisor to Chiang Kai-shek, 1938–1939; field officer, 1938–1941; CO, 2d Assault Army, 1941–1942; captured by the Germans near Sevastopol, May 1942; worked for the Reich Propaganda Ministry and led an anti-Soviet Liberation Army, 1943–1945; captured by Soviet troops at Prague, May 1945; executed for treason, August 1945
R: Lt. Gen.

Nikolai N. Voronov

B: St. Petersburg, 1899
ED: Graduate, Petrograd Artillery School, 1919; Frunze Mil. Acad., 1930
MS: Joined Red Army, 1918; fought in Civil War, 1919–1921; CO of a battery, bttn., and artillery regt., Chief of artillery, Proletarian Inft. Div., 1922–1926, 1931–1934; Head, Leningrad Artillery School, 1935–1937; Chief, Red Army Main Artillery Admin., 1937–1939; Chief of artillery, Soviet forces, Far East, 1939; CO of artillery, Karelian Front, Russo-Finnish War, 1939–1940; Chief, Red Army Main Artillery Admin., and Chief of Artillery, USSR Armed Forces, 1939–1941; Chief, Red Army Main Artillery Admin., 1941–1945; CO of Artillery, USSR Armed Forces, 1945–1950; Chief, Acad. of Artillery Science, 1950–1953; ret. 1953
RR: Chief Marshal of Artillery
A: O. Lenin (4); O. Red Banner (3); other decorations and medals
PO: Member, CPSU, 1919

Kliment E. Voroshilov

B: Lugansk Oblast, February 3, 1881
MS: Joined Red Army, 1918; CO, 5th Ukr. and 10th Armies and Tsaritsyn Front, Dep. CO and memb., Revolutionary Mil. Council, Southern Front, Dep. CO, Kharkov MD, 1918; CO, 14th Army then 1st Independent Front, 1919; memb., Mil. Council, 1st Cavalry Army and CO, suppression of Kronstadt revolt, 1920–1921; CO, North Caucasian MD, 1921–1924; CO, Moscow MD and memb., USSR Revolutionary Mil. Council, 1924–1925; USSR Pop. Comr. of Defense and Chmn., USSR Revolutionary Mil. Council, 1925–1934; USSR Pop.

Comr. of Defense, 1934–1940; Dep. Chmn. and later Chmn., Defense Council, USSR Council of Pop. Comr., 1940–1941; CO, Northwestern Salient, 1941; memb., USSR State Cmte. on Defense and Stavka rep. to Leningrad and Volkhov Fronts, 1941–1942; so, Independent Maritime Army, 1942; memb., Soviet Mil. Del., Teheran Conference, 1943; so in HQ, USSR Partisan Movement, 1944–1945; Head, Soviet Control Comm., Hungary, 1945–1947; civilian politician, 1947–1961; ret. 1961; died December 2, 1969
R: Marshal of the Soviet Union
A: Hero of the Soviet Union; O. Lenin (5); O. Red Banner (5); O. Suvurov; Hero of Socialist Labor; other decorations and medals.
PO: Member, CPSU, 1903; Chmn., Lugansk Soviet, 1905; strike leader, Ukr., 1905–1907; in prison or exile, 1907–1914; civilian, 1914–1917; Chmn., Lugansk Soviet and co-founder of CHEKA, 1917–1918; memb., CC, CPSU, 1921–1961; dep., All-USSR Supr. Sov. convoc. until 1961; Dep. Chmn., USSR Council of Ministers, 1946–1953

Pavel I. Yefimov

B: January 1906
ED: Graduate, Leningrad Mil.-Pol. Acad.; Acad. of the General Staff
MS: Joined Red Army, 1932; po, 1933–1941; memb., Mil. Council, Transcaucasian Front, 1941–1945; po, 1945–1956; memb., Mil. Council and Head, Pol. Bd., Group of Soviet Forces in Germany, 1957–1958; FDC, Main Pol. Bd., USSR Ministry of Defense, 1959–1974; Consultant, Main Inspectorate, USSR Ministry of Defense, 1974–
R: Col. Gen.
A: O. Lenin; O. Red Banner; O. Red Star; other decorations and medals
PO: Member, CPSU, 1925; del., CPSU Congress, 1956–1961; dep., USSR Supr. Sov. convoc., 1954–1962

Aleksey A. Yepishev

B: Astrakhan, May 19, 1908
ED: Graduate, Mil. Acad. of Mechanization and Motorization, 1938
MS: Joined Red Army, 1930; NCO and cadet, 1930–1938; po, 1938–1939; civilian Ukr. politician, 1939–1941; memb., Mil. Council, Stalingrad Front, 1941; USSR Pop. Comr. of Medium Machine Building, 1942; memb., Mil. Council, Steppe Front, 1943–1945; civilian government official and diplomat, 1946–1962; Head, Main Pol. Admin.,

USSR Ministry of Defense, 1962–
R: General
A: Hero of the Soviet Union; O. Lenin (2); O. Red Banner (3); O. Red Star; other decorations and medals
PO: Member, CPSU, 1929; memb., CC, Ukr. CP, 1938–1939; del., CPSU Congress, 1952, 1961–; cand. memb., CC, CPSU, 1952–1964; memb., CC, CPSU, 1964–; dep., USSR Supr. Sov. convoc., 1937, 1950–

Andrey I. Yeremenko

B: Markovka, Ukr., 1892
ED: Graduate, Higher Cavalry School, 1923; Frunze Mil. Acad., 1935
MS: Tsarist cavalry officer, 1913–1918; joined Red Army, 1919; fought in Civil War, 1919–1921; CO, 55th Regt., 14th Cavalry Div., 1923; cavalry officer, 1924–1934; DC then CO, 14th Cavalry Div., 1935–1937; CO, 6th Cossack Corps, 1938–1939; CO, 3d Mechanized Corps and 1st Far Eastern Independent Army, 1940; DC then CO, Western Front and Bryansk Front, wounded and in hospital 1941–1942; CO, 4th Strike Army, wounded and in hospital, CO, Stalingrad and Southeastern Fronts, 1942; CO, Southern and Kalinin Fronts, 1943; CO, Independent Maritime and 2d Baltic Fronts, 1943–1944; CO, 4th Ukr. Front, 1945; CO, Carpathian MD, 1945–1946; CO, West Siberian MD, 1946–1953; CO, North Caucasian MD, 1953–1958; Inspector General, Main Inspectorate, USSR Ministry of Defense, 1958–
R: Marshal of the Soviet Union
A: Hero of the Soviet Union; O. Lenin (4); O. Suvurov; O. Kutuzov; other decorations and medals
PO: Member, CPSU, 1918; dep., USSR Supr. Sov. convoc., 1946–1958; del., CPSU Congress, 1939, 1953–1958; cand. memb., CC, CPSU, 1956–1958

Mikhail M. Zaitsev

B: 1923
MS: Unknown before 1972; FDC, Bye. MD, 1972–1976; CO, Bye. MD, 1976–
R: Col. Gen. of Tank Troops
A: O. Red Star; other decorations and medals
PO: Member, CPSU, 194?; memb., CC, Bye. CP, 1976–

Matvey V. Zakharov

B: St. Petersburg, 1898
ED: Graduate, Artillery Course for Red Commanders, 1918; Frunze Mil. Acad., 1928; Acad. of the General Staff, 1937
MS: Red Guard volunteer, participated in Bolshevik uprising, 1917; CO of various artillery units, Civil War, 1919–1921; so and artillery CO, various units, 1918–1924, 1928–1935, 1937–1941; CoS, Kalinin Front, 1941; CoS, Leningrad and Steppe Fronts, 1942–1943; CoS, 2d Ukr. and Transbaikal Fronts, 1944–1945; Dep. CO, Far East MD, 1945–1947; CO, Acad. of the General Staff, 1947–1949; Dep. Chief, Soviet General Staff, 1949–1952; Chief Inspector, Soviet Ground Forces, 1952–1953; CO, Leningrad MD, 1953–1957; CO, Group of Soviet Forces in Germany, 1957–1960; Chief, Soviet General Staff and 1st Dep. USSR Minister of Defense, 1960–1963; CO, Acad. of the General Staff, 1963–1964; Chief, Soviet General Staff and 1st Dep., USSR Minister of Defense, 1965–1976; Inspector-Advisor, Main Inspectorate, USSR Ministry of Defense, 1976–
R: Marshal of the Soviet Union
A: Hero of the Soviet Union; O. Lenin (4); O. Red Star (4); other decorations
PO: Member, CPSU, 1917; dep., USSR Supr. Sov. convoc., 1954–1976; del., CPSU Congress, 1956–1976; memb., CC, CPSU, 1964–1976

Aleksey S. Zhadov

B: 1901
MS: Unknown before 1942; CO, 66th Army, 1942; CO, 5th Guards Army, 1943–1945; CoS, Central Group of Forces (Austria-Hungary), 1945–1950; Head, Frunze Mil. Acad., 1952–1953; FDC, Soviet Ground Forces, 1954–ret.
R: General
A: O. Lenin; O. Suvorov; O. Kutuzov; other decorations and medals
PO: Member, CPSU, 192?; dep., Ukr. Supr. Sov. convoc., 1955; dep., RSFSR Supr. Sov. convoc., 1963; del., CPSU Congress, 1961.

Georgiy K. Zhukov

B: Stretkovka, Kaluga Guberniya, December 1896
ED: Graduate, Frunze Mil. Acad., 1931
MS: Private and NCO, 10th Novgorod Dragoons Regt., 1916–1918;

joined Red Army, 1918; CO of a platoon and troop in Civil War, 1918–1920; CO of a troop unit, 4th Cavalry Div., 1920–1928; visited Germany to study armored tactics, 1928–1929; Dep. CO of a regt., 6th Cavalry Div., 1931–1932; CO of a regt., 6th Cavalry Div. then CO, 4th Cavalry Div., 1934–1935; volunteer-advisor, Spanish Civil War, 1936; CO, 3d Cavalry Corps, 1936–1937; DC of cavalry, Bye. MD, 1937–1939; CO, 1st Army Group, Khalkhin-Gol, 1939; Dep. CO, Kiev MD and CoS, Northwestern Front in Russo-Finnish War, 1940–1941; Chief, Soviet General Staff and Vice-USSR Comr. of Defense, later CO, Western Front, 1941–1944; CO, 1st Ukr. and 1st Bye. Fronts, 1944–1945; CO, Soviet occupation forces and Chief, Soviet Mil. Admin., Germany, 1945–1946; CO, Soviet Ground Forces, 1946; CO, Odessa MD and Urals MD, 1946–1953; 1st Dep. USSR Minister of Defense, 1953–1955; USSR Minister of Defense, 1955–1957; dismissed and ret. by Khrushchev, 1957; died June 18, 1974
R: Marshal of the Soviet Union
A: Hero of the Soviet Union (4); O. Lenin (5); O. Red Star (4); O. Suvurov; many other decorations and medals
PO: Member, CPSU, 1919, del., CPSU Congress, 1946, 1952–1956; cand. memb., CC, CPSU, 1952; memb., CC, CPSU, 1953–1957

Author Index

Author Index